THE BEST OF MGM

By JAMES ROBERT PARISH

As Author

The Fox Girls*
The Paramount Pretties*
The RKO Gals*
The Slapstick Queens
Good Dames
Hollywood's Great Love Teams*
Elvis! (and Supplement)
Great Movie Heroes
Great Child Stars
Great Western Stars
Film Directors Guide: Western Europe
Film Actors Guide: Western Europe
The Jeanette MacDonald Story
The Tough Guys*
Hollywood Character Actors*

As co-author

The Emmy Awards: A Pictorial History
The Cinema of Edward G. Robinson
The MGM Stock Company: The
   Golden Era*
The Great Spy Pictures
The George Raft File
The Glamour Girls*
Liza!
The Debonairs*
Hollywood Players: The Forties*
The Swashbucklers*
The All-Americans*
The Great Gangster Pictures
The Great Western Pictures
Hollywood Players: The Thirties*
Film Directors Guide: The U.S.
The Great Science Fiction Pictures

Hollywood on Hollywood
The Leading Ladies*
The Hollywood Beauties*
The Funsters*
The Forties Gals*
The Hollywood Reliables*

As editor

The Great Movie Series
Actors' Television Credits: 1950-72
   (and Supplement)

As associate editor

The American Movies Reference Book
TV Movies
Errol Flynn
Boris Karloff

By GREGORY W. MANK

As Author

It's Alive! The Classic Cinema Saga
   of Frankenstein
Classics of Terror* (to be published)
The Hollywood Hissables* (to
   be published)

As co-author

Hollywood Players: The Forties*
Hollywood on Hollywood

The Hollywood Beauties*
The Funsters*
The Hollywood Reliables*

*Published by Arlington House

THE BEST OF MGM

The Golden Years (1928-59)

JAMES ROBERT PARISH and GREGORY W. MANK
with Richard Picchiarini

Research Associates

John Robert Cocchi   Florence Solomon

Introduction by DeWitt Bodeen

Arlington House Publishers
Westport, Connecticut

Library of Congress Cataloging in Publication Data

Parish, James Robert.
  The best of MGM.

  Includes index.
  1. Moving-pictures—Plots, themes, etc. I. Mank,
Gregory W. II. Picchiarini, Richard. III. Title.
IV. Title: MGM: the golden years (1928-59)
PN1997.8.P3   791.43'75   81-7880
ISBN 0-87000-488-3   AACR2

Production services by Cobb/Dunlop Inc.

Dedicated to
the artistic, technical, administrative, and sales talent
who combined to make the MGM product possible

Acknowledgments

RESEARCH CONSULTANT:
Doug McClelland

Earl Anderson
Richard Braff
Kingsley Canham
Howard Davis
Morris Everett, Jr.
Film Favorites (Bob Smith, Charles Smith)

Films in Review
Focus on Film
Pierre Guinle
Ken D. Jones
William T. Leonard
David McGillivray
Albert B. Manski
Alvin H. Marill
Mrs. Earl Meisinger

Peter Miglierini
Michael R. Pitts
Screen Facts (Alan G. Barbour)
Mrs. Peter Smith
Don E. Stanke
Charles K. Stumpf
T. Allan Taylor
Lou Valentino

And special thanks to Paul Myers, former curator of the Theatre Collection at the Lincoln Center Library for the Performing Arts (New York City), and his staff: Monty Arnold, David Bartholomew, Rod Bladel, Donald Fowle, Maxwell Silverman, Dorothy Swerdlove, Betty Wharton, and Don Madison of Photographic Services.

PREFACE

In order to allow sufficient discussion of each entry detailed in this volume, it was decided to limit selections to MGM's "Golden Era," from late 1928, the start of the studio's talking feature films, to 1959, the year in which the remake of *Ben-Hur* was released to multiple Academy Award acclaim. Naturally, with such a wide spectrum to choose from, it was not possible to include as many favorite examples of the Metro-Goldwyn-Mayer product as I would have liked to include. It is hoped that the selections presented herein will offer the reader an overview of the ever changing style and personality of the Culver City studio during the four-decade period described.

JAMES ROBERT PARISH

CONTENTS

MGM—HOLLYWOOD'S OLYMPUS

Today, with the power of the movie studio gone, it is not easy to explain to those who were not around during the twenties and thirties why the dream of every film artiste, craftsman, and worker was to be under contract to Metro-Goldwyn-Mayer. MGM stood like Olympus, towering over all other studios. The contract players and workers there were like so many gods and goddesses, envious of one another, and all striving to be the studio's top attraction. To be among their number was an honor devoutly coveted.

"More stars than there are in heaven!" was MGM's proud boast, and some of those stars are still known by the sobriquets given them by an eager press department—"Lady of the Screen" (Norma Shearer), "the King" (Clark Gable), "the Great Lover" (John Gilbert), "Empress of Emotion" (Joan Crawford), "the Platinum Blonde" (Jean Harlow), "Man of a Thousand Faces" (Lon Chaney), "Sweethearts of the Screen" (Jeanette MacDonald and Nelson Eddy).

The twenties and thirties were a time of innocence, a time when the public worshipped its idols by setting them apart from commoners like thee and me. Like the ancient deities, MGM's luminaries had all the failings of humans—but always, for they were gods indeed, they had the glory of immortality. And a few of them, it seems now, really were immortals after all.

The beginnings of MGM do not trace to the early silent-film history, as do those of Paramount, Fox, and Universal. MGM stood for three separate production units, which merged in the early twenties: the old Metro Studio, which joined forces with the Samuel Goldwyn Studios, which in turn was joined by Louis B. Mayer Productions. Goldwyn bowed out of the amalgamation almost at once, although it was he who actually had more to sell than any of the others: the acreage and studio buildings themselves were his; he had a bigger list of contract players, directors, and writers; he owned some valuable story properties; and his own name as a class producer meant more than the name of any other production head at the time. Thus the studio, briefly known as Metro-Goldwyn, flourished. Within a year Louis B. Mayer joined the unit, and Metro-Goldwyn-Mayer, a subsidiary of Loew's Inc., was born.

Metro had been one of the plusher studios since its founding in 1915. It had an active studio in the East and one, both charming and complete, in Hollywood (on Romaine, west of Vine, between Santa Monica and Sunset Boulevards). Its product was always distinctly high class, and at one time it could boast of having a contract list with some of the best names in the industry. One of the first big romantic teams, which had started at Essanay, reached full flower at Metro—Francis X. Bushman and Beverly Bayne. Also enormously popular then was the team of Harold Lockwood and May Allison. Eventually, that team was broken up and both players began new careers at Metro as stars in their own right. Lockwood died in 1918, a victim of the Spanish influenza epidemic that swept America that year, but Miss Allison continued as a Metro star until the end of 1922. Bert Lytell, a matinee idol of the Broadway stage, came to Metro as a film star, and remained there for several years. He starred in such hits as **Lombardi, Ltd., A Trip to Paradise** (the first film version of **Liliom**), **The Lone**

Wolf, and a number of program features built around the adventures of Boston Blackie. Alice Lake, once a Sennett bathing girl, became Lytell's leading lady, and then was made a star at Metro. And occasionally deluxe performers came to the studio long enough to star in a single venture, Ina Claire in **Polly with a Past**, to name one. In 1921 Metro terminated its longstanding contract with Nazimova. For three years she had been the studio's most prestigious star and one of Hollywood's most engaging personalities. The biggest moneymaking star at Metro was Viola Dana, a bright comedienne who was equally at home in drama; her pictures were always immediate box-office hits.

Thus, in 1922 Metro had three stellar attractions still under contract: Viola Dana, June Mathis (one of Hollywood's top scenarists), and all-time great screen director Rex Ingram, whose masterly production of **The Four Horsemen of the Apocalypse** (1921) had brought Metro not only its finest hour, but also sizable financial returns. Ingram had his faithful entourage—his wife, actress Alice Terry, his cinematographer, John B. Seitz, and his favorite actor, Ramon Novarro.

Despite the continuing returns on **The Four Horsemen,** Metro was in dire financial trouble by 1922. Fortunately, Marcus Loew, head of Loew's Inc., a theater chain, needed a studio that would grind out products to be shown in Loew's movies houses. He therefore bought Metro. By this time, though, only Viola Dana and the Rex Ingram unit, which included Miss Mathis, were working under contract. Nevertheless, it was a coup for Loew. Jackie Coogan and Buster Keaton then joined the new Metro lot through the Joseph Schenck interests, and a few months later a separate contract was made with independent film producer Louis B. Mayer, who agreed to furnish Metro with four annual releases of high quality made under his banner. Mayer had been releasing a complete program of Anita Stewart and Mildred Harris Chaplin features at First National, and had made some excellent dramatic movies like **The Famous Mrs. Fair.**

These developments, however, were insufficient to make Metro the reigning movie monarch. So, through the machinations of Lee Shubert, a board member and big stockholder at both Loew's Inc. and Goldwyn Pictures, Marcus Loew was able in 1924 to bring Samuel Goldwyn's studio into the new setup. Although Goldwyn himself never became a part of the merger, his name became half of the company name—Metro-Goldwyn—because of his prodigious contribution to the amalgamation. The studio itself, on Washington Boulevard in Culver City, California, had been built by Thomas H. Ince and sold to Goldwyn, who then moved his eastern studio and production offices from Fort Lee, New Jersey, to the new Culver City home.

It was also in 1924 that Louis B. Mayer moved in on Marcus Loew. The latter could only admire Mayer's sagacity, and appointed him head of production, studio chief, in which capacity Mayer served with his aides Harry Rapf and Irving Thalberg. Thus the studio became Metro-Goldwyn-Mayer.

The new company now boasted an array of talent that made every other studio's roster look puny. Metro had supplied the Rex Ingram unit, with writer

June Mathis, cinematographer John B. Seitz, and players Ramon Novarro and Alice Terry; also from Metro came director Victor Schertzinger, Viola Dana, Jackie Coogan, Buster Keaton, and Monte Blue. From Goldwyn came writers Frances Marion and Carey Wilson, and the man who would become top art director of the industry—Cedric Gibbons. Directors King Vidor, Marshall Neilan, Erich von Stroheim, Robert Z. Leonard, Charles Brabin, and Victor Seastrom were a Goldwyn inheritance, and there were stars like Mae Murray, Blanche Sweet, Aileen Pringle, Eleanor Boardman, Mae Busch, John Gilbert, William Haines, and Conrad Nagel. News tycoon William Randolph Hearst also released his features through Goldwyn by way of Cosmopolitan Productions, the biggest star of which was Marion Davies. From Goldwyn also came a superlative library of unfilmed stories, the principal being General Lew Wallace's **Ben-Hur.** From Mayer came himself (which was considerable), with Rapf and Thalberg as seasoned production executives, and a roster of players that included Lon Chaney, Renée Adorée, Norma Shearer, Huntley Gordon, Hedda Hopper, plus a quartet of dependable directors: Reginald Barker, Hobart Henley, Fred Niblo, and John M. Stahl.

The gods had taken over, and from their Olympus were about to rule. For the next fifty years, from 1924 to 1974, Metro-Goldwyn-Mayer reigned, producing 1,709 feature films and establishing a record for achievement and honors in the industry that is unmatched.

In October 1924 the first of those films was released. **He Who Gets Slapped** had been adapted by Carey Wilson and Victor Seastrom from a Theatre Guild production of a Russian play by Leonid Andreyev, with Seastrom also serving as director for a cast headed by Lon Chaney, Norma Shearer, and John Gilbert. Highly artistic, moody, and intense, this film nevertheless started the studio down the road to phenomenal success by becoming a genuine success in its own right. Since the studio's motto was, grandly, **Ars Gratia Artis** ("Art for Art's Sake"), the production of **He Who Gets Slapped** was in the proper spirit, for the studio never got so arty again.

For the first decade of its existence, MGM ascended high into the heavens, with a record of one hit after another. At the same time disagreements between Mayer and Thalberg arose, for Mayer was a business executive and Thalberg an artistic man of good taste; if the disagreements got serious, Nicholas Schenck came onto the scene to smooth the discord. Both parties made compromises; a truce would be declared; and the troubled parties would work through another season to the glorification of the studio.

Both Mayer and Thalberg could be ruthless; that is, after all, a prime requisite of an executive. Mayer was a vulgarian in matters of taste, but, even though both men were perfectionists, Thalberg knew how to attain perfection,

The MGM lot.

Young actress Joyce Coad attending the MGM studio school.

and Mayer did not. Mayer had to be led, and he resented it, although he knew it was necessary. Each man knew both the value and the price of everything that could be bought, and there was little that couldn't be bought, except the signatures of the Lunts on a contract for a film after they had made one (**The Guardsman,** 1931), and the signature of an artiste like Katharine Cornell for even a single movie. Nor could money buy Mayer that innate sense of good taste in filmmaking, which Thalberg had. The productions Thalberg personally produced (and he never took credit for them) raised the standard of the entire industry, and any film he offered advice upon benefited. His untimely death, brought on by overwork, lessened the quality of MGM releases thereafter, for the company was never able to find a man who could step into his shoes.

When Thalberg died in 1936, the company had twelve remarkable years of achievement behind it, and was into a thirteenth year. Mayer resisted deciding upon another associate to follow Thalberg, because there wasn't one around whom he could trust. He therefore surrounded himself with the best that money could buy, an assemblage of producers, each with his own unit. Mayer plunged ahead doggedly, hoping he would not be double-crossed, or proved incompetent. He knew well how great the contribution of Thalberg had been during those first twelve years, and he feared any man who might gain the power to outmatch and outvote him. There was always talk of finding "another Thalberg," but nobody knew better than Mayer that Thalberg had been unique.

Mayer nevertheless successfully bluffed his way through the rest of the thirties and into the forties, carrying the power of MGM, like Atlas, on his shoulders. During the late thirties, he had the advice and help, as an assistant, of his son-in-law, David O. Selznick, no mean producer in his own right, but Selznick seized his first chance to set up a production studio of his own, and bowed out of the MGM arrangement. Later, when Selznick needed help and went to Mayer, wanting the loan of Clark Gable to play Rhett Butler in **Gone With the Wind** and also wanting MGM to put up money for additional backing for the picture, Mayer proceeded with a wiliness that would have done credit to a patriarch out of the Old Testament. He gave Selznick the loanout of Gable, and he gave him an investment check from MGM of an additional $1,250,000 for the picture's budget. For this MGM got distribution rights and half the profits from **Gone With the Wind.** When Selznick's company disbanded, MGM acquired all rights to the film, and to date that has meant at least $150,000,000, and will mean at least that much more in the next decade with television sales, reruns, and perhaps a remake or sequel.

Mayer continued to bluff his way along in total control throughout the war years, aided by the executive producers who were helping him to keep the product of the studio high. No one was blind to the fact, however, that during those years, film could be stuck together with spit and become a moneymaking feature. The test would come when the war was over, and pictures returned to a peacetime schedule. A more exacting taste would be obligatory then.

On one occasion in the forties when I was a guest at a party, I happened to overhear a discussion between Mayer and Frances Marion. Talk never strayed from filmmaking, as it never does at a Hollywood party, and Miss Marion, when asked what kind of pictures formed the backbone of a successful studio, answered promptly, "Love stories and Westerns—and they're better when you keep them apart."

Mayer frowned. "What do you mean, Frances?"

"I mean the best Westerns are really romances between two men, and..."

"Now, Frances!" Mayer waved a finger at her reprovingly, and then relaxed, beaming happily. "What about mother?" he asked.

"What about her, Mr. Mayer?"

"Stories about mothers, I mean—her sacrifices—family stories—you know, the domestic life of America—with little children—girls and boys growing up—and their pets, dogs, cats, horses? Can you name one family picture that never made money?"

"No, because they represent a dream world, and dreams always make money. The kind of picture you're talking of is about the kind of family Americans **wish** they had. But it doesn't exist. I come from a large family. I know. I also know mother never gets a decent break."

Mayer said no more, but everybody knew what he had in mind. Mayer's great weakness was the family film, and he loved to idealize the family on film. And that kind of picture did bring him money at the box office. Americans did like themselves idealized up there on the screen. Even more than he was of **Ben-Hur** (which, in its way, is a **big** family film) and of his musical spectaculars (like **The Great Ziegfeld**), Mayer was prouder of a family coming to life in an MGM film, and acting as a family should, or at least as he thought one should. He very much admired, was moved by, and laughed and cried at the Eugene O'Neill play **Ah, Wilderness!** which Frances Goodrich and Albert Hackett had fashioned for Clarence Brown. MGM bought a play, **Skidding,** by Aurania Rouverol, which was about one of those pleasant, nonexistent American families, and made it into a movie called **A Family Affair,** which was about small-town America and a certain character, played by Lionel Barrymore, named Judge Hardy and his close family. The minute Mayer saw it, he wanted more. The success of **Ah, Wilderness!** had pointed the way, but there was a mint to be made from a series based upon the exploits of Judge Hardy and his family. The very next year, 1938, saw the release of **You're Only Young Once.** Mickey Rooney had been in both **Ah, Wilderness!** and **A Family Affair,** and now in **You're Only Young Once** he was the most important member of the family, which now had Lewis Stone as the father. The Hardy family films caught on at once, and they came along regularly for the next two years, every one of them a blockbuster. Mayer proved that today he would have made a marvelous TV executive, because he no sooner had one successful series than he wanted another, and he got it with **Young Dr. Kildare,** the basis at MGM of a whole series of hospital stories involving young Dr. Kildare and his old superior Dr. Gillespie, played by Lew Ayres and Lionel Barrymore. This went on and on, resuming to go into television series production. On the theory that if two series were good, three would be better, Mayer got Mary McCall Jr. to adapt a Wilson Collison story, and the picture was called **Maisie,** starring Ann Sothern. These three series films were all from the B picture unit, and they were so popular that they sometimes saved face for the studio when too many A's flopped.

Mayer could also rate a strong A average in picking stars. He could also disparage himself later when he let one go, like Grace Moore or Deanna Durbin, and they went to other studios and made smash hits. When he fostered a star's career, his interest was benevolent and paternal. He believed in Joan Crawford as a top movie star, and when the Aphrodite of the MGM Olympus wanted help or advice, she could go directly to the sanctum sanctorum of Father Zeus. He adored lilting operetta music, and Jeanette MacDonald was one whose career he sponsored, although he didn't always think she sang with enough schmaltz, and

Judy Garland and Mickey Rooney at the MGM school in 1938.

once got down on his knees before her and to her consternation sang a Jewish lament to show her how to put feeling behind words. He liked Judy Garland, and regarded himself as her foster father, although there were times when he wished that she would don Dorothy's red shoes and become Shirley Temple, for whom he positively had a weakness. He thought Garland terribly plain and called her his "monkey," which didn't help her inborn inferiority complex. He didn't like Jean Harlow, and couldn't understand her immediate popularity at MGM; he thought her "vulgar." Clark Gable, Robert Montgomery, Robert Young, and Robert Taylor were four stars whose quick rises to fame at MGM Mayer admired, and he would listen to what they wnated, although that didn't mean they got it. He felt like a father to Mickey Rooney, and nearly every day reproved him for some misbehavior. He had a series of favorite boy stars—from Jackie Coogan to Jackie Cooper to Mickey Rooney and Freddie Bartholomew.

About the last one there is a classic story. One day Mayer summoned the young Bartholomew to his office to tell him that the studio was pleased with his film work and wished to give him a bonus. How would Freddie like the gift of a motorcar all his own? Young Freddie was, of course, delighted, but wanted a car of greater horsepower than what Mayer in the name of MGM was willing to offer.

"You don't make enough money to run such a car," Mayer explained kindly. "Just buying gas would keep you broke."

But Freddie was more than ever insistent, and, finally, Mayer brought his fist down upon the table with emphasis. "Now, Freddie," he said, "I don't want to be Scotch about this..."

The best appreciation of Mayer was expressed not long ago to a newspaperman by George Cukor: "Louis B. Mayer—he never really liked me very much—but he was a very astute man, a creative man, and a wise man; he's sorely missed. I don't think people appreciated what he and Thalberg did and created. Louis B. Mayer understood that this is a family business, and I think there is a huge public that has been alienated by what has happened here. What we need are showmen like Louis B. Mayer and Harry Cohn instead of hacks."

Even though MGM's profits in 1946 were the largest ever, the gross income was down; this was even more apparent in 1947. Other studios were obviously making better pictures. Worse, MGM had no Academy Award nominees in the Best categories those two years. The time had come when Louis B. Mayer could no longer stall about getting another Thalberg. Mayer finally chose Dore Schary for the job.

Schary had enjoyed a meteoric rise from accomplished writer to executive at MGM with his own unit, to head of production at RKO-Radio Studios. Although

The MGM studio roster in 1944.

Mayer never could trust a writer, and knew that politically Schary and he were as far apart as the two poles, he prayed for the best, vowing, nevertheless, that not for one second would he relax his vigilance. The Reds could take over!

The two men got along peaceably enough in the beginning. In 1949 they cohosted a luncheon in the fantastic commissary which featured Louis B. Mayer's favorite chicken noodle soup. There fifty-eight of the eighty contract players broke bread. They had reason to celebrate, because MGM/Loew's profits were on the rise, and they were even better in 1950, when all the other studios were on the downgrade and in the dumps. Significantly, a few awards came MGM's way in 1951, with **An American in Paris** winning for Best Picture. During that year, however, the relationship between Mayer and Schary worsened, and finally, at a meeting in 1952, Mayer got into such a tizzy that he forced Schenck to choose between him and Schary. He was absolutely stricken dumb when Schenck chose Schary to become head of the studio.

Mayer was out.

So was virtually every other big contractee from the beginning. Three years later, Gable would leave, the last of the early contract people. When he returned from the wars, his new films were not overpowering hits, and he was glad to leave the studio where he had been under contract for thirty-four years. Crawford was already gone, but a bigger star than ever freelancing. Garbo left before the war began. Norma Shearer was quietly retired. Too many were dead.

Dore Schary lasted in power only five years, stepping out with an enormous personal profit. Then a series of production chiefs took over. None of them lasted in control for very long. The inroads of television and the rising production costs were making a formidable thing of theatrical film production; the studios not only couldn't compete but couldn't even cope with the eager TV giant rising in the East. Sol C. Siegel was in the top executive chair in 1958, followed by Robert Weitman in 1962, until Herbert Solow took over and held the job down in 1969.

Everything, meanwhile, was going wrong. The days of the tycoons were gone. The federal government was no help; its enforcement of the antitrust laws caused Loew's Theatres, Inc., to divest itself of all interests in MGM as a studio making feature films.

Nobody wanted the top seat, because it was the hot seat, and burned more than the pants of those who sat in it. Schenck himself stepped down from the presidency of Loew's in 1955. Arthur Loew, his successor, lasted barely a year, and resigned to Joseph Vogel, at which time Louis B. Mayer himself tried to regain power in a grand play, but death caught up with him, and he died, a bitter and unhappy man, in 1957.

Even then, looking back, those in the industry found his days of power at MGM not so bad, after all. He may have been uncouth, but MGM made the top pictures in the twenties, the thirties, and even the forties. His worst defeat had been the demise of his dearest enemy, Irving Thalberg. The two together had made a thing of beauty out of MGM—but studios tarnish quickly when good taste goes (as it did when Thalberg died) and real executive domination ceases (as it did when Mayer was forced out). The movies, at most, in the days of the studios could hardly represent the best of the democratic processes of life; they were fashioned by a form of tyranny, and were at their best when guided by a benevolent despot. The evils of favoritism and nepotism can nip away at a tyrant's power, but those forces wrought no real havoc at MGM; they were stronger at Universal under the Laemmles, but, again, they survived. People have a way of dying, you know.

The presidency passed from Robert O'Brien to James Polk Jr. in 1969. A year later James. T. Aubrey Jr., a onetime television executive, took over. With Aubrey, in 1973, came a complete cessation of distribution of films made by MGM; a situation reversed yet again in 1980 when MGM decided to go back into active production itself.

The heartache became heartbreak as the death rattle continued. MGM had started out with the original six glass studios left it by Goldwyn and a modest acreage for the back lot exteriors. Now, inroads had already been made in that acreage by real estate developers. The street sets, the village centers of Europe, the jungles, and whatever were sold for high rises or condominiums—exactly what Culver City needs. And a hundred acres of real estate, sold!

Worse, all the wonderful storehouse of "things" which lived at MGM were turned over to an auctioneer, numbered, and sold to the highest bidder. Debbie Reynolds managed to buy a lot of loot, but when she ran out of money and couldn't borrow any more, she had to be content with the costumes she had acquired, hoping some day to start a movie costume museum of her own.

Everything at MGM went under the hammer, or by private bid. Props,

The MGM studio roster in 1949.

costumes and modern wardrobe, library, furniture, automobiles, engines from the carpenter shop, lights, cameras—all sold to the highest bidder as a sign of the times. God knows who's now wearing Dorothy's red shoes from **The Wizard of Oz.** There were, I understand, six pairs made originally (they always make more than the one), so there are six buyers around who have immortal powers if only they'll put their red slippers on—and make it all come back, or get better. And bigger. That's the way MGM did things.

Bras and lingerie were sold from the wardrobe. (Who got Lana Turner's underthings?) Male stars who made boxing films had their shorts sold, and I am told by a reliable source that somebody bought what was reputed to be Clark Gable's jockstrap, and complained, "It's not as big as I thought it would be." That's what happens when you deal with an illusion.

In the last prime years of its existence MGM had enjoyed a brief renaissance as the production center for a series of MGM-TV specials and series shows. Some of them fared very well; in fact, one of them, the "Doctor Kildare" series, is responsible for the rise of Richard Chamberlain, who has never succeeded in establishing himself in anything but an indifferent role in a prestige picture (**The Slipper and the Rose** and **The Towering Inferno**), but who has made a real place for himself as the star of TV specials and as the star of many distinguished onstage productions, both in Britain and the U.S.

The twenty-three soundstages which still occupy the MGM lot are busy with renters, filming TV and commercial products and even making an occasional MGM or independent film. They're at least turning out film.

Occasionally—even regularly—there are retrospectives of MGM films, and those attending are suddenly made aware of the wonder that was. There were wonderful film adaptations of the best in English literature (far better than those

remade by the British themselves)—**Treasure Island** (1934), **David Copperfield** (1934), **Captains Courageous** (1937), **A Tale of Two Cities** (1935), **Pride and Prejudice** (1940), **The Picture of Dorian Gray** (1945). There were the great musicals: **The Great Ziegfeld** (1936), **Meet Me in St. Louis** (1944), all of the **Broadway Melody** pictures (1928, 1936, 1938, 1940), **For Me and My Gal** (1942), **Easter Parade** (1948), **Take Me Out to the Ball Game** and **On the Town** (1949), **Singin' in the Rain** (1952), **The Band Wagon** (1953), **Kiss Me Kate** (1953), **Seven Brides for Seven Brothers** (1954), **Les Girls** (1957), **Gigi** (1958); and, as I remember now, anything at all with Astaire doing so much as a single dance from **Dancing Lady** (1933) on to the bits and pieces of the two **That's Entertainment** films that were like the pick of coming attractions (1974 and 1976).

There are all the Garbo films (even that lovely face looking puzzled as if wondering why she was present in **Two-Faced Woman** (1941), the last feature she ever made. There is the remake of **Ben-Hur** (1959), which had none of the excitement of the early silent version, but did have some rare moments of a believable performance by Charlton Heston in the leading role, very much miscast, but good actors can work miracles.

And there were the big specials of each year, like **Greed** (1924), **The Big Parade** (1925), **The Merry Widow** (1925), **La Boheme** (1925), **Tell It to the Marines** (1926), **Mare Nostrum**, Rex Ingram's greatest film achievement (1926), **The Student Prince in Old Heidelberg** (1927), **The Crowd** (1927), **Laugh, Clown, Laugh** (1928), **The Big House** (1930), **Grand Hotel** (1932), **Dinner at Eight** (1933)—and on up through the years, for every year has almost at least one production worth citing.

The comedies of the Marx Brothers are naturals for retrospectives, because

Louis B. Mayer and Mario Lanza at MGM in the late 1940s.

they have not become dated, nor have audiences changed so much as not to enjoy every moment of their madness. There was top entertainment also in the short subjects MGM put out regularly, especially the Robert Benchley pieces, the Laurel & Hardy films from Hal Roach, also the Patsy Kelly shorts, and the **Crime Does Not Pay** series, which introduced many a newcomer to film, like Robert Taylor, and made it possible for him to play in features. As for comedy, one of the real greats, Buster Keaton, was a regular star at MGM from 1924 to 1933 (**Sherlock, Jr.** and **The Navigator,** both wonderful films, to **What! No Beer?**—unfortunately, completely unfunny).

At least once every year now, there is a special showing on TV of **The Wizard of Oz,** the film that endeared Judy Garland to the world. Who will ever forget her singing "Somewhere over the Rainbow"? Incredibly, that song was almost left out. And Mayer was never reconciled to Garland's playing Dorothy; he wanted to borrow Shirley Temple!

In 1973, MGM films were turned over to United Artists in the USA and Canada, and to Cinema International Corporation in the rest of the world; it is their problem keeping them alive, as this arrangement is supposed to last until October 1983.

When Aubrey resigned, an act which was inevitable, Frank E. Rosenfelt (from MGM's legal department) was appointed president, while Kirk Kerkorian, hotel and airline financier, assumed the title of chief executive. Kerkorian's major project, since he was behind MGM's building the Las Vegas Grand Hotel with MGM financing, was apparently to make a super special of **Grand Hotel, Las Vegas,** a movie based on the 1932 all-star hit. A remake of **Grand Hotel (Weekend at the Waldorf)** had been attempted on the American plan in 1945, and there wasn't much grand about it. At least, time is kind; an original cast can never be reassembled and thus cannot flop in what they had once played with incomparable brilliance.

MAYER AND MGM—BEHIND THE SCENES

When Louis B. Mayer took over as head of production at MGM, he had with him his two loyal cohorts—Irving Thalberg and Harry Rapf. Thalberg and Mayer seldom agreed, but Rapf was easygoing enough to compromise even when he didn't agree with the master. Today, Thalberg is remembered as the man behind the most tasteful productions at the studio. Because he favored the musical, Rapf became a producer of such spectacles as **The Broadway Melody** and **Hollywood Revue,** and he stayed on as an MGM producer until his death in

1949, when the studio was under the management of Dore Schary. (Rapf passed away during the production of his Metro film **Border Incident,** a Western thriller.)

The administrative men around Mayer were known as production supervisors, and such first-rate producers were to emerge from the setup as Hunt Stromberg (**Mutiny on the Bounty**), Albert Lewin (**Our Dancing Daughters**), and Bernard Hyman and Paul Bern, two of Thalberg's closests associates. When Mayer went to Europe to find out what was really going on with the filming of the silent **Ben-Hur,** Eddie Mannix moved onto the lot, much to Mayer's original disapproval. But Mannix, a henchman of Nicholas Schenck's at Loew's Inc., stayed on the Culver City lot to become one of the "Mayer group." At the time when there was trouble on the set of **The Merry Widow,** von Stroheim was removed from the picture and his crew and the extras refused to work under anybody else, it was Mayer who went down on the set with Mannix to try and get everything in order. A worker moved closer to Mayer to hear him better. Misunderstanding this movement, Mannix slugged the worker as a protective measure toward Mayer. The incident could have meant nasty lawsuits for the studio, but Mannix's instinctive gesture was the basis of the strong attachment that grew between Mayer and Mannix.

Mayer's faithful secretary for years was Ida Koverman, who had been a secretary to Herbert Hoover at one time. She was a strong force in the Republican party, and Mayer himself soon became a power among Republicans. He hoped to get his studio solidly behind the Republican platform. Mayer received little encouragement in this regard from some of the top directors, a few

Ad for Singin' in the Rain *('52).*

xv

actors who were definitely apolitical, and almost all the writers, but he bullied and threatened his way among other employees.

Laurence Weingarten was head of publicity in the beginning for MGM, but became a full-fledged producer after his marriage to screenwriter Sylvia Thalberg, Irving's sister. Weingarten's association as producer was to last for thirty-two years at the studio. (In April 1974 he received the Irving Thalberg Award at the Academy Award show.) Howard Strickling became head of publicity after Weingarten, and remained Mayer's best and most dependable friend to the end, in 1957, when Mayer died of leukemia.

Douglas Shearer, Norma's brother, quickly moved in with the advent of sound, creating the MGM sound department, which just as rapidly topped the best in the field. It was a new development in moviemaking, needing a new kind of man, and Shearer filled the bill admirably. Year after year, Douglas Shearer won the Oscar for Best Sound, and for his sucessful engineering work at MGM, pioneering in sound.

One of MGM's best-liked producers was a man who rose from film editor to producer, Sam Zimbalist; he was in the midst of production in Rome of the remake of **Ben-Hur,** when he suddenly died of heart failure.

Margaret Booth became one of the studio's best editors and eventually succeeded to the head of the editing department. She won an Oscar for Best Editor with the first **Mutiny on the Bounty.** Other MGM editors who in the early years won Academy Awards for their work were Robert J. Kern (**David Copperfield**), Basil Wrangell (**The Good Earth**), Elmo Vernon (**Captains Courageous**), Tom Held (for both **The Great Waltz** and **Test Pilot**), and Hal C. Kern and James E. Newcom (who divided honors for **Gone With the Wind**).

Ben Piazza headed the talent and casting department, and also acted as chief scout and advised on which actor should be put under contract and groomed for stardom. Robert Taylor and Clark Gable were two of those he favored who become top stars. Benny Thau, a devoted Mayer man, later took over as head of the talent department.

MGM's cinematography department was unbeatable. George Barnes won a nomination for Best Cinematography for **Our Dancing Daughters** (1928), but Clyde Da Vinna also won an Oscar that same season for **White Shadows in the South Seas.** The very next year William Daniels gained a nomination for his camera work on Garbo's **Anna Christie.** In those early years, George J. Folsey Jr. was nominated three different seasons: **Reunion in Vienna** (1933), **Operator 13** (1934), and **The Gorgeous Hussy** (1936). Karl Freund won for **The Good Earth** (1937) as did Joseph Ruttenberg the following year for **The Great Waltz** (1938).

For years Cedric Gibbons was the king of set decoration at MGM, winning honors annually and often creating great fads in modern decoration at the same time, such as showing how to modernize a room (as he did for many a Crawford film). Gibbons won his first Oscar with **The Bridge of San Luis Rey** (1929), and a Most Popular award for **The Merry Widow** (1934), as well as a deserved nomination for **The Great Ziegfeld** (1936).

MGM was the magnet for every imaginative and creative costume designer in the world. Early in the MGM story, Erté came from Paris, but didn't stay long after the first **Ben-Hur** and **La Bohème;** André-Ani did some of the early, more bizarre Garbo creations, and then he also withdrew to Prais. Top man at the studio quickly became Adrian (Gilbert Adrian), and he drew some very talented designers like Walter Plunkett and Irene to the fold. Plunkett was magnificent with costumes (**Gone With the Wind** and **Diane**), and Irene was a mistress of the modern tailored look, while Adrian picked and chose from among the MGM ladies who were to represent Hollywood style for him, such as Garbo, Shearer, and Crawford.

Writers were always a problem to both Mayer and Thalberg. The studio operated on the principle of hiring many of them—preferably the very best in the trade—keeping them supposedly busy, and paying them top salaries on the supposition that writers could be happy with such conditions. They did not want writers to fraternize among themselves, because writers were too independent and rebellious, and sooner or later they would start agitating for a union or guild to represent them. Mayer and Thalberg fought the Writers Guild every step of the way, but finally had to give in, and let the writers make their final determination

on writing credits for each film. When the Guild won, out went all those MGM scribblers who didn't know the first thing about writing, and had been hired on the basis of favoritism or nepotism.

Kate Corbaley, top reader of the story department, was special reader to Mayer. She and Edwin Knopf, and other storytellers, would gather regularly and tell Mayer the stories of properties up for purchase. Mayer never read screenplays, treatments, or original stories and novels. It was up to Kate Corbaley and her staff to make the tales so visually exciting that he would pick up the phone and make a deal himself, or give such an order.

Male writers objected strenuously to the presence of so many females among the writing contract list, complaining that Frances Marion, Bess Meredyth, Anita Loos, Adela Rogers St. Johns, Dorothy Farnum, Josephine Lovett, Bradley King, Sonya Levien, Wanda Tuchock, Claudine West, Zelda Sears, and Sarah Y. Mason had the edge on getting the best assignments, and that the writing department of the studio was "bitch-oriented." When Marion heard of their dissatisfaction, she said cryptically, "They're very lucky to have us on their side; we've saved many a tale of theirs."

MGM—THE STARS IN THE HEAVENS

He Who Gets Slapped (1924) was the first release by the new organization, Metro-Goldwyn-Mayer, and Norma Shearer played the leading heroine's role. She was twenty-one years old at the time, and was to be a star at MGM for eighteen more years. Before MGM, she had been under exclusive contract to Louis B. Mayer, who didn't really care much for her as an actress. Mayer was about to dump her, when the company amalgamation came, and he learned that his trusted aide, Irving Thalberg, had fallen in love with Miss Shearer and was determined to make her not only his project for future stardom at the studio, but his wife as well.

Norma Shearer was born in Montreal. She wanted to be a musician, but her mother was determined that she be an actress in films, so she went to New York and got extras and bit roles and some modeling jobs. Never did one girl have so much against her physically. She had a cast in one eye, narrow shoulders, bowlegs, and heavy thighs. Great care had to be taken by the cameraman if she wore short skirts, or a bathing suit. She had an aristocratic nose, and was at her best and most beautiful in profile. Possessed with grit and determination, she was probably the hardest-working actress ever to appear in films. She met every crisis with intelligence, and became a top star in talking features when sound

The studio telephone exchange which operated on a twenty-four-hour basis, employing fourteen operators.

The MGM publicity department at work.
a) Thousand's Cheer ('43).
b) Till the Cloud's Roll By ('46).

came in, although she had never had theater experience. Her voice, in the beginning, was too high and thin, and she rushed her words, but she studied like a demon until every flaw was conquered.

In that first year, 1924, Miss Shearer appeared in the casts of four other films, the best of which was **The Snob,** which she made with John Gilbert and Conrad Nagel. One thing was clear by the end of the twenties: Thalberg was on the right track with her—she was going to get there, right to the very top. She had survived a great deal, and showed a good endurance record.

Of MGM's fifty-three releases during its second year, Norma Shearer was featured in one, which was the best, **The Tower of Lies,** and starred in three program pictures—**The Devil's Circus, A Slave of Fashion,** and **His Secretary.** She continued throughout the twenties, more or less holding her own with her starring films, most of which had a good deal of chic. Two featured roles cinched

her claim to fame as an actress. The first was as Kathy in Lubitsch's **The Student Prince in Old Heidelberg,** in which she, perhaps miscast, was entirely effective and sympathetic. The second role was in **The Actress,** an adaptation of Sir Arthur Wing Pinero's play **Trelawny of the Wells,** and in it Miss Shearer gave what is probably her best performance in silent films; it is a pity it's not shown today in retrospectives.

When talkies came in she was ready, and Thalberg had wisely chosen a courtroom melodrama as her first, **The Trial of Mary Dugan.** Thalberg had married her in 1927, and she now received full MGM treatment as First Lady of the Screen. She won the Oscar as Best Actress for her performance in **The Divorcee,** given in the 1929-30 season. That same year she was an Academy nominee for **Their Own Desire,** and she would be a nominee the next year for **A Free Soul,** in 1934 for **The Barretts of Wimpole Street,** in 1936 for **Romeo and Juliet,** and in 1938 for **Marie Antoinette.**

She bore Thalberg a son and a daughter, and was a devoted mother and wife, leaving her film work for a year when Thalberg went to Europe for a long rest. When he died in 1936, having fought for and prepared **Marie Antoinette** for her, being a movie star no longer meant that much to her, although she brought radiance to a dull role as the wife in Cukor's **The Women** (1939) and was excellent in LeRoy's gripping melodrama, **Escape** (1940). After two old-fashioned and not very funny comedies, **We Were Dancing** (1942) and **Her Cardboard Lover** (1942), Miss Shearer retired from her career. She was one of the largest stockholders, if not the largest, at MGM, and had become wealthy in her own right. She married a handsome ski instructor, Martin Arrouge, and they have lived abroad for long periods of time and followed the ski season there and here. They have a home above the Strip in Hollywood, but the last year Miss Shearer, who has been troubled with illnesses, entered a private sanatorium outside Pasadena, and in 1980 became a patient at the Motion Picture and Television Country House Hospital.

By the end of 1925, the way was clear for John Gilbert to become the great romantic star of the era. He had begun at the studio in 1924, with MGM's first release, **He Who Gets Slapped,** as the circus rider lover of the heroine, Norma Shearer, and before the year was out, he had dazzled viewers and burnt up the screen with his love scenes with Aileen Pringle in **Wife of the Centaur** and Elinor Glyn's **His Hour.** The same year (1924) he also gave evidence of his real talent as a leading actor when, with great relish, he played the unsympathetic antihero in **The Snob.**

In 1925, he had three stupendous hits in a row: his greatest film performance as the hero in King Vidor's **The Big Parade;** his work as Rudolpho, playing opposite to Lillian Gish's Mimi, in Vidor's **La Bohème;** and his dashing performance as Danilo in Erich von Stroheim's **The Merry Widow.**

In Vidor's **Bardelys the Magnificent** (1926), a costume swashbuckler, Gilbert continued his rise to fame, playing what is probably the screen's most memorable love scene with Eleanor Boardman, in a small rowboat as it drifts down a river under a line of willows. He was also excellent that year in an offbeat role as a barker in a sideshow circus, with Renée Adorée, in Tod Browning's very macabre **The Show.** That same year began his co-starring roles with Garbo in **Flesh and the Devil** (1926), **Love** (1927), and **A Woman of Affairs** (1928). Garbo and Gilbert were lovers off screen as well as on, and he wanted desperately to marry her, but she was not one to be hurried about anything, and it was obvious that although they looked well together, it was she who took any acting honors in their pictures. He made two films with Joan Crawford also—**Twelve Miles Out** (1927) and **Four Walls** (1928)—but his best release in this period was in a Monta Bell newspaper/murder drama, **Man, Woman and Sin** (1927), in which his partner was the electric Jeanne Eagels, making one of her few appearances in silent films. And in **The Cossacks** (1928), Gilbert was again the romantic lead, but the picture never really came alive although both Renée Adorée and Nils Asther were excellent in it. Much more interesting was **Masks of the Devil,** a psychological drama directed by Victor Seastrom, in which Gilbert played a rake, again an antihero. He was excellent, even if the picture was largely ignored by a public intent on hearing its movie heroes talk.

Sound technician and Mickey Rooney on the sidelines of The Devil Is a Sissy *('36).*

The public was soon to hear Gilbert's voice. He played in a skit in **Hollywood Revue of 1929,** in which Norma Shearer and he did the balcony scene from **Romeo and Juliet,** first seriously in costume, and then jazzed up in slang. Seen today, it is appalling, and one wonders why Thalberg didn't demand that it be scrapped. Both stars fared ill vocally, although Miss Shearer had fewer problems that Gilbert. Gilbert's real downfall came with his first all-talking release, the disastrous **His Glorious Night** (1929). His last silent, also that year, **Desert Nights,** with Mary Nolan, had been a very acceptable torrid romance.

Gilbert himself, although nervous about facing the microphone, was not too concerned about his vocal quality. Born in Logan, Utah, 1897, of a show-business family, he had been an actor onstage with years of experience before he even faced a silent camera. His leading lady in **His Glorious Night,** the frigid and noble Catherine Dale Owen, was not much help with her Katherine MacDonald school of reaction. In the house in Manhattan when **His Glorious Night** opened, there were nervous titters among the matinee ladies, listening to all this high-sounding nonsense, and then when Gilbert seized Miss Owen and kept saying, "I love you, I love you, I love you!" the ladies burst into helpless merriment. For a score of years no director could get an actor to say "I love you" on the screen, even in basso profundo.

Gilbert retreated, hurt and puzzled. Rumor had it that director Lionel Barrymore had been paid well to stage the scene so that it would be unconscious camp and thus send Gilbert down the drain, but it was argued that Barrymore was above anything like that, even if Mayer wasn't. Actually, Gilbert's first talkie was supposed to have been a Thalberg production of Tolstoy's play **Redemption,** but it was held up for retakes and **His Glorious Night** pushed in ahead. Something was rotten in the state of MGM. Gilbert, unhappy and frightened, started to drink.

Finally, in 1930, **Redemption** was released. For him it was the coup de grace. Audiences didn't laugh much—they walked out, or just went to sleep, bored to death. It was not Gilbert's fault; it was a turgid story that had had so many directors that it had no style at all. Fred Niblo had directed the first version, and Eleanor Boardman, Renee Adoree, and Conrad Nagel were the supporting players. Lionel Barrymore had been called in for retakes, which only supported stories that he was directing to bring Gilbert down from glory.

It was in the cards that Gilbert's career would crash. His arch-enemy was Louis B. Mayer, who was not above sabotaging a valuable studio commodity in order to get the personal revenge he coveted. Mayer and Gilbert first tangled at a party, when Mayer overheard Gilbert casually mention something about his own

mother having been a bit of a whore. In Mayer's lexicon, all motherhood was sacred, and no man categorized his mother as a prostitute, even if that was how she made her living. He pounced upon Gilbert, roaring, "What did you say?" When Gilbert repeated his statement, the fight was on. They had to be separated, and from that time on they weren't invited to the same parties.

Then when Eleanor Boardman married King Vidor at the home of Marion Davies, it was at the last minute decided to make it a double wedding, with Gilbert marrying Greta Garbo, because the silent Swede had finally said yes. The guests waited and waited—but no Garbo. She had changed her mind again, and gone off on her own. To the anxious and fretful Gilbert, Mayer callously said, "Why marry her? If you want to go to bed with her, invite her to the beach for a weekend." With a howl of rage, Gilbert was upon Mayer, punching and throttling. Again they had to be forcibly separated, Mayer, wiping the blood from his face, said "I'll ruin you if it costs me a million!" Gilbert smiled ironically, and said, "That's just what it'll cost you, Mr. Mayer, and more. Only this afternoon I signed a contract with Nicholas Schenck for six talking features at $250,000 apiece!"

Mayer was stunned. The guests composed themselves, and the wedding of Eleanor Boardman to King Vidor proceeded.

Everybody knew Mayer was out to get Gilbert, but nobody sensed the lengths to which he would go. John Gilbert was already the highest-salaried star at MGM, and his new contract would make him the richest in Hollywood. The legal department tried to buy up the contract, but Gilbert was determined not to sell out or to settle. If he never made another picture, he would make those six talkies, and let them be his swan song, even if nobody went to see them.

And nobody did after **Hollywood Revue, His Glorious Night,** and **Redemption.** Customers simply wouldn't go to a Gilbert movie. The six films he made under that new contract were **His Glorious Night** (1929), **Way for a Sailor** (1930), three in 1931—**The Phantom of Paris, Gentleman's Fate,** and **West of Broadway**—and **Downstairs** (1932). Aware of his problems, Gilbert had gone immediately to a reputable vocal coach, who brought his speaking voice down to a resonant baritone. He also developed a charm and an ease in manner. His final three of the six films were actually very good, and the last one, **Downstairs,** often revived, is a minor masterpiece. Gilbert wrote that story and played the central character, an operator and heel with all the devastating charm of a von Stroheim "man you love to hate." Hardly the type of role for a star on the downgrade to play, but he was on his way out anyway, and wanted to leave with something he could be proud of.

It was not to be his last, however, for when the studio had trouble casting

The MGM photo still laboratory.

The Metro flower shop supplies flower arrangements for modern and period films.

the male lead for Garbo's **Queen Christina** (1933), she simply said, "Get John Gilbert," and stayed home until they got him. Gilbert again played with her sensitively, and they made a handsome romantic team. But when it was over, there was nothing more, except for a part at Columbia in Lewis Milestone's **The Captain Hates the Sea** (1935). Dietrich fell in love with him and tried to get him the Gary Cooper part in **Desire**, but it came to nothing. He died of alcoholism in 1936 at the age of thirty-nine.

The star of MGM's first feature release in 1924, **He Who Gets Slapped**, was Lon Chaney, and there are few who would not argue that he was the best actor in American films. He had first come into contact with Irving Thalberg when Thalberg was Carl Laemmle's assistant at Universal, and they liked one another at once. Chaney was among those under contract to Mayer's group at the time of the amalgamation, so Thalberg had little difficulty in persuading Mayer to bring him in.

Thalberg arranged for him to return to Universal for its big special, **The Phantom of the Opera** (1925), which is the only feature film of Chaney's not released by MGM after his artistic triumph in **He Who Gets Slapped**. Everything at MGM was set up to climax Chaney's long career as an actor. He was put at ease by his remarkable compatibility with both Thalberg and Mayer. And the director whom he had met and worked with in his Universal period, Tod Browning, was now under contract at MGM, where he and Chaney first rejoined forces on **The Unholy Three** (1925), making this suspenseful crook melodrama one of Chaney's best-remembered films. That same year, for Victor Seastrom, Chaney made **The Tower of Lies**, adapted from Selma Lagerlof's **The Emperor of Portugalia**. His characterization of a simple Swedish peasant was instantly recognized as one of Chaney's most outstanding performances, largely because it was so understated that the final moments of madness were all the more shocking.

The following year, 1926, saw the release of two thrillers, both directed by Tod Browning: **The Blackbird**, in which Chaney played a dual role, actually the same man with a dual identity—the Cockney crook known as the Blackbird and the crippled Bishop of Limehouse; and **The Road to Mandalay**, in which he played a horrifying one-eyed criminal known as Singapore Joe.

Every Chaney feature at MGM made a nice profit, but one of the biggest successes was **Tell It to the Marines**, an MGM special about the U.S. Marine Corps, with Chaney, the master of makeup, using none at all to play the tough Sergeant, whose whole life has been the Marines. Eleanor Boardman played a

Marine nurse, and William Haines did some of the best work of his career as the sassy racetrack tout whom Chaney makes into a man of purpose. George W. Hill, director, made it a lusty and moving film, and for his role of Sergeant O'Hara Chaney was made an honorary member of the Marine Corps and an honor guard officer for life.

Chaney then succeeded in creating a gallery of bizarre villains: a dual role of Mr. Wu and Wu's Honorable Father in **Mr. Wu**, an oriental revenge drama; a strong man without arms known as Alonso the Armless in **The Unknown**; an ignorant serf named Sergei in **Mockery**, a Russian Revolution melodrama; and another dual role, as Scotland Yard Inspector Blake and as a Human Vampire in **London After Midnight**.

He then went back to playing two roles without makeup in 1928: a gangster named Chuck Collins in a crook melodrama, **The Big City**; and a tough plainclothes detective named Dan Callahan in **While the City Sleeps**. Also in 1928 he played his favorite role, Tito the clown, in **Laugh, Clown, Laugh**. Chaney filmed three features in 1929, to which sound effects and a music score were added. In **West of Zanzibar** he was Dead Legs, a revenge-crazed cripple in a wheelchair. In **Where East Is East**, another revenge melodrama, he played a catcher of wild animals named Tiger. His last 1929 release, and his last silent, was **Thunder**, and in it he was the sympathetic engineer Grumpy Anderson. **Thunder** had marvelous sound effects.

Of the eighteen films he made on becoming an MGM star, eight were directed by his good friend Tod Browning, who understood the exotic as well as Chaney. The leading ladies of his films were played by good actresses—Norma Shearer, Gertrude Olmstead, Mae Busch, Renée Adorée, Lois Moran, Eleanor Boardman, Joan Crawford, Barbara Bedford, Marceline Day, Betty Compson, Loretta Young, Anita Page, Mary Nolan, Estelle Taylor, Lupe Velez, Phyllis Haver, and Lila Lee.

He was to make one talking feature, a remake of what was probably his most popular success at MGM, **The Unholy Three**, in which he played his original role of Echo, the ventriloquist who masquerades as Mrs. O'Grady. He assumed five distinct character voices for this film, because it pleased him, the "Man of a Thousand Faces," to be known also as the "Man of a Thousand Voices."

Ironically, a recurring throat illness struck him following the picture's completion, and specialists confirmed that he was dying of a bronchial cancer. He died in St. Vincent's Hospital, Los Angeles, of a hemorrhage of the throat on an August morning in 1930. He was only forty-seven years old, having been born of deaf and dumb parents in Colorado Springs, Colorado, in April 1883.

The MGM property department; equipment here for Quo Vadis *('51).*

The MGM back lot-transportation department with props for *Westward the Women* *('51)*.

On location for Westward the Women *with the MGM crew.*

He was unquestionably top man among all the pantomimists in the silent films. He made his bow as a speaking actor, and was allowed time to hear the applause that greeted his efforts before the curtain came down.

Renée Adorée was probably the best instinctive actress of all those present when MGM came into being. In the very second year of the studio's growth, she came forth with one of the loveliest performances ever recorded by a camera, as Melisande in King Vidor's **The Big Parade.** Of French birth herself, she played a young French peasant in love with an American soldier. She was a special pet of Louis B. Mayer, who, whatever else might be thought of him, had an enviable instinct for the true cinematic player.

Born in Lille, France, in 1898, her real name was Janne de la Fonte. She entered movies via the circus and the Folies Bergère. Taking a new name, she came to the United States, where it didn't take her long to try her luck in movies. She did very well as a leading lady at Goldwyn's old studio in Fort Lee, New

Jersey, and on coming to the West Coast, she made a number of pictures at the old Fox studio, where she played leading lady to John Gilbert, then one of Fox's up-and-coming young players. They were a successful team before she contracted with Louis B. Mayer, who brought her to MGM. By the time she and Gilbert were again cast as lead, in **The Big Parade,** they knew one another well, and enjoyed playing together.

She had two MGM releases before **The Big Parade. The Bandolero** (1924) was shot partly in Spain, and Tom Terriss, director, saw to it that it had all the romantic elements—bandits, gypsies, and matadors. It also had Gustav von Seyffertitz. The other was Rupert Hughes' **Excuse Me** (1925), in which she had third billing, after Norma Shearer and Conrad Nagel, playing a kind of grisette.

After **The Big Parade** (1925) and her overwhelming performance and reception as Melisande, MGM didn't have anything at hand as good as that to give her as a follow-up; in fact, she never did get another role as fine as that in **The Big Parade.** She was in several inconsequential romantic farces in 1925, among them Elinor Glyn's **Man and Maid** and Hobart Henley's **An Exchange of Wives,** with Eleanor Boardman, Lew Cody, and Creighton Hale. That year she had a colorful heroine's role in Tod Browning's **The Blackbird,** in which she played with Lon Chaney and her ex-brother-in-law, Owen Moore (she was married briefly to Tom Moore when she was at Goldwyn's). Then, also in 1925, she did get the luscious supporting role of Musetta in Vidor's **La Bohème,** with Lillian Gish and John Gilbert, but one had the feeling that much of her footage must have landed on the cutting-room floor. What there was was gloriously right for Musetta.

She had the misfortune to go into the film **The Exquisite Sinner** (1926), on which Josef von Sternberg walked out, and Phil Rosen finally took over. She had a colorful gypsy role, but the picture, as exhibited, never caught fire. Another film, **Heaven on Earth,** in which she and Conrad Nagel virtually replayed their roles in **The Exquisite Sinner,** was released the following year, 1927, but most of it looked like outtakes from **Sinner.** It was also directed by Rosen, which strengthened the feeling.

The truth is, Miss Adorée, adored as she was by everybody at the studio, was besieged by bad luck. Announced to play the heroine of **The Trail of '98,** she had to withdraw and let Delores Del Rio take over, because she fell very ill from a lung ailment. This happened several times, because she was suffering from tuberculosis and never seemed to get enough rest and peace between pictures. Nothing she did could even touch Melisande. Nevertheless, she was very

The studio staff shop where workmen are fashioning a stone wall for Everything I Have Is Yours *('52).*

had a remarkable gift for creating stars from extras and beginners. Rudolph Valentino, whom he directed in **The Four Horsemen** and **The Conquering Power**, and Barbara LaMarr, whom he directed in **The Prisoner of Zenda** and **Trifling Women,** were devastatingly handsome, but they were stars who could only exist in their own orbits, and both left Ingram, to burn their candles at both ends, and meet death while still young. Valentino died in 1926, at the age of thirty-one, and Miss LaMarr was twenty-nine when she died the same year. Ingram's two greatest stars were Alice Terry, whom he married and who is still alive, and Ramon Novarro, who, at Ingram's suggestion, quit the Ingram unit in Europe after **The Arab** (1924) and returned to Hollywood, where he became a star at the new MGM that same year.

Ramon Novarro (Samaniegos) was born in 1899 in Durango, Mexico. When only a boy, he fell in love with moving pictures, and determined that he would be a star. He danced, played extras and bits, and finally, when Ingram gave him the role of Rupert of Hentzau in **The Prisoner of Zenda,** his star began to rise. He was

Hedda Hopper and designer Adrian.

effective as a young Chinese girl in Chaney's **Mr. Wu** (1927), and in W.S. Van Dyke's **The Pagan** (1929) she played a Sadie Thompson-like lady with strength and verve. Although there were sound effects and music (Novarro sang "Pagan Love Song") in that film, there was no spoken dialogue. She appeared in a speaking role in John Gilbert's ill-fated **Redemption** (1930), playing a gypsy, as she did in **Call of the Flesh,** with Novarro. That was her last film, for she became very ill and had to be put in a sanatorium, where she lingered until death took her in 1933, at age thirty-five.

Although Mayer was exceedingly fond of her and respected her talent, he did not do right by her. After the sensation she created in **The Big Parade,** she should have been starred in colorful and heartbreaking roles, but all she played were gypsies, ladies of the evening from Montmartre, and some vivacious, dizzy flirts. She got better fare on loanouts: she was very moving in two Thomas Meighan Paramount films, **Tin Gods** (1926) and **The Mating Call** (1928); and she was charming in her first talkie, Tay Garnett's **The Spieler** (1928). She never complained, but she was far too good an actress to be stuck with some of the moribund stuff into which she had to breathe life. Although a stunning star, she was seldom allowed to shine.

Metro's biggest attraction ironically never shone like the lodestar he truly was, once the amalgamation took place and MGM came into being. Rex Ingram, a sensitive director of great taste and imagination, put Metro on the map with **The Four Horsemen of the Apocalypse** and **The Conquering Power** (both 1921). In the next two years he made five other features that brought him international fame—three in 1922, **Turn to the Right, The Prisoner of Zenda,** and **Trifling Women,** and two in 1923, **Where the Pavement Ends** and **Scaramouche.** He also

Producer Carey Wilson, costume designer Walter Plunkett, Lana Turner, and costume designer Irene discussing Green Dolphin Street *('47).*

The Metro wardrobe department.

Director Frank Borzage gives approval to Ruth Hussey's gown on the soundstages for Flight Command *('40).*

dramatically poetic in **Trifling Women** for Ingram and he gave one of the most sensitive performances the screen has ever seen as the pagan native, Motauri, who falls in love with the missionary's daughter (Alice Terry) in **Where the Pavement Ends.** He then played the title role in **Scaramouche**, with Terry and Lewis Stone (another from the Ingram stock company), and was acknowledged to be the most promising romantic actor in Hollywood. "I take my hat off to him," said Pola Negri in admiration, not realizing that in America admiring ladies didn't have to doff anything to their idol.

Mayer had been responsible for Ingram's not getting the directorial assignment for **Ben-Hur**, which he was born to direct. Like all men who have nothing of the artist or the man of good taste in their natures, Mayer distrusted Ingram, who held a gloomy wake when Marcus Loew let him know that he had lost out on the assignment. When the amalgamation took place, therefore, Ingram knew well that he could never work with any sense of artistic freedom in a Hollywood studio that also housed Louis B. Mayer. He made private plans to go to Europe with his unit, and took Terry and Novarro with him to film **The Arab**. His headquarters were in the beautiful Cine Studios in Nice, and most of **The Arab** was shot on location in Africa. They were busily at work when the actual amalgamation took place in 1924. It was when shooting on the picture finished that Ingram advised Novarro to return, so that Mayer could make him an MGM star.

Novarro was costar to Enid Bennett for **The Red Lily** (1924) and **Thy Name Is Woman** (also 1924), both directed by Fred Niblo. At this time, Mayer's foolishness in not giving Ingram the directorship of **Ben-Hur** broke publicly. Shooting under Charles Brabin in Italy, the company had suffered nothing but setbacks. Production was ordered stopped, and Brabin, the director, and George Walsh and Gertrude Olmstead, two of the stars, were ordered home. Quietly,

almost as if they were being politely shanghaied, Fred Niblo was sent to direct **Ben-Hur,** and Ramon Novarro and May McAvoy to play the leads. This was entirely Mayer's doing. When he was still not satisfied with the pace of filming, the entire production was ordered back to Culver City, where two-thirds of what appeared on screen in the final cutting was shot, even most of the famous chariot race.

Mayer was very happy with Novarro's work, and naturally favored him over John Gilbert to become the romantic hope at MGM. When he negotiated a new contract with Novarro to star for him, he didn't realize what he had bargained for; the Mexican youth from Durango was as wily a contractor as the onetime Russian Jew from Boston. He kept asking for rewrites of his contract, and kept turning them back to Mayer, once saying, "Excuse me, Mr. Mayer, you haven't indicated at what times I shall be allowed to go to the bathroom."

Novarro told me once, "I was dying to have my career managed by Irving Thalberg, but I soon realized that his only star interest was his wife. If Norma needed or wanted something, I could be left sitting in his waiting room for a week until she got it. So I groaned, signed the contract, and in my opinion because I had been forced to kiss Louis B. Mayer's ass, I never made a worthwile picture again at MGM."

Of course, Novarro, in his Latin way, was exaggerating. He resented, after his triumph in **Ben-Hur**, being starred in a series of typically American films like **The Midshipman** (1925), **The Flying Fleet** (1928), and **Huddle** (1932).

"I always did the best I could, but I was hopelessly miscast as a student at the Naval Academy, and certainly as a football hero. The only things I did at MGM I liked were **The Pagan** (1929), **The Student Prince in Old Heidelberg** (1927), and parts of the two I made in 1931, **Son of India** and **Daybreak**, which Jacques Feyder directed. When talkies came, I was allowed to sing, and that I liked—from **The Pagan** to **Cat and the Fiddle** (1933) with Jeanette MacDonald, and **The Night Is Young** (1934). That one from a Pulitzer Prize novel, **Laughing Boy**, nearly destroyed me; it was the worst picture I ever made, bar none."

He left MGM after 1935, directed, made a few more movies that he didn't like, went into the theater, made a picture in France called **La Comédie du Bonheur** for Marcel l'Herbier, and then in the late forties and the fifties enjoyed a renascence of his career, this time as a character actor, in television and feature films. His last was **Heller in Pink Tights** (1960), with George Cukor directing.

He had an alcoholic problem, and several times was in the hospital at the Motion Picture Country House for treatment for a respiratory ailment. When drunk, he was prey for young men on the prowl, and in 1968 he was brutally

Makeup artist William Tuttle applying Oriental makeup to Paula Raymond.

murdered by two young hustlers he had allowed to enter his home when he was alone.

Mention Hollywood, and the one actress who symbolizes what it was in the golden era is Joan Crawford.

She came to MGM in 1925, its second year of existence. She rose to stardom there, and stayed a star until 1943, becoming the most popular of all actresses in America, as well as admired in foreign lands as a cinematic artiste.

Joan Crawford was fundamentally American, "the shopgirls' delight" in the twenties and thirties. Working girls copied her hairdress, her clothes, the tailored look with the wide shoulders, the shoes with ankle straps, the big hungry wide eyes, a body that was made to dance, a husky voice that delighted the ear, a lipsticked mouth widened without a cupid's bow that became known as something to be attained—"the Crawford smear."

She came from nothing, from nowhere. She was nothing. But in Hollywood, she had arrived. She was somebody. She was a great movie queen.

Born Lucille LaSueur in San Antonio, Texas, in 1901, her parents divorced when she was young, and she took her new father's name, Cassin, being known for a while as Billie Cassin. She survived a foot injury that kept her in bed for a year when she was a child; she survived poverty and deprivation; her education was constantly interrupted. She survived dance competitions and got a nightclub job in Chicago before J. J. Shubert hired her for the Mistinguette show, **Innocent Eyes** (1924). Harry Rapf, Mayer's other assistant, saw the show, signed her to an MGM contract, and brought her to Hollywood.

Many girls had got that far, but she was determined she would go to the top. She would be a star. She was still young and had a lot of baby fat. She went on a strict diet, and suddenly that face with the beautiful planes, the strong jaw, the wide forehead began to emerge. The fleshy thickness disappeared from her body, never to return.

She was always taking lessons. Too aware of her lack of formal education, she took private lessons from those at the top. Once, I know, she took singing lessons from Rosa Ponselle, the brilliant Metropolitan Opera soprano, and sang a duet with her for a private recording. When she made her first screen appearance, she had gone back to her first name, Lucille LeSueur, but the studio wanted something more American, something more suitable. A contest was held through a movie magazine, and some reader proposed the name Joan Crawford. She was rechristened, and the name stuck.

People admired her drive, her yearning ambition. She began to work a lot in

The MGM script department where scripts, manuscripts, and production stills are catalogued for future use.

Stewart Granger, Janet Leigh, and Mel Ferrer in Scaramouche *('52).*

program features, but when she played with Constance Bennett and Sally O'Neil in Edmund Goulding's **Sally, Irene and Mary** (1925), she made a real hit; of the trio, she is the only one called upon to meet stark tragedy and sudden death, when the car in which she is joyriding is struck by a speeding train.

She made a great many more films, but when she played in **Our Dancing Daughters** (1928) for Harry Beaumont she was on the very threshold of stardom, which she achieved in her last silent, **Our Modern Maidens** (1929). At the same time she married her first husband, Douglas Fairbanks Jr. Everything had come true. She was at the top, yet she was destined to go higher.

Her first all-talkie was **Untamed,** and in it she sang "Chant of the Jungle." The next year, 1930, she starred in **Paid,** from Bayard Veiller's Broadway hit **Within the Law,** and box-office records were broken. Her fans loved her rich, throaty voice speaking or singing. A new male rage, Clark Gable, and she played together, and were such instant dynamite that they made eight features as lovers. And then in 1932 she played, superbly, the stenographer Flaemmchen, hungry to know life and real love, in MGM's all-star **Grand Hotel,** in which she acted with John and Lionel Barrymore, Greta Garbo, Wallace Beery, Lewis Stone, and Jean Hersholt. I've seen it now a good dozen times, and I can only honestly say that Crawford's performance is the best in the film. It is amazing how she, with so little background, knew exactly what to do and how to do it, how to underplay, how to be in there holding her own with all those professionals—and as professional as any of them.

Crawford was to give many another fine performance at MGM—in **Dancing Lady** (1933), again with Gable; in **The Women** (1939), another all-star Cukor movie in which she was funny and savage in an unsympathetic role; in **Susan and God** (1940), again displaying, thanks to Cukor, that she understood how to play comedy; and in Cukor's **A Woman's Face** (1941), demonstrating that there was no better dramatic actress in Hollywood.

It may have startled her momentarily in 1938 when some exhibitor anxious for personal publicity labeled her "box-office poison." Straightaway, she gave some of her very best performances at MGM. She left the studio, however, in 1943, after eighteen years there. The war was being fought then. She signed at Warner Bros., but made no film until 1945, when she made **Mildred Pierce,** and won an Academy Award.

Her subsequent features at Warner Bros. were enormously popular. I happen to like her second one, **Humoresque,** which she did with John Garfield, better than any of the others. Everybody has his favorite, but I'd still go to see Joan Crawford in anything. And do, whenever a revival comes around, and she is the star of a retrospective.

Peter Lorre and Joan Crawford in Strange Cargo *('40).*

Joan Crawford in Dancing Lady *('33).*

Crawford was an actress who could never be idle. At her peak at MGM, she not only made movies, but did radio, often appearing for Cecil B. DeMille on his "Lux Radio Playhouse." She was likewise successful in television, and later enjoyed a very successful business executive promotion job with Pepsi-Cola.

In her last years she preferred to live quietly in Manhattan, alone and very content. She had been Mrs. Douglas Fairbanks Jr., Mrs. Franchot Tone, Mrs. Philip Terry, and divorced in all three cases. Her fourth husband, Alfred Steele, left her a widow. She had four adopted children, who all married, and she became a grandmother. Her death in May 1977 was a sad loss to show business.

Anyone interested in emulating Clark Gable should start off by being completely natural; there was not an affected bone in Gable's makeup. Once he got some footage, American moviegoers crowned him their movie king. He was king among his own profession too, which could only admire the brash, virile image he brought to the screen. Women and men, children and adults alike paid him homage. He was not an actor, but he imposed his image on every role he played, and it worked, except in one case—**Parnell** (1937), which required a sympathetic actor and might have been a good film had somebody like Robert Donat played the part.

He was born in Cadiz, Ohio, in 1901, batted around the country for a time doing rugged outdoor jobs until he got work in the theater, and in his self-mocking but determined way aimed for the top. Actresses liked him, especially older women, and a trio—Jane Cowl, Pauline Frederick, and Alice Brady—contributed to his welfare and bluff sophistication, polishing this rare diamond in the rough. Gable preferred older women as a rule; not till he married Carole Lombard in 1939, only to lose her in a plane crash in 1942, did he realize that the relationship of a man and woman belonging to the same generation might have

something more to it than sex. Their love had a maternal-paternal consideration that kept their relationship basking warmly in truth. He was lucky when he was married a fifth time to Kay Spreckels, and found love a second time before he died.

Gable knocked around on the Hollywood studio scene, playing extras and bits in feature fare, and not getting anywhere much. Lionel Barrymore got him a screen test at MGM, but the powers that be rejected him as a contract player because of his big ears; it was not only their size, but their direction—they stuck out. Ben Piazza, casting director and head of talent for MGM, pointed out that ears can be pinned back by the makeup department. A second look was taken of him, as the villain in a Western he made at RKO-Pathe in 1931, **The Painted Desert.** He was given a trial short-term contract at MGM, where he distinguished himself as a gangster in Joan Crawford's **Dance, Fools, Dance** and played a milkman in a Constance Bennett movie, **The Easiest Way.** He went over to Warner Bros. to play a hood who beat up Barbara Stanwyck in **Night Nurse.** If Warner Bros. had been smart enough to overlook his ears, it could have corralled Gable. As it was, however, the returns on the Crawford film poured in with ecstatic comments on Gable; he was given a new contract at MGM, and the era of Clark Gable began.

Frances Marion told me that as the original writer of **The Secret Six,** she was on the set daily making dialogue changes; it didn't take her long to realize that the likeliest candidate for stardom in the film was not John Mack Brown, whom the studio was pushing and had given second billing, but Gable, in one of his first tough-sympathetic parts, although far down in billing importance. With the approval of director George Hill (who was also Marion's husband), Frances hastily rewrote the Gable role on set, giving him some juicy scenes and fresh dialogue. Every critic praised his performance, and he quickly gained an adoring public, female and male.

The list of his early successes is dizzying; one wonders how he could make so many in so little time. There was **A Free Soul** (1931) with Shearer, Lionel Barrymore, and Leslie Howard, in which he was a ruthless gangster who gets slain by Howard, fiance of Shearer, when Gable makes her his mistress and mistreats her. There was **Susan Lenox, Her Fall and Rise** (1931), starring Garbo, the only time they ever appeared together, and he was one of the few actors who held his own with her. There was **Laughing Sinners** (1931), because MGM wanted him in another one with Crawford; it was by public demand, and the studio was willing to junk a good half of a feature that had been completed and previewed in order to put it back into production, replacing all scenes in which John Mack Brown had played, with Gable opposite Crawford. Then, there was

Clark Gable and Helen Hayes in The White Sister *('33).*

Possessed (1931), another Crawford vehicle, one of her very best, in which they lighted up the screen and brought in box-office gold. In 1931 also, Gable's name came first in a list of actors playing in a Kentucky Derby action film, **Sporting Blood.** At the end of 1931 MGM willingly gave Gable stardom in **Hell Divers,** in which he had his name above the title for the first time, and his supporting cast included Wallace Beery, Dorothy Jordan, Marjorie Rambeau, and Marie Prevost. Every picture thereafter starred or costarred him. He had proved himself to be the King. And for twenty-four years he reigned at MGM.

He won an Academy Award as Best Actor in 1934 for his performance in **It Happened One Night.** It was one of his few loanouts, and was made for Frank Capra at Columbia. It was the runaway year for **It Happened One Night,** which one five of the top awards—to Gable; to Claudette Colbert in the female lead; to Capra for Best Director; as Best Picture; and to Robert Riskin for Best Screenplay.

Gable's greatest triumph was his performance as Rhett Butler in **Gone With the Wind** (1939). He was nominated as Best Actor, but Robert Donat got the Oscar for **Goodbye, Mr. Chips.** The blockbuster nonetheless captured eight awards, plus the Thalberg Award for its producer, David O. Selznick. Yet everybody knew that without Gable, **Gone With the Wind** would have been an emasculated film. Although the women were very strong in it, Gable was its guts.

The best all-round male star at MGM was Robert Montgomery, who possessed intelligence, charm, and remarkable versatility as an actor. The image Spencer Tracy projected as a star was virile and true. But neither so perfectly personified the star as the King himself. Think of the biggest actor at MGM, and you can only think of Clark Gable, whether you are seeing him in **Mutiny on the Bounty** (1935), **San Francisco** (1936), **Test Pilot** (1938), **Boom Town** (1940), **Mogambo** (1953), a remake of the equally memorable **Red Dust** (1932), or even **The Misfits** (1960), his last film (not MGM). There is much that doesn't come through in that final film, but Gable does, and so does that last scene which he played with Marilyn Monroe, and **because** of him. Gable was effortlessly male, but the image he created was romantic; sensitivity and warmth marked the man to a degree unmatched by any other film hero.

There has never been such a female star in the heavens as Greta Garbo. She has not made a film since **Two-Faced Woman** (1941), the only really poor one she ever made. Four decades away from the screen, and she still represents to most film fans the ultimate in film stardom. She was the greatest international box-office attraction of all the single stars. World War II cut off her vaster foreign public, but she remains a star whose retrospectives today earn more for MGM than the violent, blood-curdling forays into pornography from which the studio has tried to make money.

Garbo is unique. She is like a goddess who occasionally descends to earth to favor us with a vision of what woman can be. She was known as La Divina abroad, and the divine one she will always remain.

She was born in Stockholm, Sweden, in 1905, and in her girlhood knew the ravages of extreme poverty. But dreams are born in poverty. And Garbo's dreams were real to her: first the theater and then films.

She was accepted as student in the Royal Dramatic Academy of Sweden's own state theater, the Royal Dramatic Theatre. There she attracted the attention of a Russian Jewish director, Mauritz Stiller, about to begin production on a version of Selma Lagerlof's **Gosta Berling's Saga.** Garbo had made only a few film commercials and one feature comedy, **Peter the Tramp.** Stiller chose her to play the Italian countess Elisabeth Donna; her surname was Gustafsson, and Stiller gave her a new name. Greta Garbo was born.

The Saga of Gosta Berling was acclaimed in Europe, and Stiller and his young protégeé went to Turkey to make a second film. But there was trouble about the money, and finally in Berlin Stiller let G.W. Pabst use the talents of his find in a film known in this country as **The Joyless Street.**

Soon after the amalgamation of Metro-Goldwyn-Mayer, Louis B. Mayer himself came to Europe on a talent hunt. It was the luckiest step he ever took, for in Europe everybody was talking about **The Saga of Gosta Berling,** its magnificent director, Mauritz Stiller, and its beautiful young Swedish actress, Greta Garbo. Mayer saw the picture, and arranged to meet them.

Chroniclers are fond of repeating that in order to get Stiller's signature on a contract, Mayer also had to sign Garbo, which he did rather than lose Stiller. I suspect, however, that Mayer was playing the wily business executive. He had seen the picture and knew that Stiller's talent was great, but he also knew that Garbo had the makings of a great star. He wanted her probably more than he ever wanted Stiller, and took them both, because neither would make a move without the other. Mayer had a sixth sense about talent, and he knew, when he wanted Garbo on the screen, that he was looking at great film talent. He had to pay for Stiller's services, but he got Garbo for a bargain. When she finally arrived in Culver City, he cast her as a femme fatale in **The Torrent,** which technically starred Ricardo Cortez, and was to be directed by Stiller. But not too many days into production Stiller was removed, to be replaced by Monta Bell. Garbo was doomed never to make another film with her mentor. Stiller was assigned to direct her in **The Temptress,** but no sooner had he begun than he ran afoul of the real star of the piece, Antonio Moreno. He was removed from the picture and Fred Niblo took over. Stiller went over to Paramount to direct Pola Negri in two of her best American films. Garbo went on alone to her place in the stars. She was always alone, and ended up alone, as goddesses do.

She made twenty-six feature films from 1925 to 1941. Ten of them were silents; fifteen were talking; and one was in the German language, the German talking version of her first English-speaking success, **Anna Christie.**

She lives in Manhattan, but she is likely to be almost anywhere, as is the wont of a Swede, especially one who radiates so divine a glow. In Olympus she would be known as the divine Androgyne, because she typifies the most beautiful in both sexes. She could be Aphrodite, and she could be Apollo. Maybe that's why in her day she was called the Sphinx. That enigmatic Mona Lisa smile suggested that she knew everything, and would say nothing.

I have limned the stories of eight stars who came to MGM in the beginning days. Five of them began when MGM began. Two, Garbo and Crawford, joined the contract ranks during the second year of the studio's existence, in 1925. The eighth, Gable, signed his first contract with the studio in 1930, and stayed there twenty-five years.

Naturally, there were many more stars in the MGM heavens, but these eight are indicative of the kind of player who attained stardom at the studio. Many others stayed long upon the scene—Marion Davies, Eleanor Boardman, William Haines, Conrad Nagal, Myrna Loy, Marie Dressler, Robert Montgomery, Jean Harlow, Rosalind Russell, Robert Taylor, James Stewart, Judy Garland, Jeanette MacDonald, Nelson Eddy, Spencer Tracy, Katharine Hepburn, Ava Gardner, Elizabeth Taylor, Lana Turner...The list could stretch across the skies.

But these eight are representative of what the studio wanted from its contract list in those golden years of the late twenties following MGM's birth. Interestingly, the eight stars came from working-class or poor backgrounds. But they were ambitious, and determined to rise to the top.

Only two remain today, both women. One is an invalid in a sanatorium, and the other still basks in her abiding glory.

THE BEST OF MGM

ADAM'S RIB

1949—101 min.

Producer, Laurence Weingarten; **director,** George Cukor; **story-screenplay,** Garson Kanin and Ruth Gordon; **art directors,** Cedric Gibbons and William Ferrari; **set decorators,** Edwin B. Willis and Henry W. Grace; **music,** Miklos Rozsa; **song,** Cole Porter; **assistant director,** Jack Greenwood; **costumes,** Walter Plunkett; **makeup,** Jack Dawn; **sound,** Douglas Shearer; **special effects,** A. Arnold Gillespie; **camera,** George J. Folsey; **editor,** George Boemler.

Spencer Tracy **(Adam Bonner)**; Katharine Hepburn **(Amanda Bonner)**; Judy Holliday **(Doris Attinger)**; Tom Ewell **(Warren Attinger)**; David Wayne **(Kip Lurie)**; Jean Hagen **(Beryl Caighn)**; Hope Emerson **(Olympia LaPere)**; Eve March **(Grace)**; Clarence Kolb **(Judge Reiser)**; Emerson Treacy **(Jules Frikke)**; Polly Moran **(Mrs. McGrath)**; Will Wright **(Judge Marcasson)**; Elizabeth Flournoy **(Dr. Margaret Brodeigh)**; Janna DaLoos **(Mary, the Maid)**; James Nolan **(Dave)**; David Clarke **(Roy)**; John Maxwell Sholes **(Court Clerk)**; Marvin Kaplan **(Court Stenographer)**; William Self **(Benjamin Klausner)**; Ray Walker **(Photographer)**; Tommy Noonan **(Reporter)**; Sid Dubin **(Amanda's Assistant)**; Joe Bernard **(Mr. Bonner)**; Madge Blake **(Mrs. Bonner)**; Lester Luther **(Judge Poynter)**; Anna Q. Nilsson **(Mrs. Poynter)**; Louis Mason **(Elderly Elevator Operator)**; Paula Raymond **(Emerald)**; Bert Davidson and George Magrill **(Subway Guards)**.

SYNOPSIS

New York County assistant district attorney Adam Bonner is happily married to lawyer wife Amanda, until they face each other as courtroom opponents. Doris Attinger attempts to murder her unfaithful husband, Warren, for his amorous interest in Beryl Caighn. Adam prosecutes Doris while Amanda defends her in a case that is difficult to contain in the courtroom. To complicate further the Bonners' marital malaise during the legal proceedings, a young composer, Kip Lurie, lavishes his attention upon Amanda.

The courtroom battle leads to violent quarrels and conditions reach such a heated state that the Bonners plan to dissolve their business affairs in preparation for a divorce. Each becomes sentimental and realizes that love and mutual concern still exist and they are reunited. Doris receives an acquittal and the victory goes to Amanda, who counters, "I wish it could have been a tie, I really do."

* * *

Though one of the most sparkling tandem vehicles of Spencer Tracy and Katharine Hepburn, **Adam's Rib** actually had an "underground" objective—to flaunt the talents of actress-comedienne Judy Holliday. At the time that Garson Kanin and spouse Ruth Gordon sold their film script, originally titled **Man and Wife,** to Metro for $175,000, Columbia's Harry Cohn was testing actresses for the role of Billie Dawn in the screen version of Kanin's Broadway hit play **Born Yesterday.** (At one point before Columbia outbid them, Metro executives had considered purchasing film rights to the play as a vehicle for Lana Turner and Clark Gable.) Cohn had ordered over thirty actresses to be tested for the part, and had narrowed the assignment down to either reigning Columbia sex queen Rita Hayworth or the play's road company star, Jean Parker. The gruff production chief re-

Advertisement for Adam's Rib *('49).*

1

fused even to test blonde, plump Judy Holliday, who had been starring with Paul Douglas and Gary Merrill in the Broadway version. "With the camera movin' in, she'd drive people out!" growled Cohn of the actress.

So to provide Judy with a showcase in a hit film that could possibly change Cohn's mind, Kanin imported Holliday to Hollywood to play Doris Attinger, the irresistible dumb blonde who tries to murder her husband (Tom Ewell) when she learns of his extramarital adventures. Director Cukor drew delightful performances from the cast, with Miss Hepburn in especially fiery form. She was seen with a new shortcut hairstyle especially designed for her by Sydney Guilaroff to enhance her interpretation of the lady lawyer. In the course of the 101-minute proceedings, she was serenaded by Cole Porter's "Farewell, Amanda" (composed especially for the film) and introduced a spectacle in the courtroom to prove woman's superior competence, by (a) reciting her endless number of academic degrees, (b) calling upon another femme to explain that she has been a plant foreman for seventeen months without a single complaint from her male working staff, and (c) by having vaudeville star Olympia LaPere (Hope Emerson) lift, effortlessly, Tracy over her head in front of the wide-eyed judge (Clarence Kolb).

The film is filled with tailor-made dialogue, suiting the stars' personalities admirably and underscoring both the offscreen personal relationship of Hepburn and Tracy and their rapport as a leading screen team. For example, as the picture's finale approaches and the couple prepare to embark for their country home, Tracy's character employs a well-timed tear to win the ultimate hand. It is a ploy his wife has used frequently in their past arguments.

> HEPBURN: All right, then. What have you proved? What does **that** show?
> TRACY: Shows the score.
> HEPBURN: Shows what I say is true. No difference between the sexes. None. Men, women. The same.
> TRACY: They are, huh?
> HEPBURN: Well, maybe there **is** a difference. But it's a **little** difference.
> TRACY: Yuh. Well, as the French say.
> HEPBURN: How do they say?
> TRACY: "Vive la difference!"
> HEPBURN: Which means?
> TRACY: Which means: "Hurray for that little difference!"

Adam's Rib was released at Christmas time of 1949; one ad heralded it as the "Funniest Picture in 10 Years! It's the Hilarious Answer to Who Wears the Pants!" More restrained but pleased was the **New York Times'** Bosley Crowther, who said that it "isn't solid food but it certainly is meaty and juicy and comically nourishing. . . . Mr. Tracy and Miss Hepburn are the stellar performers in this show and their perfect compatibility in comic capers is delightful to see." As for Judy Holliday, lavished throughout the production with flattering publicity releases at the orders of friends Kanin, Cukor, Tracy, and Hepburn, Crowther in the **Times** pronounced her "simply hilarious." Kanin obtained his objective. On the

strength of **Adam's Rib**, Judy won a Columbia contract and the Billie Dawn role in **Born Yesterday** (1950), for which she would win an Oscar.

In 1972 ABC-TV produced a made-for-television version of **Adam's Rib**, starring Ken Howard and Blythe Danner in the original Tracy and Hepburn assignments. This led to an ABC-TV Friday night series, which premiered with Howard and Danner in September 1973. However, nearly a quarter of a century had passed since the film original. Female liberation was no longer a novel theme and "Adam's Rib" died a quick network death, airing its last on December 28, 1973—two years before the defeat of the Equal Rights Amendment to the Constitution.

ALIAS JIMMY VALENTINE
1928—7,803'

Director, Jack Conway; based on the play by Paul Armstrong; **continuity,** Sarah Y. Mason; **titles,** Joe Farnham; **adapter,** A. P. Younger; **sets,** Cedric Gibbons; **wardrobe,** David Cox; **song,** William Axt, Mort Harris, Raymond Klages, and David Mendoza; **camera,** Merritt B. Gerstad; **editor,** Sam S. Zimbalist.

William Haines (Lee Randall [**alias Jimmy Valentine**]); Lionel Barrymore (**Doyle**); Leila Hyams (**Rose**); Karl Dane (**Swede**); Tully Marshall (**Avery**); Howard Hickman (**Mr. Lane**); Billy Butts (**Bobby**); Evelyn Mills (**Little Sister**).

SYNOPSIS

Jimmy Valentine, adept at cracking safes by relying on his sense of touch, arrives in a small town to rob a bank. His crony is Swede and a confederate on the job is Avery. There he falls in love with the bank president's daughter, Rose. His new romance inspires him to make a fresh start.

With his new name "Lee Randall," Jimmy secures a position with the bank and hopes to marry Rose in the near future. He has been successful in warding off pursuing detective Doyle's questioning when the film's climax occurs. His fiancée's younger sister becomes trapped in the airless safe and only Jimmy's sensitive fingers can unlock it.

Deciding to drop his defense, Jimmy turns to the detective and says, "Turn out the lights, Doyle. I can work better in the dark." Having saved the child, Valentine now fears he has lost Rose.

Then to the safecracker's surprise, Doyle turns to him and says jauntily, "Well, goodbye, Mr. Randall. Glad to have met you."

* * *

It was while Hollywood was undergoing its metamorphosis to sound with much weeping and gnashing of teeth that MGM decided to remake its 1920 silent photoplay success, **Alias Jimmy Valentine,** which had featured Bert Lytell, Vola Vane, and Wilton Taylor. The new version starred William Haines, Leila Hyams, and Lionel Barrymore in the leading parts of the charming safecracker, his fiancée, and the hounding detective.

William Haines and Leila Hyams in Alias Jimmy Valentine *('28).*

The last, in true **Les Miserables** style, allows his prey to go free in the finale.

Under Jack Conway's direction, the new **Alias Jimmy Valentine** was completed as a silent film. However, with talkies the latest rage, Metro's Irving Thalberg ordered Conway to put the feature back into production and to reshoot the last two reels with sound. Because MGM had not yet installed the necessary audio equipment, the **Valentine** company visited Paramount Studios. There, for a handsome fee, the Marathon Street lot played host to its competitor.

In retrospect, it is almost touching to view this fledgling sound effort. The presentation of the early hidden microphone concealed in flower arrangements, lamps, and under tables would later become a cliché in a spoof like **Singin' in the Rain** (1952). But the 1928 **Alias Jimmy Valentine** proved such touches were far from fiction.

Nevertheless, when MGM released its pioneer sound film in the late summer of 1928 (eleven months after the release of Warner Bros.' **The Jazz Singer**), it was proudly advertised as "synchronized with TALK, MUSIC and SOUND." Its promotional campaign boasted such lurid teasers as "Slowly . . . silently . . . ominously . . . the great steel door swung shut, locking within that airless vault a helpless little child—the sister of the girl he loved . . . ." On a more conventional note, of the film's underworld hero it was said that "he could even steal a lady's heart."

Whitney Williams (**Los Angeles Sunday Times**) compared the new, slick entry with its predecessor of 1920: "It is interesting to note, too, that the two pictures have been treated along entirely different lines. The former was strictly dramatic, the latter is a comedy, with bits of drama interpolated here and there."

While **Alias Jimmy Valentine** made a proper box-office showing, MGM was busily installing audio facilities on the Culver City lot. Two soundstages were hastily constructed and soon were filled with casts acting **and** talking to their silver screen audiences.

Ironically, although William Haines, one of Metro's most popular leading men in silents, made a smoothly stylish debut in talkies in this film, his career as an MGM star soon dimmed. It was not because of his lack of acting talent so much as his reputation around Hollywood as a noncloseted homosexual. Louis B. Mayer was so distressed over the spreading rumors about his major star that several times he called Haines to the executive suite to counsel him about his "abnormality," but to no avail. By 1931 Haines had departed MGM and by 1934 he had made his last film, Mascot's **The Marines Are Coming.** Meanwhile, he had immersed himself in the profession of interior decorating, which he very successfully and joyfully practiced until his death at age seventy-six in December 1973.

AN AMERICAN IN PARIS
1951 C—113 min.

Producer, Arthur Freed; **director,** Vincente Minnelli; **story-screenplay,** Alan Jay Lerner; **songs,** Ira and George Gershwin; **orchestrator,** Conrad Salinger; **music directors,** Johnny Green and Saul Chaplin; **choreography,** Gene Kelly and Carol Haney; **color consultants,** Henri Jaffa and James Gooch; **art directors,** Cedric Gibbons and Preston Ames; **set decorators,** Edwin B. Willis and Keogh Gleason; **costumes,** Orry-Kelly and Walter Plunkett; **Beaux Arts Ball costumes,** Plunkett; **ballet costumes,** Irene Sharaff; **makeup,** William Tuttle; **technical adviser,** Alan Antik; **sound,** Douglas Shearer; **montage,** Peter Ballbusch; **special effects,** Warren Newcombe and Irving Ries; **camera,** Alfred Gilks; **ballet camera,** John Alton; **editor,** Adrienne Fazan.

Gene Kelly (**Jerry Mulligan**); Leslie Caron (**Lise Bourvier**); Oscar Levant (**Adam Cook**); Georges Guetary (**Henri Baurel**); Nina Foch (**Milo Roberts**); Eugene Borden (**Georges Mattieu**); Martha Bamattre (**Mathilde Mattieu**); Mary Young (**Old Woman Dancer**); Ann Codee (**Therese**); George Davis (**François**); Hayden Rorke (**Tommy Baldwin**); Paul Maxey (**John McDowd**); Dick Wessel (**Ben Macrow**); Don Quinn and Adele Coray (**Honeymoon Couple**); Alfred Paix (**Postman**); Noel Neill (**American Girl**); Nan Boardman (**Maid**); John Eldredge (**Jack Jansen**); Anna Q. Nilsson (**Kay Jansen**); Madge Blake (**Edna Mae Bestram, the Customer**); Art Dupuis (**Driver**); Greg McClure (**Artist**); André Charisse (**Dancing Partner**).

SYNOPSIS
Ex-GI Jerry Mulligan remains in Paris after World War II to study art and to paint. His Montmartre bon ami Adam Cook, the world's oldest child prodigy, is also an American who appears to be on an endless scholarship in Paris.

Mulligan meets Lise Bourvier and becomes captivated with her youthful beauty and charm as well as confused by her elusiveness. Meanwhile, Mulligan finds a wealthy patroness, Milo Roberts, who purchases two of his paintings and offers to set him up in a studio. In the process Jerry would be added to her collection of lovers. He refuses.

Much to his dismay, Jerry learns later that Lise is engaged to Henri Baurel, a music-hall star who once rescued the girl from the Nazis and has grown to love her as she blossoms into womanhood. At the lavish masked ball Henri discovers that Lise loves Jerry and he steps aside nobly.

The film concludes with a ballet as the picture moves from reality to fantasy. The dance recapitulates Mulligan's plight in losing the girl he now loves. The story is danced out in six different locales, with the connecting symbol being a single rose (representing the girl). At the ballet's finale Mulligan is seen in the same position he had been previously when Lise departed. Now she returns to him. Fade-out.

* * *

It was for good reason that as a climax to the hugely popular **That's Entertainment!** (1974) MGM featured the classic ballet from **An American in Paris,** perhaps the most celebrated of all MGM musicals and the winner of several Academy Awards.

The inspiration for **An American in Paris** grew from producer Arthur Freed's attending (with Ira Gershwin) a concert in which George Gershwin's "American in Paris" suite was performed. Wanting to produce a musical set in Paris, Freed asked to purchase the title and Ira gave his consent, provided that his late brother's music would be used. Contracts were drawn and Freed appointed Vincente Minnelli to direct.

With Gene Kelly announced for the starring role of Jerry Mulligan, Freed devoted ample time to testing and searching for the perfect choices for the other major parts. The role of Henri Baurel was offered originally to Maurice Chevalier; he balked at playing a part in which he lost the girl at the picture's close, and the assignment went to Georges Guetary. Celeste Holm was considered initially for the character of wealthy Milo, but was passed over after screen tests of the less costly Nina Foch showed she had the proper screen quality. Finally, Kelly had seen Leslie Caron in Paris when she was fifteen and a dancer with the Roland Petit Company. She reported for a screen audition and received the key role of Lise Bourvier.

Kelly would speak later of the techniques and philosophies which made **An American in Paris** such a success:

> If the camera is to make any contribution to dance, the focal point must be the pure background, giving the spectator an undistorted and all-encompassing view of dancer and background. To accomplish this end, the camera must be made to move with the dancer, so that the lens becomes the eye of the spectator, your eye. Minnelli, Sharaff [costumer], Chaplin [music director], and I worked in close harmony; none of us made a move without the other. In short, we really tried to make a ballet, not just merely a dance, not a series of beautiful moving tableaux, but an emotional whole, consisting of the combined arts which spell ballet, whether on the screen or on the stage.

The ballet of which Kelly speaks is an eighteen-minute masterpiece, inspired by impressionist canvasses.[1] It employed a backdrop 300 feet long by 40 feet high for the Place de la Concorde and 500 costumes, required six weeks of rehearsals, and cost $542,000—the most expensive production number filmed to that point. The entire feature required fourteen months to shoot at a cost of $2,723,903.

Released on November 9, 1951, **An American in Paris** was immediately heralded as a masterpiece of screen musicals. Bosley Crowther (**New York Times**) insisted, "Count a bewitching French lassie by the name of Leslie Caron and a whoop-de-doo ballet number, one of the finest ever put upon the screen, as the most commendable enchantments of the big, lavish musical film. . . ." **Variety,** "Metro has another sock box-office winner in **An American in Paris.** Film is one of the most imaginative musical confections turned out by Hollywood in years. . . . Full credit goes to director Vincente Minnelli for his meritorious pacing of the story and the sharp way he reins his cast."

---

[1]The six different locales provide segments dominated by the visual styles of painters Dufy, Manet, Utrillo, Rousseau, Van Gogh, and Toulouse-Lautrec.

Gene Kelly and Leslie Caron in An American in Paris *('51).*

The film, though earning no Academy nominations for principal performers, won six Oscars: 1. Story and Screenplay—Alan Jay Lerner, 2. Color Cinematography—Alfred Gilks and John Alton, 3. Art and Set Direction—Cedric Gibbons, Edwin B. Willis, Preston Ames, and Keogh Gleason, 4. Scoring of a Musical Picture—Johnny Green and Saul Chaplin, 5. Costume Design—Orry-Kelly, Irene Sharaff, and Walter Plunkett, and 6. Best Picture.[2]

The Best Picture victory of **An American in Paris** was the first time a musical won the Oscar since **The Great Ziegfeld** (1936). Even more important to MGM, it was the first Metro picture to win in this category since **Mrs. Miniver** (1942). In addition, the Academy presented producer Freed with the Irving G. Thalberg Memorial Award, and Gene Kelly received a special Oscar statuette for "appreciation of his versatility as an actor, singer, director, and dancer, and specifically for his brilliant achievements in the art of choreography on film."

For all its glories, **An American in Paris** was more a critical success than a box-office victory. It grossed $4,000,000 in distributors' domestic rentals, but did not equal the popularity of other Metro 1951 musicals, such as **The Great Caruso** ($4,531,000, thanks to the talents of Mario Lanza) and **Showboat** ($5,533,000).[3]

As for the performing talent in **An American in Paris,** Gene Kelly would continue to shine at MGM until the mid-1950s. For Leslie Caron it was the beginning of a long-lasting international film career. As a result of her Paris screen test for this picture, she had been signed to a Metro contract. While waiting for the film to begin production, she had been cast in Barbara Stanwyck's **The Man with a Cloak** (1951), a rather dreary costume melodrama which MGM did not release until after **An American in Paris.** Of her experiences on the musical, Caron said that "dancing before a camera instead of an audience was very confusing, until I learned to imagine an audience, and then it was all right." Despite the array of mediocre dramas the studio would cast her in, Caron, the French gamine with the delightful pout, had several good musicals in store for her at the lot. Levant, the self-destructive genius of music

and wit, would make two more MGM appearances: **The Band Wagon** (1953) and **The Cobweb** (1955), the latter a study of life at a mental sanatorium. Sadly, Georges Guetary, who made such a hit in **An American in Paris,** would not make another Hollywood picture.

Over the years, **An American in Paris** has been subject to scrutiny and reevaluation by a myriad of sources. Granted it seems today far less sophisticated and innovative than when it premiered, the film nonetheless has a self-contained charm that time cannot destroy. Most sources agree that pianist Levant's self-indulgent performance of the Piano Concerto in F (Levant also is seen working assorted other instruments, conducting, and even applauding himself in the audience) is a poor imitation of a gimmick used to perfection by Buster Keaton in the silent comedy **The Playhouse.** Guetary has his solo, "I'll Build a Stairway to Paradise," which was conceived as a sendoff on the Folies Bergère format, so in conflict with Kelly's theories of the new style of blending music and dance. Kelly, Guetary, and Levant combined talents for "By Strauss," which pokes gentle fun at the old waltz tempo, and "I Got Rhythm" finds smiling Kelly at work with his favorite type of participating audience—small children. The value of having Gallic Guetary and acerbic Levant in the cast is well realized in "Tra-La-La-La-La," in which Gene exudes his joyous love for Caron while the dour cynic Levant stands by in disbelief. "'S Wonderful," on the other hand, is a duet contrasting the screen personalities of Kelly and Guetary, each in love with Caron.

---

[2]**An American in Paris** won the Best Picture Oscar over such contenders as **A Place in the Sun** (Paramount), **A Streetcar Named Desire** (Warner Bros.), and **Quo Vadis** (MGM). **An American in Paris** placed number three on the National Board of Review's Ten Best List, and number three in the **Film Daily**'s Top Ten Pictures chart.

[3]In 1960 Gene Kelly formed Voli Productions to produce telefilms. His first project was to be a thirty-minute series, "An American in Paris," starring Van Johnson. It was to be filmed in Paris, with Michel Legrand composing and conducting the music, but it never materialized.

In **Gene Kelly** (1976), Jeanine Basinger concludes:

One of the loveliest numbers in the entire musical genre is the tender dance between Kelly and Leslie Caron to "Our Love Is Here to Stay." Set in a soft blue-gray mist beside the banks of the Seine, this "falling in love" number beautifully captures the relationship of two people whose thoughts and feelings about each other have already gone beyond words. The only logical way to express their feelings is through the dance, in which they find their tentative way to touching each other, building to a lovely, shared swirl of sensuous feeling. The smoky river fog provides a romantic haze, with the warmth of their skin tones and the yellow fog lights adding color. Their slightly embarrassed conversation is perfect, with Caron's full white skirt in the blue mist a poem of movement all by itself. When Gene Kelly wanted to sing a love lyric, he knew just how to make it right, and this is one of his best vocals.

In 1973 Donald Knox's book **The Magic Factory: How MGM Made "An American in Paris"** was published. It reveals sundry data on the background and formulation of this trend-setting musical, detailing such items as that the eighteen-minute ballet was put into production to make use of the sudden delay in shooting when Nina Foch contracted chicken pox.

Kathryn Grayson, Frank Sinatra, and Gene Kelly in Anchors Aweigh *('45).*

ANCHORS AWEIGH

1945 C—145 min.

Producer, Joseph Pasternak; **director,** George Sidney; **story idea,** Natalie Marcin; **screenplay,** Isobel Lennart; **Technicolor consultants,** Natalie Kalmus and Henri Jaffa; **art directors,** Cedric Gibbons and Randall Duell; **set decorators,** Edwin B. Willis and Richard Pefferle; **vocal arranger,** Earl Brent; **orchestrator,** Axel Stordahl; **songs,** Jule Styne and Sammy Cahn; Ralph Freed and Sammy Fain; **assistant director,** George Rheim; **sound,** Douglas Shearer; **camera,** Robert Planck and Charles Boyle; **editor,** Adrienne Fazan.

Gene Kelly **(Joseph Brady);** Frank Sinatra **(Clarence Doolittle);** Kathryn Grayson **(Susan Abott);** Jose Iturbi **(Himself);** Dean Stockwell **(Donald Martin);** Carlos Ramirez **(Carlos);** Henry O'Neill **(Admiral Hammond);** Leon Ames **(Commander);** Rags Ragland **(Police Sergeant);** Edgar Kennedy **(Police Captain);** Pamela Britton **(Girl from Brooklyn);** Henry Armetta **(Hamburger Man);** Billy Gilbert **(Cafe Manager);** Sharon McManus **(Little Girl Beggar);** James Burke **(Studio Cop);** Chester Clute **(Iturbi's Assistant);** James Flavin **(Radio Cop);** Grady Sutton **(Bertram Kramer);** Tom and Jerry **(Cartoon Specialty);** Peggy Maley **(Lana Turner Double);** Sondra Rodgers **(Iturbi's Secretary);** Steve Brodie and Garry Owen **(Soldiers);** William Forrest **(Movie Director);** Renie Riano **(Waitress);** Ray Teal **(Assistant Movie Director);** Milton Kibbee **(Bartender).**

SYNOPSIS

Sailors Clarence Doolittle and Joseph Brady sing and dance their way through a four-day Hollywood leave. Shy Doolittle receives lessons in the art of the pickup from brash Brady. Among the girls they encounter is a Brooklyn waitress who works in a Mexican restaurant. She is "the kind of girl a guy brings four bottles of beer to. . . ."

Trouble arises when the duo rescue sailor-loving tyke Donald Martin and return him to his initially austere aunt, Susan Abbott. She is a movie extra with vocal ambitions. Both Clarence and Joseph fall in love with Susan and they seek to get her an audition with piano virtuoso Jose Iturbi.

In the process, Doolittle ends up with the Brooklyn waitress and Brady wins the love of Susan. Little Donald is pleased by his aunt's choice.

"What was I then? A crooner who'd been singing for a big band for seven years and whose only claim to fame was that girls swooned whenever I opened my mouth." So quipped Frank Sinatra of MGM's **Anchors Aweigh,** the film that won the singer true cinema stardom after some minor screen work mostly elsewhere.[1] The musical also established Gene Kelly as a major movie actor/

---

[1]Sinatra had appeared as a singer with Tommy Dorsey and His Orchestra in the Eleanor Powell–Red Skelton spy spoof **Ship Ahoy** (1942) at Metro.

singer/dancer/choreographer and earned him an Oscar bid. Moreover, the film boosted the stock of studio soprano Kathryn Grayson, won a Best Picture Oscar nomination, and grossed $4,500,000 in distributors' domestic rentals.

Produced by Joe Pasternak, who specialized in the boy-meets-girl film, **Anchors Aweigh** was a hodgepodge of talent: Sinatra, crooning "What Makes the Sunset?" "Brahms Lullaby," "The Charm of You," and, in the Hollywood Bowl setting, "I Fall in Love Too Easily." With Kelly he duets the mocking "We Hate to Leave," dances to "I Begged Her," and duets the comic "If You Knew Susie" (geared to remove Grayson's 4-F date Grady Sutton from the picture). The often too patrician Kathryn Grayson vocalizes "All of a Sudden My Heart Sings" and "Jalousie," and Jose Iturbi plays and conducts "The Donkey Serenade," "Piano Concerto," and "Hungarian Rhapsody No. 2."

Most memorably, within the film there is Kelly's Mexican Hat Dance with somber-faced little Sharon McManus and his famous live-action and animated dance with the "Tom and Jerry" cartoon characters. A major number is Kelly's interpretive dancing to "La Cumparsita" in which, decked out in period costume, he imagines himself to be a swashbuckling hero who climbs the balcony to claim the princess (Grayson). The sequence—shot on a movie studio Spanish village set—foreshadows Kelly's "Mack the Black" number in **The Pirate** (1948).

Within **Anchors Aweigh,** which boasted Technicolor and fine direction by George Sidney, there are many diversions: Dean Stockwell as an ingratiating child performer who had joined the MGM stock company; and character players Leon Ames as the Commander, Rags Ragland as the Police Sergeant, Edgar Kennedy as the Police Captain, Henry Armetta as the Hamburger Man, and Billy Gilbert as the Cafe Manager—all making delightful comic contributions. Not to be overlooked is the multihued photography of Robert Planck and Charles Boyle.

There were a few problems on the set, especially with Sinatra. He rebelled against a longstanding MGM mandate: that performers were not allowed to watch the daily rushes of their scenes (actors, reasoned the studio, were never pleased by the rushes, often became upset by them, and frequently demanded that certain scenes be redone). After threatening to walk off the film, Sinatra convinced Pasternak to allow him to study the dailies. The producer complied after Sinatra promised not to bring anybody else to see them. The singer arrived with six friends in tow.

Anchors Aweigh was released in August 1945,[2] near perfect entertainment for the war-winning U.S. public and a delight to most critics. **Cue** wrote, "Produced with typically lavish Technicolor musical extravagance, MGM's biggest and best musical film of the year is a generous package of mirth and music—overflowing with comedy, songs, dances, and revue numbers, with bright lines and amusing situations. . . ." The **New York Times** said, "Mr. Kelly is the Apollonian marvel of the piece, dancing, singing, and performing in a delightfully gay and graceful style. And Miss Grayson is not far behind him, with her winsome manner and truly lyric voice. But bashful Frankie is a large-sized contributor to the general fun and youthful charm of the show."

Anchors Aweigh won an Academy Best Picture nomination, but lost to Paramount's **The Lost Weekend.** And Gene Kelly received a Best Actor nomination, but bowed to Ray Milland in his **The Lost Weekend** triumph. The musical became the studio's number-two moneymaker (number one was the Garson-Peck **Valley of Decision**) of the 1944–45 season. It was a time frame in which such big grossers as the two above-mentioned entries as well as **Meet Me in St. Louis, Mrs. Parkington, Music for Millions, National Velvet, Thirty Seconds over Tokyo, Thrill of a Romance,** and **Without Love** made solid contributions to the $175,000,000 gross of Loew's Inc.

Sinatra, who gained an MGM pact as a result of **Anchors Aweigh,** was just entering his first peak period of filmmaking. He would join Gene Kelly for Metro's **Take Me Out to the Ball Game** and **On the Town,** both 1949 hit releases. His only rematch with Kathryn Grayson proved to be the nadir of his Metro tenure, the dismal **The Kissing Bandit** (1948).

---

[2]Principal photography on **Anchors Aweigh** was completed in 1944, but due to the technical requirements—especially the dancing scene between Gene Kelly and the cartoon mouse Jerry—the musical was not released until late summer of 1945.

ANNA CHRISTIE
1930—74 min.

Director, Clarence Brown; based on the play by Eugene O'Neill; **adapter,** Frances Marion; **titles,** Madeleine Ruthven; **art director,** Cedric Gibbons; **gowns,** Adrian; **sound,** G. A. Burns and Douglas Shearer; **camera,** William Daniels; **editor,** Hugh Wynn.

Greta Garbo **(Anna Christie);** Charles Bickford **(Matt);** George F. Marion **(Chris);** Marie Dressler **(Marthy);** James T. Mack **(Johnny the Harp);** Lee Phelps **(Larry).**

SYNOPSIS

When Anna is a child her father, Chris, leaves her on a farm with relatives while he follows the sailor's life. Anna runs away when she becomes older and eventually becomes a prostitute. During a low point in her existence she goes to Chris for help and he allows her to live aboard his fishing barge. There Anna meets a rough-and-tumble older version of herself, the good-natured tramp Marthy, who is Chris's mistress.

A rescued sailor, Matt Burke, falls in love with Anna. The two are happy until Anna, angry at her father's earlier negligence, reveals the truth about her sordid background. Matt departs but cannot forget Anna. He later returns and of-

Greta Garbo and James T. Mack in Anna Christie *('30).*

fers to wed her, swearing his love to her on a cross.

* * *

"GARBO TALKS!" The words became American folklore in 1930 as audiences had the opportunity of hearing as well as seeing the screen's most worshipped creature. It is many minutes into the storyline before Garbo's character makes her entrance. Sporting a world-weary smirk, her body clad in rather simplistic garb, she enters a waterfront saloon and speaks to a bored bartender and a waiting world, "Gimme a visky with chincher aile on the side—and don't be stingy, baby." Hence with her twelfth MGM feature, Garbo gracefully traversed the formidable gap between silents and talkies, a chasm into which so many of her coleads had toppled.[1] It served to perpetuate her career as Hollywood's most idolized woman.

The property selected with such care by Metro was the Eugene O'Neill drama that had premiered at the Vanderbilt Theatre on November 2, 1921, starring Pauline Lord in her greatest stage triumph. The show lasted 177 performances, winning a Pulitzer Prize for drama. In 1923 there was a silent-film version starring Blanche Sweet and released by First National.

For the new edition, Charles Bickford[2] was assigned to play Anna's tough lover. George F. Marion, who had played the ne'er-do-well Chris in both the Broadway and silent-film renditions, was hired to repeat his role, and, on the advice of scripter Frances Marion, her pal Marie Dressler was rescued from near nadir by being cast as Marthy.

Clarence Brown, who had twice before directed Garbo, was entrusted to handle this film. Irving Thalberg ordered him to supervise two weeks of script rehearsal before actual shooting began. Garbo disliked the prospect, but agreed, once promised that shooting would end each afternoon at five. (When Garbo would first hear herself in the rushes, she was not charmed by the deep, sensual tones which greeted her. The star's only comment was "My God, is that my voice?")

However, when the picture debuted in March 1930 with such ad teasers as "Caught in the throbbing current of life and love on the East River waterfront" and "A bit of human flotsam on the current of life and love," the international press and audiences were far more impressed than was Garbo. Mordaunt Hall (**New York Times**) decided, "One soon becomes accustomed to Miss Garbo's surprisingly low intonations. She is a real Anna, who at once enlists sympathy for her hard life. The words and expressions of this girl make one think of her in character, and cause one almost to forget she is Miss Garbo. . . . Here she is a Swedish girl to whom life has been anything but kind and who for that reason at the age of thirty is bitterly cynical. . . . All this is splendidly acted by Miss Garbo who proves here that she can handle a forceful role with little or no relief in its dull atmosphere just as well as she can play the part of the fashionably dressed, romantic wife of a money lawyer." Richard Watts, Jr. (**New York Herald-Tribune**) approved of Garbo's cinematic "glamour" and judged the film "accurate, handsomely produced, well acted, and faithfully managed . . . there is never anything commonplace about **Anna Christie**."

An outstanding box-office triumph,[3] **Anna Christie** placed fifth on **Film Daily**'s Ten Best List for the year, and Garbo was nominated for a Best Actress Oscar (she lost to Norma Shearer of MGM's **The Divorcee**). The film won a fresh screen career for Marie Dressler who received a new MGM contract and soon became the favorite thespian of Louis B. Mayer. For the studio it provided additional prestige, demonstrating how a film company could transform a controversial play into mature screen fare. Shot on a twenty-day schedule at a cost of $376,000, it drew a $576,000 profit.

On February 7, 1938, Joan Crawford and Spencer Tracy starred in the "Lux Radio Theatre" version of **Anna Christie**, with Marjorie Rambeau and George F. Marion in support. Although the original O'Neill play has not yet experienced another Hollywood screen version, it has remained a frequently revived play, notably: 1952, with Celeste Holm and Kevin McCarthy; 1977, with Liv Ullmann and Mary McCarty. In 1957 a musical version, **New Girl in Town**, played Broadway, with Gwen Verdon and Thelma Ritter in the leads.

---

[1] As Hollywood would do with Tallulah Bankhead, the studio attempted to raise Garbo's vocal register on the soundtrack.

[2] Bickford made his film debut in MGM's **Dynamite**, directed by Cecil B. DeMille. After a very impressive Broadway career, the actor seemed destined for great success in Hollywood. However, he was extremely outspoken and one of his prime targets was his studio boss, Louis B. Mayer. The latter retaliated by loaning Bickford to other companies for mediocre projects, or allowing him to remain idle on the home lot. The making of **Anna Christie** came during a reprieve in the Bickford-Mayer ongoing fight. The height of the feud occurred during the filming of MGM's **The Sea Bat**, during which Bickford called Mayer "a venomous little junk peddler" and a "posturing little ignoramus."

Mayer had the final word, refusing to assign Bickford to a prime role in **The Big House** or to loan him to RKO for **Cimarron** (1931) or to Warner Bros. for **The Maltese Falcon** (1931). Bickford would continue to work in Hollywood, but always as the lead of low-budget films or, later, as a featured player.

[3] Jacques Feyder directed the German-language version of **Anna Christie** (1930) which starred Garbo, Hans Junkermann (Matt), Salka Viertel (Marthy), and Theo Shall (Chris).

ANNA KARENINA
1935—95 min.

Producer, David O. Selznick; **director,** Clarence Brown; based on the novel by Leo Tolstoy; **screenplay,** Clemence Dane and Salka Viertel; **adapter-dialogue,** S. N. Behrman; **collaborator,** Erich von Stroheim; **art directors,** Cedric Gibbons and Fredric Hope; **set decorator,** Edwin B. Willis; **music,** Herbert Stothart; **ballet staged by** Margarete Wallmann; **mazurka staged by** Chester Hale; **vocal and choral effects,** Russian Symphony Choir; **consultant,** Count Andrey Tolstoy; **technical adviser,** von Stroheim; **assistant director,** Charlie Dorian; **costumes,** Adrian; **sound,** Douglas Shearer; **camera,** William Daniels; **editor,** Robert J. Kern.

Greta Garbo (**Anna Karenina**); Fredric March (**Count Alexei Vronsky**); Maureen O'Sullivan (**Kitty**); May Robson (**Countess Vronsky**); Constance Collier (**Countess Lidia**); Reginald Owen (**Stiva**); Freddie Bartholomew (**Sergei Karenin**); Basil Rathbone (**Alexei Karenin**); Phoebe Foster (**Dolly**); Reginald Denny (**Captain Nicki Yashvin**); Gyles Isham (**Levin**); Buster Phelps (**Grisha**); Ella Ethridge (**Anna's Maid**); Sidney Bracy (**Vronsky's Valet**); Cora Sue Collins (**Tania**); Olaf Hytten (**Butler**); Joseph Tozer (**Butler**); Guy D'Ennery (**Ivanovich, the Tutor**); Ethel Griffies (**Mme. Kartasoff**); Mary Forbes (**Princess Sorokino**); Mischa Auer (**Mahotin**); Dennis O'Keefe (**Best Man**); Joan Marsh (**Lily**); Sarah Padden (**Governess**); Betty Blythe (**Woman**); Robert Warwick (**Colonel**); Francis McDonald, Larry Steers, and Harry Cording (**Officers at Banquet**); Gino Corrado (**Waiter**); Mahlon Hamilton (**Colonel**).

SYPNOSIS

In nineteenth-century Russia the hauntingly lovely Anna Karenina resides with her wealthy government-official husband, Alexei Karenin. The couple's marriage has been blessed by a young son, Sergei, who is the primary joy of his mother's domestic life.

Anna goes to town to visit her philandering brother Stiva in an attempt to salvage his marriage to Dolly. While away from home, Anna meets and falls in love with handsome Count Alexei Vronsky. She returns to her husband and child but continues to rendezvous with her lover. When Anna later begs Karenin for a divorce, he refuses. He fears a scandal would taint his career and make him society's fool. He informs Anna that if she should become Vronsky's mistress, he will forbid her ever to see Sergei again. Torn between two loves, Anna cannot surrender Vronsky and she departs with her lover.

Because he has flouted polite society by his flagrant romance with Anna, Vronsky has been requested to leave the military. He and Anna spend beautiful moments together in "exile" in Italy. But he soon feels pulled toward the army again. He misses the camaraderie and the prospects of participating in the glories of the pending Turkish-Serbian war. After a quarrel with Anna he rejoins his elitist military unit. In the meantime, Anna has made a secret visit to her home to see Sergei.

Anna follows Vronsky to the train station to apologize to him for their disagreements. There she observes his stately mother introducing him to an attractive, socially proper young woman. At that moment Anna suddenly realizes she has lost everything that is important to her. Distraught, she throws herself onto the tracks in the path of an oncoming train.

* * *

Greta Garbo, May Robson, and Fredric March in Anna Karenina *('35).*

Thus it was a very unhappy David O. Selznick who went on to produce **Anna Karenina**, the intractable Greta's selection as her next Metro vehicle. The astute Selznick had carefully noted that both Garbo's **Queen Christina** (1933) and **The Painted Veil** (1934)—her latest films after returning from vowed retirement—had been disappointing; that Paramount had been indulging Marlene Dietrich in such costume entries as **Song of Songs** (1933) and **The Scarlet Empress** (1934); and that Samuel Goldwyn's **Nana** (1934) had been a disaster. Garbo, who held very fond memories of **Love** (1927),[1] the silent version of Tolstoy's tragic novel, insisted on a reprise. Fortunately, it was produced[2] with such style, taste, and elegant dramatics that it became another critical triumph for Garbo, Selznick, and the studio and one of Metro's top grossers of the 1935–36 season.

Because George Cukor was so resentful that Garbo chose not to do **Dark Victory**, Selznick thought it wise to replace him on **Anna Karenina** with director Clarence Brown. There were also scripting problems to be dealt with, as the vigilant Legion of Decency was aghast at the prospect of a new filming of Tolstoy's novel of 1875 with its daring theme of a woman sacrificing willingly her husband and position for her lover (by whom, in the book, she has an illegitimate child.) Selznick hired Clemence Dane (of **A Bill of Divorcement**) and Salka Viertel to circumvent the censors and provide an appeasing scenario.

The cast selected for the costume drama was superb. Besides the reluctant March, Selznick enlisted Metro ingenue Maureen O'Sullivan[3] as Kitty who loses her Vronsky to Anna's charms, Freddie Bartholomew (title role actor of Selznick's **David Copperfield**, 1935) as Anna's beloved tyke

---

January 7, 1935

Miss Greta Garbo
La Quinta, California

Dear Miss Garbo:

I was extremely sorry to hear this morning that you had left for Palm Springs, because we must arrive at an immediate decision, which, I think, will have a telling effect on your entire career.

As I told you the other day, we have lost our enthusiasm for a production of **Anna Karenina** as your next picture. I personally feel that audiences are waiting to see you in a smart modern picture and that to do a heavy Russian drama on the heels of so many ponderous, similar films, in which they have seen you and other stars recently, would prove to be a mistake. . . .

Mr. [George] Cukor shares my feeling and it seems a pity that we must start our first joint venture with you with such a lack of enthusiasm and such an instinct of dread for the outcome. . . .

. . . if I act very quickly, I can purchase

Dark Victory, the owners of which have resisted offers from several companies for many months. The play is at the top of the list at several studios and if we do not purchase it, the likelihood is that it will be purchased for Katharine Hepburn. . . .

Fredric March will only do **Anna Karenina** if he is forced to by his employers, Twentieth Century Pictures. He has told me repeatedly that he is fed up on doing costume pictures; that he thinks it a mistake to do another; that he knows he is much better in modern subjects. . . . We are doubly fortunate in finding in **Dark Victory** that the male lead is also strikingly well suited to Mr. March.

For all these reasons, I request and most earnestly urge you to permit us to switch from **Anna Karenina** to **Dark Victory** and you will have a most enthusiastic producer and director, respectively, in the persons of myself and Mr. Cukor.

. . . I will be very disappointed, indeed, if you do not agree with our conclusions.

Most cordially and sincerely yours,
David O. Selznick

---

[1]The original version, **Love,** was directed by Edmund Goulding. It featured John Gilbert as Vronsky, Brandon Hurst as Karenin, and Philippe DeLacy as Sergei. The film was made with alternate endings. In one, Anna commits suicide at the railroad station; in the other (used for general release and the one seen in today's television prints), Anna and Vronsky are reunited happily, when they each happen to visit her son on the same day at his military school.

[2]Richard Corliss in **Greta Garbo** (1974) was not pleased with the mounting. "To judge by his work here . . . Clarence Brown should have been directing royal wedding processions instead of movies. **Anna Karenina** is weighed down with 'living tableaux' in static long shot. Other shots are held longer than necessary so that we may appreciate Cedric Gibbons' handiwork and David O. Selznick's largesse. But this tactic backfires because the sets speak more of excess than of pure extravagance—and because we really only want to see Garbo anyway."

[3]Interviewed years later, O'Sullivan would remember, "I did not have very much contact with Garbo during the making of **Anna Karenina**. I liked her; she was nice, very beautiful. As an actress, she gave you very little. In other words, it was a love affair between her and the camera. In fact, when working with her one felt she was doing nothing really, that she wasn't even very good, until you saw the results on the screen and you realised the love affair she had with the camera. The camera with her was quite extraordinary. I think she was just a natural."

Sergei, and Basil Rathbone (**Copperfield**'s hateful Mr. Murdstone) as the unyielding and formidable Karenin. Also involved in the filming was none other than Erich von Stroheim, not as an actor but as a script collaborator and a technical adviser. In addition to the powerful acting ensemble, **Anna Karenina** features an opulent opera ballet staged by Margarete Wallmann (which few of the cast are watching when the illicit lovers Anna and Vronsky enter their opera box) and a fanciful mazurka, a lengthy but charming dance number staged by Chester Hale.

Selznick released **Anna Karenina** in the late summer of 1935.[4] He wondered fearfully[5] if critics and audiences would be too much aware of the absence of on-camera rapport between Garbo and March. (Allegedly, whenever March attempted to become too amorous on the set in preparation for a love scene, the very reserved Garbo would hastily bite on a piece of garlic to keep her screen colead at arm's length.)

Fortunately, the fourth estate was duly impressed with the presentation. Andre Sennwald (**New York Times**) was agog at the new maturity which MGM brought to Tolstoy's work:

Having put on a couple of mental years since the 1927 version of **Anna Karenina,** which called itself **Love** and meant it, the cinema now is able to stab tentatively below the surface of Tolstoy's passion tales and hint at the social criticism which is so implicit in them. . . . **Anna Karenina** widens the iris of the camera so as to link the plight of the lovers to the decadent and hypocritical society which doomed them. The photoplay is a dignified and effective drama which becomes significant because of that tragic, lonely, and glamorous blend which is the Garbo personality.

The star herself, whose acting was nearing an immaculate flawlessness, collected a bouquet of tributes: "Garbo's haunting beauty is what you'll remember about **Anna Karenina**" (**New York Sun**); "The persuasive genius of Garbo raises [the film] into the class of art" (**Photoplay**); "Garbo's greatness as supreme star of the screen is here exhibited for all who have eyes to see, ears to hear, and imagination to be stirred" (**Picture Play**).

Though there were no major Academy Award nominations for **Anna Karenina**, the motion picture supplied a potent elixir to Garbo's position as the screen's greatest beauty and actress and joined **Broadway Melody of 1936, The Great Zieg-**feld, **A Night at the Opera, Rose-Marie, San Francisco,** and **A Tale of Two Cities** as MGM's top moneymakers of the season.

Although **Anna Karenina** bequeaths to Garbo disciples some of their most cherished movie moments—especially her introduction, appearing gradually from behind wisps of train smoke, and her suicide as she disappears under the wheels of a departing train in the lonely darkness of the station—the film supplied Basil Rathbone with less-happy memories of the star. In his autobiography, **In and Out of Character** (1962), he related:

From the first day to the last we were just Anna and Karenin to one another, and I gave one of the best performances of my life, thanks largely to the inspiration I derived from Miss Garbo. On the last day that we worked together we were seated next to one another waiting to be "called." I turned ever so slightly for a last look at that beautiful face. She sat motionless, intense, there was not so much as the flicker of an eyelid. She might have been a wax figure of herself in Madame Tussaud's. Suddenly I heard myself saying desperately, but with the utmost control, "Miss Garbo, I wonder if you would grant me a very great favor. When I work with anyone I admire as much as I admire you I ask for the privilege of a signed photograph. I have one here that will help me to remember this wonderful experience in playing opposite you. Would you sign it for me?"

There was a moment's pause, and then, without a movement, she said, "I never give picture."

I was both confused and hurt, and try as I will I have never quite forgiven her. To me and to everyone else that I know who has met her, Miss Garbo remains an enigma. Perhaps it is that none of us really know her; but the most interesting aspect would seem to be, does Miss Garbo know herself?

ANNIE GET YOUR GUN
1950 C—107 min.

Producer, Arthur Freed; **director,** George Sidney; based on the play by Irving Berlin and Herbert and Dorothy Fields; **screenplay,** Sidney Sheldon; **music numbers staged by** Robert Alton; **music director,** Adolph Deutsch; **songs,** Berlin; **women's costumes,** Helen Rose and Walter Plunkett; **men's costumes,** Plunkett; **makeup,** Jack Dawn; **art directors,** Cedric Gibbons and Paul Groesse; **set decorators,** Edwin B. Willis and Richard A. Pefferle; **color consultants,** Henri Jaffa and James Gooch; **sound,** Douglas Shearer; **special effects,** A. Arnold Gillespie and Warren Newcombe; **montage,** Peter Ballbusch; **camera,** Charles Rosher; **editor,** James E. Newcom.

Betty Hutton (**Annie Oakley**); Howard Keel (**Frank Butler**); Louis Calhern (**Buffalo Bill**); J. Carrol Naish (**Sitting Bull**); Edward Arnold (**Pawnee Bill**); Keenan Wynn (**Charlie Davenport**); Benay Venuta (**Dolly Tate**); Clinton Sundberg (**Foster Wilson**); James H. Harrison (**Mac**); Bradley Mora (**Little Jake**); Diana Dick (**Nellie**); Susan Odin (**Jessie**); Eleanor Brown (**Minnie**); Chief Yowlachie (**Little Horse**); Robert Malcolm (**Conductor**); Lee Tung Foo (**Waiter**); William Tannen (**Barker**); Anne O'Neal (**Miss Willoughby**); Evelyn Beresford (**Queen Victoria**); John Hamilton (**Ship Captain**); William Bill Hall (**Tall Man**); Edward Earle (**Footman**); Marjorie Wood (**Constance**); Elizabeth Flournoy (**Helen**); Mae Clarke (**Mrs. Adams**); Frank Wilcox (**Mr. Clay**); Andre Charlot (**President Loubet of France**); Nino Pipitone (**King Victor Emmanuel**); John Mylong (**Kaiser Wilhelm II**); Carl Sepulveda, Carol Henry, and Fred Gilman (**Cowboys**).

SYNOPSIS

Headlining Buffalo Bill's Wild West Show is Frank Butler, a champion sharpshooter. When the spectacle show plays Cincinnati, Ohio, the company meets backwoods girl Annie Oakley, a crack shot.

Annie quickly falls in love with Frank and accepts a position with Buffalo Bill's show as an assistant, to be near the dashing gunman. Frank finds himself emotionally attached to Annie, but his pride is hurt when his act is superseded by Annie's extravagant new show routine.

Frank quits the act and teams with rival showman Pawnee Bill who also represents Sitting Bull. The Indian, meanwhile, becomes enamored of Annie and adopts her as a daughter. Later he provides the financial backing for a European tour. Buffalo Bill's show is a personal triumph for Annie, but the showman loses money and returns to America broke. He hopes to effect a merger with Pawnee Bill.

With the two shows merged successfully, Annie and Frank are reunited after a "rigged" shooting match results in Annie losing the contest but winning Frank.

* * *

Phoebe Annie Oakley Mozie was born in a log cabin in Ohio in 1860. By the time she expired in 1926 she had weaved for herself a legend that would make the name Annie Oakley one of the most colorful names in Western folklore.

In 1935 the cinema took its first major step in perpetuating Annie's legend with the release of RKO's **Annie Oakley,** starring Barbara Stanwyck in the title role and Preston Foster as her sharpshooting romance Frank Butler. However, it was not until eleven years later, May 16, 1946, that all of America became Oakley-conscious with the premiere of Broadway's **Annie Get Your Gun.** The musical comedy starred Ethel Merman and Ray Middleton, with tunes by Irving Berlin and a book by Herbert and Dorothy Fields. With its rousing score—boasting "Anything You Can Do," "Doin' What Comes Naturally," and "There's No Business Like Show Business" among the principal songs—and Merman's overpowering portrayal, the show played 1,147 performances and inspired endless speculation concerning a movie version.

MGM, as all expected, delivered the best offer—$650,000 for the screen rights—and pre-

---

[4]The publicity campaign for **Anna Karenina** enthused, "No one but Tolstoy could have written the tender, poignant romance of a love which knew no middle ground. No one but lovely Garbo could have portrayed the heroine with such power to thrill a romance-hungry world. No one but MGM could have given it the magnificent production it deserves."

[5]Selznick judged that the leisurely buildup of the stars' love affair was too slow-paced even for this deliberately metered photoplay. He had scenes deleted from the early segments of the feature. For example, there are extant stills of Garbo's Anna seated at a large banquet table with military officer friends of Vronsky. This scene, among others, is not in the release print.

J. Carroll Naish and Betty Hutton in Annie Get Your Gun *('50).*

pared the spectacle as a vehicle for Judy Garland[1] under the direction of Busby Berkeley. New Metro contractee Howard Keel, signed by the lot after his success as Curly in the London company of **Oklahoma!,** won the flamboyant assignment of Frank Butler. Geraldine Wall was cast as Dolly, Annie's rival for Frank's attentions; and Metro character stars Frank Morgan, J. Carrol Naish, Keenan Wynn, and Edward Arnold were added as (respectively) Buffalo Bill, Chief Sitting Bull, fast-talking agent Charlie Davenport, and competing showman Pawnee Bill.

However, as W. C. Fields would say, "Things happened." **Annie Get Your Gun** became one of the more epic of film production disasters in Metro's history. Although the motion picture was eventually completed and would earn a stout profit ($4,650,000 just in U.S. and Canadian distributors' rentals), there were many times when Culver City was about to cancel the seemingly doomed feature. The disasters, in chronological order:

1. Production on the color film began April 4, 1949. On April 5, Howard Keel's horse falls while Howard is in the saddle. The actor's ankle is shattered and director Berkeley is forced to shoot around Keel for six weeks.

2. May 3, 1949: Busby Berkeley is fired by producer Arthur Freed after the veteran MGM producer-songwriter views the rushes. "Buzz had no

conception of what the picture was all about," said Freed. "He was shooting the whole thing like a stage play. Everyone would come out of the wings, say their lines and back away upstage for their exits." Charles Walters replaces Berkeley.

3. May 10, 1949: Judy Garland is suspended from MGM for her unprofessional behavior—calling in sick (without proof of ailment), leaving work early, performing in a most disjointed, nervous fashion, etc. She is removed from **Annie Get Your Gun.** (She had already prerecorded the score, which years later would be released in an LP album; her already filmed scenes would become collectors' items in the home-movie market.) Judy enters Boston's Peter Bent Brigham Hospital for treatment of her emotional and drug-addiction problems. The studio pays her bills and sends her flowers. She is later heartbroken to discover that the film is proceeding without her.

4. Many replacements for Garland are considered, including some actresses suggested when the property was first acquired: Republic's Judy Canova, Warner Bros.' Doris Day, and MGM's own Betty Garrett (whose studio contract has just expired). Instead, MGM borrows Paramount's bombastic blonde bombshell, Betty Hutton, whose explosive, hoydenish talents have won her a large following of fans and whose blistering ego has won her a large number of enemies. Says Hutton of the stellar assignment, "Frankly, I know a lot of people don't want me to play this."

5. Mid-August 1949: Charles Walters' Metro contract expires. As he enters negotiations for a new one, George Sidney, long lusting to helm the **Annie** project, convinces Louis B. Mayer and Dore Schary to give him the directorial chores.

6. September 18, 1949: Frank Morgan, a

Metro contractee for sixteen years, suffers a fatal heart attack. Louis Calhern replaces him as Buffalo Bill and all of Morgan's footage must be reshot. Shortly afterward, Benay Venuta replaces no longer available Geraldine Wall and the original children picked to play Annie's siblings have all matured so much in the past six months that they must be replaced.

Finally, on October 10, 1949, George Sidney begins shooting the revamped picture and, forty-six filming days later, on December 16, 1949, **Annie Get Your Gun** reaches completion. Total cost: $3,768,785. The most expensive sequence is the rodeo finale which covered five and a half acres of backlot ground and demanded one of the largest Hollywood casting calls: 1,000 actors, 165 horses, 25 trick riders, and 50 sharpshooters.

Amazingly, all the headaches inspired by the **Annie** horrors were soothed when **Annie Get Your Gun** entered national distribution in the spring of 1950—almost exactly a year after its troubled beginning. **Time** magazine treated Betty Hutton to a cover story, and noted, "Thanks to the irrepressible Betty Hutton, Irving Berlin's fine ten-song score, and a showmanlike production, **Annie Get Your Gun** should leave moviegoers feeling they have been entertained. Brimming with colorful costumes and extravagant, Hollywood-style Wild West shows." All of the major supporting actors, especially J. Carrol Naish[2]—a particular joy as the red man who booms, "No put money in show business!"—were delightful, perfectly complementing Hutton's dynamics and Keel's virility.

Of Berlin's original Broadway score for **Annie,** "Moonshine Lullaby" and "I Got Lost in His Arms" were not used for the filming, and Berlin's newly created[3] "Let's Go West Again," which was added to the picture's repertoire for Garland, then Hutton, to sing, was deleted from the completed production. (If it had been up to Dore Schary, the all-important shooting-match sequence would have been cut or greatly pared down in the film. He could not comprehend its relevance to the plot-line!)

There were segments of the filmgoing audience who preferred Hutton's enthusiastic rendition of "You Can't Get a Man with a Gun," "Doin' What Comes Naturally," or "I'm an Indian Too" (the latter executed in mock Fanny Brice style). Others endorsed Keel's slick interpretation of "The Girl That I Marry" or "My Defenses Are Down." But there were few doubts among viewers that the duets[4] of Hutton and Keel were on target: "Anything You Can Do," "They Say It's Wonderful," and the crowd-pleasing finale number, "There's No Business Like Show Business."

This boisterous tribute to buckskin entertainers would receive an Oscar for Best Scoring (Adolph Deutsch and Roger Edens) for a musical

---

[1]In typical Hollywood tradition, neither the role's creator (Merman) nor her famous and talented replacement (Mary Martin) in the national road company were serious contenders for the screen role. They were not considered big enough box-office attractions nor suitably young for the part.

[2]He would again play the Indian chief in the potboiler **Sitting Bull** (1954).

[3]When **Annie Get Your Gun** was revived at Lincoln Center in New York in 1966 with Ethel Merman, Irving Berlin saluted the occasion by adding to the score "An Old-Fashioned Wedding."

[4]Actually Keel did **not** enjoy working with Hutton, finding her too ego-conscious, impetuous, and improvidently demanding.

picture. The zesty picture would help to revitalize the public's love of screen musicals, encouraging MGM to produce a host of top song-and-dance films over the next several years. While Betty Hutton would return to Paramount and then drift into later film retirement, Howard Keel would prove a boon to the Metro lot. He became a pivotal performing force in the MGM musicals of the fifties.

In 1977, the year Debbie Reynolds starred in an extensive road tour of **Annie Get Your Gun,** Barbra Streisand optioned the screen rights to the musical. It led to much controversial speculation as to how she would interpret the beloved piece of Americana. However, the Streisand version never came to be.

THE ASPHALT JUNGLE
1950—112 min.

Producer, Arthur Hornblow, Jr.; **director,** John Huston; based on the novel by W. R. Burnett; **screenplay,** Ben Maddow and Huston; **art directors,** Cedric Gibbons and Randall Duell; **set decorators,** Edwin B. Willis and Jack D. Moore; **music,** Miklos Rozsa; **makeup,** Jack Dawn; **sound,** Douglas Shearer; **camera,** Harold Rosson; **editor,** George Boemler.

Sterling Hayden (**Dix Handley**); Louis Calhern (**Alonzo D. Emmerich**); Jean Hagen (**Doll Conovan**); James Whitmore (**Gus Minissi**); Sam Jaffe (**Doc Erwin Riedenschneider**); John McIntire (**Police Commissioner Hardy**); Marc Lawrence (**Cobby**); Barry Kelley (**Lieutenant Ditrich**); Anthony Caruso (**Louis Ciavelli**); Teresa Celli (**Maria Ciavelli**); Marilyn Monroe (**Angela Phinlay**); William Davis (**Timmons**); Dorothy Tree (**May Emmerich**); Brad Dexter (**Bob Brannon**); Alex Gerry (**Maxwell**); Thomas Browne Henry (**James X. Connery**); James Seay (**Janocek**); Don Haggerty (**Andrews**); Chuck Courtney (**Red**); Helene Stanley (**Jeannie**); Jean Carter (**Woman**); Pat Flaherty (**Younger Officer**); Ralph Dunn (**Older Officer**); Strother Martin (**Doldy**); Henry Corden (**Smith**); Frank Cady (**Night Clerk**); David Hydes (**Evans**); Albert Morin (**Eddie Donato**); Eloise Hardt (**Vivian**); Saul Gorss (**Private Policeman**); Wilson Wood (**Man**); Fred Graham (**Truck Driver**); Benny Burt (**Driver**).

SYNOPSIS
Doc Erwin Riedenschneider, an ex-convict, masterminds a midwestern jewelry heist of Belletier & Co. which nets $500,000. Doc's cohorts in the caper are underlings Louis Ciavelli and Gus Minissi, bookie Cobby who finances the operation, and fast-shooting gunman Dix Handley. The last is involved with singer Doll Conovan. His dream is to buy back the family's farm in Kentucky and live there with Doll. It is disreputable lawyer Alonzo D. Emmerich who promises Doc that he will dispose of the hot jewels.

Meanwhile Emmerich plans a double-cross which will enable him to acquire the gems for himself and to enjoy further the company of his curvaceous "niece" Angela Phinlay. The double-

cross fails and the robbers are still unable to cash in on their loot.

Dix and Doc hide away at Doll's apartment. Later Doc attempts to leave for a distant city and anonymity, but the police apprehend him. In attempting his escape, Dix is wounded and Doll takes him to Dr. Swanson who calls the police. Dix dies on his way to his Kentucky retreat.

* * *

"This film . . . gives such an electrifying picture of the whole vicious circle of a crime—such an absorbing illustration of the various characters involved, their loyalties and duplicities, and of the minutia of crime techniques—that one finds it hard to tag the item of repulsive exhibition in itself," wrote the **New York Times'** Bosley Crowther after viewing **The Asphalt Jungle.** John Huston's brilliantly directed study of criminology has since become a model endlessly copied but rarely matched in underworld-centered movies and television episodes.

Adapted from the 1949 novel by W. R. Burnett (who had written **Little Caesar,** which had done so much for Warner Bros. and Edward G. Robinson back in 1931), **The Asphalt Jungle** had not enticed any director before Huston became interested. It appeared on paper to be a very routine cops-and-robbers tale with a downbeat ending. However, recognizing elements in Burnett's story that could reveal odd and novel insights into criminal thinking, Huston worked on the screenplay with Ben Maddow.

Huston met with opposition in his casting of

the project. He decided that Sterling Hayden, recently dropped by Paramount Pictures, should play Dix Handley. The studio thought a bigger box-office draw was more appropriate. Huston insisted on testing Hayden. After the celluloid audition—which proved the director had been correct in his hunch—Huston congratulated Hayden, "The next time somebody says you can't act, tell them to call Huston." There were few squabbles about selecting studio contractees Louis Calhern and James Whitmore for the role of a shyster lawyer and the getaway man, or when veteran Sam Jaffe was hired to play the aging mastermind, Doc Riedenschneider.

But there was unhappiness on the lot with the selection of the female leads. Once again, company powers determined that more celebrated performers should handle the roles. However, Huston again won his way, using twenty-two-year-old Jean Hagen (an MGM contractee) as chanteuse Doll Conovan and twenty-one-year-old Marilyn Monroe (a freelancer being promoted by agent-mentor Johnny Hyde) as sultry, shady Angela Phinlay. Commented Huston on this casting, "I chose Jean Hagen because she had a wistful, down-to-earth quality rare on the screen. A born actress. And as for Marilyn Monroe—well, it was type-casting that turned out to be inspired."

Of this excursion into tawdriness, Louis B. Mayer said, "That **Asphalt Pavement** thing is full of nasty, ugly people doing nasty, ugly things. I wouldn't walk across the room to see a thing like that." But by 1950 it did not matter very much at

Sterling Hayden, Jean Hagen, and Sam Jaffe in a publicity pose for The Asphalt Jungle *('50).*

MGM what Mayer thought. He was losing his battle to retain control of studio production, and would soon be ousted by Dore Schary, whom he had brought over from RKO to assist him in running the declining facilities.

When **The Asphalt Jungle** premiered early in the summer of 1950, **Look** magazine explained:

> **The Asphalt Jungle** has features that usually result in a mediocre movie: an average cops-and-robbers crime story and a cast of "unimportant" names. But its original-minded director, John Huston, makes them seem fresh, tense—and on most counts, "different." For Huston is a director who can put life into hackneyed characters and situations—proving once again that imagination can lift a story out of the rut of banality.

> Sam Jaffe's incisive performance won him a Best Supporting Actor Academy nomination, but he lost to George Sanders of Twentieth Century–Fox's **All About Eve.** The National Board of Review voted **The Asphalt Jungle** number three on its Ten Best list (under **Sunset Boulevard** and **All About Eve**) and named Huston the best director of the year. The Screen Directors Guild selected Huston as best director of the season.

After the fact, MGM was delighted with **The Asphalt Jungle.** Contractee Jean Hagen[1] began receiving better parts, climaxing with her unforgettable Lina Lamont of 1952's **Singin' in the Rain;** the other blonde, Marilyn Monroe, would find her great success at Twentieth Century–Fox.

The studio was also happy with the story, and has remade it three times. In 1958 it underwent a westernization as **The Badlanders** with Alan Ladd and Ernest Borgnine; in 1962 it found Egypt as a locale in **Cairo** (with George Sanders ironically situated in Sam Jaffe's old role); and in 1972 there appeared a black exploitation version, **Cool Breeze.** The popular film's title was also used by a 1961 TV series with Jack Warden, which dealt with the casework of the Metropolitan Squad, a special team of plainclothes detectives operating in Manhattan.

BABES IN ARMS
1939—97 min.

Producer, Arthur Freed; **director,** Busby Berkeley; based on the musical play by Richard Rodgers and Lorenz Hart; **screenplay,** Jack McGowan, Kay Van Riper, and **uncredited:** Florence Ryerson, Edgar Allan Woolf, Noel Langley, Joe Laurie, John Meehan, Sid Silvers, Walter DeLeon, Irving Brecher, Ben Freedman, and Anita Loos; **music adapter,** Roger Edens; **music director,** George Stoll; **orchestrators,** Conrad Salinger and Leo Arnaud; **songs,** Rodgers and Hart; Freed, Gus Arnheim, and Abe Lyman; E. Y. Harburg and Harold Arlen;

[1]When the public was so emphatically enthusiastic over Miss Monroe's presence in the film, Jean would be led to wisecrack, "There were only two girl roles, and I obviously wasn't Marilyn Monroe."

Freed and Nacio Herb Brown; **art director,** Merrill Pye; **set decorator,** Edwin B. Willis; **wardrobe,** Dolly Tree; **camera,** Ray June; **editor,** Frank Sullivan.

Mickey Rooney **(Mickey Moran)**; Judy Garland **(Patsy Barton)**; Charles Winninger **(Joe Moran)**; Guy Kibbee **(Judge Black)**; June Preisser **(Rosalie Essex)**; Grace Hayes **(Florrie Moran)**; Betty Jaynes **(Molly Moran)**; Douglas McPhail **(Don Brice)**; Rand Brooks **(Jeff Steele)**; Leni Lynn **(Dody Martini)**; John Sheffield **(Bobs)**; Henry Hull **(Madox)**; Barnett Parker **(William)**; Ann Shoemaker **(Mrs. Barton)**; Margaret Hamilton **(Martha Steele)**; Joseph Crehan **(Mr. Essex)**; George McKay **(Brice)**; Henry Roquemore **(Shaw)**; Lelah Tyler **(Mrs. Brice)**; Lon McCallister **(Boy)**; Sidney Miller, Rube Demarest, Irene Franklin, Charles Brown, Kay Deslys, Patsy Moran, and Harrison Greene **(Bits)**.

SYNOPSIS
Vaudeville's golden days are past and such veteran troupers as Joe and Florrie Moran are deemed passé. But they refuse to admit defeat and organize a revue starring other old-timers and embark on a tour.

Because they have refused to take their show business-loving offsprings with them, the talented youths decide to produce their own show. It will prove to their parents that they are worthy

Song sheet music for Babes in Arms *('39).*

of consideration and it will demonstrate to the Long Island townsfolk that they are actually very healthy and normal youths who do not belong in an institution for underprivileged children.

Mickey Moran, inspired by Patsy Barton, writes the show in which he will star as well as

Joseph Crehan, Harrison Greene, Mickey Rooney, and Judy Garland in Babes in Arms.

direct. Everyone concerned is relying on Mickey, even Judge Black who has given the teenagers a month to demonstrate their worth. Otherwise he will be forced to send them to a trade school, just as local busybody Martha Steele insists.

How to finance the musical is answered when ex-child star Rosalie Essex agrees to back the show, **if** she is assigned the starring female role. This requirement is a shock to Patsy, who is now reduced to being an understudy. It demands a good deal of explaining by Mickey and later by her mother to convince Patsy that this is the only way and that the welfare of the entire production must come before the desires of any one participant.

At the last minute Rosalie withdraws from the production and Patsy goes on in her place. The show seems to be going well, when a sudden rainstorm ruins the evening.

Later Mickey receives a letter from Madox, a New York producer, asking the novice showman to call on him in Manhattan. Madox agrees to mount Mickey's revue on Broadway. And since he is a long-time friend of Joe Moran, he arranges for Joe to be employed as consultant for the up-coming show.

* * *

Richard Rodgers and Lorenz Hart's **Babes in Arms** enjoyed a run of 289 performances on Broadway in 1937. The production, featuring Mitzi Green, Wynn Murray, Ray Heatherton, Alfred Drake, Ray McDonald, and Grace McDonald, boasted a memorable score linked with a one-dimensional storyline with the accent on youth. It was a ready-made package to emerge under the MGM banner of family-oriented features. Long-time MGM songwriter Arthur Freed, who was branching out into other areas of activities at Metro, acquired the film rights for $21,000. He began producing this, his first musical, while in the midst of completing his initial producer's assignment for the studio, **The Wizard of Oz** (1939).

In **That's Entertainment: Part One** (1974) Mickey Rooney would impishly recall the series of Metro features he made with Judy Garland, most of them involving the gee-let's-put-on-the-big-show format. A montage of clips emphasized his point about the repetition of plot structure. However, in its day, and with the new slant of magnificent talent and enthusiasm provided, the formula for **Babes in Arms** was refreshing to the majority of filmgoers. It is still a treat to see today!

Babes in Arms is something of a landmark in the history of MGM. It was the third[1] outing for Rooney and Garland, but their first major production and their first joint musical. It was to be the first of four Busby Berkeley-directed vehicles for the young screen pair, and for Berkeley it was his first full-fledged directing assignment at the Culver City lot (he previously had created and staged the finale for Jeanette MacDonald's **Broadway Serenade**, 1939). As detailed in Hugh Fordin's **The World of Entertainment** (1975), **Babes in Arms** saw the consolidation of the Arthur Freed

production unit, which over the next two decades would be responsible for the bulk of the studio's prime musical films.

Just as only three[2] songs were retained from the Broadway show original, so the play's plotline was restructured to accommodate not only the film medium, but the growing importance of Mickey Rooney as an MGM luminary. Even if his part had only been the equal of Garland's, it would have become naturally enlarged during production for at that point in his career there was no containing the super exuberance of this ultra-talented performer who could dance, sing, mimic, play the drums, carry repartee, handle drama, and nearly always steal the limelight.

Constructing the screenplay for **Babes in Arms** fell to a small task force at Metro. Florence Ryerson and Edgar Allan Woolf prepared a story outline which did not please Freed. He requested Jack McGowan to revamp it along the following lines:

I just like the premise [of the original Broadway show]. We keep that. In the play none of the older people appear. I want to change that and have the vaudevillians show that time has passed them by and that they couldn't catch up. . . . I got to thinking about George M. Cohan and his parents. He was always thinking about his father and mother, trying to do things for them. That's why in the last scene, when Mickey Rooney gets his big chance at success, I want him to send right away for his father.

Among the others who would work on the screenplay were Noel Langley, Sid Silvers, Joe Laurie, Anita Loos, and finally Kay Van Riper.

To back up the two stars, Metro employed baritone Douglas McPhail[3] and (his offscreen wife) Betty Jaynes, an MGM contract duo noted more for blandness than as the new generation's answer to Nelson Eddy and Jeanette MacDonald. Blonde June Preisser, as a marshmallow femme fatale, made her screen debut after several Broadway assignments. Among the supporting cast was Johnny Sheffield, who in 1939 joined MGM's **Tarzan** series as Boy.

Babes in Arms began filming on soundstage 3 on May 12, 1939. Berkeley, unable or unwilling to forget his trademark production number routines from his 1930s Warner Bros. musicals, went wild on some of the big vocal numbers. In staging the title tune—done in a call-to-arms format—McPhail is the leader of the youths gathering new recruits to the cause (putting on the big show). The scene climaxes at a bonfire. Later there is an

overlavish blackface routine with Rooney and Garland as interlocutors handling the top performing assignments, in an array of dancing, singing, comedy, and mimicry.

The apex of the film was E. Y. Harburg and Harold Arlen's "God's Country" production extravaganza.[4] It was shot on soundstage 27 over a three-day period, following five days of rehearsal, and one day of prerecording. Part of the $32,970 cost for the sequence went for the ten additional boys and girls, sixty-one dancers, nine children, and twenty musicians that Berkeley "needed" to make the segment come to life. (The only thing missing from the typical Berkeley touch was his array of bleached-blonde chorines.) What would distinguish this film from most of Berkeley's prior film assignments was that here the musical numbers, even the big ones, were integrated into the overall plot conception, adding to the development of characterization. Such was the power of Freed to impose his ideas on other veterans.

Only observers of the shooting of **Babes in Arms** would have been aware of the on-the-set struggle between Garland and her director. Unlike Rooney, who was a happy-go-lucky, quick-study, eager-to-rehearse individual, high-strung Judy relied on spontaneity of performance to bolster her rather undisciplined lifestyle. She hated to rehearse, was not a very good dancer, and disliked authority. With a "taskmaster" for a director she felt as if she might snap inside. She would say later of Berkeley, "I used to feel as if he had a big black bullwhip and he was lashing me with it. Sometimes I used to think I couldn't live through the day."

Judy demonstrates a (nervous) vitality in the film only partially exploited in her prior screen outings. Here she is kittenish, coy, vulnerable, dynamic, and, best of all, in marvelous voice. At the publisher's office she and Rooney harmonize on "Good Morning" in a bouncy fashion. Later with Rooney's onscreen sister (Jaynes) Judy offers the gimmicky "Opera Versus Jazz," followed by her zingy swing interpretation of "Figaro." With McPhail and Jaynes she performs "Where or When," and in a very touching rendition sings "I Cried for You." This is in marked contrast to her enthusiastic participation in the group numbers: "Babes in Arms," the minstrel show[5] and "God's Country" (wherein she does an imitation of Eleanor Roosevelt).

Babes in Arms premiered at Grauman's Chinese Theatre on October 10, 1939, and a week later opened at the Capitol Theatre in New York. The studio marketed the feature as "the musical all the world was waiting for!" Rooney's star drawing power was promoted with ads proclaiming his versatility. "You've never seen Mickey Roo-

---

[1]Rooney and Garland had appeared together in **Thoroughbreds Don't Cry** (1937) and **Love Finds Andy Hardy** (1938).

[2]From the Broadway score the filmmakers used the little tune and "Where or When" with snatches of "The Lady Is a Tramp." Not used were such hit tunes as "My Funny Valentine," "Johnny One Note," "Imagine," and "I Wish I Were in Love Again." The Harold Arlen-E. Y. Harburg song "Let's Take a Walk Around the Block" was considered for the film.

[3]McPhail would commit suicide on December 7, 1944, age thirty. He had attempted suicide in 1941 when he and Jaynes, his wife of three years, had divorced. In early 1944 he had been discharged from the Army as being emotionally unequipped for military life.

[4]MGM was never bashful about promoting its own stars and product within the context of any given Metro film. In the "God's Country" number there is the rather distasteful lyric, "We've got no Duce, no Führer [but] we've got Garbo and Norma Shearer."

[5]The minstrel show number ("My Daddy Was a Minstrel Man") includes: "Oh, Susanna" (Rooney-Garland), "Ida" (Rooney), "I'm Just Wild About Harry" (Rooney-Garland-chorus), "Do Da" (all), "Camptown Races" (all), and "On Moonlight Bay" (Rooney-Garland-chorus).

ney 'til now! He sings! He taps! He whangs the bass violins! He mimics Gable! He outgrumbles Lionel Barrymore! And with Judy's heart songs and an exciting musical comedy plot . . . no wonder it is the talk of America!"

Perhaps the **New York Daily News** best summed up the critical reaction to **Babes in Arms:** "As an entertainment, it has lost some of its original sophistication and the elastic snap with which it went over on the stage. But it has gained in comic interludes and serves to introduce several new screen personalities." The film's final cost was $748,000[6] and then it went on to gross $3,335,000 in its initial release. Sparking the word-of-mouth praise for the feature was the personal-appearance stage tour Rooney and Garland undertook around the U.S. to promote the picture.

This film would catapult Rooney into the top box-office star echelon in 1939 and resulted in his Oscar nomination as Best Actor. At the February 29, 1940, Oscar ceremony Rooney competed against such screen stalwarts as Clark Gable, James Stewart, Laurence Olivier, and Robert Donat. The last mentioned won the Academy Award for MGM's **Goodbye, Mr. Chips.** In 1938 Rooney had been given a special Oscar for his "contribution in bringing to the screen the spirit and personification of youth." The following year Rooney presented this same award to his frequent costar Judy Garland for her achievement as a screen juvenile.

"Hammy" Hammond); Donald Meek **(Mr. Stone);** James Gleason **(Thornton Reed);** Emma Dunn **(Mrs. Williams);** Frederick Burton **(Professor Morris);** Cliff Clark **(Inspector Moriarity);** William A. Post, Jr. **(Announcer);** Alexander Woollcott **(Himself);** Luis Alberni **(Nicky);** Carl Stockdale **(Man);** Dick Baron **(Butch);** Will Lee **(Waiter);** Donna Reed **(Secretary);** Joe Yule **(Mason, Aide to Reed);** Stop, Look, and Listen Trio **(Themselves);** Tom Hanlon **(Radio Man);** Renee Austin **(Elinor);** Roger Steele **(Boy);** Bryant Washburn **(Director);** Charles Wagenheim **(Composer);** Arthur Hoyt **(Little Man Customer);** Jack Lipson **(Fat Man Customer);** Dorothy Morris, Maxine Flores, and Anne Rooney **(Pit Astor Girls);** Margaret O'Brien **(Little Girl at Audition);** Sidney Miller **(Pianist);** King Baggott **(Man in Audience);** Barbara Bedford **(Matron);** Shimen Ruskin **(Excited Russian);** Jean Porter **("Hoe Down" Dancer);** Leslie Brooks **(Actress–Committee Extra).**

SYNOPSIS

The singing-dancing trio of Tommy Williams, Ray Lambert, and Morton "Hammy" Hammond are convinced they are the Great White Hope of Broadway, despite the overwhelming apathy that greets their auditions.

"The Three Balls of Fire," as they dub themselves, enjoy swapping dreams with the other young hopefuls who congregate in Times Square. At the Pit Astor Drugstore, Tommy meets a weeping Penny Morris, unsuccessful actress. Tommy comforts the distraught Penny, and learns that she is the daughter of a music teacher, Professor Morris, and that she devotes a great deal of her time to assisting at the neighborhood settlement house. Tommy develops a brainstorm—package a show with all his unemployed friends, including Penny, to raise money to send those underprivileged children to the country for a vacation.

As Tommy busily prepares the show, Miss Jones, assistant to famed producer Thornton Reed, contacts him and presents him with the opportunity to join Reed's new production, now trying out in Philadelphia. Tommy jubilantly accepts, but Penny expresses disappointment in him—what of all his friends and the children to be served by THEIR show? Tommy gives up his chance of a lifetime. By means of a block party, he earns the funds necessary to rent a theatre for the charity performance.

Meanwhile, Miss Jones, impressed by Tommy's sacrifice, succeeds in getting permission for the troupe to use one of Reed's old abandoned theatres for the show. Disaster strikes on opening night, when the fire department condemns the building. However, no member of the audience demands a refund, assuring the chil-

BABES ON BROADWAY
1941—118 min.

Producer, Arthur Freed; **directors,** Busby Berkeley and, **uncredited,** George Sidney; based on the unpublished story "Convict's Return" by Harry Kaufman; **story,** Fred Finklehoffe; **screenplay** by Finklehoffe, Elaine Ryan, and, **uncredited,** Robert Tree West, John Monks, Ralph Spence, Gertrude Purcell, Edmund Hartman, Charles Riesner, Vincente Minnelli, and Elsie Janis; **art directors,** Cedric Gibbons and Malcolm Brown; **set decorator,** Edwin B. Willis; **makeup,** Jack Dawn; **gowns,** Kalloch; **men's wardrobe,** Gile Steele; **musical presentation,** Merrill Pye; **music adapter,** Roger Edens; **music director,** George Stoll; **orchestrators–vocal arrangers,** Leo Arnaud, George Bassman, and Conrad Salinger; **songs,** Burton Lane and Ralph Freed; Edens and Freed; Lane and E. Y. Harburg; Harold Rome; Al Stillman and Jararaca and Vincente Paiva; **sound,** Douglas Shearer; **camera,** Lester White; **editor,** Frederic Y. Smith.

Mickey Rooney **(Tommy Williams);** Judy Garland **(Penny Morris);** Fay Bainter **(Miss Jones);** Virginia Weidler **(Barbara Jo Conway);** Ray McDonald **(Ray Lambert);** Richard Quine **(Morton**

---

[6]Rooney was receiving $900 per week on contract, plus a $7,500 bonus; Garland was on a $500 per week contract; Winninger received $4,000 weekly; and Guy Kibbee earned $1,600 weekly. Berkeley was hired at $1,500 per week.

Judy Garland, Mickey Rooney, Ray McDonald, and Richard Quine in a publicity pose for Babes on Broadway ('41).

dren of their vacation. Reed himself arrives. After the crowd has dispersed, he sees a special performance of the revue. So impressed is he that he engages the entire company for a Broadway edition, and Tommy and Penny win stardom.

* * *

As the third Busby Berkeley–Mickey Rooney–Judy Garland musical romp,[1] MGM and producer Arthur Freed mounted **Babes on Broadway.** In many ways it was superior to the earlier vehicles, allowing the two stars to display more versatility in a slightly more sophisticated vein.

At this juncture, Garland was receiving $2,000 weekly from Metro, while Rooney earned $1,200 weekly plus a picture bonus of $25,000. Originally, Louis B. Mayer intended that his new contractee Shirley Temple would join Mickey and Judy for this picture, but the ex-Twentieth Century–Fox sensation declined the offer, and Virginia Weidler was given the role of Barbara Jo, the good-hearted settlement youngster-worker.

Production began on July 14, 1941, and concluded on November 7, 1941. Taskmaster Berkeley put the entire cast through strenuous paces, determined to work vim into the rather naive and derivative "original" story mostly concocted by Fred Finklehoffe. During the long hours of rehearsal, Rooney could be found spending his off hours consulting assorted bookies, while Garland would frequently employ her free time on the soundstage to compose fiction. One of her efforts, "Love's New Sweet Song," would be utilized for radio's "Silver Theatre" with Judy starring in the audio drama. According to Christopher Finch in his biography of Garland, **Rainbow** (1975):

It's often been said that Judy found it difficult to work with Berkeley, but the reports seem exaggerated—at least as far as this early period is concerned. Not that their relationship was entirely congenial. Berkeley's system of intensive, repeated rehearsals was not ideal for Judy, who responded most happily to more spontaneous situations. She was not lazy, but repetition was tedious for her. Although her concentration span appeared to be short, and she was easily distracted, she had a remarkable memory and almost freaky powers of retention. She had only to walk through a routine a couple of times to have it down pat.

When Berkeley first worked with her, he was driven half-crazy by her apparent inability to listen to anything he was saying. He was partial to giving elaborate instructions and was very put out when Judy stared off into space while he was talking to her. He would then become incensed and scream that she hadn't listened to a thing he had said, whereupon Judy would repeat his instructions, word for word, unable to figure out what had provoked his outburst.

—————
[1]Berkeley had previously directed Garland and Rooney in MGM's **Babes in Arms** (1939) and **Strike Up the Band** (1940). Producer Arthur Freed had planned to team Mickey and Judy in **Good News,** but the production was delayed until 1947 and by that time it would be June Allyson and Peter Lawford who would star in the endurable college-set musical.

Bolstering the gee-let's-put-on-a-big-show formula is the array of enthusiastic musical numbers performed within the 118 minutes of entertainment. As a patriotic salute to the staunch British, Garland sings "Chin Up, Cheerio, Carry On" as a swarm of English refugee youths look on. (Another patriotic number, "Ballads for Americans," would be deleted; the outtakes would turn up in 1942's **Born to Sing,** an MGM vehicle which was originally to star Garland and Rooney, but which made do with Virginia Weidler, Ray McDonald, and Douglas McPhail.)

There is a poignant segment filmed on the dusty stage of a long-abandoned theatre, as Garland and Rooney recall various past performing greats. Mickey imitates Walter Hampden's interpretation of **Cyrano de Bergerac,** struts as Harry Lauder singing "She Is Ma Daisy," and cavorts in George M. Cohan tradition with "I'm a Yankee Doodle Boy." In this section, devised by Vincente Minnelli, Garland retorts to Rooney's display of versatility with impersonations of Sarah Bernhardt, then as Fay Templeton singing "Mary's a Grand Old Name" and as Blanche Ring performing "Rings on Her Fingers." This interlude alone demonstrated just how dynamic an entertainment team Garland and Rooney were in 1941.

If there seemed little novelty left in the possibility of having his young talent perform a "Hoe Down" on screen, Berkeley revealed once again how powerful a conceptualist he was. The sequence featured Judy and Mickey, Six Hits and a Miss and the Five Musical Maids. Its intricate camera setups and choreography brought a special vitality to the film, outreaching the parallel "Do the Conga" number from **Strike Up the Band.** This new jive number was composed by Ralph Freed and Roger Edens.

In **Strike Up the Band** there had been the Gay Nineties segment with the youths performing a Victorian melodrama **(Nell of New Rochelle)** complete with weeping-fainting heroine and hissable, moustached villain. Now in **Babes on Broadway** there is a companion piece, the sketch "The Convict's Return" which was acquired from the Broadway revue **Streets of Paris.** It allowed Mickey to play eight different roles!

Having tasted success with the minstrel show finale in **Babes in Arms** there was little doubt what the finale of **Babes on Broadway** would encompass. Freed okayed the repeat of this gimmick. At a cost of $107,000 (with nine days of rehearsal and nine days of filming), the climactic scenes were shot. They consisted of Judy performing Harold Rome's "Franklin D. Roosevelt Jones" song, and Mickey offering a banjo solo of "Swanee River" and "Alabama Bound." The entire cast (with a solo by Virginia Weidler) was utilized for a strut version of "Waiting for the Robert E. Lee" and "By the Light of the Silvery Moon." Roger Edens, who arranged this finale segment, would recall for Hugh Fordin's book **The World of Entertainment** (1975) that the expansive minstrel number was a flop in the Glendale, California, preview of the feature.

"We tried to figure out why. As it turned out we realized there was no shot of Mickey and

Judy making up in blackface, so the audience didn't know it was Judy and Mickey. And it was a very good lesson: if you ever are going to show someone in disguise, you better show them putting it on. So we did a retake showing Mickey and Judy getting into blackface so that the audience could tell it was them. And then the number went like a house on fire."

As additional bonus items for viewers of this extravaganza musical, MGM hired Broadway critic, personality, and wit Alexander Woollcott at a fee of $5,000 to spend one day (August 25, 1941) on the MGM soundstage and film a prologue for the film—a re-creation of his "Ye Town Tattler" radio program in which he suggests that the story about to unfold is typical of young America's dream for Broadway success. More invigorating than this was Mickey's impersonation—in full costume and makeup in the show-within-the-show—of Carmen Miranda singing "Mama Yo Quiero." Mickey the talented reproduced the eccentric Brazilian Bombshell's gestures, accent, and movement amazingly well, not only because he was a great student of mimicry, but also because he had the best teacher possible—Miss Miranda herself.

On New Year's Eve 1941 **Babes on Broadway** premiered at Radio City Music Hall. Audiences were agog. Critics, however, did not succumb as easily to the charms of the show. As the **New York Times** reported, "When Metro spreads itself on a production number, it invariably does a handsome job. And, it has done right nicely by the finale of **Babes on Broadway,** providing a mammoth eye-filling setting for the minstrel show which is the only racey and really entertaining episode in this otherwise dull and overly long potpourri of comedy, drama, third-rate jokes, and music." **Variety** was a bit harsher, focusing on the stars: "Both Rooney and Miss Garland, the child wonders of some years back, are fast outgrowing, at least in appearance, this type of presentation, which depends entirely on the ah's and oh's that spring from watching precocious children." Nevertheless, the picture, which cost $940,068.70 to make, grossed $3,859,000.

After this seventh teaming of Mickey and Judy, the acting pair would work together again for MGM in **Thousands Cheer** (1943), **Girl Crazy** (1943), and **Words and Music** (1948).

THE BAD AND THE BEAUTIFUL
1952—118 min.

—————

Executive producer, Dore Schary; **producer,** John Houseman; **director,** Vincente Minnelli; based on the story "Memorial to a Bad Man" by George Bradshaw; **screenplay,** Charles Schnee; **music,** David Raksin; **art directors,** Cedric Gibbons and Edward Carfagno; **set decorators,** Edwin B. Willis and Keogh Gleason; **costumes,** Helen Rose; **assistant director,** Jerry Thorpe; **hairstyles,** Sydney

Guilaroff; **makeup,** William Tuttle; **sound,** Douglas Shearer; **special effects,** A. Arnold Gillespie and Warren Newcombe; **camera,** Robert Surtees; **editor,** Conrad A. Nervig.

Lana Turner **(Georgia Lorrison);** Kirk Douglas **(Jonathan Shields);** Walter Pidgeon **(Harry Pebbel);** Dick Powell **(James Lee Bartlow);** Barry Sullivan **(Fred Amiel);** Gloria Grahame **(Rosemary Bartlow);** Gilbert Roland **(Victor "Gaucho" Ribera);** Leo G. Carroll **(Henry Whitfield);** Vanessa Brown **(Kay Amiel);** Paul Stewart **(Syd Murphy);** Sammy White **(Gus);** Elaine Stewart **(Lila);** Jonathan Cott **(Assistant Director);** Ivan Triesault **(Von Ellstein);** Kathleen Freeman **(Miss March);** Marietta Canty **(Ida);** Lucille Knoch **(Blonde);** Steve Forrest **(Leading Man);** Perry Sheehan **(Secretary);** Robert Burton **(McDill);** Francis X. Bushman **(Eulogist);** Harold Miller **(Man);** George Lewis **(Lionel Donovan);** Madge Blake **(Mrs. Rosser);** William Tannen, Dabbs Greer, Sara Spencer, and Frank Scannell **(Reporters);** Stanley Andrews **(Sheriff);** Ben Astar **(Joe);** Barbara Thatcher, Sharon Saunders, and Erin Selwyn **(Girls);** Major Sam Harris **(Party Guest);** Bess Flowers **(Joe's Friend at Party);** Louis Calhern **(Voice on Recording);** Pat O'Malley, Eric Alden, Stuart Holmes, Reginald Simpson, Jay Adler, Larry Williams, Roger Moore, and George Sherwood **(Bits).**

SYNOPSIS

Ruthless Hollywood director Jonathan Shields is out to dignify himself as the outstanding filmmaker of his generation. He teams with fledgling director Fred Amiel. After years of struggle, Shields throws over Amiel for a name director to helm his big feature film. In the same vein Shields picks up drunken extra Georgia Lorrison and builds her into a glamorous star. She makes the error of falling in love with him only to find he has used her as a packaged commodity.

Shields lures Southern professor-writer James Lee Bartlow to Hollywood to adapt his bestselling novel into a screenplay. The producer senses that the writer's wife, Rosemary, impedes James Lee's progress and therefore he coaxes Latin lover Victor "Gaucho" Ribera to entertain Rosemary. This liaison ends on a note of tragedy when she dies in a car crash.

Director, actress, and writer all relate their tales via flashback as they sit in Harry Pebbel's office. The veteran producer is hoping to entice them to pool their talents for a forthcoming Jonathan Shields production. They realize that Shields is a full-fledged heel, but a talented one. They agree to work for the filmmaker once again.

* * *

The screenplay fascinated me. It told of a film producer who uses everyone in his rise to the top: the actress he deceives by professing his love; the young director whose picture he expropriates; the screenwriter who loses his wife because the producer maneuvers her into an affair. Yet, at the end, all those who have been exploited are better off for having worked with him, their reputations established and their careers flourishing as never before. The cruelties they've suffered at his hands are un-

Dick Powell, Lana Turner, Barry Sullivan, and Walter Pidgeon in The Bad and the Beautiful *('52).*

forgivable, yet they must grudgingly admit he's largely responsible for their success. . . .

. . . a harsh and cynical story, yet strangely romantic. All that one hated and loved about Hollywood was distilled in the screenplay. . . .

The above is from Vincente Minnelli's **I Remember It Well** (1974), concerning **The Bad and the Beautiful,** which has since become a classic example of Hollywood sneering at Hollywood. While the film today emerges as something of a cliché—only because of the repetitions which followed it—it was a bold statement at the time, especially from MGM, where the cutthroat policies of rising talents had long prospered.

The film was originally titled **Tribute to a Bad Man** and was based on a short story by George Bradshaw. It was a project first of Arthur Freed, then of John Houseman. The latter producer (who has since won a Best Supporting Actor Academy Award) gained industry recognition via his theatrical and brief film association with Orson Welles of the Mercury Theatre. In the early fifties Houseman had come to Culver City on the invitation of Dore Schary, Louis B. Mayer's nemesis, and Schary enjoyed the idea of scalding Hollywood, something Mayer abhorred. (A short time before, at the premiere of Paramount's **Sunset Boulevard,** Mayer had accosted director Billy Wilder in the theatre lobby and sputtered, "You have disgraced the industry that fed you!")

Though Schary was favorable to the project, he still was surprised when Minnelli was anxious to direct what originally was conceived of as a B picture.[1] Kirk Douglas leaped eagerly at the offer to play the pivotal bastard role of Jonathan Shields. When Lana Turner learned about the female lead—loosely based on the life and bad times of Diana Barrymore—she volunteered to

play Georgia Lorrison.[2] Walter Pidgeon, aware that age was sapping away his ever-dapper image, almost received a veto from Houseman and Minnelli when he sought the part of producer Harry Pebbel who works by the creed, "Give me a picture that ends with a kiss and black ink on the books!" Both filmmakers saw Pidgeon as the perennial Clem Miniver. But Pidgeon arrived at Minnelli's office in a crumbled gray suit and a crew-cut wig. He won the part. Dick Powell (then under pact to MGM) was sought for the director part of Fred Amiel. He opted instead to appear as novelist James Lee Bartlow. Gloria Grahame was assigned as Powell's on-camera wife, and Barry Sullivan was handed the director's (thankless) role.

In his memoir, Minnelli writes that as casting continued the script lifted episodes from the lives of genuine Hollywood figures to formulate its story. "The hero would be based on David Selznick and others, the heroine would remind the audience of Diana Barrymore. The director of the cat people film and other small budget pictures would be patterned on Val Lewton." The accuracies were not very clear, perhaps fearing potential lawsuits: Selznick's ambitions never ruined him to the degree they did Shields; Diana Barrymore, who had a short film career at Universal in the forties, was not particularly exploited by any film executive, and remained her own worst enemy; Lewton, somewhat forgotten by Robert Wise and Mark Robson after he nurtured their early careers at RKO, in reality faced a far sadder end to his life than does Fred Amiel, who achieves a professional success that Lewton never did.

The most appreciated scene in this $1,500,000 production is Lana Turner's hysterical, screaming car drive after finding Shields making love to another woman. It is the histrionic highlight of the picture and a special moment in

---

[1] Minnelli turned down **Lili** (1953) to do **The Bad and the Beautiful.**

[2] Lana Turner's salary for **The Bad and the Beautiful** was $10,000 per week for four weeks, charged by MGM against Houseman's producing unit.

Turner's lengthy screen career. As Minnelli remembers:

The following sequence was probably as cinematic a piece of business as I've ever been associated with. . . . I plotted out the scene as if we were photographing a ballet. The car was on a turntable. I devised the camera's in and out movement, first zooming in on Lana's face, then on her foot as it pressed down on the accelerator, then on the back of her head so that the blurred image of the rain she had to drive through was suggested. When it was all laid out, I explained the scene to Lana. . . . Lana went through the tortured scene with the technique and instinct of the consummate actress. . . . She was a hungry kitten lapping up milk and she proved she was a very good actress . . . if only a director would take the time with her.

However, according to Lana Turner in her appearance at New York's Town Hall in the Legendary Ladies series of 1975, she was not friendly with Vincente Minnelli when the picture was shot. When she asked for direction in that demanding sequence, he replied, "I haven't a clue." Hence, Lana (so she says) "winged" the action and self-created the outstanding dramatic scene of her career. The truth?

Released with the ad lines "MGM's Drama of the Blonde and the Brute" and "No Holds Barred . . . in this story of a blonde who wanted to go places . . . and a brute who got her there . . . the hard way!" **The Bad and the Beautiful**, produced at a cost of $1.5 million, proved a blockbuster. In the words of Hollis Alpert (**Saturday Review** magazine), "[The film] provides a more complete and sociological view of the dream factory than any movie has yet attempted. . . . When one sees acting from people who were not hitherto thought to possess any marked degree of ability, the accolade is generally fixed on the director. Vincente Minnelli has undoubtedly coaxed the best out of his players, but blood does not spring from a stone, and perhaps he has utilized to the fullest what was already there." Bosley Crowther (**New York Times**), however, reported, ". . . for all this probing and all this intimate looking around amid the realistic paraphernalia and artificial clutter of Hollywood, there does not emerge a clear picture of exactly how movies are made. It is a crowded and colorful picture, but it is choppy, episodic, and vague." Perhaps this explains why **The Bad and the Beautiful** did NOT receive a Best Picture Academy Award nomination, though it **did win** five Oscars: Best Screenplay—Charles Schnee; Best Black and White Cinematography—Robert Surtees; Best Black and White Costumes—Helen Rose; Best Art and Set Direction—Cedric Gibbons, Edward Carfagno, Edwin B. Willis, and Keogh Gleason; and Best Supporting Actress—Gloria Grahame.[3]

The fact that neither Kirk Douglas nor Lana

Turner received Oscar bids surprised many, though many others felt that Grahame's Dixie-drawled sensuous spouse undercut Lana's performance.

The Bad and the Beautiful joined **The Band Wagon, Ivanhoe, Million Dollar Mermaid,** and **The Naked Spur** as one of MGM's most profitable products of the 1952–53 season.

Memorable scenes from the film include Turner's first appearance, as only her legs dangle from a loft inside her Shakespearean star father's decaying beach mansion, her voice tinged with tears and alcohol; Douglas leaving a gambling party beaming, only to reveal to his anxious friends that he lost; Turner "dying" for the sound-stage cameras à la Greta Garbo; and the three-exploited souls—Sullivan, Turner, and Powell—lifting the telephone receiver as they walk out of Pidgeon's office to overhear what the exiled Jonathan Shields is planning for his next film production.

A decade later, in 1962, producer John Houseman, director Vincente Minnelli, star Kirk Douglas, and scenarist Charles Schnee would join forces again for another acid tale of Hollywood on Hollywood. MGM's **Two Weeks in Another Town**, which featured some footage from **The Bad and the Beautiful**, Unfortunately, this distillation of Irwin Shaw's sharp novel failed to create the audience stir its predecessor had.

BAD DAY AT BLACK ROCK
1954 C—81 min.

Producer, Dore Schary; **associate producer,** Herman Hoffman; **director,** John Sturges; **story,** Howard Breslin; **screenplay,** Millard Kaufman; **color consultant,** Alvord Eiseman; **music,** Andre Previn; **art directors,** Cedric Gibbons and Malcolm Brown; **set decorators,** Edwin B. Willis and Fred MacLean; **sound,** Wesley C. Miller; **camera,** William C. Mellor; **editor,** Newell P. Kimlin.

Spencer Tracy **(John J. Macreedy)**; Robert Ryan **(Reno Smith)**; Anne Francis **(Liz Wirth)**; Dean Jagger **(Tim Horn)**; Walter Brennan **(Doc Velie)**; John Ericson **(Pete Wirth)**; Ernest Borgnine **(Coley Trimble)**; Lee Marvin **(Hector David)**; Russell Collins **(Mr. Hastings)**; Walter Sande **(Sam)**; Francis McDonald **(Bit)**.

SYNOPSIS

On a hot summer's day in 1945 a streamlined train deposits John J. Macreedy at Black Rock. Macreedy, a war veteran with a crippled left arm, hopes to deliver a war medal won by a deceased son of a Japanese-American farmer in the area.

An air of hostility welcomes Macreedy to the California desert town. When he drives to the Oriental's ranch, he discovers it to be a charred, abandoned ruin. It develops that during the aftermath of the anti-Japanese feelings surrounding the attack on Pearl Harbor, rancher Reno Smith led a mob whose work resulted in the death of the Oriental.

Aiding Smith in his terror against stranger Macreedy are sadistic Coley Trimble and telegraph operator Hastings, the latter aborting Macreedy's pleas for help. Tim Horn is the sheriff stymied by bully boss Smith, while Liz Wirth is on hand to brighten up the grim proceedings.

Eventually Macreedy succeeds in administering a beating to Trimble. Smith is killed and the other conspirators face justice.

* * *

Francis McDonald, Lee Marvin, Robert Ryan, Spencer Tracy, Ernest Borgnine, and Walter Sande in Bad Day at Black Rock *('54).*

The new regime at MGM under Dore Schary was (in the opinion of many of the old guard) a bit too liberal in its themes and philosophies. In the 1930s the lot had been one of the hotbeds of conservative Republicanism in Southern California. Louis B. Mayer organized his talents to campaign for Herbert Hoover, and Irving Thalberg actually concocted short subjects to slander the ideals of Upton Sinclair in the 1934 California gubernatorial race ("Nothing is unfair in politics," explained Thalberg).

However, as the Senator Joe McCarthy era faded in the 1950s, leaving only the casualties suffered by both the Right and the Left, Metro produced a picture that today seems more rowdy than idealistic. At the time it was deemed controversial. The title: **Bad Day at Black Rock**. The subject: racial prejudice, not against the blacks, but against the Japanese.

Few topics could have so inflamed sentiments in California. It was that state which had corralled Japanese-Americans into "camp" colonies during World War II for the protection of "good" Americans. And few pictures received such lavish treatment. On Schary's directive, **Bad Day** was allotted a cast boasting three Oscar winners (Spencer Tracy, Dean Jagger, and Walter Brennan) as well as two rising tough-character stars (Ernest Borgnine and Lee Marvin) who would soon join the Academy Award ranks.

Under the direction of John Sturges, with Metro contractee Anne Francis as the sole female principal, the cast welded strongly together. Actually Tracy had not wanted to make the film; only at the strong persuasion of Schary had he agreed. However, once he saw how the picture was shaping up at the heat-soaked location site in Death Valley, Tracy had a decided change of spirit. Suddenly the tough filming conditions during the sweltering summer of 1954 seemed worthwhile. The finale of the film finds the one-armed, aging Tracy employing karate to give the burly Borgnine a beating in one of the cinema's most fondly remembered fights.

Released very late in 1954, **Bad Day at Black Rock** was a worthy commercial attraction. It earned solid reviews. **Variety** said, "Considerable excitement is whipped up in this suspense drama, and fans who go for tight action will find it entirely satisfactory. . . . Besides telling a yarn of suspense, the picture is concerned with a social message on civic complacency whether in a whistlestop or a city. Fortunately for entertainment purposes, the makers have wisely underplayed this social angle so it seldom gets out of hand. . . ."

John O'Hara reported in **Collier's** magazine, "You are not going to see many pictures as good as **Bad Day at Black Rock**. There just haven't been many pictures as good as **Bad Day at Black Rock**, and mindful of the law of averages, I can predict there won't be many. This is one of the finest motion pictures ever made. . . . As to the acting, well, at least a gold cigarette case to everyone in the cast . . . so that in the future when Tracy runs into Robert Ryan or Robert Ryan encounters Anne Francis or Anne Francis sees Walter Brennan they can always flash the case at each other, the memento of a professional experience they can all be proud to have shared."

Besides its splendid cast, the brooding **Bad Day** benefited greatly from Eastman Color and especially from the widescreen process. Director Sturges was opposed by many when he suggested using the special filming device. "At that time CinemaScope was considered to be desirable only for thousands of people in huge spectacular productions. I thought it ought to be the other way around," related Sturges. "Some at MGM said to me, 'You poor fella, you've got nothing up there but the desert and one man and you're stuck with CinemaScope.' Well, I thought, that was about as stupid an observation as could be made—because, if you try to show the isolation of one man in the desert, it's obvious that the more space you have around him the better off you are. I liked CinemaScope and that film certainly gave me a marvelous way to use it."

Bad Day at Black Rock placed fourth in the National Board of Review's Ten Best list, and fifth in **Film Daily**'s tally. It also earned Spencer Tracy his fifth Oscar nomination. Ironically he was defeated in the Best Actor category by the coworker he had so impressively pummeled at Black Rock—Ernest Borgnine of **Marty** (United Artists).

With the exception of the narration he would provide for **How the West Was Won** (1963), **Bad Day** was Tracy's final film at MGM. He was assigned to another MGM Western, **Tribute to a Bad-man** (1956). Once again he opposed the notion, especially because of the arduous location trek he would have to undertake in the high mountains near Montrose, California. Director Robert Wise tried to cope with the unruly Tracy on location, but one day the star suddenly vanished. Production was shut down, at a cost of $30,000 a day. Tracy reappeared a week later, giving no reason for his disappearance. The veteran player then appeared on camera for three half-days of shooting but refused to heed any instructions from Wise. The final blow occurred when Tracy insisted an elaborate ranch set be moved to a lower altitude. Wise said no and had Tracy replaced with James Cagney.

Tracy, the last of the giants from Metro's golden age of the thirties, thereafter left the studio. He and his employer settled his contract, which allowed the star to partake of the company pension plan. The end of MGM's global supremacy moved another step closer to reality.

THE BAND WAGON
1953 C—112 min.

Producer, Arthur Freed; **associate producer,** Roger Edens; **director,** Vincente Minnelli; **story-screenplay,** Betty Comden and Adolph Green; **dance and music numbers** staged by Michael Kidd; **songs,** Howard Dietz and Arthur Schwartz; Schwartz and Alan Jay Lerner; **music director,** Adolph Deutsch; **music numbers designer,** Oliver Smith; **orchestrators,** Conrad Salinger, Skip Martin, and Alexander Courage; **color consultants,** Henri Jaffa and Robert Brower; **art directors,** Cedric Gibbons and Preston Ames; **set decorators,** Edwin B. Willis

and Keogh Gleason; **makeup,** William Tuttle; **costumes,** Mary Ann Nyberg; **sound,** Douglas Shearer; **special effects,** Warren Newcombe; **camera,** Harry Jackson; **editor,** Albert Akst.

Fred Astaire (**Tony Hunter**); Cyd Charisse (**Gaby Berard**); Oscar Levant (**Lester Marton**); Nanette Fabray (**Lily Marton**); Jack Buchanan (**Jeffrey Cordova**); James Mitchell (**Paul Byrd**); Robert Gist (**Hal Benton**); Thurston Hall (**Colonel Tripp**); Ava Gardner (**The Movie Star**); LeRoy Daniels (**Shoe Shine Boy**); Jack Tesler (**Ivan**); Dee Turnell, Elynne Ray, Peggy Murray, and Judy Landon (**Girls in Troupe**); Jimmie Thompson and Bert May (**Boys in Troupe**); John Lupton (**Jack, the Prompter**); Owen McGiveney (**Prop Man**); Sam Hearn (**Agent**); Herb Vigran and Emory Parnell (**Men on Train**); Ernest Anderson (**Porter**); Frank Scannell, Stu Wilson, and Roy Engel (**Reporters**); Al Hill (**Shooting Gallery Operator**); Paul Bradley (**Dancer in Park–Waiter**); Bobby Watson (**Bobby, the Dresser**); Lotte Stein (**Chambermaid**); Smoki Whitfield (**Chauffeur**); Dick Alexander and Al Ferguson (**Stagehands**); Betty Farrington (**Fitter**); Bess Flowers (**Lady on Train in "Girl Hunter" Number**).

SYNOPSIS
Dancing film star Tony Hunter has experienced a box-office slump. He returns to New York where writer friends Lester and Lily Marton have written a musical which artsy director Jeffrey Cordova attempts to transform into a modern retelling of **Faust**. Tony also experiences difficulty with choreographer Paul Byrd, and this intensifies when Tony begins to fall in love with Paul's girl, Gaby Berard, a young ballerina and the costar of the musical.

The show receives harsh out-of-town notices in New Haven and it falls on Tony's shoulders to save the production from folding on Broadway. Tony takes over the director's spot and Cordova joins the cast as a costar. They adhere to the Martons' original conception and after Tony sells his valuable collection of paintings to refinance the show, it opens. The production proves to be a hit, and so does Tony's romance with Gaby.

* * *

"It was the coldest, unfriendliest, the most terrible experience I can remember," says Nanette Fabray of **The Band Wagon**, the 1953 color musical which Archer Winsten (**New York Post**) judged "the best musical of the month, the year, the decade, or for all I know, of all time." For almost all concerned, this splendidly unique picture was a trial, hardly the series of experiences that would showcase the classic Howard Dietz-Arthur Schwartz song "That's Entertainment."[1]

Originally **The Band Wagon** was a Broadway revue of 1931, with book and lyrics by George S. Kaufman and Howard Dietz and music by Arthur Schwartz; the stars were Clifton Webb and Fred and Adele Astaire (the last time they danced together professionally). Producer Arthur Freed,

---

[1]Dietz was publicity chief at Metro, as well as a company vice president. He would write a biography of his show business years entitled **Dancing in the Dark** (1974).

MGM's undisputed genius at producing musicals, and director Vincente Minnelli decided to revamp the property and signed Betty Comden and Adolph Green to create a new script (which turned out to be somewhat autobiographical for all concerned), Michael Kidd to choreograph, Oliver Smith to design, and pooled the song catalogue of Schwartz-Dietz, retaining only three of the original revue's songs ("Dancing in the Dark," "I Love Louisa," and "New Sun in the Sky"), to which two new ones were added: "That's Entertainment" and "Girl Hunt Ballet." The latter number featured music by Schwartz and narration by Alan Jay Lerner.

Then came the myriad of problems. Twentieth Century–Fox had already filmed a version of **The Band Wagon** entitled **Dancing in the Dark,** a 1949 release starring William Powell and Betsy Drake. Fox argued that it owned the title and MGM was thus forced to buy the name back for $10,000. Star Fred Astaire was miserable during production. His wife, Phyllis, mother of his children Fred and Ava, was terminally ill (she died in 1954). After Clifton Webb, then on contract to Fox, snubbed the offer of playing Jeffrey Cordova,[2] Metro considered Vincent Price and Edward G. Robinson before signing English star Jack Buchanan—who arrived in Hollywood requiring extensive dental surgery and spent most of the filming in extreme pain. Third lead Oscar Levant, never very agreeable in the best of health, was recuperating from a heart attack and pointed to his chest whenever he wanted to avoid an undesirable chore (such as the "Triplets" number, which he was to perform with Astaire and Buchanan; Fabray replaced him). In addition to personality problems, costs became exorbitant. The fee for completing the "Girl Hunt Ballet" alone was $314,475.[3] Cinematographer George Folsey was taken off the film when the production department felt shooting was going too slowly. He was replaced by Twentieth Century–Fox's Harry Jackson.

The time factor was proving to be a sore point. Because Buchanan's contract required him to be through shooting by early December 1952, it was necessary to adopt a rather unusual filming schedule. During one week only dialogue scenes

Fred Astaire, Nanette Fabray, and Jack Buchanan in The Band Wagon *('53).*

were shot, then during the next week only musical numbers were lensed. As for the shooting of what proved to be the finale, "That's Entertainment," it was a race to see if it could be photographed before Buchanan departed from California or Levant erupted into another tirade. (When self-indulgent Levant said that striding up and down the long set ramp was against doctors' orders, an exasperated Astaire embarrassed him by carrying him down the structure.)

Finally, after a shooting schedule lasting from October 20, 1952, to January 28, 1953 (with retakes accomplished in early February 1953) and a cost of $2,169,120, **The Band Wagon** reached completion.

It was all worthwhile. Bosley Crowther of the **New York Times** heralded the film as "a wholly original and intrinsic musical show that cleverly takes advantage of the old—and two new Schwartz-Dietz tunes" and labeled **The Band Wagon** "a major achievement in a screen genre." **Cue** observed, "Star-studded musical comedy of show business—overflowing with mirth, melody, lavish production and revue numbers, bright lines, brilliant performances."

Among the many musical highlights are: Astaire, Fabray, Buchanan, Levant, and Charisse performing a rousing "That's Entertainment"; Astaire's classic "A Shine on Your Shoes"; Fabray's "Louisiana Hayride"; the comic "Triplets"; and especially the elaborate Mickey Spillane–spoofing "Girl Hunt Ballet," with Astaire finally upstaged by the beautiful and leggy Charisse,[4] and "Dancing

in the Dark," which finds Astaire and Charisse nimbly gliding through Central Park.

There were several numbers filmgoers never got to see in the release print: Astaire and Fabray in "Gotta Bran' New Suit," Astaire and Charisse dancing to "You Have Everything," Fabray and Levant performing "Sweet Music to Worry the Wolf Away," and, among others, a rendition of "Two-Faced Woman." The last song, as prerecorded by India Adams, would turn up in MGM's **Torch Song** (1953) with Joan Crawford mouthing the Schwartz-Dietz tune.

Unaided by Academy Award nominations or wins, **The Band Wagon,** which debuted at Radio City Music Hall in July 1953, earned $5,655,505, making it one of the heavier-grossing Hollywood musicals. It owed its success to the close-knit members of the Arthur Freed production unit, which was able to surmount production and personality obstacles to turn out a sparkling whole.

In his memoirs, **I Remember It Well** (1974), director Minnelli provides a postscript to **The Band Wagon**—and to the big golden days of MGM. Recalling Fred Astaire's visit to the old train set on the Culver City lot to do a narration-hosting assignment for **That's Entertainment!** (1974), Minnelli writes:

"The set was a mess," Fred says. "All the windows on the train were broken. Nobody had tried to sweep or clean up. It was just a wreck. The Twentieth Century Limited looked so black and dreary. As I walked along, I noticed that

---

[2]Comden and Green had written the part loosely based on Jose Ferrer's life, who at that point in his career was directing stage shows.

[3]Comden and Green had planned to create a whodunit-ballet for the big Astaire-Charisse number, but they were informed that the Dietz-Schwartz team was to contribute the segment. The duo submitted "The Private Eye" song, which did not appeal to choreographer Michael Kidd. Roger Edens later thought of the Mickey Spillane ballet spoof and Alan Jay Lerner, then at MGM working on Freed's **Brigadoon** (1954), agreed to provide the narration "for fun . . . no money."

Years later, Minnelli would say "it had to be a ballet with some kind of style, and it had to be popular. As Mickey Spillane's novels were very popular, I made it a satire on those novels. They're almost a satire in themselves. I made it in the spirit of Mickey Spillane, with beautiful girls and killings and private eyes."

In **The Movie Musical** (1974) Lee Edward Stern would assess, **"The Band Wagon,** with its many delights, is not perfect . . . The final ballet . . . is so convinced of its own cleverness that its effect is jarring rather than amusing."

---

[4]Although Charisse would regard Astaire as "a perfectionist" and the "most perfect gentleman I have ever known," Astaire would recently recollect that of all his

many dance partners, she was the heaviest he ever had, and he came to dread the lifts. Many regard the Astaire-Charisse team, rematched in **Silk Stockings** (1957), as the finest pairing of Astaire on screen.

the carpeting was torn and the seats of the train were missing. But I suppose nothing should last forever."

THE BARKLEYS OF BROADWAY

1949 C—109 min. (British Release Title: THE GAY BARKLEYS)

Producer, Arthur Freed; **associate producer,** Roger Edens; **director,** Charles Walters; **screenplay,** Betty Comden, Adolph Green, and, **uncredited,** Sidney Sheldon; **music director,** Lennie Hayton; **songs,** Harry Warren and Ira Gershwin; **orchestrator,** Conrad Salinger; **vocal arranger,** Robert Tucker; **music numbers staged by and directed by** Robert Alton **(choreography of** "Shoes with Wings On," Hermes Pan); **color consultants,** Natalie Kalmus and Henri Jaffa; **art directors,** Cedric Gibbons and Edward Carfagno; **set decorators,** Edwin B. Willis and Arthur Krams; **Miss Rogers' costumes,** Irene; **men's costumes,** Valles; **makeup,** Jack Dawn; **sound,** Douglas Shearer; **special effects,** Warren Newcombe; **dancing shoes effect,** Irving Ries; **camera,** Harry Stradling; **editor,** Albert Akst.

Fred Astaire **(Josh Barkley);** Ginger Rogers **(Dinah Barkley);** Oscar Levant **(Ezra Miller);** Billie Burke **(Mrs. Livingston Belney);** Gale Robbins **(Shirlene May);** Jacques Francois **(Jacques Pierre Barredout);** George Zucco **(The Judge);** Clinton Sundberg **(Bert Felsher);** Inez Cooper **(Pamela Driscoll);** Carol Brewster **(Gloria Amboy);** Wilson Wood **(Larry);** Jean Andren and Laura Treadwell **(Women);** Margaret Bert **(Mary, the Maid);** Allen Wood **(Taxi Driver);** Forbes Murray, Bess Flowers, Lois Austin, and Betty Blythe **(Guests in Theatre Lobby);** Bill Tannen **(Doorman at Theatre);** Mahlon Hamilton **(Apartment Doorman);** Hans Conried **(Ladislaus Ladi);** Sherry Hall **(Chauffeur);** Reginald Simpson **(Husband);** Esther Somers **(Sarah's Mother);** Helen Eby-Rock **(Sarah's Aunt);** Mary Jo Ellis **(Clementine);** Joyce Matthews **(Genevieve);** Joe Granby **(Duke de Morny).**

SYNOPSIS

Successful Broadway husband-and-wife team Josh and Dinah Barkley have a happy marriage except for occasional temperamental outbursts. When French playwright Jacques Pierre Barredout approaches Dinah with a dramatic role, Josh resents his wife's ambitions for thesping over terping. The fact that Dinah seems romantically attached to Jacques does not help matters.

Close friend Ezra Miller, a composer, is privy to the seesawing battle that occurs as Dinah begins preparation for her dramatic debut as the young Sarah Bernhardt. Meanwhile Josh continues to work in the medium he knows best, song and dance, using an understudy, Shirlene May, to replace his defecting wife.

Ginger Rogers and Fred Astaire in The Barkleys of Broadway *('49).*

Later Dinah's dramatic venture proves a fiasco and the Barkleys are brought together for a charity revue show. They resume their career together, reassured of their mutual love.

* * *

RKO Studios had been the site of some of the cinema's most wonderful celluloid moments as Fred Astaire and Ginger Rogers performed their tandem dancing throughout the 1930s. Their professional relationship, ever creatively splendid, often was personally nonamicable. In 1939 they made their ninth and what promised to be their last joint screen appearance together. After **The Story of Vernon and Irene Castle,** Astaire left RKO to freelance. His first assignment thereafter was **Broadway Melody of 1940** (MGM) with Eleanor Powell. That year Ginger would win an Oscar for her dramatics in **Kitty Foyle.** It seemed she might never have to rely on her dancing again. Throughout the 1940s Astaire perpetuated his dancing with such partners as Paulette Goddard **(Second Chorus),** Rita Hayworth **(You'll Never Get Rich** and **You Were Never Lovelier),** Joan Leslie **(The Sky's the Limit),** Lucille Bremer **(Yolanda and the Thief** and **Ziegfeld Follies),** etc. Meanwhile, Ginger pursued a career in "straight" assignments in such fare as **Roxie Hart** (1942), **Tender Comrade** (1943), and MGM's **Weekend at the Waldorf** (1945). The hopes for a screen reunion between the once lilting dance-and-song couple seemed more and more unlikely.

What were the events that led to the wonderful return in MGM's **The Barkleys of Broadway?** Not very pleasant ones. The success of Astaire with Judy Garland in Metro's **Easter Parade** (1948) encouraged Arthur Freed to produce another picture to showcase the two superstars. Betty Comden and Adolph Green fashioned an original screenplay which had elements of factuality in it; a Harry Warren and Ira Gershwin score was added.

The script was completed in March 1948 and the main talents involved were pleased. On May 1 Astaire began rehearsal of "Shoes with Wings On," aided by choreographer Hermes Pans, who had worked frequently with Astaire at RKO. Garland began rehearsals on June 14. By her third week on the film she began to experience the same set of physical-emotional problems that had plagued her work on **The Pirate** (1948). She "withdrew"[1] from the project and a desperate Freed had the notion of contacting Ginger Rogers (at her Oregon ranch) as a substitute. After appropriate overtures and contract negotiations, Rogers joined the cast. Astaire said he was delighted, "Gin and I had often discussed the possibility of getting together for a rematch. And here it was, out of a clear sky."

Because of the very contrasting personalities and talents of Rogers and Garland, the script and array of songs had to be altered. Such Warren and Gershwin works as the hillbilly "Courtship of Elmer and Ella," the comic ballet "Poetry in Motion," and "Natchez on the Mississip' " were deleted. The last number had been conceived with

[1] Garland would later relate of this trying period, "The rehearsals began and my migraine headaches got worse. I went for days without sleep but I kept on. Then I started to be late to rehearsals and began missing days. Finally I was fired. They didn't even give me the courtesy of a call or a meeting or a discussion. They sent me a telegram."

Garland particularly in mind. To fill in one of the gaps, Roger Edens suggested resurrecting George and Ira Gershwin's "They Can't Take That Away from Me," which had been used by Astaire and Rogers in the ferryboat scene for **Shall We Dance?** (1937). (Harry Warren was not thrilled by this addition.)

With a revised scenario and song catalog, **The Barkleys of Broadway** began filming again on August 8. The times were not always happy. One day Garland came to visit the set wearing one of her costumes from the musical. The nervous situation was made worse when she refused to leave. Finally she was led off the premises by director Walters. At this point Rogers was in her dressing room in tears, trying not to hear the insults shouted at her by Judy.

On the other hand, Astaire and Rogers found pleasure in working together again, displaying their usual keen sense of cooperation as well as competition. Fred later remembered:

When we finally got around to shooting our first dance, I thought for some reason Ginger seemed taller than usual. I asked [Hermes] Pan, "Am I crazy or is Ginger on stilts?" He said, "I know—something is different." I went to Ginger. "Hey," I said, "have you grown or have I shrunk?" She laughed and confessed she had sneaked some higher heels over on me.

As would prove true in later MGM features showcasing the wit and music virtuosity of Oscar Levant, the frenetic pessimist was a trying soul to have on the soundstages. Things were not made easier when Arthur Freed arrived on the set. According to Charles Walters:

Freed did a terrible thing regarding Levant. Right in front of him, Arthur said, "Now, Chuck, I want you to realize that Oscar is a very talented and very funny personality. And anything he wants to do, just stand back and let him go on with it." Now you just don't do that sort of thing to a director, at least not while the actor is within earshot.

Levant's fertile imagination was almost as big as his ego. He would later contend that his piano solo numbers (Khachaturian's "Sabre Dance" and excerpts from Tchaikovsky's Piano Concerto No. 1 in B-flat minor) were recorded directly as he performed them for the camera. Actually, as Hugh Fordin points out in **The World of Entertainment,** they were prerecorded under Lennie Hayton's supervision and then played back for the filmed scenes.

The film offers a fine variety of singing and dancing.[2] During the opening scene, Astaire and Rogers are shown dancing to "Swing Trot." It was a number added to the score at Astaire's insistence, thinking it would be useful later on to promote his new franchised dance schools. When the picture proved to have a plethora of routines,

rather than junk "Swing Trot" it was utilized up front.

Two numbers are employed in the film which do not fit into the rehearsing-for-the-show format. "A Weekend in the Country" allows the trio of Astaire, Rogers, and Levant to scamper about the countryside while on holiday at Billie Burke's plush suburban estate. The other is "You'd Be Hard to Replace," which Astaire sings in his bid to rewoo Rogers. This segment occurs in the duo's New York apartment with each player wearing a bathrobe!

The comic "My One and Only Highland Fling," finds the star team performing in kilts and brogues, whereas the instrumental "Bouncin' the Blues" is given an informal but precise handling by the accomplished dancers. Then there is the elegant "They Can't Take That Away from Me," danced by the couple in formal attire. For moviegoers it is the apogee of the Astaire-Rogers screen teaming, reminding viewers again of joyous past memories from the 1930s. The finale, "Manhattan Heartbeat," has the couple involved in a Gotham montage, which peaks with the team whirling about a replica of the Plaza Hotel fountain as some four dozen pairs of dancers complement the stars' movements. With the multihued lights accenting Rogers' dress and the set, the film ends.

As with so many Fred Astaire films, there is one number that causes unusual comment. Such is the case with "Shoes with Wings On." Hermes Pan would remember that the concept for the unique dance came to him from Walt Disney's screen version of **The Sorcerer's Apprentice.** (Others insist that the British-made **Red Shoes** had a strong influence on the dance's origin.) According to Ira Gershwin, he was motivated for this alternating-forms-of-dance theme by spotting a picture of the god Mercury in Bulfinch's **Mythology.** In Fordin's above-mentioned study of the Arthur Freed MGM unit, he describes the segment:

The Barkleys have split up. Astaire continues the show with Mrs. Barkley's understudy, and this is his big new solo number. It takes place on the stage; the set is a shoestore with Astaire as the shoemaker. The curtain opens on a number of customers of different types: a ballet dancer, a tap dancer, a child toe dancer, a Russian girl dancer, etc., are posed in a tableau during the introductory music. As the first rhythm chorus starts, the tableau breaks and Astaire waits on his customers, fitting ballet shoes, adjusting taps, etc. The customers leave one by one and he closes his store. As he is standing by the counter, a pair of shoes suddenly appear dancing on the counter, to Astaire's amazement. He tries to catch the shoes but they slip away. The shoes dance all around him; Astaire falls in with their rhythm, dancing with them, until momentarily the shoes disappear. At this point we hear Astaire's voice off scene reflecting his thoughts, "I've got shoes with wings on." Astaire does a pantomime to the lyric of the song, there is a wild tap dance with Astaire again dancing with the shoes until, in a frenzy, he grabs two guns from behind the counter and shoots the shoes. They disap-

pear one after another. Astaire then throws the guns into the store window—it breaks with a terrific crash—at the same time all the shoe boxes fall out of the shelves and Astaire collapses, buried under a heap of shoes.

The logistics of filming this special effects number were demanding, requiring strict discipline by every participant. For perfectionist Astaire it was a most satisfying creative peak. Audiences would reap enjoyment from his dedication.

By October 30, 1948, **The Barkleys of Broadway** had completed production at a cost of $2,325,420—amazingly under budget by some $87,000 despite the Garland-induced holdup. The entity was released to high approval. Otis L. Guernsey, Jr. **(New York Herald-Tribune)** decided, "This new musical . . . finds the movies once again relying on old hat to keep up appearances, but as long as there is a touch of **Top Hat** about it, no one can complain. . . . The accent in this picture is on flashing feet and graceful body angles rather than on singing, but in the absence of a hit tune there is a bonanza of rhythm and motion."

Bosley Crowther **(New York Times)** judged, "Next to the patching of relations between Russia and the United States, there is probably no rapprochement that has been more universally desired than the bringing back together of Ginger Rogers and Fred Astaire. . . . Metro has joined the two again in **The Barkleys of Broadway** and the health of the world should improve. . . . Age cannot wither the enchantment of Ginger and Fred." Levant received his critical due, acting as the sharp-tongued foil for Astaire (a marked contrast to the daffy friends, servants, et al., who were the dancer's confidants in past features).

The film would gross $5,421,000 in its initial release. Its enormous draw influenced the Academy of Motion Picture Arts and Sciences to present Astaire with a special Oscar statuette "for his unique artistry and his contributions to the technique of musical pictures."

The Barkleys remains the climax of the Astaire-Rogers screen teaming. There were no cinema follow-ups. Ginger attempted to return to MGM in 1950 as a replacement for ailing Judy Garland in **Annie Get Your Gun,** but Louis B. Mayer told her, "Keep your high heels and your silk stockings, you're not raucous enough." (To prove otherwise, Rogers would later headline a successful summer-stock tour of **Annie.**) Astaire remained at Metro throughout much of the fifties with such screen partners as Cyd Charisse, Vera-Ellen, and Jane Powell.

THE BARRETTS OF WIMPOLE STREET
1934—110 min. (TV Title: FORBIDDEN ALLIANCE)

Producer, Irving G. Thalberg; **director,** Sidney Franklin; based on the play by Rudolf Besier;

---

[2] The less said about Ginger Rogers' dramatics during her show-within-the-show scenes, especially her demonstrations of stanza reading in her acting school audition sequence, the better.

screenplay, Ernst Vajda, Claudine West, and Donald Ogden Stewart; **assistant director,** Hugh Boswell; **art directors,** Cedric Gibbons and Harry McAfee; **set decorator,** Edwin B. Willis; **costumes,** Adrian; **music numbers,** Herbert Stothart; **sound,** Douglas Shearer; **camera,** William Daniels; **editor,** Margaret Booth.

Norma Shearer (**Elizabeth Barrett**); Fredric March (**Robert Browning**); Charles Laughton (**Edward Moulton Barrett**); Maureen O'Sullivan (**Henrietta Barrett**); Katharine Alexander (**Arabel**); Ralph Forbes (**Captain Cook**); Una O'Connor (**Wilson**); Marion Clayton (**Bella**); Ian Wolfe (**Bevan**); Ferdinand Munier (**Dr. Chambers**); Leo G. Carroll (**Dr. Waterloo**); Alan Conrad, Neville Clark, Robert Carleton, Peter Hobbes, and Mathew Smith (**Brothers**); George Kirby (**Coachman**); Winter Hall (**Clergyman**); Lowden Adams (**Butler**); Vernon Downing (**Octavius**).

SYNOPSIS

In nineteenth-century London Edward Moulton Barrett's three daughters, Elizabeth, Henrietta, and Arabel, live like prisoners in their Victorian home as a result of their tyrannical father. Eldest daughter Elizabeth is a frail invalid who is wilting as she has lost the will to live. Her only outlet from reality is her poetry; her only object of affection is her pet dog, Flush.

Poet Robert Browning discovers Elizabeth's verse and begins a secret correspondence with her. Their letters blossom into words of love and Browning goes to Elizabeth, bringing her new hope for life. When he proposes marriage, she feels that her frailty will impede his robust life.

Later Browning meets Edward Barrett and senses the father's abnormal feeling for his daughter. Elizabeth consents to marry Browning and leave for Italy. While packing, Elizabeth encounters her father, whose profession of tenderness turns into carnal madness. Elizabeth escapes and Arabel discovers the farewell note which Henrietta presents gloatingly to their father.

* * *

"When poets love . . . heaven and earth fall back to watch" blazed the dramatic advertisement for MGM's **The Barretts of Wimpole Street.** The Rudolf Besier stage play had become a popular and enduring Broadway vehicle for Katharine Cornell in 1931,[1] and Irving Thalberg envisioned the part of aesthetic poetress Elizabeth Barrett Browning (1806–61) as an ideal assignment for his wife Norma Shearer.

William Randolph Hearst had other thoughts. The newspaper tycoon thought that the winsome Elizabeth was a perfect role for his blonde mistress, Marion Davies (born 1897), and informed Louis B. Mayer of his predilection. However, Mayer, disenchanted with the Hearst-Mayer combine on the MGM lot, backed Thalberg's choice. Like most people, Mayer could not picture Miss Davies in the sensitive part. Moreover, her films were losing appeal steadily at the box office. Miss

Fredric March and Norma Shearer in The Barretts of Wimpole Street *('34).*

Davies herself felt no resentment at Mayer's dictate ("I visited Norma Shearer on **The Barretts of Wimpole Street** set, but I was whisked right off," she recalls in her memoirs, **The Times We Had**). But Hearst harbored a bitterness over the loss. As a result he moved Cosmopolitan Pictures from MGM to Warner Bros. and ordered his newspaper chain to squelch MGM publicity, especially any references to Norma Shearer.

Thalberg, anxious to rebuild Norma's reputation after her less than stellar "comeback" picture **Riptide** (1934), assembled a stellar cast. Besides his Oscar-winning wife, there were Academy Award champs Fredric March[2] and Charles Laughton.[3] The latter was delighted to play

the monstrous, incestuous Mr. Barrett and lost fifty pounds to play the role. It amused Laughton to convey the censored areas of Barrett's perverted love for his daughter; he quipped, "They can't censor the gleam in my eye!" Director Sidney Franklin commented during production in the spring of 1934, "In such pictures as this we penetrate the heart of romance. These characters are brilliant, dashing, colorful—yet their love for each other is as deep and clear and simple as a mountain stream."

Released in the summer of 1934, **The Barretts of Wimpole Street** was an enormous success. **Variety** exulted, "Superbly acted and inspirationally directed, [it] . . . comes to the screen as powerful, absorbing drama, off the beaten track of picture entertainment, and having both the requirements of fine artistry and the earmarks of a smashing commercial success." Granted the

---

[1] Brian Aherne was Browning, and Charles Waldron was the father.

[2] Shearer and March had previously performed together in MGM's **Smilin' Through** (1932).

[3] Laughton, still under contract to Paramount, had left the U.S. and returned to England to perform in stage repertory work. When he signed for **The Barretts,** he returned to America via the ship "Berengaria," and then flew across the U.S. to California. He and his actress wife Elsa Lanchester stayed at the Garden of Allah Hotel during the spring 1934 filming.

During the shooting, director Sidney Franklin, who clearly was in awe of the austere British actor, asked Laughton how he perceived his role. The star responded, "Like a monkey on a stick." According to Norma Shearer,

when Laughton first arrived on the set, he fell at her feet and kissed her hand, while Elsa stood in the background. During the filming, there would be afternoon cast breaks with eggnog in Shearer's dressing suite. One day in the midst of shooting, Shearer and co-player Maureen O'Sullivan found Laughton's muttonchop whiskers so "amusing" and giggled so much that filming had to be halted for the day.

on-screen leads lacked the élan of the stage originals, the theatrical dimensions of their parts nonetheless fit their screen styles very well indeed. The film was voted number one in the **Film Daily** annual Ten Best list, won the **Photoplay** magazine Gold Medal as best picture of 1934, became one of the season's top grossing releases, and earned Academy Award nominations in the areas of Best Picture and Best Actress. Columbia's **It Happened One Night** won the Best Picture prize with its star, Claudette Colbert, defeating Shearer in the contest.

MGM would remake **The Barretts of Wimpole Street** in 1957, again under the direction of Sidney Franklin. However, none of the principals—Jennifer Jones as Elizabeth, Bill Travers as Browning, and John Gielgud as Mr. Barrett—could match the flamboyant charm of the star trio of the 1934 classic. A literate, well-garnished, powerful testimony to the genius and taste of Thalberg and the talents of its performers, the original **Barretts** is a neglected gem. It is televised, generally at ridiculously late hours, under the title **Forbidden Alliance** so as to avoid confusion with its inferior remake.

BATAAN
1943—114 min.

Producer, Irving Starr; **director,** Tay Garnett; **screenplay,** Robert D. Andrews; **art directors,** Cedric Gibbons and Lyle Wheeler; **set decorators,** Edwin B. Willis and Glen Barner; **music,** Bronislau Kaper; **assistant director,** William Lewis; **sound,** Douglas Shearer; **special camera effects,** Arnold Gillespie and Warren Newcombe; **camera,** Sidney Wagner; **editor,** George White.

Robert Taylor (**Sergeant Bill Dane**); George Murphy (**Lieutenant Steve Bentley**); Thomas Mitchell (**Corporal Jake Feingold**); Lloyd Nolan (**Corporal Barney Todd**); Lee Bowman (**Captain Henry Lassiter**); Robert Walker (**Leonard Purckett**); Desi Arnaz (**Felix Ramírez**); Barry Nelson (**F. X. Matowski**); Phillip Terry (**Gilbert Hardy**); Roque Espiritu (**Corporal Juan Katigbak**); Kenneth Spencer (**Wesley Epps**); J. Alex Havier (**Yankee Salazar**); Tom Dugan (**Sam Malloy**); Donald Curtis (**Lieutenant**); Lynne Carver, Mary McLeod, and Dorothy Morris (**Nurses**); Phil Schumacher (**Machine Gunner**); Bud Geary (**Infantry Officer**); Ernie Alexander (**Wounded Soldier**).

SYNOPSIS

During World War II in the Pacific theatre of war, thousands of Allied soldiers evacuate the battered Philippine community of Bataan amidst Japanese bombardment. Captain Henry Lassiter orders Sergeant Bill Dane and Corporal Jake Feingold to blow up a bridge in order to hold the area. Included in the suicide mission are sailor Leonard Purckett, Private F. X. Matowski, wisecracking Corporal Barney Todd, Private Gilbert Hardy, Private Felix Ramirez, Private Wesley Epps, Private Sam Malloy, Private Yankee Salazar, Corporal Juan Katigbak, and Lieutenant Steve Bentley.

The men prepare by digging foxholes, setting up machine guns, and organizing supplies. The group successfully blows up the target bridge but Lassiter falls when hit by a Japanese sniper. One by one, the valiant soldiers succumb to the preying enemy, yet they manage to hold their position. Finally Sergeant Dane digs his own grave and makes a final stand against the attacking Japanese, killing several in an onslaught of rapid fire before his own bullet-filled body drops, a testimony to his earlier sentiment, "It doesn't matter where a man dies so long as he dies for freedom!"

* * *

While a great deal of celluloid bilge was dumped onto the public during the World War II years by producers who equated propaganda with profits, a good number of realistic, downplayed, grim dramas also emanated from Hollywood, picturing war as a brutal necessity to end aggressions against mankind. MGM ran the gamut during these frightening times in producing war-related entertainment with films ranging from the inspiring **Mrs. Miniver** (1942), to the philosophical **Human Comedy** (1943), to the melodramatic **Hitler's Madman** (1943, starring John Carradine as the sinister Heydrich, who saves his best sneers for priests and young girls). However, occupying a special niche in Metro's 1940s propaganda was **Bataan.** It focused its 114 minutes of screen time on combat, dealing a blend of realism, sincerity, and just enough melodramatics to fill audiences with a patriotic hatred for the Axis oppressors.

Taking its cue from the great success of Paramount's **Wake Island** (a Best Picture Oscar nominee for 1942 and a favorite with marines), **Bataan** related the account of the thirteen heroes who fought to delay the Japanese invasion of the Philippines. While the MGM picture was primarily a male actor project (**Wake Island** had some early feminine footage), there were occasional audience concessions. Big box-office star Robert Taylor headlined as Sergeant Bill Dane and the screenplay provided stereotypes for easy audience identification. Dore Schary, who was involved with the production of the picture, recalls:

The stereotype always appears in war pictures. Every war picture we made had a Jew, an Italian, a Pole, a WASP. But not always a black man, because blacks weren't integrated in the army at that time. . . . I put one in **Bataan,** just put one in, that's all. I said, "To hell with it, we're going to have one black." We got a lot of letters from people complaining.

In addition to black Kenneth Spencer, **Bataan** featured a Pole (Barry Nelson), a Cuban (Desi Arnaz), a Latin (Roque Espiritu), and an Irish-accented Jew (Thomas Mitchell), as well as newcomer Robert Walker as the overtalkative green gob Leonard Purckett (the role won him a long-term Metro contract). Director Tay Garnett requested some three hundred Japanese actors for the war film—an impossibility because most Japanese had been removed to internment centers in mid-America—but had to settle for Chinese and Filipino players.

Lloyd Nolan, Robert Taylor, and Thomas Mitchell in Bataan *('43).*

The feature had its (over)doses of GI heroism, perhaps the most outrageous[1] being the sequence in which mortally wounded air force pilot Steve Bentley (George Murphy) orders his plane loaded with TNT and then, in imitation of the Japanese kamikaze pilots, crashes his craft into the enemy's bridge. It is to be noted that not all of the thirteen soldiers die at the hands of the enemy; Desi Arnaz's Felix Ramirez succumbs to a bout of malaria (in a scene which proved Arnaz had the makings of a solid actor).

Advertised as "The story America will never forget!" and "The story of a patrol of 13 heroes!" **Bataan** won both critical and public endorsement upon its June 1943 release. The **New York Herald-Tribune** reported, "**Bataan** has heroic dimensions and great melodramatic and emotional intensity . . . crowded with human and personal touches." **Variety** noted, "It's an all-male cast, but with terrific sock to women audiences in depicting front-line adventures of their sons, husbands, sweethearts." And the **New York Times,** while granting the film has a "melodramatic flaw" and "contains some admitted technical mistakes," praised MGM for making "a picture about war in true and ugly detail. . . . it doesn't insult the honor of dead soldiers, which is something to say for a Hollywood film these days."

The entire cast, especially Thomas Mitchell as a grizzled corporal, and Taylor (albeit rather dour), supplies the proceedings with virility and sincerity of sorts. Not to be overlooked is the handling of the heroes' adversary, the "beastly" Japanese. In the opening scenes the enemy is shown massacring civilians and soldiers alike in their air and land attack on the Philippines. Later, as Norman Kagan details in **The War Films** (1974), "The inhuman enemy takes on chilling forms in the Pacific, at one point drifting toward them hidden in a milky fog, another time camouflaged into sinisterly shifting trees and brush."

The latter part of the film, in which the men fall one by one to the Japanese snipers, has caused some film historians to record the picture as an "unofficial remake" of John Ford's **The Lost Patrol,** set in the Arabian desert.[2] (That 1934 RKO film was itself remade as the 1939 Western **Bad Lands.**)

As for what Allied women were doing during the Bataan conflict, MGM offered **Cry Havoc,** also in 1943, which detailed the fate of a group of nurses caught in the Axis invasion of the island. Later war action in Bataan was documented in RKO's **Back to Bataan,** starring John Wayne and Anthony Quinn.

---

[1]MGM avoided the pitfalls which would tarnish Warner Bros.' **Objective, Burma!** (1945) in which Errol Flynn's American soldier wins the battle (and war) almost single-handedly, a plot device that infuriated the British (who participated in that theatre of war) and caused the film to be yanked from English release for seven years.

[2]Critic James Agee would describe the ten-little-Indians story gimmick of **Bataan** as a ritualistic Americana folk dance that was "naive, coarse-grained, primitive, honest, accomplished, and true."

BATHING BEAUTY
1944 C—101 min.

Producer, Jack Cummings; **director,** George Sidney; based on the screen story "Mr. Co-ed" by Kenneth Earl, M. M. Musselman, and Curtis Kenyon; **screenplay,** Dorothy Kingsley, Allen Boretz, and Frank Waldman; **Technicolor consultant,** Natalie Kalmus; **music supervisor–director,** Johnny Green; **orchestrators,** Ted Duncan, Calvin Jackson, and Johnny Thompson; **choreography,** Jack Donahue and Robert Alton; **art directors,** Stephen Goosson and Merrill Pye; **set decorators,** Edwin B. Willis and McLean Nisbet; water ballet **staged by** John Murray Anderson; **songs,** Green; **assistant director,** George Ryan; **sound,** Frank B. MacKenzie, Ralph A. Shugart, and William R. Edmondson; **camera,** Harry Stradling; **editor,** Blanche Sewell.

Red Skelton **(Steve Elliott);** Esther Williams **(Caroline Brooks);** Basil Rathbone **(George Adams);** Jean Porter **(Jean Allenwood);** Jacqueline Dalya **(Maria Dorango);** Bill Goodwin **(Willis Evans);** Donald Meek **(Chester Klazenfrantz);** Nana Bryant **(Dean Clinton);** Harry James **(Harry);** Buddy Moreno **(Buddy);** Helen Forrest **(Helen);** Carlos Ramirez **(Specialty);** Ethel Smith **(Organist);** Harry James' Music Makers, Xavier Cugat & His Orchestra with Lina Romay **(Themselves);** William Hayden **(Bit);** Sarah Edwards **(Miss Phillips);** Almira Sessions **(Miss Kern);** Elspeth Dudgeon **(Miss Travers);** Ann Codee **(Mme Zarka, the Ballet Teacher);** Francis Pierlot **(Professor Hendricks);** Earl Schenck **(Professor Nichols);** Dorothy Adams **(Miss Hanney);** Shelby Payne **(Cigarette Girl);** Margaret Dumont **(Mrs. Allenwood);** Russell Hicks **(Mr. Allenwood);** Joe Yule **(Bartender);** Janis Paige **(Janis);** Dorothy Ford **(Dorothy);** Betty Jaynes, Beverly Tyler, Margaret Adams, and Ann Lundeen **(Co-eds);** Fidel Castro **(Student).**

SYNOPSIS
At a California summer resort Broadway songwriter Steve Elliott falls in love with Victoria College swimming instructress Caroline Brooks. Caroline plans to resign her teaching post and Steve decides to cancel his contract to write songs for producer George Adams' water pageant.

Learning the bad news, Adams tries to break up the marriage by having actress Maria Dorango pose as George's spouse. Convinced that Steve is a bigamist, Caroline returns to Victoria College. Steve follows and becomes the first male to enroll at the all-girls school, leading to several uproarious incidents. Adams follows the pair to the campus where Steve vows that he will not write another song until his marital mixup becomes untangled.

Finally Maria tells Caroline the truth and the pair reconcile on the night of the spectacular water pageant.

* * *

Red Skelton and Esther Williams in Bathing Beauty *('44).*

There was indeed at MGM, as at other studios, a curious and obvious caste system.[1] There was a deep, awkward gap between employees regarded as **stars** and those contractees deemed only **feature players.** The symbol of this social stigma at Culver City in the 1940s was an edifice known simply as the Stars' Building. It was a plushly furnished structure populated only by the biggest names of the lot and barred to anybody else who tried to enter without official blessing. The late Brian Donlevy once chuckled how, when visiting the Metro facility on loan from Paramount in 1941 to play in **Billy the Kid,** he drew a berth in the Featured Players Hall and quietly wondered what it was like in the noble structure his costar Robert Taylor occupied. Donlevy did not find out until almost three years later when he signed a nonexclusive pact with MGM and reported for work in King Vidor's **An American Romance.** As Lana Turner once gushed of this rather Victorian studio custom, "Believe me, when the time came for you to move from the featured players' building into the building of the stars' dressing rooms, it was a thrilling event in your life. It was like entering a new kingdom in which you were the queen."

In 1944, when wartime America was seeking relief from the agonies of global conflict by escaping to cinemas almost nightly, MGM graduated ten humble feature players into the star building. In alphabetical order they were: Laraine Day, Kathryn Grayson, Van Johnson, Gene Kelly, George Murphy, Margaret O'Brien, Susan Peters, Ginny Simms, Robert Walker, and Esther Williams. The last of these, Miss Williams, ascended to the airy company via her third feature picture, **Bathing Beauty.**

Perhaps the most beautiful and photogenic actress ever on contract at MGM, the twenty-one-year-old U.S. swimming champion had served the usual beauty apprentice period by appearing in Metro's **Andy Hardy's Double Life** (1942) and then charming fellow newcomer Van Johnson in **A Guy Named Joe** (1943). Finally, six (credited) writers concocted a "perfect" vehicle that allowed her to be pretty and charming, and, most important, to swim. With Red Skelton for box-office stability, Basil Rathbone for some acting flair,[2] and such

varied musical attractions as organist Ethel Smith (performing "Tico-Tico"), Carlos Ramirez (singing "Echo of a Serenade"), and the orchestras of both Harry James and Xavier Cugat, Esther came cinematically into her own.

After surviving two false titles—**Mr. Co-Ed** and **Sing or Swim**—**Bathing Beauty** appeared in theatres in June 1944. "If there's anything to be described as perfect hot weather entertainment, **Bathing Beauty** is it," wrote Leo Mishkin **(New York Morning Telegraph).** John T. McManus **(PM)** noted, "It has at least a hundred fabulous formfits in its water spectacle finale alone. Easily another hundred lovelies promenade promiscuously in the dry-stage backgrounds while the MGM naiads swim patterns and splashy Arabesques that make Billy Rose's late World's Fair spectacle seem like something swum in a rain barrel. In addition there is MGM's ace naiad Esther Williams, with her own amphibious retinue. And this is only the ending. . . . **Bathing Beauty** is escapism with a blue-sky vengeance." Even the **New York Times'** hard-to-please Bosley Crowther had to admit, "Miss Williams' talents as a swimmer— not to mention her other attributes—make any title the studio wants to put on it okay by us. When she eels through the crystal blue water in a rosy-red bathing suit or splashes in limpid magnificence in the gaudy water carnival which John Murray Anderson has brought to pass, she's a bathing beauty for our money, even though dragged in by the heels." And in **Variety's** words, Esther

Williams was "pulled to stardom by her swimsuit straps."

She would draw a weekly check from MGM for several years after her last film made there **(Jupiter's Darling,** 1955). MGM spent a decade hiring writers to crank out "musical splash" scripts that centered on Esther's swimming acumen; choreographers would develop dances that did not tax her limited terpsichorean skills; dubbers supplied her singing voice; and directors tried to be patient with her limited acting skills ("Wet she is a star, dry she ain't," cracked Fanny Brice). Recently the ex-aquatic star would remark cynically, "All they ever did for me at MGM was to change my leading men and the water in the pool."

BATTLEGROUND
1949—118 min.

Producer, Dore Schary; **associate producer,** Robert Pirosh; **director,** William Wellman; **story-screenplay,** Pirosh; **art directors,** Cedric Gibbons and Hans Peters; **set decorators,** Edwin B. Willis and Alfred E. Spencer; **music,** Lennie Hayton; **assistant director,** Sid Sidman; **makeup,** Jack Dawn; **sound,** Douglas Shearer and Conrad Kahn; **montage,** Peter Ballbusch; **camera,** Paul C. Vogel; **editor,** John Dunning.

Jerome Courtland and John Hodiak in Battleground *('49).*

---

[1] MGM stock company player Selena Royle would wistfully recall her tenure at MGM in the mid-1940s, where her long-time personal friend Spencer Tracy was a star. "I was quite hurt at first, for I had expected Spence and Louise to ask me to dinner, and of course they never did. I realized eventually that it wasn't anything about **me**; it was just the way things were with everybody."

[2] It should be noted that **Bathing Beauty** was one of the few MGM pictures to feature Basil Rathbone during his tenure there in the early 1940s. MGM was so busy farming out the actor to Universal for the Sherlock Holmes series and to Blue radio network for the Holmes broadcasts and to other Hollywood studios, that he appeared in only four Metro pictures during a five-year contract period there. Said Rathbone of the studio system, "I really don't mind Metro's selling my services for the Holmes pictures at a much larger fee than they're paying me. That's just good business. But what **does** gripe me is the fact that, when I do a film for them, it's always a piece of junk like **Bathing Beauty.**"

Van Johnson (**Holley**); John Hodiak (**Jarvess**); Ricardo Montalban (**Rodriguez**); George Murphy ("**Pop**" **Ernest Stazak**); Marshall Thompson (**Joe Layton**); Jerome Courtland (**Abner Spudler**); Don Taylor (**Standiferd**); Bruce Cowling (**Wolowicz**); James Whitmore (**Kinnie**); Douglas Fowley (**Kipp Kippton**); Leon Ames (**Chaplain**); Guy Anderson (**Hansan**); Brett King (**Lieutenant Teiss**); Richard Jaeckel (**Bettis**); Jim Arness (**Garby**); Denise Darcel (**Denise**); Thomas E. Breen (**Doc "Medic"**); Roland Varno (**German Lieutenant**); George Offerman, Jr. and William Self (**G.I.'s**); Dewey Martin, Tommy Noonan, and David Holt (**GI Stragglers**); Michael Browne (**Levenstein**); Jim Drum (**Supply Sergeant**); Jerry Paris (**German Sergeant**); Nan Boardman (**Belgian Woman Volunteer**); John Mylong (**German Major**); Ivan Triesault (**German Captain**); George Chandler (**Mess Sergeant**); Dick Jones (**Tanker**); Tommy Kelly (**Casualty**); Ian MacDonald (**American Colonel**); Scotty Beckett (**William J. Hopper**); Screaming Eagles of the 101st Airborne Division (**Themselves**).

SYNOPSIS

On December 17, 1944, the 101st Airborne Division dreams of the long-awaited rest in Paris, complete with clean sheets, showers, gals, and wine. Their hopes are shattered when they are assigned to the Belgian town of Bastogne. Among the 101st's motley components are girl-chasing Holley, who romances Denise, with whom he and others are billeted; the young replacement Joe Layton; Jarvess, a small-town columnist inspired to enlist by his own editorials; Rodriguez, a kid from Mexico City seeing his first snowfall in Belgium; Pop Stazak, thirty-five years old and awaiting his discharge. The platoon sergeant is Kinnie.

The "Screaming Eagles" experience a history-making week in Bastogne during the "Rundstedt offensive" as they hold their ground against the Nazis, despite being surrounded and outnumbered. At one point the Germans don GI uniforms and blow up bridges behind them to further entrap the 101st. Each day becomes more grim as the field hospital is captured, tanks run out of gas, and gunners run short of ammunition. The Germans demand an unconditional American surrender. General George McAuliffe's answer is "Nuts!"

When all seems lost, Allied tanks begin to move into the area and the sky becomes filled with Allied planes and billowing supplies: gasoline, ammunition. and rations. The battered 101st is saved.

* * *

"The guts, gags, and glory of a lot of wonderful guys!" read the famous copy that advertised **Battleground** (1949), Metro's acclaimed reenactment of the Battle of the Bulge of December 1944—some of the grimmest days of World War II.

The production itself was one of the grimmest battles ever waged at MGM. **Battleground** was a property developed by Dore Schary at RKO where studio boss Howard Hughes had forbidden the filmmaker to produce it. Hughes found the theme too depressing. When Schary joined MGM

in 1948 as vice president in charge of production, he brought the pet project with him. Louis B. Mayer agreed with Hughes that **Battleground** was not ideal cinema material. But Schary, who had pushed through the thought-provoking **Crossfire** (RKO, 1947), fought hard now for this controversial venture. He enlisted so much corporate support that he succeeded in winning his way. Schary's victory provided Hollywood with endless conversation. Many noted that the Mayer-Schary war was uncannily similar to the one of 1925, when Irving Thalberg had defeated Mayer's block of **The Big Parade.**

Battleground came from an original story by Robert Pirosh, who also prepared the screenplay. He and the director William ("Wild Bill") Wellman, former French Aviation Force pilot whose credits included **Wings** (1927), **Beau Geste** (1939), and **The Story of G.I. Joe** (1945), insisted on complete realism. (More so than had been experienced on the studio's adaptation of **Command Decision,** 1948, another account of the complexities of military life in World War II.) Bastogne was duplicated on the studio lot, with 500 trees (many giant pines) flown in from northern California; twenty paratroopers, all veterans of Bastogne and the 101st Airborne, were brought to Hollywood for six weeks to appear in the film and to offer technical advice; and no background music was to be used ("They had no eighty-piece orchestra in the foxholes," said Pirosh). Against this realism, freckle-faced Van Johnson and shapely Denise Darcel provided some nonobtrusive love interest, with John Hodiak, George Murphy, Ricardo Montalban, and James Whitmore displaying the sinewy toughness of the Airborne.

There was also something of a censorship scrape with the Breen Office during the making of **Battleground.** When the Germans had demanded that the Allies surrender at Bastogne, General McAuliffe's famous response was "Nuts!" The word heretofore had been blue-penciled by the Breen Office no matter what the connotation. In this case "Nuts!" passed the censors "to preserve historical accuracy."

Battleground, dedicated to "the Battered Bastards of Bastogne," was released in the late fall of 1949 to enormous critical and public approval.[1] Bosley Crowther (**New York Times**) declared, "MGM's **Battleground,** produced by Dore

---

[1] In **The War Film** (1974) Norman Kagan wrote: "The emphasis was on plausibility: the snow-covered battleground, the clumsy, heavy-coated dogfaces slogging along or digging foxholes or in a swift, confused firefight with English-speaking Nazi infiltrators (and a near fight with a stuffy major who can't prove his loyalty with a knowledge of baseball or movies). Van Johnson is likable as a rifleman who drags a dozen eggs through days of combat because he never has time to make an omelet. Very effective too is a chaplain [Leon Ames] whose field sermon is a simple justification of the war: 'Was this trip necessary? Thousands died because they thought it wasn't, till there was nothing left to do but fight. We must never let force impose itself on a free world. Yes, this trip was necessary. Don't let anyone say you were a sucker for fighting in a war against fascism!' But ideas are always in the background. **Battleground** is really most about the look of combat. . . ."

Schary, is **The Big Parade** of World War II. Here is the unadorned image of the misery, the agony, the grief, and the still irrepressible humor and dauntless mockery of the American G.I." Howard Barnes (**New York Herald-Tribune**) wrote, "The work steers resolutely away from a contrived romance which might have made it more popular with customers. In the same manner there is no glorification of individual soldiers. . . . **Battleground** is grimly honest. Artistic integrity has gone into nearly every foot of it."

Robert Pirosh won an Oscar for his script. **Battleground** received Oscar nominations for Best Film (losing to Columbia's **All the King's Men**) and James Whitmore received a Best Supporting Actor bid for his Platoon Sergeant Kinnie (losing to Dean Jagger of Twentieth Century–Fox's **Twelve O'Clock High**). The film did win the **Photoplay** magazine Gold Medal as best picture of the year. It grossed $5,060,000.

Besides giving the public a realistic examination of the Battle of the Bulge, **Battleground** provided Metro insiders with a glimpse of Dore Schary's swelling power at the studio. Less than two years after **Battleground**'s release, Louis B. Mayer would be forced into a bitter resignation and Schary would be the new monarch of declining MGM—for a time.

BEN-HUR

1959 C—217 min.

Producer, Sam Zimbalist; **director,** William Wyler; based on the novel **A Tale of the Christ** by Major General Lew Wallace; **screenplay,** Karl Tunberg and, **uncredited:** Maxwell Anderson, S. N. Behrman, Gore Vidal, and Christopher Fry; **associate directors,** Andrew Marton, Yakima Canutt, and Mario Soldati; **third-unit director,** Richard Thorpe; **assistant directors,** Gus Agosti and Alberto Cardone; **costumes,** Elizabeth Haffenden; **art directors,** William A. Horning and Edward Carfagno; **set decorator,** Hugh Hunt; **makeup,** Charles Parker; **music,** Miklos Rozsa; **sound,** Franklin Milton; **sound recording,** Sash Fisher and William Steinkamp; **special camera effects,** A. Arnold Gillespie, Lee LeBlanc, and Robert Hoag; **camera,** Robert L. Surtees; **second-unit camera,** Piero Portalupi; **third-unit camera,** Harold E. Wellman; **editors,** Ralph E. Winters and John D. Dunning.

Charlton Heston (**Judah Ben-Hur**); Jack Hawkins (**Quintus Arrius**); Stephen Boyd (**Messala**); Haya Harareet (**Esther**); Hugh Griffith (**Sheik Ilderim**); Martha Scott (**Miriam**); Sam Jaffe (**Simonides**); Cathy O'Donnell (**Tirzah**); Finlay Currie (**Balthasar**); Frank Thring (**Pontius Pilate**); Terence Longden (**Drusus**); Andre Morell (**Sextus**); Marina Berti (**Flavia**); George Relph (**Tiberius**); Adi Berber (**Malluch**); Stella Vitelleschi (**Amrah**); Jose Greci (**Mary**); Laurence Payne (**Joseph**); John Horsley (**Spintho**); Richard Coleman (**Metellus**); Duncan Lamont (**Marius**); Ralph Truman (**Aide to Tiberius**); Richard Hale (**Gaspar**); Reginald Lal Singh (**Melchior**); David Davies (**Quaestor**); Dervis Ward

Stephen Boyd and Charlton Heston in Ben-Hur *('59).*

(Jailer); Claude Heater **(The Christ)**; Mino Doro **(Gratus)**; Robert Brown **(Chief of Rowers)**; Tutte Lemkow **(Leper)**; Howard Lang **(Hortator)**; Ferdy Mayne **(Captain of Rescue Ship)**; John LeMesurier **(Doctor)**; Stevenson Lang **(Blind Man)**; Aldo Mozele **(Barca)**; Dino Fazio **(Marcello)**; Michael Cosmo **(Raimondo)**; Remington Olmstead **(Decurian)**; Hugh Billingsley **(Mario)**; Aldo Silvani **(Man in Nazareth)**; Cliff Lyons **(The Lubian)**; Joe Yrigoyrn **(The Egyptian)**; Joe Canutt **(Sportsman)**.

SYNOPSIS

During the seventh year of the reign of Augustus Caesar of the Roman Empire, Judah Ben-Hur is born into a rich Jewish family. About the same time Jesus Christ is born.

Years later Ben-Hur becomes reacquainted with his boyhood friend Messala, now the Roman commander of the garrison in Jerusalem. Messala's objective in his new post is to discover the Jewish patriots who oppose Roman rule, including the man known as Jesus Christ. When Ben-Hur does not inform on copatriots, Messala condemns him to being a galley slave. Ben-Hur's mother, Miriam, and his sister, Tirzah, are sentenced to a dungeon.

Three years later Ben-Hur saves the life of Roman admiral Quintus Arrius during a sea battle and gains his freedom. He returns to Jerusalem and is told by Messala that his mother and sister are dead.

Embittered by such news Ben-Hur agrees to drive the chariot in the great Jerusalem race for Ilderim, the sheik he met in the desert on the way back to his homeland. In the race at the circus arena Ben-Hur defeats Messala, the latter dying when he is thrown from his chariot. His last words reveal that Ben-Hur's mother and sister are still alive, but living in the Valley of the Lepers.

Aided by a former slave named Esther, Ben-Hur reestablishes himself in Jerusalem. He later witnesses Christ bearing His cross to Calvary prior to His crucifixion. Ben-Hur offers Christ water, much to the annoyance of the Roman guards. When he returns to his home he discovers that his mother and sister have been miraculously cured of their disease and they enjoy a happy reunion.

Ben-Hur plans his future with Esther.

* * *

The moving, spectacular epic, which **Time** magazine hailed as "the best of Hollywood's super spectacles" and **Variety** cheered as "the blockbuster to top all previous blockbusters," had been a dream of Metro producer (and onetime editor) Sam Zimbalist ever since his Rome-produced **Quo Vadis** (1951) grossed a walloping $12,500,000. However, MGM, plagued by tight money problems, and the gruesome monsters of television and Wall Street, could not plan definite production of this remake of Metro's 1925 triumph[1] until 1956. The

[1]At the time of the formation of Metro-Goldwyn-Mayer, April 17, 1924, **Ben-Hur** was shooting in Rome, with Charles Brabin directing and George Walsh playing the title role. Louis B. Mayer and Irving Thalberg had very high hopes for this beloved story; the 1880 novel by Lew Wallace had sold more copies than any other novel in printing history, and the play, first presented on Broad-

new **Ben-Hur** progressed as a spectacular which would win Zimbalist the greatest grosses and awards of his career.

It would also kill him.

Direction of **Ben-Hur** was entrusted to William Wyler, the notorious perfectionist and Oscar winner of MGM's **Mrs. Miniver** (1942). With Wyler placing heavy emphasis on characterization, a lengthy search was made for the proper cast. Originally Metro offered Universal $750,000 to secure the services of Rock Hudson for the title role; "contractual problems and conflicting schedules" prevented his casting, as did the next choices, Marlon Brando and Burt Lancaster.[2] Eventually the part went to Charlton Heston, so impressive as Moses in Cecil B. DeMille's **The Ten Commandments** (1956). An international roster filled the other major parts: Palestine's Haya Harareet as the slave girl Esther; England's Jack Hawkins as the Roman sea captain Quintus Arrius; Wales' Hugh Griffith as the belching Sheik Ilderim; Scotland's Finlay Currie as tne wise man Balthasar; Australia's Frank Thring as Pontius Pilate; America's Cathy O'Donnell (Wyler's sister-in-law), Martha Scott, and Sam Jaffe as (respectively) Ben-Hur's mother Miriam, sister Tirzah, and slave Simonides; and Ireland's Stephen Boyd as Messala—"the Roman warrior, who traded loyalty for power, and trust for treachery."[3]

Production began at the Cinecitta Studios in

way in 1899 by Klaw and Erlanger, starred William Farnum as Ben-Hur and William S. Hart as Messala. It had been playing around the world for twenty years.

Realizing the feature could be strategic in establishing MGM's industry prominence, Thalberg was distraught when the difficult epic took shape as indeed a spectacular but a dreadfully dull one. Thalberg and Mayer replaced director Brabin with Fred Niblo and star Walsh with Ramon Novarro. But production problems and poor footage still remained.

Finally, with one year's worth of work completed in Rome, $2,000,000 spent, and only half the film completed, the **Ben-Hur** company was ordered back to Hollywood where Thalberg could keep a sharper eye on the production. A replica of the Antioch Coliseum, costing $300,000 and winning the status of Hollywood's largest set (bigger than Griffith's Babylon of **Intolerance**), was erected on the lot. When the film was finally completed, the cost was $4,000,000, double that of any picture made to that date.

When premiered in New York in December 1925, **Ben-Hur** fulfilled the hopes held for it by the newly restructured studio. The performances of Novarro and Francis X. Bushman (who as Messala is not killed in this version of the chariot race, but crippled), the direction of Niblo, and the spectacle established Metro-Goldwyn-Mayer as a major Hollywood studio. Though the silent film was not extremely profitable at the time of its release—because of the overhead and because the syndicate owners of the theatrical rights earned half of the profits—it is still listed on **Variety**'s report of all-time box-office champs with a domestic gross of $4,000,000. It would be reissued in 1931 by MGM with a special sound-effects soundtrack added.

[2]Other contenders for the title role were John Gavin and Cesare Danova, the latter actor brought from Italian films to Hollywood to play the part eventually given to Heston.

[3]Other candidates for the part of Messala were Victor Mature and Steve Cochran.

Rome where, with much publicity, MGM proceeded to exhaust most of its $15,000,000 budget. There were 300 sets, 100,000 costumes,[4] 1,500,000 props, 10,000 extras, and 78 Yugoslavian horses trained for the chariot race. The crucial circus race, created by second-unit directors Yakima Canutt, Andrew Marton, and Mario Soldati, and arguably one of the most exciting episodes ever filmed, required the building of a $1,000,000 coliseum. The set was composed of 1,000,000 feet of lumber, 250 miles of metal tubing, and 1,000,000 pounds of plaster. It covered 18 acres, held nearly 10,000 extras, and contained some 40,000 tons of sand shipped from the Mediterranean beaches. The nine-minute on-camera race required a full three months of lensing. While this segment was in progress, third-unit director Richard Thorpe and cinematographer Harold E. Wellman completed the galley action sequences and some of the arena scenes, and accomplished some retakes for the other units already in progress.

Although MGM's publicity department dutifully reported these expenditures with pride, the cost was highly aggravating to the front office. MGM was no longer in solid financial shape and a failure for **Ben-Hur** could have meant the collapse of the corporation. The film, which eventually required ten months of actual shooting—despite the utilization of three shooting units—dragged on slowly. It was delayed by Wyler's methodical manner of retakes and the elephantine challenges of the enormous production. With the crushing responsibility on his shoulders, fifty-four-year-old producer Zimbalist suffered a fatal heart attack in Rome on November 4, 1958. Production was wrapped up quickly after his death and the company returned home.

When premiered in late 1959 as a roadshow attraction (in Camera 65 widescreen and stereophonic sound processes), **Ben-Hur** relieved MGM's apprehensions by becoming a sensation. Bosley Crowther **(New York Times)** acclaimed, "By far the most stirring and respectable of the Bible-fiction pictures ever made. . . . A remarkably intelligent and engrossing drama." **Films in Review** said, "A major motion picture phenomenon . . . it brings upon the wide screen virtually all the technical and artistic resources of contemporary filmmaking." **Saturday Review** wrote, "Spectacular without being a spectacle. . . . Not only is it not simpleminded, it is downright literate. . . . There are no erotic ballets in worship of some sun goddess, no slinky sirens in diaphanous silks and a few beads to lure the hero from the path of virtue.[5]

Charlton Heston, Martha Scott, Cathy O'Donnell, and Haya Harareet in Ben-Hur.

And where there are scenes of spectacular action—notably a stirring sea battle and the famous chariot race . . . (as exciting and nerve-tingling as anything ever put on the screen)—they serve the story; they do not exist as an end in themselves. . . . William Wyler has proven with **Ben-Hur** that taste and intelligence need not be lacking in a spectacle. The Academy should create some special award for that alone." There was no such special honor, but **Ben-Hur** won a record number of Oscars—eleven: 1. Best Film[6] 2. Best Actor—Charlton Heston[7] 3. Best Supporting Actor—Hugh Griffith 4. Best Director—William Wyler 5. Best Color Cinematography—Robert L. Surtees 6. Best Art and Set Direction—William A. Horning, Edward Carfango and Hugh Hunt 7. Best Sound—MGM sound department 8. Best Film Edition—Ralph Winters and John D. Dunning 9. Best Music Scoring—Miklos Rozsa 10. Best Special Effects—A. Arnold Gillespie and Robert MacDonald (visual effects), and Milo Lory (audible effects) 11. Best Color Costumes—Elizabeth Haffenden.

Ben-Hur, then the third longest film ever made,[8] went on to become the third highest-grossing picture of its time (under MGM's **Gone with the Wind** and MGM's **Doctor Zhivago,** 1965)—$36,550,000. In 1971 it drew the biggest audience of any televised film to that time—32,630,000 viewers. Its success spawned the production of a rash of historical epics: Universal's **Spartacus** (1960), with Kirk Douglas; Allied Artists' **El Cid** (1961), with Charlton Heston; MGM's **King of Kings** (1961), with Jeffrey Hunter; Columbia's **Barabbas** (1962), with Anthony Quinn. None neared the craftmanship and/or success of **Ben-Hur.** The once great MGM studio was in its final throes of glory.

No Hollywood (or other) cinema extravaganza has since come close to the artistry of **Ben-Hur:** the beauty and sensitivity in the opening nativity scenes, the breathless spectacle of its sea battle and now legendary chariot race, the creative and often moving performances (notably by Heston's searching hero and Boyd's arrogant villain), and the sweeping multichanneled score by Rozsa. While much credit must go Sam Zimbalist, who

---

[4]Under the heading of costumes: over four hundred pounds of hair were sold to the company for use in makeup by the peasant women of upper Piedmont in Italy; the luxurious hair of these women has perennially been sought by wigmakers.

[5]The British **Monthly Film Bulletin** would point out, "Freudians may find little difficulty in categorizing the relationship of Ben-Hur and Messala, as it burgeons from slow, strong handshakes to whip-slashings and a blood-drenched death scene. But in fact the whole thick and tear-bedaubed conception is a Victorian one, embracing as it does Frank Thring's portrayal of Pontius

Pilate as an exquisite, Oscar Wildean quean, Haya Harareet's dewy-eyed slave girl, a wilting orgy reminiscent of **Intolerance,** and the sudden switch in Jack Hawkins' Quintus Arrius from a sort of nineteenth-century flogging headmaster to a Dickensian uncle figure."

[6]**Ben-Hur,** in the Best Picture category, defeated **Anatomy of a Murder** (Columbia), **The Diary of Anne Frank** (Twentieth Century–Fox), **The Nun's Story** (Warner Bros.), and **Room at the Top** (Continental).

[7]Heston defeated Laurence Harvey **(Room at the Top),** Jack Lemmon **(Some Like It Hot),** Paul Muni **(The Last Angry Man),** and James Stewart **(Anatomy of a Murder).**

[8]Among the many scenes cut from the 217-minute release print of **Ben-Hur** were sequences involving Marina Berti as Flavia, the Roman temptress who attracts Ben-Hur. In the final screen version she has only one small scene remaining.

Ben-Hur *on television.*

Chester Morris and Wallace Beery in The Big House *('30).*

fought so long—and fatally—for the project (which was under the company supervision of Sol C. Siegel), perhaps the main share of credit must go to William Wyler, who insisted that this be a film of characterization, not a series of epic tableaux. At the 1976 American Film Institute Life Achievement Award tribute to Wyler, Charlton Heston commented, "Doing a picture with Willie Wyler is like getting the works at a Turkish bath. You damn near drown—but you come out smelling like a rose."

THE BIG HOUSE
1930—80 min.

Director, George Hill; **story-screenplay-dialogue,** Frances Marion; **additional dialogue,** Joe Farnham and Martin Flavin; **art director,** Cedric Gibbons; **sound,** Robert Shirley and Douglas Shearer; **camera,** Harold Wenstrom; **editor,** Blanche Sewell.

Chester Morris **(John Morgan)**; Wallace Beery **(Butch Schmidt)**; Lewis Stone **(Warden James Adams)**; Robert Montgomery **(Kent Marlowe)**; Leila Hyams **(Anne Marlowe)**; George F. Marion **(Pop Riker)**; J. C. Nugent **(Mr. Marlowe)**; Karl Dane **(Olsen)**; DeWitt Jennings **(Captain Wallace)**; Matthew Betz **(Gopher)**; Claire McDowell **(Mrs. Marlowe)**; Robert Emmet O'Connor **(Donlin)**; Tom Wilson **(Sandy, the Guard)**; Eddie Foyer **(Dopey)**; Rosco Ates **(Putnam)**; Fletcher Norton **(Oliver)**; Adolph Seidel **(Prison Barber)**; Eddie Lambert and Michael Vavitch **(Bits)**.

SYNOPSIS
Warden James Adams greets his new charge:

From now on you will be No. 48642. You ran a man down with your car and killed him. You were drunk. Your sentence can be redeemed

by good behavior. . . . I want to warn you of evil influences. Prison does not give a man a yellow streak, but if he has one, it brings it out.

With that playboy Kent Marlowe begins his ten-year manslaughter term, sharing a cell with murderer Butch Schmidt and stickup man John Morgan.

The two prison pros recognize Kent's basic cowardice and treat him brutally. He in turn pulls stunts that create problems for others; one of these leads Morgan to being placed in solitary confinement. Morgan vows revenge and later escapes. While free he encounters Kent's sister, Anne,[1] with whom he falls in love. Later Morgan is recaptured and returned to prison. He is just in time to learn about the Thanksgiving Day prison escape being engineered by Butch.

True to his style, Kent informs on his fellow prisoners, and on the day of the planned break, the guards are prepared. However, Butch and his determined gang make a solid stand and hold one wing of the prison. Kent attempts to break away and Butch shoots him. Later, a guard is killed and thrown into the courtyard. The warden refuses to accede to Butch's demands.

Morgan has not been part of the escape plot, since he had decided to complete his term and marry Anne upon his release. Butch later accuses Morgan of ratting on his pals and shoots him. The injured Morgan returns the gunfire and kills

---
[1]Frances Marion's screenplay had called originally for Leila Hyams to be Montgomery's wife.

Schmidt. The authorities regain control of the prison via the use of tanks. Later Morgan is paroled.

* * *

Wallace Beery was fat, coarse, and rude. And in 1929 he was unemployed, having been dropped by Paramount Studios after a mediocre string of somewhat popular service comedies with Raymond Hatton. However, Beery was also a powerfully effective actor, whose experience directing and starring in Essanay, Keystone, and Universal comedy shorts, as well as his acting range (from an early drag comic character called Sweedie to horrid post-World War I Huns to noble heroes), remained rooted in the memory of MGM executives. The studio signed Beery for the film. Ironically, it was to be at Metro, the home of Garbo, Shearer, Gilbert, and other pulchritudinous countenances, where uncouth Wallace Beery would gain his greatest celebrity. He began his rise to new fame with the sad chore of replacing his dying friend Lon Chaney as the glowering, bald Butch Schmidt of **The Big House.**

Though it was at Warner Bros. that the prison/gangster/moll melodramas flourished in the 1930s, it was Metro which really began the trend in the talkies. Inspired by the stage successes of such penal thrillers as **The Last Mile** and **The Criminal Code,** Frances Marion produced a script detailing the brutalities of prison life, and her husband George Hill managed to obtain a director's post. Visiting such formidable U.S. bastilles as Sing-Sing, Joliet, and San Quentin to talk with wardens, penologists, and supervisors, Hill obtained a feel for his material and the experience to supervise the building of a soundstage replica of a penitentiary, complete with cell blocks, a mess hall, a chapel, and a warden's office, all containing effective overhead lighting to supply shadow effects.

The cast was stocked with Lewis Stone as Warden Adams; new MGM contractee Robert Montgomery as Kent, the drunken driver who faces the horror of coping with prison life; and Chester Morris as the handsome crook in love with Kent's sister. Morris was under a special two-picture pact to MGM engineered by Irving Thalberg. As part of this deal he had earlier joined with Montgomery and Norma Shearer in **The Divorcee.** The part of brutal "Machine Gun" Butch Schmidt was a grotesque role worthy of Lon Chaney's unique talents. However, his throat problems—later diagnosed as cancer—fated that his only talkie would be **The Unholy Three** (1930). Beery was thus contracted and leaped at the chance.

When the production got under way, director Hill informed his largely male cast, "The first person that acts gets canned." If any performer began to overplay his part, he would be informed, "You played that like an actor in New York." In his extensive movie career, the role of John Morgan would remain Chester Morris's favorite. Years later he would say, "We all gave our roles the best that was in us, and the virility and truthfulness of the picture were more satisfying than anything else I've done."

"**The Big Parade** of men beyond the law. . . . See 3,000 desperate convicts in their break for freedom! Thrills!" was how MGM chose to promote **The Big House** when it debuted at New York's Astor Theatre on June 24, 1930. The film was released in both silent and talking versions.[2] The latter won far more playing engagements. Audiences were thrilled by the convicts' singing of "Open the Gates and Let the King of Glory In" on Thanksgiving Day as they prepare for the big break; the roar of the tanks which crash into the prison to quell the violence; and the incessant tramping of the prisoner's feet which continues even as "The End" flashes on the screen.

Reviews were enthusiastic. **New York Times:** "It is a film in which the direction, the photography, the microphone work, and the magnificent acting take precedence over the negligible story . . . a film that sweeps swiftly along . . . an insight into life in a jail that has never before been essayed on the screen." **New York Evening Post:** "Purely as a documentary film, **The Big House** should be ranked among the better achievements of Hollywood. . . . It has what they call the 'feel' of its subject; it is impossible to see it without rousing to an uncomfortable degree a personal identification with the life of the prison."

While Morris was superior as the dapper thief determined to start a new life and Montgomery offered a fine interpretation of the coward—in contrast with his usual sophisticated image—it was Beery who dominated the proceedings. As the **New York Evening Post** interpreted it, "In the

acting of **The Big House,** it is Wallace Beery who runs off with the glory. . . . Beery, in his brawling bullying way, epitomizes the underworld; he is the incarnation of a convict, and it is his motives and behavior in bringing about the desperate prison break which throw an interesting light on criminal psychology."

Nominated for a Best Picture Academy Award, **The Big House** lost to Universal's **All Quiet on the Western Front.** Oscars did go to Frances Marion (Best Screenplay) and Douglas Shearer (Best Sound Achievement). Beery himself won a Best Actor nomination (the winner: George Arliss for Warner Bros.' **Disraeli**). More important, Beery was signed by the impressed front office to an MGM contract; he stayed at the studio for the rest of his life as one of the lot's best paid and most **disliked** stars.

Though **The Big House** enjoyed a solid box-office success,[3] MGM did not choose to follow up with many more penal-genre entries; both Louis B. Mayer and Thalberg found the subject matter coarse and distasteful. Instead, Warner Bros.—home of **Little Caesar** and **The Public Enemy**—became the supreme screen interpreter of underworld mien.

THE BLACKBOARD JUNGLE
1955—101 min.

Producer, Pandro Berman; **director,** Richard Brooks; based on the novel by Evan Hunter; **screenplay,** Brooks; **art directors,** Cedric Gibbons and Randall Duell; **music adapter,** Charles Wolcott; **music,** Bill Haley and the Comets; **assistant director,** Joel Freeman; **camera,** Russell Harlan; **editor,** Ferris Webster.

Glenn Ford (**Richard Dadier**); Anne Francis (**Anne Dadier**); Louis Calhern (**Jim Murdock**); Margaret Hayes (**Lois Judby Hammond**); John Hoyt (**Mr. Warneke**); Richard Kiley (**Joshua Y. Edwards**); Emile Meyer (**Mr. Halloran**); Warner Anderson (**Dr. Bradley**); Basil Ruysdael (**Professor A. R. Kraal**); Sidney Poitier (**Gregory W. Miller**); Vic Morrow (**Artie West**); Dan Terranova (**Belazi**); Rafael Campos (**Peter V. Morales**); Paul Mazursky (**Emmanuel Stoker**); Horace McMahon (**Detective**); Danny Dennis (**DeLica**); David Alpert (**Lou Savoldi**); Gerald Phillips (**Carter**); Dorothy Neumann (**Miss Panucci**); Henny Backus (**Miss Brady**); Robert Foulk (**Mr. Katz**); Paul Hoffman (**Mr. Lefkowitz**).

SYNOPSIS

Novice New York high-school teacher Richard Dadier encounters a survival-of-the-fittest battleground, combatting student hoods Artie West, Belazi, Peter V. Morales, DeLica, and Gregory W.

Miller. Daily, classroom life becomes a student-initiated exercise in tension. Dadier is the target of both physical and verbal assaults in his attempt to conduct a class and maintain discipline. His pregnant wife Anne is also the victim of threatening notes and phone calls from a depraved student. The final confrontation occurs when Artie challenges Dadier with a knife. Miller rises to the challenge and defends the teacher.

Other teachers involved in the hellish life at the high school are cynical Jim Murdock, idealistic Joshua Y. Edwards, and comely Lois Hammond.

* * *

Today, when assorted murders, rapes, and horrors within the walls of the public schools are not only tolerated but defended by discoursers on the social scene, dramas dealing with juvenile delinquency seem embarrassingly passé. However, in the mid-1950s the image of the knife-wielding, smart-tongued, venomous self-wasters deeply distressed the silent majority. When Evan Hunter's 1954 novel **The Blackboard Jungle** became a bestseller, it was MGM—where a now exiled Louis B. Mayer had once become apoplectic whenever Andy Hardy appeared blasé about his mother's home-cooked supper—that purchased the screen rights and filmed as disturbing a chapter on perverse youth as has ever been lensed.

The Blackboard Jungle tells the sordid account of a teacher, Richard Dadier (played with excellent fiber by Glenn Ford), who finds not only himself abused by his class of hooligans, but his pregnant wife also besieged by foul notes and calls. A solid cast included Richard Kiley—a decade away from his Broadway triumph in **Man of La Mancha**—as the naively idealistic Mr. Edwards, who sees his cherished jazz record collection smashed by the vermin he defends; Vic Morrow as Artie West, the snarling head psychopath of the brood; and twenty-eight-year-old Sidney Poitier as Gregory Miller, the minority member who climactically recognizes the malignancy of his peers and aids his teacher in the compelling knife showdown.

MGM was still very much the "assembly line" of entertainment when **The Blackboard Jungle** was produced. A mere three months elapsed from the film's shooting to its release. While many teachers rushed to criticize the film—some out of stubborn dedication to the misfits they were unfortunate enough to be teaching, others out of embarrassment that their friends might see what a jungle they labored in—the critics were impressed. Wrote William K. Zinsser of the **New York Herald-Tribune,** "Educators are already up in arms over **Blackboard Jungle,** which is not exactly a nosegay to American teaching, but nevertheless it's a good movie and, purely on those terms, a good entertainment." Bosley Crowther (**New York Times**) noted, "As a straight melodrama of juvenile violence this is a vivid and hair-raising film. Richard Brooks, who wrote the screenplay and directed, departs little from Mr. Hunter's book, and he puts his principal actors through paces that would seem to leave them permanently marred and scarred." Incidentally, **The Black-**

---

[2] MGM also made Spanish, German, and French versions of the picture. The last was directed by Paul Fejos and featured Charles Boyer in the John Morgan role.

[3] With a forty-day production schedule, **The Big House** cost $414,000, and earned a $462,000 profit.

Glenn Ford in The Blackboard Jungle *('55).*

board Jungle benefited from the flavor supplied by the rock-and-roll soundtrack, particularly Bill Haley's catchy tune "Rock Around the Clock."

Released in the same year Twentieth Century–Fox distributed the saccharine, nostalgic **Good Morning, Miss Dove** (about a small-town teacher and her beloved students), **The Blackboard Jungle** reaped the profits of its sensationalism. It grossed $5,459,000 in distributors' domestic rentals.

BLOSSOMS IN THE DUST
1941 C—100 min.

Producer, Irving Asher; **director,** Mervyn LeRoy; **story,** Ralph Wheelwright; **screenplay,** Anita Loos; **art directors,** Cedric Gibbons and Urie McCleary; **set decorator,** Edwin B. Willis; **Technicolor consultants,** Natalie Kalmus and Henri Jaffa; **gowns,** Adrian; **men's costumes,** Gile Steele; **music,** Herbert Stothart; **makeup,** Jack Dawn; **sound,** Douglas Shearer; **special effects,** Warren Newcombe; **camera,** Karl W. Freund and W. Howard Green; **editor,** George Boemler.

Greer Garson (**Edna Kahly Gladney**); Walter Pidgeon (**Sam Gladney**); Felix Bressart (**Dr. Max Breslar**); Marsha Hunt (**Charlotte Kahly**); Fay Holden (**Mrs. Kahly**); Samuel S. Hinds (**Mr. Kahly**); Kathleen Howard (**Mrs. Keats**); George Lessey (**Mr. Keats**); William Henry (**Allan Keats**); Henry O'Neill (**Judge**); John Eldredge (**Damon McPherson**); Clin-

ton Rosemond (**Zeke**); Theresa Harris (**Cleo**); Charlie Arnt (**G. Harrington Hedger**); Cecil Cunningham (**Mrs. Gilworth**); Ann Morriss (**Mrs. Loring**); Richard Nichols (**Sammy**); Pat Barker (**Tony**); Mary Taylor (**Helen**); Marc Lawrence (**LaVerne**); Will Wright (**Senator**); Almira Sessions (**Woman Vase Buyer**); Frank Darien (**Accountant**).

SYNOPSIS

Edna and Charlotte—daughter and adopted daughter respectively of Mr. and Mrs. Kahly of Wisconsin—are refined young women, each of them engaged to an upstanding man. A chance encounter between Edna and the dashing Sam Gladney changes her plans. She rejects her fiancé to become betrothed to Sam, who has created a thriving flour-mill business in Texas.

Edna and Charlotte plan a double wedding. However, when Charlotte's future in-laws reveal that the mark of illegitimacy on her birth certificate makes her unacceptable as a wife for their son, the distraught bride-to-be commits suicide.

Edna weds Sam and they settle happily in Texas until a tragic accident takes their young son. The child's death almost destroys their marriage, but Edna forges a new life for herself by starting a foundling home. In the meantime, Sam has met with financial reverses and later dies. Edna continues with her efforts, despite severe hardships.

Eventually she is successful in persuading the Texas legislature to remove from birth certificates the word **illegitimate.** Despite her growing fondness for one of her young charges, she now

realizes that for his future welfare she must consent to placing him with a young couple who can afford to provide him with the benefits of their wealth. Her satisfaction must come from helping to continue the work of the Texas Children's Home and Aid Society.

* * *

I'd seen him. He lived near me when I first came out [to Hollywood] and rented a little house with my mother in Beverly Hills. I used to see this handsome gentleman two doors away weeding his lawn. (Walter loves his garden and green things.) He was so nice. When I was first brought over, Mr. Mayer said to him (Walter was coasting along at high gear at that time), "Would you be kind enough to make a test with a young lady? She has been very successful on the London stage, but we don't know what she'll be like in front of the camera. Would you make a kind of a routine test?" He said, "I'd be delighted." He was such an angel and so sweet in the test—I was understandably very nervous.

Thus in her charmingly long-winded way did Greer Garson in 1976 describe her first meeting with Walter Pidgeon on TV's "Mike Douglas Show." It was 1939 and the forty-one-year-old Pidgeon was a general service leading man at MGM after a madly diversified career ranging from Broadway leading man to Ruritanian baritone of early screen operettas to movie character parts. He had been a citizen of Hollywood for fourteen years before his thirty-one-year-old Anglo-Irish neighbor arrived.

However, in the two years that passed from their screen test to the stars' first feature together, the beautiful titian-headed Garson had been Oscar-nominated for **Goodbye, Mr. Chips** (1939) and lavishly praised for her starring with Laurence Olivier in **Pride and Prejudice** (1940). She had managed to make in two seasons a far greater industry impression than veteran Walter had made in sixteen. Hence, when Garson, now bearing the title Queen of the Metro lot—displacing Garbo, Crawford, and Shearer—began working on **Blossoms in the Dust,** she was in the position to request for her leading man the same Mr. Pidgeon who had so magnanimously tested with her a few years before.

With direction by Mervyn LeRoy, and a Technicolor production by Irving Asher, **Blossoms** was an unabashed emotional attack on moviegoers' heartstrings. To ensure an appropriately overwhelming number of adorable toddlers, MGM ran an advertisement for children—621 applicants, if press releases can be believed, stormed the studio the first day! The film eventually employed 850 kids, 100 being babies and 750 being two to eight years old.

Production of **Blossoms in the Dust** was a happy one. Garson and Pidgeon became fast friends, she a happy audience for his ribald limericks and mischievous sense of humor. Still, there was one problem which appeared insurmountable; the suave Pidgeon was inadept at dancing, making it nearly impossible for him to play a key scene waltzing with Garson. According to Pidgeon:

Ray Gordon, Felix Bressart, and Greer Garson in Blossoms in the Dust *('41).*

BOMBSHELL
1933—91 min. (a.k.a. BLONDE BOMBSHELL)

Associate producer, Hunt Stromberg; **director,** Victor Fleming; based on the unproduced play by Caroline Francke and Mack Crane; **screenplay,** Jules Furthman and John Lee Mahin; **art director,** Merrill Pye; **set decorator,** Edwin B. Willis; **gowns,** Adrian; **camera,** Chester Lyons and Harold G. Rosson; **editor,** Margaret Booth.

Jean Harlow **(Lola Burns);** Lee Tracy **(Space Hanlon);** Frank Morgan **(Pop Burns);** Franchot Tone **(Gifford Middleton);** Pat O'Brien **(Jim Brogan);** Una Merkel **(Miss Mac);** Ted Healy **(Junior Burns);** Ivan Lebedeff **(Marquis di Binelli);** Isabel Jewell **(Junior's Girl);** Louise Beavers **(Loretta);** Leonard Carey **(Winters);** Mary Forbes **(Mrs. Middleton);** C. Aubrey Smith **(Mr. Middleton);** June Brewster **(Alice Cole);** Donald Kerr **(Marty, the Makeup Man);** James Burke **(Immigration Officer);** Ed Brady **(Reporter);** Morgan Wallace **(A. G. Gilette);** Gus Arnheim and His Orchestra **(Themselves);** Dennis O'Keefe **(Dance Extra);** Ethel Griffies and Mary Carr **(Orphanage Representatives).**

SYNOPSIS

Cinema sexpot Lola Burns, longing for a new image and lifestyle, becomes engaged to the Marquis di Binelli. Lola's studio publicity agent Space Hanlon ends the engagement by arranging for the titled foreigner to be arrested as an illegal alien.

Later, film director Jim Brogan offers Lola marriage as well as a career. She rejects him and decides to adopt a child as a single parent. The antics of her father and brother, however, cause adoption agency officials to brand her home unfit for raising an infant.

Still later, Lola rushes off to Palm Springs where she meets and falls in love with Gifford Middleton. Her hopes for a future with him are dashed when Gifford's snobbish family disapproves of Lola's movie career and her father. Back at the studio Lola learns that Gifford's "family" was composed of actors whom Space had planted to show Lola that she really belongs in films. Lola finally begins to understand Space's genuine concern for her.

* * *

Poor Jean Harlow! Even after her triumph in **Red Dust** (1932) and almost stealing the honors of the star-studded **Dinner at Eight** (1933), the platinum star remained one of Hollywood's most popular inside jokes. Though she had become one of Culver City's best-liked employees—a lovable, good-natured girl who shot craps with the technical crew between takes and played jazz records in her studio bungalow at top volume (even Garbo, in a neighboring bungalow, never objected)—"the Baby" appeared to be ensnared by the trappings of being Hollywood's most unabashed sex queen.

Her mother, "Mama Jean," was always at her daughter's side, beaming at cameras and squirming into interviews; her stepfather, moustached, dapper Marino Bello, was ever ensnaring Metro

---

You know what they did? They turned me loose with an instructor on stage 15—it's four blocks long. I had to do a waltz. I could reverse—I had the whole doggone stage to do it. Now I get in with Mervyn on the picture and it's in Greer's drawing room, and I had fifteen feet to turn around in. I couldn't do it!

Invincible LeRoy henceforth decided to create a platform on skates, on which Pidgeon stood while Garson danced around him. As Garson would joke, "We were the first duet on a skateboard . . . . I think I ran around the circumference, and he stayed on the skateboard."

With the skateboard's assist, **Blossoms in the Dust** was completed on schedule and released with the teasers "Garson is gorgeous in Technicolor" and "The thrilling story of a fighting lady and the romance that inspired her."

Some critics found the confectionary script by Anita Loos hard to countenance, Bosley Crowther **(New York Times),** for one: "There is a shade too much of shining nobility in this film, too often tiny fingers tug deliberately on the heartstrings. And the dramatic continuity seems less spontaneous than contrived. The career of Mrs. Gladney is drawn out over a tedious stretch of time." **Newsweek** magazine concurred. "**Blossoms in the Dust** is an inspirational film of infrequent drama and such surcharged sentiment that its appeal will be chiefly limited to feminine audiences," but it did note that "the cast, both adult and infant, is excellent. As the indomitable woman who has found comfortable homes for more than 2,000 foundlings, Greer Garson gives a sincere and believable performance. Walter Pidgeon as her husband . . . also manages to survive the powerful competition of dozens of babies of all sizes and colors."

Blossoms in the Dust became a great audience pleaser. It drew Oscar nominations in the areas of Best Picture (Twentieth Century–Fox's **How Green Was My Valley,** in which Pidgeon starred just after completing **Blossoms,** won) and Best Actress (Garson was defeated in her second bid by Joan Fontaine of RKO's **Suspicion**). The plushly photographed picture did win Academy Awards, however, in the areas of Art Direction (Cedric Gibbons and Urie McCleary) and Set Decorator (Edwin B. Willis).

So began the tandem art of Greer Garson and Walter Pidgeon. They would repeat their **Blossoms** assignment on "Lux Radio Theatre" on April 16, 1942, and would go on to share the star billing (with Greer always on top) in seven more MGM motion picture entries. While Pidgeon's solid and sometimes stolid acting was a perfect foundation for and contrast with Garson's, the lady's capacity for snaring the best reviews, the awards, and the magazine cover stories somewhat stifled the new career lease[1] Pidgeon won via his superb dominance in Twentieth Century–Fox's **Man Hunt** (1941) and **How Green Was My Valley.** Nevertheless, they produced together some of the screen's most notable chemistry and have always retained the highest regard for each other.

---

[1]Since he was past the age for military service, Pidgeon's availability in a man-shortage Hollywood during World War II escalated his professional rise.

Lee Tracy, Louise Beavers, and Jean Harlow in Bombshell *('33).*

stars for money for fabricated investments and pursuing starlets for assorted favors. Harlow's agent, Arthur Landau, pressured her to "live like a star" and bullied her into purchasing a gaudy, glistening white mansion atop a hill in Beverly Glen. It was a luxury she could ill afford because of the insatiable money appetites of her parents. Then too the studio public relations department was always harassing her into attending premieres and personal appearances in the slinkiest of gowns, the highest of spiked heels, etc. It was Harlow's unfortunate predicament that inspired the most lethal self-parody Hollywood ever filmed, and, in the opinion of many, provided the best performance Harlow ever gave—**Bombshell.**[1]

If today's movie enthusiast believes Hollywood engaged in its dream-factory indiscretions in blissful ignorance, unaware of its shallowness and deceit, **Bombshell** demonstrates otherwise. Based on an unproduced play by Caroline Francke and Mack Crane, **Bombshell** tackles head-on a squad of cinema indelicacies: merciless agents, parasitic hanger-ons, obnoxious fans. All are lampooned by the Jules Furthman–John Lee Mahin scenario and emphasized by the stiletto direction of Victor Fleming. MGM even took the advantage of dropping into the storyline a few contractee names, such as Gable's and Lewis Stone's; there are references to **Red Dust,** and scenes shown from **Hold Your Man** (1933), featuring Harlow and Gable.

However, what really supplied **Bombshell** with a special sting and gave it an edge over previous Hollywood self-spoofs such as 1932's

Once in a Lifetime and **What Price Hollywood?** was its pungent examination of the star's entourage. The latter was inspired, of course, by Harlow's own family. Frank Morgan (based on Bello) is a bumbling con-man father, Ted Healy a freeloading brother (Harlow actually had no brother), Una Merkel a smart-mouthed servant, and, most impressive, staccato-speaking Lee Tracy an obnoxious delight as Space Hanlon, the prototype of the conniving, remorseless, ten-percenter who makes life hell for a naive star. Nasal-voiced Tracy is an unforgettable screen character, cracking such lines about his blonde employer as "Where I'll kick her the camera will never pick up the scar!"

It is Harlow, to be sure, who makes **Bombshell** transcend a mere smart-alecky thumb-nosing at Hollywood into a charming entry. As Lola Burns, the Platinum Blonde "known from Kokomo to the Khyber Pass," she provides (in a luscious parade of all-white Adrian costumes), a dazzling portrait of the adulated movie star. She is seen in all facets: as the venomous shrew screaming at her lazy servants; later as the grand celebrity primping for her public; or caught offguard as the insecure, confused young woman who witnesses her one true desire—to adopt a baby—shattered by press agent villainy.

MGM promoted the film as a Harlow vehicle, "She's sizzling! She's explosive! She'll rock the nation with laughter!... This is lovely Jean Harlow's happiest role—as the vivacious, voluptuous bombshell of Hollywood who erupted so often she blew the lid off her own private life and loves!" The public and the press responded joyfully to her on-screen vivacity. The **New York Herald-Tribune** reported:

For those of us who are enthusiasts for the increasing talents of the distinguished

Miss Harlow, **Bombshell** is chiefly important for the fact that it provides the first full-length portrait of this amazing young woman's increasingly impressive acting talents. . . . Miss Harlow reveals again that gift for an amalgamation of sophisticated sex comedy with curiously honest innocence which is the secret of her individuality. There can be no doubt now that she is a distinguished performer. **Bombshell** is important as another step in Miss Harlow's brilliant career.

Harlow's near-perfect interpretation allows the viewer almost to forget **Bombshell**'s lackluster moments, such as Pat O'Brien's appearance as a curiously colorless film director and Franchot Tone's reading of the chestnut "I'd like to run barefoot in your hair."

Jean Harlow gained much from this film. Besides the glowing reviews she received, she landed a third husband . . . MGM cinematographer Hal Rosson. The short, moustached forty-year-old was chief photographer of **Red Dust** and **Bombshell.** They would elope[2] on September 18, 1933, to Yuma, Arizona (their romance had begun in Tucson, Arizona, where the **Bombshell** company shot the desert scenes that were supposed to take place in Palm Springs). **Bombshell** also earned Jean the honor of placing her hand and spiked heel prints in the cement slabs of Grauman's Chinese Theatre on September 29, 1933. However, the film did not bring Harlow one item she did **not** want particularly anyway—the approval of Louis B. Mayer. After the premiere of **Bombshell** at Grauman's, Mayer bustled up to Harlow, began to mouth a compliment, thought better of the idea, and simply smirked, "God . . . Lee Tracy has great lines!"

BOOM TOWN
1940—116 min.

Producer, Sam Zimbalist; **director,** Jack Conway; **story,** James Edward Grant; **screenplay,** John Lee Mahin; **assistant director,** Horace Hough; **music,** Franz Waxman; **art directors,** Cedric Gibbons and Eddie Imazu; **costumes,** Adrian and Gile Steele; **sound,** Douglas Shearer; **special effects,** Arnold Gillespie; **montage,** John Hoffman; **camera,** Harold Rosson; **editor,** Blanche Sewell.

Clark Gable (**Big John McMasters**); Spencer Tracy (**Square John Sand**); Claudette Colbert (**Betsy Bartlett**); Hedy Lamarr (**Karen Vanmeer**); Frank Morgan (**Luther Aldrich**); Lionel Atwill (**Harry Compton**); Chill Wills (**Harmony Jones**); Marion Martin (**Whitey**); Minna Gombell (**Spanish Eve**); Joe Yule (**Ed Murphy**); Horace Murphy (**Tom Murphy**); Roy Gordon (**McCreery**); Richard Lane (**Assistant District Attorney**); Casey Johnson (**Little Jack**); Baby Quintanilla (**Baby Jack**); George Lessey (**Judge**); Sara Haden (**Miss Barnes**); Frank Orth

---

[1]Metro later changed the film title to **Blonde Bombshell,** fearing the public would think **Bombshell** was a war picture.

---

[2]The marriage lasted eight months.

Spencer Tracy and Clark Gable in Boom Town *('40).*

Claudette Colbert[1] (the twin Oscar winners of **It Happened One Night,** 1934), as well as the reunion of Gable and Spencer Tracy (with whom the virile chemistry had flowed in Metro's **San Francisco,** 1936, and **Test Pilot,** 1938). To complete its luminous quadrangle, Metro added spicy Hedy Lamarr to the proceedings, thereby creating the greatest all-star picture of 1940.

To properly support the prodigious lineup, MGM created a lavish setting. An entire 1919 boomtown (representing Burkburnett, Texas) was built on the Culver City lot, covering a sixty-acre tract. Included were fifty buildings, a railroad yard, and streets soaked so that the mud would be knee-deep. In addition, Metro imported 500 tons of oil equipment and 10,000 oil-associated properties—and provided the studio's technicians with the challenge of "bringing on" an oil gusher. With a supporting cast which included Frank Morgan and Lionel Atwill, along with geysers of MGM gloss, **Boom Town** cost a plump $2,000,000 to produce. (The publicity releases insisted, "Biggest All-Star Sensation! It happens once in a lifetime. Such a cast of stars. Such a show! It B-O-O-M-S with thrills.)

Tracy had been resistant about appearing in **Boom Town,** realizing from a study of the script that he would again be playing the conscience-stricken pal of **the** leading man, his task in his last two outings with Gable. It would be the last time he would team with the King. On the other hand, Gable thought the rollicking adventure picture a lark, reviving memories of his own years in the oil fields, and he found director Jack Conway as congenial as in their past projects together. Soon Gable and Conway were playing practical jokes on each other during the making of **Boom Town.**

Hollywood wags expected fireworks between the two female stars, vying for on-camera focus. However, Lamarr's role was so subordinate and sympathetic to Colbert's character that the two actresses had no real chance for celluloid competition. Lamarr would be teamed later that year with Gable in **Comrade X,** while earlier that season she and Tracy had been seen in the ill-fated, production-plagued **I Take This Woman.**

"In the manner of a 'wildcat' driller indifferent to the laws of conservation, the Culver City producers have really shot the works [in **Boom Town**]," declared the **New York Times.** Scribe Bosley Crowther continued: "With four stars in the picture, the desperate compulsions under which director and scriptwriter must have worked are obvious. . . . More colorful action in the oil fields and less agitation indoors might have made **Boom Town** a great picture. . . ." The **New York Herald-Tribune** reasoned, "There is so much spectacle in the tale of the wildcat oil operators, who become tycoons only to find they have lost touch with the abiding values in living, that only the most blasé filmgoer could fail to be impressed by it. Western high jinks, a wee child, and courtroom speeches about individual enterprise constitute the various

---

[1]Colbert only made three MGM pictures in her sixty-four film career: **It's a Wonderful World** (1939), **Boom Town,** and **The Secret Heart** (1946).

(Barber); Frank McGlynn, Jr. **(Deacon);** Curt Bois **(Ferdie);** Dick Curtis **(Hiring Boss).**

SYNOPSIS

Big John McMasters and Square John Sand meet in a Texas oil town in 1919 and form a partnership in the wildcat oil business. Square John sends for his schoolteacher sweetheart, Betsy Bartlett, who soon falls in love with Big John and marries him. But the two men manage to continue their business dealings together. Square John becomes bitter when he suspects that Big John is unfaithful to Betsy. The two men gamble for rights to their enterprise. Big John is the victor. Square John and Betsy, now broke, leave the area.

Some years later the two men cross paths again. When Square John learns that Big John is having an affair with Karen Vanmeer, he proposes marriage to the woman, hoping to save Big John's marriage to Betsy. Karen wisely refuses Square John's offer, realizing he still loves Betsy. Square John convinces Big John to return to Betsy.

Before long the two long-standing friends-rivals are brawling it out; later each man loses his wealth. When Big John is brought into court for an antitrust violation it is Square John's testimony which spares his onetime associate from a jail sentence. At the finale, both men are friends and together with Betsy they return to the oil fields where they began.

* * *

"Devil-May-Care Men Fight for Girls and Gold!" proclaimed the advertisements for this sprawling epic, employing the oil fields as a backdrop for the rematching of Clark Gable and

come-ons of the production. While they make it vastly popular, I think that they have resulted in a scrambled and inept motion picture."

Scrambled and inept, perhaps, but audiences found irresistible[2] the prospect of watching Gable and Tracy brawl, patch up, and brawl some more, while Colbert watches their fisticuffs with chic concern and Lamarr provides an alluring but temporary romantic side trip for Gable. So there would be no mistaking as to who was the major leading lady, Colbert is kissed some dozen times by the ardent Gable, while (younger) Hedy receives no busses from the King, though **she** gives **him** a single kiss.

Boom Town quite rightly received no Oscar bids in major categories. **Film Daily** did list it among the year's Ten Best, and, as all expected, it became one of the year's top grossers, reaping a husky $4,600,000 in domestic rentals. Rowdy, grandiose, constantly fun for the players and the audience, **Boom Town** is an unrefined, delightful close to the screen matching of Gable with Colbert and with Tracy. It offers a vigorous panorama of irreplaceable stars—and an irreplaceable studio regime—at their gaudy, entertaining, indiscriminating best.

BOYS TOWN
1938—96 min.

Producer, John W. Considine, Jr.; **director,** Norman Taurog; **story,** Dore Schary and Eleanore Griffin; **screenplay,** John Meehan and Schary; **music,** Edward Ward; **music arranger,** Leo Arnaud; **art directors,** Cedric Gibbons and Urie McCleary; **set decorator,** Edwin B. Willis; **montage effects,** Slavko Vorkapich; **camera,** Sidney Wagner; **editor,** Elmo Vernon.

Spencer Tracy **(Father Edward J. Flanagan);** Mickey Rooney **(Whitey Marsh);** Henry Hull **(Dave Morris);** Leslie Fenton **(Dan Farrow);** Addison Richards **(The Judge);** Edward Norris **(Joe Marsh);** Gene Reynolds **(Tony Fonessa);** Minor Watson **(The Bishop);** Victor Kilian **(The Sheriff);** Jonathan Hale **(John Hargraves);** Bobs Watson **(Pee Wee);** Martin Spellman **(Skinny);** Mickey Rentschler **(Tommy Anderson);** Frankie Thomas **(Freddie Fuller);** Jimmy Butler **(Paul Ferguson);** Sidney Miller **(Mo Kahn);** Robert Emmett Keane **(Burton);** Phillip Terry **(Reporter);** Gladden James **(Doctor);** Kane Richmond **(Jackson, the Reporter);** George Humbert **(Calateri);** Jay Novello **(Gangster with Marsh);** Johnny Walsh **(Charley Haines).**

SYNOPSIS
In an attempt to help misdirected youths, Roman Catholic priest Father Edward J. Flanagan creates a home as a refuge for tough neighborhood kids.

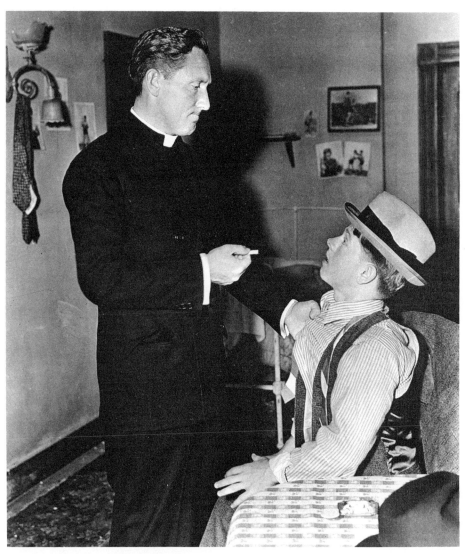
Spencer Tracy and Mickey Rooney in Boys Town *('38).*

His wards are hoodlums who would otherwise be sent to a reformatory. Flanagan believes "there isn't any such thing in the world as a bad boy. . . . But a boy left alone, frightened, bewildered . . . the wrong hand reaches for him . . . he needs a friend . . . that's all he needs."

Flanagan receives moral support from his bishop and financial aid from his pawnbroker friend Dave Morris and the shabby building is soon outgrown by its charges. One Christmas Eve finds Flanagan so overburdened with financial debts that he cannot even purchase a simple tree; however, Morris comes to the rescue again.

Later, with contributions from many sources, a new home is established on a 200-acre spread outside Omaha, Nebraska. Just before Joe Marsh is about to be sent to the state prison, he contacts Flanagan and gives him funds to take care of younger brother Whitey, an out-and-out hooligan. Whitey constantly fights Flanagan's beneficial overtures and attempts to disrupt the regulations of Boys Town. He even runs away from Flanagan's

domain. But thereafter he finds redemption. He helps the priest and the youths capture a gang of bank robbers and is later elected mayor of Boys Town. Thus, through Flanagan's guidance and his own growing maturity, Whitey emerges as an outstanding example of the rehabilitative process of Boys Town.

* * *

"More laughs than **Love Finds Andy Hardy**. . . . More thrills than **Test Pilot**. . . . More tears than **Captains Courageous** . . . with the stars that made them great . . . Spencer Tracy and Mickey Rooney!"

This was the copy that announced **Boys Town,** MGM's 1938 box-office winner. If Louis B. Mayer adored anything more than crying himself, it was making other people cry (with sentiment) and **Boys Town** was the perfect cue for tears among Great Depression audiences. In 1917, Father Edward J. Flanagan had founded Boys Town in Omaha, Nebraska, and in the ensuing years, the priest's efforts made the institution one of

---

[2] Warner Bros. that year released a very mild oil-field story, **Flowing Gold,** starring Pat O'Brien, John Garfield, and Frances Farmer.

the best-publicized charities in the country. MGM paid Father Flanagan $5,000 for the use of his and the institution's name—a sum that Boys Town, even two decades after its founding—was grateful to accept.

Delighting in the humanitarian theme, Mayer lavished the project with a budget of $1,000,000. To play the Father Flanagan of the scenario, he recruited Spencer Tracy (then in remission from his drinking problems), the Best Actor Oscar winner for **Captains Courageous** (1937) and the performer who had created the endearing characterization of Father Tim Mullin in **San Francisco** (1936). The star would comment later, "I knew Father Flanagan personally, and felt nobody could put over his warmth, inspiration, and humaneness of feeling in a picture. But I became so absorbed in the characterization that by the end of the first week I had stopped worrying."

Mickey Rooney, who appeared in eight Metro releases of 1938 and had played with Tracy in **Captains Courageous**, was ideal as the troublesome Whitey whom Flanagan transforms from a hateful punk to a model product of Boys Town.[1] Norman Taurog, a specialist with young performers, directed the production, replacing Jack Ruben who died suddenly from a heart ailment.

Distributed late in the summer of 1938,[2] **Boys Town** was released with the dedication, "In tribute to a supreme achievement based upon a noble ideal, this picture is dedicated to the Rev. Father Edward J. Flanagan, the inspired founder of Boys Town, near Omaha, Nebraska . . . and to the splendid work he is performing for homeless abandoned boys, regardless of race, creed, or color." The **New York Herald-Tribune** heralded it as "a film which is provocative as well as entertaining. It makes no bones about the fact that organized society invariably turns young tramps into hardened criminals and shows that even private charity is faced with innumerable obstacles in caring for them." The film, filled with kitsch, precocious if restrained young performers, and enhanced by on-location shooting at the actual Boys Town, became one of the top-grossing pictures of the 1938–39 season.

MGM held high hopes for **Boys Town** at the eleventh Academy Award ceremony, held at the Biltmore Bowl on February 23, 1939. The film was nominated for Best Picture; it lost to Columbia's **You Can't Take It with You**. However, Spencer Tracy won the Best Actor Oscar, becoming the first male actor to win two consecutive years. Only because of studio pressure was he present to receive the trophy in person.[3] (He had scheduled hernia

surgery the year before when he won for **Captains Courageous**.) Dore Schary and Eleanore Griffin won the Best Original Film Story Oscar. And Mickey Rooney, largely on the strength of his **Boys Town** performance, shared a miniature Oscar with Universal's Deanna Durbin for their "spirit and personification of youth."

The success of **Boys Town** would encourage Metro to film an eventual sequel, **Men of Boys Town** (1941), with Tracy back in his Father Flanagan part and Rooney returning as the "junior mayor" of the institution. Norman Taurog again directed. It was predictably popular.[4]

Boys Town continues to be popular Christmas time TV fare, despite a well-publicized account in 1972 which tarnished somewhat the image of Father Flanagan's dream. The **Sun** papers of Omaha won a 1973 Pulitzer Prize for special local reporting with a series of stories entitled "Boys Town: America's Wealthiest City?" The reporters discovered that the development was then worth over $226,000,000! Monsignor Nicholas Wegner, Father Flanagan's successor, answered the outcries with, "We're a social agency, but social welfare has to be run as a business." Nevertheless, the embarrassing news caused Boys Town to reduce severely its fund appeals and to curtail the lavish building plans it was intending.

In his book **Tracy and Hepburn** (1971), Garson Kanin quotes Tracy on his late-in-life reflections on **Boys Town**:

"I was sitting and watching **Boys Town** and there I am with this whole group and I realize that one of them a few days before—I'd seen in the paper—had been picked up for drunk driving, and one of them is off his rocker in an institution somewhere. Then there's two of them, they were friends back then, and somebody told me they've been picked up for pushing dope, and then there was poor little Mickey, and I've got my arms around all these characters and the camera's rolling in and I say 'There **are** no bad boys!' I want to tell you I nearly fell out of this chair. Nearly, hell, I **did**."

THE BROADWAY MELODY
1929—104 min.[1]

Producer, Harry Rapt; **director,** Harry Beaumont; ensemble numbers staged by George Cunningham; **screen story,** Edmund Goulding; **screenplay,** Sarah Y. Mason; **dialogue,** Norman Houston and James Gleason; **titles,** Earl Baldwin; **songs,** Nacio Herb Brown and Arthur Freed; George M. Cohan; Willard Robison; **sets,** Cedric Gibbons; **costumes,** David Cox; **sound,** Douglas Shearer, Wesley Miller, Louis

Kolk, O. O. Ceccarini, and G. A. Burns; **camera,** John Arnold; **editor: sound version,** Sam S. Zimbalist; **silent version,** William Levanway.

Anita Page **(Queenie Mahoney)**; Bessie Love **("Hank" Mahoney)**; Charles King **(Eddie Kerns)**; Jed Prouty **(Uncle Bernie)**; Kenneth Thomson **(Jack)**; Edward Dillon **(Stage Manager)**; Mary Doran **(Flo)**; Eddie Kane **(Francis Zanfield)**; J. Emmett Beck **(Babe Hatrick)**; Marshall Ruth **(Stew)**; Drew Demarest **(Turpe)**; James Gleason **(Music Publisher)**.

SYNOPSIS
Eddie Kerns, an unknown vaudeville dancer, writes a popular song and is hired by Broadway producer Francis Zanfield to perform in one of his theatrical revues.

Since he has long been in love with "Hank" Mahoney, the older half of a vaudeville sister act, Eddie now persuades her to leave her present show and come to New York with her sister Queenie.

It is not long before Eddie begins romancing Queenie. Instead of falling for his charms, she becomes the mistress of one of Zanfield's backers in order to help keep Hank and Eddie together.

When Hank learns that Eddie and Queenie are in love, she persuades him to take Queenie away from her protector. Eddie and Queenie resume their romance. As for Hank, she finds a new "sister" for her act and returns to small-time vaudeville.

*   *   *

MGM's entry in the second year of the Academy Award competition, **The Broadway Melody** was voted best film of 1928–29 over **Alibi** (United Artists), **Hollywood Revue of 1929** (MGM), **In Old Arizona** (Fox), and **The Patriot** (Paramount). Historically, **The Broadway Melody** was notable for four firsts: first original film musical, first musical to receive the Academy Award, first sound film to be similarly awarded, and the first MGM production to be cited as Best Picture.

Bessie Love would reminisce about the making of **The Broadway Melody** for John Kobal's **Gotta Sing, Gotta Dance** (1970):

"Our director, Harry Beaumont, had already directed a few sound films for Vitaphone (Warner Brothers). Arthur Freed, who wrote the songs, had been a beau of mine a few years before. Of course, at this point a great many of the sound problems with the mike hadn't been ironed out. I remember listening to the playback of one scene, and we heard this echo in the background. So the sound experts said, 'Everybody out'; they laid carpets and covered the entire area with nails. Back we went and reshot the scene; listened to the playback. The echo was still there. So out we went, in they came, hanging the place with heavy curtains and material to drown the echo. Playback, echo, out; they added something else, until finally they got it as good as they possibly could. Mind you, at this period, the sound equipment was being improved almost week to week, so that the end of **Broadway Melody** sounded much better than the beginning, but Thalberg decided against any reshooting because of the cost and time.

---

[1]Schary would recall of his $750 per week scripting assignment on **Boys Town** that producer John Considine had originally intended having a focal role in the picture for studio contractee Freddie Bartholomew, but that Schary talked him out of distorting the focal relationship between Tracy and Rooney.

[2]The studio promoted the film with "Once in a year, perhaps once in a decade, comes a picture of such heartwarming sincerity and power . . . such laughter and tears. . . ."

[3]Tracy later gave the Oscar to Father Flanagan (who died in 1948), with the added inscription, "To Father Edward J. Flanagan, whose great human qualities, kindly sim-

plicity, and inspiring courage were strong enough to shine through my humble efforts."

[4]In mid-1980 producer-director-writer Clyde Ware announced that he would film **Boys Town**, based on the founding of the institution in 1917 by Father Flanagan, with Michael Cole as the star of the production.

[1]Technicolor scenes.

Anita Page and Bessie Love in The Broadway Melody *('29).*

story for **The Broadway Melody** was Edmund Goulding, who earned greater glory as a director of such ventures as MGM's Oscar-winning **Grand Hotel** (1932).

Photoplay magazine reported:

The picture is most notable, however, because in it the talkies find new freedom and speed.

The microphone and its twin camera poke themselves into backstage corners, into dressing rooms, into rich parties, and hotel bedrooms. . . . There is one colored sequence with a new song, "The Wedding of the Painted Doll," that will start you dancing. . . . The crafty directorial hand of Harry Beaumont has tickled, teased, and whipped it into a fast, funny, sad little story, alive in turn with titters and tears.

Variety extolled the film's merit and simultaneously offered an admonition regarding the incipient talkies:

The **Broadway Melody** has everything a silent picture should have outside of its dialogue. A basic story with some sense to it, action, excellent direction, laughs, a tear, a couple of great performances and plenty of sex. It's the fastest moving talker that's come in, regardless of an anticlimax, with some of the stuff so flip and quick that when the capacity gets over 2,000 they may not catch everything.

Bessie Love enjoyed a striking comeback in the cinema with **The Broadway Melody**, marking a new high in her screen career that had begun some two dozen films earlier in 1916. She was Oscar-nominated for her role of Hank Mahoney, but lost the Best Actress Award to Mary Pickford of **Coquette** (United Artists).

Love would say years later to Kobal for **Gotta Sing, Gotta Dance:**

"After the success of **Broadway Melody**, I was cast in nothing but musicals. . . . In **Hollywood Revue**, we all just did sketches and bits. They wanted everybody at MGM to do something they had never done before. They asked me if I had ever done an acrobatic dance. I told them I hadn't; so they said, 'Okay, you're doing an acrobatic dance!' And it was fun! . . .

"I got a little fed up with doing all those musicals. Marie Dressler said she would spank me if I didn't stop them. I wanted to, but when you sign with a big studio, you must expect to do what you're given. . . .

"I wasn't really a singer, but this didn't matter for **Broadway Melody**, since the part I played didn't really require it. Nobody realized this; and when people tell me how nice I sing, I simply thank them for it. Of course, I quickly began taking singing lessons—for a time from the same person Bebe [Daniels] went to."

MGM would utilize the title tag **Broadway Melody** for a trio of revues: **of 1936, of 1938,** and **of 1940**. In 1940 the studio would also revamp the original storyline of **The Broadway Melody** for **Two Girls on Broadway** starring Lana Turner, George Murphy, and Joan Blondell.

"When we were doing the musical numbers, the orchestra was playing right along with us; it was all direct recording. By the time we did **Hollywood Revue of 1929,** though, a few months after **Broadway Melody,** we recorded the musical numbers first, and then acted to them on playback, like they do now. So you can see how fast things were happening."

The Broadway Melody cost $280,000 to make and opened at New York's Astor Theatre on February 9, 1929. Audiences willingly paid the $2 admission price to view the "100 percent talking, singing, dancing" film which averaged $27,000 per week, shattering previous box-office records. By the end of a year in release (in sound and silent versions) the film would gross $4,000,000 (largely from theatres where the admission price was 35¢ per person).

Motion Picture News would herald, "Metro-Goldwyn-Mayer have stolen a march on all their competitors in the talkie production field by being the first on the market with a combination drama and musical revue that will knock the audiences for a goal. Others have had revues and musical comedies in work but MGM is the first to hit the screen with theirs and to them will have to go the glory for all time of being the pioneers."

The film had songs[2] mostly by Nacio Herb Brown (music) and Arthur Freed (lyrics); the latter went on to be the lot's chief producer of distinguished musicals a decade later. Providing the

---

[2]The score included Brown-Freed's "The Broadway Melody," "The Wedding of the Painted Doll," "You Were Meant for Me," "The Boy Friend," "Love Boat," and "Truthful Deacon Brown," and George M. Cohan's "Give My Regards to Broadway."

BROADWAY MELODY OF 1936

1935—103 min.

Producer, John W. Considine, Jr.; **director,** Roy Del Ruth; **story,** Moss Hart; **screenplay,** Jack McGowan and Sid Silvers; **additional dialogue,** Harry Conn; **art directors,** Cedric Gibbons and Merrill Pye; **set decorator,** Edwin B. Willis; **gowns,** Adrian; **choreography,** Dave Gould; **"Lucky Star" ballet staged by** Albertina Rasch; **songs,** Nacio Herb Brown and Arthur Freed; **orchestrator,** Edward B. Powell; **music arranger,** Roger Edens; **assistant director,** Bill Scully; **sound,** Douglas Shearer; **camera,** Charles Rosher; **editor,** Blanche Sewell.

Jack Benny (**Bert Keeler**); Robert Taylor (**George Brown**); Una Merkel (**Kitty Corbett**); Eleanor Powell (**Irene [Mlle Arlette]**); June Knight (**Lillian**); Vilma Ebsen (**Sally**); Buddy Ebsen (**Buddy Burke**); Nick Long, Jr. (**Basil Newcombe**); Robert Wildhack (**Hornblow**); Sid Silvers (**Snoop Blue**); Frances Langford (**Singer**); Irene Coleman, Beatrice Coleman, Mary Jane Halsey, Ada Ford, Lucille Lund, and Georgina Gray (**Showgirls**); Paul Harvey (**Managing Editor**); Theresa Harris (**Maid**); Max Barwyn (**Headwaiter**); Bernadene Hayes (**Waitress**); Bud Williams (**Pullman Porter**); Bert Moorhouse (**Hotel Clerk**); Andre Cheron (**Hotel Manager**); Rolfe Sedan (**Assistant Hotel Manager**); Bobby Gordon (**Copy Boy**); Anya Teranda, Luana Walters, and Patricia Gregory (**Chorus Girls**).

Robert Taylor, Una Merkel, and Nick Long, Jr. in Broadway Melody of 1936 *('35).*

SYNOPSIS

Play producer George Brown is casting his new musical show financed by possessive, attractive Lillian. He receives a visit from Irene, his hometown childhood sweetheart. At first he does not recognize her, but later apologizes. She begs him to allow her to appear in his upcoming production (she is an expert dancer), but he refuses. He insists she is too nice to be mixed up in Broadway. It is not long before he realizes he loves her, as she does him, and without attempting to discover whether she has performing talents, he tells her to go home and avoid the heartaches of the profession.

But Kitty Corbett, Brown's loyal secretary, has confidence in Irene and hits on a gimmick to make her famous. She knows the extensive buildup columnist Bert Keeler has been giving a famous Parisienne singer is just a stunt to irk talent-seeking Brown. (Keeler dislikes George and wants him to waste time trying to find the elusive vocalist.)

Thereafter Kitty dresses Irene in a blonde wig, trains her to speak with a French accent, and presents her as the illustrious Gallic chanteuse Mlle Arlette. The talented performer elates George. Meanwhile, the actual Mlle Arlette cables Bert Keeler from Paris, ordering him to desist from using her name in his column.

Bert approaches Irene–Mlle Arlette and tells

her the only way he will permit her to continue in the George Brown show, without revealing the truth, is for her to tell George the actual facts. She does this, but in such a manner that George suddenly realizes how foolish he has been.

George and Irene can now marry.

* * *

LOUIS B. MAYER: My dear child, we are going to test you for the lead in this picture.

ELEANOR POWELL: Oh, Mr. Mayer, you can't do that. I don't know anything about the camera. You have a girl in this picture who dances, sings, is sexy and everything—she's magnificent. You'd be just wasting your time. You can't do that.

MAYER: You don't seem to realize, I run the studio. I press all the buttons up here, and I am going to make a test whether you like it or not. . . .

Thus does Eleanor Powell remember the circumstances that made her one of MGM's most irresistible attractions in the beguiling though contrived **Broadway Melody of 1936.**[1] The escapism was an enchanting conglomeration of Arthur Freed—Nacio Herb Brown tunes, Jack Benny's comedy, Buddy and Vilma Ebsen's hoofing, the

[1] Powell worked on this musical on a three-week, $1250 per week engagement.

vintage glamour of Robert Taylor, and the celebrated tap dancing of the glorious Miss Powell.

The new **Broadway Melody** was a follow-up but not a sequel to Metro's Oscar-winning **The Broadway Melody** (1929). The latest entry in the **Broadway** series evolved in hodgepodge fashion. Warner Bros.' veteran director Roy Del Ruth, of the Ruby Keeler–Dick Powell vehicle fame, was signed to monitor a musical feature which could mix appealing, crowd-pleasing performers with a batch of Freed-Brown songs: "Broadway Rhythm" (performed by Powell and Frances Langford), "I Got a Feeling You're Fooling" (Powell, Taylor, Langford, and June Knight), "On a Sunday Afternoon" (Buddy and Vilma Ebsen), "Sing Before Breakfast" (Powell and the Ebsens), "This Is the Night" and "You Are My Lucky Star" (Powell and Langford). Jack Benny, whose NBC Sunday night radio program was at the top of the ratings, was signed as the bitchy columnist Bert Keeler; Robert Taylor, then a $35 per week studio stock player, was cast as producer George Brown (his song-and-dance excursion here with June Knight was his first and last for the screen); the dance team of Buddy and Vilma Ebsen climbed on; and a bevy of lovely and leggy showgirls was spiked into the lively proceedings.

Meanwhile, Eleanor Powell, twenty-three-year-old veteran of such Broadway shows as Florenz Ziegfeld's **Hot Cha** and **George White's Scandals,** was preparing for her MGM debut. She had been regaled as the World's Greatest Feminine Tap and Rhythm Dancer by the Dance Masters of America, had performed a guest spot in Fox's **George White's 1935 Scandals,** and had come to the Culver City lot to try her luck in winning the role of Kitty Corbett, the switchboard operator. So impressed, however, was Del Ruth, as well as Mayer, that Una Merkel (a contract feature player on the lot) was given that comic assignment and Eleanor instead landed the plum part of Irene. It is she who, in the course of the film, dons a blonde wig to pose as the French Mademoiselle Arlette, does a Katharine Hepburn takeoff, sings, dances, and climactically shines in top hat and spangled tuxedo in the "Broadway Rhythm" finale.

To beautify Powell for the screen, MGM persuaded her to endure the painful and humiliating process of having her teeth capped, her hair tinted red, and her face extensively experimented upon by studio cosmeticians to achieve the proper glamorous effect. (It had been decided that Powell initially lacked femininity.)

Eleanor soon experienced the glories of an MGM in its greatest era. In the tap-dancing numbers (filmed without sound equipment since the tap sounds were later dubbed onto the soundtrack), the dyed and capped starlet would perform before an all-star audience including Jean Harlow, Lionel Barrymore, and Fredric March, all taking a sojourn from their respective soundstages. A full orchestra complemented the dancer's performance. Powell would recall:

When I danced at Metro, they used to build these bleachers on each side of the set just like the fans have out here when there's a big premiere. Everybody used to come over and sit. You could smoke; you could applaud; you could talk because there was no sound being picked up; just silence. It was like you were playing to a live theatre audience. You'd hear applause, and people would yell out, "Go, Ellie. Show 'em, honey. Go ahead, honey." It egged you on like a racehorse.

Eleanor, in fact, was almost **too** good. Worried that an unknown was emerging as the star of the picture, Mayer called a high-level conference midproduction and seriously considered replacing Eleanor with a name performer. As she told Jay Rubin in a **Classic Film Collector** interview:

"No matter what happens, you want people to come to the theatre. So Mr. Mayer said, 'Maybe we should put Joan Crawford in or Loretta Young and dub the dancing'—not by me, but with a long shot, a double doing the numbers—'to be assured of the people coming to the theatre to begin with.'

"Mr. Del Ruth stepped up, and he said, 'First of all, if you do that, I walk off the picture.' . . . Then he said, 'Furthermore, if she doesn't become a star overnight, I personally will do any two pictures on this lot gratis for you.'

"I don't know what Mr. Mayer thought, but I was in. I'd make it."

Del Ruth discreetly kept the topic of this top-level conference from Eleanor throughout production, only telling her of the problem after she had indeed become an "overnight" star.

When released late in the summer of 1935, **Broadway Melody of 1936** was an enormous financial success. Critics noted that the components of the film made for top screen entertainment, even if the too clichéd story did not. Andre Sennwald (**New York Times**) penned, "The faces are new, and so are the songs and dances and some of the jests, but the work is in the familiar backstage tradition of the original **Broadway Melody,** which was a model for musical comedy in the infant talkies." The **New York Post** added, "The spirited tempo of the picture will account more for its box-office success than the story, since the latter deals familiarly with the familiar material of Broadway."

Audiences did not protest the familiarity. Most agreed with columnist Walter Winchell: "Finest musical I ever saw. . . . Swelegant. . . . Orchids to Eleanor Powell." **Broadway Melody of 1936** would place number eight on **Film Daily**'s Ten Best poll. It was Academy-nominated for Best Picture, losing to Metro's own **Mutiny on the Bounty.** An Oscar did go to Dave Gould for his dance direction of "I Got a Feeling You're Fooling" of **Broadway Melody** as well as his work on the "Straw Hat" number of United Artists' **Folies Bergere.**

Eleanor Powell, of course, won the major laurels of the film. After returning to Broadway for the musical **At Home Abroad** she came back to MGM as a great studio moneymaker.[2] Metro's immensely popular **Broadway Melody** celluloid format would return, with Miss Powell, in 1938 and 1940.

BROADWAY MELODY OF 1940
1940—102 min.

Producer, Jack Cummings; **director,** Norman Taurog; **story,** Jack McGowan and Dore Schary; **screenplay,** Leon Gordon and George Oppenheimer; **costumes,** Adrian; **art director,** Cedric Gibbons; **music director,** Alfred Newman; **orchestrators,** Edward Powell, Leo Arnaud, and Charles Henderson; **music supervisor,** Roger Edens; **songs,** Cole Porter; **choreography,** Bobby Connolly; **camera,** Oliver T. Marsh and Joseph Ruttenberg; **editor,** Blanche Sewell.

Fred Astaire (**Johnny Brett**); Eleanor Powell (**Clare Bennett [Brigit Callahan]**); George Murphy (**King Shaw**); Frank Morgan (**Bob Casey**); Ian Hunter (**Bert Matthews**); Florence Rice (**Amy Blake**);

Lynne Carver (**Emmy Lou Lee**); Ann Morriss (**Pearl DeLonge**); Trixie Firschke (**Juggler**); Douglas McPhail (**Masked Singer**); Charlotte Arren (**Audition Singer**); Herman Bing (**Silhouette Artist**); Jack Mulhall (**George, the Theatre Manager**); Vera Vague (**Receptionist**); Irving Bacon (**Soda Jerk**); James Flavin (**Dancehall Worker**); Joseph Crehan (**Dancehall Manager**); Joe Yule (**Dan, the Unemployed Actor**); Hal K. Dawson (**Grady, the Press Agent**); Gladys Blake and George Chandler (**The Bride and Groom**); William Tannen (**Emmy Lou's Friend**); The Music Maids (**Singing Quartet**).

SYNOPSIS
The dance team of Johnny Brett and King Shaw is down on its luck. Because they cannot get bookings, they take temporary jobs as professional hosts at Manhattan's Dawnland Ballroom. They eventually gain permission from the dancehall manager to perform their specialty act as a bonus for Dawnland customers.

Their act is seen by Bob Casey, a philandering musical show producer. He is especially impressed by Johnny's dancing. However, thinking Casey is a process server (seeking custody of Shaw's dress suit), Johnny tells addled Casey he is King Shaw. His theory is that if he accepts the legal summons it will be void.

As a result it is King who is requested to audition as Clare Bennett's new dance partner. Johnny good-naturedly coaches King, who wins the job opposite the princess of the musical stage. Even when Casey learns of his error, Brett insists that King deserves the break.

However, Shaw and success do not mix. His ego expands to such a degree that Clare begs Bert Matthews, Casey's partner, to replace her vis-à-vis. In the meantime, Clare and Johnny meet, quickly gaining respect for one another's dance skill. It is not long before they begin to fall in love.

On opening night, King arrives at the theatre late and drunk. When Johnny cannot sober his pal, he dons his friend's costume and mask and steps out on the stage as a substitute. Later in the production, King is able to go on, and no one—except Clare—is the wiser. When the show and King receive rave reviews, he becomes more egotistical than before. Finally Clare tells King the whole story. That evening he arrives at the theatre inebriated. He orders Clare to locate Johnny at the Dawnland Ballroom. She retrieves Johnny and they reach the theatre in time for the opening number.

For the finale of the show, the trio perform together.

* * *

It took mighty MGM to bring the world's two greatest dancers together. And whata show of shows they're in! You've never seen its like . . . for song, for spectacle, for thrilling romance!

The Oscar-nominated **Broadway Melody of 1936** (1935) was such a bonanza for MGM stockholders that in 1937 there appeared another spinoff of Metro's classic **Broadway Melody** (1929), appro-

---

[2]Well camouflaged was the fact that Powell's singing in this film was dubbed by Marjorie Lane, a redheaded chanteuse of the Hollywood Trocadero Club. Lane, on contract to MGM, would also dub for Powell's **Broadway Melody of 1938** (1937) and **Rosalie** (1937).

Fred Astaire and Eleanor Powell (photo on table) in Broadway Melody of 1940 *('40).*

there is the contrasting "I've Got My Eyes on You," in which Astaire dances on an empty stage, using a sheet-music photograph of Powell as his partner. (Powell, unknown to Astaire, has watched this episode and tells him, "That was swell, Johnny, . . . swell!")

One of the more fascinating segments of the film has Powell and Astaire performing the "Juke Box Dance" to its boogie-woogie beat. It is a compliment to choreographer Bobby Connolly that its intricate execution and changes of rhythm worked so well. For the scene in which a masked Astaire substitutes for Murphy, the Cole Porter song "I Concentrate on You" (sung by Douglas McPhail) is employed.

For the film's finale, MGM allotted a generous $120,000 to create the set for the intricate "Begin the Beguine" number. (The Porter song had been used originally for his 1935 Broadway musical **Jubilee**.) The setup employed a sixty-foot-square multifaceted mirror attached to a revolving track, which was swung around to alter backgrounds within the dance. In **Starring Fred Astaire** (1974) Stanley Green and Burt Goldblatt describe the scene:

> Following a sultry vocal, the two [Astaire and Powell] appear dancing on a mirrored floor surrounded by mirrored stars and palm trees. Their elegant tapping to the throbbing melody . . . is abruptly terminated by a change of pace and scenery, as a vocal quartet—patterned after the Andrews Sisters—emerge to mangle the song through some contemporary scat singing. Led by a wailing clarinet (a la Artie Shaw), Fred and Eleanor reappear in sportier garb to resume tapping—for a spell without orchestral accompaniment—and build the number to its jubilant finish.

For the wrapup, Astaire, Powell, and Murphy appear while the orchestra reprises "I've Got My Eyes on You." Discarded from the film musical were "I Happen to Be in Love" and "I'm So in Love with You."

There were several unusual facets to **Broadway Melody of 1940.** It was the first film since MGM's **Dancing Lady** (1933) that presented Astaire in a backstage story. It was the first time on screen he had a male dance partner (Murphy). Despite this reputation for introducing some of the finest Irving Berlin and Jerome Kern songs, Astaire had little singing to do in **Broadway Melody**—one solo, and one duet. And, of course, this was his first (and only) pairing with the very talented Eleanor Powell.[2]

Watching **Broadway Melody of 1940** one can fully appreciate the individual talents involved in the picture. But somehow director Norman Taurog was unable to make everything mesh on a high level. The tandem dancing of Astaire and Powell is fun to behold, but Fred and Eleanor are **not**

priately titled **Broadway Melody of 1938.** Roy Del Ruth again directed; Arthur Freed–Nacio Herb Brown tunes again filled the score; Robert Taylor, Eleanor Powell, and Buddy Ebsen again headed the cast, assisted by George Murphy, Sophie Tucker, and a fifteen-year-old newcomer named Judy Garland (who stole the limelight with her rendition of "Dear Mr. Gable"). When the results again proved lucrative, MGM concocted yet another **Broadway Melody.** This one **of 1940** and boasting the union of the energetic Eleanor Powell and the sophisticated Fred Astaire, the latter fresh from his contract expiration at RKO.

When the film went into production in the fall of 1939, producer Jack Cummings thought of budgeting the musical to include Technicolor. However, the advent of World War II had shut off many European film release markets, causing MGM to restrict expenditures on this and other studio products.

For this latest (and final) edition of **Broadway Melody,** Cole Porter provided the score (as he had for MGM's **Born to Dance,** 1936, starring

Powell). It gave the "series" a new approach since Porter's numbers were far more sophisticated than had been those of his predecessors. For example, the opening vaudeville routine, "Please Don't Monkey with Boadway" (performed by Astaire and Murphy), is a far cry from the bravura sentiment of "Broadway Melody" **(The Broadway Melody),** "Broadway Rhythm" **(Broadway Melody of 1936),** or "Your Broadway and My Broadway" **(Broadway Melody of 1938).**

Much more than was the case in the previous **Broadways,** the song-and-dance numbers here flowed out of the plotline in a smooth fashion. The backstage story concocted by Leon Gordon and George Oppenheimer made this possible. Powell is first seen performing "I Am the Captain" in which she sings, taps, and allows herself to be tossed about by the chorus of gobs. Murphy's audition for Powell's show allows him to demonstrate the elegant "Between You and Me."[1] Then

---

[1] For this number it was intended that a specially constructed banked ramp would provide the finale for the

heel-and-toe work of Murphy and Powell. However, the performers expressed a worry that it was dangerous. Special-effects man A. Arnold Gillespie said "nonsense" and proceeded to demonstrate the feat. He slid down the ramp and broke his leg!

[2] Her singing continued to be dubbed.

really a team. She is better as a solo. He is a pleasant singer and a good actor—skills Eleanor never perfected. As **Variety** noted when the picture was released in February 1940, it "lacks ingredients to carry it into the smash hit class." It did solid business (and its display of superior dancing still is a wonder to behold), but the excitement of the prior two **Broadways** was not to be found.

Powell, the World's Greatest Tap Dancer, continued at MGM to grand effect in **Lady Be Good** (1941). She was cast as the stooge to Red Skelton in **Ship Ahoy** (1942) and **I Dood It** (1943). Also in 1943 she performed a specialty act in **Thousands Cheer.** Thereafter she departed the Culver City complex, and wed movie actor Glenn Ford (they had a son Peter in 1945; divorced in 1959; she has not remarried). She made only two more films: the mediocre United Artists release **Sensations of 1945** (1944) and a guest appearance in MGM's **Duchess of Idaho** (1950), an Esther Williams' vehicle.

CABIN IN THE SKY
1943—99 min.[1]

Producer, Arthur Freed; **associate producer,** Albert Lewis; **director,** Vincente Minnelli; based on the play by Lynn Root, John LaTouche, and Vernon Duke; **screenplay,** Joseph Schrank and, **uncredited,** Eustace Cocrell and Marc Connelly; **music adapter,** Roger Edens; **music director,** George Stoll; **orchestrators,** George Bassman and Conrad Salinger; **choral arranger,** Hall Johnson; **music number staged by** Busby Berkeley; **songs,** LaTouche and Duke; Harold Arlen and E. Y. Harburg; Duke Ellington; **art directors,** Cedric Gibbons and Leonid Vasian; **set decorators,** Edwin B. Willis and Hugh Hunt; **costumes,** Irene, and Howard Shoup; **men's costumes,** Gile Steele; **camera,** Sidney Wagner; **editor,** Harold F. Kress.

Eddie ("Rochester") Anderson (**Little Joe Jackson**); Ethel Waters (**Petunia Jackson**); Lena Horne (**Georgia Brown**); Rex Ingram (**Lucifer Jr.—Lucius**); Kenneth Spencer (**The General—Parson Green**); Louis Armstrong (**The Trumpeter**); Oscar Polk (**Fleetfoot—The Deacon**); Nicodemus (**Dude**); Ernest Whitman (**Jim Henry**); Clinton Rosemond (**Dr. Jones**); John ("Bubbles") Sublett (**Domino Johnson**); Duke Ellington and His Band (**Themselves**); Butterfly McQueen (**Lily**); Fletcher Rivers and Leon James, and Ford Washington (**Specialties**); Ruby Dandridge (**Mrs. Kelso**); Raymond Turner (**Doorman**); Mantan Moreland (**Trumpeter Imp**); Bill Bailey (**Washing Machine Salesman**); Hall Johnson Choir (**Voices**).

SYNOPSIS
Gambler, drinker, womanizer Little Joe Jackson becomes wounded in a dice game brawl and struggles between life and death. During his de-

---

[1]Filmed in Sepia.

Eddie ("Rochester") Anderson, Ethel Waters and Kenneth Spencer in Cabin in the Sky ('43).

lirium, Joe dreams that the devil, Lucifer Jr., has claimed him.

Meanwhile, Joe's devoted wife Petunia prays and the Lawd's General, an angel, grants Joe six months of life to make amends for his past sins. Aiding Lucifer in his claim for Joe's soul is the seductive Georgia Brown.

Joe does make amends and is generally content with his newfound righteousness. Whenever he longs for his former way of life, a tug-of-war occurs between the General and Lucifer. Lucifer arranges for Joe to win a sweepstakes ticket and Georgia attempts once again to lure Joe from Petunia.

Now Joe resumes his libertine ways and Petunia must woo back her husband. She follows him to John Henry's cafe and a shootout results in Little Joe and Petunia being shot. The General decides to destroy the vile cafe and sends a tornado to annihilate its occupants.

The noise awakens Joe from his dream and he vows that he will one day share a "cabin in the sky" with his beloved, patient Petunia.

* * *

Business had never been booming for the October 1940 Broadway musical **Cabin in the Sky.** It featured an all-black cast (including Ethel Waters, Todd Duncan, Dooley Wilson, Rex Ingram, and Katherine Dunham), a book by Lynn Root, lyrics by John LaTouche, music by Vernon Duke, and direction and choreography by George Balanchine. Without the minority-favoring philanthropy that in later years came to the financial aid of floundering all-black Broadway shows, **Cabin in the Sky** closed after 156 performances and a loss of $25,000.

Enter MGM. Producer Arthur Freed, excited about the idea of filming **Porgy and Bess,** learns that the Gershwin show is unavailable, so he settles on **Cabin in the Sky.** The studio purchases the film rights for $40,000, putting the New York producers $15,000 ahead. Ethel Waters and Rex Ingram are brought to Hollywood to repeat their Broadway parts. Eddie ("Rochester") Anderson (of the Jack Benny radio program and films) is signed to star as Little Joe Jackson. Lena Horne[2] is put under MGM contract. While waiting for the filming to begin, she is featured in **Panama Hattie** (1942) as a specialty performer. Added to the cast are such black character players as Oscar Polk (memorable in **Gone with the Wind** as Tara's devoted "Pork"), Ernest Whitman (earlier a stalwart hero server of such Fox films as **The Prisoner of Shark Island** and **Jesse James**), and Butterfly McQueen ("Prissy" of birthin' baby fame). In addition, there are Louis Armstrong, Duke Ellington and His Band, and the Hall Johnson Choir. Making his debut as a feature film director is Vincente Minnelli.

The musical is filmed entirely in Sepia and the song score is filled out with the Harold Arlen–E. Y. Harburg song, "Happiness Is a Thing Called Joe."[3] During the lensing there is much feuding amongst the stars. Tension is especially heavy between Ethel Waters and Lena Horne. In Hugh Fordin's **The World of Entertainment** (1975), the

---

[2]Lena Horne had very definite ideas about how a black should appear on the screen, even in white-controlled Hollywood of the 1940s. She rejected the role of Jeanette MacDonald's maid in **Cairo** (1941) as being an unflattering stereotype. She was replaced by Ethel Waters.

[3]Lena Horne's song "Ain't It the Truth" would be deleted from the release print.

author quotes several of the parties involved in the unpleasantries.

ETHEL WATERS: I objected violently to the way religion was being treated in the screenplay. All through the picture there was so much snarling and scrapping that I didn't know how in the world **Cabin in the Sky** ever stayed up there.

LENA HORNE: Unlike Miss Waters I was enjoying myself hugely on this picture. But the kids who were working in scenes with Ethel Waters told me she was violently prejudiced against me. Miss Waters was not notably gentle toward women and she was particularly tough on other singers.

VINCENTE MINNELLI: I was kind of a bulwark between them because I loved Lena and I loved Ethel . . . but Ethel didn't like Lena at all. It always seemed so ridiculous to me, because Ethel was such a great artist. In New York it was her show, but now it was divided—there was the new element of the beautiful colored girl . . . but I had my own troubles.

Apparently nobody in the cast was too charming. Butterfly McQueen would later insist that "Eddie Anderson teased Miss Waters, Lena Horne regarded her with contempt, and director Minnelli was cutting about her when she was out of sight."

Despite everything, **Cabin in the Sky,** which had begun production on August 31, 1942, was completed (with retakes) on October 28, 1942, at a cost of $662,141. The ad campaign read, "Broadway's big, fun-jammed musical show is on the screen at last! Crowded with stars—and songs—and spectacle—in the famed MGM manner." **Cabin in the Sky** became Hollywood's first[4] black major production since King Vidor's **Hallelujah!** (1929). Reviews were very flattering. Thomas Pryor (**New York Times**) offered, "The Metro picturization . . . is every inch as sparkling and completely satisfying as was the original stage production in 1940. In short, this first all-Negro screen musical in many a year is a most welcome treat." **Variety** decided, "**Cabin** is a worthwhile picture for Metro to have made, if only as a step toward recognition of the place of the colored man in American life." All the characterizations, especially Anderson's Little Joe, Waters' faithful Petunia, and Rex Ingram's Lucifer Jr., were emotionally and vividly portrayed.

Cabin in the Sky was a major contribution to at least two causes: the showcasing of black Hollywood talent, and the introduction of the directing abilities of Vincente Minnelli in feature films. "If **Cabin in the Sky** hadn't been a small picture," said Minnelli, "and a risky one too, I would have had to wait much longer for that first break."

---

[4]Also in 1943, Twentieth Century–Fox released **Stormy Weather.** Directed by Andrew L. Stone, this thinly veiled account of Bill ("Bojangles") Robinson's life featured Robinson, Lena Horne, Cab Calloway and His Band, Katherine Dunham, and Fats Waller (especially effective performing "Ain't Misbehavin' ").

CAMILLE
1936—108 min.

Producers, Irving Thalberg and Bernard Hyman; **director,** George Cukor; based on the novel by Alexandre Dumas; **screenplay,** Zoe Akins, Frances Marion, and James Hilton; **music,** Herbert Stothart; **choreography,** Val Raset; **art directors,** Cedric Gibbons and Frederic Hope; **set decorator,** Edwin B. Willis; **gowns,** Adrian; **sound,** Douglas Shearer; **camera,** William Daniels; **editor,** Margaret Booth.

Greta Garbo (**Marguerite Gautier**); Robert Taylor (**Armand Duval**); Lionel Barrymore (**General Duval**); Henry Daniell (**Baron de Varville**); Elizabeth Allan (**Nichette**); Lenore Ulric (**Olympe**); Laura Hope Crews (**Prudence**); Jessie Ralph (**Nanine**); Rex O'Malley (**Gatson**); Russell Hardie (**Gustave**); E. E. Clive (**St. Gadeau**); Douglas Walton (**Henri**); Marion Ballou (**Corinne**); Joan Leslie (**Marie Jeanette**); June Wilkins (**Louise**); Elsie Esmond (**Madame Duval**); Fritz Leiber, Jr. (**Valentine**); Edwin Maxwell (**Doctor**); Eily Malyon (**Therese**); Mariska Aldrich (**Friend of Camille**); John Bryan (**DeMasset**); Rex Evans (**Companion**); Eugene King (**Gypsy Leader**); Adrienne Matzenauer (**Singer**); Georgia Caine (**Streetwalker**); Elspeth Dudgeon (**Attendant**); Effie Ellsler (**Grandma Duval**); Olaf Hytten (**Croupier**); Ferdinand Munier (**Priest**); Zeffie Tilbury (**Old Duchess**); Guy Bates Post (**Auctioneer**); Barry Norton (**Emile**).

SYNOPSIS

In mid-nineteenth-century France, aging Parisian courtesan Marguerite Gautier—known for her love of the camellia flower—is currently involved with the arrogant Baron de Varville. She may be worldly and cynical but she is kind and generous, as re-

Greta Garbo and Robert Taylor in Camille *('36).*

vealed when she pays for the wedding of her friend Nichette.

One evening at the theatre Marguerite meets Armand Duval, a young, handsome, and naive bachelor. Soon the two fall in love. The baron reprimands her for her dalliance when he discovers that she has spent considerable time with Armand. She, in turn, tries to convince herself and the others that the romance is a frivolity; but, in reality, Armand has won her heart.

Armand's father, General Duval, comes to Marguerite and warns her that she will ruin Armand's career as well as his life if she marries him. For Armand's well-being she leaves him, explaining that she prefers her former hedonistic life of luxury. Further disaster strikes when she contracts tuberculosis and must sell all of her possessions to pay her bills. All of her former friends and acquaintances ignore her; only the faithful maid Nanine remains to comfort her.

Armand later learns of Marguerite's deteriorating health and returns to her, promising to remain by her side forever. She dies in his arms, knowing that Armand truly loves her.

* * *

Louis B. Mayer once pontificated, unaware that he would be documented, that the motion pictures had bequeathed the world only one truly great artist, "Greta Garbo—unless you count that damn mouse!" The greatest testimony to this statement lies in **Camille** (1936), in which Garbo's Marguerite Gautier, the tragic Lady of the Camellias, is generally celebrated as the single most beautiful performance of the American sound screen.

The consumptive courtesan of the Alexandre Dumas novel had long enticed actresses; the stage version of **Camille** became a favorite of such international stars as Eleanora Duse and Sarah Bernhardt. By 1936 there had also been at least four widely distributed photoplay versions: Bernhardt in 1912, Clara Kimball Young in 1917, Nazimova in 1920, and Norma Talmadge in 1927.

In searching for an appealing follow-up to Garbo's **Anna Karenina** (1935) which won her the New York Drama Critics Best Actress Award, Irving Thalberg gave director George Cukor a choice between **Manon Lescaut** and **Camille**. Cukor jumped at the latter, and Thalberg set the tone for the film:

The audience must forget within the first five minutes that this is a costume picture. It must be contemporary in its feeling, but one thing mitigates against that effect; the point that a girl's past can ruin her marriage. That problem doesn't exist any more. Whores can make good wives; that has been proven.

Hence scenarists[1] Zoe Akins, Frances Mar-

ion, and James Hilton transferred Armand Duval's agony over Marguerite's dark past to jealousy over her current relationship with the Baron de Varville.

Thalberg carefully selected the rest of the cast. As Armand, the producer chose $75 per week contractee Robert Taylor because of the actor's "pretty" handsomeness. The actor would later recall the assignment as a formidable experience. "I was a scared kid of twenty-five and she was thirty-one, in full bloom, already a fantastic legend." As the smoothly wicked Baron de Varville, Thalberg initially wanted John Barrymore, but the memories of Barrymore's drunken buffoonery on the **Romeo and Juliet** set and that actor's declining health led to the signing of Henry Daniell, the sleek, foxy English player, for the villainous characterization. Lionel Barrymore was cast as Armand's fustian father, and Laura Hope Crews, Rex O'Malley, and Lenore Ulric represented the demimonde of Paris as a cigar-smoking bawd, an effeminate gossip, and an unabashed hussy, respectively.

With sumptuous sets by Cedric Gibbons, and William Daniels angling his camera at the star with almost divine reverence, Cukor painstakingly guided Garbo through her apex performance. "She is a fascinating artist," admitted the director, "but she is limited. She must never create situations. She must be thrust into them; the drama comes in how she rides them out." Hence, Cukor scrutinized every idiosyncrasy of Garbo, trying to make each mannerism blend with an unforgettable performance.

In a **Focus on Film** article, veteran screenwriter DeWitt Bodeen recalls one such instance:

One of my favorite scenes is where Garbo, having made a rendezvous with Robert Taylor for late supper in her apartment is suddenly surprised by the unexpected return of Henry Daniell, her baronial lover. It was an added scene, and Daniell told me once how, on the morning he was to shoot it, he crossed the lot to his dressing room and encountered Garbo on the way to hers.

She smiled wanly. "How do you like the new scene, Mr. Daniell?" she asked.

"I think it's a good scene," he said cautiously, "but I'm honestly worried about it. You see, I don't laugh very well."

"I don't either," she confessed plaintively.

That, of course, was the whole point of the scene, and Cukor staged it with an electric brilliance.

That scene has become a classic, both players laughing toward a mad crescendo as the Baron sadistically plays the piano, torturing Marguerite with his knowledge of her arranged tryst. So has the lovely pastoral sequence in which Marguerite and Armand rejoice in the countryside; the heartbreaking vignette in which Camille weeps bitterly as she writes her farewell to Armand after

his father directs her to "give up" his son; and the beautifully played finale, in which a dying Marguerite tells the devoted Armand, "Perhaps it's better if I live in your heart—where the world can't see me."[2]

As **Camille** neared the end of production, Irving Thalberg died of pneumonia, on September 14, 1936. Bernard Hyman replaced him as producer. The company mourned deeply, especially Garbo, who had shortly before his demise ordered Thalberg off the set because his concerned visits made her nervous. Perhaps it was the memory of this mandate which moved Garbo from her famous seclusion to join Mayer, Nicholas Schenck, and most of the studio executives at the California premiere of **Camille** late in 1936.

When the picture opened in January 1937 in New York, it was promoted with the ad lines, "Their lips meet for the first time. . . . Supreme thrill seared in your memory forever. . . . As Garbo, the incomparable, and Robert Taylor, the screen's outstanding romantic idol, live again the love story the world has taken to its heart." For her performance in **Camille**, Garbo won her most lavish reviews:

The incomparable Greta Garbo has returned to the screen in a breathtakingly beautiful and superbly modulated portrayal of **Camille**. . . . The Marguerite she brings to the screen is not only the errant and self-sacrificial nymph conceived by the younger Dumas nearly a hundred years ago, but one of the timeless figures of all great art. . . . It is likely that Miss Garbo still has her greatest role to play, but she has made the Lady of the Camellias, for this reviewer, hers for all time. [Howard Barnes, **New York Herald-Tribune**]

Greta Garbo's performance is in the finest tradition: eloquent, tragic, yet restrained. She is as incomparable in the role as legend tells us that Bernhardt was. Through the perfect artistry of her portrayal, a hackneyed theme is made new again, poignantly sad, hauntingly lovely. . . . Miss Garbo has interpreted Marguerite Gautier with the subtlety that has

---

[1]In **The Great Romantic Films** (1974) Lawrence J. Quirk points out of **Camille**: "And that dialogue! For all its Victorian flow and voluminous phrasing, it rings true in poetic terms: 'Armand has taught me that all love is not selfish, nor goodness dull, nor men faithless. . . . Let me love you; let me live for you; don't let's ask more from Heaven than that—God might get angry. . . . I

don't suppose you can understand Monsieur, how someone unprotected as you say I am, can be lifted above selfishness by sentiments so delicate and pure.' "

---

[2]Bosley Crowther notes in **The Great Films** (1967): "Thus does this classic romance conclude, precisely as it should, with the ideal, illusory woman, still lovely and imperishable, in a bereft man's arms. This is not death as mortals know it. This is but the conclusion of a romantic ritual. Marguerite is really going to live forever, and not just in the heart of Armand."

And in **Greta Garbo** (1974) Richard Corliss observes: "To watch Marguerite's death scene as played by Garbo is to see a great actress breathe life into that soul, and then to see it extinguished with a final dying fall. . . .

"To write about a phenomenon such as this is to pin down nuances as subtle and evanescent as a butterfly with the net of clumsy words. It's an attempt to describe the ineffable, to attach nouns and adjectives to a state of beauty, an art, a vision caught on celluloid. Like Yeats' definition of poetry, Garbo's performance has 'the perfections that escape analysis.' Great acting such as this cannot be parsed. It can only be perceived, from a mortal distance, and treasured."

earned her the title "first lady of the screen." [Frank S. Nugent, **New York Times**]

Robert Taylor (whose performance won a salute from Nugent, "Taylor avoids the callousness of previous Armands") and Daniell (whose silky perversity won him a Metro player's contract and baptized him as one of Hollywood's finest heavies) shared in the glory, as did Cukor for his incisive direction. Garbo, who dominated the picture, won her third Best Actress Academy Award nomination. Her competitors were impressive: Irene Dunne for Columbia's **The Awful Truth**, Janet Gaynor for United Artists' **A Star is Born**, Luise Rainer for MGM's **The Good Earth**, and Barbara Stanwyck for United Artists' **Stella Dallas**. Many were surprised when Garbo's Marguerite lost to the O-Lan of Luise Rainer. However, Garbo's **Camille** did win the New York Drama Critics Award for best feminine performance.

Camille became Garbo's greatest box-office success. It returned a huge gross on its $1,500,000 production cost and remains today as the legendary actress's most stunning cinema achievement.

CAPTAINS COURAGEOUS
1937—116 min.

Producer, Louis D. Lighton; **directors**, Victor Fleming and, **uncredited**, Jack Conway; based on the novel by Rudyard Kipling; **story ideas, uncredited**, Howard Hawks; **screenplay**, John Lee Mahin, Marc Connelly, and Dale Van Every; **songs**, Franz Waxman and Gus Kahn; **music**, Waxman; **marine director**, James Havens; **art directors**, Cedric Gibbons and Arnold Gillespie; **set decorator**, Edwin B. Willis; **sound**, Douglas Shearer; **camera**, Harold Rosson; **editor**, Elmo Vernon.

Freddie Bartholomew (**Harvey Cheyne**); Spencer Tracy (**Manuel**); Lionel Barrymore (**Captain Disko Troop**); Melvyn Douglas (**Mr. Cheyne**); Mickey Rooney (**Dan Troop**); Charley Grapewin (**Uncle Salters**); Christian Rub (**Old Clement**); Walter Kingsford (**Dr. Finley**); Donald Briggs (**Tyler**); Sam McDaniel (**Doc**); Dave Thursby (**Tom**); John Carradine (**Long Jack**); William Stack (**Elliott**); Leo G. Carroll (**Burns**); Charles Trowbridge (**Dr. Walsh**); Richard Powell (**Steward**); Billy Burrud (**Charles**); Jay Ward (**Pogey**); Oscar O'Shea (**Walt Cushman**); Jack LaRue (**Priest**); Billy Gilbert (**Soda Steward**); Norman Ainsley (**Robbins**); Tommy Bupp and Wally Albright (**Boys**); Katherine Kenworthy (**Mrs. Disko**); Murray Kinnell (**Minister**); Gertrude Sutton (**Nate's Wife**); Dora Early (**Appleton's Wife**).

SYNOPSIS
Rich and spoiled twelve-year-old Harvey Cheyne runs away from his Connecticut school when he is rejected as a member of an exclusive club. His millionaire father, a widower, books passage on a liner for Europe and decides to take his son with him. After drinking six ice cream sodas, Harvey becomes ill, leans too far over the rail, and falls overboard near the Grand Banks, unseen by anyone!

Harvey awakens aboard the small Gloucester-based schooner **We're Here,** which was passing by the liner. Accustomed to having his own way, Harvey orders Captain Disko Troop to return home. The captain explains he cannot return to port until the schooner has its catch in the hold, which should be in three months. The captain's son, Dan, attempts to make friends with Harvey, but the stubborn boy rejects him.

Manuel is the Portuguese fisherman who had rescued Harvey and it is the older man who adopts a paternal interest towards his "leetle feesh." Soon the boy comes to idolize Manuel and becomes his dory mate during fishing treks. On the way back to Gloucester **We're Here**, races rival schooner **Jenny Cushman**, operated by Walt Cushman. Manuel volunteers to climb aloft to furl the topsail, but the mast cracks and he falls into the water in a tangle of ropes and canvas. After an attempted rescue, the crew watches Manuel sink into the sea.

The heartbroken Harvey is reunited later with his father at Gloucester. Out of the nine dollars' wages he earned aboard, the boy buys a candlestick for Manuel's father and one for Manuel. During a memorial service for sailors who have died at sea, Harvey throws a wreath on the water when Manuel's name is called. Mr. Cheyne also throws a wreath, which drifts entwined with Harvey's. For the first time Harvey turns to his father for consolation.

* * *

Powerful, moving, and splendidly entertaining, MGM's **Captains Courageous**, based on Rudyard Kipling's 1897 novel, is one of the cinema's great adventure films, grandly scaled, deeply atmospheric, admirably cast.

In October 1935 cameramen Harold Marzorati and Bob Roberts, business managers Frank Barnes and Ewing Scott, and marine technicians Jim Havens and Harry Marble traveled to Gloucester, Massachusetts, where they purchased the 110-foot schooner **Oretha F. Spinney**, which was rechristened **We're Here.** With Captain J. M. Hersey at the wheel and the filming crew aboard, the ship sailed for Newfoundland where it remained throughout December, and then headed for Nova Scotia. Shots of the fishing fleet in every type of conceivable weather were lensed for use in the picture. In March the schooner sailed south, through the Panama Canal, and on up the Pacific Coast to Los Angeles Harbor. That September, with the selected cast finally available for filming, the picture got under way. (In the meantime, the **We're Here** and John Barrymore's former yacht, rechristened **Jennie Cushman,** traveled up to Monterey and to Coos Bay, Oregon, for fog scenes.) On October 1, 1936, the cast journeyed out to Avalon, Catalina Island, for location filming.

In the course of the seven months of on-again, off-again production, the crew had to contend with fickle weather, especially in the instance of seeking a storm background used for the racing shots between the two schooners. When a terrific storm did hit, the shots were filmed near Mazatlan, Mexico. Off Cape San Lucas, lower Cal-

Freddie Bartholomew, Lionel Barrymore, and Spencer Tracy in Captains Courageous *('37).*

ifornia, the **We're Here** nearly capsized. Before the picture wound up its shooting schedule, Victor Fleming underwent surgery and during his absence Jack Conway took over direction. Back at MGM, an exact reproduction of the galley and forecastle of the schooner **We're Here** had been set up on Metro's stage 7. It was balanced on a gyroscope to tilt the set in any direction to simulate the rolling of a vessel.

Playing the major role of Harvey Cheyne was Britisher Freddie Bartholomew, patrician child star who, in the words of **Time** magazine, "gets an estimated $1,250 a week from Metro-Goldwyn-Mayer because he impersonates immature characters like the heroes of **David Copperfield, Little Lord Fauntleroy,** and **Professional Soldier,** with incongruously mature dignity." The script altered the age of Harvey from nineteen to twelve to fit the top-billed Freddie. Lionel Barrymore, less than a year away from the crippling disease that would confine him to crutches or a wheelchair, played Captain Disko Troop. Dapper Melvyn Douglas, whose Columbia contract was now being shared by MGM, was given a very subordinate role as Harvey's wealthy father. Mickey Rooney, who had just completed his first Andy Hardy venture, **A Family Affair,** in which Barrymore played his dad, was again related to the veteran actor in this seafaring yarn. Saturnine John Carradine, on loan from Twentieth Century–Fox, was properly spiteful as the superstitious Long Jack.

However, the performance everyone remembers most fondly is Spencer Tracy's Manuel, the Portuguese fisherman who scoops Harvey out of the water and teaches him to be a just man. Tracy was terribly uncomfortable in the curly-haired makeup (Joan Crawford passed him on the lot early in production and exclaimed "My God, it's Harpo Marx!") and with singing[1] the songs "Don't Cry Little Fish" and "Ooh, What a Terrible Man." He later recalled, "I used to pray that something would happen to halt production. I was positive I was doing the worst job of my life."

However, when **Captains Courageous** premiered in May 1937 critical enthusiasm for the Victor Fleming–directed saga was abundant. **Variety** labeled it "one of the best pictures of the sea ever made." Frank S. Nugent **(New York Times)** described the film as "another of those grand jobs of moviemaking we have come to expect of Hollywood's most prodigal studio. With its rich production, magnificent marine photography, admirable direction and performances, the film brings vividly to life every page of Kipling's novel and even adds an exciting chapter or two of its own." Howard Barnes **(New York Herald-Tribune)** warned, "You May find Spencer Tracy's Portuguese accent a trifle startling at first. But once he takes the little chap he fished out of the sea

in hand, he gives an impersonation that can only be called perfect." Barnes agreed with the other reviewers that **"Captains Courageous** belongs with the screen's few masterpieces. . . ."

Captains Courageous won a Best Picture Academy Award nomination but lost the prize to Warner Bros.' **The Story of Louis Pasteur.** Tracy was nominated for Best Actor. His competition was formidable: Charles Boyer (of MGM's **Conquest**), Fredric March (of United Artists' **A Star Is Born**), Paul Muni (of Warner Bros.' **The Life of Emile Zola**), and Robert Montgomery (of MGM's **Night Must Fall**). Tracy was so certain that Fredric March would win—and so certain that he would not take it like the proverbial good sport—that he arranged to go into the hospital for a hernia operation. "Can you imagine," winced Tracy years later, "what I felt like—lying there, in all those itchy bandages around my middle, and plenty of pain—when the word came through, I'd won it?" Mrs. Tracy accepted for her husband, who had a second surprise when his Oscar was mistakenly engraved to "Dick Tracy" (Tracy would receive a properly engraved Oscar the following year for his work in **Boys Town**).

As for Master Bartholomew, MGM announced it planned to star him in a version of Kipling's **Kim** with Robert Taylor as Mahbub Ali. But that project would remain a vision rather than a reality for thirteen years. Bartholomew was already beginning to outgrow his youthful appeal and was soon supplanted on the lot by popular Mickey Rooney. The latter was later scheduled to star in **Kim,** perhaps costarred with Spencer Tracy as Mahbub Ali, the Red Beard. But when Metro finally did the story in 1950, Dean Stockwell and Errol Flynn were cast in the key roles.

On December 4, 1977 ABC-TV presented a two-hour television movie version of **Captains Courageous** starring Jonathan Kahn **(Harvey Cheyne);** Karl Malden **(Disko Troop);** Richardo Montalban **(Manuel);** Fred Gwynne **(Long Jack);** Neville Brand **(Little Penn);** Jeff Corey **(Salters);** and Fritz Weaver **(Mr. Cheyne).** It led Judith Crist to write in her **TV Guide** column:

> Most movie buffs' off-the-cuff reaction to a remake of Rudyard Kipling's **Captains Courageous** is bound to be "Who needs it?" Deep in our hearts lies MGM's 1937 saltwater classic that won Spencer Tracy a best-actor Oscar for his portrait of Manuel, the Portuguese fisherman who rescues a spoiled rich kid from the briny and makes a man of him aboard a fishing schooner. It was star-studded Hollywood stuff, with Freddie Bartholomew, Lionel Barrymore, and Mickey Rooney, among others, and enough tears jerked by Manuel's demise to double the ocean's depth. On the cuff, however, and forty years later, one has to credit John Gay's new TV adaptation of the 1897 Kipling story for its shift of emphasis from sentiment to storyline and its concentration on character rather than spectacular seascapes. Small wonder that Ricardo Montalban is a far more credible Portuguese than Tracy, though in this version Manuel has secondary status and the boy's chief mentor is Disko Troop, captain of the **We're Here,** bound for the Newfoundland Banks. . . ."

---

[1] Tracy's character is fond of singing and accompanying himself on the vielle, an ancient Portuguese stringed instrument, which resembles both a mandolin and a piano-accordion. At one point Manuel tells Harvey, "I don't write songs. I just find them in my mouth. Say, sometimes a song is so big and sweet inside, I just can't get him out, and then I look up at the stars and maybe cry and feel so good."

CAT ON A HOT TIN ROOF
1958 C—108 min.

Producer, Lawrence Weingarten; **director,** Richard Brooks; based on the play by Tennessee Williams; **screenplay,** Brooks and James Poe; **art directors,** William A. Horning and Urie McCleary; **set decorators,** Henry Grace and Robert Priestley; **assistant director,** William Shanks; **wardrobe,** Helen Rose; **makeup,** William Tuttle; **sound,** Dr. Wesley C. Miller; **special effects,** Lee LeBlanc; **camera,** William Daniels; **editor,** Ferris Webster.

Elizabeth Taylor **(Maggie Pollitt);** Paul Newman **(Brick Pollitt);** Burl Ives **(Big Daddy Pollitt);** Jack Carson **(Gooper Pollitt);** Judith Anderson **(Big Mama Pollitt);** Madeleine Sherwood **(Mae Pollitt);** Larry Gates **(Dr. Baugh);** Vaughn Taylor **(Deacon Davis);** Deborah Miller, Patty Ann Garrity, Hugh Corcoran, Rusty Stevens, and Brian Corcoran **(Gooper's Children).**

SYNOPSIS
Lusty Big Daddy Pollitt owns 28,000 acres of "the richest land this side of the Valley Nile" in southern United States. Big Daddy suffers from an illness that tests at a clinic reveal to be cancer. Big Mama refuses to accept this fact and hides the truth from her husband, passing off his ailment as a spastic colon. The plantation and estate will be inherited by Big Daddy's sons Gooper and Brick. Gooper is a successful lawyer submerged in self-pity and married to shrewish Mae, whose famed fertility has produced five obnoxious "no-neck monsters" with another on the way. Brick, the "thirty-year-old boy," and his wife Maggie have produced no offspring.

Big Daddy hounds Brick about the problems existing between him and Maggie. Brick has turned to steady drinking, and this combined with a recently broken leg causes him to renege on his marital duties, a situation which makes Maggie feel like "a cat on a hot tin roof."

During a warm summer's evening Brick's earlier life and his relationship with the long-deceased Skipper surface. In a crucial confrontation with his father, Brick admits, "All I wanted was a father, not a boss—I wanted you to love me." To turn the tide in Brick's favor, Maggie announces to the family that she is carrying Brick's child. This is a fabrication that Maggie is determined to turn into a reality. At the finale she and Brick have reunited.

* * *

On March 24, 1955, Tennessee Williams' **Cat on a Hot Tin Roof** opened at the Morosco Theatre, treating Broadway audiences to a cast which included Barbara Bel Geddes **(Maggie),** Ben Gazarra **(Brick),** and Burl Ives **(Big Daddy).** The controversial production won the New York Drama Critics Award and the Pulitzer Prize. MGM promptly acquired the film rights.

The studio initially bought the property as a vehicle for Grace Kelly, who had been making millions of box-office dollars for other studios on loanout: **Dial M for Murder, Rear Window, The**

Elizabeth Taylor and Paul Newman in Cat on a Hot Tin Roof *('58).*

die Fisher–Debbie Reynolds–Elizabeth Taylor headlines. The gossip doubtlessly had a strong effect on the picture's domestic gross of $9,750,000, making **Cat** the top moneymaker of Metro's 1958 season and, at the time, the tenth biggest monymaker in the studio's history.

Cat on a Hot Tin Roof joined the Oscar contest in the categories of Best Picture (defeated by MGM's **Gigi**), Best Actor (Newman lost to David Niven of United Artists' **Separate Tables**), Best Actress (Taylor lost to Susan Hayward of United Artists' **I Want to Live!**). The Best Supporting Actor prize of 1958 was given to Burl Ives, officially for his performance in that year's **The Big Country** (United Artists), though many cited his **Cat** performance as a major factor in the voters' decision.

Of the 1950s cinema versions of such Tennessee Williams plays as **The Glass Menagerie** (1950, Warner Bros.), **A Streetcar Named Desire** (1951, Warner Bros.), **The Rose Tattoo** (1955, Paramount), **Baby Doll** (1956, Warner Bros.), and **Suddenly, Last Summer** (1959, Columbia; also with Miss Taylor), Metro's **Cat** is perhaps the most satisfying work. It is rich with the playwright's undisguised bitterness and crammed with full-dimensional performances. Metro took a cue from the hefty proceeds. As the decade of the 1960s began, the studio's direction took a decided turn toward the controversial and the sometimes sordid properties that most appealed to the increasingly "aware" new generations of viewers.

The 1976 Canadian TV production (starring Laurence Olivier, Natalie Wood, and Robert Wagner) proved by contrast how vibrant the 1958 film still is. Granted, censorship of the screen has loosened up tremendously in the last two decades, but the Taylor-Newman-Ives feature is still a powerful entertainment package.

THE CHAMP
1931—87 min.

Producer-director, King Vidor; **story,** Frances Marion; **screenplay-dialogue,** Leonard Praskins; **additional dialogue,** Wanda Tuchock; **art director,** Cedric Gibbons; **sound,** Douglas Shearer; **camera,** Gordon Avil; **editor,** Hugh Wynn.

Wallace Beery (**Andy Purcell**); Jackie Cooper (**Dink Purcell**); Irene Rich (**Linda Carlton**); Rosco Ates (**Sponge**); Edward Brophy (**Tim**); Hale Hamilton (**Tony**); Jesse Scott (**Jonah**); Marcia Mae Jones (**Mary Lou Carlton**); Lee Phelps (**Louie, the Bartender**); Frank Hagney (**Manuel Caroza**).

SYNOPSIS

In Tijuana Andy Purcell, an ex-prizefighter champion, is down on his luck and in the thrall of

Bridges at Toko-Ri, To Catch a Thief, and her Oscar-winning **The Country Girl** (1954) for Paramount. George Cukor was set to direct the Metro screen version of the Williams drama. However, when the homosexuality theme[1] proved a problem in formulating a workable script, Cukor backed away from the project (in December 1957), and studio chief Dore Schary assigned the film to Richard Brooks. With the assistance of James Poe, Brooks fashioned a scenario that contained but a hint of the homosexuality that was quite overt in the Broadway production. To broaden the film's appeal, the play's third act was revamped to provide a more positive finale, one in which there is no ambiguity that Maggie and Brick will once again enjoy connubial bliss in the bedroom.

Meanwhile, time had passed, and Grace Kelly had in April 1956 become the Princess of Monaco. Hence, after a youthful MGM tenure with dogs and horses, Elizabeth Taylor (replacing Ava Gardner) was cast in the feline role of Maggie the Cat. Paul Newman was contracted for the part of bitter Brick (replacing Anthony Franciosa), Burl Ives signed to re-create his stage triumph as Big Daddy, Judith Anderson replaced Mildred Dunnock as Big Mama, Jack Carson substituted for Pat Hingle as Gooper Pollitt, and Madeleine Sherwood retained her stage assignment as Gooper's obnoxious, grasping, ever-fertile spouse Mae.

Cat began shooting on March 12, 1958. On March 19 Miss Taylor did not report to the Culver

City soundstages, citing illness as the excuse for her absence. Two days later, on Friday, March 21, her husband Mike Todd died in an airplane crash. (Taylor had been scheduled to join him on the New York–bound trip, but canceled out because of a cold.) A very shattered Elizabeth attended his funeral on March 25 and did not return to **Cat** until April 14. By then the emotionally drained star was eight pounds thinner and very weak. Nevertheless, Brooks managed to keep the actress emoting with fiery results and the picture was completed on May 16, 1958.

Cat on a Hot Tin Roof was released in September 1958 and received copious critical acclaim. Bosley Crowther (**New York Times**) reported, "As a straight exercise in spewing dirty linen, this fine Metro-Goldwyn-Mayer production in color would be hard to beat. It is done by superior talents, under the driving direction of Richard Brooks, making even the driest scenes drip poison with that strong, juicy Williams dialogue." Though all the performances were superb—Newman broodingly excellent, Ives bombastic, Anderson surprisingly effecitve at barking with a Southern accent, Carson and Sherwood perfectly vulgar—the top plaudits were snared by Miss Taylor. The **New York Times** exclaimed, "She is terrific," and **Films in Review** judged her Maggie "the best performance of her career."

As it turned out, Miss Taylor was also the top drawing card for the picture at the box office.[2] The film's premiere competed with the Ed-

---

[1]Metro had "conquered" a similar problem in translating Robert Anderson's **Tea and Sympathy** onto the screen in 1956, and thereby drained the drama of much of its homosexual material.

[2]Years later costumer Helen Rose would say that one of her most satisfying MGM assignments was dressing Miss Taylor for this film. Although Taylor spent a goodly

portion of the picture parading about in a slinky slip, her tailored, full-skirted white dress was so popular with filmgoers that Miss Rose was able to start a private dressmaking company, manufacturing copies of the outfit.

alcohol and gambling. When the Champ divorced his wife Linda, the custody of their child Dink went to the then champion pugilist.

Now Linda is wealthy through remarriage, whereas Andy struggles to provide a life for his son. Andy gives Dink a racehorse as a gift for looking after him, and the boy dubs the animal Little Champ. On the day of Little Champ's first race, Andy encounters Linda at the track. On seeing Dink, she suddenly becomes very maternal and later has her husband, Tony Carlton, ask Andy to give up custody of the boy. He refuses, but thereafter gambles away the ownership of Little Champ.

To rebuy the horse, Andy borrows money from Linda, which she loans on condition that Dink come live with her. Andy pretends not to care for the boy anymore, and the youth goes off to reside with the Carltons. However, on the train up the California coast, Dink disembarks at San Diego and returns to Tijuana, where he finds the Champ training in earnest for a big comeback bout. Dink spots Manuel Caroza, Andy's opponent, during a workout, and realizes that his dad cannot win the match. But Andy is insistent upon the contest and in the ring, despite a heavy battering, emerges as the champion. Thereafter, while in his dressing room, the victorious champ suffers a fatal heart attack. The Carltons appear on the scene and the stunned boy goes off again with them.

* * *

For Louis B. Mayer, a motion picture could receive no higher accolade than that of its audience's tears. Sentimentality was the favorite emotion of the mogul. With this lachrymose point of view, Mayer directed his ace scenarist Frances Marion to produce the storyline that first teamed Wallace Beery and Jackie Cooper. It would set the pattern for Beery's seemingly endless reprisals of the good-hearted ne'er-do-well. The enormously popular feature won Oscars for Beery and for Miss Marion.

While the tale of a washed-up Tijuana fighter excited Mayer's emotions, not many in Hollywood shared his initial enthusiasm. In fact, the director, King Vidor, would not even mention **The Champ** in his autobiography, **A Tree Is a Tree**. As British **Monthly Film Bulletin** critic Tony Rayns pointed out in a recent retrospective study of the picture, "the film is pitched at a modest enough level to suggest that he [Vidor] undertook it as a mere programmer. MGM presumably conceived it as the latest of a growing line of vehicles for their star Wallace Beery, and as a chance to match him with the up-and-coming child star Jackie Cooper."

The nine-year-old Cooper, a veteran of **Our Gang**–Hal Roach comedies and Paramount's **Skippy** (1931), for which he was Oscar-nominated, was indeed the antithesis of the grizzly, burly, middle-aged Hollywood veteran Beery, fresh from his Oscar-nominated triumph as prisoner Butch in Metro's **The Big House** (1930). However, on screen, their chemistry was quite remarkable. Scenes such as the one in which Beery, as the drink- and gambling-plagued Champ, heartbreakingly pretends that he dislikes his little son, led MGM executives to stand in the back of the theatres

Jesse Scott, Wallace Beery, and Jackie Coope in The Champ *('31).*

and proudly gauge the audience's weeping. And the climax, in which the Champ battles his way back to the championship as Dink throbs with hero-worshipping excitement, inspired moviegoers to cheer.[1] Location filming was accomplished in Tijuana and at Cliente racetrack.

While the pairing of the two male stars would be repeated in **The Bowery** (1933, United Artists), and MGM's **Treasure Island** (1934) and **O'Shaughnessy's Boy** (1935), Cooper would relate years later that Beery off camera was determined to live up to his on-screen Hollywood image—as one of the cinema colony's rudest and most disagreeable men.[2] Cooper remembers that he once impulsively threw his arms around Beery after an especially well-played tender scene and that the gruff Beery yanked the boys's arms off him and pushed him away. The episode caused the child thespian to produce genuine tears.

When released in November 1931, **The Champ** did **not** receive lavish critical acclaim from most reviewers. The **New York Times** noted, "While the incidents are strewn with tears and intermittent

comedy, the story is not apt to awaken any great respect. . . . But while the sum total of the narrative is old-fashioned and forced, one can always appreciate Mr. Beery and Master Cooper, even though it may cause one to wish that the producers had put them into something with real artistry." Critical reservations aside, **The Champ** was a box-office champion. During its very successful engagement at Grauman's Chinese Theatre in Hollywood, Charles Chaplin and Vidor would stand across Hollywood Boulevard and enjoy the sight of the crowd as they sobbed their way out of the movie house.

So successful was the popular response to **The Champ** that, despite lukewarm reviews, the film was nominated for the Best Picture of 1931–32 (Metro's **Grand Hotel** won).[3] Frances Marion won an Oscar for her screenplay, and Wallace Beery was placed in competition with Frederic March (for Paramount's **Dr. Jekyll and Mr. Hyde**) and Alfred Lunt's (for MGM's **The Guardsman**) for the Best Actor prize. At the November 18, 1932, Academy Award ceremonies at Hollywood's Ambassador Hotel, Mayer and friends were confident that Beery would win. However, Fredric March was announced Best Actor and the aghast Mayer stomped into the back room with his cronies to see what happened to the balloting. Learning that March had defeated Beery by one vote, Mayer persuaded the Academy executives that a second prize should be presented because of the close competition. Thus Lionel Barrymore (winner of the

---

[1] In the original cut of the film, the Champ was to lose the fight. The scene was reshot in order to balance the tragic ending of the fighter's heart attack in the dressing room.

[2] Cooper remarked recently in a newspaper interview with the **New York Daily News**, "Beery was a sad man," hypothesizing that the then childless actor was frightened at becoming close to a child who was not his own. "That had a lot to do with his unhappiness—plus, I think, the fact that he started out in this business as a female impersonator. This also might have haunted him." Cooper rarely discusses Beery because he does not wish "to put him down."

[3] Shot on a thirty-two-day production schedule at a cost of $356,000, **The Champ** earned a profit of $561,000.

previous year's Oscar for MGM's **A Free Soul**) presented the proud-appearing Beery with a statue.

Over the years **The Champ** has been often analyzed as to its moral point of view. Although the film obviously shows partiality for the carefree, reckless life in Tijuana as compared with the middle-America lifestyle represented by the Carltons, both the picture and Vidor's direction reveal an ambivalence that suggests, at times, that each lifestyle is equally virtuous. Tony Rayns remarks in his **Monthly Film Bulletin** essay:

[Vidor] characteristically introduces a number of recurrent motifs that link otherwise disparate or incompatible circumstances: both Dink's parents, for instance, try to undress him for bed, and his reactions (he refuses help from the Champ because he's angry with him at the time, and sends Linda out of the sleeper compartment to assert his own adulthood) evidence the undercurrents that inevitably flow through his relationships with both parties. Vidor's "realism" is marked throughout by just such touches of unforced intimacy, as well as by his complete suppression of sentimentality in all the more emotionally charged scenes. Another such motif is used in the final scene, when the impasse over Dink's future is cruelly, arbitrarily resolved by the Champ's death; Dink, finding no comfort from any of his onlooking friends, pounds the wall of the dressing room, just as the Champ pounded the wall of his prison cell after telling Dink that he had to join his mother. Linda's arrival on the scene does provide the solace that Dink needs (he races into her welcoming arms), but the hysterical intensity of his reaction to his father's death keeps the drama open-ended, in a sense, by demonstrating how much like his father Dink can be.

Retaining its audience appeal, **The Champ** was remade by MGM as **The Clown** (1953) with Red Skelton and Tim Considine in the Beery-Cooper roles. Beery himself revived his Oscar-winning palooka on two separate occasions on Cecil B. DeMille's "Lux Radio Theatre" (November 13, 1939, and June 29, 1942). In April 1977 MGM announced that it had authorized yet another version of **The Champ**. The new MGM/United Artists edition, produced by Dyson Lovell, scripted by Walter Newman, and directed by Italian filmmaker Franco Zeffirelli, was released in the spring of 1979. It starred Jon Voight as the ex-champ, Ricky Schroder as the boy, and Faye Dunaway as the ex-wife. It led critic Charles Champlin to report in the **Los Angeles Times:**

What survives in Franco Zeffirelli's warm-toned, leisurely and unstintingly romantic remake of **The Champ,** set in the here and now, is Frances Marion's steel-strong basic story of a boy's love (by no means blind) for his endearing bum of a father, a wandering mother's discovery of all she's lost, and the father's grand and heroic repayment of the son's devotion. . . . The principal difference is that Vidor's classic was a fast-moving (but never hurried) 86 minutes long. Zeffirelli's is more than a half-hour longer (122 minutes). The added length, even if it provides an operatic richness of decor, can be felt. And, since doing a sentimental piece like **The Champ** is a manipulative business however much we choose to believe it's all happening before our dampened eyes, the pace in its slowest stretches makes you aware of the hand more than the sleight of.

CHINA SEAS
1935—89 min.

Producer, Albert Lewin; **director,** Tay Garnett; based on the novel by Crosbie Garstin; **screenplay,** Jules Furthman and James McGuinness; **song,** Arthur Freed and Nacio Herb Brown; **costumes,** Adrian; **art directors,** Cedric Gibbons, James Havens, and David Townsend; **set decorator,** Edwin B. Willis; **camera,** Ray June; **editor,** William Levanway.

Clark Gable (**Captain Alan Gaskell**); Jean Harlow (**China Doll [Dolly Portland]**); Wallace Beery (**James MacArdle**); Lewis Stone (**Tom Davids**); Rosalind Russell (**Sybil Barclay**); Dudley Digges (**Dawson**); C. Aubrey Smith (**Sir Guy Wilmerding**); Robert Benchley (**Charlie McCalleb**); William Henry (**Rockwell**); Live Demaigret (**Mrs. Volberg**); Lillian Bond (**Mrs. Timmons**); Edward Brophy (**Wilbur Timmons**); Soo Yong (**Yu-Lan**); Carol Ann Beery (**Carol Ann**); Akim Tamiroff (**Romanoff**); Ivan Lebedeff (**Ngah**); Hattie McDaniel (**Isabel McCarthy**); Donald Meek (**Chess Player**); Emily Fitzroy (**Lady**); Pat Flaherty (**Second Officer Kingston**); Forrester Harvey (**Steward**); Tom Gubbins (**Ship's Officer**); Charles Irwin (**Bertie, the Purser**); Willie Fung (**Cabin Boy**); Ferdinand Munier (**Police Superintendent**); Chester Gan (**Richshaw Boy**); John Ince (**Pilot**).

SYNOPSIS

Alan Gaskell is the captain of the **Kin Lung,** which sails the China Seas and which now is carrying a gold shipment from Hong Kong to Singapore. Gaskell fears a pirate attack and another worry appears when China Doll, his former mistress, books passage aboard his vessel. Also on the voyage is aristocratic Britisher Sybil Barclay, a past romance who has married another man. Now widowed, Sybil begins to fall in love with Gaskell anew. China Doll, hoping for a rerun herself, receives a rejection from the virile captain. To console herself, she engages in a session of cards and drink with trader Jamesy MacArdle, who loves her. When China Doll learns that MacArdle is in league with the pirates, she goes to Gaskell, who turns her away before she can relate this discovery.

Now bitter, China Doll teams with MacArdle in executing the daring caper. Third officer Davids sacrifices himself by falling into the pirates' junk with a bag of grenades. Rather than suffer punitive consequences, MacArdle poisons himself, and China Doll is arrested for her conspiracy. Sybil later convinces Gaskell that he would be happier on the China Seas with his past mistress. He agrees, and informs China Doll that he will aid her at the trial and then wed her.

* * *

Though Irving Thalberg was deeply proud of the honors he had won as the producer of such artistic triumphs as **A Free Soul** (1930), **Grand Hotel** (1932), and **The Barretts of Wimpole Street** (1934), he realized better than anyone else the strain of being known as Hollywood's unimpeachable producer of the highest standards. With this in mind, Thalberg announced to his surprised staff, "To hell with art this time. I'm going to produce a picture that will make money." Thus was formed the concept for "a seagoing **Grand Hotel** melodrama of pirate waters, hidden gold, and a Gable-esque captain, a Harlow-esque voluptuary, and a Beery-esque rascal." The formula of the picture, as accurately described by Bob Thomas in his biography, **Thalberg: Life and Legend** (1969), "was to fill the screen with bright personalities, give them pseudosophisticated dialogue to talk at a rapid rate, and play the whole thing so fast and furiously that the audience had no time or inclination to question the inadequacies."

Even Irving Thalberg, it appears, was sometimes susceptible to "fugging it."

With Tay Garnett at the director's helm, Thalberg was happy to note that his three stars—Gable, Harlow, and Beery (all coplayers in 1931's **The Secret Six,** along with featured performer Lewis Stone)—were happy to join the unpretentious shenanigans. Gable, who had just separated again from his wife Ria, was feeling particularly boisterous. In fact, during the film's arduous action scenes, he frequently demanded to do his own stunts. As Garnett would recall, "When Gable decided to risk his neck, his neck got risked." Harlow, after a short-lived marriage to Hal Rosson and two lesser vehicles—**The Girl from Missouri** (1934) and **Reckless** (1935)—was anxious to get back to the type of role that pleased her audiences. As for gruff Beery, he was happy not to be cast again with young scene-stealer Cooper, and delighted that his fishing-hunting pal Gable would be his costar (even if it meant working again with Harlow, whom he detested).

Though a lark for cast and crew, **China Seas** had its share of on-the-set temperament, feuding, and actual physical danger. Garnett was annoyed by Thalberg's constant presence and interference on the set. When Gable insisted on performing the film's most breathtaking stunt—dodging a five-ton steamroller (packed with hidden gold) that breaks loose and rolls amok about the wet deck—the star was almost killed. So were his double (Chick Collins) and Harlow's (Loretta Rush) when the special-effects team unleashed fifty tons of water too soon, gushing both doubles into a maze of water-soaked cables where electrocution was avoided by a chillingly narrow margin. On March 3, 1935, Harlow turned twenty-four and the company treated her to a birthday party, which Beery did not attend. Some nineteen months elapsed between the preproduction conferences to the final takes, but **China Seas** was at last completed.

Wallace Beery, Clark Gable, and Ivan Lebedeff in China Seas *('35).*

Released in July 1935, the film mostly delighted the major reviewers. **Variety** observed, "This is a story of love—sordid and otherwise—of piracy and violence and heroism on a passenger boat run from Shanghai to Singapore. Somehow it manages to give the three starring players an even shake in time allotment, lines, and general importance." Regina Crewe **(New York American)** reported, "As for the principals, none of the three has ever been better. Miss Harlow, in particular, is at her best, while both Messrs. Gable and Beery add to their already weighty laurels." Indeed, it was the "blonde bombshell" who garnered the most ardent praises, so much so that **Time** magazine presented her as the cover girl of its August 19, 1935, issue.

Despite the generally hospitable reviews, **China Seas'** tawdriness did rate one strong editorial sermon, from **Photoplay:** "Action and thrills, striking photography and the glitter of the well-known team of Gable and Harlow only partly obscure the sordidness of this tale of a white man's deterioration in the fetid moral atmosphere of the Orient. It is not sufficiently adroit in its handling to make its coarseness and brutality even slightly palatable."

As expected, **China Seas,** along with **Forsaking All Others, David Copperfield,** and **Mutiny on the Bounty,** became one of Metro's top grossers of the season. The box office for **China Seas** was aided by the guesting of Gable, Harlow, and Russell on Louella Parsons' "Hollywood Hotel" on CBS radio, August 6, 1935, to reprise some major **China Seas** scenes.

THE CITADEL
1938—110 min.

Producer, Victor Saville; **director,** King Vidor; based on the novel by A. J. Cronin; **screenplay,** Ian Dalrymple, Frank Wead, and Elizabeth Hill; **additional dialogue,** Emlyn Williams; **art directors,** Lazare Meerson and Alfred Junge; **music,** Louis Levy; **assistant director,** Pen Tennyson; **sound,** C. C. Stevens and A. W. Watkins; **camera,** Harry Stradling; **editor,** Charles Frend.

Robert Donat **(Dr. Andrew Manson);** Rosalind Russell **(Christine Manson);** Ralph Richardson **(Dr. Philip Denny);** Rex Harrison **(Dr. Lawford);** Emlyn Williams **(Owen);** Penelope Dudley-Ward **(Toppy Leroy);** Francis L. Sullivan **(Ben Chenkin);** Mary Clare **(Mrs. Orlando);** Cecil Parker **(Charles Every);** Nora Swinburne **(Mrs. Thornton);** Edward Chapman **(Joe Morgan);** Athene Seyler **(Lady Raebank);** Felix Aylmer **(Mr. Boon);** Joyce Bland **(Nurse Sharp);** Percy Parsons **(Mr. Stillman);** Dilys Davis **(Mrs. Page);** Basil Gill **(Dr. Page);** Joss Ambler **(Dr. A. H. Llewellyn).**

SYNOPSIS

Dr. Andrew Manson is appointed community doctor of Blaenelly, a depressed mining town deep in the South Wales mountains. He takes his work seriously, even refusing to carry on the old practice of issuing false certificates to miners so they might receive wages while pretending to be ill and not working. This antagonizes some of the miners.

In Blaenelly he meets Dr. Philip Denny, a surgeon who has come to this obscure village to forget his wife's infidelity. Manson also meets and falls in love with the local schoolteacher, Christine. Only when she threatens to depart for another teaching assignment does he gather courage to ask her to wed him. Meanwhile, Dr. Manson carries on his research work in the field of tuberculosis, using the coal-mine dust as the basis of his studies. But the superstitious antagonism of local physicians and the ignorant miners soon disgusts him.

Andrew and Christine leave for London. But again Dr. Manson is disappointed: no patients, no practice, and no money. One day, he meets an old school friend, Dr. Lawford, who has become a wealthy society doctor. He introduces Dr. Manson to other physicians, who carry on the unethical practice of splitting fees obtained from wealthy patients. Rather promptly Dr. Manson becomes one of them, despite Christine's objections. In a short time he is well-to-do.

But the death of his best friend, Denny, at the untalented hands of one of his incompetent confreres makes Dr. Manson realize how he has degenerated. He abandons everything and joins an unlicensed but highly competent researcher in tuberculosis work. He permits the man to operate on the young daughter of a friend. The girl's life is saved, but the medical association brings a charge against Dr. Manson for working with an unlicensed surgeon. Andrew pleads his case eloquently, but leaves with Christine without awaiting the verdict. He now plans to establish the Philip Denny Memorial Clinic.

* * *

MGM entertained high hopes for the lucrative operation of its new English base of operations, headquartered at London's Denham Studios. Encouragement was supplied by **A Yank at Oxford** (1938), the first Metro production filmed there. It starred Robert Taylor, Maureen O'Sullivan, Lionel Barrymore, and (against the wishes of an unimpressed Louis B. Mayer) Vivien Leigh. It was the second offering of the British unit, however, which won the studio lavish praise. Moreover, it served to invigorate the careers of director King Vidor, actor Robert Donat, and actress Rosalind Russell. **The Citadel** is one of the finest-played and best-remembered cinema excursions of the 1930s.

The A. J. Cronin novel on medical idealism had become an international bestseller, and captivated King Vidor. He had not made a film for MGM since **The Stranger's Return** (1933), which he also produced. In the meantime, he had toiled at Paramount for a trio of films, at United Artists for **Our Daily Bread** (1934), and more recently at United Artists for Samuel Goldwyn's remake of **Stella Dallas** (1937). Robert Donat, whose sole Hollywood credit was **The Count of Monte Cristo** (1934), had just signed with MGM a lush six-picture contract that covered an unspecified amount of time because of his asthmatic condition, which seriously handicapped his career. Vidor initially wanted Spencer Tracy for the part of Denny, Man-

Rosalind Russell and Robert Donat in The Citadel *('38).*

son's best friend, whose death[1] opens his eyes to the the brutality of the medical profession. But Tracy was unavailable, so the part went to London and British film favorite Ralph Richardson. As Manson's wife Christine, Elizabeth Allan was initially selected, but was replaced by Rosalind Russell after Vidor informed producer Victor Saville that Miss Allan was not suitable for the role. The dismissed actress filed—and won—a $17,000 breach-of-contract suit against MGM. Rex Harrison, twenty-nine-year-old London stage and film player, was hired as Dr. Lawford, the money-loving Harley Street society doctor.

Vidor was greatly impressed by all the talents associated with this fine production—especially Donat's, and later recollected for the TV interview series **The Men Who Made the Movies:**

The Citadel I made in England for Metro-Goldwyn-Mayer. I had seen Robert Donat on the screen as a romantic type of hero, and when I met him he was far from that. He had a concave chest and slender little arms, but as he started to get interested in the film, he blossomed out and filled out—he had ways of making himself look robust. And he was the only actor I ever knew who wanted to go out looking for locations with the director. He wanted to know all about the scenes; he wanted to look at them too—and study the people. We went to Wales to-

gether. And he laid out his entire emotional rise and fall, how he would play each scene. It was interesting that he would have a mirror right on his lap and keep working on his makeup—the makeup around his eyebrows and hair and all that—right up until the cameras were going, and then he'd drop it and immediately give a superb performance. I was never more pleased with anybody's performance than I was with his. I said to him one time, "I can't help but think what would happen if you didn't keep the mirror up there until the last minute." He said, "I'd probably be worse." And I said, "Well, I don't want to change anything. You're too good." He was a superb fellow, very much like Tyrone Power, who was also a wonderful guy to work with—a real gentleman. . . . But in that film were Rex Harrison and Ralph Richardson and Rosalind Russell and a whole lot of wonderful actors. At that time, in England, you could go to the theatre and if you saw somebody playing the lead in the theatre, you could get them to come out in the morning or afternoon and work in the films. That was a great thing for casting. I thought **The Citadel** told a good story . . . I was very much interested, and I felt very good about it. I thought it would win an Academy Award, and it almost did. It just missed by a few votes.

The Citadel was released late in 1938 with the following ad campaign, "Torn from the pages of a great novel. Now brought thrillingly to life on the screen. . . . Secrets of a doctor as told by a

doctor. . . . A story 10,000,000 people have read! . . . Now after a year's preparation . . . MGM's greatest production."

The film won lavish acclaim. Frank S. Nugent **(New York Times)** endorsed **The Citadel** "as one of the best screen dramas of the year. . . . There is no doubt . . . of the film's superiority to the bestselling novel from which it came. Nor is there any doubt about its containing some of the finest scenes in contemporary history." Archer Winsten **(New York Post)** reported, "When all performances rise to such a level, one must look beyond the actors to the director, in this case King Vidor. He has made many fine pictures, but none so perfect as this."

The Citadel won the best picture of the year citation from the New York Film Critics, the National Board of Review, and **Look** magazine. It placed eighth in **Film Daily**'s Ten Best picture poll. And, as Vidor stated, it almost won the Oscar for Best Picture. It lost narrowly to Columbia's **You Can't Take It with You**. Donat was nominated for the Best Actor Oscar, losing to Spencer Tracy of **Boys Town** (MGM), while Vidor lost to Frank Capra of **You Can't Take It With You**, and the scenarists lost to the screenwriters of **Pygmalion** (British-lensed and acquired for distribution by MGM).

Of enormous aid to the international prestige of MGM, **The Citadel** reinstated Vidor at the studio's main lot in Hollywood. He soon began work on **Northwest Passage** (1940). It also boosted the stock of the London MGM headquarters and of Robert Donat, both of whom achieved even greater success the following year with the release of **Goodbye, Mr. Chips**. The picture served to demonstrate to MGM and to the industry that Rosalind Russell was continuing to grow as a dramatic actress and no longer should be regarded as merely a Myrna Loy substitute. As for Rex Harrison, he was offered a seven-year Hollywood contract by MGM. However, he refused to journey to far-off California for such a horrendously long period, especially with England fast becoming involved in World War II.

COMMAND DECISION
1948—112 min.

Producer, Sidney Franklin; **director,** Sam Wood; based on the play by William Wister Haines; **screenplay,** William R. Laidlaw and George Froeschel; **art directors,** Cedric Gibbons and Urie McCleary; **music,** Miklos Rozsa; **sound,** Douglas Shearer; **camera,** Harold Rosson; **editor,** Harold F. Kress.

Clark Gable **(Brigadier General K. C. "Casey" Dennis);** Walter Pidgeon **(Major General Roland Goodlow Kane);** Van Johnson **(Technical Sergeant Immanuel T. Evans);** Brian Donlevy **(Brigadier General Clifton I. Garnet);** John Hodiak **(Colonel Edward Rayton Martin);** Charles Bickford **(Elmer Brockhurst);** Edward Arnold **(Congressman Arthur**

---

[1] In Cronin's novel it is not Denny who dies, but Manson's wife Christine; the filmwriters deemed this overly tragic and henceforth made the convenient change.

Sam Flint, Edward Earle, Henry Hall, Hank Daniels, Edward Arnold, Clark Gable, and Moroni Olsen in Command Decision *('48).*

Malcolm); Marshall Thompson (**Captain George Washington Bellpepper Lee**); Richard Quine (**Major George Rockton**); Cameron Mitchell (**Lieutenant Ansel Goldberg**); Clinton Sundberg (**Major Homer V. Prescott**); Ray Collins (**Major Desmond Lansing**); Warner Anderson (**Colonel Ernest Haley**); John McIntire (**Major Belding Davis**); Michael Steele (**Captain Incius Malcolm Jenks**); Mack Williams (**Lieutenant Colonel Virgil Jackson**); Moroni Olsen (**Congressman Stone**); John Ridgely (**James Carwood**); Edward Earle (**Congressman Watson**); William Lester (**Parker, the Chauffeur**); Henry Hall and Sam Flint (**Congressmen**); Holmes Herbert (**Chairman**); John James (**Officer**); Pete Martin (**Command Sergeant**); Barry Nelson (**Loudspeaker Voice**); Wilson Wood, Arthur Walsh, and J. Lewis Smith (**Photographers**); Hank Daniels (**Bit**).

SYNOPSIS

Brigadier General K. C. ("Casey") Dennis, commander of an American bomber base in England in 1943, orders a top-secret bombing mission under the code name Operation Stitch. The mission involves destroying plants manufacturing a new German jet plane. The controversial issue centers around the excessive number of lost men and planes it will cost to destroy the target. War correspondent Elmer Brockhurst opposes the operation on this basis, but Dennis continues his offensive command with the advent of favorable weather.

Entering the conflict are Dennis's superior,

Major General Roland Goodlow Kane, and Brigadier General Clifton I. Garnet. Kane favors delaying the raids pending a congressional committee visit.

On the second day of the raid, Dennis must "talk in" a bombardier whose pilot and copilot have been killed. Thereafter Dennis convinces Kane that the mission must be completed, but the revelation from Colonel Edward Martin that a town other than the target—Schweinhafen—has been hit by mistake, causes Kane to cancel the military project.

Later Kane requests that the officer-nephew of Congressman Malcolm be decorated, but Dennis reveals that the man had been arrested for refusing to make the last raid. In exchange for granting the decoration, Dennis is allowed to continue his bombing strikes. Finally the target is destroyed at heavy costs and Malcolm denounces Dennis. The latter had hoped to continue the operation by bombing Fendelhorst. Kane relieves Dennis of his command and replaces him with Garnet, who intends to carry out the Fendelhorst bombing. Dennis assumes a Pacific command, content in knowing that his operation will be realized.

* * *

On October 1, 1947, **Command Decision**, William Wister Haines' play based on his novel on the pressures of wartime decisions, opened on Broadway at the Fulton Theatre, starring Paul Kelly as Brigadier General Casey Dennis, a man tortured by his obligations to send men to almost

certain death in bomber missions over Germany. The drama ran for an acclaimed 409 performances. Like R. C. Sherriff's 1928 play and 1930 film **Journey's End** and the 1930 and 1938 movie versions of **The Dawn Patrol, Command Decision** did not attack the pride and radicalism that necessitated a war. Instead, it focused on the heartache suffered by men who control the daily destiny of thousands of young men. Impressed by the New York success of this deglamorized version of the world crisis, MGM purchased the screen rights and prepared a major production.

To retain the virility of the stage production, MGM kept the all-male-cast idea and lensed the picture in stark black and white. Clark Gable, climbing back to box-office royalty after the disaster of **Adventure** (1945) with his successes in **The Hucksters** (1947) and **Homecoming** (1948), was assigned the Kelly part; stalwart Walter Pidgeon portrayed the conniving General Kane. To bolster the marquee appeal even further, MGM added Van Johnson and Brian Donlevy in major roles, as well as character favorites Edward Arnold and Charles Bickford. The cast worked well together; the only difficulty was Gable, who, still morose over his sobering war experiences and the 1942 death of wife Carole Lombard, was engaging in heavy drinking that required short camera setups and constant retakes. Then too, Gable was being asked to shape a very interior characterization, a portrayal quite in contrast with his extrovert personality and past acting experience.

Released in December 1948 with the ad copy "Heroes, cowards, fighters, braggarts, liars, lovers . . . and what goes on in their hearts," **Command Decision** won major critical ovations. Two scenes in particular—Gable's talking down the bombardier of a B-17 plane in which he is the only living crew member, and Pidgeon's beautifully sustained speech rationalizing his deceit with the press in regard to losses in the raids— supplied fine, grim stuff for post-World War II audiences. **Variety** noted, "Sam Wood's direction is articulate in endowing the film with the toughness of war and, at the same time, a sentiment that will click with the femmes. There are no phony touches in this drive for drama." The **New York Times** praised the manner in which the film "looks with a cynical repugnance upon the seamy side of war," and **Newsweek** magazine complimented the entire cast, noting that "all contribute to a script that is worthy of their most valiant efforts."

One faction **not** endeared to the picture was the English critics, who like their countrymen were sensitive concerning the United States' contributions to the war. The London press labeled the movie "contemptuous" and "insulting" regarding Britain's war efforts, feeling the movie suggested that U.S. bombardiers had defeated Germany single-handedly. (Warner Bros. had suffered a similiar English attack after the release of **Objective, Burma!**, 1945, starring Errol Flynn.)

Despite the praise engendered by **Command Decision**, it was not a major contender in the Academy Award sweepstakes. However, it did inspire Twentieth Century–Fox to push ahead with its **Twelve O'Clock High** (1949), a drama with a similar theme, and led MGM to embark on **Battleground** (1949).

DAVID COPPERFIELD
1935—133 min.

Producer, David O. Selznick; **director,** George Cukor; based on the novel by Charles Dickens; **adapter,** Hugh Walpole; **screenplay,** Howard Estabrook; **art directors,** Cedric Gibbons and Merrill Pye; **set decorator,** Edwin B. Willis; **costumes,** Dolly Tree; **assistant director,** Joe Newman; **sound,** Douglas Shearer; **special effects,** Slavko Vorkapich; **camera,** Oliver T. Marsh; **editor,** Robert J. Kern.

W. C. Fields (**Mr. Micawber**); Lionel Barrymore (**Dan Peggotty**); Maureen O'Sullivan (**Dora Spenlow**); Madge Evans (**Agnes Wickfield**); Edna May Oliver (**Aunt Betsey**); Lewis Stone (**Mr. Wickfield**); Frank Lawton (**David Copperfield as a Man**); Freddie Bartholomew (**David Copperfield the Child**); Roland Young (**Uriah Heep**); Elizabeth Allan (**Mrs. Copperfield**); Elsa Lanchester (**Clickett**); Basil Rathbone (**Mr. Murdstone**); Jessie Ralph (**Nurse Peggotty**); Jean Cadell (**Mrs. Micawber**); Lennox Pawle (**Mr. Dick**); Violet Kemble-Cooper (**Jane Murdstone**); Una O'Connor (**Mrs. Gummidge**); John Buckler (**Ham**); Hugh Williams (**Steerforth**); Ivan Simpson (**Limmiter**); Herbert Mundin (**Barkis**); Fay Chaldecott (**Little Em'ly as a Child**); Florine McKinney (**Little Em'ly as a Woman**); Marilyn Knowlden (**Agnes as a Child**); Harry Beresford (**Dr. Chillip**); Mabel Colcord (**Mary Ann**); Hugh Walpole (**The Vicar**); Renee Gadd (**Janet**); Arthur Treacher (**Donkey Man**).

SYNOPSIS

In early nineteenth-century England, six months after the death of his father, David Copperfield is born. His young life is soon an unhappy one as his gentle mother remarries. Her new spouse is the austere Mr. Murdstone, who beats David with a whip and soon becomes a widower when Clara dies in childbirth.

Murdstone sends David to make something of himself at his export warehouse in London. There David stays with the crafty Mr. Micawber and his sprawling family. When Micawber is hauled off to debtor's prison, David runs away to Dover and takes refuge with his Aunt Betsey and her bizarre friend, Mr. Dick. The delightful Aunt Betsey chases Murdstone and his sister away when they come to claim David. The boy's new protectors see to it that he receives a decent schooling. After graduation he becomes a writer.

He also falls in love and inspires love. He weds the sickly Dora Spenlow, not aware that Agnes Wickfield, daughter of Mr. Wickfield, the man who gave him lodging during his college days, is already in love with him. Dora soon dies.

Mr. Wickfield, meanwhile, calls on David. He has been cheated by a business associate, Uriah Heep. David enlists the aid of Micawber to defeat Heep's machinations and to restore Wickfield's happiness. David now realizes that Agnes loves him. He asks her to become his wife.

* * *

It appeared to be Louis B. Mayer's lot in life to carry the cross of brilliant—and ambitious—producers. If the Mayer versus Irving Thalberg battles were nasty, the Mayer versus David O. Selznick conflicts were worse, for Selznick was Mayer's son-in-law.

David Copperfield represented one of these battles—an Olympian one indeed. In the beginning, Mayer vetoed Selznick's dream of cinematizing the English novel which was the favorite book of Selznick's immigrant father. He had taught himself English by it, and had instructed his children to read with it. Mayer opposed the idea of classics on the screen. He felt they were automatic box-office disasters. Nevertheless, Selznick bullied the film into production throughout 1934.

George Cukor was selected to direct the version of Charles Dickens' beloved classic. Cukor commented on the project,

> You must get the essence of the original, which may involve accenting some of the weaknesses. When you read **David Copperfield,** you know why it lasted. There's too much melodrama and the second half is unsatisfactory, but there's this underlying vitality and invention. For me, that determined the style of the picture.

As casting began, another front office squabble erupted. Mayer wanted contractee Jackie Cooper to play the title role. He hoped his star quality would boost the film's revenue. However, both Cukor and Selznick protested. They argued that an American actor was out of the question. Cukor went to England where a talent scout referred young Freddie Barthlomew to the director. As legend has it, Cukor was impressed enough by Freddie that the boy's ambitious Aunt Cissie took the youth to Culver City, California. There she attired the lad in Dickensian togs, complete with a tall beaver hat. She propelled the child into a meeting with Selznick himself. "I am David Copperfield, sir," said Freddie. "Right you are," said Selznick and Bartholomew was signed for the leading part.

Little expense was spared to corral an all-star cast. From the home lot the producer and director selected: Lionel Barrymore as old Peggotty, Charles Laughton as Mr. Micawber, Maureen O'Sullivan,[1] Madge Evans and Elizabeth Allan as the women in David's life; feisty Edna May Oliver as the cantankerous Aunt Betsey, comic Roland Young in a very change-of-pace role as Uriah Heep, Basil Rathbone as the sadistic Mr. Murdstone, et al.

After a week's work, Laughton, ever suffering

[1]Decades later Maureen O'Sullivan would admit that she "just could not get those tears" for Dora's deathbed finale in **David Copperfield,** so director George Cukor "sat at the end of the bed twisting my feet until the tears came."

self-torture because of his failure to reach acting perfection, had to withdraw from the film. By this point he had devised a marvelous makeup based on the original Cruickshank drawings and had secured several painfully authentic costumes. As noted by Charles Higham in his biography **Charles Laughton** (1976), Cukor and Laughton clashed constantly over interpretation: "Charles suffered agonies between the scenes, and kept fluffing lines, begging for retakes. After three days he asked Cukor to release him, and have W. C. Fields take on the role. Two miserable days later, Cukor agreed." (This did not preclude Laughton's wife, Elsa Lanchester, from continuing in her part of Clickett, the Micawbers' maid.)

Borrowing W. C. Fields from Paramount turned out to be inspired casting. It was worth all the problems he created. He battled for a time for Selznick to allow him to perform his juggling and pool table comedy routines. He had to read his prose lines from cue cards as his memory for dialogue was slight, especially after years of relying on ad-libbed line readings. But he toiled conscientiously. Cukor would recall, "He only worked for about two weeks and he was an absolutely charming man. He was born to play the part; he **was** Mr. Micawber . . . he was marvelous, hard-working and would try anything . . . he realized he was working with something that was a classic and he behaved that way."

At least one other actor was having trouble with his role, Basil Rathbone. The lean, gregarious Basil, one of the film colony's most outgoing and friendliest men, was here beginning a Hollywood stay during which he would come to be recognized as the cinema's greatest all-time villain. He would report in his memoirs, **In and Out of Character** (1962):

> One morning at MGM I thrashed the living daylights out of poor little Freddie Bartholomew as David Copperfield.
>
> It was a most unpleasant experience, for I was directed by Mr. George Cukor to express no emotion whatsoever—merely to thrash the child to within an inch of his life: I had a vicious cane with much whip to it, but fortunately for Freddie Bartholomew and myself, under his britches and completely covering his little rump, he was protected by a sheet of foam rubber. Nevertheless, Freddie howled with pain (mostly anticipatory I presume) and in his "closeups" his face was distorted and he cried real tears most pitifully. . . .
>
> . . . When it was over I rushed over to Freddie and took him in my arms and kissed him. We had become great friends, and he was often over to our house for a swim in the pool and dinner. This made the playing of Mr. Murdstone all the harder for me. . . .

When completed, **David Copperfield,** all two and a half hours' worth, was previewed in Bakersfield and later Santa Ana. Mayer pressured Selznick to shorten the picture. The producer decided to eliminate Barrymore's work as Dan Peggotty after the cool reception to his scenes in Bakersfield. When four lady schoolteachers at a later screening protested Peggotty's absence,

Herbert Mundin, Freddie Bartholomew, Jessie Ralph (on couch), and Elizabeth Allan in David Copperfield ('35).

Selznick restored the missing two reels. In its 133-minute version, **David Copperfield** was released in 1935. The public response vindicated Selznick and relieved Mayer (although he was annoyed simultaneously that the fought-against picture was a success). Andre Sennwald (**New York Times**) reported:

Although it is a film of enormous length, according to screen standards . . . Hugh Walpole's screenplay has been arranged with such uncanny correctness and each of the myriad episodes which go into the making of the varied canvas has been performed so perfectly, that the photoplay slips by in an unwearying cavalcade. . . .

Like Dickens himself, it is able to invest each character in this complex story with such a completeness of personality that none is too minor to take his place in the unforgettable gallery. Certainly it is in the great narrative tradition of the cinema. . . .

All the actors won glory. Some of the performances (Young's unctuous Uriah Heep, Fields' Micawber, Rathbone's Murdstone) over the years have become picaresque classics themselves. MGM signed Freddie Bartholomew and proceeded to build him into a major star. He soon reported for work opposite Greta Garbo and with chum Basil Rathbone in Selznick's **Anna Karenina** (1935). The "older" David Copperfield, Britisher Frank Lawton, also experienced a career boost.

A great commercial and critical success,

David Copperfield joined **China Seas, Forsaking All Others,** and **Mutiny on the Bounty** as a major Metro grosser of 1935. The film placed number one on **Film Daily**'s Ten Best Picture poll, and fourth in the National Board of Review's Ten Best, and was nominated for the Best Picture Academy Award, losing to **Mutiny on the Bounty.** The success of **David Copperfield** also supplied Selznick with the courage and stimulation to break away from his father-in-law. After 1935's **Vanessa, Her Love Story, Reckless, Anna Karenina,** and **A Tale of Two Cities,** he would form his own filmmaking company.

DINNER AT EIGHT
1933—110 min.

Producer, David O. Selznick; **director,** George Cukor; based on the play by George S. Kaufman and Edna Ferber; **screenplay,** Frances Marion and Herman J. Mankiewicz; **additional dialogue,** Donald Ogden Stewart; **art directors,** Hobe Erwin and Fred Hope; **camera,** William Daniels; **editor,** Ben Lewis.

Marie Dressler (**Carlotta Vance**); John Barrymore (**Larry Renault**); Wallace Beery (**Dan Packard**); Jean Harlow (**Kitty Packard**); Lionel Barrymore (**Oliver Jordan**); Lee Tracy (**Max Kane**); Edmund Lowe (**Dr. Wayne Talbot**); Billie Burke (**Millicent Jordan**); Madge Evans (**Paula Jordan**);

Jean Hersholt (**Jo Stengel**); Karen Morley (**Lucy Talbot**); Louise Closser Hale (**Hattie Loomis**); Phillips Holmes (**Ernest DeGraff**); May Robson (**Mrs. Wendel, the Cook**); Grant Mitchell (**Ed Loomis**); Phoebe Foster (**Miss Alden**); Elizabeth Patterson (**Miss Copeland**); Hilda Vaughn (**Tina, Kitty's Maid**); Harry Beresford (**Fosdick**); Edwin Maxwell (**Mr. Fitch, the Hotel Manager**); John Davidson (**Mr. Hatfield, the Assistant Manager**); Edward Woods (**Eddie**); George Baxter (**Gustave, the Butler**); Herman Bing (**The Waiter**); Anna Duncan (**Dora, the Maid**).

SYNOPSIS

Fluttery New York socialite Millicent Jordan is obsessed with playing hostess to a perfect dinner. Her mania prevents her from displaying sympathy for her husband Oliver, owner of a shipping line who faces bankruptcy and is the victim of a heart condition that just might kill him. The Jordans' daughter, Paula, is involved in an affair with drunken ex-matinee idol Larry Renault. As Oliver keeps his illness a secret and Paula conducts her furtive romance, Millicent proceeds merrily to fill her guest list.

Invitations are extended to blustery Dan Packard, the very tycoon who is trying secretly to gobble up Jordan's business, and his wife Kitty, a platinum-blonde floozy whom Packard had first met in the hat check room of the Hottentot Club. Packard's guilty conscience dictates he not go, but socially ambitious Kitty accepts. Also invited is Carlotta Vance, a stage star of the Gay Nineties who has lost her famed beauty but not her candor or wit. She is an old romance of Oliver's. Also included on the guest list are dapper Dr. Talbot— then in the midst of an affair with Kitty Packard— and his wife Lucy. Learning that Larry Renault is in town, Millicent calls him—Paula is there when she does—and he too accepts, encouraged by Paula. To complete the guest list, Millicent expects Lord and Lady Ferncliffe, an internationally prominent couple.

But things happen. Renault, reprimanded by his agent Max Kane for getting drunk and insulting producer Jo Stengel who might have offered him a small part, kills himself—illuminating his profile under a lamp as gas pervades his apartment. Lucy Talbot, aware of her spouse's affair with Kitty (as well as with others), has a showdown with him; Dr. Talbot vows to reform. And Kitty, swearing that "I'm gonna be a lady if it kills me!" demands that Dan escort her to the party and that he call off his attack on Jordan's business, or she will expose the details of his sordid business deals.

Eight o'clock arrives and so do the guests— but not the British Ferncliffes, who have accepted another engagement. Carlotta, learning of Renault's death, tells Paula, and encourages her to accept the attentions of Ernest DeGraff, a smitten suitor. Oliver, becoming very ill, is treated by Talbot, who in turn tells Millicent of the seriousness of her husband's condition. Finally realizing where her sense of values really rests, and realizing her husband's troubles for the first time,

Jean Harlow and Marie Dressler in Dinner at Eight *('33).*

attractive. Harlow was very soft about her toughness.

If **Grand Hotel** had a bumpy creation, **Dinner at Eight** was the perfect example of on-set tranquility, coasting to a finish on April 17. While Cukor was impressed by the cooperation of all the name performers, none pleased him as much as John Barrymore (with whom Cukor had worked at RKO the year previous in **A Bill of Divorcement**). Recalled Cukor on the NET 1970s teleseries "The Men Who Made the Movies":

In **Dinner at Eight** he played a second-rate cheapish actor, which God knows he wasn't. And he did it with enormous wit and very subtly. . . . I remember the very touching end. . . . I said, "I think he [Renault] can't even die satisfactorily . . . something awkward and awful should happen to him, even though he was imagining this great death scene where he was going to kill himself. . . . I think it would be awfully interesting if he did this very ugly, middle-aged awkward sprawl," and he did this so wonderfully. And then he pulled himself together and died showing his profile. Jack was a man with no vanity, and enormous knowledge and humor as all the Barrymores had. They were all fascinating creatures. They were really magical people.

When released in August 1933, **Dinner at Eight** was, in the words of Bland Johaneson **(New York Daily Mirror),** "wholly splendid." Cukor had injected pace into the proceedings without succumbing to temptations to overcinematize the stage story. Each star enjoyed at least one special vignette that lingered after the viewing: Dressler clucking in embarrassment as her dog has an "accident" in the hotel corridor; Lionel Barrymore chuckling in sad nostalgia as he remembers his juvenile love for Carlotta; Burke going to hysterical pieces when she learns that the Florida-bound Ferncliffes will not be attending her dinner; Tracy's powerfully sustained tongue-lashing of Barrymore when the latter destroys a job possibility; and producer Hersholt spitting, "You **sag,** Renault, like an old woman. . . . You're a corpse . . . go get yourself buried!"

However, special salutes must go first of all to John Barrymore for his superb portrayal of the tragic Renault, played almost in black-comedy style as he misquotes Ibsen, soliloquizes on his ex-wives with punctuations of muggings and raspberries. He also creates one of the screen's most vivid—and pathetic—suicides. Some critics insisted that Barrymore was merely playing himself—or, rather, playing the drunken man he would later become—but this is not so. The real-life inebriate was a foul, frightening, self-waste who urinated in restaurant lobbies and appeared to glorify his own ruin. But in **Dinner at Eight** Barrymore is in complete control of his deft characterization, which he patterned after his father-in-law, actor Maurice Costello; his brother-in-law, actor Lowell Sherman; and, last, himself.

The other huzzahs go to Beery and, even more so, to Harlow. Whenever the feature is revived, audience response, as it was in 1933, favors most strongly the Olympian insult slaughters that erupt

Millicent vows to be a better wife and to reform her socially snobbish ways. And Packard, understanding that Kitty is sincere in her threats, tells Jordan that his business is safe. "I've been looking the proposition over . . . I was just saying to my wife tonight, it looks like a good place for me to sink a little dough, didn't I, honey?" Meanwhile, his blonde spouse makes conversation with Carlotta: "I was reading a book the other day . . . it's all about civilization or something, a nutty kind of book. Do you know that the guy says that machinery is going to take the place of every profession?" "Oh, my dear," replies Carlotta, eyeing Kitty's obvious physical charms, "that's something you'll never have to worry about!"

* * *

When MGM shot **Grand Hotel** (1932), the gathering of a superstar cast was thought an audacious challenge. It proved both a critical and a financial success. The studio, thrilled with the Oscar winner's box-office record, sought another vehicle in which to package as many stars as possible.[1] The studio located the proper showpiece playing at Broadway's Music Box Theatre—George S. Kaufman's and Edna Ferber's comedy **Dinner at Eight.**[2]

With Frances Marion, Herman J. Mankiewicz, and Donald Ogden Stewart making scenario adjustments (including the now classic closing exchange), **Dinner at Eight** started production under the aegis of Mayer's fiercely ambitious son-in-law David O. Selznick (imported from his former base at RKO) and youngish director George Cukor. Production commenced on March 16, 1933, with a gaggle of the studio's most lustrous stars in roles which might have been conceived just for them: Mayer's "pet" Marie Dressler as former great beauty Carlotta Vance; John Barrymore as the strutting, eye-rolling, alcoholic ex-idol Larry Renault; Wallace Beery as bombastic, shady tycoon Dan Packard; Jean Harlow as his venomous-tongued, up-from-the-gutter spouse Kitty; Lionel Barrymore as a dying (again!) businessman; Billie Burke as an especially fluttery socialite; Lee Tracy as a fast-talking show business agent; and in less-sizable but nicely spotted assignments, Madge Evans, Jean Hersholt, Karen Morley, Phillips Holmes, and Edmund Lowe. Despite the seeming perfection of casting, Mayer did not like Jean Harlow and thought she would suffer in comparison to Dressler, the Barrymores, et al. Director Cukor felt differently:

I'd seen her in **Public Enemy** and **Hell's Angels,** where she was so bad and self-conscious it was comic. She got big laughs when she didn't want them. Then I saw **Red Dust**—and there she was, suddenly marvelous comedy. A tough girl, yet very feminine, like Mae West. They both wisecrack, but they both have something vulnerable, and it makes them

---

[1]Also that year MGM would package the all-star **Rasputin and the Empress** starring the three Barrymores (Ethel, John and Lionel) and **Night Flight,** which boasted a cast including: Clark Gable, Helen Hayes, John and Lionel Barrymore, Myrna Loy, Robert Montgomery, and William Gargan. The latter was produced by David O. Selznick and directed by Clarence Brown; box-office response was lukewarm.

[2]The original Broadway production opened on October 22, 1932 and ran for 243 performances, starring Constance Collier (Carlotta Vance), Conway Tearle (Larry Renault), Paul Harvey (Dan Packard) Judith Wood (Kitty),

Malcolm Duncan (Oliver Jordan), Anne Andrews (Millicent Jordan), Sam Levene (Max Kane), Austin Fairman (Dr. Talbot), and Olive Wyndham (Mrs. Talbot).

between the two performers. The gruff, notoriously unlikable Beery and the breezy, happy Harlow had no love for one another in actual life,[3] and Cukor allowed them free rein to spew their harangues.

HARLOW: Who do you think you're talkin' to, that first wife of yours out in Montana? That poor mealy-faced thing with her flat chest that didn't have nerve enough to talk up to ya', washin' out your greasy overalls and cooking and slavin' in some mining shack? No wonder she died. . . . Ya' big windbag!

BEERY: Listen, you little piece of scum you . . . You can go back to that sweet-smelling family of yours—back of the railroad tracks in Passaic! And get this—if that sniveling, money-grubbing, whining old mother of yours comes fooling around my offices anymore, I'm going to give orders to have her thrown down those sixty flights of stairs, so help me . . . !

In fact, not only did Harlow hold her own in the distinguished cast, proving Mayer's apprehension unnecessary, but she nearly stole the picture. The **New York Daily Mirror** reported, "Among all those great performers it is little Jean Harlow who stands out. . . . Harlow is magnificent." And the **New York Herald-Tribune** wrote, "Of them all I think the amazing Miss Jean Harlow gives the grandest show . . . among a congress of stars doing their best she is quite the hit of the evening."

Surprisingly, **Dinner at Eight** won no Oscars, nor even any major Academy nominations. But there were many career benefits from the project. The film was a professional triumph for Selznick, who would continue to win accolades at Metro until he split from his aghast father-in-law to form his own film production company. Cukor's work was highly regarded by the Culver City staff and the director would go on to direct some of the lot's more illustrious features. With **Dinner at Eight**, Jean Harlow finally snared acceptance from the Metro hierarchy as a talent deserving top treatment and respect.

One of the most popular and frequently revived products of the Metro Golden Age, **Dinner at Eight** remains a favorite with film enthusiasts, a delightful, magical picture that defies any producer to dare a remake. In 1966, a restaging of the play did brave Broadway, but reviews were cold and the play limped through an unspectacular 127-performance run.[4] Wrote critic Gary Carey in his incisive text **Cukor & Co.**, "The memory of the film strangled the production like a resentful ghost."

---

[3]An actual quote of Beery on Harlow, "That woman! If I had to spend the rest of my life on a desert island and I had to choose between the two of them, I'd pick Marie Dressler rather than Harlow." Harlow on Beery, "He's a mean old son-of-a-bitch whose grave I'd love to piss on."

[4]The revival opened at the Alvin Theatre on September 27, 1966, with Arlene Francis (Carlotta), June Havoc (Millicent Jordan), Darren McGavin (Renault), Walter Pidgeon (Oliver Jordan), Pamela Tiffin (Kitty), Robert Burr (Dan Packard), Jeffrey Lynn (Dr. Talbot), and Phil Leeds (Max Kane).

THE DIVORCEE
1930—84 min.

Producer-director, Robert Z. Leonard; based on the novel **Ex-Wife** by Ursula Parrott; **treatment,** Nick Grinde and Zelda Sears; **continuity-dialogue,** John Meehan; **art director,** Cedric Gibbons; **gowns,** Adrian; **sound,** J. K. Brock and Douglas Shearer; **camera,** Norbert Brodine; **editors,** Hugh Wynn and Truman K. Wood.

Norma Shearer **(Jerry)**; Chester Morris **(Ted)**; Conrad Nagel **(Paul)**; Robert Montgomery **(Don)**; Florence Eldridge **(Helen)**; Helene Millard **(Mary)**; Robert Elliott **(Bill)**; Mary Doran **(Janice)**; Tyler Brooke **(Hank)**; Zelda Sears **(Hannah)**; George Irving **(Dr. Bernard)**; Judith Wood **(Dorothy)**.

SYNOPSIS
When Paul crashes his automobile resulting in the disfiguring of Dorothy, he marries her, thinking it the only gentlemanly thing to do. The marital infectiousness spreads to Ted and Jerry, a pair of modern young lovers. Ted, a newspaperman, believes that infidelity cannot disrupt true love.

Later, on their third wedding anniversary, Jerry realizes that Ted is having an affair. She is crushed, despite Ted's avowal that the woman means nothing to him. In an attempt to test Ted's code, Jerry has an affair with Don, reasoning that this will even the score. Ted is furious with Jerry's reciprocal conduct and leaves her.

After their divorce Ted turns to drink and desolation while Jerry flits from flirtation to flirtation. Paul confesses his love for Jerry and offers to divorce the disfigured Dorothy and take Jerry to China as his wife. Jerry realizes Dorothy's dependency and nobly rejects his offer. She then journeys to Paris where Ted has sunk into disillusionment. On New Year's Eve, the pair reunite amidst a French cabaret setting.

* * *

NEW YORK SUN: Norma Shearer is the American beauty rose of the Metro-Goldwyn-Mayer nurseries.

JOAN CRAWFORD: Well, she sleeps with the boss.

Thus spun the conflicting sentiments toward Norma Shearer, an aristocratic actress who earned a tremendous film following (despite her physical handicap of being wall-eyed and her occasional lapses into overtheatrics). Miss Shearer had been on the Metro lot since 1923, surviving the assorted corporate mergers, the appearance of new actress rivals, and the public's very fickle taste. In 1927 she had married Irving Thalberg, which had ensured her position in the studio hierarchy, but had done nothing to endear her to company and industry factions who disputed her talents as a performer. Then in 1930 she stilled—at least temporarily—the jeers of her opponents when she won the Academy Award for Best Actress for her portrayal of loose-living Jerry in **The Divorcee.**

By 1930 standards, **The Divorcee** was very tawdry stuff (although only a pale shadow of its book original). It was a sensual soap opera incorporating young love, disfigurement, drink, dissipation, and infidelity, all encased in a sophisticated setting. It was distilled from a highly controversial bestseller, **Ex-Wife,** a book deemed so "wicked" that the author, Ursula Parrott, published it anonymously, adding her name to the dust jacket only after thousands of copies had been sold. MGM purchased the screen rights for $25,000. It seemed a rather superfluous gesture since Metro did not mention the bestseller in its publicity and Nick Grinde and Zelda Sears so deviated from the novel in their scenario that the film could easily have been made without the book rights.

Originally the project was announced as a Garbo vehicle. But the Swedish actress was offended by the material and refused the assignment. The next choice mentioned was Joan Crawford. In the meantime, Shearer, weary of the "lady" parts she had been playing in such successes as **The Last of Mrs. Cheyney** (1929) and **Their Own Desire** (1929), eagerly hunted the role of Jerry, a modern-moral girl who seeks vengeance on her philandering husband by tallying affairs of her own. The star reputedly told her spouse, "Irving, the public is getting tired of me being the lady in every picture. I've **got** to play something more daring!" With much reluctance, Thalberg agreed, "Well, after all, Norma is a very strong-minded girl and she knows what she wants. Not only does she usually get it; she is usually right."

With a bitter Joan Crawford out of the picture—along with Nick Grinde and John Meehan, each of whom had been announced as director—**The Divorcee** began production with Robert Z. Leonard (doubling as the film's producer) directing. Thalberg took intense care to ensure that Norma was properly showcased. Three leading men were assigned to the project: dapper Chester Morris, suave Conrad Nagel, and sophisticated Robert Montgomery. The flattering camera work of Norbert Brodine favored Norma's left profile, and Adrian's more sumptuous frocks added to her screen allure.

On April 19, 1930, **The Divorcee** premiered. Though the **New York Times** was lukewarm in its appraisal ("It is a competently acted production, with good direction in some of its scenes, but it is virtually a suspenseless affair, particularly as it is garnished with the inevitable embrace on the

Chester Morris and Norma Shearer in The Divorcee *('30).*

final fade-out"), most reviewers shared the sentiments of **Billboard:** "MGM, through the capable direction of Robert Z. Leonard and an extraordinary treatment of its story, extraordinary in its subtlety and meticulous handling of risqué situations, has turned out an exceptional talking picture." When box-office business proved outstanding and Norma won laurels for her latest characterization, Thalberg was delighted with his wife's astuteness. And with the son she bore him on August 25, 1930, named Irving Grant Thalberg, Jr.

On November 5, 1930, at the $10.00 a plate Academy Award Ceremony Banquet at the Ambassador Hotel, **The Divorcee** was a candidate for Best Picture, but lost to Universal's **All Quiet on the Western Front.** In the Best Actress category, Norma was nominated for **The Divorcee** and **Their Own Desire.** Her competition included Metro's Greta Garbo (nominated for **Anna Christie** and **Romance**). Conrad Nagel presented Shearer with the Oscar.

Filmed on a twenty-two-day schedule at a cost of $341,000, **The Divorcee** earned a profit of $335,000.

EASTER PARADE
1948 C—103 min.

Judy Garland and Fred Astaire in Easter Parade *('48).*

Producer, Arthur Freed; **associate producer,** Roger Edens; **director,** Charles Walters; **story,** Frances Goodrich and Albert Hackett; **screenplay,** Sidney Sheldon, Goodrich, Hackett, and, **uncredited,** Guy Bolton; **music numbers** staged and directed by Robert Alton; **music director,** Johnny Green; **orchestrators,** Conrad Salinger, Mason Van Cleave, and Leo Arnaud; **vocal arranger,** Robert Tucker; **songs,** Irving Berlin; **Technicolor consultants,** Natalie Kalmus and Henri Jaffa; **art directors,** Cedric Gibbons and Jack Martin Smith; **set decorators,** Edwin B. Willis and Arthur Krams; **women's costumes,** Irene; **men's costumes,** Valles; **makeup,** Jack Dawn; **sound,** Douglas Shearer; **special effects,** Warren Newcombe; **camera,** Harry Stradling; **editor,** Albert Akst.

Judy Garland (**Hannah Brown**); Fred Astaire (**Don Hewes**); Peter Lawford (**Jonathan Harrow III**); Ann Miller (**Nadine Gale**); Clinton Sundberg (**Mike, the Bartender**); Jules Munshin (**François, the Headwaiter**); Jeni LeGon (**Essie**); Jimmy Bates (**Boy with Don**); Richard Beavers (**Leading Man**); Dick Simmons (**Al, the Stage Manager**); Dee Turnell (**Specialty Dancer**); Lola Albright and Joi Lansing (**Showgirls**); Robert Emmet O'Connor (**Cop Who Gives Johnny a Ticket**); Wilson Wood (**Marty**); Lynn and Jean Romer (**"Delineator" Twins**); Peter Chong (**Valet**); Nolan Leary (**Drug Clerk**); Benay Venuta (**Bar Patron**); Frank Mayo (**Headwaiter**); Doris Kemper (**Mary**); Hector and His Pals [Carmi Tryon] (**Dog Act**).

SYNOPSIS
It is New York around 1912. Nadine Gale informs her dance partner Don Hewes that she has signed a contract for a Broadway show and that she intends to be a solo act from now on. Their present professional commitments as a team mean nothing to her. As she tells him, "I'm not being selfish, I'm just thinking of me." Nevertheless, Don still loves Nadine. But her affections are reserved for Don's buddy, Jonathan Harrow.

Don decides to continue his act and explains that he will make a star of any chorus girl he chooses. He selects Hannah Brown, a virtual novice currently performing in an unimpressive cafe. At first Don attempts to mold Hannah into another Nadine—even changing her name—but soon realizes that she is a very individualistic performer. Don and Hannah are to appear in the **Follies,** but he rejects the job offer when he learns that Nadine will be the star of that Ziegfeld revue.

Hannah, by now in love with Don, knows he is still emotionally involved with his ex-partner. Completing the triangular pattern is Jonathan, who admits his attraction for Hannah. Eventually Don realizes that it is Hannah and not Nadine whom he adores.

Don and Hannah earn their own Broadway show, **Walking Up the Avenue,** during which they perform "A Couple of Swells." The hit cements their status as stars. Nadine temporarily separates them when she lures Don into dancing their old number "It Only Happens When I Dance with You" at the **Midnight Follies** after the evening show.

Later Hannah clears up the misunderstanding by presenting Don with a hat to wear in the Easter Parade, which occurs on the first anniversary of their meeting.

*   *   *

When MGM completed production of **Easter Parade** in March 1948 studio optimism was so high regarding the film's enormous appeal that the executives wanted to employ the description, "The **Gone With the Wind** of musicals." Composer Irving Berlin talked them out of it, "Just say that it's a very enjoyable show." Nevertheless, so warm was the audience response to this charming Technicolor melodic adventure that Metro probably could have devised such an ad campaign without any embarrassment. **Easter Parade** remains one of the studio's greatest musical moments.

The film developed as a collaboration between Irving Berlin and storywriter Frances Goodrich and her spouse Albert Hackett. Producer Arthur Freed initially announced that the cast would include Judy Garland, Gene Kelly, Frank Sinatra, Kathryn Grayson, and Red Skelton. As plans developed the lineup was changed to Garland, Kelly, Peter Lawford, Ann Miller and Jules Munshin (as François, the headwaiter).

Rehearsal began in mid-September 1947 with Kelly's "Drum Crazy" number. Then Kelly broke his ankle during a game of touch football in his own backyard. Seeking a replacement, all immediately thought of Fred Astaire.[1] However, he had retired in 1946, taking a "mental" vacation after years of devising new dance techniques. Nevertheless, a call to Astaire's San Diego county ranch with the blessing of Kelly returned Astaire

---
[1]Fred Astaire was making his sixth appearance in an Irving Berlin song-filled picture; his most recent ones had been Paramount's **Holiday Inn** (1942) and **Blue Skies** (1946).

to the soundstages after a thirteen-month absence.

At first Vincente Minnelli was thought ideal for directing **Easter Parade** since he had been guiding his wife Judy Garland and Kelly through the trouble-plagued **Pirate** (1948). Then it was decided, for everyone's emotional welfare, not to have him remain on the Berlin project. Thus after five days on the new entry he was replaced by Charles Walters. The latter had joined Metro in 1942 as a choreographer and occasional screen dancer. He had made his directorial bow with **Good News** (1947). That movie established him as the first artist to both direct and choreograph a major Hollywood musical feature.

Molding a film into a shootable format is always a creative effort filled with the unexpected. Such was the case with **Easter Parade.** Director Walters was dissatisfied with the shooting script provided by the Hacketts and requested several rewrites. These were contributed by Sidney Sheldon and Guy Bolton. Their aim was to give the scenario more levity and raise it further from the genesis of a **Pygmalion**-like plotline.

Not the least of problems was selecting the song-and-dance numbers from Berlin's vast catalog. Roger Edens was primarily responsible for that. As tunes were employed from Berlin's distant past, they required new arrangements. One case in point was "Shaking the Blues Away" (from the **Ziegfeld Follies of 1927**). Also picked from Berlin's repertoire were: "I Want to Go Back to Michigan," "I Love a Piano," "Snooky Ookums," "Ragtime Violin," "When the Midnight Choo Choo Leaves for Alabam'," "The Girl on the Magazine Cover," "Beautiful Faces Need Beautiful Clothes," "Everybody's Doing It Now," and "Easter Parade." The **new** numbers composed by Berlin were "Better Luck Next Time," "Drum Crazy," "It Only Happens When I Dance with You," "I Love You—You Love Him," "A Fella with an Umbrella," "Steppin' Out with My Baby," "Mister Monotony,"[2] and "Let's Take an Old-Fashioned Walk." The last novelty number did not meet Freed's expectation, and Berlin jovially sat down and (allegedly) an hour later came back with "A Couple of Swells."

Easter Parade, which had started shooting in late November 1947 (after the usual prerecording sessions), completed production on February 9, 1948.[3] For the final scene of this period musical, the setting was to be Fifth Avenue in the midtown area. Art director Jack Martin Smith utilized an available paved section on lot 3 to construct approximately two city blocks, including the lower portion of St. Patrick's and other edifices associated with Fifth Avenue. Since only one side of the street (with ten-foot-high sections of buildings) had been built, the missing other side was added to the film by means of a technical process. The end result allowed for the breathtaking shot of seven hundred extras, buggies, cars, conveyances, parading down Manhattan's famed elite way, period 1912.

Easter Parade was previewed in February 1948 and released that July. The ads: "Judy pours out her heart in glorious love songs . . . and inspires debonair Astaire to his greatest triumph . . . in a musical romance as gay and tender as Irving Berlin's melodies." Wrote **Cue** magazine, "Splendiferously Technicolored, fancily decorated, it is probably the most elaborate package of musical entertainment since MGM's **Ziegfeld Follies.** The plot is familiar but funny, the lines and lyrics are comic, and the direction light and quick." The **New York Times** wrote, "If the screenplay were something more original than a conventional backstage romance, **Easter Parade** easily could have been a great musical instead of just a good one." The **New York Herald-Tribune** observed, "**Easter Parade** is a bit thin on plot, but it has music and dancing to delight the most captious screengoer." The picture, which cost $2,503,654 to produce, grossed $6,803,000 in its initial release. Johnny Green and Roger Edens would win Oscars for the Best Score of a musical film.

Over the years, two numbers[4] in **Easter Parade** have become classics. One, "Shaking the Blues Away," shows Ann Miller at her sexy, gyrating best.[5] An unusual aspect of this offering is that the performer is not surrounded by a legion of chorus boys but performs the dynamic solo on a bare stage, supported only by billowing translucent curtains and a chorus of voices. The other highlight is "A Couple of Swells," with Garland and Astaire in hobo attire planning a droll stroll up famous Fifth Avenue.

When **Easter Parade** opened, **Newsweek** magazine reported, "The important thing is that Fred Astaire is back again with Irving Berlin calling the tunes." MGM was so pleased with the results of the venture and the teaming of Astaire and Garland that it immediately set about to schedule a new tandem celluloid vehicle. The project selected by the Freed unit was **The Barkleys of Broadway** (1949). However, Judy's recurrent illnesses and erratic behavior occasioned her removal from the picture. Her happy replacement: Ginger Rogers.

EDISON THE MAN
1940—107min.

Producer, John W. Considine, Jr.; **associate producer,** Orville O. Dull; **director,** Clarence Brown; **story,** Dore Schary and Hugo Butler; **screenplay,**

---

[2]It was deleted from the release print; it was sung by Garland. Also cut was "I Love You—You Love Him" and "A Pretty Girl Is Like a Melody."

[3]During filming of **Easter Parade** Garland had to return to **The Pirate** set for constant retakes.

[4]Not to be overlooked is Astaire's "Steppin' Out with My Baby," his trick number for this picture. In the course of the choreographed routine he performs a ballet of sorts, a blues dance, and a jitterbug. For each he has a different gorgeous partner. Thanks to MGM's industrious technical department—another first was created by Metro—the initial use of slow motion synchronized with sound allowed the dancer to perform a slow-motion solo dance finale while the chorus behind him continued performing at regular speed.

[5]Berlin was initially opposed to casting Ann Miller in the film.

Talbot Jennings and Bradbury Foote; **assistant director,** Robert A. Golden; **music,** Herbert Stothart; **art directors,** Cedric Gibbons and John S. Detlie; **set decorator,** Edwin B. Willis; **women's costumes,** Dolly Tree; **men's costumes,** Gile Steele; **makeup,** Jack Dawn; **technical advisers,** William A. Simonds, the Edison Insitute, and Norman R. Speiden, director of historical research, Thomas A. Edison, Inc.; **sound,** Douglas Shearer; **camera,** Harold Rosson; **editor,** Frederick Y. Smith.

Spencer Tracy (**Thomas Alva Edison**); Rita Johnson (**Mary Stilwell**); Lynne Overman (**Bunt Cavatt**); Charles Coburn (**General Powell**); Gene Lockhart (**Mr. Taggart**); Henry Travers (**Jim Els**); Felix Bressart (**Michael Simon**); Peter Godfrey (**Ashton**); Frank Faylen (**Galbreath**); Byron Foulger (**Edwin Hall**); Guy D'Ennery (**Lundstrom**); Addison Richards (**Dr. Johnson**); Milton Parsons (**Acid Graham**); Arthur Aylsworth (**Bigelow**); Gene Reynolds (**Jimmy Price**); Grant Mitchell (**Shade**); Donald Douglas (**Jordan**); Harlan Briggs (**Bisbee**); Charles Trowbridge (**Clark**); Harold Minjir (**Blair**); George Meader (**Minister**); Charles Waldron (**Commissioner**); Charles Lane (**Lecturer**); Irving Bacon (**Sheriff**); Edward Earle (**Broker**); Joe Whitehead (**Man**); Emmett Vogan (**Secretary**); Tom Mahoney (**Policeman**); Bruce Mitchell (**Coachman**); Milton Kibbee (**Workman**); Nell Craig (**Woman**).

SYNOPSIS
In 1929, eighty-two-year-old Thomas Alva Edison is to be honored on the fiftieth anniversary of his invention of the incandescent light. Before attending the testimonial dinner, the venerable elder citizen is interviewed by two enthusiastic high school students. He tells the youths, "One percent inspiration is very important. . . . You cannot invent it. . . . You have to have it."

Once at the Golden Jubilee Celebration, Edison begins to think back on his life while the testimonial speeches are in progress.

He recalls coming to New York at the age of twenty-five and working at numerous menial jobs. A defective umbrella brings Mary Stilwell into his life, and they eventually wed. Meanwhile, he has gone to work for Western Union and has begun experimenting with a stock tickertape machine. He sells the invention to General Powell and Mr. Taggart. With the money he opens a laboratory at Menlo Park. Meanwhile, Edison marries Mary and they later have two children.

Among Edison's fifteen hundred inventions are the electric light bulb and the phonograph. Still later, despite great odds and many adversaries, he is permitted a charter to light a New York City district if he meets a prescribed six-month deadline. He and his staff complete the task on schedule and from his Pearl Street station, Edison demonstrates that his electrical lighting plan can and does work.

The scene flashes ahead to the banquet where the chief speechmaker is toasting the guest of honor and pleading that mankind not destroy itself with its own inventive genius. A morally concerned Edison asserts, "What man's mind can conceive, man's character can control."

* * *

Felix Bressart and Spencer Tracy in Edison the Man *('40).*

really a bad picture at all; it's just that the same formula has been used so often with these lives-of-the-great-men films that it has become stereotyped. Spencer Tracy, one of Hollywood's most capable and sincere actors, is well cast as the struggling inventor who works against all odds." Howard Barnes (**New York Herald-Tribune**) penned, "For almost any player except Tracy, the role would be thankless. Edison is shown as an irascible, stubborn, insatiably curious man whose personal existence was exceedingly mundane, and whose professional achievements defy dramatic projection. Nevertheless, by the sheer persuasion of his acting Tracy makes the film definitely worth seeing. It is a relief to find an actor relying on his own artifice, not grease paint, to bring a great figure to life. It is a completely credible portrayal."

Without the topicality of Twentieth Century–Fox's **The Story of Alexander Graham Bell** (1939), which blended much fiction with romance, plus the box-office draw of Don Ameche, Loretta Young, and Henry Fonda; or the star-packed cast of Warner Bros.' **Juarez** (1939—Paul Muni, Bette Davis, Brian Aherne, John Garfield, et al.); or the lavishly praised outstanding performance of Raymond Massey in RKO's **Abe Lincoln in Illinois** (1940—Massey won an Oscar nomination), **Edison the Man** did not place high with the public in 1940. : was a case of integrity obscuring commercial-ess.

EDWARD, MY SON
1949—112 min.

Producer, Edwin C. Knopf; **director,** George Cukor; based on the play by Robert Morley and Noel Langley; **screenplay,** Donald Ogden Stewart; **music,** John Woodridge; **music director,** Sir Malcolm Sargent; **art director,** Alfred Junge; **sound,** A. W. Watkins; **special effects,** Tom Howard; **camera,** Freddie Young; **editor,** Raymond Poulton.

Spencer Tracy (**Arnold Boult**); Deborah Kerr (**Evelyn Boult**); Ian Hunter (**Dr. Woodhope**); Leueen MacGrath (**Eileen Perrin**); Felix Aylmer (**Mr. Hanray**); Walter Fitzgerald (**Mr. Kedner**); Tilsa Page (**Betty Foxley**); Ernest Jay (**Detective**); Colin Gordon (**Ellerby**); Harriette Johns (**Phyllis Mayden**); Julian d'Albie (**Summers**); Clement McCallin (**Sergeant Kenyon**).

SYNOPSIS

Edward Boult is the son of Englishman Arnold Boult, the latter an ambitious monster of a man who vows to make his son a success. Over the years Arnold's various tactics to pave a golden path for his Edward include arson, bribery, and driving two people to suicide.

Arnold's ambition finally alienates even his wife, Evelyn. She asks for a divorce, but her proud husband refuses and threatens to smear her reputation if she initiates such an action. Her attempts to stop her spouse's activities fail and she

What studio could resist a stirring biography of a great humanitarian? Surely not MGM, as proven in 1940 when the film company released not one but two patriotic biographies based on the life of Thomas Alva Edison (1847–1931).[1] The first, **Young Tom Edison,** appeared in February 1940, starring Mickey Rooney and directed by Norman Taurog. Three months later there appeared the more prestigious, bigger-budgeted **Edison the Man,** with Spencer Tracy in the title role.

Edison the Man, directed by Clarence Brown, covers the major years of the man's creativity, from twenty-two to thirty-five. (Edison was thirty when he invented the talking machine, thirty-two when he perfected the electric light, and thirty-five when he successfully "lighted" New York. Interestingly, the picture does not deal with his work on the motion picture camera.) Though MGM's **Edison** films were **not** to be regarded as a series—they exist as separate entries, with **Edison the Man** not fashioned as a sequel to **Young Tom Edison**—several things linked the two chronicle features: Edison's slight deafness, his lack of formal schooling, his enjoyment of apple pie and milk, and the song "Sweet Genevieve."

Tracy was particularly aware of the acting challenge when he accepted the assignment. He would reveal later:

I gradually worked out of my feeling of being afraid I wouldn't do everything that the char-

acter merited and just went ahead from day to day, trying my best. I lived in the Edison atmosphere as much as I could for a couple of months ahead of production. In these days, when you run into some kind of "ism" everywhere you turn, I think Edison's life is the best ·case history, in a dramatic form, American young people could possibly get on the things this country makes possible and stands for.

MGM took pains to reproduce in Culver City Edison's Menlo Park laboratory in its entirety, and also made reproductions of Edison's various key inventions. In the scenario Butler sought to be faithful to the spirit of the simple, earnest American without succumbing too much to the Hollywood malady of overromanticizing.

As might be expected, ·the publicity department felt compelled to titillate would-be viewers with its advertising slogans: "A story of love and courage—stranger than fiction . . . the most exciting picture of the year" and "The love of a woman . . . the courage of a fighting America . . . lifted him from obscurity to thrilling fame!"

The black-and-white feature drew respectful reviews. Archer Winsten (**New York Post**) noted, "Though handicapped by a subject more devoted to wrinkling the brow than performing photogenic oddities, **Edison the Man** can be safely placed among the best of the screen biographies." William Boehnel (**New York World-Telegram**) championed, "Dore Schary and Hugo Butler have fashioned a fine original story about the Wizard of Menlo Park, which is human, charming, and engrossing, without ever becoming maudlin." Philip T. Hartung (**Commonweal** magazine) was more restrained in his praise, "**Edison the Man** isn't

---

[1]Both features were supervised by producer John W. Considine, Jr. and associate producer Orville O. Dull. Dore Schary, Hugh Butler, and Bradbury Foote were the writing team on **Young Tom Edison** and they were joined by Talbot Jennings for **Edison the Man.**

Spencer Tracy and Deborah Kerr in Edward, My Son *('49).*

mer of 1948, but it was nearly a year later before it was released. The studio had rightfully feared the reaction of the critics[3] and the mass public. "That peculiarly fascinating fable of a devilishly cruel British lord which was played with such wit and finesse by Robert Morley on the stage in **Edward, My Son**," wrote Bosley Crowther of the **New York Times**, "has been drained of its most trenchant poison in its transference to the screen and with the plainly un-British Spencer Tracy acting the principal role." It was clear that the aging Tracy was less suited to villainy than ever, and the star soon compensated for this disappointing film with his comic performances in **Adam's Rib** (1949) and **Father of the Bride** (1950). (It was also in this period that he made **Malaya** (1950) with James Stewart, an only sporadically interesting World War II melodrama instigated by Dore Schary, the new executive in charge of production at Metro.)

In his memoirs, **Robert Morley: A Reluctant Autobiography** (1966), that actor writes of the cinema version of the drama in which he played for three years:

> I used to be asked in those days whether I wouldn't have liked to play in the film myself, but I think I much preferred to sell it to Metro for Spence. A fine actor, he was criticized for his performance in the film because he played it too straight. I am not sure there was much alternative. When some years later ["U.S. Steel Hour," CBS-TV, December 7, 1955] I did it myself on television in the States, it was not very successful. It was much easier to play on the stage with scenery than it was to act in the more realistic settings which are necessary on the screen. A great deal of its initial success depended, too, on my speaking directly to the audience, and this device loses it spontaneity when attempted in the cinema."

If **Edward, My Son** is remembered for Kerr's impressive histrionics and not for Tracy's dramatic attempts, it should be noted the film also served to inspire Jack Benny's scripters. It provided them with material for an amusing parody on the comedian's Sunday night radio program shortly after the film's general release.

takes to alcohol—finally drinking herself to the grave.

But all of Arnold's deviousness and cruelty are naught when Edward is killed in a motoring accident. Thereafter, Arnold is convicted of previous atrocities of his devising and sent to prison. Upon his release, he begins an apparently doomed search for the illegitimate child his prized Edward sired before his demise.

* * *

"The dramatic story of a man who loved too much" and "Broadway's No. 1 Stage Play Is Now on the Screen" appeared to promise a solid motion picture. The prospects for a substantial entry seemed excellent with a cast[1] headed by Spencer Tracy and Deborah Kerr and direction by George Cukor. However, such was not the case. **Edward, My Son** emerged a very interesting failure in MGM's postwar period. It displayed flashes of talent here and there, but it fell far below expectations in both critical and commercial appeal.

The drama, by Robert Morley and Noel Langley, had been a great London success. It also had played 260 Broadway performances at the Martin Beck Theatre, where it opened September 30, 1948. Morley himself portrayed the leading part of destructively ambitious Arnold Boult, with Peggy Ashcroft as his dipsomaniac wife and Ian Hunter as his doctor friend. When MGM purchased the screen rights to the property, it proudly announced that **Edward, My Son** would be the first production filmed at Metro's new Borehamwood Studios near London.

There were several blunders in the production, beginning with Donald Ogden Stewart's screenplay. Initially it changed the lead character from an Englishman to a Canadian immigrant so the star would not have to simulate a British accent. Stewart's adaptation mellowed Boult's villainy, a move which muddled the story, especially since Tracy was miscast in the first place as a man who placed ambition above everything else. As in the stage play, the son Edward **never** appeared, but was only spoken about, a theatrical device which frustrated moviegoers. Within the film, Tracy's character spoke directly to the audience (as did Morley in the play), a structural gimmick which appeared artificial and specious to film fans.

The salvation of **Edward, My Son** rested partially on the supporting players who had played their roles on stage (Ian Hunter as the understanding Dr. Woodhope and Leueen MacGrath as Boult's mistress Eileen Perrin). In this outing Deborah Kerr would again prove her dramatic mettle.[2] As the tormented wife driven to alcoholism and death by her cold husband she would be Oscar-nominated. However, she lost the Best Actress award to Olivia de Havilland of **The Heiress** (Paramount).

Edward, My Son had been filmed in the sum-

EXECUTIVE SUITE

1954—104 min.

Producer, John Houseman; **director,** Robert Wise; based on the novel by Cameron Hawley; **screenplay,** Ernest Lehman; **art directors,** Cedric Gibbons and Edward Carfagno; **assistant director,** George Rhein; **camera,** George Folsey; **editor,** Ralph E. Winters.

---

[1]Leueen MacGrath, as Tracy's mistress, was the only player to portray her part in London, in New York, and in the film. She later became Mrs. George S. Kaufman.

[2]Originally it had been suggested that Katharine Hepburn play the role of Tracy's wife on screen.

[3]In England, Dilys Powell carped in the **London Sunday Times**, "I might add that the story of a British tycoon whose life is ruined by adoration of the spoiled son we never see might as well, for all the feeling it has of England, have been made in Ecuador."

Nina Foch, Barbara Stanwyck, Walter Pidgeon, William Holden, Dean Jagger, Louis Calhern, and Fredric March in Executive Suite *('54).*

William Holden (**McDonald Walling**); June Allyson (**Mary Blemond Walling**); Barbara Stanwyck (**Julia O. Tredway**); Fredric March (**Loren Phineas Shaw**); Walter Pidgeon (**Frederick Y. Alderson**); Shelley Winters (**Eva Bardeman**); Paul Douglas (**Josiah Walter Dudley**); Louis Calhern (**George Nyle Caswell**); Dean Jagger (**Jesse Q. Grimm**); Nina Foch (**Erica Martin**); Tim Considine (**Mike Walling**); William Phipps (**Bill Lundeen**); Lucille Knoch (**Mrs. George Nyle Caswell**); Mary Adams (**Sara Asenath Grimm**); Virginia Brissac (**Edith Alderson**); Edgar Stehli (**Julius Steigel**); Harry Shannon (**Ed Benedeck**); Charles Wagenheim (**Luigi Cassoni**); May McAvoy (**Grimm's Secretary**); Robin Camp (**Mailroom Boy**); Ray Mansfield (**Alderson's Secretary**); Bert Davidson and A. Cameron Grant (**Salesmen**); Mimi Doyle (**Telephone Operator**); Faith Geer (**Stork Club Hatcheck Girl**); David McMahon and Ralph Montgomery (**Reporters**); Raoul Freeman (**Avery Bullard**); Bob Carson (**Lee Ormond**); Ann Tyrell (**Shaw's Secretary**); Carl Saxe and Dick Landry (**Workers**); Mike Lally (**Spectator at Ball Game**); Matt Moore (**Servant**); Phil Chambers (**Toll Station Attendant**); Chet Huntley (**Narrator/Tredway**).

SYNOPSIS

When the long-time president of a giant furniture manufacturing company dies suddenly of a heart attack, his vacancy hurls the corporation bigwigs into competition to fill the post. Among the candidates for the powerful position are senior vice president Frederick Y. Alderson, aged and fatigued; Jesse Q. Grimm, company veteran hitherto eager to retire; sales manager Josiah Walter Dudley; vice president George Nyle Caswell; controller Loren Phineas Shaw; and young executive McDonald Walling. Carefully watching the battle for power are Julia O. Tredway, the dead president's hypertense ex-mistress, and Erica Martin, the late man's secretary who has been overcome with grief at his passing.

While young Walling continues in his usual work, enjoying his off hours with wife Mary and son Mike, Shaw pursues a bitter and unscrupulous drive to obtain his goal. His machinations include blackmailing Dudley when he learns of his love affair with Eva Bardeman, and forcing Caswell to join his ranks after learning of the vice president's past efforts to sell the corporation short.

Despite Shaw's ambition, the major stockholders, including the suicidal Julia, recognize in Walling's young idealism a choice candidate for the presidential position. After Walling presents an eloquent speech in the board of directors' room, regarding company pride and continuity, the board votes Walling into power.

* * *

In the 1953–54 movie season Metro-Goldwyn-Mayer placed five releases in the enviable list of the twenty-five top moneymakers. Four of the huge grossers were **Mogambo,** with its alluring star trio of Clark Gable, Ava Gardner, and Grace Kelly; **Knights of the Round Table,** a lavish costume epic (in CinemaScope and color) starring Robert Taylor and Ava Gardner; **The Long, Long Trailer,** with television deities Lucille Ball and Desi Arnaz; the exuberant musical romp **Seven Brides for Seven Brothers,** with appealing Jane Powell and Howard Keel and a bevy of marvelous young dancers. The fifth film, however, contained a theme which appeared to hold no lucrative cinematic appeal: the world of big business.

But MGM succeeded in proving false the theory that the intricate machinations of business would make moviegoers somnolent. **Executive Suite,** produced with elegance (in black and white) by John Houseman (who was responsible for the studio's laudatory **Julius Caesar,** 1953), was directed with zest by Robert Wise, and boasted a high-priced cast ($700,000).[1] The Oscar-holding actors of the troupe were: William Holden (1953's **Stalag 17**), Fredric March (1932's **Dr. Jekyll and Mr. Hyde** and 1946's **The Best Years of Our Lives**), and Dean Jagger (1949's **Twelve O'Clock High**). MGM favorites June Allyson (completing her Metro contract with this film), Walter Pidgeon, Louis Calhern, and Nina Foch joined the proceedings as did Paul Douglas, Shelley Winters, and Barbara Stanwyck.[2]

Based on the 1950 novel by Cameron Hawley, **Executive Suite** was filmed by Metro at a very transitional time in the corporation's history. Freelance arrangements, percentage-of-profit deals, and a withering filmmaking climate were slowly killing the grand studio style of motion picture production which could cram a cargo of stars into a single picture.[3] As such, **Executive Suite** represented one of MGM's—and Hollywood's—last all-star films of the **Grand Hotel** and **Dinner at Eight** tradition. For some, however, the depth and nuance of **Grand Hotel,** the thespianic flamboyance of **Dinner at Eight,** or even the gaudy high spirits of **China Seas** were lacking in this entry.

For many filmgoers—perhaps expecting perfection—the acting ensemble (with the exception of Stanwyck's hysterical stockholder and Nina Foch's weepy secretary) lacked the energy one might have expected, and the script reflected less dimension than there could have been. Did Ernest Lehman really believe it necessary to paint so black and white a picture of the business world in order to rivet moviegoers' attention for 104 minutes? He presented a narrow-lapeled Lancelot in the form of William Holden, content to caress warm wife June Allyson and play ball with son Tim

---

[1]According to producer John Houseman in his autobiography, **Front and Center** (1979), director Robert Wise's fee was $30,000 and the remaining production costs, after paying the stars, was less than $500,000.

As an economy measure, Houseman decided to ignore the use of soundtrack music in the film. For the film's opening titles showing the Sub-Treasury Building in Wall Street, one hears the sound of heavy chimes of a neighboring clock as each of the stars' names appears on the screen.

[2]Regarding her brief but telling assignment in the picture, Stanwyck would say, "Size has never bothered me. If it had, I would not have done **Executive Suite.** I liked the role and I wanted to do it, no matter how short it was. I think I worked all of seven days."

[3]William Holden would recollect, "Everybody was so good—so on his toes—that when you went in there in the morning you had to put on your best. It was a great experience."

Considine while his Attila-like foe Fredric March sprinkled evil glitter over the costars.

Whatever its artistic faults (far more evident in reviewing the film today), **Executive Suite** succeeded in luring box-office dollars and many critical huzzahs. After its May 1954 release (bowing at Radio City Music Hall), the film placed number five on the National Board of Review's Ten Best Film List, and number eight on **Film Daily**'s poll. For an all-star venture, **Executive Suite** nearly became a one-man show through the calculating performance of Fredric March. As the shameless schemer, he upstaged the script weaknesses and gave the production a tense, sometimes fascinating aura of cutthroat deceit. March deserved Academy Award consideration for this study of repellent behavior, but only Nina Foch entered the Oscar sweepstakes. (She was defeated in the Best Supporting Actress category by Eva Marie Saint of **On the Waterfront**.)

While many critics cheered the film,[4] Bosley Crowther **(New York Times)** was one of the few to pinpoint the feature's major flaw: "The only trouble with all of these people, as directed by Robert Wise, is that they are strictly two-dimensional. They are what you might call prototypes. . . . They give no substantial illusion of significance, emotion, or warmth."

The commercial success of **Executive Suite** led to a Twentieth Century–Fox fascimile, the CinemaScope and color **Woman's World** (1954), in which automobile corporation tycoon Clifton Webb had to pick a successor from such competitors as Van Heflin and Fred MacMurray as concerned wives June Allyson and Lauren Bacall anxiously watched, with more empathy than most audiences.

A pathetic footnote to **Executuve Suite** was added in the fall of 1976. CBS-TV began, on Monday night at ten o'clock, a network program, "Executive Suite," officially based on the novel but depending more on the 1954 feature for commercial inspiration. The hour-long weekly show wasted the talent of such performers as Mitchell Ryan, Stephen Elliott (in the Fredric March part), and Madlyn Rhue, forcing them to deal with tired and ridiculous clichés such as a kidnapping scheme, overly complicated interracial romances, and a suicidal lesbian. When ratings quickly sagged for the new venture, MGM veteran Ricardo Montalban was rushed into the cast as a little-theatre Lothario, but nothing could help the show. "Executive Suite" was canceled midseason, leaving the original feature film version an almost untampered happy memory for many moviegoers.

FATHER OF THE BRIDE
1950—93 min.

Producer, Pandro S. Berman; **director,** Vincente Minnelli: based on the novel by Edward Streeter;

[4]**Newsweek** magazine lauded, "Built around a situation in which six men and one woman are involved in a struggle for power in a corporation, **Executive Suite** moves with the pace and tension of a fine detective story. . . ."

screenplay, Frances Goodrich and Albert Hackett; **music,** Adolph Deutsch; **art director,** Cedric Gibbons and Leonid Vasian; **set decorators,** Edwin B. Willis and Keogh Gleason; **costumes,** Helen Rose and Walter Plunkett; **assistant director,** Marvin Stuart; **makeup,** Jack Dawn; **sound,** Douglas Shearer; **camera,** John Alton; **editor,** Ferris Webster.

Spencer Tracy **(Stanley T. Banks)**; Joan Bennett **(Ellie Banks)**; Elizabeth Taylor **(Kay Banks)**; Don Taylor **(Buckley Dunstan)**; Billie Burke **(Doris Dunstan)**; Leo G. Carroll **(Mr. Massoula)**; Moroni Olsen **(Herbert Dunstan)**; Melville Cooper **(Mr. Tringle)**; Taylor Holmes **(Warner)**; Paul Harvey **(Reverend A. I. Galsworthy)**; Frank Orth **(Joe)**; Rusty Tamblyn **(Tommy Banks)**; Tom Irish **(Ben Banks)**; Marietta Canty **(Delilah)**; Willard Waterman **(Dixon)**; Nancy Valentine **(Fliss)**; Mary Jane Smith **(Effie)**; Jacqueline Duval **(Peg)**; Fay Baker **(Miss Bellamy)**; Frank Hyers **(Duffy)**; Chris Drake, Floyd Taylor, Don Anderson, William Mahan, Walter Kelly, Peter Thompson, and Charleton Carpenter **(Ushers)**; Lucille Barnes, Erin Selwyn, Janet Fay, and Wendy Waldron **(Bridesmaids)**; Douglas Spencer **(Organist)**; Stuart Holmes, Anne Kunde, Ella Ethridge, William Bailey, and Dorothy Phillips **(Bits in Dream Sequence)**; William "Bill" Phillips **(Movers' Foreman)**.

SYNOPSIS
Stanley T. Banks is sitting amidst an awesome pile of postwedding debris. He looks directly at the audience and speaks, "I would like to say a word about weddings. I've just been through one."

Stanley then proceeds to relate the account of how his beautiful daughter Kay, having fallen in love with young Buckley Dunstan, becomes engaged to be wed and how Stanley, carrying on the tradition of the expense-paying father of the bride, nearly topples into the poor house living up to the custom and expectations. Those who look on as Stanley struggles are wife Ellie, sons Tommy and Ben, and the imperious prospective in-laws, Herbert and Doris Dunstan.

For all the financial horrors, the wedding eventually comes off, and Stanley survives to smile at it, now that it thankfully is in the past.

* * *

"MGM announces the event of the season! . . . The bride gets the THRILLS! Father gets the BILLS!" was how Metro hawked its profitable comedy, **Father of the Bride.** Based on the 1948 short novel by Edward Streeter (which was bolstered with Gluyas Williams' comic illustrations), it was produced by Pandro S. Berman and directed by Vincente Minnelli. The comedy mixed the star skills of Spencer Tracy as a harassed father, Elizabeth Taylor as his blushing, beautiful, chatter-box daughter, and Joan Bennett as the "perfect" wife and mother. The excursion into domestic fun would reap $4,150,000 in distributors' domestic rentals.

Production of this film brought about several coincidences. Tracy and Bennett were being reunited on screen after eighteen years: they had

Paul Harvey, Tom Irish, Don Taylor, Spencer Tracy, and Elizabeth Taylor in Father of the Bride *('50).*

costarred together as Fox contract players in 1932's **She Wanted a Millionaire** and **Me and My Gal.** Bennett, as Taylor's mother, had a memorable screen role in common with her celluloid daughter. Both had played Amy in **Little Women**, Joan in the 1933 RKO version and Elizabeth in the 1949 MGM rendition. Receiving the most publicity, however, was the fact that Elizabeth Taylor at the time of production was seriously dating Nicky Hilton of the hotel-chain family. They became engaged as the picture was shooting and Metro merrily spent $50,000 ballyhooing the marriage in tandem with the Berman production. The marriage, incidentally, did not last a month.

One of the few sour notes on the black-and-white production was the part that Jack Benny did **not** play in the proceedings. The media star learned of the project and asked MGM's Dore Schary for the key part of Stanley T. Banks. Schary promptly awarded him the job. Berman protested that Benny was a comedian without the necessary dramatic skills to interpret the focal role and threatened to tear up his own MGM contract if Schary mandated Benny's casting. Hence Minnelli, knowing Benny was not to have the role, had to direct him in a face-saving screen test. The erratic Tracy, who had gone to New York City angry because he had not been asked first to play Stanley, learned the true situation. He returned to begin shooting in January 1950.

In **I Remember It Well** (1974) Minnelli chooses to overlook the unpleasant aspects of the above-mentioned episode and describes this film as "the shortest and sweetest experience I'd ever encountered." The feature glided to completion in an economical twenty-eight days, with the set a very happy one. Minnelli describes Tracy thus:

Spencer was an inspiration. His instincts were infallible. . . .

There wasn't a better man at comedy. He wasn't a mugger, at least never in scenes with other actors. The facial contortions came when he was alone and unobserved.

One scene in particular revealed his brilliant comic flair. His daughter and her fiancé have had a fight. The boyfriend comes to the house, but the daughter won't see him. The father takes over. He knows exactly how the situation should be handled. He patronizingly asks the young man to come back another time, speaking with the quiet authority of a man who, after all, should know his own daughter better than anyone. She simply cannot see him now. But before the young man can take leave, the girl accidentally enters the room. That's all they need. They rush into each other's arms. The father is left standing there, the unwanted third man, trying to figure out a way to gracefully exit.

The brilliant way Spencer played the scene [was a joy]. Jack [Benny] had done the same scene for his test, and the contrast between the two performances was easily discernible to even the most uneducated eye. Spencer's reading was the essence of comedy, because it was achingly true.

Father of the Bride opened in 1950 to terrific business. Taylor was beautiful in her Helen Rose–

Walter Plunkett $1,800 wedding gown, Joan Bennett was appropriately charming and unruffled,[1] and Billie Burke, as ever, was a delight as the addled mother of the groom. Rusty Tamblyn, who would graduate to become an MGM dancer in several mid-1950s outings, was appropriately disinterested in his older sibling's problems. However, it was Tracy who scored the big hit of the comedy. **Newsweek** magazine assessed:

The film, while it packs all the satire of our modern tribal matrimonial rite that was richly contained in the original, also possesses all the warmth and poignancy and understanding that make the Streeter treatise much beloved. . . . As a father, torn by jealousy, devotion, pride, and righteous wrath, Mr. Tracy is tops. . . . And right beside him are Joan Bennett as the typical mother of the bride, Elizabeth Taylor as the happy little lady, and Don Taylor as the overshadowed groom. . . . Yes, **Father of the Bride** is a honey of a picture of American family life. It shouldn't discourage matrimony but—well, this reviewer is certainly happy to have all sons.

The **New York Times** placed **Father of the Bride** third on its 1950 Ten Best Picture list; the Academy nominated it as Best Film (it lost to Twentieth Century–Fox's **All About Eve**); and Tracy received his fourth Oscar nomination (losing to Jose Ferrer of Columbia's **Cyrano de Bergerac**).

On February 25, 1951, Tracy, Taylor, and Bennett re-created their film roles to the "U.S. Steel Theatre Guild of the Air." Because of the enormous response to the original, MGM produced a sequel in 1951. Entitled **Father's Little Dividend**, it was again produced by Berman, with Tracy, Bennett, Taylor (Elizabeth and Don), Burke, Olsen, Canty, Tamblyn, Irish, and Paul Harvy recreating their original parts. As all expected, box-office business was powerful and **Father's Little Dividend**—the dividend, of course, being a baby—placed among the studio's bigger moneymakers of that year.

In 1957 the team of Alan Jay Lerner and Frederick Lowe had the concept of doing a musical film based on this property. Herman Levin, producer of Broadway's **My Fair Lady**, also considered a stage production of the venture and discussed the same with Lerner and Lowe. Neither version materialized.

MGM produced a thirty-minute comedy series version of "Father of the Bride" for the 1961–62 CBS-TV season. The thirty-four episodes starred Leon Ames (Stanley Banks), Ruth Warrick (Ellie Banks), Myrna Fahey (Kay Banks), Burt Metcalfe (Buckley Dunstan), Ransom Sherman and Lurene

Tuttle (The Dunstans), and Rickie Sorensen (Tommy Banks). The storyline covered Kay's engagement, wedding, and her months of struggle to adjust to marital life.

THE FIREFLY
1937—138 min.[1]

Producer, Hunt Stromberg; **director,** Robert Z. Leonard; based on the musical play by Otto Harbach and Rudolf Friml; **screenplay,** Frances Goodrich and Albert Hackett; **adapter,** Ogden Nash; **music director,** Herbert Stothart; **songs,** Friml and Harbach; Bob Wright, Chet Forrest, and Friml; **art directors,** Cedric Gibbons and Paul Groesse; **set decorator,** Edwin B. Willis; **choreography,** Albertina Rasch; **gowns,** Adrian; **technical adviser,** George Richelavie; **sound,** Douglas Shearer; **montages,** Slavko Vorkapich; **camera,** Oliver Marsh; **editor,** Robert J. Kern.

Jeanette MacDonald (**Nina Maria Azara**); Allan Jones (**Don Diego Manrique de Lara–Captain François Andre DeCoucourt**); Warren William (**Colonel de Rougemont**); Billy Gilbert (**Innkeeper**); Henry Daniell (**General Savary**); Douglass Dumbrille (**Marquis de Melito**); Leonard Penn (**Etienne**); Tom Rutherfurd (**King Ferdinand**); Belle Mitchell (**Lola**); George Zucco (**St. Clair, Chief of French Secret Service**); Corbett Morris (**Duval**); Matthew Boulton (**Duke of Wellington**); Robert Spindola (**Juan**); Ian Wolfe (**Izquierdo, the Minister**); Manuel Alvarez Maciste (**Pedro**); Frank Puglia (**Pablo**); John Picorri (**Cafe Proprietor**); James Carson (**Smiling Waiter**); Jason Robards, Sr. (**Spanish Patriot**); Ralph Byrd (**French Lieutenant**); Dennis O'Keefe (**French Soldier, Admirer**); Sam Appel (**Fruit Vendor**); Rolfe Sedan (**Hat Vendor**); Hooper Atchley (**French Officer**); Stanley Price (**Joseph Bonaparte**); Theodore von Eltz (**Captain Pierlot**); Eddie Phillips (**Captain**); Robert Z. Leonard and Albertina Rasch (**Cafe Extras**); Sidney Bracy (**Secretary**); Lane Chandler (**Captain of the Guard**); Pedro DeCordoba (**Spanish General**).

SYNOPSIS

In the lusty Madrid of 1808, the beautiful Nina Maria, "the Firefly," a singing, dancing, flirtatious redheaded entertainer, performs in a cafe. Unknown to Nina's infatuated band of admirers is that she is actually a Spanish spy in the employ of the Marquis de Melito, adviser to King Ferdinand VII. Her task is to discover Napoleon's invasion plans. To rid herself of an ardent admirer named Etienne, Nina flirts with Don Diego Manrique de Lara, a wealthy and handsome young Spaniard. She departs the next morning for Bayonne to carry out her mission.

The enchanted Don Diego follows Nina, and insists upon accompanying her through the Pyrenees. When they arrive in Bayonne, Nina instantly turns her charms on Napoleon's staff of-

---

[1]Off camera, Bennett, then wed to producer Walter Wanger, was involved in a raging battle with gossip columnist Hedda Hopper. When Wanger had produced **Vogues of 1938**, Hopper had an acting role in it and had requested her close-up be deferred to the following morning when she would look fresh. Wanger refused. A similar situation occurred with Bennett during the making of **Father of the Bride;** Hopper focused on the episode in her column, and Bennett retaliated with a two-page trade advertisement, besides sending a live, deodorized skunk to Hopper.

---

[1]Filmed in Sepia.

Jeanette MacDonald and Theodore von Eltz in The Firefly *('37).*

ficer, Colonel de Rougemont. However, the apparently smitten Don Diego still woos the lady until she admits to being in love with him. But when Nina appeals to Don Diego for aid in obtaining a letter of De Rougemont's, which will result in the arrest of Ferdinand, the "Spaniard" reveals himself to be a French spy. He is actually Captain François Andre DeCoucourt, who has the job of following the wily Nina.

Five years of war elapse before Nina again meets de Rougemont, the latter recently promoted to general and still infatuated with her. For patriotic reasons she agrees to carry on a romance. But then Don Diego appears again, proving Nina to be a spy. She is arrested and sentenced to death.

The heartbroken Don Diego comes to Nina's cell. He laments that his duty has forced him to betray a woman he truly loves. As he speaks, the Battle of Vitoria begins. It is then learned that Nina had been a component of the British-Spanish strategy. She had deliberately been caught with the maps so the French would change their impregnable positions. Don Diego rushes to join his regiment, but is wounded en route.

Later Nina finds Don Diego in a field hospital. With Napoleon repulsed from Spain and the English and the Spanish exulting in victory, peace is again restored. The young lovers are now free to heed their hearts. They embark on the same Pyrenees mountain path where their love affair had blossomed years before.

* * *

Scarcely any other topic of gossip was more popular with MGM staffers than the passions of the boss, Louis B. Mayer. Veterans of the studio recall that it was virtually common knowledge that Mayer was attracted—strongly—to his "class" female stars, especially Myrna Loy and Jeanette MacDonald. Hence there were many smug grins around the lot when the front office announced the news that the redheaded Iron Butterfly's plea for a film sans Nelson Eddy had been granted.[2] The property: **The Firefly.**

The Otto Harbach–Rudolf Friml operetta had opened on Broadway on December 2, 1912. It starred Emma Trentini, Roy Atwell, and Melville Stewart, and ran for 120 performances. Even then the romantic melodrama of the Napoleonic Wars struck some audiences as pretty dated material. Nevertheless, Hunt Stromberg, producer of **The Great Ziegfeld** (1936) and many other Metro pictures, went to work. He assigned Ogden Nash to adapt, Frances Goodrich and Albert Hackett to write the screenplay, and Allan Jones to serve as Jeanette's new leading man.[3]

Stromberg spared little expense to provide MGM's leading soprano with a lavish vehicle, and Mayer vetoed few extravagances. There were location trips to Europe by the technical department—despite ominous rumblings of approaching

warfare—to study settings and to purchase needed props and costume materials. Some seventeen hundred special costumes were required for the picture, with fourteen ensembles especially designed for Jeanette by Adrian. Lot 2's "Verona Square," so beautifully created for **Romeo and Juliet** (1936), was redecorated to give the feeling of romanticized Madrid. The battle of Vitoria was expensively re-created on stage 11. In all there were thirty major sets for the film (shot in Sepia). The two chief outdoor locations for **The Firefly** were in the Lone Pine Mountains.

In preparation for **The Firefly,** MacDonald underwent rigorous dance instruction from Albertina Rasch, so that she could execute the intricate steps of the bolero, tango, flamenco, and fandango. To complicate her working schedule, she was then engaged to actor Gene Raymond. In the final period of production—on Wednesday, June 16, 1937—she and Raymond were wed at the Wilshire Methodist Church in Beverly Hills. The lavish affair cost approximately $25,000; Louis B. Mayer was in charge of the gilt-edge arrangements. The lucky three hundred invited guests included her two screen leading men, Nelson Eddy and Allan Jones. The day following the wedding, Jeanette was back at MGM to complete **The Firefly.**

"It will make 1937 remembered always as the year of the first romantic dramatic musical film!" said the teaser ad for **The Firefly,** which debuted in late summer 1937. The critics were not pleased with the alterations of the stage original, which, in the first place, they felt was too archaic a property for contemporary audiences. Stated Kate Cameron **(New York Daily News),** "The production is pretentious and overlong. . . ."

Yet for all its overblown theatricality and the oversized performances of such supporting players as Billy Gilbert, Henry Daniell, George Zucco, and Warren William, **The Firefly** was irresistible to most audiences. The beautiful Jeanette, swirling[4] and singing, performed such songs as "Sympathy," "Giannina Mia," and "Love Is Like a Firefly." The stalwart, handsome Jones had his highlight when he performed a rendition of "The Donkey Serenade" (developed from a Friml piano piece). It became the most popular song of the picture and would be the actor-singer's trademark song for decades to come. With **Test Pilot** and **Rosalie, The Firefly** became a Metro top grosser of the 1937–38 season.

After **The Firefly** Jeanette hoped to reteam with Jones in **Girl of the Golden West** (1938), but Louis B. Mayer was insistent she reunite with Eddy. There were three reasons for his decision. Mayer's fiercely loyal secretary-confidante Ida Koverman was a great enthusiast of Eddy and persuaded Mayer that the baritone had a lot more box-office appeal than Jones. Second, Mayer and

---

[2]Eddy had already costarred with MacDonald in **Naughty Marietta** (1935), **Rose-Marie** (1936), and **Maytime** (1937). While she was making **The Firefly,** he was teamed with Ilona Massey and Eleanor Powell in **Rosalie** (1937).

[3]Louis B. Mayer had tried to sign Jones a few years before to a Metro contract, but the tenor was then under contract to the Broadway Shuberts, a situation which cost him the lead opposite MacDonald in **Naughty Marietta.** Later he appeared in such MGM films as the Marx Brothers' **A Night at the Opera** (1935), had a smallish role in **Rose-Marie,** and been loaned to Universal for **Show Boat** (1936) with Irene Dunne.

[4]For the sequence in which Jeanette is seen dancing on a table top in the cafe, cinematographer Oliver Marsh developed a special trick. The camera-crane apparatus was suspended through a circular hole in the ceiling of the Madrid set, and revolved around on a metal pole, which resembled a piece of oil-well tubing. This "merry-go-round shot" allowed Marsh to photograph MacDonald in a 360-degree circle four times as she danced around a round table.

Jones never enjoyed a cordial working or social relationship. The tenor was too independent for company-man Mayer, and the employee soon found himself suffering the brunt of the mogul's wrath. He would be benched for much of the remainder of his Metro term contract. Third, Mayer was coming to believe that his beloved soprano had transferred to MGM from Paramount only at the request of her pal Irving Thalberg. According to Mayer's way of thinking, any friend of that (late) producer could be no true comrade of the boss on high. Mayer confirmed these suspicions of her disloyalty when MacDonald maneuvered behind his back to re-record her soundtrack for **The Firefly**'s French version. It was a custom she had long followed, but one that increasingly and inexplicably annoyed the dogmatic corporation executive.

For the time being he decided to continue pampering Jeanette, who was earning "the top half of a million dollars a year," but she must follow his orders more closely. Thus it was decreed that she and Eddy (each could live nicely without the other) must work again on the Metro soundstages.

Ben Blue, George Murphy, Gene Kelly, and Judy Garland in For Me and My Gal ('42).

FOR ME AND MY GAL
1942—104 min.

Producer, Arthur Freed; **director,** Busby Berkeley; based on the story "The Big Time" by Howard Emmett Rogers; **screenplay,** Richard Sherman, Fred Finklehoffe, and Sid Silvers, and **uncredited:** Jack McGowan and Irving Brecher; **technical adviser,** Elsie Janis; **music adapter,** Roger Edens; **music director,** George Stoll; **choreography.** Bobby Connolly and Gene Kelly; **vocal arrangers-orchestrators,** Conrad Salinger, George Bassman, Leo Arnaud, and Edens; **art directors,** Cedric Gibbons and Gabriel Scognamillo; **set decorators,** Edwin B. Willis and Keogh Gleason; **musical presentation,** Merrill Pye; **gowns,** Kalloch; **men's costumes,** Gile Steele; **makeup,** Jack Dawn; **sound,** Douglas Shearer; **montage,** Peter Ballbusch; **camera,** William Daniels; **editor,** Ben Lewis.

Judy Garland (**Jo Hayden**); George Murphy (**Jimmy K. Metcalfe**); Gene Kelly (**Harry Palmer**); Marta Eggerth (**Eve Minard**); Ben Blue (**Sid Simms**); Richard Quine (**Danny Hayden**); Keenan Wynn (**Eddie Milton**); Horace [Stephen] McNally (**Mr. Waring**); Lucille Norman (**Lily Duncan**); Betty Welles and Anne Rooney (**Members of Jimmy's Company**).

SYNOPSIS

In the pre–World War I days of vaudeville, Jo Hayden is part of a song-and-dance act composed of Lily Duncan, Sid Simms, and Jimmy K. Metcalfe. Jo endures the rigors of the vaudeville circuit in order to send her younger brother Danny to medical school. She also hopes to work her way to the top—the Palace Theatre in New York.

Jo meets handsome, fast-talking Harry Palmer, who urges her to break from the act to join

him. At first she is reluctant to leave her partners, but stoic Jimmy convinces her to team with Harry. After two years, Jo and Harry are still playing the small time, whereas Sid and Jimmy have experienced rising success.

On the circuit Harry meets Eve Minard, internationally famous singing star. Harry is captivated by her and soon ignores Jo whenever he is offstage. She, unfortunately, has fallen in love with him. Jo arranges for Eve to help Harry's career and Harry jumps at the opportunity. Upon disclosing his show business break, Harry finds Jo in tears. They realize their love and plan to wed.

Just as Harry's career is on the brink of blossoming, World War I begins and Harry receives his draft notice. To avoid going into the service, Harry smashes his hand in a trunk. It is at this time that Jo learns her brother has been killed in front-line action. She leaves Harry. He then tries to enlist but is rejected as he has permanently maimed his hand. Not knowing Jo's whereabouts, Harry joins a YMCA unit and serves in France, where he finds Jo singing to the troops.

Harry displays his bravery by saving the lives of a company of wounded men. Harry and Jo reunite. Armistice. Next stop—the Palace Theatre.

* * *

For Me and My Gal retains a special place in MGM lore for two reasons: it was the first adult, dancing, solo star-billing screen role for Judy Garland; and it provided the screen debut of Gene Kelly.

Designed as an answer to Twentieth Century–Fox's **Alexander's Ragtime Band** (1938) starring

Alice Faye, Tyrone Power, and Ethel Merman, **For Me and My Gal** was originally conceived by producer Arthur Freed as a vehicle for Garland and George Murphy. The latter was to interpret the colorful part of hoofer Harry Palmer. However, in studying the script, Freed noted how similar the part of Harry was to the Broadway character in **Pal Joey,** which had starred Gene Kelly.

Kelly himself was now in Hollywood following his success in that Broadway hit, on contract to David O. Selznick.[1] Playing his hunch, Freed shifted Murphy to the part of docile Jimmy K. Metcalfe (although the actor maintained second billing). Freed arranged for MGM to purchase fifty percent of Kelly's contract from Selznick International. The result was considerable friction between Kelly and Murphy, as well as between Kelly and director Busby Berkeley, who had favored Murphy for the Palmer part.[2]

In his autobiography, **Say . . . Didn't You**

[1]After Louis B. Mayer had seen **Pal Joey** on the Broadway stage he invited Kelly to join the MGM family, promising that no screen test would be required. Later Kelly was ordered to make one; he lost his temper and wrote Mayer a strong letter rescinding the agreement. Then David O. Selznick put Kelly under an exclusive contract, although allowing him to complete his **Pal Joey** stage assignment and to choreograph the Broadway show **Best Foot Forward.** When Kelly did arrive in California, Selznick thought of casting him as the priest (or later as the drunken doctor) in **Keys of the Kingdom.** Kelly dissuaded the producer from these notions.

[2]Arthur Freed later recalled the matter of selecting a director for **For Me and My Gal:** "Since this was a story about vaudeville and the struggles of a young couple to

Used to Be George Murphy? (1970), the actor-turned-politician has vivid recollections of the making of this Metro picture. He hated being "relegated to the part of the schnook who never gets the girl. . . . I'd begun to develop a phobia about this state of affairs." He also relates that he told Freed the script was in trouble since Kelly's character was basically unsympathetic. Nobody paid him any heed. But, the day following the preview, he encountered Louis B. Mayer at the MGM annual golf tournament and the mogul said, "You spoiled the picture." Mayer explained that "about eighty-five percent of the preview cards said Murphy, not Kelly, should have gotten the girl." Murphy then adds:

On his [Mayer's] order, the entire cast of For Me and My Gal was recalled for what turned out to be twenty-one days of retakes. Two big scenes were added to make Gene a hero. The toughest part for me was when they shot the whole finale over again—without me. . . . This really upset me because everyone involved—including Mayer—conceded that I had done a more than adequate job. It wasn't pleasant to discover that my efforts had wound up on the proverbial cutting-room floor. But that's Hollywood, as I used to tell fledgling actors when I was president of the Screen Actors Guild.

On the other hand, Kelly—with good reason—has pleasant memories of his film debut:

Of all the actors in Hollywood who had seen me or known me from my Broadway days, Judy was my first booster. I was a very lucky fellow to be selected by Arthur Freed to do my first picture opposite her, and don't think that she didn't have a lot to do with that. The greatest thing I remember about Judy during the shooting of For Me and My Gal was her kindness. I was a good stage performer, but the movies threw me. . . . Judy never mentioned this to me, but very quietly helped me. I'll never forget how much I learned about movies during that first picture.

Although a backstage story, For Me and My Gal took full opportunity to become a flag-waving propaganda piece, dredging up a slew of vaudeville numbers circa World War I. In the score were such old favorites as "For Me and My Gal," "After You've Gone," "Ballin' the Jack" "Till We Meet Again," "Oh, You Beautiful Doll," "When You Wore a Tulip," "Where Do We Go from Here?" "What Are You Going to Do to Help the Boys?" "How You Gonna Keep 'em Down on the Farm?" "Smiles," "Over There," "There's a Long, Long Trail A-winding," "Oui, Oui, Marie," and "You Asked Me If I Love You."

reach the top, we needed someone who knew the route, someone who knew about the hard work and heartaches that went with this way of life. The obvious choice was Buzz, who had lived this kind of story himself—it was his own background. Our only reservation in choosing him was that this was not simply a musical but an emotional story with some pathos and drama. It also contained a great deal of music, and we were a little afraid he might concentrate on that rather than the story. But he didn't. He came up with a very warm and human picture."

For Me and My Gal opened at the New York City Astor Theatre on October 21, 1942. Among the ads: "They love! It's a swift-paced romance of vaudeville's golden days! He was a fresh guy but he stole his way into her heart," and "Step out with Judy and a screenful of entertainers in her grandest hit! Nineteen great songs! A love story that brings tears! It's got everything . . . for you and your gal."

Howard Barnes (New York Herald-Tribune) noted, "The best parts of For Me and My Gal have to do with a vanished era of showmanship. The reconstructed variety turns, with appropriate musical accompaniments, are eminently satisfying." As for the star, Barnes wrote, "Miss Garland is someone to reckon with. Of all the youngsters who have graduated into mature roles in recent years, she has the surest command of her form of make-believe." Variety noted, "Like vaudeville itself, this Metro musical about the old two-a-day is hokey, but undeniably appealing. Miss Garland is a knockout as the warmhearted young song-and-dance girl. Kelly gives a vividly drawn portrayal of the imperfect hero, practically another Pal Joey." At a production cost of $802,980, For Me and My Gal grossed $4,371,000.

MGM took cognizance of the success of For Me and My Gal. It vindicated the studio's hopes for Judy Garland, permitting it to overlook the approximately four weeks of sick leave she took during the filming. The picture's popularity inspired Metro to buy all of Kelly's Selznick contract and to make him an MGM star, a status he would enjoy for the next fifteen years. Garland and Kelly would be reteamed for The Pirate (1948) and Summer Stock (1950), and each appeared separately in the all-star Thousands Cheers (1943) and Ziegfeld Follies (1946).

Murphy would remain at MGM for another decade; his two best remaining films for the studio were Bataan (1943) and Battleground (1949). In 1944 he succeeded another MGM star, Robert Montgomery, as president of the Screen Actors Guild. In 1947 he and Montgomery helped to found the new Hollywood Republican Committee, and in 1952, 1956, and 1960 he was in charge of the entertainment for the Republican National Convention. The Academy of Motion Picture Arts and Sciences awarded the actor a special Oscar in 1950 for "services in correctly interpreting the film industry to the country at large." Although Murphy's last feature was Metro's Talk About a Stranger (1952), he remained as a full-time company employee acting as "official ambassador as a liaison between MGM and the unions." In the late 1950s Murphy left the studio, having clashed once too often with arch Democrat Dore Schary. In 1965 he became a member of the Eighty-ninth Congress, as a Republican senator from California.

FREAKS
1932—64 min.

Director, Tod Browning; based on the story "Spurs" by Tod Robbins; **screenplay,** Willis Gold-beck and Leon Gordon; **dialogue,** Edgar Allan Woolf and Al Boasberg; **sound,** Gavin Burns; **camera,** Merritt B. Gerstad; **editor,** Basil Wrangell.

Wallace Ford (**Phroso**); Leila Hyams (**Venus**); Olga Baclanova (**Cleopatra**); Rosco Ates (**Rosco**); Henry Victor (**Hercules**); Harry Earles (**Hans**); Daisy Earles (**Frieda**); Rose Dione (**Madame Tetrallini**); Daisy and Violet Hilton (**Siamese Twins**); Edward Brophy and Matt McHugh (**Rollo Brothers**); Olga Roderick (**Bearded Lady**); Johnny Eck (**Boy with Half a Torso**); Randian (**Hindu Living Torso**); Schlitzie, Elvira, and Jennie Lee Snow (**White Pin Heads**); Pete Robinson (**Living Skeleton**); Koo Coo (**Bird Girl**); Josephine-Joseph (**Half-Woman—Half-Man**); Martha Morris (**Armless Wonder**); Frances O'Connor (**Turtle Girl**); Angelo Rossito (**Midget**); Zip and Pip and Elizabeth Green (**Specialties**); Albert Conti (**Landowner**); Michael Visaroff (**Jean, the Caretaker**); Ernie Adams (**Sideshow Patron**); Louise Beavers (**Maid**).

SYNOPSIS

Hans, a midget in Mme Tetrallini's French circus, is engaged to Frieda, a midget bareback rider. However, Cleopatra, the physically normal trapeze artist, is the object of Hans' infatuation. Meanwhile, the unscrupulous Cleopatra is involved in a love affair with Hercules, the strongman, and laughs derisively at Hans' pathetic attentions. When she learns later that the midget has inherited a fortune from a rich uncle, she plans to marry him, then poison him, and run away with Hercules.

The now rejected Frieda confides her plight to Phroso and Venus, the clown and seal tamer who also plan to marry. Despite attempts to warn Hans of the malicious Cleopatra, the midget marries the circus vamp. At their wedding banquet, she mocks her husband by carrying on with Hercules. She antagonizes the freaks by dismissing them with drunken epithets when they invite her to join them.

The freaks discover Cleopatra's plot and avenge her insults by mutilating her and placing her on exhibition (as a bizarre human chicken) in one of the sideshow pits that she had loathed earlier. Hans marries Frieda, and Phroso and Venus too are united.

* * *

On Valentine's Day 1931 Universal Studios released **Dracula,** the horror classic directed by Tod Browning and starring Bela Lugosi as the Continental bloodsucker. The picture grossed $500,000, a tidy sum in those depression days. When Universal released a Christmas follow-up in the haunting form of **Frankenstein** (1931), directed by James Whale and with Boris Karloff as the bewildered creature, the grosses more than doubled those of **Dracula.** Irving Thalberg carefully noted the success of Universal producer Carl Laemmle, Jr., and determined that MGM should be the leading studio of any genre, no matter how odd. Thalberg summoned writer Willis Goldbeck into his office and dictated, "I want to give me something even more horrible than **Frankenstein.**" He got it—**Freaks.**

Based on Tod Robbins' story "Spurs," **Freaks**

Angelo Rossito, Johnny Eck, director Tod Browning, the Pin Heads, Pete Robinson, Josephine-Joseph, and Olga Roderick (the Bearded Lady) on the set of Freaks *('32).*

told the morbid account of the macabre revenge obtained by circus oddities when one of their own, a wealthy midget, is exploited and almost murdered by a wicked lady trapeze artist. When Louis B. Mayer learned what Thalberg planned to put into production on his "family entertainment" lot, he exploded with objections. But Thalberg could not be dissuaded. The producer even went so far as to assign director Tod Browning—billed by MGM as "the Edgar Allan Poe of the screen"—to deliver the horror as chillingly as possible.

Browning assembled an entire coterie of circus "freaks" to flesh out the tale: Daisy and Violet Hilton, the Siamese twins; Randian, the Hindu living torso; Olga Roderick, the bearded lady; Johnny Eck, the boy with half a torso; Koo Coo, the bird girl; Josephine-Joseph, the half-woman–half-man; Pete Robinson, the human skeleton; and others. This sideshow menagerie provided a striking contrast with the usual glamorous personalities who strutted or sashayed across the Culver City lot. When Browning one day insisted on taking all the freaks to lunch in the studio commissary, F. Scott Fitzgerald, among others, beat a hasty retreat, leaving his appetite behind him.

To give the unique story a proper framework and the audience a few characters with whom they might identify, Wallace Ford was starred as a clown and pretty Leila Hyams as his seal tamer girlfriend, both sympathetic to the freaks. But this did not block Browning from focusing with uncomfortable scrutiny on the melodramas of

Hans and his marriage to the vamp trapeze artist Cleopatra (played with monstrous sexuality by Olga Baclanova). The director mixes sickly amusing touches (a stuttering suitor proposes to one of the Siamese twins while the other one reads; when he kisses his fiancée, the other twin reacts swooningly). There are moments of disturbing sadism as Cleopatra's eyes gleam as she laughingly watches her strongman lover beat a defenseless freak. The climax spotlights the freaks as they crawl, wriggle, and caper through a violent storm armed with knives and guns in pursuit of Cleopatra and the strongman. The denouement, in which Cleopatra is revealed as a twisted, bleating, web-footed freak, is a masterpiece of the cinema of the grotesque.

Freaks was released in the summer of 1932 with the promotional teaser "Can a full-grown woman truly love a midget? Here's the strangest romance in the world—the love story of a giant, a siren, and a midget!" Critical response was one of stunned horror. One trade journal termed the film "so loathsome that I am nauseated thinking about it." MGM retaliated by adding a lengthy preface to the film, stating, among many other things, that "history and religion, folklore and legend abound in tales of misshapen misfits who have altered the world's course. Goliath, Caliban, Frankenstein, Gloucester, Tom Thumb, and Kaiser Wilhelm, are just a few."

But audiences of the day had no stomach for **Freaks,** and the outcries of social groups and crit-

ics persuaded MGM to withdraw it quickly from release.[1] Some years later the studio snuck the film back into spotty release under the title of **Nature's Mistakes.** The ad lines read, "Do Siamese twins make love? . . . What sex is the half-man–half-woman?" However, for the most part, **Freaks** remained locked in the studio vaults, a controversial and somewhat shameful memory to the studio even today. It is shown at occasional theatre revivals, but **never** on television. Bearing this in mind, the next time Louis B. Mayer allowed such physically unusual performing talent on the back lot, he made sure it was for an entirely different type of project: **The Wizard of Oz** (1939). And even then he would have problems, this time from the Singer Midgets, hired to play the Munchkins. As for returning to the horror genre, Metro's flirtations thereafter were few and very far between.

In recent years, **Freaks** has won a few critical cheers. In 1963 Penelope Gilliat wrote in the **London Observer,** "The film is moving, harsh, poetic, and genuinely tender . . . the sort of thing that can be done only by art." Noted critic Vincent Canby **(New York Times)** in 1974 judged **Freaks,** "One of the perhaps half-dozen great horror films of all time." However, the actual "freak" community is yet to be impressed. In 1971 Colonel Montague Addison, a dwarf, wrote to **Films in Review,** "I avoided seeing **Freaks** for years on the advice of my freak friends. When I finally did see it my worst fears were realized. While pretending sympathy and understanding for a defenseless minority group, **Freaks** actually exploits and degrades us, in a manner that is hokey as well as offensive."

In the summer of 1976 a Los Angeles theatre booked a double-bill, Paramount's **Dr. Jekyll and Mr. Hyde** (1932) and **Freaks.** The audience of primarily young, dungaree-wearing buffs loudly Bronx-cheered March's Oscar-winning emoting in the first film. But as **Freaks** unreeled, they became deathly quiet and even emitted a few sincere gasps. **Freaks** has not lost its power.

A FREE SOUL
1931—91 min.

Director, Clarence Brown; based on the novel by Adela Rogers St. John and the play by Willard Mack; **adapter,** John Meehan; **art director,** Cedric Gibbons; **gowns,** Adrian; **sound,** Anstruther MacDonald; **camera,** William Daniels; **editor,** Hugh Wynn.

Norma Shearer **(Jan Ashe);** Lionel Barrymore **(Steve Ashe);** Clark Gable **(Ace Wilfong);** Leslie Howard **(Dwight Winthrop);** James Gleason **(Eddie);** Lucy Beaumont **(Grandmother Ashe);** Claire Whitney **(Aunt Helen);** Frank Sheridan **(Prosecuting Attorney);** E. Alyn Warren **(Bottomley, Ace's**

[1]Filmed on a thirty-six-day production schedule, **Freaks** cost $316,000 and drew a $164,000 loss in its initial release.

Chinese Servant); George Irving (**Johnson, the Defense Attorney**); Edward Brophy (**Slouch**); William Stacy (**Dick**); James Donlin (**Reporter**); Sam McDaniel (**Valet**); Lee Phelps (**Court Clerk**); Rosco Ates (**Men's Room Patron**); Henry Hall (**Detective**); Francis Ford (**Skid Row Drunk**); Larry Steers (**Proprietor of Casino**).

SYNOPSIS

Jan Ashe, a modern, independent woman, has a refined, polo champion sweetheart, Dwight Winthrop, a drunken, sporadically brilliant lawyer father, Steve Ashe, and an undeniable craving for macho Ace Wilfong, a smirking gangster whom Ashe successfully defends on a murder charge. At the birthday party of her grandmother, Jan announces her engagement to Dwight—just before an inebriated Steve and a natty Ace crash the scene. The abashed family, who have long disowned Steve, snub the pair. An angered Jan, in her broad-minded fashion, sympathizes with the outcasts and departs with Ace in his roadster, ending the evening at his hideout.

Jan soon discovers Ace to be "a new kind of man." One evening Steve, unaware of his daughter's affair, visits Ace's speakeasy. Police raid the joint and Steve takes refuge in Ace's adjacent apartment. There he comes face to lacquered face with his daughter, seductively clad in a slinky gown. Disgusted that his daughter would become infatuated with a man like Ace ("The only time I hate democracy is when one of you mongrels forgets his place"), Steve takes her home. Jan makes a bargain. She will stop seeing Ace if Steve gives up alcohol (a disease that drove his father to insanity).

Father and daughter begin camping in Yosemite, experiencing three months of happiness before Steve succumbs to his old urge, buys liquor, and disappears. Refused by her family, Jan returns to Ace. Soon, however, she discovers what a ruffian he can be and she tries to escape. In the midst of a fight at her apartment, Dwight arrives to witness her being abused. Later he tracks Ace down and shoots him dead.

Dwight faces a murder charge and refuses to defend himself. Jan searches for her father and locates him in a flophouse. At the eleventh hour in the courtroom, a scrubbed-up Ashe arrives, takes over Dwight's defense, and calling Jan to the stand, has her relate to the court the sordid tale of her affair with Ace. In a passionate speech, Ashe blames himself for his daughter's scandal and Dwight's offense. He implores the jury, "There is only one breast that you can pin the responsibility for this murder on . . ." and then falls dead to the floor. The jury finds Dwight not guilty. The polo player promises to follow Jan to New York City as she departs to start a fresh life.

* * *

In 1931 the idea seemed ludicrous that any male actor on screen could batter about Norma Shearer—Academy Award winner for **The Divorcee** (1930), socially popular wife of Irving Thalberg, and a pedestaled MGM female attraction with a following of great magnitude.

Yet it happened. The film was **A Free Soul**

Clark Gable and Norma Shearer in A Free Soul *('31).*

and the rogue was a relatively unknown Metro contract player who would become the greatest male draw in MGM's history—Clark Gable.

Based on the novel[1] by Adela Rogers St. John,[2] **A Free Soul** appealed to Irving Thalberg because of the sensual character of Jan Ashe. The producer envisioned the "loose" lady as a plum part for his wife Norma. The John Meehan screenplay contained another dynamic character, Steve Ashe, the heroine's father. Both Louis B. Mayer and Thalberg immediately thought of Lionel Bar-

[1]Willard Mack's dramatization of Miss St. John's book opened on Broadway at the Playhouse Theatre on January 12, 1928, for 100 performances. Kay Johnson was the San Francisco society girl, Lester Lonergran was her father, and Melvyn Douglas was Ace Wilfong.

[2]Miss St. John's book was based on her real-life relationship with her father, noted criminal lawyer Earl Rogers. The latter was as notorious for his heavy drinking as for his courtroom gimmicks.

rymore. By this point the veteran actor had turned to behind-the-camera pursuits and had vowed that his acting days were over. But the acting challenges of the characterization were too much for Barrymore to resist.

Thalberg assigned Britisher Leslie Howard the role of refined Dwight Winthrop, Jan's beau. But the role of animalistic Ace Wilfong, brutal gangster, was less easily cast. There was on the lot at the time a thirty-year-old, $350 a week contract player named Clark Gable. He had scored in a Los Angeles stage production of **The Last Mile** as Killer Mears. His glowering won him a Metro screen test that was disastrous.[3] Bits and small roles at various studios followed. It was a role in MGM's **The Easiest Way** (1930) that later impressed the Culver City lot to sign the newcomer to a two-year contract.

Gable approached the project with great trepidation. In his book **Thalberg: Life and Legend** (1969), Bob Thomas quotes Gable on the challenge of his major part and the prospect of working with highly regarded Metro director Clarence Brown:

> "I don't know what I'll do if Brown stops me in the middle of a speech. I've got a photographic memory, and I think of everything in one piece—that's my stock company training. If I'm stopped I'll have to go back to the beginning again."

However, everything went smoothly on the soundstage. When Thalberg witnessed the scenes of Gable pushing Norma about, he personally gave orders that director Brown heighten the tough scenes to ensure that the audience emotion created was sympathy for the "heroine" and not awe of the racketeer. (The fact that Ace Wilfong's character undergoes an unexplained personality change from breezy to Neanderthal did not phase Thalberg's artistic sense.) Barrymore's major concern, of course, was his jury speech. Brown realized the mechanics of Lionel's theatre background and arranged for him to rehearse it all in one nonstop take. The actor flung himself into the speech with such barnstorming glee that, after one run-through, he informed Brown he had exhausted himself and doubted if he could do it again. Brown then revealed that he had had three cameras running during Barrymore's histrionics, and the first take was printed.

When premiered in June 1931—three nights before the Thalbergs departed on a trip to Europe—**A Free Soul** was a sensation.[4] Leslie Howard, again bland and stiff as the proper beau, caused little audience impact. But Shearer, Barrymore, and Gable were magnificent. Lionel's rampant theatrics captured the major share of critical hurrahs and led to his being Oscar-nominated. On the evening of November 10, 1931, at Los Angeles' Hotel Biltmore, Mr. George Arliss announced Barrymore as the year's Best Actor.

Norma Shearer reaped accolades as the voluptuary Jan. Almost four decades after the picture's shooting, John Baxter in **Hollywood in the Thirties** (1968) would appraise her work as

> superb. Striking rather than beautiful, her ferocious squint neatly camouflaged by Brown, she wears Adrian's gowns with the erotic flair that a lack of underwear could inspire. Only Jean Harlow was able more effectively to suggest nudity beneath the draped silk. . . . Later

scenes exhibit her frank sexual hunger. . . . Though the film degenerates later . . . nothing can detract from the intensity of its early scenes, nor from Shearer's magnificent picture of arrogant female sensuality.

For her performance Shearer garnered her third Academy nomination. She did not win but did present—as the previous year's winner—the Oscar to Marie Dressler (for MGM's **Min and Bill**).

Finally, Gable himself triumphed via his Ace Wilfong. As Shearer herself said later, "It was Clark who made villains popular. Instead of the audience wanting the good guy to get the girl, they wanted the heavy to win her." Cinema fans were stunned by Gable's sexy violence. Lyn Tornabene would observe in her book **Long Live the King** (1976):

> Clark Gable was the man the world was waiting for. At just the right moment he stepped out of a telephone-booth-sized dressing room and appeared on the screen, unrealized superman of a traditional era. . . . In his arms, queens and goddesses became women. Cocksure, but not arrogant, he was the man every woman wanted, and every man wanted to be. As Fairbanks was assumed to be a real swashbuckler and Chaplin really a sad clown, when movies absorbed logic like a sponge, so audiences assumed Gable was really Gable.

A Free Soul produced many ramifications at MGM. Mayer, thrilled by Barrymore's Award-winning performance, offered the actor a lifelong studio contract. The ever-insolvent Barrymore accepted. Shearer's on-screen carnality gave a new dimension to her screen image and won her more admirers in the studio hierarchy. As for Gable, the studio renegotiated his contract, offering him $1,150 weekly. Soon he would be playing opposite Greta Garbo in **Susan Lenox—Her Fall and Rise** (1931). In years to come he would play opposite Shearer again, in **Strange Interlude** (1932) and **Idiot's Delight** (1939).

As for **A Free Soul**, an adaptation was aired on "Lux Radio Theatre" on November 1, 1937, starring Ginger Rogers and Don Ameche. In 1953 MGM made a rather lackluster new version of the property, entitling it **The Girl Who Had Everything**. The glossy sixty-nine-minute black-and-white programmer starred Elizabeth Taylor, William Powell (in the Barrymore role), Fernando Lamas (as an underworld figure named Victor Ramondi), and Gig Young as the heroine's old beau. Of this remake, **Variety** reported, "Armand Deutsch's production guidance drew on expert technical assists to dress up the physical look of the film, but shortchanged the paying customers on story value and entertainment."

---

[3]In 1926 Gable had toured with Barrymore in **The Copperhead**. It was Barrymore who directed Gable's wretched MGM screen test. Reputedly as a joke, Barrymore dressed Gable as a native. Gable would later reminisce: "Lionel was fidgety as a cat. He insisted on supervising the makeup job in his own office. As an Indian warrior, of course, I wore a minimum of clothing. When Lionel started walking me to the stage out on the lot where the test was to be made I created the sensation of all time. Guys were whistling at me, and the girls coming out of the commissary were yoo-hooing. I was never so embarrassed in my life. I whispered to Lionel, Let me go back to the dressing room and get a top coat. 'The hell with all of them,' Lionel said. 'Haven't they ever seen feathers before?' "

[4]Filmed on a thirty-one-day production schedule, **A Free Soul** cost $529,000 and earned a profit of $244,000.

FURY
1936—90 min.

Producer, Joseph L. Mankiewicz; **director,** Fritz Lang; **story,** Norman Krasna; **screenplay,** Bartlett Cormack and Lang; **assistant director,** Horace Hough; **music,** Franz Waxman; **art directors,** Cedric Gibbons and William A. Horning; **set decorator,** Edwin B. Willis; **wardrobe,** Dolly Tree; **sound,** Douglas Shearer; **camera,** Joseph Ruttenberg; **editor,** Frank Sullivan.

Sylvia Sidney (**Katherine Grant**); Spencer Tracy (**Joe Wilson**); Walter Abel (**District Attorney**); Bruce Cabot (**Kirby Dawson**); Edward Ellis (**Sheriff**); Walter Brennan (**Bugs Meyers**); George Walcott (**Tom**); Frank Albertson (**Charlie**); Arthur Stone (**Durkin**); Morgan Wallace (**Fred Garrett**); George Chandler (**Milton Jackson**); Roger Gray (**Stranger**); Edwin Maxwell (**Vickery**); Howard Hickman (**Governor**); Jonathan Hale (**Defense Attorney**); Leila Bennett (**Edna Hooper**); Esther Dale (**Mrs. Whipple**); Helen Flint (**Franchette**).

SYNOPSIS
Garageman Joe Wilson drives south to meet his fiancée Katherine Grant. En route he is mistaken for a kidnapper as a result of several chance details: his taste for salted peanuts, his possession of a five-dollar bill from the original ransom money, etc. Because he slept on the open road, he has no hotel records to establish a legitimate alibi.

The fair-minded sheriff recognizes the evidence as merely circumstantial, and feels Wilson may be innocent. However, an angry crowd spawns rumors that Wilson is a Chicago mobster and feels the sheriff is too weak to deal with the syndicate. Fearing Wilson might be freed, the crowd becomes an ugly mob and storms the jailhouse where Wilson is housed—burning it to the ground. A terrified Katherine watches the tragedy, horrified that her fiance is trapped in the blazing building.

However, Wilson miraculously escapes. Secretly he works to bring the mob to trial for its seemingly murderous act. The jury finds the mob guilty, but Joe accedes to his fiancée's wishes by appearing in court and saving the mob from death.

* * *

That **Fury** was ever made at MGM was a minor miracle; that the studio released the picture was even more of a "divine" blessing.

In 1934 MGM producer David O. Selznick was in Paris and signed German director Fritz Lang to an MGM pact. The Continental director had recently left his homeland (unattracted by life under the Third Reich) and in France directed **Liliom** (1934). When the monocled foreigner reached Culver City, no one seemed to know what to do with him, or how to utilize his talents. He was treated with suspicion, many feeling he might be another Erich von Stroheim. Eventually the studio put him to work on several projects, none of which was realized. They included a modern version of **Dr. Jekyll and Mr. Hyde**, a screen version of James Warner Bellah's short story "The Man Behind You," and a story involving the disaster aboard the SS **Morro Castle**. When not devoting time to these diversions, Lang traveled about the country, getting to know America, Americans, and their language.

When he returned to Metro, writer Norman Krasna mentioned a screen story he was preparing entitled **Mob Rule**. From this four-page outline,

Mannix called Lang into his office and said, "Look, you put something into this picture that wasn't in the script." After the executive reread the script, he had to admit that Lang was right; he had added nothing. But, insisted the hard-to-please Mannix, "it **sounds** different on the screen!"

When **Fury** was being readied for release, the studio planned to dump it onto the double-bill market, hoping to push the picture into oblivion. Then W. R. Wilkerson, publisher of the **Hollywood Reporter,** learned that Metro was to preview the film in some obscure theatre and inquired about the showing. "Oh, don't go . . . it's a lousy picture," said one executive. But Wilkerson persisted; he wanted to see any film directed by Lang. He was but the first of many to laud the completed work.

As a result of word-of-mouth enthusiasm, MGM opened **Fury** as a first-run attraction in New York. The critical reaction was generally positive. The **New York American** labeled it "a tremendously vital film saga that shatters the shackles of conventional motion picture entertainment to blast its way through a terribly tense drama of mob violence." The very Hollywoodish ingredients that Lang fought against including in the film were the sole elements that came under artistic attack. At the finale, for example, after the hero has delivered an impassioned speech, he and the heroine come together in a kiss-laden reunion. Such contradictions moved critics like Otis Ferguson (**New Republic**) to write, "[It] is a powerful and documented piece of fiction about a lynching for half its length, and for the remaining half a desperate attempt to make love, lynching and the Hays Office come out even."

Social significance was **not** a major product of MGM, and despite the overall critical success of **Fury**, Metro saw no reason to pursue the genre further. Lang departed MGM thereafter for United Artists, to film his next picture **You Only Live Once** (1937), with Henry Fonda and Sylvia Sidney (whose only MGM film was **Fury**). Lang would not return to MGM until 1955, when he directed the cinemascope feature **Moonfleet,** with Stewart Granger. For Lang, who had been banned from the lot for two decades, "it was a kind of satisfaction to come back."

As for Spencer Tracy, **San Francisco,** which the actor had completed just before he embarked on **Fury,** was released several weeks after the Lang picture. On the basis of the critical and public endorsement of Tracy in both of these features, his position as a rising MGM star was apparent.

Spencer Tracy and Sylvia Sidney in a publicity pose for Fury ('36).

Lang and Bartlett Cormack proceeded to devise a fleshed-out scenario. All the while studio executive Eddie Mannix—egged on by Louis B. Mayer—was hopeful that the project would flop and that this strange person could be written off as a contractual mistake of impulsive Selznick.

But Lang persisted and the scenario took shape. Lang and Cormack utilized the details of an actual lynching in San Jose, California, to supply the basis for their tale. Only after the screenplay was partly done did anyone bother to tell Lang that his "hero" could **not** be a lawyer as intended. It had to be a man of the street if the public was to empathize with the character.

Still no one was very impressed with the prospects of this project. It was regarded as a throwaway vehicle. As such, Joseph L. Mankiewicz, previously a Paramount contract writer and freshly moved to MGM, was assigned as producer of the project. What difference did it matter if he

flopped on his maiden effort? The same attitude applied to the casting of the relative studio newcomer Spencer Tracy.

During filming Lang encountered a good deal of difficulty. He was used to the European style of filmmaking, according to which the troupe in front of and behind the camera worked each day until the job was finished. He was unaware of union rules and ran into a great many problems with the extras when he persistently forgot to give them food or rest breaks, or both. Tracy took the side of the bit players, and the set was unharmonious.

Several of the scenes Lang intended to use (or did shoot), which involved blacks as the victims of white mob rule, were deleted by order of Louis B. Mayer. According to the mogul, his studio's function was to make a profit on entertainment, not provide social commentary.

When the film finished production, Eddie

GASLIGHT
1944—114 min. (British Release Title: THE MURDER IN THORNTON SQUARE)

Producer, Arthur Hornblow, Jr.; **director,** George Cukor; based on the play by Patrick Hamilton; **screenplay,** John Van Druten, Walter Reisch, and John L. Balderston; **music,** Bronislau Kaper; **art directors,** Cedric Gibbons and William Ferrari; **set decorators,** Edwin B. Willis and Paul Huldschinsky; **assistant director,** Jack Greenwood; **sound,** Joe Edmondson; **special effects,** Warren Newcombe; **camera,** Joseph Ruttenberg; **editor,** Ralph E. Winters.

Charles Boyer (**Gregory Anton**); Ingrid Bergman (**Paula Alquist**); Joseph Cotton (**Detective Brian Cameron**); Dame May Whitty (**Miss Thwaites**); Barbara Everest (**Elizabeth Tompkins**); Angela Lansbury (**Nancy Oliver**); Eustace Wyatt (**Budge**); Emil Rameau (**Mario Guardi**); Edmond Breon (**General Huddelton**); Halliwell Hobbes (**Mr. Muffin**); Terry Moore (**Paula at Age Fourteen**); Tom Stevenson (**Williams**); Heather Thatcher (**Lady Dalroy**); Harry Adams (**Policeman**); Charles McNaughton (**Wilkins**); Bobby Hale (**Lamplighter**); Alix Terry (**Girl of Ten**); Eric Wilton (**Valet**); Simon Oliver (**Boy in Museum**); Alec Craig (**Turnkey**); Leonard Carey (**Guide**).

SYNOPSIS

In 1870 young and impressionable Paula Alquist, who has studied opera in Italy, meets older, sophisticated Gregory Anton. After a two-week courtship they wed and embark on a short Italian honeymoon. Then he insists they move into Paula's late Aunt Alice Alquist's London home. Aunt Alice, a famous opera singer, was a murder victim in her house many years before, and it had been little Paula who had discovered her corpse. The case remains unsolved by Scotland Yard. Tending to No. 10 Thornton Square are, among others, the cook Elizabeth and the flirtatious cockney maid Nancy.

Suave Gregory constantly nags his wife and accuses her of increasing memory lapses. Paula believes him. He also divulges that Paula's mother ended her life in an insane asylum and that she is headed in the same direction.

Youngish Scotland Yard detective Brian Cameron witnesses Gregory upbraiding Paula and takes an interest in their situation as well as the unsolved murder. Giving the law enforcer some little-known facts is neighborhood gossip Miss Thwaites.

After several futile attempts, Brian gains access to Paula's home and explains his position, reassuring her that she is **not** going insane. Brian also discovers objects reported "misplaced" by Paula, actually locked in Gregory's desk. An incriminating letter also links the diabolical husband to Aunt Alice's murder some twenty years earlier.

Just as Anton discovers the sought-after jewels—sewn into a stage costume that Aunt Alice had worn—Cameron overcomes him and ties him to a chair. While awaiting the police, Paula has her moment of emotional triumph. She refuses to heed his begging to be freed. She spits out, "I hate you! Without a shred of pity . . . without a shred of regret . . . I watch you go with glory in my heart!"

* * *

Patrick Hamilton's chilling melodrama of a husband intent on driving his wife insane, titled **Angel Street** on the stage, opened on Broadway (after a very successful London run) in December 1941 with a cast featuring Judith Evelyn as the

Ingrid Bergman and Charles Boyer in Gaslight *('44).*

tortured wife, Vincent Price as the wicked spouse, and Leo G. Carroll as the detective. The play's great success (it eventually tallied 1,293 performances) impressed Hollywood filmmakers, despite the fact there was already a British film version (1940) in release abroad. Columbia Pictures bought the screen rights, intending it as a vehicle for Irene Dunne. Later the rights were resold to MGM, under the proviso that the negatives to the British film be destroyed.[1]

At first MGM intended to star Hedy Lamarr in the thriller, but it was fast losing faith that the temperamental European beauty could be a dramatic actress of much import. Instead, Metro borrowed from David O. Selznick the services of Ingrid Bergman, fresh from the triumph of **For Whom the Bell Tolls** (1943). Also from the Selznick stable came Joseph Cotten, making his MGM debut as Detective Cameron.[2] (The film's credits would read, "Miss Bergman and Mr. Cotten appear through the courtesy of David O. Selznick.") Continental Charles Boyer was cast as the sinuous Gregory Anton, and Angela Lansbury, daughter of British character actress Moyna MacGill, took time off from her parcel-wrapping job at Bul-

lock's Wilshire Department Store to test for the part of low-life maid Nancy. She won the part (despite front office concern over her lack of sex appeal) and celebrated her eighteenth birthday on the set. No British-set picture of the World War II years would be complete without the presence of Dame May Whitty, and so MGM cast its distinguished veteran contractee as the garrulous Miss Thwaites. It is she who punctuated her every statement with "Well" and who provided the film with moments of comedy relief.

Gaslight was directed by George Cukor, who later recalled:

Ingrid Bergman had no difficulty in grasping the character of Paula Alquist's essential frailty, but she would complain, "Oh, I look so **healthy.**" However, I think healthy people can be frightened. In fact, very often it's perhaps more moving. . . . [The film] was helped too by Charles Boyer's unorthodox style in the role of Paula Alquist's tormentor, Gregory Anton; he has a kind of line, a manner of implacable coldness, and he kept that up all the time. . . . This was Angela Lansbury's very first picture . . . from the day she started she was so completely professional and authoritative that she absolutely **was** that girl Nancy. She could also sing and dance and was altogether enormously gifted.

In preparing for her role Ingrid was advised by director Cukor that she should visit a mental institution to observe patients who have been driven to the brink of insanity and beyond. The

---

[1]The British film version of **Gaslight** starred Diana Wynward, Anton Walbrook, and Frank Pettingell. In 1952 surviving prints were utilized for its U.S. release, distributed under the title **Angel Street.**

[2]Cotten's role on stage, as played on Broadway by Leo G. Carroll, was that of a colorful eccentric. The part lost a great deal in its metamorphosis to young romantic.

Swedish actress later remarked, "one young woman there interested me and much of her strange qualities went into my characterization."

When **Gaslight** opened at New York's Capitol Theatre on May 4, 1944, the play **Angel Street** was still playing just a few blocks away. One of the ad lines used to promote the film was "This is love . . . clouded by evil . . . darkened by a secret no one dared to guess! . . . The strange drama of a captive sweetheart!" The love themes interpreted in the motion picture are not of the usual Hollywood variety. As Curtis Brown details in **Ingrid Bergman** (1973):

> Cukor, who gave the film its inner pulse, sees to it that the theme — the kinds of love—is distinctly revealed in the way each of the two principals reacts in the presence of the beloved. For Bergman, it is love devoid of experience, as well as sexual dependence on a "matinee idol" husband. For Boyer, it is love of jewels. The expression of rapture on Boyer's face, seen in close-up, as he describes the crown jewels in the Tower of London, is, along with the scene in which he discovers the jewelry he has almost driven a woman to madness for, the only moment of real love in the film. Both Boyer and Cukor make these episodes memorable.

Journals such as the **New York Times** expressed regret that the movie version strayed from the play's structure (that is, expanding the original plot's time lapse from twelve hours to several years, and extending the story locale from the house itself to many settings). The **Times** thought these changes caused the film to lose "much of the fearful immediacy of the play." However, the **New York Sun,** with others, was more impressed, "**Gaslight,** with its luscious costumes, striking photography, good acting, sinister atmosphere, and a plot that depends upon a gradual accumulation of detail, is heavy melodrama, so well produced that it makes absorbing entertainment." **Variety** penned, "It is an apparently expensive production in the usual Metro tradition, and Boyer, as the homicidal husband, Miss Bergman, as the wife, Cotten, the detective, have given carefully studied, restrained performances that have captured the full intent of the script."

It would be the **New York Post**'s Archer Winsten who pointed out the film's two best performances. Of Miss Bergman's interpretation of the young woman who finds confidence through love, then is driven almost to insanity, and who finally gains the upper hand over her persecutor, the critic wrote, "[Her] mingling of love, terror, and the growing sense of her own mind's failure represents one of the better achievements of the season." As for Miss Lansbury, who portrayed the bold tart (and who sang the teasing "Up in a Balloon, Boys"), Winsten observed, "[She] calls to mind one of Bette Davis's most famous efforts in **Of Human Bondage.**"

In the 1944 Oscar contest, **Gaslight** was well represented. It was nominated for Best Picture (the winner: Paramount's **Going My Way**); Best Actor (Boyer lost to Bing Crosby of **Going My Way**); and Best Supporting Actress (Lansbury lost to Ethel Barrymore of RKO's **None but the Lonely Heart**). But the production had several victories: Ingrid Bergman (who defeated an impressive lineup of Best Actress nominees: Claudette Colbert of United Artists' **Since You Went Away,** Bette Davis of Warner Bros.' **Mr. Skeffington,** Greer Garson of MGM's **Mrs. Parkington,** and Barbara Stanwyck of Paramount's **Double Indemnity**); and Cedric Gibbons, William Ferrari, Edwin B. Willis, and Paul Huldschinsky (Best Black-and-White Interior Design).

In a year when Victorian costume melodrama had high appeal for audiences (Twentieth Century–Fox's **The Lodger;** Producers Releasing Corporation's **Bluebeard,** etc.), **Gaslight** was the major success. It also began the start of a MGM contract for Angela Lansbury, who recently remarked, "I happened to see **Gaslight** not long ago on television. I was amazed. I thought, My God, how did I have all that assurance!"

As often befalls classics—and **Gaslight** is a minor one—it served later as the basis of satire. In the mid 1950s Jack Benny decided to parody the MGM film in a skit on his TV comedy show. The takeoff, titled "Autolight," costarred him with Barbara Stanwyck. The segment led to a complex infringement lawsuit, hinging on whether a large piece of copyrighted material might be used in a parody. After many rounds in the courts, the program was eventually telecast.

GIGI
1958 C—116 min.

Producer, Arthur Freed; **directors,** Vincente Minnelli and, **uncredited,** Charles Walters; based on the novel by Colette; **screenplay-lyrics,** Alan Jay Lerner; **music,** Frederick Loewe; **music supervisor/director,** Andre Previn; **orchestrator,** Conrad Salinger; **vocal supervisor,** Robert Tucker; **costumes, production designer, scenery,** Cecil Beaton; **art directors,** William A. Horning and Preston Ames; **set decorators,** Henry Grace and Keogh Gleason, **color consultant,** Charles K. Hagedon; **assistant directors,** William McGarry and William Shanks; **makeup,** William Tuttle and Charles Parker; **hairstyles,** Sydney Guilaroff and Guillaume; **sound,** Dr. Wesley C. Miller; **camera,** Joseph Ruttenberg and Ray June; **editor,** Adrienne Fazan.

Leslie Caron **(Gigi);** Maurice Chevalier **(Honoré Lachaille);** Louis Jourdan **(Gaston Lachaille);** Hermione Gingold **(Mme Alvarez);** Eva Gabor **(Liane d'Exelmans);** Jacques Bergerac **(Sandomir);** Isabel Jeans **(Aunt Alicia);** John Abbott **(Manuel);** Monique Van Vooren **(Showgirl);** Lydia Stevens **(Simone);** Edwin Jerome **(Charles, the Butler);** Dorothy Neumann **(Designer);** Marilyn Sims **(Redhead);** Richard Bean **(Harlequin);** Pat Sheahan **(Blonde);** Leroy Winebrenner **(Lifeguard),** Marya Ploss **(Model);** Jack Trevan **(Coachman).**

SYNOPSIS
In 1900 Paris, Gaston Lachaille, dapper, bored bon vivant, finds relief from his constant tedium of elegant soirées and beautiful women in the humor of his confidant and playboy uncle, Honoré Lachaille. Gaston is also amused by the innocence of a young acquaintance named Gigi. The French girl is in the midst of an arduous training program, courtesy of her grandmama, Mme Alvarez (an old flame of Honoré's),[1] and her Aunt Alicia, a retired courtesan.

After being cuckolded by his lady of the moment, Liane d'Exelmans, when she embarks on a tryst with her handsome skating instructor Sandomir, Gaston takes Gigi and Mme Alvarez on a vacation to Trouville—and finds himself attracted to the blossoming young lady whom he had always regarded as a child.

Upon returning to Paris, Gaston begins squiring Gigi about the city and plans to make her his mistress. However, the naive Gigi, lacking the cattiness of most of her peers, fails in her attempts to be a "woman of the world." Gaston retracts his mistress arrangement and proposes marriage to Gigi. She accepts.

* * *

In May 1958 **My Fair Lady,** in its third year on Broadway, was playing to capacity at New York's Mark Hellinger Theatre on 51st Street. Meanwhile, six blocks away, at the Royale Theatre on 45th Street, MGM's new cinema musical **Gigi** was playing to a full house, where audiences applauded the glamorous maturing of the title character (Leslie Caron), the elegant ennui of her beau (Louis Jourdan), the Alan Jay Lerner–Frederick Loewe score, and the beautiful Cecil Beaton costumes. The close similarities between the two musicals, which shared identical composers, costumers, and plot parallels, escaped few. As Bosley Crowther wrote in his **New York Times** review of **Gigi,** "There won't be much point in anybody trying to produce a film of **My Fair Lady** for a while, because Arthur Freed has virtually done it with **Gigi** . . . a musical film that bears such a basic resemblance to **My Fair Lady** that the authors may want to sue themselves."[2]

Gigi, of course, was more than a mere Parisian-set parroting of the Shavian musical: it was by itself a glittering jewel of a color film, the winner of nine Oscars and, in many ways, the apex of Arthur Freed's musical reign at MGM.

"Why does Arthur want to make a picture about a whore?" was the battle cry of many MGM potentates who opposed Freed's expansive plans to bring Colette's novel through a grand musical evolution. The charming French tale of a young girl trained to be the perfect mistress who instead finds matrimony had already been adapted into an acclaimed French film (1948) and a 1951 Broadway show (which made an American star of Audrey Hepburn). Freed, however, had solid faith in the film's potentialities, a belief he very much needed as **Gigi** slowly formulated.

Adaptation. The initial enemy to Gigi's emergence was the film industry censorship of-

---

[1]Gigi's mama, who also resides with Mme Alvarez, is a minor performer at the Comique Opera. She is heard rehearsing vocal exercises, but is never seen throughout the proceedings.

[2]Leslie Caron's song "Say a Prayer for Me" within **Gigi** had originally been created for the stage version of **My Fair Lady.**

Louis Jordan, Leslie Caron, and Maurice Chevalier in Gigi *('58).*

fice, which objected to the scenario on five points, the first and major one being, "**All** the characters in this story participate, or did participate, or intend to participate, in a man-mistress relationship." MGM's clever adaptation was contrived to emphasize Gaston's boredom at his easy-virtue life; and Gigi's reaction to his suggestion that she become his mistress was to be one of horror, thereby making the denouement perfectly aboveboard. The naughty tones of the original tale were thus whitewashed satisfactorily for the censors.

After the original French film (to which the late Colette herself had contributed some of the dialogue) had been studied, Alan Jay Lerner began writing the screenplay. At first he opposed writing the lyrics, but the enthusiasm of his collaborator Frederick Loewe for the film and his own joy as the movie progressed soon convinced him otherwise. There was one costly sidelight at this point. Stage producer Gilbert Miller and his associates (including writer Anita Loos, who was the first to interest Freed in the project when she discussed its controversial sex theme in a letter to him) also owned rights to the Colette property, which they hoped to transform into a Broadway musical. Freed had to pay them $87,000 to abort their already announced show. (Colette's widower received $125,000 for the screen rights from Metro.)

Casting. From the beginning there was a disagreement as to which actress should interpret the title role. Lerner wanted Audrey Hepburn of the Broadway cast; some at MGM touted Pier Angeli, Freed wanted Leslie Caron, the French actress who had scored in MGM's **An American in Paris** (1951) and **Lili** (1953), and who had recently

played in the non-musical version of **Gigi** with great success on the London stage. The argument was settled when Miss Hepburn declined the role; Betty Wand would dub Caron's on-camera vocals. For the part of Honoré, Gaston's aging roué adviser, Maurice Chevalier was a natural choice, and immediately accepted. (He had been a personal friend of Colette's and an admirer of both the French film and Lerner-Loewe's **My Fair Lady.**) Gaston was less easily cast. Lerner suggested Dirk Bogarde, but he was unavailable. The role was finally taken on by Louis Jourdan with much reluctance—he feared the demands of the singing assignment. Hermione Gingold, then a popular favorite with late-night audiences because of her spots on Jack Paar's TV talk show, landed the part of Gigi's grandmama; Isabel Jeans, the veteran actress, was suggested by George Cukor for the part of Aunt Alicia, Gigi's tutor. Eva Gabor was assigned to be Liane, Gaston's amoral mistress, and Jacques Bergerac (Ginger Rogers' ex-spouse), at the insistence of Miss Gabor, played Sandomir, the lascivious skating instructor. Bergerac replaced actor Richard Winckler and earned $5,000 for three days' work.

Shooting. There were twenty-four days of location filming in France to ensure proper settings and atmosphere. Among the sights captured on screen: the Bois de Boulogne, Palais de Glace, Montfort-l'Amaury, Musée Jacquemart-André, Maxim's, La Grande Cascade Restaurant, Court de Rohan, Avenue Rapp, Jardin des Tuileries, Place Furstenburg, Place du Palais Bourbon, Jardin du Luxembourg, Jardin de Bagatelle, Pont Alexandre, and Trouville. When production ran close

to $500,000 over budget, the company was forced to return to the MGM Culver City lot for thirty-five days of additional shooting.

Problems. There were many. The hot August weather repeatedly caused the many beautiful showgirls, in heavy 1900s Parisian fashions and tight corsets, to faint; foul weather plagued the lensing of the Trouville beach sequence;[3] director Vincent Minnelli (who would have an uncredited assist from Charles Walters) became very ill after a swan bit him in the Jardin de Bagatelle; Jourdan walked off the picture temporarily after Freed said his singing sounded "just like [Rex] Harrison's." Even after these difficulties were solved, Freed was not satisfied with the superior results of the previews, and **Gigi** went back into production at Metro for eleven days of retakes and added scenes. Finally, after a cost of $3,319,335, **Gigi** was completed.

All the turmoil in achieving the final results was justified when **Gigi** played its new previews. Metro rented Broadway's Royale Theatre, a stage house, for the film's premiere engagement. While there was some critical carping, notably from **Time** magazine ("If all the French finery impresses the customers, it also smothers the story . . . the physical exuberance of the production flusters the pensive sensuality of Colette's mood"), the film reaped mainly huzzahs: "An exquisite work of art" (**New York Herald-Tribune**); "One hundred percent escapist fare. . . . Replete with taste from its sartorial investiture to the ultimate histrionic performances" (**Variety**); "One of the most elegant and tasteful musicals that MGM has ever turned out . . . a hugely enjoyable show" (**Saturday Review**).

The film collected nine Oscars: Best Film, Best Director (Minnelli), Best Writing based material from another medium (Lerner), Best Color Cinematography (Joseph Ruttenberg), Best Art and Set Direction (William A. Horning–Preston Ames, Henry Grace–Keogh Gleason), Best Song ("Gigi"), Best Scoring (André Previn), Best Costume Design (Cecil Beaton),[4] Best Film Editing

---

[3]In the beach sequence of "I Remember It Well" the lifeguard is played by Leroy Winebrenner, known in the 1930s as Paramount's Baby Leroy, and as such, a one-time costar of Chevalier.

[4]Stanley Kauffmann (**The New Republic**) would insist, "**Gigi** is consistently pleasant, but is extraordinary in only one way. Do not be deceived by the advertising; the real star is Cecil Beaton, who designed the costumes and scenery. When the story ambles and the songs don't quite soar, the clothes and settings continue to enchant. A deaf man could enjoy **Gigi**. . . . There is, beyond Beaton's designs, one unmixed blessing in the picture. Someone had the happy thought of writing in an uncle for Gaston, an aging philosophical **boulevardier**, and of giving the part to Maurice Chevalier. Every time Chevalier approaches, one mutters, 'No, it's too silly, I'm not going to be charmed by a man who deliberately sets out to charm me'; and every time, Chevalier prevails. . . . It is interesting to note how any hint of distastefulness—in the idea of the two old women raising a girl to be a courtesan, in Chevalier's waiting around for little girls to grow up, in Jourdan's financial offer—has been kept out of the film. The movie-makers have caught Colette's flavor in the matter. The boundaries of the story are firmly marked and, within them, the char-

(Adrienne Fazan), making **Gigi** the most Academy Award–lauded musical in history. In addition, Chevalier received a special Oscar ("for his contribution to the world of entertainment for more than half a century"). **Gigi** also won the **Photoplay** magazine Gold Medal, placed third in the **Film Daily** Ten Best picture poll and tenth in the National Board of Review's Top Ten pictures, and grossed $7,263,000 in U.S. and Canadian distributor rentals.

A none too impressive footnote to **Gigi**: In May 1973 the San Francisco–Los Angeles Civic Light Opera mounted a stage version of the Lerner and Loewe classic; it premiered on Broadway at the Uris Theatre on November 16, 1973. The all-star cast included Alfred Drake as Honoré, Daniel Massey as Gaston, Agnes Moorehead as Aunt Alicia, Maria Karnilova as Grandmama, and newcomer Karen Wolfe as Gigi. It was an unhappy production; Miss Moorehead was dying of cancer, and there were problems with a male star's egomania. The show closed on February 10, 1974, but did receive a major Tony Award for best musical score.

GIRL CRAZY
1943—99 min.

Mickey Rooney, Judy Garland, and Tommy Dorsey and His Orchestra in Girl Crazy *('43).*

Producer, Arthur Freed; **directors,** Norman Taurog and, **uncredited,** Busby Berkeley; based on the musical play by George and Ira Gershwin, Guy Bolton, and John McGowan; **screenplay,** Fred F. Finklehoffe and, **uncredited:** William Ludwig, Dorothy Kingsley, and Sid Silvers; **assistant director,** Joseph Boyle; **music adapter,** Roger Edens; **music director,** George Stoll; **orchestrators,** Conrad Salinger, Axel Stordahl, and Sy Oliver; **vocal arrangers,** Hugh Martin and Ralph Blane; **dance director,** Charles Walters; "I Got Rhythm" number directed by Berkeley; **art director,** Cedric Gibbons; **set decorators,** Edwin B. Willis and Mac Alper; **costume supervisor,** Irene; **costume associate,** Irene Sharaff; **sound,** Douglas Shearer; **camera,** William Daniels and Robert Planck; **editor,** Albert Akst.

Mickey Rooney (**Danny Churchill, Jr.**); Judy Garland (**Ginger Gray**); Gil Stratton (**Bud Livermore**); Robert E. Strickland (**Henry Lathrop**); Rags Ragland (**Rags**); June Allyson (**Specialty Number**); Nancy Walker (**Polly Williams**); Guy Kibbee (**Dean Phineas Armour**); Tommy Dorsey and His Orchestra (**Themselves**); Frances Rafferty (**Marjorie Tait**); Howard Freeman (**Governor Tait**); Henry O'Neill (**Mr. Churchill, Sr.**); Sidney Miller (**Ed**); Eve Whitney (**Brunette**); Carole Gallagher and Kay Williams (**Blondes**); Jess Lee Brooks (**Buckets**); Roger Moore (**Cameraman**); Charles Coleman (**Maitre d'Hotel**); Harry Depp (**Nervous Man**); Richard Kipling (**Dignified Man**); Henry Roquemore (**Fat Man**); Alphonse Martel (**Waiter**); Barbara Bedford (**Churchill's Secretary**); William Beaudine, Jr. (**Tom**); Irving Bacon (**Reception Clerk**); Katherine Booth (**Girl**); Hazel Brooks, Noreen Nash, Natalie Draper, Inez Cooper, and Linda Deane (**Showgirls**); Don Taylor, Jimmy Butler, Peter Lawford, John Estes, and Bob Lowell (**Boys**); Sarah Edwards (**Governor's Secretary**); William Bishop, James Warren, and Fred Beckner, Jr. (**Radio Men**); Spec O'Donnell (**Fiddle Player**).

SYNOPSIS
Young Manhattan playboy Danny Churchill, Jr. makes a habit of squiring pretty girls to posh nightclubs, a situation his newspaper publisher father abhors. When Danny's photo appears in a newspaper depicting him being kissed by a bevy of beauties, the elder Churchill orders his son to Cody College, an all-male institution in the hinterlands of Arizona.

At Cody, Danny meets Dean Phineas Armour and his granddaughter Ginger Gray (who also runs the local post office). Among his costudents are Henry Lathrop and Bud Livermore. Danny takes an immediate dislike to the rigors of the Arizona college. His only friend is Rags, the school caretaker and a former Manhattanite. Ginger later convinces Danny to remain at Cody. He, in turn, declares his love for her.

Bad news comes in the form of a state legislative decision to close Cody College because of the enrollment decline. Ginger and Danny visit Governor Tait, who agrees to refrain signing the bill for two months while the students prepare a Western rodeo to attract publicity as well as more applicants. While visiting the state capital, Danny attends the coming-out ball for the governor's comely daughter Marjorie.

Danny lures all of the area's debutantes to Cody's rodeo by promising each one that she will be rodeo queen. This guarantees that "one hundred beautiful girls" will be in attendance. At the rodeo the contest is narrowed down to Ginger and Marjorie. Aware of the publicity involved in naming the governor's daughter rodeo queen, Danny crowns Marjorie while Ginger stands by nobly, concealing her hurt and disappointment.

Later Danny explains his strategy, and the incoming mail reveals hundreds of new applicants, a fact which boosts Ginger's spirits.

* * *

"Hold your hats, folks!" said the **New York Times'** Theodore Strauss after watching **Girl Crazy.** "Mickey Rooney and Judy Garland are back in town. And if at this late date there are still a few diehards who deny that they are the most incorrigibly talented pair of youngsters in movies, then **Girl Crazy** should serve as a final rebuttal." The ninth[1] Rooney-Garland opus had opened, and as the ads proclaimed,

Judy and Mickey!
Joy and Music!

---

[1]Plans for Rooney and Garland to star in 1941 in **Good News** failed to materialize; **Born to Sing** (1942) was originally intended for the duo, but it was reduced to a B musical, featuring Virginia Weidler, Ray MacDonald, and Douglas McPhail.

---

acters take their ethics seriously, different from ours though they may be. . . ."

They're Together Again and When They're Together It's a Grand, Happy Show!
It's Got Rhythm!
It's Got Comedy!
It's Got G-A-L-S!

With the old George and Ira Gershwin show[2] tailored for the talents of Mickey and Judy, MGM set out to prove again that the movies had no more talented a pair of performing youths.

Mickey and Judy agreed wholeheartedly.

By 1943 Rooney was twenty-two (already married and divorced from Ava Gardner), Garland was twenty (in the midst of an unsuccessful marriage to David Rose). Both players were fast maturing to their performing peaks. But just as their talents were sharpening, their egos were enlarging. As such, **Girl Crazy** became one of the most headachy productions of the Arthur Freed unit as Judy and Mickey began tossing about their power on the Metro lot.

The film used the full Gershwin score: "Sam and Delilah," "Treat Me Rough," "Bidin' My Time," "Embraceable You," "Do," "Barbary Coast," "But Not for Me," and "I Got Rhythm." "Fascinating Rhythm" was borrowed from the Gershwins' **Lady Be Good,** and Roger Edens added "Happy Birthday, Ginger." The Gershwin tunes "When It's Cactus Time in Arizona" and "Boy, What Love Has Done for me" were employed as background music. A raucous number, "Bronco Busters," featuring Garland, Rooney, and Nancy Walker, would be recorded, but deleted from the feature.

Girl Crazy began production on January 4, 1943, and almost immediately there were apparently insurmountable problems. Berkeley began three weeks of rehearsals and shooting for the big "I Got Rhythm" number, which was to feature Garland, Rooney, Tommy Dorsey and His Orchestra, and numerous dancers. Musical adapter Roger Edens later commented on his disagreements with Berkeley:

We disagreed basically about the number's presentation. I wanted it rhythmic and simply staged; but Berkeley got his big ensembles and trick cameras into it again, plus a lot of girls in western outfits, with fringe skirts and people cracking whips, firing guns . . . and cannons going off all over my arrangement and Judy's voice. Well, we shouted at each other, and I said, "There wasn't enough room on the lot for both of us."

The number was completed (at an extra cost of $97,418.99 to the budget, which eventually soared to $1,410,850.85, some $323,000 over its estimated cost). Freed then shut down the pro-

duction and dismissed Berkeley from the unit (he would be loaned to Twentieth Century-Fox for Alice Faye's **The Gang's All Here**). A month later **Girl Crazy** resumed shooting, this time with Norman Taurog as director. Garland, who could not (would not) cope with dictatorial, precision-oriented Berkeley, got along much better with "Uncle" Norman.

This was not the end of the troubles. Rooney, meanwhile, had grown fond of Palm Springs, and requested—and then demanded—that the company report there for a ten-day location shooting junket (for filming of the "Could You Use Me" automobile song number). Off went the troupe into the 112-degree heat of that desert resort, only to have Rooney contract a painful sunburn. Not idle during all of this was Judy Garland. She had become enmeshed in a new romance. One night on location, she left without word for a Los Angeles rendezvous. The cast and crew were left to cope with a particularly nasty example of one of Palm Springs' notorious windstorms. While Judy was AWOL, the company generally spent the time cursing and getting drunk at the Desert Inn, the only "luxury" hotel there at the time. Ironically, in the sandstorm part of the equipment was damaged, and eventually a goodly portion of the number had to be restaged back at the studio.

By May 14, 1943, the film was through shooting. It proved to be quite a show. There were the Tommy Dorsey orchestra, Freed's beautiful "Du Barry" girls (who had sent a letter to the producer requesting a pay raise from $60 to $75 per week), and dozens of attractive hopefuls as the college kids—including Peter Lawford and Don Taylor. On tap were June Allyson in a bouncy specialty club number, Nancy Walker as a wise-cracking zany on the campus, and Frances Rafferty as the governor's daughter (who towers over Rooney in height and refinement). Especially effective in the film was Rags Ragland, MGM's ex-burlesque comedian contractee. His stereotyped portrayal of the dumb but sensitive handyman was a standout, especially in the tender sequence wherein he consoles Garland, she being convinced she has lost Rooney's affections forever.

Some critics agreed with Wanda Hale's **(New York Daily News)** reservations about the film: "Not one of Mickey's, Judy's, or MGM's best musicals, it will do quite nicely until a better one comes along." But Otis L. Guernsey, Jr. **(New York Herald-Tribune)** cheered: "Chalk up another musical comedy triumph for the Rooney-Garland team," and **Time** magazine approved Rooney as "a natural dancer and comedian. . . . [Garland's] presence is open, cheerful, and warming. If she were not so profitably good at her own game, she could obviously be a dramatic cinema actress with profits to all." The audience found little over which to quibble, and **Girl Crazy** grossed $3,771,000 in its initial release.

Memorable scenes included: Rooney performing imitations of a tennis match announcer and boxing announcer, Judy waltzing with Chuck Walters (her dance partner of **Presenting Lily Mars,** 1943) for "Embraceable You"; Judy's solos of "Embraceable You" and "But Not for Me"; Judy teaming with Mickey for "I Got Rhythm" (the fi-

nale) and "Could You Use Me"; and the above-mentioned Allyson rendition of "Treat Me Rough," in which nightclub patron Mickey becomes entangled in a vigorous onstage workout.

Girl Crazy was the last vehicle built around the team of Garland and Rooney. In 1944 Rooney joined the army and when he returned to MGM, he had outgrown some of his typical juvenile roles (although he would be sandwiched in one more 1940s **Andy Hardy** picture). While he was the co-star of the highly fictional and ludicrous biography of Richard Rodgers (Tom Drake) and Lorenz Hart (Rooney), **Words and Music** (1948), Judy appeared in the film only as a special performer. During Garland's 1963–64 CBS-TV variety show series, Rooney appeared as one of her guests.

MGM remade **Girl Crazy** as **When the Boys Meet the Girls** (1965), a dull reworking of the plot line, starring Connie Francis and Harve Presnell.

GONE WITH THE WIND
1939 C—219 min.

Producer, David O. Selznick; **directors,** Victor Fleming and, **uncredited:** George Cukor and Sam Wood; based on the novel by Margaret Mitchell; **screenplay,** Sidney Howard and, **uncredited:** Jo Swerling, Charles MacArthur, John Van Druten, Oliver H. P. Garrett, Winston Miller, John Balderston, Michael Foster, Edwin Justus Mayer, and F. Scott Fitzgerald; **production designer,** William Cameron Menzies; **interiors,** Joseph B. Platt; **art director,** Lyle Wheeler; **set decorator,** Edward G. Boyle; **makeup** and **hairstyling,** Monty Westmore, Hazel Rogers, Ben Nye; **historian,** Wilbur G. Kurtz; **technical advisers,** Susan Myrick and Will Price; **second-unit director,** Reeves Eason; **research,** Lillian K. Deighton; **Technicolor supervisors,** Natalie Kalmus and Henri Jaffa; **assistant directors,** Eric G. Stacey and Ridgeway Callow; **music,** Max Steiner; **choreography,** Frank Floyd and Eddie Prinz; **special effects,** Jack Cosgrove and Lee Zavitz; **sound,** Frank Maher; **camera,** Ernest Haller, Ray Rennahan, and **uncredited:** Lee Garmes; **editors,** Hal C. Kern and James E. Newcom.

Clark Gable **(Rhett Butler);** Vivien Leigh **(Scarlett O'Hara);** Leslie Howard **(Ashley Wilkes);** Olivia de Havilland **(Melanie Hamilton);** Hattie McDaniel **(Mammy);** Thomas Mitchell **(Gerald O'Hara);** Barbara O'Neil **(Ellen O'Hara);** Laura Hope Crews **(Aunt Pittypat Hamilton);** Harry Davenport **(Dr. Meade);** Ona Munson **(Belle Watling);** Evelyn Keyes **(Suellen O'Hara);** Ann Rutherford **(Careen O'Hara);** Butterfly McQueen **(Prissy);** Alicia Rhett **(India Wilkes);** Everett Brown **(Big Sam);** Eddie Anderson **(Uncle Peter);** Rand Brooks **(Charles Hamilton);** Carroll Nye **(Frank Kennedy);** Jane Darwell **(Mrs. Merriwether);** Mary Anderson **(Maybelle Merriwether);** Isabel Jewell **(Emmy Slattery);** Victor Jory **(Jonas Wilkerson);** Yakima Canutt **(Renegade/Double for Clark Gable);** Cammie King **(Bonnie Blue Butler);** Lillian Kemble-Cooper **(Bonnie's Nurse);** Ward Bond **(Tom, a Yankee Captain);** Paul Hurst **(Yankee Deserter);** George Reeves **(Stuart Tarleton);** Fred Crane **(Brent Tarleton);**

---

[2]**Girl Crazy,** with book by Guy Bolton and John McGowan, lyrics by Ira Gershwin, and music by George Gershwin, had played 272 Broadway performances, with a cast featuring Ginger Rogers, Willie Howard, and Ethel Merman. It debuted on October 14, 1930. In 1932 RKO had released a film version, revamping it as a vehicle for the comedy team of Bert Wheeler and Robert Woolsey and employing only a small fraction of the marvelous Gershwin score. In 1939, MGM announced plans to star Eddie Cantor in the property but the concept was shelved.

Marcella Martin (**Cathleen Calvert**); Jackie Moran (**Phil Meade**); Cliff Edwards (**Reminiscent Soldier**); Ed Chandler (**The Sergeant**); George Hackathorne (**Wounded Soldier in Pain**); Roscoe Ates (**Convalescent Soldier**); John Arledge (**Dying Soldier**); Eric Linden (**Amputation Case**); Guy Wilkerson (**Wounded Card Player**); Tom Tyler (**Commanding Officer During Evacuation**); Frank Faylen (**Soldier Aiding Dr. Meade**); Lee Phelps (**Bartender During Siege**); Ernest Whitman (**Carpetbagger's Friend**); William Stelling (**Returning Veteran**); Louis Jean Heydt (**Hungry Soldier**); Irving Bacon (**Corporal During Reconstruction**); Si Jenks (**Yankee on Street**); Harry Strang (**Tom's Aide**); Mickey Kuhn (**Beau Wilkes**); Marjorie Reynolds and Tom Seidel (**Guests**).

Vivien Leigh at Tara in Gone with the Wind *('39).*

SYNOPSIS

It is April 1861 and still the most glorious era of the South. And no other plantation in Clayton County, Georgia, is more bountiful than Tara, the cherished and realized dream of Irish immigrant Gerald O'Hara and his wife Ellen. "Land is the only thing worth living for, worth dying for," he informs his family, including daughters Scarlett, Suellen, and Careen, "for it's the only thing that lasts."

Such words mean little to the eldest daughter, sixteen-year-old Scarlett O'Hara. Fiery and flirtatious, she captivates the attentions of most of the eligible young men of northern Georgia. She, however, is most obsessed with Ashley Wilkes, the blond, sensitive aristocrat. Much to Scarlett's anxiety, he is deeply in love with his selfless cousin Melanie Hamilton. The incensed Scarlett vows to herself that some day she will snare Ashley from the trusting arms of the gentle Melanie.

Meanwhile, war talk has inflamed the passions of the South and there comes to Tara one Rhett Butler—the roguish, dapper black sheep of a Charleston family that has acquired a glamorously amoral reputation. Rhett irks the Southern gentlemen by professing little optimism in Dixie's chances against the well-equipped Northern armies, but he captivates Scarlett, who impresses Rhett as a perfect lover—spirited, self-centered, arrogant, and ruthless. Yet Scarlett, flushed by Ashley's marriage to Melanie, forgets Rhett as she weds Melanie's bland brother Charles in an attempt to end the rumors circulating about her and Ashley.

War breaks out and Ashley leaves for the battles, Charles ungallantly dies in training camp, and Melanie in Atlanta survives a rugged pregnancy, abetted by Scarlett and hysterical slave Prissy.

When General Sherman begins his bloody bombardment of Atlanta, Scarlett, who has been living there with Melanie and her Aunt Pittypat, seeks to escape and return to Tara. Fate propels her into the protection of Rhett Butler, now a very successful war profiteer. He aids Scarlett, Melanie (and her young infant), and Prissy in escaping the conflagration. Once again, Scarlett is strongly drawn to the virile Captain Butler, but

they separate after the escape. She returns to Tara.

The war has transformed Tara into a grotesque nightmare. Scarlett's mother has succumbed to typhoid, her father has gone insane, and the Union army has reduced the estate to a shambles. The weak-willed younger sisters are unable to stop the deterioration, so Scarlett takes the challenge upon herself. There are hideous disasters: a Union looter attempts to shoot Scarlett, and she shoots him in the face; Jonas Wilkerson, Tara overseer-turned-carpetbagger, tries to snare the estate for himself and his white-trash bride Emmy; and Gerald O'Hara dies from a horse fall suffered as he dementedly chases Wilkerson off the property. Notwithstanding, Scarlett vows, "I'll never be hungry again!" and conquers the obstacles before her.

With Tara "saved," Scarlett hurls herself into business deals during Reconstruction, and traps a wealthy businessman husband, Frank Kennedy, who had been her sister's beau. Still foremost in her mind, however, is to claim Ashley, who has returned from the war completely crushed spiritually. When Scarlett is later attacked by a squad of white-and-black-trash as she brazenly drives about in her carriage—and is saved by the intervention of former slave Big Sam—Kennedy, Ashley, and some others form a posse. Their aim is to drive the undesirables out. In the effort Ashley is wounded and Kennedy is killed. Thereafter Rhett Butler arduously courts Scarlett until she agrees to be his wife.

Rhett does everything he can to make Scar-

lett happy. He restores Tara to exquisite beauty, presents his wife with lavish gifts, and becomes a doting father to their little daughter Bonnie. However, Scarlett's quest for Ashley continues—and plagues Rhett. One night, after Scarlett calls Rhett a "drunken fool," he forcibly lifts her into his arms and carries her upstairs to the boudoir.

The death of Bonnie in a fall from her horse, leads to the dissolution of Rhett and Scarlett's marriage. Soon after Bonnie's death, Melanie, always weak, dies. Now Scarlett finally realizes that Ashley had only one genuine love in his life, Melanie; that she had been foolish ever to think otherwise. But this insight comes too late. Rhett has packed his bag and is leaving his wife forever. Scarlett sobs, "What will become of me?" Rhett turns in the doorway and replies, "Frankly, my dear, I don't give a damn."

Alone, Scarlett bitterly weeps, then controls herself, remembering her watchword of survival, "Tomorrow is another day."

* * *

Forget it, Louis. No Civil War picture ever made a nickel.
> Irving Thalberg to Louis B. Mayer
> May 1936

Have gone over and carefully thought about **Gone With the Wind** . . . its background is very strongly against it . . . most sorry to have to say no in face of your enthusiasm for this story.
> David O. Selznick to literary agent
> Katharine Brown
> May 1936

Vivien Leigh and Leslie Howard at Twelve Oaks.

I don't want the part for money, chalk, or marbles.

> Clark Gable to David O. Selznick
> 1938

This woman is a terrible bitch!

> Vivien Leigh on Scarlett O'Hara
> 1939

I haven't the slightest intention of playing another weak, watery character such as Ashley Wilkes. I've played enough ineffectual characters already.

> Leslie Howard to David O. Selznick
> 1938

Oh, you don't want to be in **Gone With the Wind**; it's going to be the biggest bust of all time.

> Jack L. Warner to Olivia de Havilland
> 1938

Don't be a damn fool, David. This picture is going to be one of the biggest white elephants of all time.

> Victor Fleming to David O. Selznick
> 1939

When one considers the glories accrued over the past four decades to the now legendary **Gone With the Wind**, it is difficult for new generations to believe the amazing odyssey of this 1,037-page novel by Margaret Mitchell from hefty tome to laureled film. The movie won a record bevy of Oscars when originally released (ten, bested only by 1959's **Ben-Hur** with eleven), ranked high on Va-

riety's all-time film champs list (with a gross of over $76,700,000 in distributors' domestic rentals), reaped the highest price to date ($5 million) paid by a network (NBC-TV) for a single feature film program, and drew the largest TV audience (130 million) ever attracted by a television film. And in 1977 the classic was dubbed, by an official tabulation of the voting members of the American Film Institute, "The Greatest Film Ever Made."

The film was an incredible awesome gamble at the time. It was birthed amid expensive publicity campaigns, exploding tempers, nervous breakdowns, at least one suicide attempt, seemingly endless in-fighting, walkouts, and a heartbreaking sellout of one producer to another to achieve the prime ingredient to the motion picture's success—Clark Gable.

MGM is certainly due some of the accolades connected with this cinema milestone. The lot provided about thirty percent of the financing and the services of Gable, a product of the company's incredible starmaking system. However, the film version of **Gone With the Wind**, is, more than anything else, a tribute to the tenacity and perfectionism of David O. Selznick, who surmounted the idiosyncrasies of the world's most difficult if divine people—artists—to complete "The Greatest Film Ever Made."

Margaret Mitchell had little interest in motion pictures. In 1936, when David O. Selznick, after extensive thought and discussion, reversed his refusal of her novel (originally titled **Tomorrow**

Is Another Day) and purchased the screen rights for $50,000,[1] she was asked whom she envisioned in the leading part. Rhett Butler should be played by Groucho Marx, she replied. (Her actual choice for the part was Basil Rathbone, who genuinely pictured himself in the heroic role and coveted it greatly.)

Still, Selznick faced a problem. **Gone With the Wind** could not be filmed before 1939 because of the other studio commitments he had: 1936's **The Garden of Allah**, 1937's **A Star Is Born, The Prisoner of Zenda,** and **Nothing Sacred,** 1938's **The Adventures of Tom Sawyer** and **Young in Heart,** and 1939's **Made for Each Other.** How to keep public interest in the property was a major concern. Over the next two years, while a slew of scriptwriters came and went,[2] Selznick, aided in his crafty, elaborate campaign by public relations ace Russell Birdwell, conducted a "search" for the actress to play Scarlett O'Hara. It generated the anticipated excitement.

Over $92,000 was spent on this talent hunt: 1,400 women were interviewed before the cameras; 149,000 feet of black-and-white film and 13,000 feet of Technicolor film were shot; and $10,000 was spent to audition 59 candidates. Among the first of the major celebrities to test was Tallulah Bankhead, who was too old, too flamboyant and stagy, and certainly too acidy. Even a telegram from the governor of Alabama failed to convince Selznick that Miss Bankhead was an appropriate choice for the female lead. Many followed, including Frances Dee, Susan Hayward, Lana Turner, Lucille Ball, and Katharine Hepburn,[3] but none matched the fire and deadly coyness of Paulette Goddard. Selznick allegedly suggested to contractee Goddard that the part was hers, on one now famous condition: inform the press of her marriage **if** she was genuinely married to Charlie Chaplin. Paulette's tart reply—"It's none of their goddamn business." On went the search.

Meanwhile, there was little need to search for the proper Rhett Butler. With George Cukor set in late 1936 as director, Selznick wrote to chief aide Daniel T. O'Shea on January 4, 1937: "For your confidential information, Cukor and I jointly feel that the choice is in the following order: (1) Gable, (2) Gary Cooper, (3) Errol Flynn."[4] As the

---

[1]Selznick later paid the author another $50,000 after the enormous success of the feature film.

[2]Sidney Howard was the major writer, though Jo Swerling, Charles MacArthur, John Van Druten, Oliver H. P. Garrett, Winston Miller, John Balderston, Michael Foster, Edwin Justus Mayer, and F. Scott Fitzgerald worked from time to time on the script.

[3]Hepburn, who had been brought initially to the screen by Selznick and director George Cukor refused to test for the part, but agreed to be the unpublicized stand-by should the filmmakers fail to locate the proper actress in time to start filming.

[4]There is the oft-told story of how Jack L. Warner, in order to placate a rebeling Bette Davis, had offered to option **Gone With the Wind** as a vehicle for her, but that the actress, unaware of the potential of the yet to be published novel, rejected the bid; later she is said to

Harry Davenport, Vivien Leigh, and Laura Hope Crews.

film neared shooting, Selznick and staff realized that Gable's casting as Rhett was absolutely necessary to the commercial success of the film. However, Gable's screen services belonged to MGM, where Selznick had surmounted the "son-in-law-also-rises" jokes (he was wed to Mayer's daughter Irene) to produce such splendid feature films as **Dinner at Eight, David Copperfield, Anna Karenina, Viva Villa!** and **A Tale of Two Cities.**

Metro's terms for **Gone With the Wind** were stringent: Gable would be loaned to Selznick, and the studio would provide one-half of the estimated $2.5 million production cost, in exchange for which MGM would have releasing rights of the film and receive one-half of the profits. A humbled Selznick accepted this bargain easier than Gable. The star was determined not to play the part (he had suffered at the box office in the historical drama **Parnell,** 1937) the public had cast him in years before. (Spencer Tracy had enjoyed irking Gable on the Metro lot by greeting him with a beaming "Hi ya, Rhett!") As Clark later remarked, "I was scared when I discovered that I had been cast by the public. I felt that every reader would

have rejected a Warner Bros. packaging which would have included Errol Flynn as her leading man (she disliked him professionally) and Olivia de Havilland as Melanie. The making of **Jezebel** (1938) at Warner Bros. has long been regarded as her studio's consolation prize for losing out in the sweepstakes. Davis has long claimed that it was George Cukor, who had directed her in the 1920s in stock in Rochester, New York, who convinced Selznick she was not suitable for the role of Scarlett.

have a different idea as to how Rhett should be played on the screen, and I didn't see how I could please everybody." When press photographs were snapped on August 25, 1938, as Gable signed for the role, the weak smile on his face was more because of the $100,000 bonus he would receive for his work on **Gone With the Wind** than for the part itself. The money would enable him to divorce spouse Ria Lingham Gable and wed lover Carole Lombard.

In the meantime, the other leading roles were cast. Leslie Howard reluctantly agreed to perform as Ashley (a part almost won by either Melvyn Douglas or Jeffrey Lynn) after Selznick promised Howard he could function as associate producer on **Intermezzo** (1939). Olivia de Havilland signed to play Melanie after recruiting Jack L. Warner's wife to support her demand to be loaned to Selznick for the assignment. Other major players assembled included Thomas Mitchell (fresh from playing ever-inebriated Doc Boone in John Ford's **Stagecoach,** a performance which won him 1939's Best Supporting Actor Oscar) as Gerald O'Hara; Hattie McDaniel as Mammy (Hattie Noel and Louise Beavers were her principal competition), Barbara O'Neil as Mrs. O'Hara (Lillian Gish and Cornelia Otis Skinner were among the few considered for the part), Laura Hope Crews as Aunt Pittypat (Selznick was initially interested in Billie Burke for the role), Harry Davenport as Dr. Meade (originally considered was Lionel Barrymore), Ona Munson as Belle Watling (Selznick had asked Katharine Brown to ask Tallulah Bankhead, his rejected Scarlett, if she would be interested in this

showy role—"and for God's sake, don't mention my name in connection with it," he ordered—but Tallulah declined), Evelyn Keyes (a Cecil B. DeMille discovery) as Suellen O'Hara, Metro contractee Ann Rutherford as Careen O'Hara (a role Selznick previously envisioned for Judy Garland), and Butterfly McQueen as slow-witted Prissy. Even the smaller roles were cast with care: ever-glowering Victor Jory as wicked Jonas Wilkerson, familiar blonde screen tart Isabel Jewell as his white-trash wife, towering Ward Bond as Captain Tom, plump Jane Darwell as Mrs. Merriwether, and B cowboy player Tom Tyler as the commanding officer during Atlanta's evacuation.

Despite all these preparations, the key part of Scarlett was not yet cast. On November 21, 1938, Selznick confided to aide O'Shea that it should be "made clear" to Jean Arthur, Joan Bennett, Loretta Young, and (standby) Katharine Hepburn that they were "in the small company of final candidates.[5] Twenty days later, on the old Pathé lot, production began with the monumental burning of Atlanta, where old film scenery (including the gates of the native village from Selznick's **King Kong,** 1933) represented the bombarded city. As the flames illuminated the Culver City sky, David's brother, Myron Selznick, arrived with twenty-five year-old English actress Vivien Leigh. His famous words were, "Dave, I want you to meet Scarlett O'Hara."

On December 12, 1938, Selznick sent off a new memo, this time announcing that Scarlett was "narrowed down to Paulette, Jean Arthur, Joan Bennett and Vivien Leigh." (Obviously, Goddard's quality in the two tests was enough to torture Selznick with second thoughts, for he had earlier excluded her from the final lists.) On January 13, 1939, the search for Scarlett was officially ended when Vivien Leigh signed a pact with Selznick to play the cherished role (she had long coveted). Her fee: $30,000.

On January 26, 1939, principal shooting began on **Gone With the Wind;** on July 1, 1939, it ended. Between these dates problems erupted which had caused many lesser motion pictures to collapse. Among them:

Director problems. On February 13, 1939, less than three weeks after principal shooting

---

[5]Also considered from time to time during the hooplah of the Scarlett search were Miriam Hopkins, Claudette Colbert, Margaret Sullavan, Carole Lombard, and Ann Sheridan. As soon as MGM had signed the contractual papers with Selznick in August 1938, column items and studio announcements insisted that Norma Shearer would play Scarlett opposite Gable (her leading man in the soon to be filmed **Idiot's Delight**). Some insisted this was merely a studio ploy to shame the widow Thalberg into closing her career at Metro sooner than expected. When Shearer reportedly demanded that the second half of the storyline be revamped to make Scarlett a more sympathetic character, it was her death knell. She eventually withdrew, graciously smiling, "The one I'd like to play is Rhett Butler." At one point, Metro tried pressuring Selznick into casting Joan Crawford as Scarlett, Maureen O'Sullivan as Melanie, and Melvyn Douglas as Ashley, but the producer argued, "They would all be miscast."

The burning of Atlanta.

commenced, Selznick issued to the press this statement regarding George Cukor: "As a result of a series of disagreements between us over many of the individual scenes of **Gone With the Wind,** we have mutually decided that the only solution is for a new director to be selected at as early a date as is practicable. . . . Mr. Cukor's withdrawal . . . is the most regrettable incident of my rather long producing career. . . ." Cukor's reputation as a "woman's director" and his penchant for delving deeply into Scarlett's and Melanie's characters while "neglecting" the scope of the film were cited as a major cause. Less publicized at the time was the fact that Cukor made Gable uncomfortable. It irked Gable that Cukor was spending more time with the ladies in the cast than with him. It was Gable who was allotted the final word on selecting the new director from candidates Robert Z. Leonard, Jack Conway, King Vidor, and Victor Fleming. He chose crony Fleming, who proclaimed after perusing the script and the completed footage to date, "I'm going to make this picture a melodrama." Gable

was delighted; Leigh and de Havilland were aghast, and would meet Cukor at his home and out-of-the-way restaurants throughout the shooting for coaching in their roles.[6]

Script problems. Despite the surplus of able craftsmen who had worked on **Gone With the Wind** over a two-year span, there was still no fully authorized shooting script (part of Selznick's dissatisfaction with Cukor was that the director was shooting pages of dialogue and sequences the producer had not yet approved). Fleming's estimation of the script, "David, your f—— script is no f—— good." Ben Hecht was rushed in, at $15,000 a week to supply desperately needed color and continuity to the screenplay.

Personality problems. Ill feeling among the major talents was rampant throughout the filming of the epic. Gable had his agent bombard Selznick with memos listing complaints on everything from Cukor to his costumes. The star had little empathy for Britisher Leigh. Anne Edwards, in her book **Vivien Leigh: A Biography** (1977), notes that "Gable admired his leading lady's vocabulary,[7] as did Fleming, but otherwise he was a bit put off by her intellect and her dedication to work." As for Leigh's feelings toward Gable, Edwards notes, "She regarded Gable as lazy, not too bright, and an unresponsive performer (though she was always laudatory about his kindness and good manners to her). . . . A sense of competition grew between the two that carried over into their scenes together. . . . But it was Gable's bad breath caused by his false teeth that was the most unpleasant aspect of their working together for Vivien."

Fleming was severely taxed by the shooting—

---

[6]Cukor stated recently, "I believe all the stuff I shot is still in the picture. As I remember, it included the opening scene on the steps of Tara, the bazaar, and the scene where Vivien Leigh came downstairs and slapped Butterfly McQueen."

[7]Vivien's salty vocabulary included her popular lament "What are you f—— about for?" whenever Gable indulged in a break on the set.

he had, after all, come onto the project after just completing most of the enormously challenging **Wizard of Oz**—and continually demanded Leigh to "ham it up." After one volatile exchange, in which Fleming informed the actress, "Miss Leigh, you can take this royal script and shove it up your royal British ass!" the director departed for his home. A few days later he nearly drove his car off a cliff in Malibu and was hospitalized with a nervous breakdown. Selznick rushed Sam Wood into service, who remained to assist Fleming when the director returned to complete the filming four weeks later.

Finally on July 1, 1939, after 140 days of shooting (Gable worked 71 days; Leigh worked 125 days), **Gone With the Wind** ended with a retake (later discarded) of the opening scene of Scarlett and the Tarleton twins. The tasks remained of editing the film into a proper length (it emerged as three hours and thirty-nine minutes) and creating a musical score (provided by Max Steiner, with motifs for the four major characters and several Civil War songs interpolated into the 282 separate musical passages). The most publicized problem at this point was Rhett's famous closing line, "Frankly, my dear, I don't give a damn." Although deemed very mild by today's public's standards, at the time **damn** was a word whose use was forbidden on screen. Rather than weaken the popular finale, Selznick paid the Producers Association $5,000 for the on-screen offense of using profanity. The cost of making **Gone With the Wind** was marked at $3,957,000.

When **Gone With the Wind** was about to be released in December 1939, MGM publicity wizard Howard Dietz sent a memo to company advertising, exploitation, and publicity departments, advising them of particular "Don'ts" in promoting the blockbuster feature.

- Don't prepare publicity stories about Margaret Mitchell, since the studio has an official biography available and since the authoress has approval of all stories about her.
- Don't publish any kind of a synopsis of the film.
- Don't permit any publication outlet to have such a variety of scene stills that they might be able to tell the storyline via stills.
- Don't ignore Victor Fleming's participation as sole credited director.
- Don't call this Selznick International Production a Metro-Goldwyn-Mayer picture ("release" is permitted).
- Don't alter the official advertising billing on the film.
- Don't refer to the Tarleton boys/brothers as the "twins."
- Don't refer to the burning of Atlanta since only the firing of particular buildings in Atlanta is shown in the picture.
- Don't refer to the film's title as deriving from the poem "Cynara"; actually it is from Ernest Dowson's poem about "Cynara."
- Don't indicate specifically which portions of the book's dialogue have been used in the picture; refer to it as "a large part of the dialogue from the book. . . ." or ". . . most of the dialogue . . ." etc.

Vivien Leigh, Clark Gable, and Olivia de Havilland in Gone with the Wind *('39).*

On December 15, 1939, **Gone With the Wind** premiered in Atlanta. The ill feelings engendered during production carried over to the premiere. Gable initially refused to attend the gala, when it was touted that three directorial talents, not just Fleming, were responsible for the film's completion. But Gable was finally persuaded to appear, along with wife Carole Lombard, in the company of the major figures involved.

Soon after its bow, the critics were heralding the achievement of **Gone With the Wind.** "The picture is an event, the greatest ever to date, in motion picture production" **(Hollywood Reporter)**; "Mightiest achievement in the history of the motion picture" **(Film Daily)**; "It is a monumental picture! . . . defies a reviewer to put into print its fabulous achievement" **(New York Herald-Tribune)**; "A first-rate piece of Americana . . . unforgettable climaxes. . . . The best of Gable's career without a doubt" **(Time)**; The greatest motion mural we have seen and the most ambitious filmmaking venture in Hollywood's spectacular history" **(New York Times)**. And so on.

"Isn't it wonderful—this benefit for David O. Selznick!" quipped Bob Hope as master of ceremonies of the Oscar festivities on February 29, 1940. The film won nine Oscars: Best Production Design (William Cameron Menzies), Best Film Editing (Hal C. Kern and James E. Newcom), Best Interior Decoration (Lyle Wheeler), Best Color Cinematography (Ernest Haller and Ray Rennahan), Best Writing (Sidney Howard, who died in August 1939), Best Director (Victor Fleming), Best Supporting Actress (Hattie McDaniel, first black Os-

car recipient—she beat out Olivia de Havilland in the acting category), Best Actress (Vivien Leigh), and Best Picture.

In the face of posterity, it still appears ludicrous that Gable, whose larger-than-life, epic performance of Rhett Butler has itself become a piece of Americana, was defeated in the Oscar race by the deeply moving but largely forgotten performance of Robert Donat in **Goodbye, Mr. Chips.**

Among the many other awards bestowed on **Gone With the Wind** was the **Photoplay** magazine Gold Medal prize.

For many years, **Gone With the Wind** rested on the honor of being the most profitable motion picture made: by July 1943 it had tallied a domestic gross of $32 million (number two being Walt Disney's **Snow White and the Seven Dwarfs** with $8 million). In 1954 the classic MGM release was reissued in a remasked, widescreen version with "Perspecta" stereophonic sound. For the Civil War centennial in 1961, **Gone With the Wind** was given a spectacular gala in Atlanta. Vivien Leigh, Olivia de Havilland, David O. Selznick, and Stephens Mitchell (brother of the authoress, who died in 1949) were among the notables in attendance.[8] The reissue did enormously well, leading **Time**

[8]Gable died in 1960 of a heart attack; Leslie Howard was killed in a plane crash in 1943; Hattie McDaniel passed away in 1952; Ona Munson committed suicide in 1955; Victor Fleming had died in 1949. (Vivien Leigh would pass away in 1967, two years after the death of Selznick and five years after the demise of Mitchell.)

Leslie Howard, Olivia de Havilland, Thomas Mitchell, Barbara O'Neill, Vivien Leigh, and Rand Brooks.

magazine to print, "Hollywood itself is practically dead but **Gone With the Wind** goes on forever." By the end of 1961 **Gone With the Wind** had grossed a domestic total of $41,200,000. In 1967 the feature was released nationally for the sixth time; Metro enlarged the print from 35 mm to 70 mm and added stereophonic sound (and lowered Vivien Leigh's bodice on the posters). These touches offended many purists, but the film continued to reap huge grosses.

Although shown on "Home Box Office" in Los Angeles and New York, **Gone With the Wind** did not appear on nationwide television until November 6 and 7, 1976, on NBC-TV as a special bicentennial attraction (the network paid $5,000,000 for the rights). The film drew an estimated 130 million viewers despite the breaks in continuity for commercials and being split in two parts. A less than pleased Olivia de Havilland vetoed the network's request that she hostess the event. The actress complained, "For this film to be shown in such a crude manner in this bicentennial year is, I think, most insensitive and very foolish. . . . I'm quite sure that Clark Gable, Vivien Leigh, Leslie Howard, and Victor Fleming are up there on some celestial veranda right now, sipping mint juleps, incensed over the proceedings." In April 1978 CBS-TV paid $35,000,000 for a twenty-year leasing agreement with MGM to annually air the classic feature.

Much attention in the fall of 1978 focused on Tara: **The Continuation of Gone With the Wind,** a brainchild of cinema producers Richard Zanuck

and David Brown.[9] Margaret Mitchell's brother, Stephens, now in his eighties, finally consented to the offer to permit a sequel to be filmed. He explained, "I figured I might as well let them have a go at it. Nobody can write like Margaret could anyway." Initially hired for the project was Award-winning scenarist James Goldman, who insisted the continuation would **not** be campy. "I take these people very, very seriously. . . . They

---

[9]In the late 1950s David O. Selznick hoped to mount a stage version of the play, even planning on constructing his own Broadway theatre to house the huge concept he had in mind. But nothing came of the idea. In November 1966 a five-hour dramatic version of the novel was produced in Japan; the following summer, a second installment (covering the later portions of the novel) debuted at the Imperial Theatre in Tokyo. In the fall of 1967 a six-hour condensation of both dramas premiered on the Tokyo stage. On January 2, 1970, a musical entitled **Scarlett,** with music and lyrics by Harold Rome and a book by Kazuo Kikuta, premiered at Tokyo's Imperial Theatre, directed by Joe Layton. On May 3, 1972, an English-language version bowed at London's Drury Lane Theatre, budgeted at approximately $450,000. It did not fare well. A variation of the British edition played in Los Angeles (August 1973) and San Francisco (October 1973), starring Pernell Roberts and Leslie Ann Warren, but it failed to win sufficient critical or public endorsement to make a Broadway goal a reality. (The show would later tour in the South and the Midwest with David Canary and Sherry Mathis.) There were LP cast albums of the musical versions, but none of them equaled the continued popularity of the Max Steiner soundtrack (and re-recorded) score.

are wonderful characters in spite of the fact that they've become as popular as they. . . . One wants to sit down to these people and have a meal. You want to feel that you've been served a proper portion of Scarlett and a proper portion of Rhett and also have a feel for what happens during the Reconstruction period. . . . So my job is to invent a story which fulfills the audiences' expectations and I think they have very particular expectations. Scarlett and Rhett are very real to people. They know what these two would do and so there are various limits in constructing the narrative. . . ."

At another juncture Anne Edwards, the biographer of **Vivien** (Leigh), was assigned to write the project, and then the projected sequel dropped from the news. Its likely reemergence as a viable commercial project diminished as inflation made the practicality of filming a historical epic unprofitable.

On December 28, 1979, the Los Angeles County Museum of Art held a fortieth anniversary celebration of the Hollywood premiere of **Gone With the Wind.** Hostessing the event was Olivia de Havilland. Among those in attendance were: Danny Selznick, son of the late producer, costume designer Walter Plunkett, art director Lyle Wheeler, film editor Hal Kern, actresses Evelyn Keyes and Ann Rutherford, actors Rand Brooks and Patrick Curtis, assistant director Ridgway Calloway, production manager Ray Klune, still photographer Fred Parrish, and stunt man Yakima Canutt.

It was Miss de Havilland who said not too long ago about this landmark film, "Every time I see it, I find something fresh, some shade of meaning, that I hadn't noticed before. It's such

Gone with the Wind premiering on television in November 1976.

a rich movie. You know, in our business, careers were supposed to be very short and a film could disappear without a trace in a year. What you hoped for was one piece of work that would somehow live on." How fortunate that so many gifted people found artistic immortality in **Gone With the Wind**.

GOODBYE, MR. CHIPS
1939—114 min.

Producer, Victor Saville; **director**, Sam Wood; based on the novel by James Hilton; **screenplay**, R. C. Sherriff, Claudine West, and Eric Maschwitz; **art director**, Alfred Junge; **music director**, Louis Levy; **special music**, Richard Addinsell; **sound**, A. W. Watkins and C. C. Stevens; **camera**, Freddie Young; **editor**, Charles Frend.

Robert Donat **(Mr. Chipping)**; Greer Garson **(Katherine Chipping)**; Terry Kilburn **(Peter Colley II–Peter Colley III–Peter Colley IV)**; John Mills **(Peter Colley as a Young Man)**; Paul Henreid **(Staefel)**; Judith Furse **(Flora)**; Lyn Harding **(Wetherby)**; Milton Rosmer **(Charteris)**; Frederick Leister **(Marsham)**; Louise Hampton **(Mrs. Wickett)**; Austin Trevor **(Ralston)**; David Tree **(Jackson)**; Edmond Breon **(Colonel Morgan)**; Jill Furse **(Helen Colley)**; Scott Sunderland **(Sir John Colley)**.

Greer Garson and Robert Donat in Goodbye, Mr. Chips *('39).*

SYNOPSIS
It is the first day of the new term at England's Brookfield School. The students file into the main building as a master takes a roll call. The setting then flashes back to 1870.

Mr. Chipping has arrived at Brookfield to teach Latin. At first he is overly lenient with his pupils, but the headmaster informs him that he must be sterner. He transforms into a strict disciplinarian, alienating students and masters alike. When promotions are given, he is overlooked.

At the age of forty he embarks on a climbing holiday in the Tyrol with a German colleague, Staefel. There he meets the young, beautiful, pert Katherine. They fall in love, marry, and return to Brookfield, where Chips' life takes on greater meeting.

After three years of bliss, Chips loses Katherine and their infant son in childbirth. Valiantly Chips continues on at the school, trying to remember all the humanizing touches Katherine taught him. Later Ralston, the new headmaster, suggests that Chips should retire because his teaching methods are now too old-fashioned. But the alumni and faculty back Chips and he remains for more terms.

Later, upon his retirement, Chips chooses to live nearby the campus. He continues to meet each year's new crop of students. When the headmaster is inducted into the army, Chips is recalled to Brookfield to become temporary headmaster.

Still years later, when Chips is on his deathbed, he overhears a master and the physician discussing him. They are regretting his lonely life. "Poor fellow," they say. "Never had any children." Chips rises to the occasion with his dying retort: "You're wrong. I have . . . thousands of them, thousands of them—and all boys."

A montage of generations of Brookfield chaps then file by, climaxing with the appearance of little Peter Colley, the offspring of four generations of Brookfield students. As he reaches front and center, he speaks forth, "Goodbye, Mr. Chips—goodbye."

* * *

It is quite amazing how many film enthusiasts insist that Clark Gable won a second Academy Award for his role of Rhett Butler in **Gone With the Wind**. The fact is, Gable lost to Britisher Robert Donat, who claimed the 1939 prize for his interpretation of the meek Mr. Chipping of **Goodbye, Mr. Chips**.

The genesis of the film occurred in 1934 when a London magazine requested writer James Hilton to prepare a piece of fiction for its ᴄ..ristmas number. Hilton obliged with a 20,000-word sketch of a professor in an English boys' school. The author would later deny that the "hero" was based on his own father, an aged schoolmaster. When the novelette was published in the United States, critic Alexander Woollcott endorsed it enthusiastically. The book's success led Irving Thalberg to purchase the screen rights for MGM.

Scenarists R. C. Sherriff, Claudine West,

and Eric Maschwitz fleshed out Hilton's sparse work with touching episodes of the assorted pupils who encounter Chips over the years. To enhance the film's realism, the picture was shot in England, partly at MGM's studio[1] in Denham, and on location at Repton College, where many of the students and some faculty acted as extras. The foremost problem was in casting the lead role, which required an actor to age from twenty-four to eighty. Hilton had his own ideas:

I would rather have an American who can feel what it ought to be than an Englishman who is selected just because he has the English accent. Now Wallace Beery has the warmth for it. Some people think that an extraordinary casting. So many people think of Chips as a little wispy man.

Among the potential candidates for the role was Charles Laughton. However, in the end MGM decided to utilize the services of Robert Donat, who had signed a six-picture pact with the studio and who had appeared already in Metro's **The Citadel** (1938). For the telling but brief assignment of Kathy, the girl who so dramatically alters Chips' life, the studio selected Irish-born Greer Garson, who had been in Hollywood for the better part of a year waiting for a screen assignment from her MGM bosses.[2] She returned to England,

[1]The biggest sets for any British-made film at the time were constructed there.

[2]According to legend, Miss Garson was already packed

the situs of her stage successes, to embark on her motion picture debut.

When released in May 1939 **Goodbye, Mr. Chips** won as sterling a set of notices as any MGM picture to that time, with most reviewers paraphrasing the **New York World-Telegram**'s critique, "A hauntingly beautiful production with Robert Donat giving a brilliant characterization. It is one of the few really great photoplays the screen has so far produced. **Goodbye, Mr. Chips** is one of those rare offerings in which story, direction, and acting have been blended so skillfully that it becomes a perfect unit." Even the British were pleased with the production. "The school atmosphere is perfect . . . . and the poignant sequences during the war period are restrained and effective in their sentimental appeal. In fact, sentiment, which is prominent throughout, always rings true and avoids being mawkish. This is a picture of which MGM may well be proud" (**Picturegoer**).

At the 1939 Academy Awards **Goodbye, Mr. Chips** was in the running for Best Picture (defeated by MGM's **Gone With the Wind**, Best Actress (Garson lost to Vivien Leigh of **Gone With the Wind**), and Best Actor. In the last category Donat was in competition with Gable (of **Gone With the Wind**), Laurence Olivier of United Artists' **Wuthering Heights**, Mickey Rooney of MGM's **Babes in Arms**, and James Stewart of Columbia's **Mr. Smith Goes to Washington**. While Donat's victory was cheered by most,[3] it deeply upset David O. Selznick, who, despite the ten Oscars earned by his classic, brooded that his publicity directives should have promoted Gable to a greater degree, in order the better to ensure his win.

MGM had great hopes for Donat and Garson after their triumphs in **Goodbye, Mr. Chips**. Garson and her mother heeded the call to Hollywood and the actress soon began her ascent to the pinnacle of Metro stardom with **Pride and Prejudice** (1940), **Blossoms in the Dust** (1941), **Random Harvest** (1942; from another James Hilton work), and her Oscar-winning **Mrs. Miniver** (1942). She also became the pet of a wide-eyed, adoring Louis B. Mayer. However, Donat proved less cooperative. His MGM contract promised script approval and his standards caused him to reject many scripts (including **Dr. Jekyll and Mr. Hyde**, 1940, and the Robert Taylor role in 1942's **Stand by for Action**). He would play in only two more Metro pictures: **Adventures of Tartu** (1943) and **Perfect Strangers** (a.k.a. **Vacation from Marriage**, 1945). Donat died in 1958 after a life handicapped by serious asthma and recurrent professional indecision.

There appeared in 1969 a musical film re-

make of **Goodbye, Mr. Chips**, produced by Metro in England. There were many preproduction problems. Original stars Richard Burton and Samantha Eggar were replaced by Rex Harrison and Lee Remick and they, in turn, by Peter O'Toole and Petula Clark. Composers Andre and Dory Previn were replaced by Leslie Bricusse (who also choreographed). Initial director Gower Champion was replaced by Herbert Ross, the latter making his directorial debut. The rather amiable, if ponderous and synthetic, film updated the story from World War I to World War II and proved a box-office disappointment. Plans for a Broadway musical of **Goodbye, Mr. Chips** were announced in the mid-1970s but failed to materialize.

THE GOOD EARTH
1937—138 min.[1]

Producer, Irving G. Thalberg; **associate producer,** Albert Lewin; **director,** Sidney Franklin; based on the novel by Pearl S. Buck; and the play by Owen and Donald Davis; **screenplay,** Talbot Jennings, Tess Schlesinger, and Claudine West; **music,** Herbert Stothart; **art directors,** Cedric Gibbons, Harry Oliver, and Arnold Gillespie; **set decorator,** Edwin B. Willis; **wardrobe,** Dolly Tree; **montage,** Slavko Vorkapich; **camera,** Karl Freund; **editor,** Basil Wrangel.

Paul Muni (**Wang Lung**); Luise Rainer (**O-Lan**); Walter Connolly (**Uncle**); Tillie Losch (**Lotus**); Lotus Lui (**The Voice of Lotus**); Charley Grapewin (**Old Father**); Keye Luke (**Elder Son**); Harold Huber (**Cousin**); Roland Got (**Younger Son**); Soo Young (**Old Mistress Aunt**); Chingwah Lee (**Ching**); William Law (**Gateman**); Mary Wong (**Little Bride**); Charles Middleton (**Banker**); Suzanna Kim (**Little Fool**); Caroline Chew (**Dancer**); Chester Gan (**Singer in Teahouse**); Olaf Hytten (**Liu, the Grain Merchant**); Miki Morita (**House Guest of Wang**); Philip Ahn (**Captain**); Sammee Tong (**Chinaman**); Richard Loo (**Farmer/Rabble-Rouser/Peach Seller**).

SYNOPSIS
Dawn. The young Wang Lung awakes, and rejoicing, "This is the day!" sets off to the great house of the village to obtain his appointed bride O-Lan, a humble slave girl whom he discovers huddled by a stove. O-Lan follows her spouse home, and that night, after the wedding feast, she retrieves a peach seed which Wang happily tossed into a rice field earlier in the day. The bride tenderly plants it outside their home.

Wang soon discovers how stoical and sacrificing O-Lan is. When she is about to give birth to their first child, she begs Wang not to go for a midwife but, instead, to rescue the crop from a violent storm. When famine later sweeps the land, O-Lan supports Wang's decision not to sell

the land as directed by his uncle. During this period of impoverishment, she cooks earth to feed their growing family of two sons and a daughter.

When they eventually are forced to leave the land, planning to return in better times, O-Lan teaches her children to beg in the city streets. Later revolution develops. O-Lan is almost shot as a looter, but the soldiers are called away and O-Lan returns home with a bag of precious jewels she has discovered in the street. The delighted Wang allows O-Lan to keep two pearls and uses the newly won wealth to purchase the great house of his native village and the fertile fields about it.

With wealth comes arrogance. Wang Lung soon becomes infatuated with the teahouse dancer Lotus and takes her as a second wife. He gifts her with the two pearls formerly owned by the hurt but silent O-Lan. The promiscuous Lotus soon seduces Wang's son and Wang discovers them making love. As he beats his errant son, a horrible locust attack begins. O-Lan and the workers rush to the fields in defense but all appears lost. Then the elder son, educated at an agricultural college, directs the people to dig ditches and create fire lanes until the wind changes. Thanks to his learning, the crops are saved and Wang is saved from ruin.

O-Lan's attempts to save the crops have critically exhausted her. At the wedding feast of her son, she lies, smiling, in the back of the hall while family and friends celebrate. Sensing her fatal illness, Wang goes to her side, begging her to live on. As a goodwill gesture he returns to her the pearls she so treasured. Finally realizing she is loved and wanted, O-Lan dies, asking her grieving husband, "Forgive me."

Wang Lung leaves her bedside and goes outdoors—to the peach tree O-Lan planted so many years before on their wedding night. Caressing the tree, he thinks of his late, beloved mate and speaks, "O-Lan. Thou art the Earth!"

* * *

By the mid-1930s Hollywood and the moviegoing world had come to expect at least one cinema blockbuster to issue annually from Culver City under the guiding genius of Irving Thalberg. In 1935 it was **Mutiny on the Bounty;** in 1936, **Romeo and Juliet.** In 1937 it was **The Good Earth.** It bore the following inscription in the credits:

> To the Memory of
> Irving Grant Thalberg
> We Dedicate This Picture
> His Last Great Achievement

Thalberg's delicate health had collapsed under a pneumonia attack, which killed him in his Santa Monica beach mansion on September 14, 1936. **The Good Earth,** then in the closing stages of production (Bernard Hyman would oversee its completion), would stand as the final tribute to his ability and tenacity.

Pearl Buck had completed **The Good Earth** in 1930 and it was published in 1931. It was on the American bestseller lists for twenty-one months, received the Pulitzer Prize, and was translated into more than twenty languages, including the

---

and ready to return home to England in defeat when director Sam Wood saw her screen test and decided that he had found the right actress to play Kathy.

[3]Former child actor Terry Kilburn would recall of the film's star, "[Donat] made a deep impression on me by always remaining in character as the old Mr. Chips, even when he was off-camera. Many people thought this was rather affected of him, but it was a deep dedication he felt toward the role and I thought it was splendid."

[1]Filmed in Sepia.

Walter Connolly, Paul Muni, and Luise Rainer in The Good Earth *('37).*

Chinese, of which there were three different versions. In 1933 it was adapted by Owen and Donald Davis as a stage play and presented by the Theatre Guild on Broadway, starring Nazimova and Claude Rains.

Since 1933 Thalberg had been enamored of the idea of cinematizing Pearl Buck's massive book. Louis B. Mayer was dismayed. "Irving, the public won't buy pictures about American farmers. And you want to give them **Chinese** farmers?" Mayer knew better than to hope to dash Thalberg's enthusiasm. Late in 1933 Thalberg dispatched director George Hill to China to shoot exteriors. Hill's wife, Frances Marion, was preparing the screenplay. Both Irving and Frances hoped the task would encourage Hill to reform his alcohol-spattered reputation.

Hill photographed reels of countryside and appeared to be fulfilling the studio's trust. Shortly after his return to Hollywood, he attended a production-story conference, on August 10, 1934. He was so intoxicated he could scarcely keep from falling down. Observing the shocked faces of his wife and Thalberg, Hill left. He returned to his South Venice oceanside home and shot himself in the head with his army revolver.

Thalberg replaced Hill with Victor Fleming. The distraught Frances Marion was relieved by Talbot Jennings, Tess Schlesinger, and Claudine West. Meanwhile, an enormous set was built in the San Fernando Valley, some fifty miles outside of Hollywood. Included were 500 acres of Chinese farms, bamboo and cabbage gardens, rice fields, and a Chinese irrigation ditch. During this period Thalberg searched painstakingly for the proper principals.

Since there was no actor under MGM contract who could play Wang Lung, the simple Chinese lad who matures from a young man on his wedding day to a wealthy, middle-aged landowner, Thalberg sought the services of Warner Bros.' Paul Muni.[2] Muni was regarded as Hollywood's "Actor's Actor" following such vivid characterizations as **Scarface** and **I Am a Fugitive from the Chain Gang,** both 1932 releases. Sixty English-speaking Chinese actors were sought, although such Occidentals as Walter Connolly, Jessie Ralph, and Charley Grapewin were cast in major supporting roles.[3] Luise Rainer, the Viennese discovery who had made only two motion pictures for MGM, including **The Great Ziegfled** (1936), was cast as O-Lan.

Then Victor Fleming's illness caused yet another delay. Sidney Franklin replaced him as Fleming entered the hospital for an operation. Production finally began in February 1936.

Franklin at the helm was aided (to a degree)

[2] As part of the deal, MGM agreed to loan Clark Gable's services to Warner Bros. for one picture, while Warner's was to provide Metro not only with Muni's presence for **The Good Earth,** but with Leslie Howard for an MGM picture as well.

[3] One of James Stewart's favorite stories concerns his screen test for a Chinese role in **The Good Earth.** Stewart's height, 6'4", caused endless problems as the scene was shot, and nobody was surprised when he lost the job.

by coach Oliver Hinsdell, who coordinated the various accents of the cast, and by General Ting-Hsiu Tu. The latter was assigned to the epic by the Nanking government to ensure the fidelity of settings and historical incidents. It would be Tu, according to press releases, who coached the army used in the revolution scenes. The animal contingent for the film included twenty donkeys, sixteen mongrel dogs, two hundred ducks, a flock of pigeons, chickens, ten Cochin hogs, an ox, two dozen horses, and six water buffaloes.

Rainer and Muni accepted no shortcuts in preparation for their demanding roles. Muni devoted months observing San Francisco's Chinatown, studying Oriental posture and accents, while the actress visited the Chinese settlements in both San Francisco and Los Angeles. The European actress would later reflect that although she and Muni both used similar researching facilities, their acting styles were indeed different: "He knew what he wanted to do in each scene. By what door he would enter, how he would make an exit, where each piece of furniture must be. When something was changed, that was difficult for him. He had to change his idea of the scene. But as for me, I didn't care. I never knew how I was going to walk on or off the set, or just what I would do when I got there."

The Good Earth emerged as a truly magnificent spectacle. The performances of Muni and Rainer were enhanced by scenes of famine (a special fascination for Depression audiences as Muni feeds his family cooked earth to save them from starvation), a chilling looting episode, and a locust plague. The last sequence was a magnificent combination of trick photography, recutting, and a blending of Chinese location shooting with closeups of locusts on a miniature soundstage as well as on-film special-effects painting. This locust attack remains one of the most memorable epic scenes of 1930s cinema.

At a cost of $2,816,000 **The Good Earth** was the most expensive Metro production since its silent **Ben-Hur** (1925). When the Pearl Buck epic was in general release in 1937, MGM's publicity department was able to boast that the film starred two major Academy Award winners; Muni and Rainer had earned Oscars in the 1936 sweepstakes, he for Warner Bros.' **The Story of Louis Pasteur** and she for **The Great Ziegfeld.**

At 138 minutes and shot in Sepia, **The Good Earth** proved engrossing, if not always meaningful, film fare. A tone of excessive piety marked the film; the prologue, for instance, stated, "The soul of a great nation is expressed in the life of its humble people." Overall, though, the film generated tremendous enthusiasm from the fourth estate. The **New York Times** championed it as "one of the finest things Hollywood has done this season or any other." **Time** decided, "A real cinema epic. . . . Sure to rank as one of the great pictures of all time."

The film grossed $3,557,000, placed second on the **Film Daily** Ten Best picture poll and sixth on the National Board of Review's Ten Best Picture list, and was nominated by the Academy for the Best Picture of the year prize. It lost to Warner

Bros.' **The Story of Emile Zola** (starring Muni). Karl Freund won an Oscar for his cinematography. In the acting categories, Luise Rainer captured her second consecutive Oscar, for her moving portrayal of O-Lan. Although this was a surprise—she had heavy competition from Irene Dunne **(The Awful Truth)**, Janet Gaynor **(A Star Is Born)**, Barbara Stanwyck **(Stella Dallas)**, and Greta Garbo **(Camille)**—it was not unexpected. Sidney Franklin was regarded as a woman's director and the focus of the story was on O-Lan rather than on Wang Lung. Therefore, it was not so unexpected when Muni[4] was **not** even nominated for **The Good Earth.** (He was nominated for **The Life of Emile Zola,** but lost to Spencer Tracy of MGM's **Captains Courageous.**)

Ironically, when Rainer accepted her second Oscar at the Biltmore Bowl on March 10, 1938, her tenure at MGM was nearing an end. Following **The Good Earth** she made only five more films at the lot, including **The Great Waltz** (1938). Near the end of her stay at the studio, Mayer, who had been paying her $250 a week during the filming of **The Good Earth,** would snap at the artistically temperamental actress, "We made you and we're going to kill you." In her cool Continental way, the star replied, "God made me."

When Thalberg died three MGM projects were still in some stage of production: **Maytime** (1937), a Hunt Stromberg production starring Jeanette MacDonald and Nelson Eddy; **A Day at the Races** (1937), produced by Laurence Weingarten and starring the Marx Brothers; and **Marie Antoinette** (1938), Thalberg's long-nurtured dream vehicle for his wife Norma Shearer, also produced by Stromberg.

Thalberg's dedication to principle and artistry made a permanent mark at MGM. His loss was sincerely mourned by the entire lot, although there was at least one superficial mourner. After calling on the widowed Norma Shearer to express his sorrow, Louis B. Mayer, for years upstaged at the studio by his young protégé's ambition and genius, departed for a Hollywood nightclub and merrily danced himself into a frenzy.

As for MGM, it would translate another Pearl Buck novel into a film. In 1944 it adapted **Dragon Seed** to the screen and Katharine Hepburn starred. The venture proved far less artistically viable.

GOOD NEWS

1947 C—93 min.

Producer, Arthur Freed; **associate producer,** Roger Edens; **director,** Charles Walters; based on the play by Lawrence Schwab, Lew Brown, Frank Mandel, B. G. DeSylva, and Ray Henderson; **screenplay,** Betty Comden and Adolph Green; **color consultants,** Natalie Kalmus and Henri Jaffa; **songs,** DeSylva, Brown, and Henderson; Comden and Green; Edens; Hugh Martin and Ralph Blane; **music director,** Lennie Hayton; **vocal arranger,** Kay Thompson; **art directors,** Cedric Gibbons and Edward Carfagno; **set decorators,** Edwin B. Willis and Paul G. Chamberlain; **women's costumes,** Helen Rose; **men's costumes,** Valles; **makeup,** Jack Dawn; **production numbers** staged by Robert Alton; **sound,** Douglas Shearer; **camera,** Charles Schoenbaum; **editor,** Albert Akst.

June Allyson **(Connie Lane);** Peter Lawford **(Tommy Marlowe);** Patricia Marshall **(Patricia McClellan);** Joan McCracken **(Babe Doolittle);** Ray McDonald **(Bobby Turner);** Mel Torme **(Danny);** Robert Strickland **(Peter Van Dyne III);** Donald MacBride **(Coach Johnson);** Tom Dugan **(Pooch);** Clinton Sundberg **(Professor Burton Kehnyon);** Loren Tindall **(Beef);** Connie Gilchrist **(Cora, the Cook);** Morris Ankrum **(Dean Griswold);** Georgia Lee **(Flo);** Jane Green **(Mrs. Drexel);** Anne Taylor **(Daisy);** Mary Stuart and Janet Winkler **(College Girls);** Wheaton Chambers **(Doctor);** Sarah Edwards **(Miss Pritchard).**

SYNOPSIS

In 1927 the captain of Tate College's football team, Tommy Marlowe, can have his choice of any girl on the campus. His vanity suffers a severe blow with the arrival of Patricia McClellan, a vivacious coed who vamps all the boys but rebuffs Tommy. She even uses her meager knowledge of French to belittle him.

The smitten Marlowe enlists the aid of Connie Lane, a librarian working her way through college, to coach him in French so that he might make his conquest of Patricia. Connie and Tommy find themselves attracted to each other and arrange to go to the prom dance as a couple. But he breaks the date when Patricia belatedly decides she wants him to be her escort. Connie is devastated.

As time passes, Patricia keeps Tommy in a whirl and eventually agrees to wed him—on condition that he win the big football game. But Tommy fails his French examination and is disqualified from playing in the decisive game. The professor in question is pressured by the students and agrees to allow Tommy to take a reexamination. Although Connie is peeved at Tommy, she agrees to coach him in the language—for the sake of school morale.

Tommy passes the examination and at the same time comes to the realization that he loves Connie, not Patricia. He is thus in a dilemma. If he wins the football game, he must wed Miss McClellan and lose Connie; if he does not come through for Tate, he will lose the admiration of his schoolmates. Making his decision, Tommy plays slovenly. A teammate learns of his predicament and relays the information to Connie. She in turn tricks Patricia into giving up Tommy for a supposedly wealthy student. When Tommy learns of his newfound freedom, he leads his team to victory, and ends up with Connie happily in his arms.

* * *

"I always say, the three greatest pictures are **Birth of a Nation, Potemkin,** and **Good News,**" laughs Betty Comden, who, with cohort Adolph Green, overhauled this old musical favorite for the brisk, happy Arthur Freed color movie of 1947.[1] The original musical, which opened at Chanin's 46th Street Theatre on September 6, 1927, and ran for 551 performances, had originally been purchased by MGM in 1929, at a price of $50,000. In 1930 **Good News** was released as a film, with Nacio Herb Brown and Arthur Freed tunes added to the Buddy DeSylva–Les Brown–Ray Henderson score. The cast of that screen version included Bessie Love as the ingenue, Stanley Smith as the hero, Lola Lane as the vamp, and Dorothy McNulty (later Penny "Blondie" Singleton) as the top practitioner of "The Varsity Drag."

For years Freed, harboring warm sentiments towards the show, which had been performed by virtually every high school and little-theatre group extant since its Broadway run, wanted to make a new movie version. In 1941 he thought of costarring Judy Garland and Mickey Rooney in the musical, but the talented pair were scheduled for other projects and the concept was shelved. Then, in a post–World War II period of heightened productivity he slated **Good News** for filming. He gave Comden and Green their first Hollywood job, following their Broadway hits of **On the Town** (1944) and **Billion Dollar Baby** (1945).

Charles Walters, following a stay at MGM as a choreographer, made his directorial debut with this feature. The leading part of sweet Connie Lane was assigned to pert June Allyson, who had reservations about Walters' capacity to handle the proceedings. Freed convinced her to give him a chance. The original choice for vampy Patricia McClelland was Gloria DeHaven, but she accepted a suspension rather than portray the unsympathetic part; relative unknown Patricia Marshall

---

[4]Muni was forty when he undertook the role of Wang Lung. He was so concerned that he would not be able properly to convey the youthful "hero" in the earlier portions of the films that he concentrated mostly on those scenes. He seemed to lose control in the later portions of the picture. He would say later, "**The Good Earth,** while I considered myself very, very badly chosen for that role—I didn't do a good job in it—the film itself was very worthwhile."

[1]In his extensive article on the cinematic art of Charles Walters in **Focus on Films** (1977), Douglas McVay observes: "if this movie has any real flaw, it lies in the script. Comden and Green (whether because this was their first Hollywood assignment, or because they were constrained by the previous Broadway and screen versions) scarcely achieve here a level of wit comparable with their finest work **(On the Town, Singin' in the Rain, The Band Wagon).** Nevertheless, by comparison with the scripts of other college musicals such as **Old Man Rhythm** [RKO, 1935] and **Too Many Girls** [RKO, 1940], their scenario for **Good News** appears positively sparkling. And they bring off at least a few moments of humor which are treasurable by any standard: for instance, Patricia Marshall as the affectedly French-spouting gold-digger on a twenties American campus, declaiming, "Quel fromage!" instead of "Quel dommage!" (June Allyson maliciously points out to her the howler, by translating it: "What cheese!"); Miss Allyson herself, lovelorn, announcing her intention of staying home and reading her favorite book—**Les Miserables;** and best of all, Joan McCracken, emerging hobbling with back bent double after being sat upon during a jalopy ride, gamely pretending to be a senior citizen and quavering: "My, the old campus hasn't changed much . . . I wonder if McKinley is still the president?"

June Allyson and Peter Lawford in Good News *('47).*

Released during the holiday season of 1947, **Good News** was rather coolly received by most critics, who had seen the whole variation done many times since MGM's 1930 version reached the screen (especially by Paramount in its array of 1930s college musicals). Noted a jaded Bosley Crowther in the **New York Times,** "It is just another college musical in which the invariable gold-digging vamp goes after the big football hero, to the anguish of the little true-love blonde, while high-spirited choruses rush on briskly between the plot scenes to sing of love and like pursuits." Despite such adverse notices, and the sight of the painfully uncomfortable Lawford hoofing abashedly, audiences thoroughly enjoyed seeing the old standby delivered with such élan and high spirits. **Good News** grossed $2,956,000 in its initial release.

Ironically, **Good News** should have been the launching pad for, or the escalation of, the film musical careers of many of its principals, but it was not. Allyson would make one more genre picture at MGM, a guest appearance in **Words and Music** (1948). She was scheduled to join with Fred Astaire in **Royal Wedding** (1951), but her pregnancy necessitated her dropping out. Mel Torme, who had been in several 1940s musicals, including **Higher and Higher** (RKO, 1943), continued having small roles at MGM. He had a tiny part in **Words and Music.** For the Esther Williams' aquacade **Duchess of Idaho** (1950), he was paid $30,000 to speak a few lines and to sing "Cold Hands, Warm Heart." When the picture premiered, Torme's song had been cut, and his acting role shredded. He would prove more adept in nightclubs and on TV than in films; some insist it was because of his volatile soundstage nature. Ray McDonald, who had been in an array of Metro musicals (**Babes on Broadway,** 1941; **Presenting Lily Mars,** 1943; **Till the Clouds Roll By,** 1946; etc.), should have gravitated to bigger and better assignments, but he faded out of show business, committing suicide in 1959 at the age of thirty-eight. As for Joan McCracken, who had previously been in the Warner Bros. film **Hollywood Canteen** (1944), **Good News** was her last foray into films. She returned to Broadway to appear in **Bloomer Girl, Me and Juliet, Galileo** (with Charles Laughton), and **The Big Knife** (with John Garfield). She died in 1961 of a heart ailment at the age of thirty-nine.

On the plus side, **Good News** led director-

earned the role. To enact the dense but lovable football star, Freed initially wanted Van Johnson but he was unavailable. Mickey Rooney was now deemed unsuitable for the part, so the nod went to Peter Lawford, who accepted the news with horror.[2] Hugh Fordin notes in **The World of Entertainment** (1974):

> That night Lawford telephoned Comden and Green: "You've got to get me out of this picture! I'll make an absolute ass of myself. After all, I'm English, I have a British accent, I'm **not** your all-American 'Joe College.' I'm stupefied. Get me out of this!" Both of them were giggling, but they convinced him that not only did he have to do it, but it would be good for him.

Rounding out the principals were: Joan McCracken (who had scored as a Broadway dancer in **Oklahoma!** and **Billion Dollar Baby**) as Babe Doolittle, talented Ray McDonald as Bobby Turner, Mel Torme as Danny, and MGM regular Clinton Sundberg as football-hating Professor Burton Kenyon.

Freed employed much of the old, beloved score: "Tait Song" (which received some additional lyrics from Roger Edens and vocal arranger Kay Thompson), "He's a Ladies Man" (title changed to "Be a Ladies Man"), "Lucky in Love," "The Best Things in Life Are Free," "Good News," "Just Imagine," and "The Varsity Drag." To distract Lawford, it was decided to revamp the script and have him have scholastic problems with French and not astronomy. The plan backfired; he spoke perfect French, and Edens, Comden, and Green wrote "The French Lesson." (The rumor still persists that it was Lawford who taught his on-camera teacher Allyson the proper pronunciation of French so she could teach him on screen.) Also added to the score was "Pass That Peace Pipe" (by Edens, Hugh Martin, and Ralph Blane), which had been prerecorded by Allyson, Nancy Walker, and Gene Kelly for **Ziegfeld Follies** (1946) but not used. A background number added was the standard "My Blue Heaven" by Walter Donaldson. Deleted from the release print was "An Easier Way," another new Edens-Comden-Green song, performed by Allyson and Marshall. Bob Alton directed the production numbers, and director Walters brought the show in at a cost of $1,662,718, under budget by $135,270.[3]

[2] In **That's Entertainment!** (1974) cohost Peter Lawford walks amidst the ruins of the Tate College set on the MGM back lot and chuckles about the studio having cast him in musicals, apparently even today refusing to believe that he was far more than adequate in the song-and-dance requirements of **Good News, Easter Parade** (1948), etc.

[3] In his article on Walters, McVay says: "The delightfully buoyant and melodious "Lucky in Love" receives the most elaborate treatment of all the numbers in the movie: the song is taken up by individuals, couples, groups, and choruses, dotted about and strolling, in and out of doors. Marshall, Lawford, Allyson all at different times join in; so does McCracken. . .; Torme contributes a share, strumming a banjolele like a kind of troubadour-cum-sardonic commentator—and indeed, after the rendition briefly halts to accommodate a short amatory spat, the song is ironically resumed before being concluded on a closeup of the banjo strings being mockingly plucked, Torme being virtually the only figure left on the scene as the others all slowly drift off about their separate businesses."

McVay then praises McCracken's enthusiastic performance of "Pass That Peace Pipe" and concludes by examining "The Varsity Drag" finale: "It is begun by Allyson, who starts to sing the ditty to Lawford with an ebullient unexpectedness . . . and develops into an intoxicating vocal and choreographic free-for-all, with Lawford and Allyson kicking up their heels in gallant and increasingly adept fashion, while the girls in ravishing pastel dresses and boys in their formal black college-prom outfits strut and swirl separately and in unison, behind and around the two stars. . . . As the camera swoops forward into a fade-out close shot of Allyson and Lawford smiling and embracing, and the end-title hits the screen and the house lights go up, we are left irresistibly grinning in our turn: grinning with the glow of sensory bliss, and with the satisfaction of long-held hopes and dreams gratified."

choreographer Charles Walters on to several other MGM musicals, including **Easter Parade** (1948), **The Barkleys of Broadway** (1949), **Summer Stock** (1950), **Lili** (1953), and **High Society** (1956). The film itself remains a delight to see.[4]

GRAND HOTEL
1932—105 min.

Director, Edmund Goulding; based on the play **Menschen im Hotel** by Vicki Baum and on her novel; American play version by William Drake; **screenplay,** William A. Drake; **art director,** Cedric Gibbons; **gowns,** Adrian; **camera,** William Daniels; **editor,** Blanche Sewell.

Greta Garbo (**Grusinskaya**); John Barrymore (**Baron Felix von Gaigern**); Joan Crawford (**Flaemmchen**); Wallace Beery (**General Director Preysing**); Lionel Barrymore (**Otto Kringelein**); Lewis Stone (**Dr. Otternschlag**); Jean Hersholt (**Senf**); Robert McWade (**Meierheim**); Purnell B. Pratt (**Zinnowitz**); Ferdinand Gottschalk (**Pimenov**); Rafaela Ottiano (**Suzette**); Morgan Wallace (**Chauffeur**); Tully Marshall (**Gerstenkorn**); Frank Conroy (**Rohna**); Murray Kinnell (**Scweimann**); Edwin Maxwell (**Dr. Waitz**); Mary Carlisle (**Honeymooner**); John Davidson (**Hotel Manager**); Sam McDaniel (**Bartender**); Rolfe Sedan and Herbert Evans (**Clerks**); Lee Phelps (**Extra in Lobby**); Bodil Rosing (**Bit**).

SYNOPSIS

The luxurious Grand Hotel in Berlin is bustling with activity, intrigue, and assorted interrelationships.

Ambitious young Flaemmchen, a stenographer at the cosmopolitan hotel, enters into a liaison with Herr Preysing, a married industrialist. Although she finds him abhorrent, she appreciates the financial and social gain she can attain with him. (She is unaware of the textile magnate's precarious monetary status. He is engaged in a shaky merger deal with an English outfit which will bring him ruin if it fails.)

Then there is bookkeeper Otto Kringelein, an employee of Preysing. He is suffering from an incurable disease. Intent on ending his days in luxury, he engages a suite in the Grand Hotel. He is rejected by Flaemmchen, who realizes he cannot advance her status, but he is offered friendship by the roguish, impoverished Baron von Gaigern (who at one point attempts to steal Kringelein's wallet).

Another hotel guest is Grusinskaya, the famous but aging ballerina who has lost confidence in her professional expertise. That night, after being coaxed to perform at the theatre, she re-

turns to her suite to encounter the baron in her rooms searching for jewelry. The baron pretends to be an admirer of the dancer and the pair soon find a new outlook on life. The lovers plan to rendezvous later in Vienna.

However, the baron's financial situation remains grim. He plots to rob Preysing's suite, but the industrialist returns with Flaemmchen, surprising the robber in the act. Preysing kills the baron in a scuffle. Kringelein intercepts Flaemmchen and leads her from the scene, while the confused Preysing is arrested. The incident gives Flaemmchen cause to reevaluate her life and she and Kringelein set out for Paris to find a cure for him. Meanwhile, Grusinskaya with [to accommodate] her entourage leave the hotel. She is unaware that the baron has been killed and will never meet her.

War-scarred physician Dr. Otternschlag asks for messages at the reception desk throughout the film, somberly observing the activities in the lobby. At the finale he comments, "Same thing every day. . . . They come and go. . . . The Grand Hotel. . . . Nothing ever happens."

* * *

In the early 1970s when Metro-Goldwyn-Mayer abandoned most of its film production to find more profitable ventures, it was no coincidence that the corporation dubbed its new multi-million-dollar Las Vegas resort hotel "The MGM Grand Hotel." For no other motion picture in the company's history is more representative of the awesomely creative powers of that studio in its prime. Even now, some fifty years after its release, no other feature film has ever so effectively assembled as dazzling a cast of legendary players as **Grand Hotel** did.

Progression toward this celluloid milestone began when German novelist Vicki Baum wrote **Menschen im Hotel** (1930), which overnight became a bestseller. Miss Baum then wrote a play version that garnered much acclaim on the German stage under the direction of Max Reinhardt. Displaying its wonted awareness of the latest show business phenomena worldwide, MGM became interested in the property and agreed to finance a Broadway version, holding an option for the film rights. As translated by William A. Drake, the drama opened at New York's National Theatre on November 13, 1930. It was staged by Herman Shumlin and featured:

Grusinskaia	Eugenie Leontovitch
Baron von Gaigern	Henry Hull
Flaemmchen	Hortense Alden
Preysing	Sigfried Rumann
Otto Kringelein	Sam Jaffe
Dr. Otternschlag	Romaine Callender
Senf, the Porter	Walter Vonnegut
Suzette, the Maid	Rafaela Ottiano

By the time **Grand Hotel** played the last of its 444 performances, MGM was diligently preparing the cinema version, under the supervision of Paul Bern, Irving Thalberg's top producer. The project was festooned with a lavish $700,000 budget. As the **coup de grace,** Metro announced an all-star cast of such magnitude that almost everybody within range of the Culver City publicity

department was impressed—save for the cast itself.

Greta Garbo faced the prospect of playing aging Grusinskaya with her usual trepidation and brooding. The script altered the character to a younger woman but she still feared the task of conveying the grace of a ballet artist (her notoriously large feet had already become a favorite Hollywood joke). To play the dashing jewel thief, Baron von Gaigern, Metro originally considered John Gilbert. But few were surprised when the front office, nursing its hate of that once great attraction, removed his name from the projected cast list and replaced him with John Barrymore. The latter despised playing such clotheshorse heroes, once equating such parts with "male impersonations of Lilyan Tashman." Joan Crawford, as the sexy stenographer Flaemmchen, feared that she would be overlooked in the proceedings when compared to such seasoned costars. She entered the production with fists raised (despite much later protestations of being overjoyed at the opportunity of finally working with Garbo). Wallace Beery had seen the Broadway play, and as he left the theatre after the performance, the first thing he said to his wife Rita was how much he detested the character of Preysing. "He doesn't murder women," said Wally, "but he's lower than anybody I've ever played." Having scored so heavily as the hero of **The Champ** (1931), Beery greeted his casting as the show's heavy by pounding on the doors of everybody on the lot in hopes of shedding the unwanted assignment. Lionel Barrymore, as the dying Kringelein, at least liked his part but could not see the appeal of an all-star movie—actors, he reasoned, were not zoo animals. Only Lewis Stone as the scarred and bitter Dr. Otternschlag and Jean Hersholt as the expectant father-porter Senf entered the film in a relaxed manner.

Therefore, when **Grand Hotel** began shooting in January 1932, with Edmund Goulding directing, Metro ordered the publicity department to issue as many reports as possible reflecting the good humor and cooperation on the set.[1] The public "learned" that John Barrymore greeted Garbo by kissing her hand and saying, "My wife and I think you are the most beautiful woman in the world"; that, after they completed their famous love scene, Garbo impulsively kissed Barrymore, exclaiming, "You have no idea what it means to me to play opposite so perfect an artist!"; that Joan Crawford was moved to genuine tears by Lionel's emotional scenes and remarked, "Every single day, Mr. Lionel Barrymore would say something nice to me. He'd say, 'How are you, baby? I never saw you look so beautiful,' he'd tell me that I had acted better than any other day that week. I know he didn't mean it, but it was nice to hear"; that John Barrymore told Wallace Beery, "Not that I'm falling in love with you or anything, but I'd like to make a statement. You're the best actor on this set"; that Beery lent Garbo the keys to his mountain cabin near Yosemite, where she "could **really** be alone."

---

[4]The less said, the better about the diluted 1974 road-and-Broadway revival of **Good News**, which featured John Payne as the football coach and Alice Faye as the astronomy instructor.

[1]**Grand Hotel** was in production for forty-nine days.

Ferdinand Gottschalk, Greta Garbo, Bodil Rosing, and Rafaela Ottiano in Grand Hotel *('32).*

However, things were **not** entirely peaceful. At times the soundstage air was heavy with animosity. Garbo was fearful that Crawford could and would steal the picture. Beery embarked on a two-day strike when shooting began ("I hate the lousy part I'm playing in **Grand Hotel.** I told 'em I didn't want to do it. I shot my mouth off to everyone in power on the lot and it didn't do a hell of a bit of good!"); when he did report for work, John Barrymore greeted him with a cocked eyebrow, perusing Beery as if he were an amusing grotesque. It began a feud that lasted until Barrymore terminated the anger with the previously mentioned praise on the eighth day of shooting.

But it was Crawford who really came in fighting. After a lengthy delay in properly lighting the Barrymore brothers, Joan snapped, "Okay, boys, but don't forget that the American movie public would rather have one look at my back than watch both of your faces for an hour." In addition, she reported every day with a secretary who carried a phonograph, playing moody pieces to place the actress in the conducive state of mind for her more powerful vignettes. (According to legend, she would frequently play Marlene Dietrich recordings, to remind Garbo of the powerful European rival at Paramount.) This record playing incensed no-nonsense Beery, who plotted revenge. One day he asked Joan if **he** could have a little mood music to help him get conditioned for a difficult scene. As Beery would recollect with delight, "So I raised my hand, giving the signal, and in marched two big guys, in blue uniforms, covered with gold braids, one banging a bass drum and the other playing 'Marching Through Georgia' on a piccolo. Joan wouldn't speak to me, except professionally, for a week!"

Nevertheless, Goulding kept temperaments to a minimum, shrewdly constructing the shooting to have all the stars together on the set as infrequently as possible. (In the end, for example, when Beery is taken out of the hotel lobby handcuffed as Garbo watches, the two stars had played their business in that scene on different days, a mechanical fact skillfully handled by the editor.) Goulding well deserved the nickname "Lion Tamer"—**Grand Hotel** was completed on schedule after forty-eight days of shooting.

On April 16, 1932, MGM premiered **Grand Hotel** at Sid Grauman's Chinese Theatre on Hollywood Boulevard and the evening was a triumph for all concerned. MGM withheld general national release of the film for several months until September 1932, allowing word of the great achievement to precede its appearance. Critics cheered the film. The **New York Times** reported, "It is a production thoroughly worthy of all the talk it has created and the several motion picture luminaries deserve to feel very proud of their performances, particularly Greta Garbo and Lionel Barrymore. . . . Miss Garbo, possibly appreciating that she was supported by a galaxy of efficient performers, decided she would do her utmost to make her role shine. And she succeeds admirably. . . . Mr. Barrymore is superb. . . . If ever an actor got under the skin of a character, Mr. Barrymore does here." Though Garbo and Lionel did win the major share of plaudits, all the leads won praise. Richard Watts, Jr. **(New York Herald-Tribune)** wrote of John Barrymore, "In the more conventional role of the unscrupulous baron he succeeds in being so charming and engaging a hero that he makes one forget that his part really is merely that of a conventional leading man. Here is Barrymore magic

to an almost miraculous extent." Ed Sullivan in his syndicated column avowed that the entire picture belonged to Joan Crawford.

Grand Hotel deservedly became a box-office bonanza. It grossed $1,594,000 and won the 1931–32 Best Picture prize. Ironically, for all the impressive histrionics provided by the stellar cast, **none** of the principals received Academy Award nominations.

The success of **Grand Hotel** was far reaching. It encouraged MGM to film other all-star blockbusters—**Dinner at Eight** (1933), **Night Flight** (1933), **Romeo and Juliet** (1936), etc.—inspired other studios to copy the plot formula, and spawned in audiences a love for all-star formula pictures that continues to this day (**The Towering Inferno, Earthquake, Airport,** etc.). The original film itself received an official remake in 1945 by Metro in the 130-minute, less moody, more glossy **Weekend at the Waldorf.** (A far less ostentatious remake of the property was the 1959 West German version featuring Michele Morgan and O. W. Fischer.)

In 1958 a musical play version of **Grand Hotel** began a pre-Broadway tour in Los Angeles starring Paul Muni (Kringelein) and Cesare Danova (the Baron), and Neile Adams, David Opatoshu, Joan Diener, and Valdimir Sokoloff. With songs by Robert Wright and George Forrest, the show entitled **At the Grand** earned no plaudits and was summarily closed after its California engagements.

Then in late 1976 Metro released news that it would remake **Grand Hotel,** to be produced by Martin Elfand and directed by Sydney Pollack. The David Zelag Goodman script, said to contain "more than a dozen star roles," would be set against the background of the MGM Grand Hotel in Las Vegas and would be a coproduction of MGM and Warner Bros. It remained a pipedream venture.

THE GREAT CARUSO

1951 C—109 min.

Producer, Joe Pasternak; **director,** Richard Thorpe; based on the story by Dorothy Caruso; **screenplay,** Sonia Levien and William Ludwig; **costumes,** Gile Steele and Helen Rose, **art directors,** Cedric Gibbons and Gabriel Scognamillo; **music supervisor,** Johnny Green; **sound,** Douglas Shearer; **camera,** Joseph Ruttenberg; **editor,** Gene Ruggiero.

Mario Lanza **(Enrico Caruso);** Ann Blyth **(Dorothy Benjamin);** Dorothy Kirsten **(Louise Heggar);** Jarmila Novotna **(Maria Selka);** Richard Hageman **(Carlo Santi);** Carl Benton Reid **(Park Benjamin);** Eduard Franz **(Guilio Gatti-Casazza);** Ludwig Donath **(Alfredo Brazzi);** Alan Napier **(Jean de Reszke);** Paul Javor **(Antonio Scotti);** Carl Milletaire **(Gino);** Shepard Menken **(Fucito);** Vincent Renno **(Tullio);** Nestor Paiva **(Egisto Barretto);** Peter Edward Price **(Caruso as a Boy);** Mario Siletti **(Papa Caruso);** Angela Clarke **(Mrs. Caruso);** Ian Wolfe **(Hutchins);** Yvette Duguay **(Musetta);** Argentina Brunetti **(Mrs. Barretto);** Maurice Samuels **(Papa Gino);**

Mario Lanza in The Great Caruso *('51).*

Edit Angold **(Hilda)**; Peter Brocco **(Father Bronzetti)**; David Bond **(Father Angelico)**; Matt Moore **(Max)**; Anthony Mazola **(Fucito at Age Eight)**; Mae Clarke **(Woman)**; Sherry Jackson **(Musetta as a Child)**; Blanche Thebom, Teresa Celli, Nicola Moscona, Giuseppe Valdengo, Lucine Armara, Marina Koshetz, Gilbert Russell, and Robert E. Bright **(Opera Singers)**.

SYNOPSIS

Enrico Caruso is born in Naples in 1873 to poor parents. As a young boy he is shown as having a gifted voice and singing in a church choir. Grown into manhood he sings in cabarets for whatever money is thrown to him. His magnificent voice eventually comes to the attention of two opera singers, who launch him on a singing career by getting him a job in an operatic chorus. His rise in the opera world is swift and before long he makes a triumphant concert tour of Europe and is proclaimed as the world's greatest tenor. Now wealthy, he returns to Naples to marry the girl he loves, only to learn she has not waited for him. He then heads for America, accompanied by a retinue of friends who have helped his career over the years. There is operatic debut is marred by the powerful influence of Park Benjamin, a wealthy patron of the arts whom he has innocently offended. Despite the man's opposition, Caruso not only becomes the idol of music lovers but even wins the love of Benjamin's daughter, Dorothy. Enrico and Dorothy eventually marry and the couple later have a child. Then the great singer becomes ill with a throat ailment. He refuses to

heed the pleadings of his wife and friends that he stop singing. He eventually collapses on the stage and dies at the age of forty-seven.

* * *

Mario Lanza! Some two decades after the drink-and-drug demise of the movies' most charismatic tenor, his glories are perpetuated by fan clubs who cherish his handful of cinema starring roles. He is remembered as the greatest opera star of the movies, as one of Metro's most dynamic screen personalities, and as one of the most temperamental monsters ever loosed in Culver City.

Lanza's greatest MGM triumph, **The Great Caruso,** had long been a pet dream of Louis B. Mayer. Caruso's widow, Dorothy, had written the story of her husband's life (1873–1921) and sold the screen rights to MGM. But Mayer was on his way out of power and there was considerable controversy among the bigwigs as to the merits of the projected Caruso feature. Lanza, who had been signed by Mayer after a 1947 concert at the Hollywood Bowl, and had scored in MGM's **That Midnight Kiss** (1949) and **The Toast of New Orleans** (1950) was the prospective choice to play the title role. He aired his views on the matter: "Those bastards in New York with all the dough don't think I'm good enough to star in Caruso's life story. Who the hell do they think can play Caruso? Nelson Eddy? There is nobody but me who can play that role. I am Caruso!"

Production was finally approved; Joseph Pasternak produced and Richard Thorpe directed. The film contained twenty-seven vocal items, nine operatic scenes, and ten opera stars. It boasted the following pieces among the richly cultural score:

"The Loveliest Night of the Year" (popular American song)
"Vesti la Giubba" (from the opera **I Pagliacci)**
"The Last Rose of Summer" (from the opera **Martha)**
"M'Appari" (from **Martha)**
"Celeste Aida" (from the opera **Aida)**
"Numi, Pietà" (from **Aida)**
"La Fatal Pietra" (Finale of **Aida)**
"Sweethearts" (from the operetta of the same name)
Sextet (from the opera **Lucia di Lammermoor)**
"La Donna à Mobile" (from the opera **Rigoletto)**
"Che Gelida Manina!" (from the opera **La Bohème)**
"E Lucevan le Stelle" (from the opera **Tosca)**
"Ave Maria" (German song)
"Mattinata" (Italian song)
"Because" (popular American song)

Before its completion, **The Great Caruso** had become a classic on the lot. Its legendary standing was not because of Lanza's talents or the appeal of his costar Ann Blyth (who performed the great hit "The Loveliest Night of the Year"), but due to the star's uniquely crude behavior. Emulating Caruso's grand style, Lanza reported to the lot each day garbed in the great tenor's favorite outfit of homburg hat, cane, and spats. Lanza developed a style all his own of alienating and incensing the cast, crew, and front office with vulgar on-the-set activities.

In a **Focus on Film** magazine interview with Scott Eyman, veteran cinematographer Joseph Ruttenberg recalled of Lanza:

"Such bursts of ego, of self-inflation I have rarely seen on a movie set. He would demand the most outrageous things simply for the sake of demanding outrageous things. . . . I made seventy-nine pictures at MGM with practically every director on the lot and I didn't have trouble with but two or three people. Doris Day I didn't get along with—and Lanza was a royal pain."

Lanza's eating habits also generated problems. After a festive weekend gluttonous Mario would report to work pounds heavier, causing hysteria among the costumers, who would be forced to alter immediately all his costumes (dieting during production was out of the question). The star, self-nicknamed "Tiger Boy," frequently kept the entire company waiting while he dallied in his dressing room with assorted starlets. His personal habits and attitudes, which included an apparent antipathy toward soap and water and a disbelief in the necessity of bathrooms, were sufficiently erratic to keep the commissary constantly buzzing about the explosive tenor.

When **The Great Caruso** opened in May 1951 at the Radio City Music Hall, Lanza was professionally vindicated. The picture grossed $1,500,000 in ten weeks there—a house record. "Undoubtedly," reported **Variety,** "Hollywood amplification builds up a voice, but Lanza's talent is obvious, of high artistic caliber and quite stirring. The top notes are clear, sonorous, and ringing. Musically, he's a treat." Beautiful Ann Blyth, who had been borrowed from Universal when none of Metro's leading ladies had the courage to work opposite Lanza, was exceptional. But it was predominately Mario who parlayed **The Great Caruso** into a smash hit, which grossed $4,531,000 in distributors' domestic rentals.

Many opera critics have suggested that Lanza was every bit the equal of Caruso. This comparison always upset Caruso's widow, who later regretted selling the rights to the book. As for Lanza, he insisted he was better than the Metropolitan opera star.

There was only one more Metro film for Lanza on his term contract. **Because You're Mine** (1952) was successful but his outrageous treatment of his leading lady,[1] Doretta Morrow, and his assorted outbursts made MGM wonder if he was indeed worth the trouble. After later recording the songs for MGM's **The Student Prince** (1954), he walked out on the production. Metro sued him for $5,000,000, then solved the problem by having Edmund Purdom lip-synch the songs to Lanza's voice tracts. Only three more films[2] were to come and then he died in Rome on October 7, 1958, after a bloodclot moved from his leg to his heart. He was only thirty-eight years old.

Although while Mario Lanza's popularity continues—his RCA recordings reputedly reap $100,000 in royalties a year—his legacy is mainly a tragic one. In the words of Joseph Ruttenberg, "That idiot Lanza! He had the greatest opportunities in the world, but he just couldn't handle success."

THE GREAT ZIEGFELD
1936—180 min.

Producer, Hunt Stromberg; **director**, Robert Z. Leonard; **story-screenplay**, William Anthony McGuire; **art director**, Cedric Gibbons; **costumes**, Adrian; **music director**, Arthur Lange; **ballet music**, Con Conrad; **choreography**, Seymour Felix; **orchestrator**, Frank Skinner; **songs**, Walter Donaldson and Harold Adamson; Irving Berlin; Harriet Hoctor; **ballet lyrics**, Herb Magidson; **sound**, Douglas Shearer; **camera**, Oliver T. Marsh, Ray June, George Folsey, and Merritt B. Gerstad; **editor**, William S. Gray.

William Powell (**Florenz Ziegfeld**); Luise Rainer (**Anna Held**); Myrna Loy (**Billie Burke**); Frank Morgan (**Billings**); Reginald Owen (**Sampston**); Nat Pendleton (**Sandow the Great**); Virginia Bruce (**Audrey Lane**); Ernest Cossart (**Sidney**); Robert Greig (**Joe**); Raymond Walburn (**Sage**); Fanny Brice (**Herself**); Jean Chatburn (**Mary Lou**); Ann Pennington (**Herself**); Ray Bolger (**Himself**); Harriet Hoctor (**Herself**); Gilda Gray (**Herself**); Charles

Trowbridge (**Julian Mitchell**); A. A. Trimble (**Will Rogers**); Joan Holland (**Patricia Ziegfeld**); Buddy Doyle (**Eddie Cantor**); Charles Judels (**Pierre**); Leon Errol (**Himself**); Marcelle Corday (**Marie**); Esther Muir (**Prima Donna**); Herman Bing (**Customer**); Paul Irving (**Erlanger**); William Demarest (**Gene Buck**); Stanley Morner [Dennis Morgan] (**Vocalist in "Pretty Girl" Number**); Allan Jones (**Voice Dubber in "Pretty Girl" Number**); Alfred P. James (**Stage Doorman**); Sarah Edwards (**Wardrobe Woman**); Suzanne Kaaren (**Miss Blair**); Mickey Daniels (**Telegraph Boy**); Alice Keating (**Alice**) Charles Coleman (**Carriage Starter**); Mary Howard (**Miss Carlisle**); Evelyn Dockson (**Fat Woman**); Susan Fleming (**Girl with Sage**); Charles Fallon (**French Ambassador**); Adrienne d'Ambricourt (**Wife of French Ambassador**); Edwin Maxwell (**Charles Frohman**); Ruth Gillette (**Lillian Russell**); John Hyams (**Dave Stamper**); Wallis Clark (**Broker**); Ray Brown (**Inspector Doyle**); Pat Nixon (**Extra**).

SYNOPSIS

Florenz Ziegfeld amasses a large amount of money from his exploitation of Sandow the strongman at the Chicago Fair. Later Ziegfeld loses his small fortune gambling in Monte Carlo. Assuaging his

Fanny Brice in The Great Ziegfeld *('36).*

---

[1]Kathryn Grayson, Lanza's leading lady in his first two films, refused to work with him ever again.

[2]The last films were Warner Bros.' **Serenade** (1956) and two made on special deals abroad and released through MGM: **The Seven Hills of Rome** (1958) and **For the First Time** (1959).

Luise Rainer and William Powell in The Great Ziegfeld.

opt for the rights to a screen biography of Florenz Ziegfeld (1869–1932). Universal made the first successful bid, but that lot's ever-shaky financial standing soon canceled plans and Metro acquired the screen rights for $250,000. The price included the screenplay written by William Anthony McGuire. He had been a longtime friend and confidant of Ziegfeld and was able to present his consumptive, dallying ladies' man chum in an attractive light rather than in a sordid one.

Producer Hunt Stromberg proceeded to spend every cent of the $2,000,000 budget on the spectacle. William Powell was starred as Ziegfeld, with his very popular screen vis-à-vis Myrna Loy[1] shrewdly added as Billie Burke. (Miss Burke, who had been set by Universal to play herself in that company's version, was awarded an MGM player's contract **not** to appear as herself and to serve instead as the film's "technical adviser.") The role of the great Anna Held, temperamental Continental star who refused to cope with Flo's womanizing, was assigned to Viennese actress Luise Rainer. She had made her debut at Metro with Powell in **Escapade** (1935), in which she replaced Loy. In addition to Frank Morgan (as Ziegfeld's old competitor Billings, who later joins the rival fold), there were Virginia Bruce (as hard-drinking bitch Audrey Lane), Nat Pendleton (Sandow the Great), and such Ziegfeld stage performers as Ray Bolger, Gilda Gray, Harriet Hoctor, Leon Errol, and Fanny Brice as themselves. One of Ziegfeld's greatest attractions, Marilyn Miller, demanded such a high price for her services that MGM canceled her appearance in the picture. A. A. Trimble was signed to play the late Will Rogers and Buddy Doyle impersonated the too high-priced Eddie Cantor.

Every effort was made through production to ensure opulence. The most celebrated number of the outing, "A Pretty Girl Is Like a Melody" (from Ziegfeld's 1919 **Follies**), has become a classic. The lavish segment boasted a huge revolving pillar of 175 steps decorated with 192 girls; a stunning Virginia Bruce lolled atop the lovely heap while Stanley Morner (later known as Dennis Morgan) "sang" with the dubbed voice of Allan Jones. This delicious scene, filmed near the close of shooting almost as an afterthought, was too large to be housed on a soundstage and was moved into an oversized circus tent on the lot. Cost of the number: $240,000.

In April 1936 the 180-minute **Great Ziegfeld** made its bow. Critical reaction was one of extravagant praise. **Variety:** "The Great Ziegfeld as a film property can be said to be the reincarnation of a theatrical tradition, fresh in memory of most theatregoers. As such . . . here is an almost contemporaneous personality. For Ziegfeld is the symbol of a tradition of show business." **New York American:** "The Great Ziegfeld is pretty nearly everything such an extravaganza should be. There are romance and reality, song and dance, gaiety and beauty, pathos and bathos which is the restless heart of Broadway." **New York World-Telegram:** "Acted with spirit and understanding by an

bad luck is the discovery of actress Anna Held, who signs a performing contract with Ziegfeld, much to the dismay of his rival Billings.

Eventually Ziegfeld weds Anna, but their marriage is plagued by his extravagances and her jealousy. Though his marriage ends in divorce, Ziegfeld continues his successful theatrical ventures. He soon marries actress Billie Burke and they have a daughter, Patricia. When Ziegfeld suffers a financial reverse, Billie offers her jewels to her husband to help recoup his former show business status. Within short order he boasts four concurrent Broadway hits: **Rio Rita, Rosalie, The Three Musketeers,** and **Showboat.**

The Depression reduces Ziegfeld to near bankruptcy and the weakening producer soon dies.

* * *

"You will never see another musical film that exceeds it in opulence, in visual inventiveness, in Babylonian splendor," cheered Thornton Delehanty of the **New York Evening Post.** He was referring to MGM's **The Great Ziegfeld,** which was playing to packed houses at New York's Astor Theatre with a top-price ticket of $2.20. Along with **Grand Hotel** (1932), **The Great Ziegfeld** is perhaps Metro's most glorious achievement of the 1930s. The film has become almost as legendary as the great showman himself, thanks to the majestic aplomb of William Powell, the heralded tears of Luise Rainer, the smart direction of Robert Z. Leonard, and the unabashedly acknowledged $2,000,000 budget that won the Oscar-earning opus the status of being MGM's costliest production since **Ben-Hur** (1925).

MGM was **not** the first Hollywood studio to

---

[1]Powell and Loy had already appeared together in **Manhattan Melodrama** (1943), **The Thin Man** (1934), and **Evelyn Prentice** (1934).

"A Pretty Girl Is Like a Melody" sequence from The Great Ziegfeld *with Virginia Bruce at top.*

ficates on the art of show business from his celestial retreat.[3]

THE GUARDSMAN
1931—83 min.

Director, Sidney Franklin; based on the play by Ferenc Molnar; **adapters**, Ernst Vajda and Claudine West; **camera**, Norbert Brodine; **editor**, Conrad A. Nervig.

Alfred Lunt **(The Actor)**; Lynn Fontanne **(The Actress)**; Roland Young **(The Critic)**; ZaSu Pitts **(Liesl, the Maid)**; Maude Eburne **(Mama)**; Herman Bing **(Creditor)**; Ann Dvorak **(A Fan)**.

SYNOPSIS

The "happiest married couple on the stage" have fallen to caustically attacking each other's thespian endeavors. Their six-month marriage is not the blissful romanticism audiences view upon the stage.

The actor feels his wife has romantic interests in a soldier, a guardsman. Later the stage star poses as a guardsman and begins to court his wife with letters and flowers. Disguised as a soldier, he arranges for a rendezvous, during which he plans to seduce her.

The actress wife does not succumb to the guardsman's advances and the husband is inwardly delighted by her display of fidelity.

Thereafter the wife coyly admits she knew it was her husband in disguise.

"How did you know?" he inquires.

"My dear, no one can kiss as you do."

* * *

"Alfred and I will not do any swimming, high diving, fast horseback riding, or any of those

expertly directed cast, the film projects itself across the screen without losing a whit of its theatrical effectiveness."

On March 4, 1937, the Ninth Annual Academy Awards Banquet was held at the Biltmore Bowl, where **The Great Ziegfeld** was named Best Picture of the year.[2] Seymour Felix received an Oscar for Dance Direction, and Luise Rainer won her first of two Oscars for her theatrically played telephone vignette in which Anna congratulates Flo, with

poignantly controlled tears, on his new marriage. Her Anna Held is perhaps the shortest Best Actress Oscar-winning role in Academy history. (She also won the New York Film Critics Circle Award for her Anna.) Strangely, neither Myrna Loy (as the fluttery Billie Burke) nor Powell (as the flamboyant and very human producer) was Oscar-nominated; each had a major assignment.

So overwhelming was audience response to **The Great Ziegfeld** that MGM could not resist continuing in the mold. **Ziegfeld Girl** (1941) would focus on the lives and times of three contrasting Ziegfeld showgirls, without presenting the great producer on camera; and **Ziegfeld Follies** (1946) would call William Powell back into service, this time playing the deceased showman who ponti-

---

[2]**The Great Ziegfeld** defeated MGM's own **Libeled Lady, Romeo and Juliet, San Francisco,** and **A Tale of Two Cities,** as well as **The Story of Louis Pasteur** (Warner Bros.), **Dodsworth** (United Artists), and **Mr. Deeds Goes to Town** (Columbia).

[3]On May 21, 1978, a three-hour NBC-TV television movie **Ziegfeld: The Man and His Women,** costing over $3 million was produced and directed by Buzz Kulik. It featured Paul Shenar (Ziegfeld), Barbara Parkins (Anna Held); Samantha Eggar (Billie Burke), Valerie Perrine (Lillian Lorraine), Pamela Peadon (Marilyn Miller), and Inga Swenson (Nora Bayes). The script by Joanna Lee dealt with the showman's life from boyhood during the Chicago fire of 1871 through his Broadway years and until his death in 1932. Ziegfeld's daughter, Patricia Ziegfeld Stevenson, served as technical adviser on the production. The production proved to be less than memorable. The **Hollywood Reporter** explained that the special ". . . has all the glimmering ingredients essential to recreating the life of showman Florenz Ziegfeld—the production is opulently lush and evidently no expense has been spared to capture the flamboyant world in which Ziegfeld made his mark in theatre history. However, this comes to naught because the film's center—the man himself—is curiously cool. Writer Joanna Lee's inventive book reveals Ziegfeld through three of the more prominent women in his life. . . . These differing viewpoints depict Ziegfeld as an opportunist, an insensitive cad, and a man susceptible to feminine wiles; indeed, the man is discussed by everyone except the source himself. . . . Lee's script is responsible and hard but lacks that connection to Ziegfeld's psyche that's so essential."

Lynn Fontanne and Alfred Lunt in The Guardsman *('31).*

other things that you do out there in movies," intoned the imperious Lynn Fontanne to Irving Thalberg. The MGM producer had come to Chicago where the Lunts were starring in **Elizabeth the Queen.** Thalberg's aim was to have the acclaimed stage stars appear together in a Metro film. Ever seeking to add "legitimacy" to the cinema, Thalberg was convinced the spectacle of the Lunts playing together in a film would gain MGM new respect and profits.

The Lunts agreed and Thalberg was delighted, even though the very outspoken Miss Fontanne took the opportunity in the hotel suite to lecture Mrs. Thalberg (Norma Shearer) on her thespian defects. "My dear, I have something to tell you. I recently saw you in one of your comedies, and I would like to give you some advice: you must not laugh at your lines after you deliver them!"

The vehicle selected for the Lunts was **The Guardsman.**[1] It was adapted from the French play by Ferenc Molnar, in which they had opened at New York's Garrick Theatre on October 13, 1924, for the first of 274 performances. The screen fee promised the team was $60,000. "Alfred and I were prepared to work for less but nobody asked us," said Lynn after their arrival in Culver City. This was only the first of embarrassments caused the studio by the loose-lipped, unabashedly flamboyant Lunts, who refused to be intimidated by any sacred cows—including Louis B. Mayer himself, whom they called "Mr. Meyers." After director Sidney Franklin worked out an elaborate set scheme that would allow Fontanne to play her bathtub scene with her back to the crew, thereby shielding her nude chest from view, the actress pivoted her bare breasts right into the camera. Her response to the unsettled Franklin was that it was the only logical thing to do; the phone had rung downstage from her.

The theatrics of the husband-wife team somewhat amused Hollywood. In his book **Mayer and Thalberg: The Make-Believe Saints** (1975), former MGM story editor Samuel Marx relates a favorite story:

When production of **The Guardsman** started, Miss Fontanne looked at the rushes; Lunt did not. After seeing them, she told him,

"You're wonderful, Alfred. You're manly, dashing, and glamorous. Your makeup is perfect, except in one short scene where the lips aren't straight. But I look frightful, I'm old, haggard, my costumes don't fit, my shape is ghastly. I photograph like a witch." According to the story, now considered a classic of actor behaviorism, Lunt brushed a finger across his mouth and murmured, "So the lips weren't straight."

The Guardsman was completed in a very economical twenty-one days; a Thalberg-ordered retake was scuttled when Lunt, opposed to the retake, used one of his tricks and "rolled out" one eye in the scene so as to appear quite peculiar. ("It always happens when I am fatigued," sniffed Lunt to the angry Thalberg.)

When the film premiered in the late summer of 1931, critical praise was abundant.[2] Irene Thirer of the **New York Daily News** reported, "Lunt and Fontanne, besides being superb artists, take splendidly to the camera. He is handsome, she beautiful; both are fascinating and glamorous." The **Times** (London) noted, "It has wit and subtlety, and perfection is somehow too harsh and brittle a word to describe the delicate interplay of thought, gesture, and voice by which Miss Lynn Fontanne and Mr. Alfred Lunt build up the characters of the Actress and the Actor." However, as Richard Watts, Jr. of the **New York Herald-Tribune** pointed out in his review, "[Though] admirable entertainment . . . it is far from exceptional as a motion picture. It has been directed with a conscientious, though unalluring, regard for the methods of the stage." Audiences for the most part found the theatricality and sophistication not to their liking, and **The Guardsman,** while a critical success, did not score at the box office.

Both Lunt and Fontanne were Oscar-nominated for their work in the film. He lost to Wallace Beery of **The Champ** and Fredric March of **Dr. Jekyll and Mr. Hyde,** she to Helen Hayes of **The Sin of Madelon Claudet.** Neither member of the starring team had any enthusiasm for movies. After **The Guardsman,** they rejected Thalberg's offer of a contract, a pact that would have netted them a million dollars.[3] The couple would appear together in only one more film, **Stage Door Canteen** (1943), in which they made patriotic cameos.

When MGM filmed **The Chocolate Soldier** in 1941 with Nelson Eddy and Rise Stevens, it did not utilize the plot of the Strauss operetta, but instead used the storyline of **The Guardsman.** On March 2, 1955, on CBS-TV's "The Best of Broadway" series, Mary Boland and Franchot Tone starred in a video version of **The Guardsman.**

---

[1] The Lunts had appeared together in the film **Second Youth** (Metro-Goldwyn, 1924); Lunt had acted without Fontanne in **Backbone** (1923), **Ragged Edge** (1923), **Lovers in Quarantine** (1925), and **Sally of the Sawdust** (1925), the last with W. C. Fields. Fontanne had acted without Lunt in **The Man Who Found Himself** (1925).

[2] Promotional copy for **The Guardsman** boasted, "Idols of the American stage at last in Talkies . . . it is the privilege of Metro-Goldwyn-Mayer to bring the aristocrats of the American stage to you in the talkie of their greatest stage success."

[3] Thalberg would have starred them in **Elizabeth the Queen** and **Reunion in Vienna.** The Lunts stated about their rejection of the studio contract, "We would just be their puppets. This we didn't do in the theatre and we couldn't do in the films." (It was in this period that Carl Laemmle at Universal offered the Lunts $250,000 to star in **Tristan and Isolde.**)

A GUY NAMED JOE
1943—120 min.

Producer, Everett Riskin; **director,** Victor Fleming; based on an unpublished story by Chandler Sprague, David Boehm, and Frederick H. Brennan; **screenplay,** Dalton Trumbo; **song,** Roy Turk and Fred Ahlert; **music,** Herbert Stothart; **art directors,** Cedric Gibbons and Lyle Wheeler; **set decorators,** Edwin B. Willis and Ralph Hurst; **assistant director,** Horace Hough; **sound,** Charles E. Wallace; **special effects,** Arnold Gillespie, Donald Jahraus, and Warren Newcombe; **camera,** George Folsey and Karl Freund; **editor,** Frank Sullivan.

Spencer Tracy **(Pete Sandidge)**; Irene Dunne **(Dorinda Durston)**; Van Johnson **(Ted Randall)**; Ward Bond **(Al Yackey)**; James Gleason **("Nails" Kilpatrick)**; Lionel Barrymore **(The General)**; Barry Nelson **(Dick Rumney)**; Don DeFore **("Powerhouse" O'Rourke)**; Henry O'Neill **(Colonel Hendricks)**; Addison Richards **(Major Corbett)**; Charles Smith **(Sanderson)**; Mary Elliott **(Dancehall Girl)**; Earl Schenck **(Colonel Sykes)**; Maurice Murphy **(Captain Robertson)**; Gertrude Hoffman **(Old Woman)**; Mark Daniels **(Lieutenant)**; William Bishop **(Ray)**; Eve Whitney **(Powerhouse's Girl)**; Esther Williams **(Ellen Bright)**; Kay Williams **(Girl at Bar)**; John Whitney and Kirk Alyn **(Officers in Heaven)**; Gibson Gowland **(Bartender)**; Edward Hardwicke **(George)**; Yvonne Severn **(Elizabeth)**; Christopher Severn **(Peter)**; Frank Faylen and Phil Van Zandt **(Majors)**; Matt Willis **(Lieutenant Hunter)**; Jacqueline White **(Helen)**.

Barry Nelson, Spencer Tracy, Van Johnson, Irene Dunne, and Ward Bond in A Guy Named Joe *('43).*

SYNOPSIS
Daring World War II combat pilot Pete Sandidge wins notoriety for his reckless bravery. His heroism excites fellow pilots but worries fiancée Dorinda Durston, a ferry command pilot. Her fears turn to grief when Pete crashes his plane into an enemy aircraft carrier, dying a hero's death.

Pete's soul travels to a militarylike heaven where "the General" dispatches the ectoplasmic Peter on a mission—to watch over fledgling pilots such as Ted Randall as well as his bereaved Dorinda. Returning to the base operated by "Nails" Kilpatrick, Pete carries out his duties. But a perplexing entanglement develops when Ted falls in love with Dorinda.

Ted soon draws the challenge of a dangerous bombing mission. However, the night before he is scheduled to take off, Dorinda, with Pete as her "copilot," steals the plane. The ghost and his ex-fiancée conduct the mission themselves and achieve their goal.[1]

* * *

Dore Schary once reflected on the peculiar tastes of the World War II public in regard to

---

[1]The original ending for **A Guy Named Joe** had Dorinda killed while successfully completing the mission. Thereafter Ted returns to his former love, Ellen Bright. Dorinda and Pete enter Paradise together. The MGM hierarchy determined this was too morbid a finale for the feature and ruled that a happier finale should be shot and spliced onto the picture.

martial wartime entertainment: "Oddly enough, the documentaries, which were made available to exhibitors for free, were not popular; the exhibitors would offer them but the public would not go to see them. Now they **would** go the next day to a picture with Errol Flynn in which he killed eighty-seven million Germans, because fiction was more interesting even though it was not pertinent to the war."

In fact, not only was fiction preferable to the horrors of watching **real** people dying, but out-and-out **fantasy** scored at the box office during the war years, as proven by Metro's **A Guy Named Joe,**[2] a rather outrageous blend of combat action, love, drama, comedy, and fantasy.

The tale of a slain fighter pilot who is dispatched from heaven to watch over a rookie was developed by talents who had experience in manufacturing cinema ghosts. Producer Everett Riskin had produced Columbia's very popular **Here Comes Mr. Jordan** (1941), which starred Robert Montgomery in a celestial mission. Dalton Trumbo, who wrote the MGM scenario, had scripted Paramount's hit **The Remarkable Andrew** (1942), with Brian Donlevy as the rye-guzzling ghost of Andrew Jackson.

A Guy Named Joe had its share of production problems both on and off the set. It was Irene Dunne's first MGM picture since **The Secret of Madame Blanche** (1933). She valued the assign-

---

[2]The film's title derives from a remark made by General Claire Chennault during the early stages of World War II: "When I'm behind the stick, I'm just a guy named Joe."

ment enough to accept second billing to Tracy. The cantankerous male star had already been spoiled by his enjoyable working relationship with Katharine Hepburn and he immediately indicated to all concerned (including Dunne) that he was not thrilled to be cast opposite such a high-toned "lady." Filming continued, and then chaos erupted. Van Johnson was involved in a serious accident when, driving friends Keenan and Eve Wynn to a preview of MGM's **Keeper of the Flame** (1942, starring Tracy and Hepburn), a car ran a stop light and smashed into Johnson's convertible. He was hospitalized and a metal plate inserted into his smashed forehead (a 4-F military deferment resulted). With the company facing an indeterminable delay until he recovered, Louis B. Mayer announced intentions of replacing Johnson. Candidates for the role of the young pilot were contractees Peter Lawford and John Hodiak. Tracy, Johnson's favorite actor, insisted he would walk off the film unless Mayer waited for Johnson to recover. Mayer agreed on the proviso that Tracy treat Dunne with more respect. Tracy agreed.

Because of the delay of **A Guy Named Joe,** Dunne was forced to start filming on **The White Cliffs of Dover** (1944) on the Culver City lot. When **A Guy Named Joe** resumed filming, the actress was obliged to perform in two big-budgeted movies at once. "I always lived the characters I played," Dunne admitted later, "and to have to be those two entirely different women at the same time was unbearable. And yet I think **A Guy Named Joe** is one of the finest pictures I ever made."

A Guy Named Joe was released on Christmas Eve 1943. **Newsweek** magazine reported, "As a war film, it combines excellent intentions and superb aerial combat shots with too much talk and an overcharge of sentiment. Call it a promising try that misses the boat but won't miss the box-office bull's-eye." Indeed, it was popular! The unapologetic attitude that there existed life after death, guardian angels, and the immortality of true love is a universal attitude. It was a soothing treat to worry-ravaged wartime families and fiancées. Even the rather ludicrous triangle and the preposterous finale in which Dunne and Tracy complete a bombing mission over the Pacific were overshadowed by the film's central transcendental appeal, and the sincere performances of all the players.

A Guy Named Joe placed eighth on **Film Daily's** Ten Best pictures list of 1944, (the year of its general release), and grossed $4,070,000 in distributors' domestic rentals. It ranked third, behind **Mrs. Miniver** (1942) and **Thirty Seconds over Tokyo** (1944, also with Tracy and Johnson and scripted by Trumbo), among Metro's most successful service films of the World War II period. Incidentally, there is no "Joe" in the picture; as explained in the storyline, "In the Army Air Corps, any fellow who is a right fellow is called 'Joe.'"

This film would serve to boost Van Johnson's stock with filmgoers. Before this big break he had fluctuated between B leads (such as in **Dr. Gillespie's New Assistant,** 1942, as Dr. Red Adams) and bits (a reporter in **Madame Curie,** 1943). In 1945 he would be listed as the number-two moneymaking star of Hollywood, preceded by Bing Crosby, and followed by Greer Garson, Spencer Tracy, Bob Hope, Judy Garland, Margaret O'Brien, and Roy Rogers. **A Guy Named Joe** was Esther Williams' second feature, following her role in **Andy Hardy's Double Life** (1942). From nineteenth spot as Ellen Bright, in **A Guy Named Joe** she would move to major billing in her next film, **Bathing Beauty** (1944). (When **A Guy Named Joe** was re-released in 1955, both Johnson and Williams were boosted to major star billing.) As for Tracy, he would make two more World War II–set features—1944's **The Seventh Cross** and **Thirty Seconds over Tokyo**—and then return to playing with Hepburn in **Without Love** (1945) and **The Sea of Grass** (1947).

HALLELUJAH!
1929—109 min.

Producer-director-story, King Vidor; **screenplay,** Wanda Tuchock; **dialogue,** Ransom Rideout; **titles,** Marian Ainslee; **treatment,** Richard Schayer; **art director,** Cedric Gibbons; **songs,** Irving Berlin; **assistant director,** Robert A. Golden; **wardrobe,** Henrietta Frazer; **sound,** Douglas Shearer; **camera,** Gordon Avil; **editors,** Hugh Wynn and Anson Stevenson.

Daniel L. Haynes **(Zeke);** Nina Mae McKinney **(Chick);** William E. Fountaine **(Hot Shot);** Harry Gray **(Parson);** Fannie Belle DeNight **(Mammy);** Everett McGarrity **(Spunk);** Victoria Spivey **(Missy Rose);** Milton Dickerson, Robert Couch, and Walter Tait **(Johnson Kids);** Dixie Jubilee Singers **(Themselves).**

SYNOPSIS
Zeke is the son of a black family with a small cotton plot on the Mississippi River. Zeke and his younger brother Spunk travel to the cotton market to sell the crop for $100, which will support the family during the coming year.

Once there Zeke encounters Chick, a dance-hall vamp, at a gambling casino. Trying to impress her, he is easily lured into a crap game with her lover, Hot Shot, a professional gambler. Using loaded dice, Hot Shot cheats Zeke out of his funds. Zeke and Hot Shot engage in a scuffle. Zeke grabs Hot Shot's gun, and firing into the crowd, accidentally shoots his brother.

A heartbroken Zeke returns home and later discovers religion. He becomes a traveling evangelist to spread God's work. Meanwhile plantation girl Missy Rose aids Zeke in his work and also falls in love with him.

Some time later Zeke encounters Chick, who quickly deserts Hot Shot to go with her new man. Zeke goes to work in a sawmill. When Hot Shot comes back, the self-indulgent Chick returns to him, tired of her impoverished existence with

Daniel L. Haynes and Nina Mae McKinney in Hallelujah! *('29).*

Zeke. Zeke follows them and later Chick is killed when Hot Shot's buggy overturns. Zeke follows Hot Shot into a swamp and murders him.

After enduring life on a chain gang, Zeke returns home to the farm, where the faithful Missy Rose awaits him.

* * *

"This amazing motion picture captures the rhapsody and religion of the colored race and unfolds a story that has an intensely dramatic pitch! Its dialogue is earthy and true. Its motion picture quality is such as only King Vidor can impart."

Judging by the pride inherent in this ad copy, one might think that Metro believed in King Vidor's project from its conception. Truth is, its execution experienced one of the greatest front office-versus-director battles ever waged on the Culver City facilities.

King Vidor, director and producer of Metro classics **The Big Parade** (1925) and **The Crowd** (1928), would relate of his first sound feature:

I was born and raised in southern Texas and my father had sawmills in Louisiana and East Texas, and I had been wanting to do a film about blacks. I'd been in Arkansas, I'd been to the churches, been all around—and been raised with them. I had all these memories, and I'd been trying to do it in a silent film. Well, I was always turned down, turned down repeatedly by the studio. Then I was in Paris and **Variety** magazine had a big headline; it said "Hollywood Goes 100 Percent Sound." I moved up my ship reservation by two or three weeks, got back in a hurry, went to the head office in New York to Nicholas Schenck and said, "Now I must make this film." I was still turned down and I said, "I will put my salary in with yours." And that appealed to him and he said, "I'll let you make a picture about whores, if that's what you are going to do."

Vidor still had many obstacles to surmount. There were very few black actors in Hollywood at the time. Most of the cast was gathered from black districts in New York and Chicago. Some came from the theatre: Daniel Haynes had been an understudy in **Showboat**; young Nina Mae McKinney had been in the chorus of **Blackbirds**, etc. Moreover, it was necessary to do location filming in Tennessee and Arkansas, but the heavy, cumbersome sound equipment was not transportable. Hence Vidor had to shoot the film silent and add sound later. Cameras would run at different speeds, synchronization processes were still very primitive, and many other technical complexities cropped up in preparing **Hallelujah!** for release.

The film was completed at a cost of $600,000, and utilized the black populace of a Mississippi River town as extras and the Irving Berlin songs "Waiting at the End of the Road" and "Swanee Shuffle." Adding sound to the film's climax, especially the pursuit through a gloomy swamp, proved an especially memorable experience for the iconoclastic film director:

To a motion picture studio in 1929 this [sound synchronization] was a fresh and unexplored adventure. We found ourselves making big puddles of water and mud, tramping through them with a microphone . . . rotting branches and fallen trees were crawled over; strange birds flew up from the morass. Never one to treat a dramatic effect literally, the thought struck me—why not free the imagination and record the sequence impressionistically? When someone stepped on a broken branch, we made it sound as if bones were breaking. As the pursued victim withdrew his foot from the stickiness of the mud, we made the vacuum sound strong enough to pull him into impending doom. . . . In my first desperation with sound, I believed that this nonfactual use of it was ideally suited to my film.

Hallelujah! proved very popular with the critics. Richard Watts **(New York Herald-Tribune)** offered, "**Hallelujah!** must certainly be one of the most distinguished and exciting motion pictures ever made . . . its poetry, drama, and pictorial magnificence combined in one stalwart whole and the result is something that constitutes a definite contribution to the local strivings for artistic expression." Mordaunt Hall **(New York Times)** wrote, "Although it is a talking venture, Mr. Vidor has not permitted sound to interfere with chances for telling photography, and several of the sequences are set forth with flashes of uplifted hands and magnified shadows. . . . As for the vocal tones, they are splendid and the dialogue contributed by Ransom Rideout is free from forced phrases or superfluous words. It tells the story succinctly, in most cases, and the actions and expressions of the players are suited to their utterances."

Despite the critical applause—it managed to place tenth in the **Film Daily** poll of 1929 and third in the **New York Times'** Ten Best Picture List—**Hallelujah!** received only limited bookings in the South. It fell flat financially in other areas, and never recouped its cost.[1]

Probably the I-told-you-so faction at Metro was too busy chanting to appreciate the continual array of prestigious reviews achieved by this trend-setting film. When it opened in England in early 1930 **Film Weekly** observed:

It is difficult to overpraise Vidor's handling of the mass scenes in which religious converts work themselves into frenzies of repentance . . . sound and singing have been used with great power to supplement the appeal of the spectacular, gesticulating crowds. This singing and shouting has waves and crests; it is not merely a babel, but it has a rhythmic power which is largely responsible for the great force of these scenes. . . .

. . . It is a film the faults of which are easily forgotten, because they are not faults which touch any of the essentials. It remains, as a whole, one of the most enterprising and impressive of all talkies.

In his book **Toms, Coons, Mulattoes, Mammies, and Bucks** (1973), black author Donald Bogle assesses:

In due time, **Hallelujah!** became not only an American classic, but the precursor of all-Negro musicals, setting the tone for the treatment of Negro casts and themes. Vidor, himself an idealist, had presented the Negroes in an idealized, isolated world. By having his blacks battle it out among themselves rather than with any white antagonists, he created an unreal universe and consequently divorced himself from real issues confronting blacks and whites in America. . . . **Hallelujah!** remains the first of Hollywood's attempts to deal with the black family, and is directly related to subsequent black family dramas such as **The Learning Tree** (1969) and **Sounder** (1972).

However **Hallelujah!** is regarded today, in 1929 it was a revolutionary step for a major studio (for whatever assortment of reasons) to undertake an expansive motion picture dealing with an all-black cast. The venture was all the more unusual when one takes into account that it was conservative MGM that produced and released it.

THE HARVEY GIRLS
1946 C—104 min.

Producer, Arthur Freed; **associate producer,** Roger Edens; **director,** George Sidney; based on the book by Samuel Hopkins Adams and the unpublished story by Eleanore Griffin and William Rankin; **screenplay,** Edmund Beloin, Nathaniel Curtis, Harry Crane, James O'Hanlon, and Samson Raphaelson; **additional dialogue,** Kay Van Riper, Guy Bolton, and Hagar Wilde; **Technicolor consultants,** Natalie Kalmus and Henri Jaffa; **art directors,** Cedric Gibbons and William Ferrari; **set decorators,** Edwin B. Willis and Mildred Griffiths; **costume supervisor,** Irene; **costumes,** Helen Rose; **men's costumes,** Valles; **makeup,** Jack Dawn; **songs,** Johnny Mercer and Harry Warren; **music director,** Lennie Hayton; **orchestrator,** Conrad Salinger; **vocal arranger,** Kay Thompson; music numbers staged by Robert Alton; **sound,** Douglas Shearer; **special effects,** Warren Newcombe; **camera,** George Folsey; **editor,** Albert Akst.

Judy Garland **(Susan Bradley)**; John Hodiak **(Ned Trent)**; Ray Bolger **(Chris Maude)**; Preston Foster **(Judge Sam Purvis)**; Virginia O'Brien **(Alma)**; Angela Lansbury **(Em)**; Marjorie Main **(Sonora Cassidy)**; Chill Wills **(H. H. Hartsey)**; Kenny Baker **(Terry O'Halloran)**; Selena Royle **(Miss Bliss)**; Cyd Charisse **(Deborah)**; Ruth Brady **(Ethel)**; Catherine McLeod **(Louise)**; Jack Lambert **(Marty Peters)**; Edward Earle **(Jed Adams)**; Virginia Hunter **(Jane)**; William "Bill" Phillips and Norman Leavitt **(Cowboys)**; Ray Teal **(Conductor)**; Horace [Stephen] McNally **(Golddust McClean)**; Jack Clifford **(Fireman)**; Vernon Dent **(Engineer)**; Paul "Tiny" Newlan **(Station Agent)**; Jim Toney **(Mule Skinner)**; Morris Ankrum **(Reverend Claggett)**; Ruth Brady, Lucille Casey, Mary Jo Ellis, Dorothy Gilmore, Gloria

---

[1]Shot in seventy-seven days, **Hallelujah** cost $320,000 to produce and lost $120,000 in its release.

Judy Garland (center), Beverly Tyler (directly behind Garland), Cyd Charisse, and Catherine McLeod in The Harvey Girls *('46).*

Hope, Mary Jean French, Daphne Moore, Joan Thorson, Dorothy Tuttle **(Harvey Girls)**; Hazel Brooks, Kay English, Hane Hall, Vera Lee, Peggy Maley, Erin O'Kelly, Dorothy Van Nuys, Eve Whitney, Dallas Worth **(Dance Hall Girls)**; Ben Carter **(John Henry)**; Byron Harvey, Jr., and Beverly Tyler **(Bits)**.

SYNOPSIS

A train arrives in the New Mexico wilds of 1890 carrying ten waitresses who will work at the Harvey Restaurant in Sandrock under the supervision of Miss Bliss. Also aboard the train is Susan Bradley, who is traveling to meet her mailorder fiancé. Upon arriving Susan discovers the letters were a hoax initiated by gambling-hall proprietor Ned Trent. Susan's fiancé turns out to be the town drunk, H. H. Hartsey. Stranded in Sandrock, Susan agrees to become a Harvey girl.

Trouble arises when Judge Sam Purvis attempts to evict the girls because their puritanical, pulchritudinous presence detracts from the Alhambra saloon traffic presided over by songand-dance girl Em. The crooked judge attempts to scare the girls away by shooting out their rooming-house lights and placing rattlesnakes in their closets. The girls retaliate by sponsoring a dance where they introduce the waltz to the untamed townsmen. This proves a real threat to the saloon trade.

By now Trent has fallen in love with Susan but decides they are mismatched. He intends to move his saloon operation to Flagstaff to end their emotional conflict. Meanwhile, Purvis and his henchmen set fire to the Harvey House. Trent and Purvis thereafter engage in a violent battle.

The next morning the Harvey House is relocated in Trent's garish saloon. Later Trent, Em, and the saloon girls board the train for Flagstaff, but Trent has a change of heart and remains in Sandrock to be with Susan. Unaware of this, Susan also boards the train to follow Trent, determined to be even a saloon girl to be near the man she loves. Em explains Trent's feelings and stops the train, allowing Susan to disembark. At that moment, Trent arrives by horse to carry her back to Sandrock.

The finale is their wedding with the Harvey girls as bridal attendants.

* * *

"MGM Gives You Technicolor! Judy Garland! 11 Song Hits! Wild West Thrills! Girls! Dances! Lusty Romance!" roared the posters for **The Harvey Girls,** Metro's 1946 Western musical. It was inspired by the Broadway phenomenon, Richard Rodgers and Oscar Hammerstein II's **Oklahoma!**

In May 1943 Arthur Freed's righthand man, Roger Edens, had seen **Oklahoma!** in its New Haven stage tryout. He encouraged his superior to produce a musical set in the West. Meanwhile, MGM producer Bernard Hyman had died in September 1942, and that canceled the production of a dramatic film, **The Harvey Girls,** to star Lana Turner. The project was to be based on the book by Samuel Hopkins Adams and the unpublished

story by Eleanore Griffin and William Rankin. After Hyman's demise Metro attempted to sell the story rights to another studio. However, Fred Harvey's family stated they would allow only MGM to produce a picture dealing with the formation of the Harvey restaurants. The project was then reassigned to Arthur Freed's unit.

Over subsequent months many scripters worked on the project, while Harry Warren and Johnny Mercer collaborated on the score.[1] At this point Freed decided to cast Judy Garland in the lead. However, she was interested in accepting the lead in Freed's musical fantasy **Yolanda and the Thief** (1945), which was to costar Fred Astaire. Garland was eventually persuaded to accept **The Harvey Girls,** and Lucille Bremer, Freed's new protégée, went into **Yolanda.**

Production began on January 12, 1945, with Edens handling most of the producer's chores. In contrast to her generally stable condition in **The Clock**—she proved an emotional life support for erratic Robert Walker—Garland was upset and extremely fatigued during much of **The Harvey Girls** lensing. She would be late constantly for morning calls, or not appear on the set at all. (Her situation was aggravated by dental problems and by Decca recording sessions.)

There were assorted mishaps on the set. During one scene Ray Bolger was scalded by steam from a locomotive. On another occasion, John Hodiak was injured in a fight scene during which a blazing beam fell on him. One of the extras caused a fire when he dropped a lighted pipe on a coworker dressed in a Victorian outfit. During filming it was discovered that married Virginia O'Brien was pregnant, and the number ("It's a Great Big World"), in which she was to shoe a horse, had to be delicately handled. Her love scenes with Bolger were deleted from the shooting schedule and she emerged as merely a specialty performer in the picture. Then there was the constant harassment of the Breen Production Code Office, which uncovered a myriad of details over which it agonized, such as whether in the cancan number the saloon chorus girls could have garters above their stockings (which must be full length). Not least, the Fred Harvey organization had an attentive representative on the set to ensure proper respect for historical fact.

But not all was negative, cinematographer George Folsey would recall:

> There was some fun too. We used to play baseball with Judy and John Hodiak on location [at Chatsworth in the San Fernando Valley]. Judy was a southpaw. . . . I had a very efficient crew and these capable guys went about their business and once we were established they'd go ahead and do it and it left me without apparently having anything to do. One day we

---

[1]The Mercer-Warren songs included: "In the Valley (Where the Evening Sun Goes Down)," "Wait and See," "On the Atchison, Topeka, and Santa Fe," "Oh, You Kid," "It's A Great Big World," "Swing Your Partner Round and Round." Also included were the "Training Sequence" by Roger Edens, "Judy's Rage" by orchestrator Conrad Salinger, and "Honky Tonk." Cut from the release print were these Mercer-Warren efforts: "March of the Doagies," "Hayride," and "My Intuition."

were sitting at lunch and Belt said, "George, I know what Howard does, and what Fenton does, and what Bobby does, and what Charlie does, but I don't know what you do." And I looked at him and said, "Well, Mr. Belt, I don't do anything. I'm not supposed to do anything. I'm just here to add class and distinction to the company!" Of course, we had a big time with that joke.

Two of the film's big sequences had their moments of concern. One sequence, the shooting of the train number on lot 3, director George Sidney remembered:

It was the weirdest thing. I turned on my radio [on the way to the set] and what did I hear? [Bing] Crosby singing . . . [that tune]. It was funny hearing the song and going out to shoot the number! That day Judy came in at one o'clock. She went through the whole thing and said, "I'm ready!" We shot it and she did it as if she had been rehearsing it for six months. It was sheer genius!

Another major sequence was the burning of the Harvey House, executed at night on lot 3. The MGM police were at full force to keep out passersby and firemen stood ready in case the flames should flare out of control and damage other sets. Judy's double—a rather husky stuntman—was garbed and wigged, ready to take over when in the storyline she is trapped within the burning structure. As Hugh Fordin relates in **The World of Entertainment** (1974):

Sidney and his camera crew, the actors, the stunt people, the extras, were ready to shoot. "Pour it on, boys!" Sidney shouted. Crouching under the eaves, a handful of brave men poured gasoline on the roof of the house, jumped off and the flames sprang up, ignited by a torch. "Action!" shouted Sidney. Hodiak and Foster started slugging each other, fell down and in a split second the stuntmen were in their places while they ran for cover, hidden by clouds of smoke. Screams were heard. In Judy's white satin gown the bowlegged stuntman leaped out of camera range, his skirt raised above his knobby knees. "Cut!" shouted Sidney. "Fire out!" he yelled at the top of his lungs. With that, dozens of firemen jumped from their hiding places, spouting oceans of water over the burning structure.

The scene had to be reshot the next night, after the building had cooled down, and the framework had been refurbished.

Production on **The Harvey Girls** was completed on June 4, 1945, a few days after Garland's divorce from David Rose. June 10 was her twenty-third birthday; five days later she wed director Vincente Minnelli.

The film's final cost was $2,524,315.06, a sizable investment in those World War II days. However, because the MGM product was then glutting the Loew's theatres, it would not be until January 1946 that **The Harvey Girls** would premiere in New York. It was a big hit. Wrote Howard Barnes (**New York Herald-Tribune**), "The Harvey Girls** is a perfect demonstration of what Hollywood

can do with its vast resources when it wants to be really showy. A skeleton of a horse opera has been clothed sumptuously with pretty girls, period sets and costumes, brawls, and conflagrations. . . . It has about as much to do with the Fred Harvey chain of railroad restaurants which followed the Atchison, Topeka, and Santa Fe across the country as a commercial calendar, but it is bustling and beautiful." The public agreed; **The Harvey Girls** grossed over $5,175,000 in its initial release.

"On the Atchison, Topeka, and Santa Fe" won an Academy Award as the best song of the year. However, there are other merits worthy of note within **The Harvey Girls**. Marjorie Main (the raucous cook) and Ray Bolger provide their brand of humor, Kenny Baker adds a vocal touch, and John Hodiak proves he can be an appealing leading man (instead of the general utility performer his contract employer, MGM, branded him). An especial delight of the film is Angela Lansbury's performance as the tightly corseted Em, the decadent Alhambra dancehall hostess who personifies the wickedness of the untamed West. Lavishly coiffed and garishly costumed, she provides a gawdy characterization in stark contrast to the sophisticated star of today.

HIGH SOCIETY
1956 C—107 min.

Producer, Sol C. Siegel; **director,** Charles Walters; based on the play **The Philadelphia Story** by Philip Barry; **screenplay,** John Patrick; **art directors,** Cedric Gibbons and Hans Peters; **set decorators,** Edwin B. Willis and Richard Pefferle; **costumes,** Helen Rose; **assistant director,** Arvid Griffen; **color consultant,** Charles K. Hagedon; **music numbers** staged by Charles Walters; **songs,** Cole Porter; **music supervisors-adapters,** Johnny Green and Saul Chaplin; **orchestra director,** Green; **orchestrators,** Conrad Salinger, Nelson Riddle, Robert Franklyn, and Albert Sendrey; **sound,** Dr. Wesley C. Miller; **special effects,** A. Arnold Gillespie; **camera,** Paul C. Vogel; **editor,** Ralph E. Winters.

Bing Crosby (**C. K. Dexter-Haven**); Grace Kelly (**Tracy Lord**); Frank Sinatra (**Mike Connor**); Celeste Holm (**Liz Imbrie**); John Lund (**George Kittredge**); Louis Calhern (**Uncle Willie**); Sidney Blackmer (**Seth Lord**); Louis Armstrong (**Himself**); Margalo Gillmore (**Mrs. Seth Lord**); Lydia Reed (**Caroline Lord**); Gordon Richards (**Dexter-Haven's Butler**); Richard Garrick (**Lord's Butler**); Richard Keene (**Mac**); Ruth Lee and Helen Spring (**Matrons**); Paul Keast (**Editor**); Reginald Simpson (**Uncle Willie's Butler**); Hugh Boswell (**Parson**).

SYNOPSIS
Tracy Lord, one of the gentry of Newport, Rhode Island, receives a surprise visit from ex-husband C. K. Dexter-Haven near the day of her society wedding to aristocratic and stuffy George Kittredge. Dexter is a popular composer involved with the Newport Jazz Festival and some of its prime

performers, including Louis Armstrong and His Band. The Lords also host reporter Mike Connor and photographer Liz Imbrie, who work for a less than savory national magazine which is eager to have exclusive inside coverage of the mating of the year.

In the course of events, Tracy comes to realize that she does not really love George or the values he endorses so pompously. She is pushed to this conclusion by her abortive romance with carefree Mike. The latter proposes to her, but she instinctively knows he belongs to the loyal Liz.

Finally, just when it seems that the gathered wedding guests will have no ceremony to view, Tracy and her ex-spouse decide to remarry.

* * *

A musical remake of **The Philadelphia Story** (1940)? Ardent disciples of that classic film to this day blaspheme the name of producer Sol C. Siegel. It was he who concocted this idea which skimmed much of the wit from the Philip Barry original to make room for a Cole Porter score and plush closeups of Grace Kelly. Still, it should be noted that **High Society** was Metro's most successful movie of 1956. It reaped $5,782,000 in box-office receipts—and this a year following the supposed demise of Hollywood musicals.

The Philadelphia Story, with its near perfect performances by Katharine Hepburn, Cary Grant, and James Stewart, had continued winning revenue for the studio via the reissue market. It was producer Siegel who plotted the metamorphosis and paid Cole Porter $250,000 to devise nine songs to carry along the story—switched, incidentally, from Philadelphia to Newport, which allowed for the "logical" inclusion of Jazz Festival participants Louis Armstrong and His Band. The film was geared to be a showcase for MGM's most important contractee, Grace Kelly. Ironically, the tremendously popular actress had earned most of her fan following on loanouts to other studios, including her Oscar-winning performance in Paramount's **The Country Girl** (1954) opposite Bing Crosby.

Supporting the enticing starring team of Kelly and Crosby (who had dated off camera) was Frank Sinatra in the somewhat subordinate role of the love-struck newspaper reporter. Others included in the upper-class proceedings were Celeste Holm as the thoughtful, sideline-waiting photographer, John Lund as the would-be groom, Louis Calhern as the twinkling Uncle Willie, and Margalo Gillmore and Sidney Blackmer as Kelly's parents.

For devotees of jazz, **High Society** provided plenty of opportunities to study the craftsmanship of Armstrong and his famed musicians. The screenplay for the musical was provided by John Patrick, author of **The Teahouse of the August Moon.** To direct **High Society,** producer Siegel assigned MGM contract employee Charles Walters, who had displayed his own brand of originality (never fully appreciated) to such studio products as **Good News** (1947), **Easter Parade** (1948), **Summer Stock** (1950), and **Lili** (1953).

Porter, a perfectionist, was not too pleased with the score he provided for **High Society.** But he was being overly self-critical. The joyous score

Frank Sinatra and Grace Kelly in High Society *('56).*

included "High Society Calypso"[1] (Armstrong and His Band), "(I Love You) Samantha" (Crosby), "Little One" (Crosby to Kelly's precocious younger sister, Lydia Reed), "Who Wants to Be a Millionaire?" (Sinatra and Holm), "True Love" (Crosby and Kelly), "You're Sensational" (Sinatra), "Now You Has Jazz" (Crosby, Armstrong and His Band), "Mind If I Make Love to You?" (Sinatra), and "Well, Did You Evah!" (Sinatra and Crosby; originally sung by Betty Grable to Charles Walters in Porter's 1939 Broadway musical, **Du Barry Was a Lady**). The last number was the film's only non-original vocal tune. (There were musical snatches from such past Porter songs as "I've Got My Eye on You" from **Broadway Melody of 1940** and "Easy to Love" from **Born to Dance**, (1936).

When released in August 1956, the color and VistaVision musical[2] received a snub from many critics who opposed the idea of tampering with a screen classic—especially one as sophisticated as **The Philadelphia Story**. William K. Zinsser of the **New York Herald-Tribune** shrugged indifferently, "John Patrick's screenplay lacks the brittle wit of Barry's original, and the actors are almost too casual about their work. They seem to be making up the words as they go along. But they are

attractive people, and on the whole **High Society** is an entertaining film." Bosley Crowther **(New York Times)** opined, **"High Society** . . . is as flimsy as a gossip-columnist's word, especially when it is documenting the weird behavior of the socially elite. And with pretty and ladylike Grace Kelly flouncing lightly through its tomboyish Hepburn role, it misses the snap and the crackle that its unmusical predecessor had." The critical reservation hurt the film not one whit. The star lineup, as well as the hit record of "True Love" (which became a standard at weddings), proved irresistible bait as **High Society** landed on **Variety's** roster of all-time box-office champs.

In assessing the virtues of **High Society** and director-choreographer Walters, Douglas McVay stated in a 1977 **Focus on Films** article:

> There are nonmusical delights in **High Society** too (quite apart from Miss Kelly's loveliness); delights of humor and charm and romanticism in writing, playing, and direction. One thinks of Kelly's first great encounter with Sinatra and Holm; of her deliciously unexpected pronounciation of "choo-choo mama"; of her later alcoholically declamatory quotation of "Not sleeping sire, but dead"; of Louis Calhern's measured, erect, tottering, monumentally hungover advance in long-shot on the morning after the night before, shouting to a deafening twittering bird, "Oh, shut up, you fool!" (although this, like Kelly's encounter with Holm and Sinatra, owes much to Walters' choreographic instinct).

Perhaps the biggest joy of the musical interludes of the film—both at the time of release and now in retrospect—is the charming blending

of captivating singing partners: Crosby and Kelly, Crosby and Sinatra, Crosby and Armstrong, and Sinatra and Holm. Walters craftily employs his cast to maximum advantage in their song segments. Holm and Sinatra (who had teamed in MGM's **The Tender Trap**, 1955, directed by Walters) give the proper insouciance to "Who Wants to Marry a Millionaire?" as they nose about the reception room studying the array of often impractical but ultraexpensive wedding gifts. Sinatra's rendering of "You're Sensational" evokes the sensuality of Kelly and causes the "fair Miss Frigidaire" to warm up. Just as Crosby has a fling with Armstrong's troupe in "Now You Has Jazz," so the veteran crooner joins with his younger rival Sinatra in the bouncy "Well, Did You Evah!" This interlude appropriately combines zippy visuals with the irreverence of the lyrics and the exaggerated gestures of the two singers.

If any number caused a sensation—before, during, and after its execution on screen—it was Crosby and Kelly dueting "True Love." MGM took elaborate efforts to promote the singing debut of its Miss Kelly, who, while admitting she was no great songstress, managed to give poise and phrasing to the love paean. As McVay relates in his survey study of this film:

> This [flashback] sequence (significantly not present in **The Philadelphia Story**) in which the newly married couple quietly and blissfully duet "True Love" on board their yacht of that name, invests the love between Tracy and her former husband with a sense of physical truth, and thus makes their movements toward reconciliation in the rest of the film equally credible. . . . The "True Love" duet . . . emerges as one of the most persuasive illustrations of the power of song (or dance) to convey sexual passion and affection more intensely than any exchange of spoken words or fervent embraces can do.

High Society and The Swan (1956), earlier released, would be Grace Kelly's final films before her marriage to Prince Rainier, which established her as queen of Monaco. Cole Porter would contribute one more original score for an MGM musical, **Les Girls** (1957). Walters would direct seven more features at MGM, including two musicals: **Billy Rose's Jumbo** (1962) and **The Unsinkable Molly Brown** (1964). Crosby and Sinatra would each continue on with their array of screen musicals and dramas, and eighteen years later would reteam as cohosts of **That's Entertainment!** (1974)).

HOLLYWOOD REVUE OF 1929

1929—11,669'[1]

Producer, Harry Rapf; **director**, Charles Reisner; **dialogue**, Al Boasberg and Robert Hopkins; **skit,**

---

[1]This number with the catchy beat opens the film, as the trumpeter-bandleader-singer and his crew reach Newport in their bus caravan. The lyrics of the calypso song set the stage for the action, and conclude with the raspy Armstrong saucily querying "Can you dig old Satch-mo swingin' in the beautiful high so-ci-et-tee?"

[2]MGM was so enamored of the title **High Society** it paid Allied Artists a hefty fee for appropriating the title employed for one of the latter company's 1955 Bowery Boys features.

---

[1]Technicolor sequences.

Joe Farnham; **art directors,** Cedric Gibbons and Richard Day; **songs,** Arthur Freed and Nacio Herb Brown; Raymond Klages and Jesse Greer; Andy Rice and Martin Broones; Joe Trent and Louis Alter; Fred Fisher; Joe Goodwin and Gus Edwards; **music score arrangers,** Arthur Lange, Ernest Klapholtz, Ray Heindorf; **dance ensembles,** Sammy Lee and George Cunningham; **assistant directors,** Jack Cummings, Sandy Roth, and Al Shenberg; **costumes,** David Cox, Henrietta Frazer, and Joe Rapf; **camera,** John Arnold, Irving Ries, Maximilian Fabian, and John M. Nickolaus; **editors,** William S. Gray and Cameron K. Wood.

Conrad Nagel and Jack Benny **(Masters of Ceremonies);** John Gilbert, Norma Shearer, Joan Crawford, Bessie Love, Lionel Barrymore, Cliff Edwards, Stan Laurel and Oliver Hardy, Anita Page, Nils Asther, Brox Sisters, Natacha Natova and Company, Marion Davies, William Haines, Buster Keaton, Marie Dressler, Charles King, Polly Moran, Gus Edwards, Karl Dane, George K. Arthur, Ann Dvorak, Gwen Lee, Albertina Rasch Ballet, The Rounders, The Biltmore Quartet **(Specialties).**

SYNOPSIS

With Jack Benny and Conrad Nagel as masters of ceremony, the film contains the following skits and numbers:

• "I've Got a Feeling for You" sung and danced to by Joan Crawford, joined by the Biltmore Quartet
• "Your Mother and Mine" sung by Charles King with a minstrel chorus
• "You Were Meant for Me" sung by Conrad Nagel to Anita Page
• "Nobody but You" sung by Cliff Edwards as he strums his uke
• Comedy sketch by Jack Benny and William Haines
• "I Could Never Do a Thing Like That" sung by Bessie Love with male chorus
• "For I'm the Queen" a comedy song performed by Marie Dressler and Polly Moran
• Magicians' sketch by Laurel and Hardy
• "Tommy Atkins on Parade" sung and danced to by Marion Davies, joined by male chorus
• Song-and-dance ensemble led by the Brox Sisters
• "The Tableau of Jewels"
• "The Dance of the Sea" skit with Buster Keaton
• "Lon Chaney" sung by Gus Edwards
• Adagio dance by Natova company
• "Romeo and Juliet" balcony scene with Norma Shearer and John Gilbert; with Lionel Barrymore as the film director, and with Shearer and Gilbert doing a takeoff of the classical scene thereafter
• "Singin' in the Rain" sung by Cliff Edwards, joined by dance ensemble
• "Charlie, Ike and Gus" comedy song routine by Charles King, Cliff Edwards, and Gus Edwards
• "Marie, Polly, and Bess" comedy song routine by Marie Dressler, Polly Moran, and Bessie Love
• "Strolling Through the Park"
• "Orange Blossom Time" sung by Charles King
• Dance routines by the Albertina Rasch Ballet
• "Singin' in the Rain" sung by Buster Keaton,

Marion Davies in Hollywood Revue of 1929 *('29).*

Marion Davies, Joan Crawford, George K. Arthur, the Brox Sisters, et al.

* * *

The many audiences who applauded throughout MGM's 11,669-foot all-star parcel of all-singing, all-talking, all-dancing **Hollywood Revue of 1929,** left the theatre aware of three things: (1) MGM truly had the right to boast that the Culver City lot contained more stars than were in the heavens; (2) the benefits of the talking picture, not to mention the glories of color which splashed the screen in two sequences, were wonderful to hear and behold; and (3) John Gilbert's tenure as a great star of Hollywood was nearing an end.[2]

Encouraged by the receipts of **The Broadway Melody** after its acclaimed release early in 1929, producer Harry Rapf perceived the appeal of a series of musical sketches and bits, all featuring the top stars of the Metro lot letting their perfumed hair down in crowd-pleasing, unpretentious vignettes.

So, under the direction of Charles Reisner and the choreography of Broadway dance director Sammy Lee, all the MGM attractions (with the notable exceptions of Garbo, who was above such carryings-on, and Lon Chaney,[3] whose contract called for $150,000 for any film appearance no

matter the size of his role) took part in the boisterous proceedings. The newly expanded songwriting department of Metro was told to create ninety new songs, from which twenty would be picked for use in the film. One of the winners was Arthur Freed's and Nacio Herb Brown's "Singin' in the Rain" ("I don't think I spent more than an hour and a half writing the lyrics for that song," laughed Freed many years later). Many hundreds of flappers sashayed through the Culver City gates to audition for the 125 showgirl roles, and Conrad Nagel (noted for his fine profile and speaking voice) and Jack Benny (already a leading stage comedian) were signed to alternate as masters of ceremonies.

The production of the potpourri film caused many Metro stars, busy during the day with their own starring pictures, to work the night shift, Nonetheless, high spirts prevailed and showed when **Hollywood Revue** premiered in the summer of 1929. There was, however, a jarring problem. Thalberg noticed at the preview that audiences jeered at the immodestly pitched tones of John Gilbert in his **Romeo and Juliet** sketch (filmed in color) with Norma Shearer. Baffled by the filmgoers' reaction to the screen's great lover, and distraught by the recorded sound of Gilbert's voice which had never struck him before as being so unvibrant, Thalberg cautiously ordered the sketch cut from the release print. But Nicholas Schenck (president of MGM's parent company, Loew's) and Louis B. Mayer, fearing a slump in box-office appeal if the segment were removed, vetoed Thalberg's excision. Gilbert himself soon became aware of the rumors on the lot and he quickly bargained for a new four-year, $1,000,000 a year

---

[2]The musical was shot on a twenty-five-day production schedule at a cost of $426,000 and earned a profit of $1,135,000.

[3]The film did contain a "Lon Chaney" song number, sung by Gus Edwards and with an extra parading about in a mask reminiscent of Chaney's **London After Midnight** (1927).

contract before the jokes about his undramatic voice tones became any nastier.

Audiences did indeed laugh as Gilbert delivered his iambic pentameter, but the **Hollywood Revue of 1929** was so engaging a mélange—by standards of the day—that it did not much matter. As Mordaunt Hall wrote in the **New York Times,** "Brimming over with good fun and catchy music, Metro-Goldwyn-Mayer's ambitious audible picture, **The Hollywood Revue** . . . won frequent outbursts of genuine applause. It is a talking and singing film free from irritating outpourings of coarse slang or a tedious, sobbing romance. . . . It has no story, which is to its credit, for every one of its sketches that comes to the screen leaves one hungry for more."

In reassessing the segments of **Hollywood Revue of 1929,** John Kobal in **Gotta Sing, Gotta Dance** (1970) evaluates:

> The film's pleasure is that of seeing stars doing the unexpected, such as Bessie Love's furiously acrobatic dance with a male chorus, in which she is hung by her leg like a human pendulum. Norma Shearer and John Gilbert (another colored sequence which has them flushing furiously from red to pale to redder) do the balcony scene from **Romeo and Juliet.** This turns out to be a film-within-the-film with Lionel Barrymore playing the director, whisky-gruff and bushy-browed. Then Norma and Gilbert do a slangy send-up of the previous scene. It isn't good as acting, and it isn't very funny, but they were awfully big stars. . . . [Gilbert's] voice is low, pleasant enough but completely undistinguished—mocking his physical appearance by contrast. Watching the chorus girls . . . one remembers Bessie Love's story that Metro was hiring its girls from all walks of life—since they were not very adept at keeping step. Other items include songwriter Gus Edwards coming on in a girls' dormitory to lecture them in song that "Lon Chaney will get you, if you don't watch out!" The imaginatively designed Jewel Box set, used as background for an exotic dance, also does service for Buster Keaton's delightful underwater hootchie-kootch dance.

Regarding the technical aspects of the film, Kobal writes:

> The camera varies little from its three restricted positions: closeup, medium long shot, and long shot. Most sequences appear to have been filmed in a single camera setup. There are some awkward, though for the time, daring attempts at unexpected angles that the sound experts must have objected to, including some overhead shots of chorus girls . . . creating flower patterns. . . . The large finale, in two-tone color, begins with Miss Rasch's girls, partially invisible, in green tutus against a green orchard. The orchard is dotted with brilliant oranges. The ballet over, the scene shifts to a shot of Noah's Ark on Mount Ararat . . . and as the storm clouds clear and the sun emerges, the MGM parade of stars, dressed in transparent plastic raincoats and hats, troupes on for the grand finale, led by Ukelele Ike in the song "Singin in the Rain."

This financial winner won an Academy Award nomination as Best Picture of the 1928–29 season. It was defeated by Metro's own **The Broadway Melody.**

The commercial concept of the all-star revue captured the fancy of other Hollywood studios, and **Hollywood Revue** was promptly followed by Warner Bros. **Show of Shows** (1929), Fox's **Happy Days,** Universal's **The King of Jazz** (1930), Paramount's **Paramount on Parade** (1930), and more—until the novelty wore out.

HONKY TONK
1941—105 min.

Producer, Pandro S. Berman; **director,** Jack Conway; **screenplay,** Marguerite Roberts and John Sanford; **music,** Franz Waxman; **songs,** Jack Yellen and Milton Ager; **art directors,** Cedric Gibbons and Eddie Imazu; **set decorator,** Edwin B. Willis; **gowns,** Kalloch; **men's costumes,** Gile Steele; **sound,** Douglas Shearer; **camera,** Harold Rosson; **editor,** Blanche Sewell.

Clark Gable (**Candy Johnson**); Lana Turner (**Elizabeth Cotton**); Frank Morgan (**Judge Cotton**); Claire Trevor (**Gold Dust Nelson**); Marjorie Main (**Reverend Mrs. Varner**); Albert Dekker (**Brazos Hearn**); Chill Wills (**The Sniper**); Henry O'Neill (**Daniel Wells**); John Maxwell (**Kendall**); Morgan Wallace (**Adams**); Douglas Wood (**Governor Wilson**); Betty Blythe (**Mrs. Wilson**); Hooper Atchley (**Senator Ford**); Harry Worth (**Harry Gates**); Veda Ann Borg (**Pearl**); Dorothy Granger (**Saloon Girl**); Sheila Darcy (**Louise**); Cy Kendall (**Man with Tar**); Erville Alderson (**Man with Rail**); John Farrell (**Man with Feathers**); Don Barclay (**Man with Gun**); Ray Teal (**Poker Player**); Esther Muir (**Blonde on Train**); Francis X. Bushman, Jr. and Art Miles (**Dealers**); Anne O'Neal (**Nurse**); Russell Hicks (**Dr. Otis**); John Carr (**Brazos' Henchman**); Art Belasco, Frank Mills, Syd Saylor, Ralph Peters, Eddie Gribbon, and Harry Semels (**Pallbearers**); Lew Kelly, Charles McAvoy, Joe Devlin, Malcolm Waite, Earl Gunn, Ted Oliver, Charles Sullivan, Monte Montague, William Haade, and Al Hill (**Miners**); Eddy Waller (**Train Conductor**); Heinie Conklin (**Dental Patient**); Tiny Newlan (**Gentleman**).

SYNOPSIS

Candy Johnson, a gambler with a shady past, sets himself up in Yellow Creek, Nevada, with an ersatz mayor and judge. Candy is aided by the Sniper and others. When the judge's lovely Boston-bred daughter, Elizabeth Cotton, arrives, Candy cannot determine whether she is prettier by lamplight or by daylight. They soon fall in love and wed after a stormy, if not exciting, courtship.

Meanwhile, Candy has established a mission, a schoolhouse, and a fire department, and begins to benefit personally from the town's success. Judge Cotton attempts to alert the townspeople to Candy and his men, but the old man is murdered. This act jolts Candy into sensibility and he returns the control of the town to the citizens and plans to leave the area. In the meantime, Elizabeth has lost her first child as a result of her distress over the judge's death. When she recovers sufficiently, she follows after her adored Candy.

* * *

Metro savored enticing advertising copy. Rarely did a film poster leave the publicity department without some dramatic copy festooned atop or below the title. However, few slogans carried the attention-getting punch of the words promoting **Honky Tonk**—"Clark Gable Kisses Lana Turner and It's Screen History!"

The greatest honor (and career boost) for any Metro actress was to be paired with Clark Gable. In his decade at the studio he had already starred opposite every major female attraction: Garbo, Shearer, Crawford, Loy, Harlow, and Lamarr. Most recently, Rosalind Russell had experienced the honor in **They Met in Bombay** (1941).

Back in 1938 Gable had tested with novice Lana Turner when she first came to the lot accompanied by her producer-director mentor from Warner Bros., Mervyn LeRoy. The King performed a scene from **Red Dust** with Lana auditioning in Harlow's old Vantine role. Gable's estimation of Lana was, "She couldn't read lines; she didn't make them mean anything. It was obvious she was an amateur. . . ." However, Lana had developed well via the MGM method of starlet grooming. She had been showcased in one of Mickey Rooney's popular Hardy series films, **Love Finds Andy Hardy** (1938), had several B film leads; and then had a climactic stellar performance as the consumptive showgirl of the plush **Ziegfeld Girl** (1941). Metro was now ready to attempt a repeat of the audience-drawing Gable-Harlow chemistry. However, Gable was not enthusiastic, remembering the young lady as she had been when she initially came to the lot. But his estimations in 1940 soon changed. "She was so much better an actress. Gone was the amateur . . . she had learned so much about acting."

Lana had also learned many other things since 1938. She had become the undisputed "Queen of the Nightclubs" and had tallied over one hundred fifty big-name males as her dates. Her companions ranged from Howard Hughes (whom she wanted to marry) to Artie Shaw (whom she did—briefly). Her wiles were reputed to be well-nigh irresistible. When production began under Jack Conway's direction, with a supporting cast of some of MGM's most picturesque character performers (including Frank Morgan, Claire Trevor, Marjorie Main, Chill Wills, and Albert Dekker), there appeared on the set a visitor, Mrs. Clark Gable.

Despite her status as one of the most adored stars in Hollywood, thirty-three-year-old Carole Lombard was an insecure beauty who feared the effect the much younger Lana might have on her very desirable husband. Some years later Lana would recall:

Marjorie Main and Clark Gable in Honky Tonk *('41).*

mance about the globe. Although production was delayed by the death of Carole Lombard on a war-bond-selling flight, the new film duplicated the torrid chemistry of before. **Somewhere I'll Find You** joined **Mrs. Miniver, Woman of the Year,** and **Honky Tonk** as Metro's top grossers of the 1941–42 season.

THE HUCKSTERS
1947—115 min.

Producer, Arthur Hornblow, Jr.; **director**, Jack Conway; based on the novel by Frederic Wakeman; **adapters**, Edward Chodorov and George Wells; **screenplay**, Luther Davis; **art directors**, Cedric Gibbons and Urie McCleary; **set decorators**, Edwin B. Willis and Jack D. Moore; **music**, Lennie Hayton; **assistant director**, Sid Sidman; **sound**, Douglas Shearer; **special effects**, Warren Newcombe and A. Arnold Gillespie; **camera**, Harold Rosson; **editor**, Frank Sullivan.

Clark Gable (**Victor Albee Norman**); Deborah Kerr (**Kay Dorrance**); Sydney Greenstreet (**Evan Llewellyn Evans**); Adolphe Menjou (**Mr. Kimberly**); Ava Gardner (**Jean Ogilvie**); Keenan Wynn (**Buddy Hare**); Edward Arnold (**Dave Lash**); Aubrey Mather (**Gaines, the Valet**); Richard Gaines (**Cook**); Frank Albertson (**Max Herman**); Clinton Sundberg (**Michael Michaelson, the Photographer**); Douglas Fowley (**Georgie Gaver**); Gloria Holden (**Mrs. Kimberly**); Connie Gilchrist (**Betty, the Switchboard Operator**); Kathryn Card (**Regina Kennedy**); Lillian Bronson (**Miss Hammer**); Vera Marshe (**Secretary**); George O'Hanlon (**Freddie Callahan**); Ransom Sherman (**George Rockton**); Anne Nagel (**Teletypist**); John Hiestand (**Radio Announcer**); Robert Emmet O'Connor (**Doorman**); Florence Stephens (**Secretary**); Gordon Richards (**Kimberly Butler**); Marie Windson (**Girl**); Billy Benedict (**Bellboy**); Chief Yowlachie (**Indian**).

SYNOPSIS
Vic Norman, former radio advertising executive, has been discharged from the army following the end of World War II. Seeking a job in the Madison Avenue advertising field, he joins the prestigious "Kimberly Tower," operated by Mr. Kimberly. The latter lives in mortal fear of gross Evan Llewellyn Evans, an uncouth soap tycoon who bullies the New York–based agency into performing the near impossible in hawking the glories of his seven-cents-a-bar Beautee Soap. When Norman meets Evans in the latter's opulent lair, he is disgusted by the man's grotesqueness. However, hopeful of finding an avenue back to success after his war service, he begins work on the $10 million Beautee Soap account.

Vic's travels reintroduce him to beautiful Jean Ogilvie, a nightclub chanteuse. Though chemistry is strong between them, Vic really becomes infatuated with Kay Dorrance, the English widow of an American general, Francis X. Dorrance. Vic wants to contract the lovely Kay to endorse Beau-

We rehearsed our first love scene—ours was a wonderful chemical rapport which came over on film—and suddenly I turned around and froze. There was beloved Carole Lombard, Mrs. Gable! . . . Well, it's one thing to work with a King but quite another to have his lady there. I retreated to my dressing room and when director Jack Conway came to say we were ready to shoot, I wailed, "I can't!" Whether Jack told Clark, I don't know. I just know that while I sat in my dressing room suffering, beautiful Carole disappeared."

Carole also took the occasion to invade Louis B. Mayer's office to swear havoc if she heard of any scandal between her spouse and MGM's young sex goddess. Mayer had heard much the same threats when Gable was working with widowed Norma Shearer on **Idiot's Delight** (1939) and patiently weathered the storm.

Nevertheless, **Honky Tonk** glided to a swift conclusion.[1] The 105-minute feature contained no less than eleven Gable-Turner screen kisses scattered amidst the audience-titillating dialogue

(Gable to Turner, "You're prettier than a little white kitten with a ribbon on it." Turner to Gable, "I haven't had much practice, but I can kiss a man").

Honky Tonk opened in October 1941. "To be specific, they're terrific," promised the ads. **Life** magazine featured the star duo on its October 13, 1941, cover, calling the **Honky Tonk** leads "the hottest, most electric combination of movie personalities since Boyer and Lamarr." **PM** critiqued, "MGM, with its own trick of sewing diamonds on cheesecloth, has given **Honky Tonk** some elegant settings, billowed Lana Turner in ribbons, laces, and black chiffon, and has cunningly contrived a perfect Gable-Turner courtship." The **New York Daily News** aired a pique shared by several other reviewers, "The doublebarrel 'oomph' of Clark Gable and Lana Turner is not magnetic enough to draw **Honky Tonk** from the mediocre level of its banal writing and ordinary script." Few were the film fans who shared such sentiments and **Honky Tonk** did enormous box-office business. (Gable and Turner later re-created their roles on "The Screen Guild Playhouse" in 1950, and in 1974 Metro produced a TV pilot called **Honky Tonk** starring Richard Crenna.)

Whatever the motive which impelled MGM to delight in pairing screen couples, Metro took the cue from **Honky Tonk** to add Gable-Turner to the lucrative couplings of Garson-Pidgeon, Rooney-Garland, Powell-Loy, and others, and began production on **Somewhere I'll Find You** (1942). In it war correspondent Gable and nurse Turner ro-

---

[1]Veteran screen performer Claire Trevor does not remember **Honky Tonk** kindly. She was Gold Dust Nelson, a rather amoral pal of hero Gable, and complains Trevor: "I had some great scenes in **Honky Tonk**. At least I *thought* I had them until I went to the press preview of it. My scenes had been scissored. 'Where am I?' I kept asking myself as I watched it on the screen. 'What happened to me?' I cried all the way home and swore I'd never make another picture."

Clark Gable and Connie Gilchrist in The Hucksters *('47).*

tee Soap. She has two growing children, Ellen and Hal. As Vic and Kay's romance develops, Evans terrifies Kimberly further by promising to withdraw his lucrative account unless a novelty occurs soon in the agency's marketing methods. Vic flies to Hollywood, signs comic Buddy Hare for a radio show and hires Jean for a recording session. Pleased with his success, Vic returns to Manhattan to learn Evans' formal response.

In an awesomely arrogant display, Evans smashes Vic's record disc to show his contempt. Then he voices his approval, having indulged in one of his favorite horrific business tactics—surprise. Outraged, Vic tells Evans the world is finished with fascists such as he, and paraphrasing one of Evans' remarks, adds, "You're all wet." Vic punctuates the point by pouring a pitcher of water over the man's panama-hatted dome. Kimberly stares in disbelief as Vic stalks out of the conference room.

The disillusioned Vic informs Kay that he is so deeply upset with the unethical advertising world,

he now wants to run off to a remote island somewhere—anywhere. Kay tells him, "You're too good for that," and, promising her trust and love, encourages him to seek new agencies to employ his creative abilities.

* * *

Nobody at MGM after 1944—least of all Clark Gable himself—seemed to realize that, no matter how poor a picture Metro found for the King, a loyal following would flock to see it. Proof positive was **Adventure** (1945) in which "Gable's Back and Garson's Got Him." That film had an infelicitous blend of romance and transcendentalism and it completely miscast the stars, but it grossed $4.5 million. The receipts failed to convey the point to the film company, and again the executives took an inordinate amount of time in selecting a new Gable vehicle.

Finally MGM settled on **The Hucksters**, the Frederic Wakeman bestseller about the cutthroat world of New York advertising. The novel, containing liberal doses of sexual play, had achieved

a certain notoriety. When Gable was informed of the project, he balked. He rightly insisted that playing in such film fare was inconsistent with his winning prewar image. MGM had no choice: it very nearly emasculated the script. But Gable still balked. Metro then began negotiations with Warner Bros. to borrow Errol Flynn to star in the pivotal role. Finally, Gable acquiesced and began work on the character of Vic Norman, the "hero" who revolts at being a yes-man at the eleventh hour.

With Gable set, MGM cast Deborah Kerr in her first Hollywood role. She had made her London screen debut in George Bernard Shaw's **Major Barbara** (1941) for producer-director Gabriel Pascal. He put her under contract and kept her employed on loanout to other British filmmaking units, including MGM's English division, for **Vacation from Marriage** (1945) with Robert Donat. Two J. Arthur Rank films (**The Adventuress**, 1946, and **Black Narcissus**, 1947) gave her international prominence, and Louis B. Mayer signed her to a seven-year Hollywood contract. Allegedly he paid Pascal $200,000 to release Kerr from her pact and offered the actress a salary beginning at $3,000 weekly and escalating to $7,000 weekly during the final two years. The ad campaign used to promote the imported actress was "Kerr rhymes with star."

For the other major female role, Ava Gardner was used. Before her accoladed siren's part on loanout to Universal for **The Killers** (1946), she had mainly won attention as a Metro contract starlet for her brief and stormy marriage to Mickey Rooney. She was awarded the part of sultry chanteuse Jean Ogilvie, even though she was not a vocalist. Corpulent Sydney Greenstreet was borrowed from Warner Bros. to portray flamboyantly odious Evan Llewellyn Evans, a man who thinks nothing of spitting on a conference table or removing his dentures in public—if it makes a point. Suave Adolphe Menjou, no longer handsome enough to avoid being upstaged by his finely tailored suits, was the cringing Kimberly.

When released in August 1947—twenty months after the premiere of **Adventure**—**The Hucksters** benefited not only from the notoriety of the novel and the screen presence of Gable, but also from the reviews. The **Hollywood Reporter** applauded, "Clark Gable zooms back to the preeminent place he long held in Hollywood with this smash performance. . . . He takes with him the charming English star Deborah Kerr, a delightful personality in her American debut. Together they manage a compelling love story that supersedes the satire of the original bestselling novel upon which the picture is based." The **New York Herald-Tribune** noted, "The Gable-Kerr team is ideal. Gal makes an impressive bow on the U.S. screen, and nobody is going to mind that a few liberties have been taken with the book to build up her role. Greenstreet is great as Evan Llewellyn Evans, who thinks of America as a blank space between New York and Hollywood where people buy soap." In fact, Greenstreet virtually stole the show as the obese tycoon, his performance sparkled with the perfect satirical bite as he spat on the glossy table, removed his teeth at a conference finale, and fumed during Gable's climactic cascade. For many filmgoers he was and is the best-remembered ingredient of a very slick, well-mounted feature.

The Hucksters grossed $4.35 million in distributors' domestic rentals, making it the studio's third biggest coin gatherer of the season (after **The Yearling** and **Till the Clouds Roll By**). Mayer directed a big-star buildup for Kerr and for Gardner. The latter reteamed later with Gable in Metro's **Lone Star** (1952) and **Mogambo** (1953). However, for Gable, who had suffered through production with the "shakes," alcohol and Benzedrine side effects, there began another painstaking search for another "right" property. The choice: **Homecoming** (1948), opposite Lana Turner.

IDIOT'S DELIGHT
1939—105 min.

Producer, Hunt Stromberg; **director,** Clarence Brown; based on the play by Robert Sherwood; **screenplay,** Sherwood; **art directors,** Cedric Gibbons and Wade B. Rubottom; **set decorator,** Edwin B. Willis; **gowns,** Adrian; **music director,** Herbert Stothart; **song,** Gus Kahn and Stothart; **choreography,** George King; **montage,** Slavko Vorkapich; **sound,** Douglas Shearer; **camera,** William Daniels; **editor,** Robert J. Kern.

Norma Shearer (**Irene Fellara**); Clark Gable (**Harry Van**); Edward Arnold (**Achille Weber**); Charles Coburn (**Dr. Walderace**); Joseph Schildkraut (**Captain Kirvline**); Burgess Meredith (**Quillery**); Pat Paterson (**Mrs. Cherry**); Laura Hope Crews (**Madame Zuleika**); Virginia Grey (**Shirley Laughlin**): William Edmunds (**Dumptsey**); Skeets Gallagher (**Donald Navadel**); Fritz Feld (**Pittatek**); Edward Raquello (**Chiari**); Lorraine Kreuger (**Bebe Gould**); Paula Stone (**Beulah Tremeyne**); Joan Marsh (**Elaine Messiger**); Bernadene Hayes (**Edna Creesh**); Virginia Dale (**Francine**); Frank Orth (**Benny Zinssar**); Peter Willes (**Mr. Cherry**); George Sorel (**Major**); Hobart Cavanaugh (**Frueheim, the Theatre Manager**); Bernard Suss (**Auguste**); William Irving (**Sandro**); Harry Strang (**Sergeant**); Emory Parnell (**Fifth Avenue Cop**); Bud Geary (**Ambulance Driver**); Mitchell Lewis (**Indian**); Joe Yule (**Comic**); Gertrude Bennett (**Woman with Powders**); Jim Conlin (**Stagehand**); Bonita Weber (**Woman with Catsup**); Rudolf Myzet (**Czech Announcer**).

SYNOPSIS
Back from World War I, Harry Van attempts to break into show business but finds himself hoofing in an Omaha vaudeville act and later working with a mind-reading act. Here Harry meets Irene, a member of an acrobatic troupe, and their encounter results in a brief romance concluded when their booking ends.

Several years later Harry is touring Europe with a six-girl song-and-dance act. En route to Geneva, Harry is stopped at a border hotel, the

Lorraine Krueger, Virginia Grey, Clark Gable, Bernadene Hayes, Paula Stone, and Virginia Dale in Idiot's Delight *('39).*

Monte Gabrielle, where he finds Irene disguised as a Russian countess, complete with blonde wig and thick accent. Traveling with Irene is international munitioneer Achille Weber. Irene denies knowing Harry and this byplay dominates much of the remainder of the storyline.

Later Weber deserts Irene and she finally admits that she was the trapeze artist from Omaha. She even remembers the number of Harry's hotel room from those long-ago days. Harry leaves for his train, but an air raid sends him back to the Monte Gabrielle. As the bombing begins, Harry and Irene plan a new act together.

* * *

Robert E. Sherwood's Pulitzer Prize–winning play, starring Alfred Lunt and Lynn Fontanne, had opened at Broadway's Shubert Theatre on March 24, 1936, running for 300 performances. When MGM purchased the screen rights, the studio planned a deluxe production, assigning Hunt Stromberg to produce, Clarence Brown to direct, and Sherwood himself to write the screenplay. The famed author even agreed to adjust the story to the more euphoric demands of Hollywood, modifying the play so that there were now (1) a prologue—3 reels' worth! (2) a moderation of the antiwar dialogue, (3) a benevolent elimination of identifying countries participating in the European war that starts at the end of the play, (4) a happy ending, and (5) more emphasis on romance and less on propaganda.

The crowning glory of the property came via its stars. Norma Shearer, despite her sagging box office and near debacle of **Marie Antoinette** (1938), won top billing as Irene Fellara with Clark

Gable as her leading man, Harry Van. Shearer caressed the part delightfully, being especially irresistible in her scenes as the Russian countess, flamboyantly sashaying about in a full blonde wig, imperiously waving her cigarette holder, and matchlessly delivering Sherwood's tangy dialogue with a rich Russian accent. (Many who had seen the stage production would comment how faithfully the actress had aped Miss Fontanne's stage performance.) As for Gable, whom Shearer requested for her vis-à-vis, he approached the assignment with more trepidation than the widowed Mrs. Thalberg. As hoofer Harry Van, Gable used George M. Cohan as a model. He rehearsed six weeks with dance coach George King to master the steps and rhythms and later called the part the most difficult he had ever undertaken.[1] (He wore a size 11-C shoe.) Audiences later delighted at his hoofing, and would applaud it again when MGM spliced a section of Gable's "Puttin' on the Ritz" number into **That's Entertainment!** (1974).

While Shearer and Gable worked well to-

[1]Several stories have passed down over the years regarding Gable's dancing role. When Gable was worried about the hoofing scenes, director Clarence Brown told him allegedly, "Hold onto the trapeze with your teeth." Said the denture-wearing star, "What do I hold onto my teeth with?"

The November 7, 1938, issue of the **Hollywood Reporter** carried the following item: "That big burly cop standing guard over the door to stage 1A at MGM is there because Clark Gable said he didn't want anyone watching him rehearse dance steps for his part as a song and dance man in **Idiot's Delight**."

gether on camera, their off-screen relationship during production was delicate. In his biography, **Gable and Lombard** (1974), Warren G. Harris relates that actress Carole Lombard, then Gable's lover and soon to become his bride, disliked Shearer, and suspected her of having romantic notions about Gable. Furthermore, wrote Harris,

Now that her mourning period for Irving Thalberg was over, Shearer was known around Hollywood as the Merry Widow. Her steady companion was George Raft, but she was also dating others as well.

It was obvious to some people working on **Idiot's Delight** that Shearer was pursuing Gable. At one point Gable got so fed up with the situation that he told a photographer, "I wish this broad would get the hell out of here." Shearer might not have been Gable's type, but a more urgent reason for his keeping his distance was that he feared Lombard's censure.

With director Brown's incisive direction (and his supervised background location shots of St. Moritz during the winter season), strong supporting performances from Edward Arnold (as munitions baron Achille Weber) and Laura Hope Crews (as Madame Zuleika), in addition to the stars' portrayals,[2] **Idiot's Delight**'s only troublesome spot was its ending. Originally filmed with a happy finale, the picture underwent the shooting of several variant tragic finales on Stromberg's orders, all of which proved unacceptable at sneak previews. The final print retained the simplistic but audience-pleasing finish of Shearer and Gable surviving the bombing raid, planning a new act together, and joining in the singing of a hymn.

Tapping the public's warm memories of the costars past teaming[3] in **A Free Soul** (1931) and **Strange Interlude** (1932), the MGM copy department cranked out such teasers as "Shearer is in Gable's arms again! . . . Thrilling news . . . as their great romantic adventure thunders from the screen." **Idiot's Delight** was released in January 1939 and the **Hollywood Reporter** rejoiced, "Surefire box office in a big way and certainly one of the most potential grossers of the year." The **New York Herald-Tribune**'s Howard Barnes praised the film's "refreshing vitality which sets it clearly apart from the remakes, extensions of cycles and never-never land offerings . . . generally treated by Hollywood." One advantage the film (which utilized a mythical European nation where Esperanto is spoken) held over the play was its timeliness; the play of 1936 seemed an exaggerated picture of things to come. But in 1939 the film was awfully close to the truth.

[2]In his book **Clark Gable** (1973), René Jordan observes, "In **Idiot's Delight**, Gable is in top form. The eyebrows have become independently mobile and operate as restless circumflex accents, rising higher and higher as Shearer escalates her outrageous repertory of lies. She is also perfect for a part that absorbs every mannerism, making the Shearer fakery no longer a curse but a blessing."

[3]Gable and Shearer might have been teamed again in 1939 had plans for her to play Scarlett O'Hara to his Rhett Butler jelled.

Idiot's Delight won no major Oscar nominations, although Shearer especially deserved a place on the ballot. But it did prove a top grosser. Unfortunately, Shearer's charming histrionics did not rescue her completely from her descent into early retirement, though Gable's hoofing and wry line delivery stand as an excellent companion piece to the Rhett Butler he would portray later in 1939.

Idiot's Delight would provide the spinoff basis for a short-lived TV comedy (!) series, "Harry's Girls" (NBC-TV, 1963), with Larry Blyden as the leader of a song-and-dance act. On March 17, 1979, Jack Lemmon and Rosemary Harris opened in a revival of the play in Los Angeles. The stage production did top business and caused many to remember the frothy exchanges of Gable and Shearer in their most engaging cinema match.

I'LL CRY TOMORROW
1955 C—117 min.

Producer, Lawrence Weingarten; **director,** Daniel Mann; based on the book by Lillian Roth, Mike Connolly, and Gerold Frank; **screenplay,** Helen Deutsch and Jay Richard Kennedy; **art directors,** Cedric Gibbons and Malcolm Brown; **music,** Alex North; **music director,** Charles Henderson; **costumes,** Helen Rose; **assistant director,** Al Jennings; **camera,** Arthur E. Arlings; **editor,** Harold F. Kress.

Susan Hayward **(Lillian Roth)**; Richard Conte **(Tony Bardeman)**; Eddie Albert **(Burt McGuire)**; Jo Van Fleet **(Katie)**; Don Taylor **(Wallie)**; Ray Danton **(David Tredman)**; Margo **(Selma)**; Virginia Gregg **(Ellen)**; Don Barry **(Jerry)**; David Kasday **(David as a Child)**; Carole Ann Campbell **(Lillian as a Child)**; Peter Leeds **(Richard)**; Tol Avery **(Fat Man)**; Guy Wilkerson **(Man)**; Tim Carey **(Derelict)**; Ken Patterson **(Director)**; Voltaire Perkins **(Mr. Byrd)**; Nora Marlowe **(Nurse)**; Harlan Warde **(Stage Manager)**; Anthony Jochim **(Paul, the Butler)**; Veda Ann Borg **(Waitress)**; Vernon Rich **(Club Manager)**; Cheerio Meredith **(Elderly Lady)**.

SYNOPSIS
In the 1910s child star Lillian Roth is pushed into a theatrical life by stage mother Katie. At eight the child is appearing on Broadway and beginning a career as a singer-actress.

As a young woman Lillian attempts to find personal happiness with David Tredman. They become engaged, but he dies. Alone and frightened, Lillian embarks upon a sixteen-year bout with alcoholism during which she marries a drunken soldier named Wallie. The marriage dissolves and Lillian soon weds alcoholic sadist Tony Bardeman, who beats her during their drunken sprees.

Once again alone, Lillian drifts to the bottom in a San Francisco gutter. She is sent back to her mother in New York and attempts suicide. Finally she reaches Alcoholics Anonymous and the cure

that allows her comeback as a nightclub singer and marriage to AA member Burt McGuire.

* * *

The year 1955 was one for tragic women screen biographies at Metro-Goldwyn-Mayer. Doris Day and James Cagney dramatized the strange relationship of Ruth Etting and "The Gimp" in **Love Me or Leave Me**; Eleanor Parker was superb as polio-stricken soprano Marjorie Lawrence in **Interrupted Melody**; and, most shatteringly, Susan Hayward portrayed alcohol-haunted Lillian Roth in **I'll Cry Tomorrow**, the most honest and in many ways the most disturbing of the based-on-life soap-opera trio released by Metro in that twelve-month span.

The property was based on Roth's own memoirs, **I'll Cry Tomorrow** (1954, written with Gerold Frank and Mike Connolly), which detailed the career that she began at age eight on the 1918 Broadway stage and that proceeded to glorious highs and sordid booze-soaked lows. The book sold some seven million copies in twenty languages. After producer Lawrence Weingarten signed director Daniel Mann, speculation rested on several actresses as "the" choice to portray Roth on camera, including June Allyson and Jane Russell. But it was three-time Oscar nominee Susan Hayward who was the winner. As Roth explained later:

After the book came out almost every studio in town wanted the story. But, at an earlier date, I had given MGM a verbal option and I held to my word. Also, they had promised that Susan Hayward would be given the title role, as I had requested. I had followed her career and thought she was an extremely skilled and sensitive actress.

I met Susan Hayward first in Las Vegas, where I was working. . . . About a month later she visited me again at the Beverly Hills Hotel in Hollywood. It was in the early afternoon and she arrived in her black Chinese pajamas with a coat thrown over them. We talked for several hours. By the time she left, I didn't know whether she was imitating me or I was emulating her. We were both so emotional about things that when we faced each other it was amost like looking into a mirror; I was looking at Lillian and she was looking at Susan.

Surrounded by a cast that included Richard Conte as a vicious spouse, Jo Van Fleet (a little younger than Hayward) as Lillian's stage mother,[1] and Eddie Albert (who had been with Hayward in **Smashup—The Story of a Woman**, 1947) as a helpful AA member, Hayward had a part of which actors' dreams are made. She also had to sing,

[1]Regarding Van Fleet's overly intense stage mother performance, Roth said, almost too kindly: "I thought Jo Van Fleet did a fine job, though she was directed to act the part in a way that was not quite true to fact. In the picture, my mother spoke with a foreign accent, whereas she was actually born in Boston and justifiably proud of her speech. There is nothing wrong with a foreign accent; our ancestors were all immigrants, but it just wasn't the way my mother spoke. Nor did she go around in furs and jewels. She was always neatly and modestly dressed, not at all an extrovert."

Eddie Albert and Susan Hayward in I'll Cry Tomorrow *('55).*

which the star did herself, reprising such Roth favorites as "Sing You Sinners," "When the Red Red Robin Comes Bob, Bob, Bobbin' Along," "Happiness Is a Thing Called Joe," "The Vagabond King Waltz," and (cut from the release print) "I'm Sittin' on Top of the World." Hayward recalled that every effort was made to evict Hollywood gloss and present the bare, sad facts without benefit of widescreen or color:

Danny Mann checked every detail. He wouldn't let me cheat with lipstick or even a curl. If he thought my hair wasn't mussed enough, he put water on his hands and mussed it down. . . . I read the book several times, and before we started filming, Danny, the producer, Lawrence Weingarten, and I went to jails and hospitals and even AA meetings, because I had to know that woman's life and what it had been.

Studio music supervisor Johnny Green would tell Doug McClelland for his book **Susan Hayward . . . Immortal Screen Star** (1975):

"We had planned to dub her but just for the hell of it, I asked the front office how much it would add to the grosses if we could say she did her own singing. They told me a couple of million. No matter what she might sound like, it was our policy to get a recording track of the actress whose voice was to be dubbed so we could get a dubber to match it. Suse arrived at my office to make the tape, scared to death of singing, this great big star—with that self-confident image. I got her to the piano, but she froze, just stood there. Finally, I said, 'Make a sound, any sound!' . . . Well, she started to sing and we got the recording. She sounded

great! I played the tape for the big brass, and at my suggestion they decided to let her do her own songs. We worked hard and everything came out fine. Suse can do anything she sets her mind to—once she sets her mind to it."

Allegedly Roth was angered that MGM did not allow her to provide the song dubbing, but denied that she was parodying Hayward's impersonation of her in her own club act then.

The results were obvious. When released in very late 1955, **I'll Cry Tomorrow** won a bouquet of notices from critics grateful to MGM for not glittering an unpretty story. Wrote William K. Zinsser (**New York Herald-Tribune**), "Most movie biographies are so sugary that the subjects don't even recognize themselves. Nobody will make that complaint about **I'll Cry Tomorrow**. . . . MGM has wrapped it up in a movie that has raw power and unusual honesty. There is nothing flabby or maudlin about it." **Variety,** "Metro has come up with a biopic that deals in realities, not storybook success values."

Hayward won the best actress prize at the Cork and Cannes Film Festival for her agonized delineation of Roth. She was also nominated for the Best Actress Oscar (as was Eleanor Parker for her tour de force in **Interrupted Melody**). But the Academy winner that year was Anna Magnani of Paramount's **The Rose Tattoo.**

I'll Cry Tomorrow became an MGM crowd-pleaser in its initial release, grossing $6,004,000 in distributors' domestic rentals. Besides enriching the studio, the film provided an opportunity for Hayward to have some of her songs from the film released as records, and provided marvelous public relations for Alcoholics Anonymous and for

Lillian Roth. In 1956, at the age of forty-five, Miss Roth made a comeback as a nightclub singer. In 1958 there appeared in bookshops a sequel, **Beyond My Worth,** which did not do nearly as well as **I'll Cry Tomorrow.**

For the record, it was just before beginning work on **I'll Cry Tomorrow** that Hayward took an overdose of sleeping pills and had to be hospitalized. One of those to offer comfort was the equally volatile Miss Roth.

INTRUDER IN THE DUST
1949—89 min.

Producer-director, Clarence Brown; based on the novel by William Faulkner; **screenplay,** Ben Maddow; **music,** Adolph Deutsch; **art directors,** Cedric Gibbons and Randall Duell; **set decorators,** Edwin B. Willis and Ralph S. Hurst; **assistant director,** Marvin Stuart; **makeup,** Jack Dawn; **sound,** Douglas Shearer; **camera,** Robert Surtees; **editor,** Robert J. Kern.

David Brian (**John Gavin Stevens**); Claude Jarman, Jr. (**Chick Mallison**); Juano Hernandez (**Lucas Beauchamp**); Porter Hall (**Nub Gowrie**); Elizabeth Patterson (**Miss Habersham**); Charles Kemper (**Crawford Gowrie**); Will Geer (**Sheriff Hampton**); David Clarke (**Vinson Gowrie**); Elzie Emanuel (**Aleck**); Lela Bliss (**Mrs. Mallison**); Harry Hayden (**Mr. Mallison**); Harry Antrim (**Mr. Tubbs**); Dan White (**Will Legate**); R. X. Williams (**Mr. Lilley**); Edmund and Ephraim Lowe (**Gowrie Twins**); Jack Odom (**Truck Driver**); John Morgan and James Kirkwood (**Black Convicts**); Ben Hilbun (**Attendant**); Ann Hartsfield (**Girl**).

SYNOPSIS
In the South black landowner Lucas Beauchamp is arrested for the murder of Vinson Gowrie, a local lumberman. Beauchamp had been found near the body and he had in his possession a revolver from which a bullet had been fired.

As he is led to jail he calls out to Chick Mallison, a white boy he had once befriended. He tells Chick he wants to see John Gavin Stevens, the boy's lawyer uncle. Stevens is reluctant to defend Beauchamp because of the high feeling in town. But he sees the prisoner at the insistence of Chick. Thereafter Stevens is jeered at by the townsfolk, who take their cue from Crawford Gowrie, the dead man's brother. Gowrie contends that Beauchamp should be dragged from jail and burned alive.

Beauchamp is unable to make Stevens agree to undertake a chore for him, one which he feels is pertinent to the case. As for what transpired at the time of the murder, Beauchamp reveals that Vinson Gowrie had beaten him to make him identify the culprit who had been stealing lumber from Gowrie. Now Beauchamp will not say who the thief is and Stevens leaves the jail in a huff.

Later Chick asks Beauchamp what the "chore"

Harry Antrim, David Brian, and Claude Jarman, Jr. in Intruder in the Dust *('49).*

is. It is then that the prisoner asks him to dig up the murdered man's body to prove that the fatal bullet was not fired from Beauchamp's gun. The lad is aided in the task by old Miss Habersham and by a young black boy. They find that the coffin is empty.

This discovery convinces lawyer Stevens and Sheriff Hampton of the accused man's probable innocence. They set out to find the corpse, and with the help of Nub Gowrie, the dead man's father, locate it in the quicksand of a nearby creek. The bullet extracted from the body proves Beauchamp was right. The Sheriff is now determined to trap the killer. As such he announces to one and all that Lucas Beauchamp has been freed and that he has returned to his cabin.

Actually he keeps the man in jail. Meanwhile, he stations himself at the cabin with Nub Gowrie. As expected, the real killer arrives to silence Beauchamp forever. It develops that the murderer is Crawford Gowrie. As Crawford is brought to jail, the townsfolk shamefacedly walk away from the building.

* * *

Throughout the 1930s MGM shied from "message" pictures of social consciousness; Fritz Lang's **Fury** (1936) was a rare exception for the slick studio. However, by the mid-1940s, sociological studies were no longer so scarce an item, especially when they could be exploited at the box office. Post–World War II audiences cheered such (commercial) studies as Paramount's **The Lost Weekend** (1945; alcoholism); Twentieth Century–

Fox's **Gentleman's Agreement** and RKO's **Crossfire** (both 1947; anti-Semitism); and Fox's **The Snake Pit** (1948; mental illness). It was in the late 1940s that Metro began making its way slowly into socially concerned filmmaking (with such entries as **Command Decision**), much to the consternation of Louis B. Mayer and the approval of increasingly powerful MGM executive Dore Schary. An outstanding example of the new direction was **Intruder in the Dust,** as striking a delineation of racial prejudice as has ever been filmed.

Based on William Faulkner's 1948 novel, **Intruder in the Dust** was produced and directed by Clarence Brown. His lengthy tenure at MGM had seen him virtually every type of picture and work with almost every great star on the lot. The film was shot almost entirely on location in Oxford, Mississippi. Of the five hundred people who passed before the cameras, fourteen were professional actors. Among them: Claude Jarman, Jr., a discovery of Brown's in **The Yearling** (1946); top-billed David Brian as the lawyer who gallantly defends a black man accused of murder and is thereafter threatened by the violent lynch mob; and Juano Hernandez, whose performance as Lucas Beauchamp rates as one of the American cinema's first important portraits of the black man as a proud and complete counterpoint to the stereotyped Stepin Fetchit–Mantan Moreland comic image. Hernandez's character is so contemptuous of the accusing white trash that he refuses to defend himself.

"Producer Clarence Brown has made a brilliant, stirring film," wrote Bosley Crowther **(New York Times)** when **Intruder in the Dust** opened in November 1949. He added, "Without one mo-

ment's hesitation, this corner, still shaking, proclaims that it is probably the year's preeminent picture and one of the great cinema dramas of our time." Crowther rated the interpretations of Brian and Jarman "excellent," praised Elizabeth Patterson as "a moving symbol of Southern delicacy and strength," and especially saluted the "staunch and magnificent integrity" of Hernandez' performance.

Other critics paraphrased Crowther's sentiments, but **Intruduer in the Dust** did not become a commercial hit. As anticipated, business—where there was any—was abysmal in the South. Moreover, **Intruder** suffered somewhat in distribution because it followed, by less than two months, Twentieth Century–Fox's **Pinky,** Elia Kazan's craftily "entertaining" study of a black girl passing for white. That highly promoted feature contained a big-name cast, including Jeanne Crain, Ethel Barrymore, and Ethel Waters[2], and its treatment of racial intolerance was less bitter and more disguised within the storyline—hence more palatable to most audiences. Metro's worthy feature rated **no** Academy Award nominations and only the rather unorthodox National Board of Review and the **New York Times**' Ten Best Pictures List accorded honor status to **Intruder in the Dust** (numbers three and ten respectively).

In his pungent study of blacks on screen, **Toms, Coons, Mulattoes, Mammies, and Bucks** (1973), Donald Bogle writes, "Tough minded and complex, **Intruder in the Dust** unearthed, among a number of things, a sombre piece of Americana; a black man on trial has little chance for justice in our country, said the film, more than twenty years before such statements were fashionable."

Intruder in the Dust was a far cry from Metro's Arthur Freed–produced all-black confectionary musical **Cabin in the Sky** (1943); rather, it recalled King Vidor's critically acclaimed MGM release **Hallelujah!** (1929). Actually it would be the mid-1960s before MGM really capitalized on the black-film craze; then **A Patch of Blue** (1965), starring Sidney Poitier, would fill theatres and earn Shelley Winters a Best Supporting Actress Oscar.

IVANHOE

1952 C—106 min.

Producer, Pandro S. Berman; **director,** Richard Thorpe; based on the novel by Sir Walter Scott; **screenplay,** Noel Langley; **adapter,** Aeneas MacKenzie; **art director,** Alfred Junge; **costumes,** Roger Furse; **makeup,** Charles Parker; **music,** Miklos Rozsa; **sound,** A. W. Watkins; **camera ef-**

---

[1]In the novel, when Vinson's body is found, Crawford is arrested and once in jail commits suicide. The film version ends just as Crawford is being brought to jail.

[2]For **Pinky,** Jeanne Crain was nominated for a Best Actress Oscar, and both Ethel Barrymore and Ethel Waters were nominated for Best Supporting Actress. Crain lost to Olivia de Havilland of **The Heiress** (Paramount), while Barrymore and Waters were beaten by Mercedes McCambridge of Columbia's **All the King's Men** (a trenchant study of political corruption in the South).

fects, Tom Howard; **camera,** Freddie Young; **editor,** Frank Clarke.

Robert Taylor (**Wilfred of Ivanhoe**); Elizabeth Taylor (**Rebecca**); Joan Fontaine (**Rowena**); George Sanders (**Sir Brian DeBois-Guilbert**); Emlyn Williams (**Wamba**); Robert Douglas (**Sir Hugh De-Bracy**); Finlay Currie (**Cedric**); Felix Aylmer (**Isaac of York**); Francis DeWolff (**Font DeBouef**); Guy Rolfe (**Prince John**); Norman Wooland (**King Richard**); Basil Sydney (**Waldemar Fitzurse**); Harold Warrender (**Locksley**); Patrick Holt (**Philip de-Malworsin**); Roderick Lovell (**Ralph DeVipont**); Sebastian Cabot (**Clerk of Copmondurst**); John Reedclock (**Hundebert**); Michael Brennan (**Baldwin**); Megs Jenkins (**Servant to Isaac**); Valentine Dyall (**Norman Guard**); Lionel Harris (**Roger of Bermondsey**); Earl Jaffe (**Austrian Monk**).

Robert Taylor, Emlyn Williams, and Finlay Currie in Ivanhoe *('52).*

SYNOPSIS

Having bravely served King Richard in the Third Crusade, Wilfred of Ivanhoe returns to England where troubles greet him, both personal and political. His father Cedric has disowned him because of his loyalties to the king. A plot is afoot to place the sinuous John on the throne while Richard is imprisoned in Austria. Nevertheless, the irrepressible Ivanhoe manages to sneak into Cedric's house to romance his love Rowena. She emphasizes the danger that surrounds Ivanhoe.

To finance the rescue of Richard, Ivanhoe seeks Isaac of York, a wealthy Jew loyal to the king. While Isaac supports the cause, his daughter Rebecca captivates Ivanhoe, despite the realization that religious differences doom their romance. Meanwhile, Prince John sends the arrogant Sir Brian DeBois-Guilbert to destroy Ivanhoe's campaign. Sir Brian stunningly succeeds, imprisoning the survivors of his attack on Torquilstone Castle. A daring raid later by Locksley sets Ivanhoe and his forces free and forces Sir Brian to retreat. Striking a villainous last blow, the knight kidnaps Rebecca and carries her back to the Royal Court.

Prince John is delighted by the idea of vengefully condemning Rebecca as a sorceress and burning her at the stake. Sir Brian is less keen—he has fallen in love with her. However, at news of her fate, Ivanhoe braves to appear. He challenges Sir Brian to fight for her and the archenemies engage in a spectacular tournament match of broad swords, mace, and chain. Ivanhoe emerges the victor after a long and bloody fight. As Sir Brian lies dying on the field, King Richard and his army arrive.

Political order is soon restored. Rebecca and her father are promised safe exodus. And Ivanhoe, returning to his faithful Rowena, takes a high place in the new Saxon England.

* * *

Sir Walter Scott's epic tale of knighthood, **Ivanhoe,** contains an enticing formula of chivalry, romance, villainy, and adventure that should be irresistible to Hollywood filmmakers. Yet by 1952 a definitive celluloid version had not reached the screen. (In 1913 two short silent editions appeared, one produced by Americans on location

in England with King Baggott and Leah Baird, the other a British rival entry with Lauderdale Maitland and Edith Bracewell. In 1935 producer Walter Wanger insisted he would film the story with Gary Cooper, Sylvia Sidney, and Madeleine Carroll starred, but the project never materialized.)

However, that year, 1952, MGM released **Ivanhoe,** and with it a grand transformation of Scott's masterly yarn. As Tony Thomas assesses in **The Great Adventure Films** (1976), "What producer Pandro Berman and director Richard Thorpe put on the screen is, so far, the finest of medieval swashbucklers, a truly spectacular picturization of the age of chivalry, with splendid scenery, castles, regal courts, and halls, jousting tournaments and beautifully costumed knights and ladies."

Ivanhoe was produced in England. MGM's profits in Great Britain from its releases had swelled over the years, so much so that a government decree tied up a large chunk of the money, forcing the studio to spend it **in** England.[1] Hence, Metro set production at the Boreham Wood Studios, although it assigned the major roles to its Hollywood-based stars. There was no question that Robert Taylor would play the swashbuckling lead. But there was some seesawing in the cast-

ing of the female roles. At one point Ava Gardner was announced to play Rebecca, but she decided the part was too unimportant. Then the studio, hoping to break up Elizabeth Taylor's romance with director Stanley Donen, willed that she go abroad to play the part. She rebelled, and it was then decided to cast Deborah Kerr (Rebecca) and Margaret Leighton (Rowena) in the pivotal distaff roles. Later Elizabeth Taylor agreed to the part of Rebecca and freelancing Joan Fontaine was contracted to play Rowena. George Sanders, who would specialize in costume drama villains in the 1950s, was admirably suited to play the sneering but daring Sir Brian.

The film was long in production. Sets sprawled all over Boreham Wood's 120 acres, the chief attraction being the massive Torquilstone Castle. Construction on the castle began two years before a single scene was shot, and it idled a year before any filming began. The castle even contained a moat, twenty feet wide and ten feet deep. There was a model erected of the Ashby-de-la-Zouche jousting fields, and MGM artists and designers studied drawings of medieval armor and weapons to provide exact reproductions.

The wedding of the epic story, the stellar cast, the meticulous detail, the sprawling action scenes, and the effective score of Miklos Rozsa made for major box-office fare. The **New York Times** paid tribute:

Out of Sir Walter Scott's gloriously panoramic novel, **Ivanhoe,** which also contains an ample measure of twelfth-century social overtones, producer Pandro S. Berman and Metro-Goldwyn-

---

[1]The British, usually sensitive to Hollywood interpretations of English classics, widely acclaimed the production of **Ivanhoe.** The trade paper **Kiné Weekly** reported, "**Ivanhoe** takes a few liberties with history and its illustrious author, yet all are justified by results. History book and spellbinding hokum in one, it cocks a snook at the purists without risking ridicule."

Mayer have fetched a motion picture that does them, Scott, and English history proud . . . it must be ungrudgingly agreed that those who emerge more triumphant are the producers of the film—they and the myriad of able craftsmen and actors who helped to achieve their brilliantly colored tapestry of drama and spectacle, now on the Music Hall's screen. . . . A grand picture, told in what Sir Walter himself called his "big bow-wow style."

The film's top drawing card was its cast, with Robert Taylor, fresh from his **Quo Vadis** triumph, in fine form as the heroic Ivanhoe, Sanders his most purringly antagonistic, and Elizabeth Taylor and Fontaine perilously lovely. But the most compelling aspect of the production was the combat scenes. Thomas describes them in **The Great Adventure Films:**

The action sequences of **Ivanhoe** called for from 500 to 1,000 extras each day and the training required was nothing less than military. Dozens of men were drilled in the use of lances, spears, and maces for the jousting scenes, and squads of men were given instruction in the use of the longbow and crossbow. The filming also required 100 suitably handsome and spirited horses, a requirement more difficult to fill than those unfamiliar with horses might imagine. Equine experts scouted England to find them and then spent time training them. The long filming provided the stuntmen with a number of field days, with falls from horses and plunges from parapets into moats. The man in charge of the military aspects was Col. Linden White, who said at the time, "How any old-time knight fought for years without injury is a mystery. The chain-mail armor of Ivanhoe's time was like the mesh rings in a modern woman's purse. A pointed barb could go through. The twelve- and fifteen-foot lances were lethal weapons. We made them as replicas, but with hollow centers and rubber ends. We had to design special saddles so that a falling rider wouldn't be trampled by a horse, and we had one of the hardest jobs teaching players how to charge at full speed with a forty- to sixty-pound suit of armor. We had some accidents, but luckily nothing too serious."

Ivanhoe was a commercial bonanza, grossing $6,258,000 in distributors' domestic rental. It placed fifth on the **Film Daily** Ten Best Picture List of 1952 and was Oscar-nominated as Best Picture of the year (but lost to Paramount's **The Greatest Show on Earth**). It inspired the studio to produce, as its first CinemaScope film, **Knights of the Round Table** (1953), also directed by Richard Thorpe and starring Robert Taylor. This time Ava Gardner did play his leading lady, cast as Queen Guinevere to his Sir Lancelot. In 1955 director Thorpe and star Taylor would team yet again, for MGM'S **Quentin Durward**, based on the Sir Walter Scott novel. In this widescreen, color exercise, Kay Kendall was the fair damsel in distress. In 1957 there would be the British-made television series "Ivanhoe" starring Roger Moore.

JOHNNY EAGER
1942—107 min.

Producer, John W. Considine, Jr.: **director,** Mervyn LeRoy; based on the novel by James Edward Grant; **screenplay,** John Lee Mahin and Grant; **art directors,** Cedric Gibbons and Stan Rogers; **set decorators,** Edwin B. Willis; **music,** Bronislau Kaper; **gowns,** Kalloch; **sound,** Douglas Shearer; **camera,** Harold Rosson; **editor,** Albert Akst.

Robert Taylor **(Johnny Eager)**; Lana Turner **(Lisbeth Bard)**; Edward Arnold **(John Benson Farrell)**; Van Heflin **(Jeff Hartnett)**; Robert Sterling **(Jimmy Courtney)**; Patricia Dane **(Garnet)**; Glenda Farrell **(Mae Blythe)**; Henry O'Neill **(Mr. Verne)**; Diana Lewis **(Judy Sanford)**; Barry Nelson **(Lew Rankin)**; Charles Dingle **(Marco)**; Paul Stewart **(Julio)**; Cy Kendall **(Halligan)**; Don Costello **(Billiken)**; Lou Lubin **(Benjy)**; Joseph Downing **(Ryan)**; Connie Gilchrist **(Peg)**; Robin Raymond **(Matilda)**; Leona Maricle **(Miss Mines)**.

SYNOPSIS
Parolee Johnny Eager pretends to be a taxi driver to appease his parole board. Actually he is the chief racketeer who operates from the posh offices of a dog track, a front for his monopolistic vices.

Johnny is a ruthless racketeer. He has elusive powers over women such as Lisbeth Bard, the socialite adopted daughter of the prosecuting attorney, John Benson Farrell, who sent Johnny to jail. As Lisbeth, a sociology student, spends more time in Johnny's company, she becomes aware of his double dealings. Later, to insure her silence, Johnny "stages" a murder to make the blue-blooded girl think she has killed one of his henchmen.

Finally Jeff Hartnett, Johnny's alcoholic lawyer pal, causes Eager to see his errors and directs him toward regeneration. Johnny demonstrates to Lisabeth that she did not kill his hireling and then, in a rare act of unselfishness, sends her away with her fiancé.

Thereafter Johnny dies a hero's death as he is gunned down in a back alley, proving that "crime does not pay."

* * *

"What use is a script when you have twin-stars like those on the company payroll?" piqued Milton Meltzer of the **Daily Worker** after viewing Metro's **Johnny Eager.** The film was a bid to re-create the Turner–Clark Gable screen excitement of **Honky Tonk** (1941), with Robert Taylor scorching Lana's lips. As the ad copy promised, "TNT—Taylor 'n' Turner—Together They're Terrific!"

For some time Robert Taylor, one of the studio's most cooperative stars, had suffered under the pretty-boy image that plagued his triumph as Armand in **Camille** (1936). **Billy the Kid** (1941) did not really accomplish transforming Taylor into a major screen tough, so the studio tried again by casting Taylor in the title role of this John Lee Mahin–James Edward Grant mixture of psycholog-

Van Heflin and Robert Taylor in Johnny Eager *('42).*

ical drama. It was a role worthy of a James Cagney, a George Raft, or an Edward G. Robinson, climaxing with the antihero being gunned down in an alley. With Lana Turner costarring as Johnny's socialite lover, who inconveniently happens to be the stepdaughter of prosecutor Edward Arnold, director Mervyn LeRoy[1] modulated the accent between crime melodrama and Taylor's romancing. The results were box-office explosives, but many critics thought the plot an artistic misfire.

New York World-Telegram: "Johnny Eager is synthetic, at times preposterous underworld melodrama, freighted with phony psychological implications. But any film which has sense of humor enough, if not sense of humor at least temerity enough, to offer Lana Turner as a student of sociology deserves to be treated kindly."

New York Morning Telegraph: "Here is the star system in all its glory, with plot, action, situation, and dialogue all subordinated to the idea of showing the principal players off to their best advantage."

Baltimore Sun: "If you want crime wrapped in cellophane and attractively packaged, here it is."

Actually, it was Metro newcomer Van Heflin who stole the limelight of this posh gangster yarn. As Jeff Harnett, Johnny Eager's Shakespeare-quoting, ever-drunk "conscience," he proved a dramatic standout. He was nominated for a Best Supporting Actor's Oscar, competing against William Bendix of **Wake Island** (Paramount), Walter Huston of **Yankee Doodle Dandy** (Warner Bros.), Frank Morgan of **Tortilla Flat** (MGM), and Henry Travers of **Mrs. Miniver** (MGM). Heflin won. Sadly, MGM did not know how to use the actor thereafter. He was assigned to **Kid Glove Killer** (1942), a B film that turned out far better than anticipated. If anything, it was his lead in the uncommercial **Tennessee Johnson** (1943) which convinced the studio that Heflin did not have marquee magic. With time out for three years as a combat cameraman with the Ninth Air Force during World War II, he returned to Metro, completing his contract with such entries as **Green Dolphin Street** (1947) and **The Three Musketeers** (1948)—both opposite Lana Turner. After **Madame Bovary** (1949) and **East Side, West Side** (1949) he left the studio.

Though Robert Taylor and Lana Turner both remained with MGM well into the 1950s, and well after the glitter had faded, they would never again be teamed in a picture. Plans to unite them in **The Three Musketeers, The Cobweb** (1955), and United Artists' **By Love Possessed** (1961) failed to materialize.

Johnny Eager would enjoy a national reissue in 1949.

---

[1]This was the first time that Mervyn LeRoy, who had brought Lana to MGM with him in 1938, had directed her at that studio. In **The Films of Lana Turner** (1976), Lou Valentino, an authority on the actress, reports, "It's a particular favorite among Turner fans since it so beautifully displays her at the peak of young loveliness."

JOURNEY FOR MARGARET
1942—81 min.

Producer, B. P. Fineman; **director,** W. S. Van Dyke II; based on the book by William L. White; **screenplay,** David Hertz and William Ludwig; **art directors,** Cedric Gibbons and Wade B. Rubottom; **set decorators,** Edwin B. Willis and Dick Pefferle; **music,** Franz Waxman; **gowns,** Kalloch; **sound,** Douglas Shearer; **camera,** Ray June; **editor,** George White.

Robert Young **(John Davis)**; Laraine Day **(Nora Davis)**; Fay Bainter **(Trudy Strauss)**; Margaret O'Brien **(Margaret)**; Nigel Bruce **(Herbert Allison)**; William Severn **(Peter Humphreys)**; G. P. Huntley, Jr. **(Rugged)**; Doris Lloyd **(Mrs. Barrie)**; Halliwell Hobbes **(Mr. Barrie)**; Jill Esmond **(Susan Fleming)**; Charles Irwin **(Fairoaks)**; Elisabeth Risdon **(Mrs. Bailey)**; Lisa Golm **(Frau Weber)**; Herbert Evans **(Man)**; Clare Sandars **(Child)**; Leyland Hodgson **(Censor)**; Anita Sharp Bolster **(Woman)**; Matthew Boulton **(Warden)**; Lilyan Irene **(Nurse)**; John Burton **(Sergeant)**; Jimmy Aubrey **(Porter)**; Heather Thatcher **(Mrs. Harris)**; Cyril Delevanti **(Stage Manager)**; Jody Gilbert **(Mme. Bornholm)**; Crau-

Fay Bainter, Margaret O'Brien, Laraine Day, Robert Young, and William Severn in a publicity pose for Journey for Margaret *('42).*

furd Kent (**Everton**); Keye Luke (**Japanese Statesman**); Henry Guttman (**Polish Captain**).

SYNOPSIS

In 1940, American journalist John Davis and his wife Nora are in World War II London where their first child will be born. While covering an air raid, John encounters Peter Humphreys, a child left parentless by the bombings. John takes him to a home for war orphans.

When John returns to his hotel, he discovers it has been hit by German bombs. Nora is hospitalized and loses the baby. Her injuries will prevent her from having children. After her hospital release, Nora returns to her Winstock, Connecticut home while John remains in London fulfilling his writing responsibilities.

Upon a visit to young Peter, John discovers the boy's sister, Margaret, a frightened little child who wears an empty incendiary bomb casing around her neck. Soon John and the two children develop a mutual attachment. John later proposes that he and Nora adopt the parentless youngsters. Nora readily agrees and he plans the trip to the United States.

Problems arise when he can take only one child in lieu of forty pounds of luggage. John decides that Margaret is more in need of leaving the war-torn city. At the last minute, a passenger, Mrs. Bailey shows up with Peter in tow. John and the two children reach America where Nora is waiting for them.

* * *

"Meet Margaret O'Brien. The most amazing new child star in the history of the screen," read Metro's ad line for **Journey for Margaret**, the cinema version of foreign correspondent William L. White's book (of the same name) relating the life stories of two blitz orphans.

Five-year-old Angela Maxine O'Brien, the modeling daughter of circus performers (her father had died four months before her birth), had already visited Metro at the age of four to appear as an auditioning cherub in **Babes on Broadway**. When director W. S. Van Dyke II began testing children for the title role in the war drama, Angela returned to Culver City to audition for the part and won it, though she was **not** surprised. "I knew I'd get it. I prayed for it."

Still, the freckle-faced discovery, who would win a special 1944 Oscar and a tribute from Lionel Barrymore, "She's the only actress outside of Ethel who's made me take out my handkerchief in thirty years," had to surrender the star billing to Robert Young and Laraine Day. The talented tyke received a special screen credit, "And presenting Margaret O'Brien."

Released late in the fall of 1942, **Journey for Margaret** joined **Mrs. Miniver** as one of Hollywood's most effectively produced pieces of Allied propaganda. The **Brooklyn Citizen** reported, "One of the least heralded and most unpretentious efforts by the screen to picture the London blitz, **Journey for Margaret** will sear your flesh with its utter truthfulness and simplicity." Wanda Hale, in her three-and-a-half star **New York Daily News** review, decided of this modestly budgeted black-

and-white feature, "Tightening up in spots would have helped, rather than hurt, this Metro-Goldwyn-Mayer production but, even with its too gradual presentation, the drama will tug at your heartstrings continuously."[1] The tiny O'Brien, of course, snared the acting plaudits. Her screen "brother," William Severn, drew no comparable response, despite his impressive juvenile charms.

MGM began a campaign to make Margaret O'Brien the movies' most beloved child since the maturing Shirley Temple. Margaret and Robert Young would be costarred again in MGM's **The Canterville Ghost** (1944). Thereafter, twenty-eight years would pass before the two performers would reunite, this time on Young's ABC-TV series, "Marcus Welby, M.D." On the December 19, 1972, episode, O'Brien would play a very overweight wife in need of medical help.

A sad footnote to **Journey for Margaret**: This was the last feature film of Major "Woody" Van Dyke, who died at age fifty-three on February 5, 1943. He had spent sixteen of his twenty-five years as a director at Culver City, where he made forty-seven of his eighty-one motion pictures.

JULIUS CAESAR
1953—120 min.

Producer, John Houseman; **director**, Joseph Mankiewicz; based on the play by William Shakespeare; **adapter**, Mankiewicz; **art directors**, Cedric Gibbons and Edward Carfagno; **set decorators**, Edwin B. Willis and Hugh Hunt; **assistant director**, Howard W. Koch; **technical adviser**, P. M. Pasenette; **costumes**, Herschel McCoy; **music**, Miklos Rozsa; **makeup**, William Tuttle; **special effects**, Warren Newcombe; **camera**, Joseph Ruttenberg; **editor**, John Dunning.

Marlon Brando (**Marc Antony**); James Mason (**Brutus**); John Gielgud (**Cassius**); Louis Calhern (**Julius Caesar**); Edmond O'Brien (**Casca**); Greer Garson (**Calpurnia**); Deborah Kerr (**Portia**); George Macreedy (**Marullus**); Michael Pate (**Flavius**); Richard Hale (**Soothsayer**); Alan Napier (**Cicero**); John Hoyt (**Decius Brutus**); Tom Powers (**Metellus Cimber**); William Cottrell (**Cinna**); Jack Raine (**Trebonius**); Ian Wolfe (**Ligarius**); Morgan Farley (**Artemidorus**); Bill Phipps (**Antony's Servant**); Douglas Watson (**Octavius Caesar**); Douglass Dumbrille (**Lepidus**); Rhys Williams (**Lucilius**); Dayton Lummis (**Messala**); Edmund Purdom (**Strato**); Paul Guilfoyle, John Doucette, Lawrence Dobkin, and Jo Gilbert (**Citizens**); John Parrish (**Titinius**); O. Z. Whitehead (**Cinna, the Poet**); John Lupton (**Varro**); Lumsden Hare (**Publius**); Ned Glass (**Cobbler**): Victor Perry (**Popilius Lena**).

SYNOPSIS

Scoffing at the words of the soothsayer, "Beware the Ides of March," proud, vain conqueror Julius

---

[1] The film had been tightened with the elimination of several scenes, including those involving Signe Hasso as Anya.

Caesar revels in his colossal power as emperor of Rome. He is unaware that his assassination is being plotted by Brutus, Cassius, and Casca. Recognizing the danger of his immense power, the trio has united to destroy his tyranny.

Caesar's wife Calpurnia is haunted by a terrible dream detailing her spouse's demise. She begs Caesar not to go to the Senate on the Ides of March. He laughs at her concern, and also ignores Artemidorus, who warns him of his pending doom.

Upon his arrival at the Senate, Caesar is indeed welcomed by the daggers of the conspirators; the bleeding emperor staggers to the once devoted Brutus and asks, "Et tu, Brute?" before receiving the lethal slash from Brutus' dagger.

Caesar's devoted Marc Antony rushes to the Senate and beholds the massacred corpse. He affects the posture of sympathy with the conspirators, while simultaneously plotting with Octavius Caesar to avenge the assassination. Brutus wins the cheers of the people when he passionately explains his actions, but Antony follows Brutus with so stinging an indictment of the murderers that the crowd reverses its sympathies. The two factions raise armies.

On the battlefield of Philippi it soon appears that the fates favor the avenging forces of Antony. Cassius forces his slave to stab him, and Brutus, ravaged by horrible visits from Caesar's vindictive ghost, kills himself.

The triumphant Antony, discovering Brutus' body, orates, "This was the noblest Roman of them all."

* * *

In 1953 the name of William Shakespeare still evoked fear and trembling in Hollywood. Hollywood had yet to translate the Bard to the screen with any happy mixture of acclaim and profits resulting, though the British had succeeded nobly with Laurence Olivier's **Henry IV** (1945) and his Oscar-winning **Hamlet** (1948). In the seventeen years since MGM had rationalized the financial loss of Thalberg's cherished **Romeo and Juliet** as a prestige success, no other major Hollywood studio had turned to the Bard. However, in 1953 **Julius Caesar** appeared. It was a beautifully acted version of the Shakespearean classic, which not only pleased critics and made money for MGM, but won the acclaim of the **London News Chronicle**: "It is maddening to be forced to admit it, but it has been left to Hollywood in this **Caesar** to make the finest film version of Shakespeare yet to be seen on screen."

The Metro production was inspired by an exceptionally well-made 16-mm version, shot in six months at a cost of $15,000 by David Bradley using the crew from Northwestern University (including Charlton Heston as Marc Antony). **Julius Caesar** was produced at MGM by John Houseman, Orson Welles' coproducer of the famed Mercury Theatre. He had recently overseen the highly regarded **The Bad and the Beautiful** (1953), justifying the esteem in which studio head Dore Schary had long held him.

Some fifteen years earlier Houseman had produced Orson Welles' modern-dress stage version of **Julius Caesar** on Broadway, and he had

Louis Calhern and James Mason in Julius Caesar *('53).*

since wanted to undo the "wrong" which he felt director-star Welles (who played Brutus) had done to the "correct" conception of Shakespeare.[1] "After all," Houseman told the wary front office at MGM, "**Julius Caesar** is just a big political gangster story!" In a more intellectual vein, Houseman spoke of the drama, "Of all Shakespeare's plays, this one is probably the most modern. It's a melodrama about the lust for power which breeds dictatorship and political violence, about the twin tyrannies of totalitarian government and mob rule, and about the human conflict of people who are caught between such forces." Such sociological depiction appealed to Schary and the production was approved.

At first it was thought that either Charlton Heston or Britisher Leo Genn would interpret the pivotal role of Marc Antony. However, Houseman was adamant; he wanted Marlon Brando for the part. The industry joked that the very mannered Brando would probably appear on screen in a torn toga mumbling the Bard's famous words. To direct the vehicle, Joseph L. Mankiewicz, who had won Oscars as writer-director of **A Letter to Three Wives** (1948) and **All About Eve** (1950), was selected. Here he would not have the opportunity (or be allowed) to play with the dialogue in his talented way. Louis Calhern, who had triumphed on Broadway in 1950 as **King Lear,** was assigned the title role; James Mason was cast as Brutus (Paul Scofield had been earlier considered); John Gielgud was signed to make his Hollywood debut

as Cassius; and Edmond O'Brien joined the troupe as the fiery Casca. Happy to be part of the production were Greer Garson, as Caesar's Calpurnia, and Deborah Kerr, as Portia, Brutus' wife. Though each role was small, both ladies were pleased at the prospect of participating in so exciting a project.

Throughout production, Mankiewicz's direction and Joseph Ruttenberg's camera sought to avoid the sensational.[2] It was a black-and-white production, and there were few attempts by the studio to graft onto the film the splendor of such recent epics as Metro's **Quo Vadis** (1951) with its Technicolor panoramas of Rome.[3] The **Julius Cae-**

sar company never left Hollywood. The battle of Philippi was shot in Bronson Canyon, just minutes from busy Sunset Boulevard. Standing sets from past MGM historical productions were stripped down and simplified for this budget-conscious MGM entry.

Before the film's release some in the MGM front office, as expected, were fidgety about the film's potential. Thus the advertisements for **Julius Caesar** would boast of pomp and sinful decadence: "Thrill to ruthless men and their goddess-like women in a sin-swept age!" "Thrill to traitors and heroes . . . killings and conspiracies . . . passions and violence in Rome's most exciting era!"

The reviews, regardless of the misguided publicity, were ecstatic. The **New York World-Telegram** reported "An admirable achievement by everyone concerned, by far the best Shakespeare ever turned out by Hollywood!" **Variety:** "Metro has pulled out all the stops to fashion a socko filmization of the Shakespearean classic. A triumphant achievement in filmmaking, it will be rated one of the great pictures of Hollywood." The National Board of Review voted **Julius Caesar** the best picture of 1953. The film was Oscar-nominated as Best Picture but lost to Columbia's **From Here to Eternity.** Brando, in a superb delineation, lost the Best Actor Oscar to William Holden of **Stalag 17** (Paramount). **Julius Caesar** did win an Academy Award for Best Black-and-White Art Direction and Set Direction (Cedric Gibbons, Edward Carfagno, Edwin B. Willis, and Hugh Hunt).

Julius Caesar proved a watershed for several of the film's troupe. Brando would star in Columbia's **The Wild One** (the same year) and **On the Waterfront** (1954), winning an Oscar for the latter. He would return to the MGM fold twice more: as Sky Masterson in Samuel Goldwyn's musical **Guys and Dolls** (1955) and as the star of the extravagant, trouble-plagued remake of **Mutiny on the Bounty** (1962). For Greer Garson, **Julius Caesar** would be her final Metro picture. She negotiated the termination of her sixteen-year contract, preferring to freelance elsewhere. She later made a guest appearance as the Mother Superior in Metro's **The Singing Nun** (1966). Edmond O'Brien, a solid actor in so many forties and fifties films, would win a Best Supporting Actor Oscar in 1954 for his agent's part in **The Barefoot Contessa** (United Artists). As for director Joseph L. Mankiewicz, he would direct the above-mentioned **Guys and Dolls** and in the early 1960s cope with Richard Burton's Marc Antony and Rex Harrison's Julius Caesar in Twentieth Century–Fox's "disaster" epic **Cleopatra** (1963), starring Elizabeth Taylor. He did have the opportunity to tinker with the dialogue.

In 1971 American International Pictures released in the U.S. a new **Julius Caesar,** produced by Commonwealth United on location in Spain with interiors filmed at MGM's Boreham Wood

---

[1]At the time the Houseman/MGM production was getting under way, Orson Welles in Rome was planning a version of the Shakespearean drama in Italy. The latter project was dropped in the face of the Hollywood version.

[2]Years later composer Miklos Rozsa would relate his experiences in supplying the background music for the film. Beyond a boy's song in the tent at night, there was very little music in the picture. It was Rozsa who suggested an overture be used. Since Mankiewicz had completed his work on **Julius Caesar** and had gone to New York, Rozsa consulted mostly with Houseman. The expense of the recording session was approved by Schary and the studio's music director. Rozsa's composition was duly recorded, receiving plaudits from the music director. Later the music director decided on a new overture. He wanted to have a full symphonic orchestra filmed in a concert-hall decor, playing Tchaikovsky's **Capriccio Italien.** In fury Rozsa went to Houseman who in turn made demands on Schary, telling him if the new overture was employed for the premiere, he would tell the press the machinations behind its use. As a result, neither overture was heard, although Rozsa's composition was later recorded for an LP album.

[3]In **Marlon Brando** (1973), René Jordan noted, "The studio aimed at an intellectual follow-up to **Quo Vadis,** and the sets looked too clean, tidy, and stagy for the surreptitiously modern conception. Performances like Brando's and O'Brien's would have worked better in a seedy, crabby Rome." Jordan would also observe, "**Julius**

Caesar was caught between realism and pageant, but the final flaw in the film's structure is Shakespeare's. The climax comes midway with the funeral oration, and Brando delivers an actor's coup that knocks the film out."

Studios in England. Despite a big-name cast, including Charlton Heston as Marc Antony (very good), Jason Robards as Brutus (very bad), and John Gielgud[4] as Caesar (flawless), the production as a whole failed, and was unfavorably compared by most major critics with the 1953 version.

KING SOLOMON'S MINES
1950 C—102 min.

Producer, Sam Zimbalist; **directors,** Compton Bennett and Andrew Marton; based on the novel by Sir Henry Rider Haggard; **screenplay,** Helen Deutsch; **art director,** Cedric Gibbons; **songs,** Eric Maschwitz and Mischa Spoliansky; **camera,** Robert Surtees; **editors,** Ralph E. Winters and Conrad A. Nervig.

Deborah Kerr (**Elizabeth Curtis**); Stewart Granger (**Allan Quartermain**); Richard Carlson (**John Goode**); Hugo Haas (**Van Brun**); Lowell Gilmore (**Eric Masters**); Kimursi (**Khiva**); Siriaque (**Umbopa**); Sekaryongo (**Chief Gagool**); Baziga (**King Twala**); Corporal Munto Anampio (**Chief Bilu**); Gutare (**Kafa**); Ivargwema (**Blue Star**); Benempinga (**Black Circle**); John Banner (**Austin**); Henry Rowland (**Traum**).

Siriaque, Deborah Kerr, Richard Carlson, and Stewart Granger in King Solomon's Mines *('50).*

SYNOPSIS
Britisher Elizabeth Curtis enlists the aid of white African hunter Allan Quatermain to search for her husband, Henry, who has been lost on the Dark Continent while searching for the legendary King Solomon's diamond mines. He disappeared some two years before, leaving only a map as a clue.

Also making the safari is Elizabeth's brother, John Goode. Their quest takes them through the deepest sections of Africa where they encounter stampeding animals, cannibals, lack of water, cobras, and crocodiles. They finally discover the remains of Elizabeth's husband. During their long period together, Elizabeth and Allan grow to love one another and begin their trek back to civilization, having survived an attack by the Watusi tribe.

* * *

"Metro's lion has every right to growl proudly. For this is a jewel of a movie," reported Hollis Alpert in the **Saturday Review** magazine after viewing the spectacle of **King Solomon's Mines.** It is one of the greatest adventure features ever made and one of MGM's greatest moneymakers of the 1950s.

Based on the 1885 novel by Sir Henry Rider Haggard, **King Solomon's Mines** had been previously filmed by Gaumont-British. The 1937 release starred Cedric Hardwicke, Anna Lee, and Paul Robeson. When Metro planned a remake, producer Sam Zimbalist determined to produce the thriller completely in Africa. For his cast he

chose Deborah Kerr, the British import who was being cast continually as the cool, beautiful lady. Originally Zimbalist thought of employing Warner Bros.' Errol Flynn to play the hero, but he was shunted aside to the less-prestigious **Kim** (1950), and Stewart Granger[1] was assigned to portray the great white hunter. (For the role, Metro's makeup artists silvered Granger's temples to provide him with a look of maturity.) Richard Carlson, handsome juvenile of the late thirties and forties, was awarded the role of Kerr's brother, John Goode.

Much as Duncan Renaldo, Harry Carey, and Edwina Booth had done in 1930 for MGM's **Trader Horn,** the cast of **King Solomon's Mines** embarked for the Dark Continent. They would cover 14,000 miles of Africa while filming in Kenya, Tanganyika, and the Belgian Congo, battling 152-degree temperatures, mosquitoes, tsetse flies, malaria, amoebic dysentery, and fatigue. The natives worked as extras for thirty cents a day, with a seven-foot Watusi named Kimursi employed as Khiva, gunbearer of the safari.

A number of the artists who endured the hardships of the location filming, recorded their recollections of the trip.

RICHARD CARLSON: The sun was our absolute mas-

ter in Africa. It ruled our lives much more than in just a physical sense. Its presence or absence dictated whether, at the end of the day's work, elation or gloom pervaded our camp. For when you're using color film no outdoor work can be done without full brilliant sunlight. For this reason, people who see **King Solomon's Mines** will conclude, I suppose, that tropical Africa is a land of perpetual sun. It isn't. . . . [Deborah Kerr's] good nature always astonished cast and crew alike. We were all convinced that no other girl in the picture business would have taken the beating she had to take on this African safari. . . . We would smear our shirts with oil to stimulate sweat, slash our trousers at the knee, and rip off shirt buttons with the greatest of abandon. Stars Deborah Kerr and Stewart Granger were not exempt. The Africans, to whom such clothing represented undreamed of luxury, watched our acts of vandalism wide-eyed and solemnly. They never laughed at us or scowled at us. But they must have thought that the ways of the white man were more insane than they had theretofore suspected.

CAMERAMAN ROBERT SURTEES: Sure it was tough. Many of us became ill—at one time we had just four members of the crew left behind the cameras, and 500 natives in front of it. All of us must have been homesick many times. But there was always Deborah, ready for whatever was next, with never a complaint of any sort. A man just couldn't gripe.

CODIRECTOR COMPTON BENNETT: We had our camp at the foot of the [Murchison] Falls. Every morning

---

[4]During the making of MGM's **Julius Caesar,** Gielgud had coached Brando in the "proper" interpretation of Shakespearean dialogue.

[1]Thirty-six-year-old Granger was signed to an MGM pact in 1949, after years on the British stage and screen. He would tell the press, "I made all those pictures for [J. Arthur] Rank at a time when we were trying to make too many, and there aren't many of them that I am proud of. Except in a few localities like New York, nobody knows me in America, and actually, I can start all over again."

we spent nearly two hours crawling up to the top—a distance of some 500 feet. Then we'd work on a love scene between Deborah and Stewart Granger in 140-degree heat. We were using Technicolor film, so the reflectors had to be just twice as close to the principals. This threw more light and heat into their faces. It's a wonder they are not both blind.

There was also much public conjecture on the personality of MGM's intended new superstar, Stewart Granger. Codirector Bennett claimed he was difficult to handle during the five months of African location work, while codirector Andrew Marton would say, "In my opinion, he's got guts in proportion to his ego." Deborah Kerr added, "Women sense that there's a bit of the brute in him. A woman's intuition tells her that being a gentleman hasn't watered down his virility, and that he would as soon thwack her on the rear as not." Carlson would add, "Everything about him is on a huge scale—his physique, his voice, his laugh, his enthusiasm, his frustrations, his temperament and his generosity. I often had the feeling he would have been happier as an Elizabethan."

At a cost of $3,500,000, **King Solomon's Mines** premiered in November 1950. It was a sensation! Howard Barnes **(New York Herald-Tribune)** wrote, "To support the fictional fancy, Metro has brought into the film such a riot of ethnic illustration, natural history, and anthropology that a skeptic can go with the safari just for the sights to be seen." Alpert of the **Saturday Review** labeled the film "one of the most remarkable pictures ever made, one that offers the kind of excitement and entertainment that movies alone can provide."[2]

The Academy listed **King Solomon's Mines** as one of the Best Picture nominees of 1950. The winner was Twentieth Century–Fox's **All About Eve.** However, the adventure tale did win Oscars in the categories of Best Color Photography (Robert Surtees) and Best Film Editing (Ralph E. Winters and Conrad A. Nervig).

A profitable marvel, **King Solomon's Mines** grossed $5,586,000 in distributors' domestic rentals. It was the start of a cycle of invigorating swashbuckling films for MGM, with Granger cast in many of them. The excess safari footage inspired MGM later to write a script around it, entitled **Watusi** (1959), starring George Montgomery. Other Metro films to use the same ploy were: **Tarzan the Ape Man** (1959) with Denny Miller, **Drums of Africa** (1963) with Frankie Avalon and Mariette Hartley, and **Trader Horn** (1973), the remake of the MGM classic with Rod Taylor, Anne Heywood, and Jean Sorel. In 1977 producer Harry Alan Towers filmed **King Solomon's Treasure** based on Henry Rider Haggard's novel **Allan Quartermain.** The picture, starring Britt Ekland and

---

[2]Typical of most adventure epics, some portions of the dialogue could not bear too close a scrutiny. For example, there is the exchange between Granger and Kerr.

    Granger: This is not the kind of journey one undertakes with a . . . shall we say . . . overwrought woman.

    Kerr: "You expect me to back out, don't you."

    Granger: "Frankly, yes."

David McCallum, carried on the African adventure story with far less spectacular results than MGM's 1950 entry.

KISS ME KATE
1953 C—109 min.

Producer, Jack Cummings; **director,** George Sidney; based on the play by Samuel and Bella Spewack and Cole Porter, derived from the play **The Taming of the Shrew** by William Shakespeare; **screenplay,** Dorothy Kingsley; **choreography,** Hermes Pan; **music director,** Andre Previn; **associate music director,** Saul Chapin, **songs,** Porter; **art directors,** Cedric Gibbons and Urie McCleary; **camera,** Charles Rosher; **editor,** Ralph E. Winters.

Kathryn Grayson **(Lilli Vanessi–Katherine);** Howard Keel **(Fred Graham–Petruchio);** Ann Miller **(Lois Lane–Bianca);** Tommy Rall **(Bill Calhoun–Lucentio);** Bobby Van **(Gremio);** Keenan Wynn **(Lippy);** James Whitmore **(Slug);** Kurt Kasznar **(Baptista);** Bob Fosse **(Hortensio);** Ron Randell **(Cole Porter);** Willard Parker **(Tex Callaway);** Dave O'Brien **(Ralph);** Claud Allister **(Paul);** Ann Codee **(Suzanne);** Carol Haney and Jeanne Coyne **(Specialty Dancers);** Hermes Pan **(Specialty Sailor Dance);** Ted Eckelberry **(Nathaniel);** Mitchell Lewis **(Stage Doorman).**

SYNOPSIS

Lilli Vanessi and Fred Graham are a divorced show business couple who suffer the pangs of jealousy and realize they are still in love after Lilli announces her pending marriage to Tex Callaway, a wealthy Texan. On the other hand, Lilli is irked when Fred reveals he is engaged to flashy dancer Lois Lane.

By pretending he intends to offer Lois the pivotal female role of Katherine in a musical version of **The Taming of the Shrew,** Fred inveigles Lilli into accepting the lead. He is scheduled to play Petruchio. During the arduous days of rehearsals the couple find their love reawakening, sparked by their onstage roles of fiery courtiers.

Several misunderstandings involving Fred and Lois cause Lilli to quit the show on opening night. However, Fred is indebted to a gambler, who has placed two thugs, Lippy and Slug, at the theatre. They compel Lilli to remain so that the show can go on and their boss be paid Fred's "IOUs." At the end of the premiere performance Fred and Lilli realize they belong to one another.

* * *

Cole Porter's zesty stage musical **Kiss Me Kate** was inspired by Shakespeare's **The Taming of the Shrew.** The tuneful revamping opened at the New Century Theatre on Broadway on December 30, 1948, starring Alfred Drake, Patricia Morison, Harold Lang, and Lisa Kirk. The musical ran for 1,077 performances and appeared a natural for MGM's cinematic slate of rousing song-and-dance entertainments in the early fifties. The studio purchased the film rights.

With the celebrated Arthur Freed unit busy with other musical projects, production of **Kiss Me Kate** was entrusted to Jack Cummings. George

Keenan Wynn, James Whitmore, Howard Keel, Kathryn Grayson, and Bob Fosse (with curly hair) in Kiss Me Kate *('53).*

Sidney was set to direct, and the Morison stage role of Lilli Vanessi/Katherine was assigned to Kathryn Grayson. She had left the company after **Lovely to Look At** (1952) and signed a four-picture pact with Warner Bros. That deal ended after only two moderately interesting 1953 releases. She returned to her old home lot to match vocal tones and dramatics with Keel, her rousing teammate from **Showboat** (1951) and **Lovely to Look At.** (Actually producer Cummings had hoped to contract Laurence Olivier for the role of Fred Graham/Petruchio, and planned to dub his singing voice.) The Harold Lang part of Bill Calhoun/Lucentio went to dancer Tommy Rall, and Lisa Kirk's Lois Lane/Bianca role was set for vivacious Ann Miller.

Cummings, impressed by the visual gimmick of the 3-D process so profitably employed by a wide variety of pictures after the success of **Bwana Devil** (1952) and **House of Wax** (1953), decided to film **Kiss Me Kate** using this flash-in-the-pan process. Director Sidney ensuingly worked into the film some appropriate touches (such as Ann Miller's legs kicking into the camera).

If anything was amiss with this delightful show, it was the sheer quantity of hit music. There were thirteen numbers in all, most of them of show-stopping quality. Not satisfied with this cornucopia of audio treats, the filmmakers added "From This Moment On," which had been composed for, but was deleted from, Porter's 1950 Broadway show **Out of This World**. In the film it would be sung and danced to by Miller, Rall, Bobby Van, and Bob Fosse. While most Metro musical aficionados have a special regard for Miller's torrid rendition of "Too Darn Hot," the picture boasts many other favorite moments: Keel and Grayson dueting "Wunderbar" and "So in Love," Grayson's sardonic "I Hate Men!" Keel (in especially excellent form as the swaggering Shakespearean) vocalizing "Where Is the Life That Late I Led?" and the comic duet of James Whitmore and Keenan Wynn, "Brush Up Your Shakespeare." (Both actors—herein playing Damon Runyonesque mugs—fondly recall the many weeks they were given to learn the steps for this number and the many handball matches and naps that precluded their rehearsing.)

When **Kiss Me Kate** opened at Radio City Music Hall in November 1953, the 3-D craze was nearly over and the film was shown in a 2-D (flat) version. (For the West Coast bow, at Loew's State Theatre in Los Angeles, the 3-D version was used.) The **New York Times** praised the entry as "one of the year's most magnificent musical films . . . better, indeed, if one may so, than the same frolic that was on the stage." **Variety** thought the film a "sweetheart of a musical."

Because of the wealth of vocal material in this picture, reviewers tended to overlook the quality dancing that abounded in the proceedings. The hoofers included Rall, who would be seen the next year in MGM's **Seven Brides for Seven Brothers**; Van, who in 1953 would be paired at MGM with Debbie Reynolds in **The Affairs of Dobie Gillis** and with Jane Powell and Ann Miller in **Small Town Girl**; and Fosse, who made his major mark later as a Broadway-television-film cho-

reographer and director. In the dancing chorus was Carol Haney, who would leap to Broadway fame in **The Pajama Game** (1954).

Regarding the ever-effervescent Ann Miller, Richard Oliver later wrote in the program notes for a reissue of the MGM soundtrack album:

With **Kiss Me Kate**, it was evident that Ann Miller had come a long way in films. Always providing zing, pzazz, and fun in her roles, she was usually cast as a not particularly bright character who had a healthy yearning for the opposite sex, especially if they were rich. In **Kiss Me Kate**, her role had more dimension but still gave her ample opportunity to flash, beginning with her opening number, "Too Darn Hot." She appears in a brief phosphorescent red outfit showing those famous legs and doing 500 taps a minute on tables, chairs, and anything else sturdy enough. From there, it was performing another showstopper, "Why Can't You Behave?" on the theatre roof under clothes lines and around chimneys in an outstanding dance routine with her partner, Tommy Rall. The two also had things well in hand in an alley setting for the comedic "Always True to You in My Fashion." During the onstage festivities, Ann Miller was in full glory trying to choose among three men in "Tom, Dick or Harry."

LADY IN THE LAKE
1946—105 min.

Producer, George Haight; **director,** Robert Montgomery; based on the novel **The Lady in the Lake** by Raymond Chandler; **screenplay,** Steve Fisher; **art directors,** Cedric Gibbons and Preston Ames; **set decorators,** Edwin B. Willis and Thomas Theuerkauf; **music,** David Snell; **assistant director,** Dolph Zimmer; **sound,** Douglas Shearer; **camera,** Paul C. Vogel; **editor,** Gene Ruggiero.

Robert Montgomery (**Philip Marlowe**); Lloyd Nolan (**Lieutenant DeGarmot**); Audrey Totter (**Adrienne Fromsett**); Tom Tully (**Captain Kane**); Leon Ames (**Derace Kingsby**); Jayne Meadows (**Mildred Haveland**); Morris Ankrum (**Eugene Grayson**); Lila Leeds (**Receptionist**); Richard Simmons (**Chris Lavery**); Ellen Ross (**Elevator Girl**); William Roberts (**Artist**); Kathleen Lockhart (**Mrs. Grayson**); Cy Kendall (**Jaibi**); Ralph Dunn (**Sergeant**); Wheaton Chambers (**Property Clerk**); Robert B. Williams (**Detective**); Ellay Mort (**Chrystal Kingsby**); Fred Sherman (**Reporter**); Robert Spencer (**Marlowe's Double**); John Webb Dillon (**Policeman**); Billy Newell (**Drunk**); Eddie Acuff (**Coroner**); Nina Ross, Charles Bradstreet, George Travell, Fred Santley, Laura Treadwell, Sherry Hall, Roger Cole, and Ann Lawrence (**Christmas Party Guests**); Frank Orth (**Greer**).

SYNOPSIS
Private investigator Philip Marlowe sits at his desk and relates to the audience his adventures in a recent homicide caper. The action dissolves

into flashback, with the camera becoming Marlowe's eyes and the viewer generally seeing only what the detective can.

Marlowe, who would rather be writing pulp novels than sleuthing, is retained by Adrienne Fromsett, editor at Kingsby Publications. His task is to locate Chrystal Kingsby, the missing wife of her publisher, Derace Kingsby. Marlowe learns that Adrienne has hopes of someday wedding Kingsby herself. It develops that previously Adrienne was interested in playboy Chris Lavery but that he jilted her.

Marlowe then visits Lavery, who denies having seen Chrystal. Later Lavery knocks out the detective; the latter regains consciousness in Bay City jail. Captain Kane and Lieutenant DeGarmot insist that Marlowe was arrested for drunken driving. After much explaining, Marlowe is released.

Clues lead Marlowe to Little Fawn Lake, where a woman's body has been found. It is thought to be that of Muriel Chess, but later Marlowe realizes that the victim—or so he is now convinced—is Mildred Haveland, who has wed Bill Chess to hide from an unspecified pursuing policeman. It seems that both Adrienne and Mildred had vied for Lavery's affections. Later Lavery is found shot to death. When Adrienne thereafter fires Marlowe, Kingsby rehires him to find Chrystal.

As the case continues, DeGarmot appears constantly on the scene, often hampering Marlowe's investigation. In fact, Marlowe later finds that DeGarmot and the real Mildred Haveland have been having an affair and have engaged in blackmail. At one point the crooked cop tries to frame Marlowe for the assorted killings, but he explains his way out of the situation. He deduces eventually that the female corpse found at Little Fawn Lake was that of Chrystal Kingsby. It seems that Lavery had known Mildred in El Paso and he was the only one who understood her true identity, so she shot him. Just after Marlowe takes away Mildred's gun, DeGarmot arrives and shoots her. DeGarmot then plans to murder Marlowe but the police arrive and in the scuffle the lieutenant is killed.

Marlowe and Adrienne, who have fallen in love, go off together.

* * *

Perhaps Basil Rathbone's Sherlock Holmes was the most familiar detective to mid-1940s audiences in the United States. Not only did he churn out potboilers based on the character for Universal Pictures, but he could be heard in Sunday night radio broadcasts dealing with the famed sleuth. However, tough, glib Philip Marlowe appeared to be of greater interest to the public at large in that decade. Raymond Chandler's snap-brimmed detective, besides being the "hero" of several stories and novels, had been personified on screen by Dick Powell in RKO's **Murder, My Sweet** (1944)[1] and by Humphrey Bogart

---

[1]Chandler's **Farewell, My Lovely** had been filmed first as part of the Falcon series at RKO. It was titled **The Falcon Takes Over** (1942) and had George Sanders' sleuth undertake the activities Chandler had written about Marlowe.

play his mettle, as in **Yellow Jack** (1938), **The Earl of Chicago** (1940), and **Rage in Heaven** (1941). After completing his naval duty in World War II, he starred with John Wayne in MGM's **They Were Expendable** (1945). When director John Ford suffered a fractured leg three weeks before the completion of that filming, Montgomery took over as director. Ford, MGM, and the public were pleased with the results. As a reward the studio allowed their serious-minded star to proceed with a new vehicle which he could direct, on condition that he star in same.

Since 1938 Montgomery had been eager to do a film utilizing a subjective point of view. As Stephen Pendo describes in **Raymond Chandler on Screen** (1976), the Metro authorities were baffled, afraid, and resentful of this innovative concept of filmmaking. In the Fisher rewrites of the scenario (which eliminated the Little Fawn Lake sequence from the novel), Montgomery's character is visible in only four narration scenes—to explain material cut from the script. When Montgomery's Marlowe kisses Adrienne Fromsett, played by Audrey Totter,[3] it is the only time Montgomery's antihero and another character are viewed from the third-person camera.

For a studio thriving on Esther Williams and Van Johnson confections, Montgomery's project was indeed alien to the company bosses. As production was about to get under way, the front office had further reservations. It decreed that only the first reel of the film could be shot. From this test footage, a decision would be made if the picture should be made. As Fisher relates to Pendo in his book on Chandler, an executive from the top level "saw the reel, then turned to us (we almost fainted) and said, 'It's fine, just fine, but where's Bob Montgomery.'" According to Fisher, that unnamed executive never did comprehend what the **Lady in the Lake** troupe was doing.

Employing the "camera I" approach, **Lady in the Lake** opens with Marlowe telling the audience, "You'll see it [the caper] just as I saw it. You'll meet the people; you'll find the clues. And maybe you'll solve it quick and maybe you won't." For Totter, being cast in this picture was a breakthrough. She had been in a dozen films at Metro, ranging from the sexy off-screen voice of **Bewitched** (1945) to one of Lucille Ball's clawing felines of **Ziegfeld Follies** (1946), to being John Garfield's waitress pickup of **The Postman Always Rings Twice** (1946). Her hair color and accent varied so from film to film that she dubbed herself "the feminine Lon Chaney of the MGM lot." Montgomery chose her as the gold-digging tigress Adrienne Fromsett not only because of her impressive screen work, but because of her versatility as a radio actress. He felt her familiarity with the all-important radio microphone would stand her in good experience for coping with the now-very-subjective camera.

The real villainess of this celluloid adventure

Lloyd Nolan and Jayne Meadows in Lady in the Lake *('46).*

in Warner Bros.' **The Big Sleep** (1946), both box-office draws. In this third screen appearance, Marlowe received a totally different treatment in MGM's **Lady in the Lake,** the most fascinating, if least commercially successful, of Chandler's Marlowe melodramas to reach the screen at the time.

MGM purchased the screen rights to Chandler's **Lady in the Lake** for $35,000.[2] It would be

the only time that Chandler, who would script Paramount's **Double Indemnity** (1944) and **The Blue Dahlia** (1946), would adapt one of his own works to the screen. However, the 175-page screenplay he presented was too loosely organized and some fifty pages too long. Producer George Haight hired Steve Fisher to revamp it and before MGM was to release the film, the studio requested Fisher to share script credit with Chandler. Fisher objected but later acceded to pressure. However, by then Chandler refused to have any proprietorship in the scenario credit.

Since **Night Must Fall** (1937), debonair contract star Robert Montgomery had displayed an antipathy to typecasting. The studio had hoped he would flop in that atypical role, but he proved adroit at heavy dramatics. Occasionally over the succeeding years he had the opportunity to dis-

[2]Chandler's novel (itself based on short stories he had written) underwent several changes for the screen version. The the of the title was dropped. For some reason the cast listing for the film has Marlowe's first name spelled with two l's, but in the film it is spelled with one l. Typically, many of the book's characters underwent alterations. DeGarmot in the book had been Lieutenant DeGarmo. The changes in this and other names—according to coscripter Steve Fisher—were "instigated by a nervous legal department at MGM, always afraid of being sued." Also the time frame of the narrative was changed from July (in the book) to Christmas (in the

film), to coincide more with the picture's planned winter release.

[3]According to Audrey Totter this scene was included because after the picture was previewed three times, each set of viewers stated on their reaction cards that they missed seeing Montgomery and Totter kiss. The desired scene was shot and added to the picture.

was played by Jayne Meadows. Doug McClelland wrote of this Metro contractee, "Meadows had one of the most unique supporting roles on record, one that, in limited screen time, allowed her to play—with manic relish—essentially three different women. First, she was seen as a peculiar landlady, then masquerading as publisher Leon Ames' long-missing wife, and in the denouement she was exposed as the murderer of three people." Second-billed Lloyd Nolan appeared as grasping police detective Lieutenant DeGarmot, Meadows' accomplice in murder. One cast member mentioned in the credits baffled less astute filmgoers. The opening credits insisted that Chrystal Kingsby was portrayed by Ellay Mort. It was Montgomery's little joke. **Ellay mort** is a phonetic spelling of the French phrase "she is dead." As indeed the character Chrystal Kingsby was; nor did she appear in the storyline.

The filming of this offbeat detective yarn required some technical maneuvering.[4] According to author Pendo:

Special camera harnesses had to be developed to facilitate the filming. In addition, every set had to be constructed in a "breakaway" fashion to allow the camera and necessary equipment complete freedom of movement. For example: As the hero (camera) gets into his auto and looks around, the car is broken away to permit the camera to circle in the same way. Even something as simple as lighting a cigarette required one man for the right hand, one for the left, and a third lying on his stomach under the camera blowing smoke under the lens. Montgomery conceded that he spent three-quarters of **Lady in the Lake**'s shooting time on his stomach.

When released, the film, which cost $1 million to make, enjoyed positive critical response. Bosley Crowther noted in the **New York Times,** "Mr. Montgomery has the least acting to do, but his scenes are played with ease and conviction. His Phillip Marlowe is somewhat more cynical[5]

and sneering—a characteristic which is developed more by the tone of his voice than anything else—than the previous conceptions of the detective we got from Dick Powell . . . and Humphrey Bogart. . . . You can take your choice of the three and still be happy." Unfortunately, the convention-bound audiences of the forties did not much care for the "camera I" approach; most preferred a charismatic star like Powell or Bogart to root for, and **Lady in the Lake,** one of MGM's most artistically adventurous offerings, rated poorly in the financial sweepstakes.[6]

Thereafter Montgomery was ordered to revert to form. He was cast in **Desire Me** (1947) opposite Greer Garson. When the actor rebelled at the sluggishness of the film as directed by George Cukor, it led to a shakeup on the project. Montgomery withdrew from the cast and was replaced by Richard Hart. Jack Conway was brought in to redirect the film (for which no one took directorial credit). It was a box-office failure. Outside of providing some of the narration for Metro's **The Secret Land** (1948), a U.S. naval documentary, Montgomery would not act again at the Culver City lot. He would turn more and more to directing, both in films and on television, later serving for a time as President Eisenhower's TV appearance consultant.

Lady in the Lake was not to be the end of Philip Marlowe's on-camera adventures. Twentieth Century–Fox's **The Brasher Doubloon** (1947) starred George Montgomery as the tough private eye. Later screen Marlowes would be: James Garner in **Marlowe** (MGM, 1969), Elliott Gould in **The Long Goodbye** (United Artists, 1973), and Robert Mitchum in **Farewell, My Lovely** (Avco Embassy, 1975) and **The Big Sleep** (1978). Van Heflin and Gerald Mohr played Marlowe in the forties on screen and in a radio series, Philip Carey was seen in the 1959–60 TV version, and Powell returned to his former characterization in an adaptation of **The Long Goodbye** in a 1954 "Climax" series episode.

LASSIE COME HOME
1943 C—89 min.

Producer, Samuel Marx; **director,** Fred M. Wilcox; based on the novel by Eric Knight; **screenplay,** Hugh Butler; **Technicolor consultants,** Natalie Kalmus and Henri Jaffa; **music,** Daniele Amfitheatrof; **art directors,** Cedric Gibbons and Paul Groesse; **set decorators,** Edwin B. Willis and Mildred Griffiths; **assistant director,** Al Raboch; **sound,** J. Edmondson; **special effects,** Warren Newcombe; **camera,** Leonard Smith; **editor,** Ben Lewis.

Roddy McDowall (**Joe Carraclough**); Donald Crisp (**Sam Carraclough**); Edmund Gwenn (**Rowlie**); Dame May Whitty (**Dolly**); Lassie (**The Dog**); Nigel Bruce (**Duke of Rudling**); Elsa Lanchester (**Mrs. Carraclough**); Elizabeth Taylor (**Priscilla**); J. Patrick O'Malley (**Hynes**); Ben Webster (**Dan'l Fadden**); Alec Craig (**Snickers**); John Rogers (**Buckles**); Arthur Shields (**Jock**); Alan Napier (**Andrew**); Roy Parry (**Butcher**); George Broughton (**Allen**); Howard Davies (**Cobbler**); John Power (**Miner**); Nelson Leigh (**Teacher**); May Beatty (**Fat Woman**); Larry Kert (**Stunt Boy for Roddy McDowall**).

SYNOPSIS

During the depression following World War I, a poor Yorkshire, England, couple, the Carracloughs, in the village of Greenal Bridge, are forced to sell their son Joey's beloved collie dog, Lassie. The collie is bought by the neighboring Duke of Rudling, who owns large kennel properties.

The brown and white collie successfully escapes twice, returning to the Carracloughs. Eventually the Duke takes Lassie to Scotland for the shooting season. There the canine is released by the Duke's compassionate granddaughter, Priscilla.

Lassie begins the long trek (nearly a thousand miles) back to his Yorkshire home. His travels introduce him to an old farm couple, Dolly and Dan'l, as well as to an itinerant tinker, Rowlie. Lassie valiantly fights his way to Greenal Bridge through storms, friends, and foes (a gun-toting sheep farmer) before reaching her beloved Carracloughs.

A solution to everyone's problems is found when the Duke hires Sam Carraclough as kennel keeper on his estate.

* * *

Of all the wondrous dogs of Hollywood celluloid fame (including Nick and Nora Charles' Asta, Our Gang's Pete, Mascot Pictures' Rinty, and Rin-Tin-Tin) none matched the prowess and perennial popularity of Lassie. Though recalled best today by means of the long-running CBS-TV series, Lassie was, of course, a major cinema phenomenon of 1940s Hollywood. "She"[1] became

---

[4] Robert Montgomery would relate to author Jon Tuska for his **The Detective in Hollywood** (1978): "The real challenge was the filming itself. We had to do a lot of rehearsing. Actors are trained **not** to look at the camera. I had to overcome all that training. I had a basket installed under the camera and sat there so that at least the actors could respond to me even if they couldn't look directly at me. Jayne Meadows, who played the landlady, had a very difficult scene with a half page of dialogue delivered to the camera without being able to look away once. The head of the camera department had to mount the camera on a boom to get me standing up from a sitting position. But the most complicated scene, as I remember, was that where Marlowe crawls to the telephone booth. It took four people just to handle the action. We had to remove all the walls of the booth after Marlowe gets inside."

[5] Fisher would relate to Pendo, " 'If Montgomery's Marlowe's sarcasm came out pessimistic, it wasn't intended, instead: bitterness at being broke, shoved around, etc., laced with a sort of acid humor, which in any case was always Robert Montgomery's bag.' "

To be noted in **Lady in the Lake** is that Montgomery's Marlowe is always anxious to abandon sleuthing for a more lucrative writing career, and he is constantly remarking within the film how seedy and unpromising the detective field is. The wisecracking, very rude Marlowe (very ungentlemanly to Totter—as witness the sequence in which he tells her her lipstick is painted crooked) is a departure from the past presentations of Marlowe on screen.

[6] While **Newsweek** magazine lauded the film as "a fascinating experiment in moviemaking," the **New York Times'** Thomas Pryor had reservations about the "different" and "fresh" film. He thought Montgomery had "failed to exploit the full possibilities suggested by this unusual technique."

In 1949 a rather jaded and understandably annoyed Raymond Chandler would reflect on **Lady in the Lake:** "The camera-eye technique of **Lady in the Lake** is old stuff in Hollywood. Every young writer or director has wanted to try it. 'Let's make the camera a character'; it's been said at every lunch table in Hollywood one time or another."

---

[1] Actually Lassie, a female animal, was played on screen by a total of five dogs—all male and standing in lineal

one of MGM's most prized properties. It was no accident or mere formality that had Lassie posing handsomely between Edward Arnold and Mary Astor at the studio's 1949 silver jubilee company portrait, or that had the canine's descendant among the prestigious alumni who were on hand for the premiere festivities of **That's Entertainment!** (1974).

The original **Lassie Come Home** in 1943 was inspired by Eric Knight's 1938 **Saturday Evening Post** short story, which was expanded in 1941 into a novel. Producer Samuel Marx recognized the property as a fine entry for Metro's B unit, which had been recently prospering with such 1942 films as **Joe Smith, American, Journey for Margaret,** and **The War Against Mrs. Hadley.** So successful were these modestly budgeted (at least by MGM standards) entries that the expensive process of Technicolor could be used for the **Lassie** film. With Fred M. Wilcox set to direct, a successful search was made for the proper juveniles. Producer Marx met Elizabeth Taylor's father during one of the latter's tours of duty as a civilian air-raid warden. The proud father spoke enthusiastically to the producer about his eleven-year-old daughter, who had failed to impress Universal as another Deanna Durbin. (She was dropped by that studio after one film, 1942's **There's One Born Every Minute.**) Marx agreed to test her and young Elizabeth was soon signed to a one-picture deal.

Roddy McDowall, the British lad who had been in the very popular **My Friend Flicka** (1943) for his home lot, Twentieth Century–Fox, was borrowed, and treated to top billing. A party of fine character stars, mostly from the MGM roster, were used for colorful support: Donald Crisp, Edmund Gwenn, Dame May Whitty (and her husband Ben Webster), Nigel Bruce, and Elsa Lanchester. The trouble lay in finding the dog.

Hearing of Metro's hunt for the right canine, trainer Rudd Weatherwax, whose film experience included such stints as training Corky, Wallace Beery's dog in **The Champ** (1931) and Jackie Cooper's in **Peck's Bad Boy** (1934), brought his male collie Pal to the Culver City lot. The studio disliked the fact that Pal was male, as well as the white blaze on his muzzle. However, the lot did hire Weatherwax to assist in picking Lassie from the legion of collies selected as finalists. Weatherwax picked a female. But when production began, she was shedding so badly that he brought in Pal to double for her (male collies' coats are fuller and healthier). After the dog played to perfection a scene in which "she" had to swim 100 yards, roll over, and collapse, director Wilcox awarded Lassie the part for good. In a **Film Fan Monthly** magazine interview, McDowall remembered Pal with great fondness:

Roddy McDowall and Lassie in Lassie Come Home *('43).*

"The original Lassie was a lot smarter than a lot of people I know. He was unbelievable. He remembered me four years later. The horses [in my movies] were different. There were six Flickas and nine Thunderheads. After that many, one loses rapport. I loved Lassie, but I hated the main Flicka horse. She was mean; kept stepping on my feet."

Lassie Come Home was a delight for audiences tired of the grim war news and yearning for a warm and sentimental drama. Archer Winsten of the **New York Post** commented, "As far as production is concerned, **Lassie Come Home** is an outstanding work. The Technicolor effects, whether in closeups of the mobile-faced Lassie or long shots of rural Yorkshire, Scotland, and points between, are excellent." Kate Cameron (**New York Daily News**) wrote, "It is a sentimental story of a dog's devotion to his young master and has been beautifully transposed to the screen in Technicolor under the sympathetic direction of Fred M. Wilcox." Bosley Crowther (**New York Times**) observed, "It is really the collie, Lassie, which is the most remarkable performer in the film. The beauty of this dog and her responsiveness go far to make the picture a thorough delight." Just as few people were aware that Lassie was actually a male, so not many were cognizant that Roddy McDowall did not perform his own stunts in the film (they were accomplished by the equally young Larry Kert, who went on to become the star of Broadway's **West Side Story**).

Elizabeth Taylor's nonprecocious work in the film won her a one-year contract with MGM, later extended after her success in **National Velvet** (1944). She would be reunited with Roddy McDowall in a segment of the sentimental saga **The White Cliffs of Dover** (1944). The studio launched a new and very popular series with the **Lassie** films: **Son of Lassie** (1945) retained Donald Crisp and Nigel Bruce in their original parts, with Peter Lawford and June Lockhart replacing McDowall and Taylor; **Courage of Lassie** (1946) gave Taylor her first top-billing role, and Tom Drake and Frank Morgan supported (interestingly, the dog in the film was called not Lassie, but Bill); **Hills of Home** (1948), which brought back Donald Crisp and Tom Drake; **The Sun Comes Up** (1949) with Lassie sharing honors with Jeanette MacDonald in her last film; **Challenge to Lassie** (1949), with Crisp making his fourth appearance in the series; and **The Painted Hills** (1951), with Lassie as Shep.

Beginning in September 1954, "Lassie" became a television[2] fixture, MGM having sold Weatherwax the rights to **Lassie** for a minuscule $2,000. The first segments—later syndicated as "Jeff's Collie"—featured Tommy Rettig, Jan Clayton, and George Cleveland. This cast was replaced in 1957 (for "Timmy and Lassie," a later syndicated title) with Jon Provost, Cloris Leachman

---

succession. The original Lassie (Pal) lived to be nineteen, his son lived to be eighteen, the third Lassie died prematurely of cancer when he was seven, the fourth Lassie was retired by 1972, and the fifth Lassie in 1972 was seven years old.

[2]"Lassie" had been an ABC network radio show as of 1947. Weatherwax's prized collie would bark on cue for the program, but the other dog sounds were performed by animal imitator Earl Keen.

(later June Lockhart), and George Chandler, a setup which ran until 1964. (A feature version of some episodes from this go-round of the show was released by Twentieth Century–Fox in 1963 as **Lassie's Great Adventure.**) In 1964 format number three was instituted, with Lassie becoming the pal of forest ranger Robert Bray. In September 1968 the canine wonder took off on her own, helping whomsoever she found in distress; and in the syndicated series beginning in 1972, Lassie, still the wanderer, finds a temporary home at the ranch of Keith Holden (Larry Pennell). There has even been an animated cartoon series, "Lassie's Rescue Rangers," which ran from 1973 to 1975. Producer Robert Maxwell, who had acquired the TV rights in 1954 to "Lassie," sold the program in 1956 to Jack Wrather for $3.5 million. Wrather's ex-actress wife, Bonita Granville, became associate producer of the TV series. It has been estimated that the **Lassie** property over the years has grossed some $60 million.

On September 19, 1977, a new **Lassie** theatrical feature began shooting at Valley of the Moon in Sonoma County, California. It was produced by Bonita Granville Wrather and William Beaudine, Jr., and directed by Don Chaffey. Set in a north California winery, with all new characters save for Lassie, the film was not a remake of any previous Lassie story. The stars of the feature were Metro veterans Jimmy Stewart and Mickey Rooney with a guest appearance by another former movie star, Alice Faye. The critics were not enthusiastic about **The Magic of Lassie** (1978). **Variety** judged, ". . . this heavy-handed attempted throwback to the tradition that began with Metro's **Lassie Come Home** in 1943 has less substance, imagination, or honest emotion than a typical half-hour episode of the longrunning TV series." The Wrather Corp.-Lassie Productions also provided "Lassie: The New Beginning" for 1978-ABC-TV which did not fare well in the ratings. It featured David Wayne, Jeanette Nolan, Gene Evans and Lee Bryant, and was judged "rather tame stuff."

LES GIRLS
1957 C—114 min.

Producer, Sol C. Siegel; **associate producer,** Saul Chaplin; **director,** George Cukor; based on the story by Vera Caspary; **screenplay,** John Patrick; **art directors,** William Horning and Gene Allen; **set decorator,** Edwin B. Willis; **costumes,** Orry-Kelly; **choreography,** Jack Cole; **songs,** Cole Porter; **music adapter–conductor,** Adolph Deutsch; **orchestrators,** Alexander Courage and Skip Martin; **sound,** Wesley C. Miller; **camera,** Robert Surtees; **editor,** Ferris Webster.

Gene Kelly **(Barry Nichols);** Mitzi Gaynor **(Joy Henderson);** Kay Kendall **(Lady Wren);** Taina Elg **(Angele Ducros);** Jacques Bergerac **(Pierre Ducros);** Leslie Phillips **(Sir Gerald Wren);** Henry Daniells **(Judge);** Patrick Macnee **(Sir Percy);** Stephen Vercoe **(Mr. Outward);** Philip Tonge **(Associate Judge);** Owen McGiveney **(Court Usher);** Francis

Ravel **(French Stage Manager);** Adrienne d'Ambricourt **(Wardrobe Woman);** Maurice Marsac **(French House Manager);** Cyril Delevanti **(Fanatic);** George Navarro **(Waiter)** Nestor Paiva **(Spanish Peasant Man);** Maya Van Horn **(Stout French Woman);** Louisa Triana **(Flamenco Dancer);** Genevieve Pasques **(Shopkeeper);** Lilyan Chavuin **(Dancer);** Dick Alexander **(Stagehand).**

SYNOPSIS
Popular Continental act "Barry Nichols and Les Girls" breaks up after too many romantic entanglements.

Several years later Sybil, now Lady Wren, wife of an English peer, Sir Gerald Wren, pub-lishes her scandalous memoirs of her life as a showgirl. Her bestselling book leads her to court on a libel suit when she claims coperformer Angele Ducros attempted suicide when Barry once rejected her romantically.

Angele takes the stand and claims it was Sybil who had attempted self-destruction because of unrequited love. Finally Barry is sworn in and testifies that he was never interested in either Sybil or Angele, but was always romantically inclined toward Joy Henderson, to whom he is currently wed. Furthermore, he explains to the court, neither girl attempted suicide. Instead, they were victims of gas fumes from a faulty heater.

Flashbacks trace the act throughout Europe and provide the setting for the musical numbers.

* * *

Kay Kendall in Les Girls *('57).*

Constance Tomkinson, an English showgirl who had worked in France, wrote a book of her adventures and misadventures; the title was **Les Girls**. The saucy sound of the Gallic title impressed the ears of MGM producer Sol C. Siegel, who purchased the book—for the title alone. He transformed her story into the film **Les Girls**, the musical hailed by **Time** magazine as "easily the best that Hollywood has put together since **An American in Paris** and **Seven Brides for Seven Brothers.**"

Soon after Siegel obtained the rights, MGM issued in October 1955 a press release stating that **Les Girls** was to be the story of four stage high kickers: Leslie Caron, Cyd Charisse, Carol Haney, and Jean Simmons. Things soon changed. The four girls were cut down to three, in the shapely, leggy forms of Mitzi Gaynor, Taina Elg, and, in her U.S. debut, Kay Kendall. Gene Kelly, in his final film under his MGM pact, was starred as Barry Nichols, the charming male leader of the act and a sort of den mother to the chorines. He is the one who advises them to be "prompt, persistent, and perfect" if they're to remain in his troupe, and not to consider marriage while in show business. "If you want a home, you go to a real estate agent."

For Cole Porter, **Les Girls** would be his final original motion picture score. (His final work would be the musical contributions for a 1958 TV special, **Aladdin**.) His songs included: "Ça, c'est l'amour" (Elg), "Les Girls" (Kelly, Gaynor, Elg, and Kendall), "Ladies in Waiting" (Gaynor, Elg, and Kendall), "Why Am I So Gone (About That Gal)?" (Kelly and Gaynor), and "You're Just Too, Too!" (Kelly and Kendall).

The John Patrick screenplay (which added to the source confusion by acknowledging Vera Caspary as the story writer) related the narrative in the fashion of **Rashomon**, the Japanese film which won a 1951 foreign-film Oscar for its storytelling method of varied viewpoints. George Cukor was signed to direct. **Les Girls** was only his second experience with a musical film.[1]

Although the motion picture had European settings, especially locales in and about Paris, it was shot at the Culver City lot. As Richard Oliver observed in his liner notes for the soundtrack album of **Les Girls**:

Many musicals have used Paris as a setting, but never as freshly as **Les Girls**. As opposed to the ususal never-never land romantic vision of Paris, this picture captures a special essence of its own. . . . [Cukor] and his art directors went to Paris and researched the environment thoroughly from tiny cramped apartments to the Folies Bergere with its chorus girls scurrying into place just in time for a musical number. All of this is in **Les Girls**, even down to the tacky-witty costumes as seen in the "Ladies in Waiting" number.

George Cukor recalled this chic film:

I thoroughly enjoyed making **Les Girls** with that girl Kay Kendall. It was very jolly. In a stylized way, I think we managed to capture the essence of Paris without using any genuine Parisian shots—although later, against my better judgment, I let them put in a couple of long shots of the real city. Gene Allen and I had been all through the city gathering material for the rooms and apartments to be used in the film: it was he who very carefully put together the Cezanne-like arrangements of bread and wine on tables, and things like that.

Certainly one or two things went wrong, such as the technicians' passion for using a lot of colored lights which we don't use any more.

When completed, **Les Girls** received a special honor. It was the first musical to be selected for Britain's Royal Command Performance, a unique honor bestowed upon one film annually. Reception was not the best, and the reaction of London reviewers would annoy Cukor even years later: "It irked me terribly when the London critics . . . said they thought it [the color] looked like tomato ketchup. 'You've got a hell of a nerve,' I thought. 'You're just poor cornball provincial people, you critics; you just don't know what the hell you're talking about.' "

In the United States, critical response wildly varied.

Christian Science Monitor: "Les Girls applies the **Rashomon** technique—contradictory, eyewitness versions of the same event—to the Hollywood musical. There all resemblance ends, fortunately for both Japan and the USA."

Cue magazine: "**Les Girls** is just about the brightest, wittiest, tunefullest, danciest and by all odds the most entertaining mirth-and-melody mixture of just about any movie season within recent memory."

New Yorker magazine: "The dances, invented by Jack Cole, and the music and lyrics, invented by Cole Porter, never quite manage to overcome the beat, beat, beat of the dialogue, which, even for a movie musical comedy, is extraordinarily long-winded and simple-minded."

In the meantime, while the fourth estate argued over the film's merit, the public at large ignored **Les Girls**, leaving it a commercial failure. Which is a shame, for the picture has many intrinsic virtues. The contrasting qualities of the three showgirls (especially Kendall and Gaynor) are a constant joy as each vies for the limelight in the act and with their employer Kelly. For many filmgoers in America, this was their first introduction to sprightly Kendall, a brilliant, elegant comedienne who could modulate her style from high to low comedy at the flick of a finger. Within **Les Girls** she enjoys a raucous number with Kelly entitled "You're Just Too, Too!" a mixture of wry self-pity ("I feel like a banjo . . . everyone's picking on me") and sophisticated adoration of her boss. When drunk she does a marvelous version of "La Habanera."

For ex—Twentieth Century—Fox musical leading lady Gaynor, **Les Girls** provided a remarkable change of format. She switched from the titillating, sometimes brassy showgirl type to the wholesome gal à la Doris Day. Her highlight in the picture is the satiric "Why Am I So Gone (About That Gal)?" a witty send-up of the Marlon Brando—**The Wild One** motif. With Kelly as a black leather-clad motorcyclist who woos flashy Gaynor, the number ranges from jocular to somber, employing the brash sounds of 1950s music to enhance the choreographed courtship of the two love-struck souls.[2]

The third member on the **Les Girls** ensemble was Finnish ballerina Taina Elg, who unfortunately could not compete with the stronger personalities of her coplayers. It is she who courts her **Pal Joey**-ish boss with "Ça C'est L'amour," the most enduringly popular number from the score. The scene for the interlude is a little boat gliding down a tree-lined river.

Proving that age had not withered Porter's ability to create a lively, ribald piece, "Ladies in Waiting" is executed in a mock **Folies Bergere** format, as the trio of courtesans within the number declare, "When we're on the spot . . . we've got to give the King everything." Interestingly, in the other ensemble number, "Les Girls," straw-hatted Kelly is not the focal point, but, instead, the singing personification of a high-class sideshow barker presenting his latest merchandise (the girls).

Les Girls won an Oscar for Orry-Kelly's costumes. Over the years the film has gained a small but enthusiastic cult of supporters. At the time of its release **Variety** thought it was "in the best tradition of the studio . . . a major effort in the art of the film musical." Some believed that **Les Girls** might occasion a renaissance of (MGM) song-and-dance motion pictures in Hollywood. It was not to be however. An age was passing.

LIBELED LADY
1936—98 min.

Producer, Lawrence Weingarten; **director,** Jack Conway; **story,** Wallace Sullivan; **screenplay,** Maurine Watkins, Howard Emmett Rogers, and George Oppenheimer; **art directors,** Cedric Gibbons and William A. Horning; **set decorator,** Edwin B. Willis; **music,** Dr. William Axt; **wardrobe,** Dolly Tree; **sound,** Douglas Shearer; **camera,** Norbert Brodine; **editor,** Frederick Y. Smith.

Jean Harlow (**Gladys Benton**); William Powell (**Bill Chandler**); Myrna Loy (**Connie Allenbury**); Spencer Tracy (**Warren Haggerty**); Walter Connolly (**James B. Allenbury**); Charley Grapewin (**Hollis Bane**); Cora Witherspoon (**Mrs. Burns-Norvell**); E. E. Clive (**Evans, the Fishing Instructor**); Bunny Lauri Beatty (**Babs Burns-Norvell**); Otto Yamaoka (**Ching**); Charles Trowbridge (**Graham**); Spencer Charters (**Magistrate McCall**); George Chandler (**Bellhop**); Greta Meyer (**Connie's Maid**); William

---

[1]He had previously directed **A Star Is Born** (1954) and would later direct **Let's Make Love** (1960) and **My Fair Lady** (1964).

[2]Jack Cole became ill during production and Kelly would complete the choreography for **Les Girls**.

Myrna Loy, Eric Lonsdale, Olaf Hytten, and William Powell in Libeled Lady *('36).*

Benedict (**Joe**); Hal K. Dawson (**Harvey Allen**); Fred Graham (**Press Man**); William Stack (**Editor**); Selmer Jackson (**Adams, the Editor of the Washington Chronicle**); William Newell (**Divorce Detective**); Duke York (**Taxi Driver**); Pat West (**Detective**); Edwin Stanley (**Clerk**); Wally Maher (**Photographer**); Tom Mahoney (**Alex**); Libby Taylor (**Tiny, Gladys' Maid**); Myra Marsh (**Secretary**); Howard Hickman (**Cable Editor**); Ralph Brooks (**Dance Extra**); Charles Croker-King (**Charles Archibald, the Lawyer**); Ines Palange (**Fortune Teller**); Richard Tucker, Charles King, Jack Mulhall, and Dennis O'Keefe (**Barkers**); Eric Lonsdale and Olaf Hytten (**Bits**).

SYNOPSIS

News editor Warren Haggerty prints a story in his paper that socialite Connie Allenbury is cavorting with another woman's spouse across the European continent. Since the account is a fabrication, Connie sues the newspaper for $5 million.

Warren learns of the libel suit just as he is to marry Gladys Benton. He postpones his nuptials and hires Bill Chandler to marry Gladys in name only, then to turn his affections toward Connie. This will allow Gladys the opportunity to sue Connie for alienation of affections, he hopes, and cause the libel claim against the newspaper to be dropped.

All works as planned until Bill actually begins to fall in love with Connie. He tries to dissuade her in her suit against the paper. Warren

convinces Gladys to pursue her case. The situation is rectified when it becomes established that Gladys and Bill must be divorced before (and so) Bill and Connie can marry.

* * *

Jean Harlow, lounging in bed in negligee and high heels, viciously determines to become a bride. William Powell is an imperious libel expert of shyster tactics. Myrna Loy, a cool millionairess with a tongue as sharp as her taste in clothes, is fighting mad. Spencer Tracy is a pugnacious newspaper troubleshooter in the Hildy Johnson tradition. Mix these four stars together—in this order of billing—and the result is a pungent farce that rates as one of MGM's top comedies of the 1930s.

Libeled Lady is a "screwball" comedy in the raucous fashion of such hits as Universal's **My Man Godfrey** (1936) and United Artists' **Nothing Sacred** (1937), and was actually a studio concession to Jean Harlow. She had reached her top salary option of $5,000 per week. After an exceptionally well-played drama comedy role in **Riff-Raff** (1935), a charming and docile performance with Gable and Loy in **Wife Versus Secretary** (1936), and some feeble espionage with Cary Grant in **Suzy** (1936), she yearned to return to comedy. And she wanted to return to the genre in the company of William Powell.

Urbane Powell, at his apex after glowing screen performances in Metro's blockbuster **The Great Ziegfeld** and Universal's **My Man Godfrey**, had become Harlow's great romance, treating the

actress to some of her happiest days. While the Harlow-Powell screen combination was certain to be profitable (as had been even their dullish 1935 musical **Reckless**), Metro added to the box-office insurance. Powell's "perfect wife" Myrna Loy and Spencer Tracy (costar of Harlow's **Riff-Raff**) were cast in the comedy package.

Under Jack Conway's direction, **Libeled Lady** raced from one hilarious episode to another: Harlow, resplendent in her wedding gown, storming into the newspaper office to retrieve her errant bridegroom (Tracy) as he leaps into the libel adventure; the contrived marriage of Powell and Harlow as she labels him "an ape" and "a baboon" ("an old friend of the family" explains the smiling "groom" Powell to the justice of the peace as Tracy gives his freshly "married" fiancée a long congratulatory kiss, "a **very** old friend!" adds Powell as the kiss grows more passionate); Powell and Harlow's overplayed farewell as man and wife, for the benefit of the gaping bellboy, as a "telegram" calls Powell on his mission to slander Loy's character (HARLOW: I'll miss my little Billykins; POWELL: I'll miss my little fuzzy-face); Loy's exquisite boredom and Powell's contained snideness as their first meeting goes sour (POWELL: Your eyes . . . remind me of. . .; LOY: Yes, yes, I know. Sparkling diamonds . . . pink sapphires. . .; POWELL: No . . . no. They remind me of —angry marbles!); Powell's floundering midstream to catch a fish worthy of impressing Loy's fishing-addicted dad (Walter Connolly); and the finale, in which Powell and Tracy fake fisticuffs to impress the ladies and to place them in the respective arms of Loy and Harlow for a happy finale. Adding to the joy of the proceedings were fine comic character performances from Connolly, Charley Grapewin as a bucolic newspaper editor, and E. E. Clive as a fishing instructor whose lessons to Powell result in a fishhook in one of Harlow's more sensitive areas.

Libeled Lady premiered in October 1936. All the principals and talents involved won critical salutes. Bland Johaneson (**New York Daily Mirror**) wrote, "Handsomely mounted and produced, lavishly costumed, cleverly written and artfully directed, **Libeled Lady** is entirely worthy of the noble comedians who head its cast." But it would be Harlow who was most praised: "We are so pathetically grateful to Metro for restoring Miss Harlow to her proper métier" (**New York Times**); "Miss Harlow, heaven be praised, is again a luminous comedienne" (Leo Mishkin, **New York Telegraph**); "She proves anew that she is a really fine comedienne" (Howard Barnes, **New York Herald-Tribune**). As **Variety** reported, "Metro has not only filled the bases, as well as the marquee . . . but it has brought in a sockeroo of a comedy."

Libeled Lady joined the MGM extravaganzas **The Great Ziegfeld, Romeo and Juliet, San Francisco,** and **A Tale of Two Cities** among the candidates for Best Picture of 1936. **The Great Ziegfeld** won. The comedy placed among MGM's highest moneymakers of the season. It was later remade by the studio as the Technicolor **Easy to Wed** (1946), with Lucille Ball, Van Johnson, Esther Williams, and Keenan Wynn in the Harlow, Powell, Loy, and Tracy parts respectively.

LILI
1953 C—81 min.

Producer, Edwin H. Knopf; **director,** Charles Walters; based on the story by Paul Gallico; **screenplay,** Helen Deutsch; **art directors,** Cedric Gibbons and Paul Groesse; **set decorators,** Edwin B. Willis and Arthur Krams; **assistant director,** Al Jennings; **makeup,** William Tuttle; **costumes,** Mary Anne Nyberg; **choreography,** Walters and Dorothy Harnac; **song,** Deutsch and Bronislau Kaper; **Technicolor consultants,** Henri Jaffa and Robert Brower; **sound,** Douglas Shearer; **special effects,** Warren Newcombe; **camera,** Robert Planck; **editor,** Ferris Webster.

Leslie Caron (**Lili Daurier**); Mel Ferrer (**Paul Berthalet**); Jean-Pierre Aumont (**Marc**); Zsa Zsa Gabor (**Rosalie**); Kurt Kasznar (**Jacquot**); Amanda Blake (**Peach Lips**); Alex Gerry (**Proprietor**); Ralph Dumke (**Monsieur Carvier**); Wilton Graff (**Monsieur Tonit**); George Baxter (**Monsieur Enrique**); Eda Reiss Merin (**Fruit Peddler**); George Davis (**Workman**); Mitchell Lewis (**Concessionaire**); Fred Walton (**Whistler**); Richard Grayson (**Flirting Vendor**); Dorothy Jarnac (**Specialty Dancer**).

SYNOPSIS

Young French waif Lili Daurier arrives at a bakery where she is to work, only to discover it has gone out of business. She turns to suave carnival magician Marc for help and he secures a waitress job for Lili. Soon the young orphan becomes infatuated with the magician, unaware that he is married to his stage assistant Rosalie.

Later Lili loses her job as a waitress and puppeteer Paul Berthalet cheers her with his philosophizing puppets. Soon he works this impromptu performance into his act while falling in love with Lili. Later he experiences jealousy when he realizes her feelings for Marc.

When the magician and his assistant leave the show for a better offer, Lili plans to depart. She is shattered to have discovered they are married. Her world seems ended. Paul, long bitter because an injured leg has ended his dancing career and forced him to refuse a **Folies Bergere** offer, slaps Lili. She leaves the carnival and in her wanderings her thoughts drift. She soon finds herself in a ballet (sequence) with Paul's puppets. The latter turn into Paul himself.

She returns to the carnival and to Paul's waiting arms.

* * *

Waifish Leslie Caron was so charming a discovery in **An American in Paris** (1951), it was nothing short of tragic that her subsequent MGM pictures were so dismal. The putrid melodrama **The Man with a Cloak** (1951), made before the musical, left what little audience came to view it apathetic. **Glory Alley** (1952) was a Raoul Walsh–directed New Orleans yarn about boxing. It also did little business. **The Story of Three Loves** (1953), directed with charm by Vincente Minnelli, met with audience resistance—they found its multiepisode tales (Leslie was in a vignette with

Farley Granger) too precious. However, there came to Leslie's rescue as charming a musical film as was ever photographed in Hollywood. **Lili** was and remains an enchanting account of the French gamine and the bitter puppeteer, the latter able to express his love for her only through the mouths of his puppets.

Based on a story by Paul Gallico (screenplay by Helen Deutsch), **Lili** was initially offered to Vincente Minnelli. He found the aura too similar to that of his **An American in Paris** and chose to direct **The Bad and the Beautiful** (1952) instead. Charles Walters replaced him. In addition to Caron's happy casting, Mel Ferrer, who had scored as the sword-flashing villain of **Scaramouche** (1952), played Paul Berthalet, the handsome but crippled dancer whose affliction has turned him to puppetry. Jean-Pierre Aumont, just recently resuming his career after the tragic death of mate Maria Montez, portrayed with élan the dashing magician Marc who dazzled Lili into infatuation; Zsa Zsa Gabor, in her fourth film assignment, was Rosalie, Marc's alluring assistant (and wife). Kurt Kasznar was Jacquot, Paul's sympathetic fellow puppeteer, and Amanda Blake (later to gain fame as Kitty of TV's "Gunsmoke" series) was on camera as Peach Lips.

The music used for **Lili** was compact. There was no intrusion of songs into the gentle narrative, no razzle-dazzle accoutrements (as with **The Band Wagon,** 1953). Instead, Lili employed only three musical interludes: an instrumental number called "Adoration," a lovely ballet simply entitled "Lili and the Puppets," and the very popular "Hi-Lili, Hi-Lo" by Bronislau Kaper and Helen Deutsch. There were no gimmicks in **Lili;** the story relied on

its sentiment, its principals, and the marvelous puppets: Carrot-Top, the little boy; Bernardo, the vain ladies-man fox; and the other little figures whom Paul uses to express his deep, tender feelings.

* * *

"You'll laugh, you'll cry, you'll love **Lili!**" promised the poster copy when the film premiered in July 1953. Some MGM executives were concerned that the simple story filmed in color would not attract sufficient customers. But critical and audience response was enthusiastic. **Punch** magazine, "One can recognize the commercial sentimentality and calculated artificial charm of Lili and still find plenty in it to enjoy." **Variety** endorsed, "Sentiment, done with an air of charm, is the principal entertainment ingredient in **Lili.**" Bosley Crowther (**New York Times**) judged, "A lovely and beguiling little film, touched with the magic of romance, the shimmer of masquerade."

Lili placed sixth in the **Film Daily** Ten Best Picture Poll of 1953. Bronislau Kaper won an Oscar for Best Scoring of a dramatic or comedy film. Leslie Caron, her career supplied with splendid impetus by this triumph, was Academy Award–nominated for Best Actress for her touching portrayal. She lost to **Roman Holiday**'s Audrey Hepburn, who then was the wife of **Lili**'s Mel Ferrer.

Perennially popular as it played re-release engagements, **Lili** later served as the inspiration of the Broadway musical **Carnival.** With a book by Michael Stewart, and lyrics and music by Bob Merrill, the show opened on April 13, 1961, and played 720 performances. Anna Maria Alberghetti starred as Lili, with Jerry Orbach as Paul, James Mitchell as the magician (here called Marco the

Leslie Caron and Mel Ferrer in Lili *('53).*

Magnificent), Kaye Ballard as a vulgarized Rosalie, Pierre Olaf as Jacquot, and Henry Lascoe as a new principal, Schlegal, the shyster carnival owner. The show won the New York Drama Critics Circle Award as best musical of the season (even if for copyright reasons the score could not contain the beloved "Hi-Lili, Hi-Lo"). MGM held the option for a screen version of **Carnival** for many years, but never turned it into a feature. It was far simpler and less expensive to continue to reissue **Lili**.

LITTLE WOMEN
1949 C—121 min.

Producer-director, Mervyn LeRoy; based on the novel by Louisa May Alcott; **screenplay,** Andrew Solt, Sarah Y. Mason, and Victor Heerman; **Technicolor consultants,** Natalie Kalmus and Henri Jaffa; **art directors,** Cedric Gibbons and Paul Groesse; **set decorators,** Edwin B. Willis and Jack D. Moore; **music,** Adolph Deutsch; **assistant director,** Al Raboch; **costumes,** Walter Plunkett; **makeup,** Jack Dawn; **sound,** Douglas Shearer and A. Norwood Fenton; **special effects,** Warren Newcombe; **camera,** Robert Planck and Charles Schoenbaum; **editor,** Ralph E. Winters.

June Allyson (**Jo**); Peter Lawford (**Laurie**); Margaret O'Brien (**Beth**); Elizabeth Taylor (**Amy**); Janet Leigh (**Meg**); Rossano Brazzi (**Professor Bhaer**); Mary Astor (**Marmee March**); Lucile Watson (**Aunt March**); Sir C. Aubrey Smith (**Mr. Lawrence**); Elizabeth Patterson (**Hannah**); Leon Ames (**Mr. March**); Harry Davenport (**Dr. Barnes**); Richard Stapley (**John Brooke**); Connie Gilchrist (**Mrs. Kirke**); Ellen Corby (**Sophie**); Will Wright (**Mr. Grace, the Storekeeper**); Harlan Briggs and Frank Darian (**Cronies**); Arthur Walsh (**Young Man**); Eloise Hardt (**Sally Gardiner**); Isabel Randolph (**Mrs. Gardiner**); Olin Howlin (**Schoolteacher**).

SYNOPSIS
While their father is away at the Civil War, the four daughters—Jo, Meg, Amy, and Beth—remain with their mother, Marmee. The girls busy themselves nursing the sick, aiding the impoverished, and singing Christmas carols.

When Mr. March returns safely, Jo moves to New York to try for success as a writer. She encounters Professor Bhaer, a German maestro who wins her heart. Meg also marries and gives birth to twins. Amy marries Laurie, Jo's former suitor, and the frail Beth eventually succumbs to her ailments.

* * *

"It is . . . possible that the calculated coyness and naiveté of this candy-tinted Technicolor tearjerker may meet with some forthright resistance from our modern hard-boiled Young Lollipop Set," speculated **Cue** magazine upon the release of Metro's **Little Women.** To be sure, it took trust in the sentimentality of the moviegoing public to film a story which was not only required school

June Allyson, Elizabeth Taylor, Mary Astor, Margaret O'Brien, Janet Leigh, and Elizabeth Patterson in Little Women *('49).*

reading for generations of Louisa May Alcott–exposed students, but already familiar film fare. In 1919 Paramount had released a silent version; and in 1933 David O. Selznick produced and George Cukor directed RKO's classic edition with Joan Bennett as Amy, Jean Parker as Beth, Frances Dee as Meg, and Katharine Hepburn in a triumphant performance as Jo.

For years, Selznick himself had planned to produce a color remake, with wife Jennifer Jones as Jo. In the late summer of 1946 it seemed this would become a reality. Others scheduled for the new rendition were: Diana Lynn (Amy), Bambi Linn (Beth), Rhonda Fleming (Meg), John Dall (Laurie), Anne Revere (Marmee), Charles Coburn (Laurie's Grandfather), Philip Friend (Brooke), Constance Collier (Aunt March), and Elizabeth Patterson (Hannah). Technicolor wardrobe and set tests were completed, but then a combination of post–World War II retrenchment within the industry and threatened craft worker strikes led the producer to cancel the project. He sold the remake rights to MGM.

Mervyn LeRoy, a producer-director strongly faithful to Louis B. Mayer, who then was losing his grasp of studio power, shared Mayer's affection for the bittersweet classic. He proceeded to produce and direct the family-oriented picture.

Public favorite June Allyson was top-billed as Jo, maturing Margaret O'Brien[1] played Beth, Janet Leigh was Meg, and a blonde-wigged Elizabeth Taylor appeared as Amy. Italian-import Rossano

Brazzi made his U.S. cinema debut in the part of the German Professor Bhaer (performed with striking sensitivity by Paul Lukas in the 1933 film). Peter Lawford, slowly gaining stardom at the studio, played Laurie (re-creating Douglass Montgomery's past assignment). The studio proudly noted the film brought together four members from the **Meet Me in St. Louis** (1944) family: O'Brien, Mary Astor (as Marmee, the mother), Leon Ames (as Mr. March, the father), and Harry Davenport (as Dr. Ames).

Mary Astor, who wrote contemptuously of this era of her career as "Mothers for Metro," shared some reminiscences in her book **A Life on Film** (1971):

My approach to the part of Marmee was not an enthusiastic one. Everybody else had fun. The girls all giggled and chattered and made a game of every scene. Taylor was engaged, and in love, and talking on the phone most of the time (which is fine normally, but not when that production clock is ticking away the company's money). June Allyson chewed gum constantly and irritatingly, and Maggie O'Brien looked at me as though she were planning something very unpleasant.

In the scene where Jo got her hair cut, Peter Lawford was supposed to arrive at the house and say, "What have you done! You look like a porcupine!" Except that for some reason the pronunciation of porcupine eluded him. It came out "porkypine." It took an entire afternoon, and everyone, even Mervyn LeRoy, was doubled up with laughter. The scene would begin, with Peter insisting, "I've got it! I've got it now!" and then, nearly at the end of the

---
[1]Margaret O'Brien would appear in a musical version of **Little Women** on CBS-TV on October 16, 1958, joined by Rise Stevens, Jeannie Carson, Zina Bethune, and Florence Henderson.

scene, he would burst in the door and say, "What have you done! You look like a porkypine!" And everybody went to pieces.

My sense of humor, my sense of fun, had deserted me long ago. And it just wasn't all **that** funny.

MGM's trust paid off when **Little Women** was released and drew great reviews. **Time** magazine: "A shade less ambitious than its 1933 predecessor, it still jerks tears with easy efficiency." The **Baltimore Sun**: "It is not a realistic portrayal of family life at the time of the Civil War, it is an idealized one; it has the quality of a pleasant and nostalgic daydream." **Variety**: "Greatly abetting the studio in catching the feeling and taste of the 1860s is the use of color in the film. In this instance, the Technicolor tinting is a pure asset lending accuracy, charm, and powerfully nostalgic allure to the old-fashioned story related in celluloid."

Drama students with good memories might have found Allyson's bubbly Jo a thespianic letdown after Hepburn's well-shaded portrayal; been overwhelmed by O'Brien's schmaltz-reeking death scene; puzzled by Brazzi's non-Germanic interpretation of Professor Bhaer; and distracted by the gloriously Technicolor rainbow which loomed over the March home just before the fade-out. However, **Little Women** attracted an enormous audience and joined Metro's array of top money earners for the season: **Command Decision, Julia Misbehaves, Neptune's Daughter, The Stratton Story, The Barkleys of Broadway, Take Me Out to the Ball Game, Words and Music,** and **The Three Musketeers**. As such, **Little Women** became an ally of Louis B. Mayer against the "modernist" movement of Dore Schary, which was slowly overtaking control of the lot.

Little Women also demonstrated some other studio transitions. The picture was the final assignment for the stalwart Britisher Sir C. Aubrey Smith, who played Mr. Lawrence. At age eighty-five, he died shortly after completing his scenes. This would be Margaret O'Brien's final film for her home company. Walt Disney had asked to borrow her thereafter for its **Alice in Wonderland** and she refused, an assignment MGM thought she should take. Thereafter the studio decided it had no further need for the fast-growing adolescent actress. As for Elizabeth Taylor, who played the flighty, often-selfish Amy, **Little Women** represented the finale of her flirtatious child-woman roles. No longer would she interpret the innocent minx on screen. With her next role—opposite Robert Taylor in **Conspirator** (1950)—she graduated to adult assignments.

LOVE FINDS ANDY HARDY
1938—91 min.

Producer, Carey Wilson; **director,** George B. Seitz; based on characters created by Aurania Rouverol; **screenplay,** William Ludwig; **songs,** Mack Gordon and Harry Revel; Roger Edens; **music,** David Snell; **vocal arranger,** Edens; **art directors,** Cedric Gibbons and Stan Rogers; **set decorator,** Edwin B. Willis; **wardrobe,** Jeanne; **sound,** Douglas Shearer; **camera,** Lester White; **editor,** Ben Lewis.

Lewis Stone (**Judge Hardy**); Mickey Rooney (**Andy Hardy**); Judy Garland (**Betsy Booth**); Cecilia Parker (**Marian Hardy**); Fay Holden (**Mrs. Hardy**); Ann Rutherford (**Polly Benedict**); Betty Ross Clarke (**Aunt Milly**); Lana Turner (**Cynthia Potter**); Marie Blake (**Augusta**); Don Castle (**Dennis Hunt**); Gene Reynolds (**Jimmy MacMahon**); Mary Howard (**Mrs. Tompkins**); Frank Darian (**Bill Collector**); George Breakston (**Beezy**); Raymond Hatton (**Peter Dugan**).

SYNOPSIS

Andy Hardy has purchased a secondhand car on the installment plan in order to take his girl, Polly Benedict, to the Carvel Christmas dance. Only $8 remains between Andy and the roadster.

Polly is called out of town suddenly and Andy is left without a date. Soon his buddy Beezy offers him the $8 to take his steady, Cynthia Potter, since he too cannot attend the dance.

Complications further arise with the arrival of young Betsy Booth, who visits her grandmother—the next-door neighbor of Judge Hardy and family. Betsy soon harbors a crush on Andy but he only offers her his romantic and financial tales of woe.

When Polly returns home unexpectedly, Andy breaks their date because of his commitment to squire Cynthia. Then Breezy changes his mind about the $8 and Andy has no date until he asks Betsy to escort him.

Later Betsy, realizing how "mature" Andy feels about Polly, arranges to bring the two of them together before she returns to Manhattan. The Hardy family's peace of mind is complete when Mrs. Hardy, who had been away caring for her sick mother, sends word to Judge Hardy that she will be home in time for the holiday festivities.

* * *

In 1974 a mild controversy erupted in the erudite pages of **Films in Review** magazine. MGM's veteran story editor—producer—chronicler Samuel Marx took great exception to the journal's printing of the following studio legend, attributed to the imagination of Ben Hecht and submitted by a Los Angeles contributor:

Hecht, who disliked Mayer, arranged an appointment to discuss with LBM a verbal outline of an original screenplay. Mayer listened as Hecht outlined the plot:

Andy Hardy finds a stray dog named Lassie, which he attempts to return to its owner and encounters Maisie Revier from whom he contracts a venereal disease that is treated by young Dr. James Kildare who is so alarmed at the number of such cases he has treated lately that he calls on Nick and Nora Charles to track down the original source which turns out to be an African couple, Tarzan and Jane.

After hearing this plot, Mayer had Hecht thrown out of his office and his contract canceled.

True or false, this story contains a basic truth: Louis B. Mayer had great respect for the high-moral family entertainment that had earned the studio such nice annual dividends. And nothing delighted him more than the **Andy Hardy** series. Of the fifteen Hardy episodes produced between 1937 and 1946, none other pleased the public or exhibitors more than **Love Finds Andy Hardy**. It contained most of the members of the popular Hardy family,[1] as well as two ladies who were being carefully groomed for bigger and better celluloid entries: Judy Garland and Lana Turner.

The evolution of the Hardy series, and Mayer's love for it, developed gradually. On May 21, 1928, **Skidding,** a play by Aurania Rouverol opened at Broadway's Bijou Theatre.[2] Reviewed by the **New York Times,** "The play was about the difficulty of keeping the family homogeneous, of keeping it from skidding, thereby giving rise to the title." The show ran for 448 performances and the screen rights were purchased by MGM, where the property rested until the great success of the American comedy **Ah, Wilderness!** (1935). Two years later, Metro fashioned **A Family Affair** (1937) with **Ah, Wilderness!** veterans Lionel Barrymore (Judge Hardy), Mickey Rooney (son Andy), Spring Byington (Mrs. Hardy), and Eric Linden, engineer boyfriend of Marian Hardy (Cecilia Parker). The film was a box-office sleeper and the studio decided to perpetuate the family series.

In the second entry, **You're Only Young Once** (1938), Lewis Stone took over for an ailing Lionel Barrymore as Judge Hardy and appeared in the opening of the film to explain that the viewers were about to witness the beginning of the series.[3] The Hardy family regulars became Stone, Fay Holden (as Mrs. Hardy—Byington was then involved with Twentieth Century-Fox's Jones family series), Sara Haden (usually as Aunt Milly), Parker (Marian), and Rooney (Andy). Julie Haydon's role of Joan Hardy, the elder sister in **A Family Affair,** was deleted from the storyline. Other regulars in the series were added: Ann Rutherford as Andy's on-again, off-again romance Polly Benedict, and George Breakston as Andy's classmate Beezy.

Judge Hardy's Children (1938), the third in the series, was equally profitable, leading to **Love Finds Andy Hardy**. It was the first of the entries to receive wide acclaim and to enjoy a decent budget. By this time Mayer had taken a strong interest in the property, recognizing Andy and his sagacious Pop as the perfect mouthpiece for his theories on his pet sacred institution, The Family.

---

[1] In most of the entries Sara Haden portrayed Aunt Milly Forrest; however, in **Judge Hardy's Children** and **Love Finds Andy Hardy**, both 1938 releases, Betty Ross Clarke played the aunt.

[2] In this original play production, Andy was played by Charles Eaton, Judge James Hardy by Carleton Macy, and Mrs. Hardy by Clara Blandick.

[3] Lewis Stone became so strongly identified with his characterization of Judge Hardy that Metro rewrote his contract. He was committed to work twelve weeks a year and to make two Hardy pictures per annum at a large salary, similar to Wallace Beery's studio deal in the forties at MGM.

Judy Garland and Mickey Rooney in Love Finds Andy Hardy *('38).*

As explained by Bosley Crowther in his book **Hollywood Rajah** (1960):

In a way he [Mayer] became the Hardy's mentor, and worked harder than anyone to maintain the character of the series and hold it to a form. He transmitted his thoughts through Carey Wilson, who was the primary idea man and general factotum of the productions. Wilson had to bear the brunt of Mayer's frequent objections and ultimatums on how Andy should behave.

In **Love** Rooney (by now a major juvenile attraction through such films as **Captains Courageous** and **Boys Town**—and soon to be earning more than $300,000 yearly) had three young ladies to squire: Judy Garland, as adolescent Betsy Booth, the visitor from New York who develops a crush on the boy and sings "Meet the Beat of My Heart," "It Never Rains but It Pours" (both by Mack Gordon and Harry Revel), and "In Between" (by Roger Edens);[4] Lana Turner, as sexpot Cynthia Turner whose favorite sport is neither swimming nor tennis, but kissing (later Andy rationalizes her as "just one of the errors of my childhood"); and Ann Rutherford, as true love Polly Benedict (played throughout the series by Rutherford). Interpolated between these romantic escapades were serious heart-to-heart chats between the Judge and Andy ("Dad, can I talk to you man to man? Can a guy be in love with two girls at

once?") and Andy's purchasing of an old jalopy ("The thing to remember," counseled Mayer to the entry's creators, "is that he wants the jalopy more than he wants the girl".)

Released July 22, 1938, **Love Finds Andy Hardy** attracted a large number of studio executives at its Hollywood premiere; word was out that Mayer was directly concerned with the series. Wanda Hale of the **New York Daily News** approved. "Like the preceding Hardy films, it is as welcome as the sunshine . . . refreshing entertainment." It became the biggest hit of the Hardy series at the time and was instrumental in establishing Garland and Turner at the studio. While the sweater girl would not be reunited with Rooney on screen again,[5] Garland would appear in two[6] more **Andy Hardy** entries: **Andy Hardy Meets Debutante** (1940) and **Life Begins for Andy Hardy** (1941). In neither case did she win the girl-chasing hero.

The **Andy Hardy** entries went on to become one of the most popular of all cinema series, buoyed by star attraction Rooney, who became in

---

[4]Garland's rendition of Cole Porter's "Easy to Love" was cut from the release print.

[5]In **Andy Hardy Meets Debutante,** the face of Cynthia Potter is shown on the cover of the Carvel High School newspaper. In **Love Laughs at Andy Hardy** (1946) her portrait is among those stashed in his bedroom gallery. In **Andy Hardy Comes Home** (1958), two scenes featuring Lana Turner's Cynthia Potter are used.

[6]Judy Garland had already appeared with Rooney in **Thoroughbreds Don't Cry** (1937); and they would appear together in the following non–Hardy family pictures: **Babes in Arms** (1939), **Strike Up the Band** (1940), **Babes on Broadway** (1941), **Girl Crazy** (1943), and **Words and Music** (1948).

1938 the country's number-one box-office star. That year the Academy Awards deciders presented both him and Deanna Durbin with Oscars for "the spirit and personification of youth" they presented on screen. At the 1942 Oscar ceremonies the series itself won an award certificate: "To Metro-Goldwyn-Mayer studio for its achievement in representing an American Way of Life in the production of the **Andy Hardy** series of films."

During its run the series gave screen exposure to such fledgling contract starlets as Esther Williams, Kathryn Grayson, Susan Peters, and Donna Reed. In his **I.E. an Autobiography** (1965), Rooney writes:

There was in fact a standard studio recipe. Take one young actress, pluck her eyebrows, cap her teeth, shape her hairline, pad as required and throw her into the ring with Andy Hardy. Then wait and see. If the public responded, the starlet became a star [and grossed for the lot in the vicinity of $73,000,000].

Throughout the run of the **Andy Hardy** series, Mayer insisted that a first-class director would ruin the pictures and he generally assigned efficient rather then inspired directors to the property. Most entries were helmed by George B. Seitz; W. S. Van Dyke handled **Andy Hardy Gets Spring Fever** (1939) and Willis Goldbeck guided **Love Laughs at Andy Hardy** (1946).

When the maturing, rebellious Mickey Rooney returned to MGM after military service in World War II, it was almost inevitable that he and paterfamilias Mayer would come to a final breaking of the way. Years later Rooney would admit that the mogul was only trying to curb the actor's ego excesses. However, at the time the pint-size star thought he could do better freelancing and producing films on his own.

In 1958, with Louis B. Mayer and his successor Dore Schary gone from the scene, the sadly decaying MGM threw together **Andy Hardy Comes Home** with a portly Rooney resuming his part[7] along with Fay Holden, Cecilia Parker, and Sara Haden. Rooney's son Tim appeared in the cast as the next generation of Hardy stock. The black-and-white programmer was not a success, merely a sad reminder of past glories. (As late as 1978 there was still trade talk of Rooney starring in a teleseries, entitled "Judge Andy Hardy" but it never came to be.

In 1972 MGM tore down most of the Carvel street sets.[8] TV showings of the series testify to an era of very different societal values—and to a very different Hollywood.

---

[7]In the late 1940s "The Hardy Family" radio series had been syndicated by MGM, starring Rooney, Stone, and Holden.

[8]In **That's Entertainment!** (1974) a still puckish Rooney, one of many hosts, parades down the remnant of the Carvel sets and reminisces about the golden days of the **Andy Hardy** series, Judy Garland, et al.

LOVE ME OR LEAVE ME
1955 C—122 min.

Producer, Joe Pasternak; **director,** Charles Vidor; **story,** Daniel Fuchs; **screenplay,** Fuchs and Isobel Lennart; **art directors,** Cedric Gibbons and Urie McCleary; **music director,** George Stoll; **Miss Day's music,** Percy Faith; **choreography,** Alex Romero; **music adviser,** Irving Aaronson; **songs,** Ted Koehler and Rube Bloom; Joe McCarthy and James Monaco; Jack Palmer and Spencer Williams; Walter Donaldson; B. G. DeSylva, Lew Brown, and Ray Henderson; Gus Kahn and Donaldson; Roy Turk and Fred Ahlert; Richard Rodgers and Lorenz Hart; Irving Berlin; Chilton Price; Nicholas Brodsky and Sammy Cahn; **costumes,** Helen Rose; **sound,** Dr. Wesley C. Miller; **special effects,** Warren Newcombe; **camera,** Arthur E. Arling; **editor,** Ralph E. Winters.

Doris Day (**Ruth Etting**); James Cagney (**Martin "The Gimp" Snyder**); Cameron Mitchell (**Johnny Alderman**); Robert Keith (**Bernard V. Loomis**); Tom Tully (**Frobisher**); Harry Bellaver (**Georgie**); Richard Gaines (**Paul Hunter**); Peter Leeds (**Fred Taylor**); Claude Stroud (**Eddie Fulton**); Audrey Young (**Jingle Girl**); Dorothy Abbott (**Dancer**); Phil Schumacher, Otto Reichow, and Henry Kulky (**Bouncers**); Jay Adler (**Orry**); Mauritz Hugo (**Irate Customer**); Veda Ann Borg (**Hostess**); Claire Carleton (**Claire**); Benny Burt (**Stage Manager**); James Drury (**Assistant Director**); Richard Simmons (**Dance Director**); Roy Engel and John Damler (**Reporters**); Robert Stephenson (**Waiter**); Chet Brandenberg (**Chauffeur**); Jimmy Cross and Henry Randolph (**Photographers**).

Robert Keith, James Cagney, and Doris Day in Love Me or Leave Me *('55).*

SYNOPSIS
In the Roaring Twenties chorus girl Ruth Etting is determined to crash into theatrical stardom. She meets Chicago racketeer Martin Snyder known as "Moe the Gimp" because of a lame leg.

In short order the coarse, bombastic hoodlum falls in love with the plucky would-be singing star. He blackmails certain "customers" into giving Ruth solo billing. Next, he promotes Ruth until she arrives on Broadway. All the while she pretends not to know his unsavory motives. He finally forces her into paying the price and they eventually legalize their relationship in marriage.

Their stormy union takes them from Broadway to Hollywood where Snyder succeeds in making her a film star. When he suspects piano accompanist Johnny Alderman of making love to Ruth, he shoots the man. Ruth divorces the Gimp and later marries the wounded piano player.

Returning to Chicago after his jail term, the Gimp opens a nightclub. Ruth offers her aid in a forgive-and-forget gesture.

* * *

Love Me or Leave Me is a Hollywood paradox: a CinemaScope musical that has the bite of authenticity. In telling the story of Ruth Etting, the famed torch singer of the 20's, the film rings true just by following the broad outline of her career as it was carried in the tabloid headlines of the day. [*Time* magazine]

The sordid story of chanteuse Etting and her lover, the Gimp, was a departure for Hollywood—and a very well-acted, directed, and profitable one.

Originally the production was envisaged as being directed by George Cukor and starring Ava Gardner. But that actress, fearful MGM would again dub her soundtrack voice as it had with **Showboat** (1951), rejected the major assignment. Instead, the Daniel Fuchs–Isobel Lennart screenplay was assigned to director Charles Vidor. The film was produced by Joe Pasternak previously, noted for his sugary Esther Williams, Deanna Durbin, Jane Powell, and Van Johnson outings.

There were problems in packaging the entity. Metro had to pay $50,000 to clear the rights to the songs employed in the film, and the three principals—Ruth Etting, Martin ("the Gimp") Snyder, and Harry Myrl Alderman (called Johnny Alderman in the film)—were all still living at the time of the production. Each had to be paid undisclosed amounts for the rights to use their names in the film. All three, however, were impressed by the Hollywood choices to represent them in the picture: Doris Day, James Cagney, and Cameron Mitchell.

Neither Day nor Cagney, both products of the Warner Bros. star system, had previously worked at MGM. Day sang a score of Etting standards such as "Mean to Me," "Everybody Loves My Baby," "Shaking the Blues Away" (previously done by Ann Miller in **Easter Parade,** 1948), "Ten Cents a Dance," and the title song. Never before, and not since has so dramatic a part come into Day's interpretive hands. As for Cagney, he leaped into the project with great enthusiasm. He consulted with several doctors regarding the Gimp's affliction, deciding the character had been lame from birth. (Unfortunately, along the way someone overlooked the fact that the racketeer had a bad left leg, not a game right one as demonstrated in the film.) Cagney created one of his most vivid characterizations in this feature and he worked well in tandem with the toughened Miss Day.[1]

"It's a powerful, turbulent drama of real people and a picture that's tops in entertainment," read MGM's ad copy when **Love Me or Leave Me** was released in 1955. **Cue** magazine observed, "It's all quite a departure for Hollywood, for MGM, and producer Joseph Pasternak." **Variety:** "While it's not the usual songsmith cavalcade, it does blend so rich a medley of some of the more popular standards of the 1920s that it's virtually a salute to ASCAP."

The film won Cagney another Oscar nomination, but he lost the Best Actor prize to Ernest Borgnine of **Marty** (United Artists). Day, who turned in a sterling performance—so different from her cotton-candy roles of before—was not nominated. However, that year MGM did have two

[1]Years later (March 1974), when Cagney was honored by the American Film Institute as the second recipient of the Life Achievement Award, Day was so eager to pay tribute to her costar that she was the only celebrity to attend the rehearsal.

actresses up for Oscars for playing vocalists in other musical biographies: Susan Hayward as Lillian Roth in **I'll Cry Tomorrow** and Eleanor Parker as Marjorie Lawrence in **Interrupted Melody.** The distaff category would be won by Anna Magnani of **The Rose Tattoo** (Paramount). But Daniel Fuchs, who wrote the story for **Love Me or Leave Me,** and coauthored the screenplay, did win an Oscar. **Love Me or Leave Me** placed eighth on the **Film Daily** Ten Best Picture Poll and grossed $4,153,000 in distributors' domestic rentals.

Although the public enthusiastically endorsed this slick rags-to-gaudy-riches study of a Prohibition-era songstress, one person was unhappy with the screen results—Ruth Etting herself. "Oh, what a ————mess that was. . . . I was never at any time a dancehall girl. It was just a means of working in 'Ten Cents a Dance.' They took a lot of liberties with my life, but I guess they usually do with that kind of thing." In **Ginger, Loretta and Irene Who?** (1976), George Eels devotes a chapter to songstress Etting (born November 23, 1896) and remarks many discrepancies between the film biography and reality: "In the interest of melodrama the scriptwriters reduced Ruth to a clichéed, hard-drinking, lusty, amoral opportunist. The result was an effective formula drama that dismissed the most interesting aspects of her character."

According to Eels, "Doris Day, who never knew Ruth, claims in her autobiography that Ruth clawed her way to the top and was a kept woman. Ruth laughed and said, 'I never was that lucky.' Urged by friends to sue, she recalled that June and Walter Winchell had always said litigation only brought the gossip to the attention of those who hadn't seen it the first time."

Eels adds:

> Snyder's characteristics were heightened for theatrical effect. . . . The time span was compressed radically; instead of meeting Myrl [Alderman] in 1935, when her career was almost finished, he was her accompanist-tutor-suitor in the 1920s. Yet the portrayals by James Cagney, Doris Day, and Cameron Mitchell of Snyder, Ruth, and Alderman were so vivid and the gritty subject matter so much more pertinent than the perennial will-they-or-won't-they get the show on or be reunited that accuracy—or lack of it—bothered only those personally involved.

LUST FOR LIFE
1956 C—122 min.

Producer, John Houseman; **associate producer,** Jud Kinberg; **director,** Vincente Minnelli; based on the novel by Irving Stone; **screenplay,** Norman Corwin; **art directors,** Cedric Gibbons, Hans Peters, and Preston Ames; **music director,** Miklos Rozsa; **camera,** Freddie Young and Russell Harlan; **editor,** Adrienne Fazan.

Kirk Douglas **(Vincent Van Gogh);** Anthony Quinn **(Paul Gauguin);** James Donald **(Theo Van Gogh);** Pamela Brown **(Christine);** Everett Sloane **(Dr. Gachet);** Niall MacGinnis **(Roulin);** Noel Purcell **(Anton Mauve);** Henry Daniell **(Theodorus Van Gogh);** Madge Kennedy **(Anna Cornelia Van Gogh);** Jill Bennett **(Willemien);** Lionel Jeffries **(Dr. Peyron);** Laurence Naismith **(Dr. Bosman);** Eric Pohlmann **(Colbert);** Jeanette Sterke **(Kay);** Toni Gerry **(Johanna);** Wilton Graff **(Reverend Stricker);** Isobel Elsom **(Mrs. Stricker);** John Ruddock **(Ducrucq);** Julie Robinson **(Rachel);** David Leonard **(Camille Pissarro);** William Phipps **(Emile Bernard);** Frank Perls **(Pere Tanguy);** Rex Evans **(Durand-Ruel);** Marion Ross **(Sister Clothilde);** Belle Mitchell **(Mme Tanguy);** Jerry Bergen **(Lautrec);** Mickey Maga **(Jan);** Norman MacCowan **(Pier).**

SYNOPSIS
Vincent Van Gogh, an intense young man, leaves his native Holland in 1878 to carry the word of God to the coal-mining region of Le Borinage in Belgium. The sad plight of the miners moves him and when his evangelistic superiors reprimand him for giving away everything he owns to help the poor families, he denounces the proselytizers for their hypocrisy and gives up his official duties.

Vincent falls into a period of mental and physical decline and months later is found living in squalor by his brother Theo. Theo persuades him to return to their parents' home in Holland to regain his strength. There he pursues an interest in art and at the same time falls madly in love with a visiting cousin, who rejects him even when he follows her back to The Hague. Humiliated, he goes to a cafe to drown his sorrow in drink. He meets there Christine, a lost woman of the slums. She becomes his model and mistress and keeps home for him while he tries to master the craft of oil painting.

When Van Gogh's father dies, Vincent is compelled to return home. This causes Christine to part from him. Having settled family matters, Vincent uses the countryside and peasants of his native land as subjects for his work, but goes to Paris when his eccentric ways prove an embarrassment to his prim family. There he is exposed to the impressionist school of painters. He is guided by Theo, now an art dealer. Vincent plunges into the new art movement and becomes drawn to flamboyant impressionist Paul Gauguin.

The Bohemian lifestyle of Paris interferes with Vincent's work, so he goes to southern France. There he regains his creative ability and induces Gauguin to join him. Their friendship turns into a nightmare when their temperaments clash. When Gauguin leaves Van Gogh, the latter suffers a mental attack and mutilates his own ear with a razor. He goes to a mental institution voluntarily and after partial recovery returns to his painting. But he creates with such intensity that he has another breakdown. Months later, when he feels a third attack coming on, he shoots himself. He dies unaware of his impact on the contemporary or future art world.

Vincent Van Gogh (1853–90) created some sixteen hundred paintings and drawings within a ten-year period. He then shot himself, at age thirty-seven, after uttering, "There will never be an end to human misery." In 1956 his surviving creative work was estimated to be worth $30 million.

Hollywood had been much interested in Van Gogh since the bestselling novel by Irving Stone, published in 1934. But how to present the painter's complex life on screen in a commercial manner? Hence the concept remained dormant until summer 1946, when the MGM story department presented MGM musical producer Arthur Freed with a synopsis of Stone's book. Freed became excited and said, "I want to buy **Lust for Life** and I want Stone to write the screenplay." The studio complied, and the property was optioned and Stone contracted to adapt the project for the screen. This was accomplished in mid-1947. But then a demanding production schedule caused Freed to shelve the property. It was eventually turned over to producer John Houseman, who joined MGM for **The Bad and the Beautiful** (1952), **Julius Caesar** (1953), **Executive Suite** (1954), and others.

It was while making **The Bad and the Beautiful** that producer Houseman, director Vincente Minnelli, and star Kirk Douglas all determined to take action to see Van Gogh's life cinematized. Actually **Lust for Life** became a reality because of the musical film version of **Kismet** (1955). When Freed acquired the screen rights to that Broadway musical, he requested Minnelli to direct the vehicle. The latter said. "I hated the show, I don't want to do it!" MGM studio head Dore Schary was aware of Minnelli's enthusiasm for the **Lust for Life** project and told him that if he would helm **Kismet,** he could make the Van Gogh picture. Minnelli agreed.

Minnelli said later, "Once we received the green light to proceed with the picture, there was no question that Kirk would play Van Gogh. No other actor was ever considered for the part." The tough star explained his attraction for the assignment, "Aside from his burning genius, the thing that attracted me to Van Gogh was his loneliness. Anyone who has experienced loneliness can understand his story. Van Gogh's tragedy was that of a man who needed other people so badly that he couldn't admit it even to himself."

Production began only after several artistic battles with the front office by Minnelli (he lost a fight to avoid CinemaScope, out of deference to the paintings; but he won a bout to substitute Ansco color for Eastman color, which would better capture the paintings). Supported by an excellent team of technicians (including cinematographers Freddie Young and Russell Harlan, and art directors Cedric Gibbons, Hans Peters, and Preston Ames), the troupe went to Europe for actual Van Gogh backdrops. Dynamic Douglas allowed his beard to grow and with the hair on his head lightened, he bore an uncanny resemblance to the impressionistic painter. The star hired a French artist to teach him to paint crows, "The director has told me that he wanted me to add crows to a painting of a wheatfield [on camera]—crows in the manner of Van Gogh. In practice sessions I painted more than 900 crows. I am not one of the art world's immortals, but at least I can now

Anthony Quinn and Kirk Douglas in Lust for Life *('56).*

catch a crow in flight." Douglas's wife, Anne, later wrote an article for the **Saturday Evening Post** about her celebrity spouse, admitting, "Kirk always brings his roles home with him. . . . He came home in that red beard of Van Gogh's, wearing those big boots, stomping around the house—it was frightening."

Critics found much to cheer in **Lust for Life,** much enhanced by its location filming in Holland, Belgium, Paris and the south of France. Said **Newsweek** magazine, "Hollywood's most profound exploration of the artistic life." **New York Times:** "Mr. Houseman and Vincente Minnelli . . . have wisely relied upon color and the richness and character it gives images to carry their tortured theme." A few critics carped about the sensationalistic aspects of the Van Gogh narrative. **Time** magazine noted, "Because the Hollywood story builds relentlessly to Van Gogh's ear-slicing for its climax, **Lust for Life** falls midway between being a first-rate art film and high-pitched melodrama."[1]

The two-hour feature benefited greatly, from a commercial and critical point of view, from the strong performances of Kirk Douglas and Anthony Quinn. Douglas's starring portrayal, arguably his greatest screen characterization, won him the

New York Film Critics Circle Award for best actor, the Foreign Press Award, and a Best Actor Oscar nomination. He lost the prize to Yul Brynner of **The King and I** (Twentieth Century–Fox). On the other hand, Quinn did win the Supporting Actor Oscar for his relatively brief but overpowering delineation of eccentric Paul Gauguin.

In **I Remember It Well**, his 1974 autobiography, Minnelli sums up **Lust for Life:**

> The reviews in general were the best of my life. **Lust for Life** was variously called the finest film about painting ever shot and the best biography. But the great satisfaction was an entirely personal one. I knew the challenges that had been surmounted, and found it an enormous triumph for us all. It remains my favorite film, simply because it contains more of my favorite moments than any other film I've directed.

MADAME CURIE
1943—124 min.

Producer, Sidney Franklin; **director,** Mervyn LeRoy; based on the book by Eve Curie; **screenplay,** Paul Osborn and Paul H. Rameau; **music,** Herbert Stothart; **art directors,** Cedric Gibbons and Paul Groesse; **set decorators,** Edwin B. Willis and Hugh Hunt; **assistant director,** Al Shenberg; **sound,** W. N. Sparks; **women's costumes,** Irene Sharaff; **men's costumes,** Gile Steele, **special effects,** Warren Newcombe; **camera,** Joseph Ruttenberg; **editor,** Harold F. Kress.

Greer Garson **(Mme Marie Curie);** Walter Pidgeon **(Pierre Curie);** Robert Walker **(David LeGros);** Dame May Whitty **(Mme Eugene Curie);** Henry Travers **(Eugene Curie);** C. Aubrey Smith **(Lord Kelvin);** Albert Basserman **(Professor Perot);** Victor Francen **(President of University);** Reginald Owen **(Dr. Henri Becquerel);** Van Johnson **(Reporter);** Elsa Basserman **(Mme Perot);** Lumsden Hare **(Professor Reget);** James Hilton **(Narrator);** Charles Trowbridge, Edward Fielding, James Kirkwood, and Nestor Eristoff **(Board Members);** Moroni Olsen **(President of Businessmen's Board);** Miles Mander, Arthur Shields, and Frederic Worlock **(Businessmen);** Alan Napier **(Dr. Bladh);** Ray Collins **(Lecturer's Voice);** Almira Sessions **(Mme Michaud);** Margaret O'Brien **(Irene at Age Five);** Dorothy Gilmore **(Nurse);** Gigi Perreau **(Eva at Age Eighteen Months);** Ruth Cherrington **(Swedish Queen);** Wyndham Standing **(King Oscar).**

SYNOPSIS
In turn-of-the-century Paris, Marie Sklodowska, a Polish student, receives an offer to study steel magnetism as a means of supporting herself. Professor Perot sets up the appointment and Marie finds herself sharing a laboratory with Professor Pierre Curie, a brilliant yet reticent scientist.

Pierre grows to love Marie and is saddened when she plans to return to Poland to teach after she passes her university examinations. He finally bolsters enough courage to propose marriage and she accepts. On returning from their honeymoon the scientists explore the mysteries of pitchblende, which they had first observed under Dr. Henri Becquerel's guidance.

After five years of concentrated study and experimentation, Marie discovers the miracle of radium. Further tests follow and the couple experiences periods of hardship and personal suffering. Their ultimate triumph occurs when their experimentation with tons of pitchblende produces a single decagram of radium. They receive worldwide honors and retire to the quiet of the country to vacation with their two children. Pierre is tragically killed in a traffic accident on the day he is to be recognized by the university.

A lonely and saddened Marie continues her experimentation and advances the existing knowledge of radium.

* * *

Louis B. Mayer loved a humanitarian theme as much as (or more than) the next film producer. When in the late 1930s smiling Jack L. Warner began reaping global accolades for producing such screen biographies as **The Story of Louis Pasteur** (1936) and **The Life of Emile Zola** (1937), Culver City began searching for equally stirring historical drama.

The studio discovered the appropriately inspirational material in Eve Curie's 1937 biography of her radium-discovering mother, Marie Curie. Universal had acquired the screen rights to the book, seeing it as a likely vehicle for Irene Dunne, but when she went on to other projects, the company sold its rights to MGM. Metro assigned Aldous Huxley and F. Scott Fitzgerald to prepare a

---

[1]Minnelli said of the ear-slicing scene, "Van Gogh, still smarting from his argument with Gauguin, goes through various stages. He stands before the mirror and looks at himself with total loathing. He makes a tortured face and grinds his nose in the mirror. He steps away, and the lamp is reflected in the mirror for a while. There is no sound. Then Van Gogh screams in pain. The scene is still reflected in the mirror. He is seen staggering by, holding his bloody hand to the side of his head."

Walter Pidgeon, Reginald Owen, and Greer Garson in Madame Curie *('43).*

screen treatment of the life of the famous lady scientist, hoping to lure Greta Garbo into starring in the project. But the Swedish actress became involved in other productions on the lot and the property was shelved. Came World War II and the studio deemed the story "too somber" for wartime audiences and the idea of any eventual production seemed highly dubious.

However, the very successful teaming of Greer Garson and Walter Pidgeon in **Blossoms in the Dust** (1941) and **Mrs. Miniver** (1942) led Metro officials to seek another vehicle to reteam the marquee attractions. MGM rediscovered its **Curie** script and Paul Osborn and Paul H. Rameau were told to polish the narrative to suit the Garson-Pidgeon personae. To ensure the "class appeal" of the production, Louis B. Mayer appointed producer Sidney Franklin and director Mervyn LeRoy to repeat the collaboration they had so well handled in **Random Harvest** (1942).

Madame Curie began production in mid-1943, almost a year after the triumph of **Mrs. Miniver**. Metro took every well-publicized opportunity to promote the picture into a surefire success. Dr. R. M. Langer of the California Institute of Technoloy stood by on the set as technical adviser, novelist James Hilton was hired to supply the narration, studio newcomer Robert Walker was given a featured role as David LeGros, and the lot's stock company was called upon to fill important subordinate parts. Spotted within the proceedings were two future MGM luminaries: Van Johnson as a reporter and Margaret O'Brien as the Curies' child Irene at age five.

And, of course, Garson and Pidgeon (wearing a beard for this outing) undertook their assignments with their wonted high professionalism and dedication—which did not mean the set was morose or dull. Director LeRoy would recollect in his autobiography, **Take One,** (1974), that Pidgeon's sense of mirth often pervaded the somber mood of the soundstage. He recalled the shooting of the telling scene of the discovery of radium:

Naturally, this was a scene that needed great drama. We rehearsed it so the audience would have goose bumps when it flashed on the screen.

I called for action, and the cameras were rolling—and then, from out of the darkness, I heard Greer laugh.

"Cut," I yelled. "Come on, Greer, what's so funny? Why the big laugh?"

"I couldn't help it," she said. "Walter just told me the funniest joke!"

The tension that had built up during the long rehearsal period was gone. I waited about fifteen minutes, until Greer and Walter stopped their giggling, and then shot the scene. It worked perfectly.

Madame Curie enjoyed a Radio City Music Hall premiere on December 16, 1943, and critical response was generally enthusiastic, albeit reserved about the "dramatic" embellishments to the life story of the great scientist. The **New York Herald-Tribune** became the picture's most ardent champion, saluting the 124-minute drama as "a staunch and brilliant motion picture account of things which are generally considered outside the realms of dramatic revelation." Pidgeon was especially well cast as Pierre Curie. The **Tribune**'s Howard Barnes complimented his characterization

as "a real and recognizable figure, who can never be confused with Pidgeon himself." Garson, whose British-Hollywood mien bore little resemblance to the Polish-born scientist, also enjoyed her emotionally overwhelming moments. The sequence in which she learns of Pierre's death, her eyes tear-laden as she longingly touches his possessions, was presented with enough genuine sentiment to reduce most wartime audiences to weeping. Still later in the lengthy production, Garson enjoys an on-camera speechmaking session as the elderly female scientist (who would win two Nobel Prizes) addresses a gathering of researchers at the University of Paris. She urges her fellow scientists to "take the torch of knowledge, and behold the palace of the future."

Forgetting the conservative returns the studio had earned on its last inventor-researcher biography project (Spencer Tracy's **Edison the Man** in 1940), Metro hoped that the Garson-Pidgeon romantic teaming would guarantee hefty profits for this elaborate project, which had long been regarded by apprehensive studio powers as an unprofitable topic. There were profits, but they were moderate. In the Oscar race, the film was nominated in the categories of Best Picture (Warner Bros.' **Casablanca** won), Best Actress (Jennifer Jones defeated Garson through her performance in Twentieth Century–Fox's **The Song of Bernadette**), and Best Actor (Pidgeon's close friend Paul Lukas triumphed for Warner Bros.' **Watch on the Rhine**).

An interesting side effect of the MGM screen biography occurred decades later when British Broadcasting Corporation producer Bob Reid set out in 1970 to make a TV documentary about Madame Curie. He wanted to portray the "real" Marie Curie, who, unlike the Greer Garson portrayal, encompassed stubbornness and bitterness. Reid's research led him to discovering in French newspapers of 1911 that the Nobel Prize winner, then five years a widow, had become involved with a married colleague. Eventually Reid decided not to do the biographical documentary but to write a book about the scientist. It was published in 1974 and four years later the British-made mini-series based on the book was shown on American PBS television. It was a distinct contrast to the legend perpetrated by the Metro film factory many years earlier.

MAISIE
1939—74 min.

Producer, J. Walter Ruben; **director**, Edwin L. Marin; based on the novel **Dark Dame** by Wilson Collison; **screenplay**, Mary C. McCall, Jr.; **art directors**, Cedric Gibbons and Malcolm Brown; **set decorator**, Edwin B. Willis; **men's costumes**, Valles; **women's wardrobe**, Dolly Tree; **sound**, Douglas Shearer; **camera**, Leonard Smith; **editor**, Frederick Y. Smith.

Robert Young **(Slim Martin)**; Ann Sothern **(Maisie Ravier)**; Ian Hunter **(Clifford Ames)**; Ruth

Ann Sothern and George Tobias in Maisie *('39).*

Hussey (**Sybil Ames**); John Hubbard (**Dick Raymond**); Cliff Edwards (**Shorty**); George Tobias (**Rice**); Richard Carle (**Roger Bannerman**); Minor Watson (**Prosecuting Attorney**); Harlan Briggs (**Sheriff**); Paul Everton (**Judge**); Joseph Crehan (**Wilcox**); Frank Puglia (**Ernie**); Willie Fung (**Lee**); Emmett Vogan (**Court Clerk**); Mary Foy (**Sheriff's Wife**); Art Mix (**Red**); C. L. Sherwood (**Drunk**); Anthony Allan and Robert Middlemass (**Bits**).

SYNOPSIS

Showgirl Maisie Ravier is stranded in a small Western town. She attaches herself to ranch foreman Slim Martin after he has wrongfully accused her of stealing his wallet. She insists that he put her up at the ranch for the night. She promises to leave in the morning.

But the next day when the ranch owner, Clifford Ames, and his wife, Sybil, arrive for a visit, Maisie pretends to be the maid. Thus she forces Slim to keep her there. Later Maisie tries to win Slim's interest, but he, having had a sad experience with one woman, is reluctant to acknowledge her charms. However, he eventually ·succumbs.

Thereafter Maisie discovers that Mr. Ames is unhappy because he knows his wife has been unfaithful. As a matter of fact, she finds Sybil at a cabin with Dick Raymond, who had followed her out West. Disgusted, Maisie decides to leave. Sybil leads Slim to believe that Maisie's departure is because of the girl's unsuccessful attempt to win Clifford Ames' affection. As a result, Slim and Maisie quarrel and part.

Meanwhile, Clifford, having found out about his wife's lover, kills himself after writing a letter to his lawyer. The sheriff arrests Slim on a murder charge. But the lawyer and Maisie arrive in time to clear Slim of the alleged crime. The letter in question indicates Ames' intent to kill himself and in it he also wills the ranch to Maisie. Finally Maisie and Slim are united in love.

* * *

"Don't let all this talk about 'Maisie, the Explosive Blonde' (emanating from the Capitol Theatre) mystify you too unbearably. It's just Ann Sothern, who is probably already one of your favorite flouncers, flouncing," wrote Bosley Crowther (**New York Times**) in his June 23, 1939, review of **Maisie**. It was the start of a new MGM series, which joined **Tarzan, Andy Hardy,** and **Dr. Kildare** as one of the studio's most prolific and popular continuing properties.

The character of Maisie Ravier, a brassy, hip-wiggling, tantrum-tossing chorine with gypsy wanderlust, was based on the Wilson Collison 1935 novel **Dark Dame.** When acquired by MGM, it was targeted as a property for Jean Harlow. After the Blonde Bombshell's tragic death in the summer of 1937, however, **Maisie** went into temporary limbo. There the property remained until early 1939, when a series of events occured which sparked warfare between Metro and Twentieth Century–Fox.

After an unhappy stay at RKO, Ann Sothern was at liberty. The curvaceous blonde actress-songstress had recently stolen United Artists' **Trade Winds** (1938) out from under the black wig of star Joan Bennett. Fox, in hopes of luring Sothern into a long-term contract, offered her a spicy

part in **Elsa Maxwell's Hotel for Women** (1939). However, after completing the assignment, she irked studio mogul Darryl F. Zanuck by accepting a contract offer from Metro. Fox vindictively butchered her **Hotel for Women** part on the cutting-room floor while Sothern reported to MGM for work on **Maisie.**

Producer J. Walter Ruben combined opulence and economy in handling **Maisie.** A Wyoming-style ranch was built on the back lot, with stables, pastures, and a ranch house, all surrounded with livestock. The cast was plucked largely from the contract roster: ever ingratiating Robert Young (who, incidentally received top billing), Ian Hunter, and Ruth Hussey, the last then in the process of an MGM star buildup. The thin script provided for comedy (Sothern's attempts to impersonate a maid), melodrama (Hussey's cuckolding of Hunter, who ultimately kills himself), and romance (with Sothern appearing in court in the final reel just in time to save Young, accused of Hunter's murder, from a guilty verdict).

As Crowther elaborated in his **Times** review, "**Maisie** remains technically a comedy . . . of course, it has moments which are touchingly sad and sentimental, and other moments which are as dramatic as the dickens—as when Miss Sothern bursts in upon Ian's wife kissing another man in the old ranch house, while Ian lies five miles down the mountain, pinned beneath an overturned station wagon. . . . Incidentally, the character of Maisie is, as promised, 'explosive.' Miss Sothern, hitherto a reasonably restrained actress, throws left hooks, gags, and fits of temperament with surprising abandon."

Something of a distant relative to Glenda Farrell's **Torchy Blane** series at Warner Bros., Sothern's **Maisie** was a great charmer to exhibitors and audiences. Metro went on with plans for a modestly budgeted series. Like the **Hardy** and **Kildare** series, these programmers gave opportunities to newly signed contractees, besides providing perennial top revenues on relatively low budgets.

The sequels were: **Congo Maisie** (1940; actually a revamping of 1932's **Red Dust,** with Sothern taking the Jean Harlow part and John Carroll and Rita Johnson taking Gable's and Astor's); **Gold Rush Maisie** (1940; with Lee Bowman); **Maisie Was a Lady** (1941; with Lew Ayres of **Kildare** and Maureen O'Sullivan of **Tarzan**); **Ringside Maisie** (1941; with George Murphy and Robert Sterling[1]); **Maisie Gets Her Man** (1942; with Red Skelton); **Swing Shift Maisie** (1943; with James Craig); **Maisie Goes to Reno** (1944; with John Hodiak and Tom Drake); **Up Goes Maisie** (1946; with George Murphy); and **Undercover Maisie** (1947; with Barry Nelson).

In addition, Sothern, who never quite achieved major MGM stardom,[2] performed **Maisie** on radio.

---

[1] In 1943 Sterling and Sothern wed; their daughter Tisha became an actress.

[2] Sothern appeared with distinction in such non-**Maisie** vehicles as **Lady Be Good** (1941; with Eleanor Powell, Robert Young, and Red Skelton) and **Panama Hattie** (1942; with Red Skelton and Rags Ragland).

On July 5, 1945, the show aired on CBS network for two years; beginning November 24, 1949, the studio's WMGM began syndicating the property, again starring Sothern for a three-year run. As John Dunning relates in his tome **Tune in Yesterday,** "The opening was sheer 1940s; the click-click of Maisie's heels, followed by the long slow whistle of a wolf. A fresh voice: 'Hi-ya, babe! Say, how about a lit——' A sharp slap, a pained 'Ouch!' and Sothern with the putdown—'Does that answer your question, buddy?' " In the mid-1950s Sothern thought of bringing **Maisie** to television, but proper rights could not be obtained for the venture. A pity.

MANHATTAN MELODRAMA
1934—93 min.

Producer, David O. Selznick; **directors,** W. S. Van Dyke II and **uncredited,** Jack Conway; based on the story "Three Men" by Arthur Caesar; **screenplay,** Oliver H. P. Garrett and Joseph L. Mankiewicz; **song,** Richard Rodgers and Lorenz Hart; **art directors,** Cedric Gibbons and John Wright; **set decorator,** Edwin B. Willis; **wardrobe,** Dolly Tree; **special effects,** Slavko Vorkapich; **camera,** James Wong Howe; **editor,** Ben Lewis.

Clark Gable (**Edward "Blackie" Gallagher**); William Powell (**Jim Wade**); Myrna Loy (**Eleanor Packer**); Leo Carrillo (**Father Pat**); Nat Pendleton (**Spud**); George Sidney (**Poppa Rosen**); Isabel Jewell (**Annabelle**); Muriel Evans (**Tootsie Malone**); Thomas Jackson (**Richard Snow**); Claudelle Kaye (**Miss Adams**); Frank Conroy (**Blackie's Attorney**); Noel Madison (**Mannie Arnold**); Mickey Rooney (**Blackie at Age Twelve**); Jimmy Butler (**Jim at Age Twelve**); Vernon Dent (**Dancer on Boat**); Pat Moriarity (**Heckler**); Leonid Kinskey (**Trotskyite**); Edward Van Sloan (**Yacht Captain Swenson**); George Irving (**Politician**); Sam McDaniel (**Black Convict**); John Marston (**Coates**); Shirley Ross (**Cotton Club Singer**); Samuel S. Hinds (**Warden**); Lee Phelps (**Bailiff**); Emmett Vogan (**Assistant Prosecutor**).

SYNOPSIS
A maritime disaster aboard the SS **Slocum** in 1904 causes East Side youngsters Jim Wade and "Blackie" Gallagher to become orphans. As adults Jim becomes the assistant district attorney and Blackie heads a casino which caters to high-society clientele.

Eleanor Packer, Blackie's chic mistress, implores him to terminate his racket association, but he feels the straight and narrow path is not for him. Eleanor meets Jim and falls in love with him. Eventually she leaves Blackie.

Jim becomes New York City's district attorney. He fires a corrupt assistant, Richard Snow, who plans revenge through a smear campaign which will impair Jim's position in the gubernatorial race. Eleanor goes to Blackie for help. He

Clark Gable, Nat Pendleton, and John Marston in Manhattan Melodrama ('34).

obliges by shooting Snow. Blackie is apprehended and Jim finds himself in the uncomfortable situation of proscuting his longtime chum. Eleanor confesses that Blackie killed Snow to protect Jim.

With plans to lighten Blackie's sentence, Jim rushes to the prison but finds that the racketeer will not allow the district attorney to commute the sentence. Blackie, accompanied by Father Pat, walks nobly to his death. Jim returns to Eleanor, focusing away from politics.

* * *

On the evening of Sunday, July 22, 1934, infamous American gangster John Dillinger was shot to death when a G-man task force gunned him down under the marquee of Chicago's Biograph Theatre. The underworld figure had just enjoyed his favorite actress, Myrna Loy, in her latest release—**Manhattan Melodrama.**

Though footnoted in Americana mainly because of its relationship to Dillinger's demise, **Manhattan Melodrama** possessed many cinema-related reasons for distinction in MGM's history. Produced by aggressive David O. Selznick, directed with impact by W. S. Van Dyke II, and uncredited by Jack Conway with a tight screenplay by Oliver Garrett and Joseph L. Mankiewicz and title song by Rodgers and Hart, the picture was the initial teaming of debonair William Powell and Myrna Loy. The dapper actor was making his debut on the lot as a contract star, following years of service at Paramount and then at Warner Bros. Loy, a young veteran of the MGM stock company, had only just recently escaped her "type" of the exotic, oversexed, often Oriental femme fatale by

the mercy of loanouts to RKO for **The Animal Kingdom** and **Topaze.** In **Manhattan Melodrama,** however, both stars were relegated to billing below Clark Gable, himself the stellar male property then at MGM. He had just returned from a disciplinary "exile" to Columbia for a Frank Capra picture called **It Happened One Night.**

Taking a cue from the success Warner Bros. was enjoying with its gangland epics, MGM fashioned **Manhattan Melodrama** as action-filled, hard-hitting stuff, but staked its success mostly on the performances of the star trio. As Blackie Gallagher, Gable is appropriately surly, sexy, and ruthless without ever becoming boorish or losing that special screen magnetism. Powell is polished and smart while avoiding the imperiousness that sometimes colored his portrayals. Loy is the "good girl" heroine (albeit Blackie's onetime mistress) without ever becoming a cliché. Also notable in the cast is young Mickey Rooney, cast as Blackie as a child. The climax, in which Gable marches nobly to the electric chair, content knowing that his ex-girl Loy and old pal Powell face a lifetime of happiness together, gives the film a bitter-sweet sentimentality that interweaves nicely with the alternating toughness and romanticism of the storyline.

With ad copy reading "A lady with a past . . . torn between love and loyalty," **Manhattan Melodrama** debuted in May 1934.[1] Though many

---

[1]Shot on a twenty-four-day schedule, **Manhattan Melodrama** cost $355,000 and earned a $415,000 profit.

motion picture critics had wearied of the gangster formats by this time, the film received strong endorsements: the **New York World-Telegram** called the picture "a keen, adult exciting melodrama" and the **New York Evening Post** reported, "**Manhattan Melodrama**, if you leave out a couple of murders, is actually a love idyll, as tender as **Little Women**; a nostalgic adieu to the good old days of Al Capone and Arnold Rothstein." Though not nominated for any of the major awards, **Manhattan Melodrama** did receive an Oscar for Best Original Story. (Its formula of two young pals growing up on the opposite side of the law would emerge in many films—for example, James Cagney and Pat O'Brien in Warner Bros.' **Angels with Dirty Faces**, 1938.)

Noting the flair with which Powell and Loy volleyed their comic lines (HE: "I was born at home because I wanted to be near mother." SHE: "Nothing like a district attorney to keep a girl in shape. We must have a good wrestle some day."), MGM rushed Powell and Loy into **The Thin Man** (1934), Powell and Loy faced thirteen more screen unions after **Manhattan Melodrama**, and on September 9, 1940, reprised their **Manhattan Melodrama** characterizations on "Lux Radio Theatre," with Don Ameche in the Blackie Gallagher role.

MARIE ANTOINETTE
1938—160 min.

Producer, Hunt Stromberg; **directors**, W. S. Van Dyke II, and **uncredited**, Julien Duvivier; based on part of the book by Stefan Zweig; **screenplay**, Claudine West, Donald Ogden Stewart, Ernst Vajda and, uncredited, F. Scott Fitzgerald; **art directors**, Cedric Gibbons and William A. Horning; **set decorator**, Edwin B. Willis; **gowns**, Adrian; **men's costumes**, Gile Steele; **choreography**, Albertina Rasch; **music**, Herbert Stothart; **song**, Bob Wright, Chet Forrest, and Stothart; **sound**, Douglas Shearer; **montage**, Slavko Vorkapich; **camera**, William Daniels; **editor**, Robert J. Kern.

Norma Shearer (**Marie Antoinette**); Tyrone Power (**Count Azel de Fersen**); John Barrymore (**King Louis XV**); Gladys George (**Mme DuBarry**); Robert Morley (**King Louis XVI**); Anita Louise (**Princess de Lamballe**); Joseph Schildkraut (**Duke of Orleans**); Henry Stephenson (**Count Mercy**); Reginald Gardiner (**Artois**); Peter Bull (**Gamin, the Blacksmith**); Albert Dekker (**Provence**); Barnett Parker (**Prince de Rohan**); Joseph Calleia (**Drouet**); Cora Witherspoon (**Mme de Noailles**); Henry Kolker (**Court Aide**); Marilyn Knowlden (**Princess Theresa**); Ivan Simpson (**Sauce**); George Meeker (**Robespierre**); Scotty Beckett (**Dauphin**); Henry Daniell (**LaMotte**); Alma Kruger (**Empress Maria Theresa**); Leonard Penn (**Toulan**); George Zucco (**Governor of Conciergerie**); John Burton (**La Fayette**); Ian Wolfe (**Herbert, the Jailer**); Mae Busch (**Mme LaMotte**); Cecil Cunningham (**Mme DeLerchenfeld**); Ruth Hussey (**Mme Le Polignac**); Claude King (**Choisell**); Walter Walker (**Benjamin Franklin**); Barry Fitzgerald (**Peddler**); Rafaela Ottiano (**Louise**); Olaf Hytten (**Bit**).

SYNOPSIS
As is the custom in eighteenth-century Europe, the lovely Marie Antoinette of the Austrian House of Hapsburg is forced into marriage with France's Louis August, Dauphin of France where the wizened King Louis XV reigns. Marie finds her new husband to be clumsy, cloddish, insipid, and usually impotent. But he is also sincere, confessing on their wedding night that he too was forced into the marriage. He wins her sympathy, if not her love.

Marie is soon introduced to the myriad of court intrigues. The intricate politics are personified by the fickle fop, the Duke of Orleans, and by the bitchy gossip Madame DuBarry. Marie also meets Count Azel de Fersen. Soon they fall in love, entering a life of Parisian gaiety. Marie vows she will renounce the throne for the dashing count.

However, DuBarry has meanwhile convinced the king that Marie, since she is childless, should be banished for her follies. But before he can do so, Louis XV dies of smallpox and Marie finds herself the Queen of France. Impressed by the honor of the monarchy, she gives up her count and joins her husband in ruling France. She bears him two children and devotes her energies to being a good wife, mother, and monarch.

However, comes the revolution and despite Marie's magnanimity as she sacrifices wealth out of deference to the starving masses, the royal family become refugees. Disguising themselves as Russians, they begin a journey to Varennes. But the King errs while being questioned on the highway and the family is arrested. They are sentenced to the guillotine.

As Marie is driven to her decapitation, she finds bravery in the thought that she will be loved always by Count de Fersen, who listens miles away to the drums signaling the death of Queen Marie Antoinette. Just before the blade falls on her neck, Marie recalls her girlhood in Austria, and in a repeat of the film's initial scene, she is seen bubbling to her mother, the Empress Maria Theresa, "Just think, Mama. . . . I shall be a queen. I shall be Queen of France!"

* * *

"Those who have glimpsed the almost completed **Marie Antoinette** (Norma Shearer, Tyrone Power) are breathless with the anticipated thrill that brings back to audiences the First Lady of the Screen. . . . How fitting that America's Beloved First Star returns to millions of picturegoers in the role of the warm, vital young beauty who became queen of France in an era that shook the world.

So read the sprawling trade advertisement MGM planted in 1938. As most of the Culver City hierarchy was well aware, the words were lies. The long-nurtured dream project of Irving Thalberg, designed to ease Norma into graceful retirement, had after Thalberg's demise in 1936 become a gaudy backdrop against which Louis B. Mayer waged a vindictive campaign to devastate Mrs. Thalberg's screen career.

Of the many schemes hatched in the offices of Mayer and company, **Marie Antoinette** was one of the nastiest.

Since 1933 Thalberg had planned to produce **Marie Antoinette** as a magnificent spectacle of the French Revolution and a deluxe vehicle for Norma's patrician beauty and regal histrionics. There were many delays, not the least of which was Norma's pregnancy with daughter Katharine (born June 13, 1935). During this Thalberg went on to plan his other pet project for his wife, **Romeo and Juliet** (1936). **Marie Antoinette** remained on the studio schedule and appeared to hold such promise that, even after Thalberg's demise on September 14, 1936, Mayer retained the costly epic, though many expected him to scrap it.

Then came the problems. In the settling of Thalberg's more than four-million-dollar-estate, Shearer's lawyers noted contract stipulations which they insisted entitled Thalberg's widow and children to a large slice of profits then being reaped by Mayer and his cronies. The studio chief, long resentful of the industry glories heaped on Thalberg, ordered his attorney to battle this claim. The resulting fracas became so publicly unpleasant that Loew's president, Nicholas Schenck, intervened from New York City. Quite shocked by Mayer's attitude, and concluding that the studio was abusing Norma and "attempting to do her in," Schenck demanded that a liberal share of the profits in question go to Norma. He also advised the studio to award her a new contract. With a fresh six-picture agreement at $150,000 per film, Norma began the three months of costume fittings for the long-awaited **Marie Antoinette** (which had already gone through many costly script revisions).

It indeed appeared that MGM had only the best hopes for this mammoth costume epic. In a deal with Twentieth Century–Fox that would send Spencer Tracy to that studio for **Stanley and Livingstone** (1939), Metro obtained the screen services of Tyrone Power as Count Axel de Fersen. It was actually a subordinate role, rather than a costarring one, but the part was enlarged out of historical proportions in deference to Fox's new screen hero. A fast-declining John Barrymore rallied gloriously to play a marvelous King Louis XV; Robert Morley was imported from England for the part of King Louis XVI;[1] Anita Louise was borrowed from Warner Bros. to play the Princess de Lamballe;[2] and such colorful players as Gladys George (as the venomous Mme DuBarry), Joseph Schildkraut (as the beauty-marked dandy, the Duke of Orleans), and Henry Daniell (as LaMotte) joined the scores of supporting characters set against the sumptuous Cedric Gibbons sets and the props which studio set designer (and prop acquirer) Edwin B. Willis devoted three months collecting from the more exclusive Parisian antique shops. Adrian (women's costumes) and Gile Steele (men's costumes) outdid themselves in

---

[1] Thalberg had initially wanted Charles Laughton for King Louis XVI and Elsa Lanchester for Princess de Lamballe; they were unavailable after the delay occasioned by Shearer's pregnancy.

[2] Anita Louise had herself played Marie Antoinette in Warner Bros.' **Madame DuBarry** (1934). Maureen O'Sullivan was to play the princess in the MGM epic, but pregnancy intervened.

Mae Busch, Anita Louise, Olaf Hytten, and Norma Shearer in Marie Antoinette *('38).*

transforming expensive European laces and silks into bedazzling period garb. Choreographer Albertina Rasch used two hundred dancers for the ballroom scenes.

However, Mayer in the meantime had been festering over the Schenck decision, and Hollywood scuttlebutt had it that he was trying to sabotage the large-scale project. His aim was to scare Shearer into selling out her Loew's stock. In his memoirs, **Robert Morley: A Reluctant Autobiography** (1966), the British actor recalls:

How true the rumors were I have never been able to decide, but certainly Miss Shearer's director, Sidney Franklin, was taken off the picture almost the night before it was due to start, and the job was handed to W. S. Van Dyke with, it was alleged, a large sum to be paid to him for every day he was behind schedule. Franklin had worked on the picture for two years; Van Dyke had never seen the script before he started shooting and knew apparently nothing whatever about the French, or their revolution.

Van Dyke, noted for his "one-take" direction of such contemporary stories as **Manhattan Melodrama** (1934), **The Thin Man** (1934), and **They Gave Him a Gun** (1937), had also helmed several of Jeanette MacDonald's costumed musicals, including **Naughty Marietta** (1935), **Rose-Marie** (1936), and **San Francisco** (1936). So he was not entirely inappropriate for the assignment. Van Dyke did clash (as Mayer hoped) with Shearer. She stormed off the set one day, to much on-the-lot publicity, when Van Dyke refused to shoot another take of a particular scene (he had already shot four). The star soon returned to the soundstage, determined to make peace with Van Dyke. They soon were getting along splendidly.

But Norma still worked in an aura of animosity. This reached a peak when the crew laughed out loud when one day Norma tripped over a hoop in her costume dress and performed a perfect pratfall. She had no alternative but to laugh along with the others. To her credit Shearer (although it was later disclosed that the Mayer harassment almost plunged her into nervous exhaustion) never flared up publicly after that walk-off. She contented herself in trying moments with her love of the intricate costumes, even wearing a beloved gown and white wig to an "all-American" costume party hosted by her neighbors William Randolph Hearst and Marion Davies.[3]

The vagaries of the MGM film factory were not entirely directed toward Miss Shearer. Another "sufferer" in the production was Britisher Peter Bull who had been imported to California along with his friend Robert Morley. Upon arrival at the

---

[3]This visit to the Hearst party was of special significance. Thalberg and Hearst had battled so bitterly for the property of **Marie Antoinette** that Hearst's loss (along with the similar battle over **The Barretts of Wimpole Street**) caused his and Davies' exit from MGM.

Culver City lot, Bull, who was to play the French blacksmith Gamin, was advised that he must learn to speak the American dialect properly so he could portray the Frenchman. Bull would recall later that his instructor turned out to be a lady of Swedish extraction. In the initial first two months of production, Bull was only on call for two days of shooting. Eventually, when the revolutionary scenes at Versailles were to be shot, Bull reported to the enormous set to discover one of the extras dressed precisely as he was. He asked the extra what his role was to be and the latter told Bull that he was a stunt man and would do the "dangerous bits" for Bull. As it turned out Bull suffered a minor fracture and several abrasions from the on-camera foray. What happened to the stunt man he could not determine. Finally there was the scene in which Bull was to be stabbed in the back by Barry Fitzgerald (playing a French peddler). According to Bull, "I was given small bags of chocolate sauce to bite on at the crucial moment, so that it spurted attractively out of my trap." While this was occurring, one production worker was carting around a replica of the head of Anita Louise (who played Princess de Lamballe). According to Bull's recollection, it was a long time before he could deal with chocolate again. The ironic finale to Bull's six months of work on **Marie and Toilette** (a name Morley gave to the film) was that the bulk of his screen scenes were deleted and his MGM career never materialized.

Finally, after sixty-seven days of shooting, **Marie Antoinette** completed filming. MGM boasted to the public that the film cost $1.8 million, contained three star roles and 152 speaking parts, employed 500 yards of white satin in the costume department, etc. One of the more "daring" ad campaigns read, "Scandals of a glamorous queen! With escapades that rocked a nation, as an adventurous beauty seeks romance!"

The film had its world premiere on July 12, 1938, at Hollywood's Cathay Circle Theatre. Los Angeles radio stations KFI and KECA refused Metro's request to donate air time for this "historical event." The studio was asked to pay regular commercial rates. It did. The epic film made its East Coast bow on August 16, 1938, at the Astor Theatre where it was roadshown on a two-a-day performance schedule.

The **New York Times** reported:

The splendors of the French monarchy in its dying days have not simply been equaled, they have been surpassed by Metro-Goldwyn-Mayer's film biography. . . . Only Tyrone Power as the romantically rather farfetched Count Axel de Fersen is permitted to approach the luminous bounds of that divinity which hedges the Shearer throne, and he does so timidly, with due deference, and with the tender consciousness not so much of love as of second-billing in his eyes.

Howard Barnes (**New York Herald-Tribune**) endorsed,

The most sumptuous historical spectacle of the year. . . . A poignant portrayal by Norma

Shearer and the equally fine characterization of the doomed Louis by Robert Morley give eloquence and dramatic power to what might have been merely an elegant costume show.

Years later Lawrence J. Quirk offered his appraisal in **The Great Romantic Films** (1974):

Miss Shearer dominates the film throughout, not only because scriptwriters, director, and all concerned have focused on her but because her beauty and talent magnetize the attention. It takes a true star to shine amidst so much glittering splendor and mammoth production opulence; there is pageantry; there are revolutionary onslaughts, palace-stormings, court balls, crowded theatre scenes—in all of them the star is the centerpiece.

Both Norma Shearer (who reprised her Marie characterization in September 1938 on "The Maxwell House Coffee Radio Hour") and Robert Morley won Oscar nominations. She lost in the Best Actress category to Bette Davis for Warner Bros.' **Jezebel,** and he lost in the Best Supporting ranks to Walter Brennan of Twentieth Century-Fox's **Kentucky.** The film itself, with a rousing yet sensitive score by Herbert Stothart, choreography by Albertina Rasch, and carefully composed cinematography by William Daniels, placed fifth on **Film Daily's** Ten Best list of 1938. Although respectably popular at the box office, it failed to match the grosses earned by the studio's **Sweethearts, Boys Town, Test Pilot,** and **Rosalie.** It was an offering both too rich and rarefied to please general audiences and to earn back the cost of its expensive mounting.

Regarding the principals, Shearer continued to receive superstar treatment at the home lot. She would next choose Clark Gable as her second-billing leading man in **Idiot's Delight** (1939). But it was obvious to all after **Marie Antoinette** that her status was declining. As for Tyrone Power, Fox studio head Darryl F. Zanuck was so angered that his prize male lead received such second-rate showcasing in **Marie Antoinette** that he vowed never to loan out Power's screen services again. He held fast to this dictum for fifteen years.

MAYTIME
1937—132 min.

Producer, Hunt Stromberg; **director,** Robert Z. Leonard; based on the operetta by Rida Johnson Young and Sigmund Romberg; **screenplay,** Noel Langley; **music adapter—music director,** Herbert Stothart; **songs,** Romberg and Young; Stothart, Bob Wright, and Chet Forrest; Stothart; James A. Bland; Young, Cyrus Wood, and Romberg; **operetta adapted by** Wright and Forrest; **adapter of French libretto,** Gilles Guilbert; **vocal arranger,** Leo Arnaud; **opera sequences directed by** William Von Wymetal; **art directors,** Cedric Gibbons and Fredric Hope; **set decorator,** Edwin B. Willis; **gowns,** Adrian; **sound,** Douglas Shearer; **camera,** Oliver T. Marsh; **editor,** Conrad A. Nervig.

Jeanette MacDonald (**Marcia Mornay [Miss Morrison]**); Nelson Eddy (**Paul Allison**); John Barrymore (**Nicolai Nazaroff**); Herman Bing (**August Archipenko**); Tom Brown (**Kip Stuart**); Lynne Carver (**Barbara Roberts**); Rafaela Ottiano (**Ellen**); Charles Judels (**Cabby**); Paul Porcasi (**Composer Trentini**); Sig Rumann (**Fanchon**); Walter Kingsford (**Rudyard**); Edgar Norton (**Secretary**); Guy Bates Post (**Emperor Louis Napoleon**); Iphigenie Castiglioni (**Empress Eugenie**); Anna Demetrio (**Madame Fanchon**); Frank Puglia (**Orchestra Conductor**); Adia Kuznetzoff (**Czaritza's Minister—Student at Café**); Howard Hickman, Harry Hayden, Harry Davenport, and Robert C. Fischer (**Opera Directors**); Harlan Briggs (**Bearded Director**); Frank Sheridan (**O'Brien, a Director**); Billy Gilbert (**Drunk**); Ivan Lebedeff (**Empress's Dinner Companion**); Leonid Kinskey (**Student in Bar**); Don Cossack Chorus (**Singers**); Mariska Aldrich (**Opera Singer**); Alexander Schoenberg (**French Proprietor**); Henry Roquemore (**Publicity Man**); Russell Hicks (**Bulliet, the Voice Coach**).

SYNOPSIS

The elderly Miss Morrison attends an American May Day celebration in 1906. She meets Kip Stuart and learns that his fiancée Barbara Roberts yearns for a singing career in New York.

Later the elusive Miss Morrison speaks with the girl and confides that she is the once famous opera diva Marcia Mornay. The older woman relates how she became a star in 1865 under the training of Nicolai Nazaroff, during the days of Louis Napoleon's French reign. Marcia feels utmost respect and gratitude to her exacting mentor and accepts his proposal of marriage.

A short time before the nuptials, she encounters Paul Allison, an American singer enjoying the Bohemian life in Paris. They soon fall in love, but Marcia feels bound by her vows to wed Nazaroff. The young lovers sadly part and the wedding takes place.

Years later in New York Marcia and Paul are thrown together when he is chosen to sing opposite her at the Metropolitan Opera. Their emotion-charged love duet reconfirms their undying love and they vow never to part again. Nazaroff, maddened by the thought of losing the woman he loves so dearly, goes to Paul's quarters and shoots him.

The story fades back to the present as Kip joins Barbara and Miss Morrison. The young lovers agree to remain together. In the final scene the spirit of Marcia Mornay rises from the aged frame of Miss Morrison and meets the spirit of Paul singing to her from the garden gate. Marcia drifts toward him and they join in singing "Sweetheart (Will You Remember?)."

* * *

In the year 1937, Metro-Goldwyn-Mayer offered audiences a wide range of impressive and enticing motion pictures. There were **The Good Earth,** the sprawling adaptation of Pearl Buck's novel starring the heralded Paul Muni and Luise Rainer; **Captains Courageous,** a stirring adventure true to the spirit of Rudyard Kipling and sparked by Spencer Tracy's Oscar-winning perfor-

Nelson Eddy and Jeanette MacDonald in Maytime *('37).*

mance; **Saratoga,** an all-star yarn which offered the public its last look at the irreplaceable, glorious Jean Harlow; and **Rosalie,** the gaudy songfest with the dancing legs of Eleanor Powell, the operatic voices of Nelson Eddy and Ilona Massey, and the music of Cole Porter. However, the studio's greatest moneymaker of the year—indeed, the greatest worldwide money earner of 1937—was **Maytime.** It was the third screen union of Jeanette MacDonald and Nelson Eddy and a beautifully produced, brilliantly creative, $1.5 million production. It so enchanted audiences over the decades that it is still specially televised every May Day in many U.S. cities.

Based on the 1917 Sigmund Romberg operetta **Maytime,** with book and lyrics by Rida Johnson Young, the story had first reached the screen as a silent feature, released by B. P. Schulberg's Preferred Pictures in 1923. When MGM first announced plans to produce the picture—on the heels of the MacDonald-Eddy hits **Naughty Marietta** (1935) and **Rose-Marie** (1936)—Irving Thalberg was to produce the venture personally. Edmund Goulding was set to direct and the Technicolor production was to costar Paul Lukas and Frank Morgan. However, filming was interrupted by Thalberg's death on September 14, 1936. Along with that of other Thalberg-supervised films **(The Good Earth, Camille,** and **A Day at the Races), Maytime**'s production temporarily collapsed.

When filming resumed, Hunt Stromberg was in charge and Robert Z. Leonard (of **The Great Ziegfeld,** 1936) occupied the vacancy left by

Goulding. The Technicolor footage from **Maytime** was scrapped, including a ten-minute vignette of MacDonald and Eddy performing from **Tosca,** as well as "Farewell to Dream" (which the artists would record for RCA). Morgan and Lukas, with other acting obligations to fulfil, left the production and Herman Bing replaced Morgan while no less than John Barrymore filled Lukas' vacancy. With an estimated loss of $500,000 on the original color version, Leonard embarked on completing the film with a brisk lushness. Plot changes were instituted at Louis B. Mayer's orders. In the new scenario MacDonald and Eddy do not wed. They endure the more tragic fate of being unfulfilled lovers who remain young eternally and together always. In the original format, much of the storyline had taken place in America.

In **Gotta Sing, Gotta Dance** (1970) John Kobal writes:

All the resources of the world's most powerful film studio were lavished on the film. The "Empress Eugenie" dresses, designed by Adrian, almost move themselves; Cedric Gibbons' reconstruction of the last days of the Third Empire, requiring ballrooms, period apartments, Parisian Bohemian quarters, and then the early American small town at the turn of the century, are uniformly superlative. Sydney Guilaroff designed the magnificent hairstyles, William Daniels' photography glows.

There is a wide variety of musical offerings within the tear-drenched feature. Eddy sings the "Students' Drinking Song," harmonizing with the

tavern group; he and MacDonald render "Carry Me Back to Ole Virginny" and later the two perform "Sweetheart (Will You Remember?)." The last number is executed in a fabulously romantic setting of St. Cloud's May Day country fair. As Eddy gently pushes MacDonald to and fro in a lofty swing, their love is confirmed. They wander amidst the crowd and later, at sunset, find a quiet forest area where they sing the song which would become their trademark number.

Not wishing to miss an opportunity to present MacDonald in operatic numbers, Metro smartly wove an array of numbers into the story. At the palace reception for Louis Napoleon she performs for the French ruler. Later at the opera house she is seen and heard rendering a selection on stage while in the attentive on-camera audience Eddy and Bing are being ejected from their wrongfully gained front seats. After MacDonald and Eddy go their separate paths, she pursues her vocal career, which is highlighted in a montage of operatic arias. But the selections from Bizet's **Les Filles de Cadiz** and Meyerbeer's **Les Huguenots** are only a warm-up for the impressive **Czaritza** segment. (This "shadow opera" was especially created for **Maytime** by Herbert Stothart and was based on Tchaikovsky's Symphony No. 5.)

Most critics were totally susceptible to **Maytime**'s romantic and musical charms. Bland Johaneson **(New York Daily Mirror)** wrote, "Abandoning the mood of light frivolity which pervaded their previous hits, **Maytime** is a perfect romance, a little sad, greatly charming and tender." Eileen Creelman **(New York Sun):** "**Maytime** is a real joy, a picture which does Jeanette MacDonald honor and which she in turn graces each moment she appears on the screen." Frank S. Nugent, **New York Times:** "The screen can do no wrong while these two are singing: when, in addition, it places a splendid production behind them, the result approaches perfection."

There would be five more screen teamings of MacDonald and Eddy: **The Girl of the Golden West** (1938), **Sweethearts** (1938), **New Moon** (1940), **Bitter Sweet** (1940), and **I Married an Angel** (1942). None of these entries would reach the creative peak attained in **Maytime,** or be as big at the box office. On September 4, 1944, MacDonald and Eddy would reprise **Maytime** on "Lux Radio Theatre." Once again audiences were wooed by the special chemistry of the operetta team and by the lilting magic of the story.

MEET ME IN ST. LOUIS
1944 C—113 min.

Producer, Arthur Freed; **director,** Vincente Minnelli; based on the book by Sally Benson; **screenplay,** Irving Brecher, Fred Finklehoffe, and uncredited: Benson, Doris Gilbert, Sarah Y. Mason, Victor Heerman, and William Ludwig; **Technicolor consultants,** Natalie Kalmus and Henri Jaffa; **music adapter,** Roger Edens; **music directors,** George Stoll and Lennie Hayton; **orchestrator,** Conrad Salinger; **choreography,** Charles Walters; **songs,**

Hugh Martin and Ralph Blane; **art directors**, Cedric Gibbons, Lemuel Ayers, and Jack Martin Smith; **set decorators**, Edwin B. Willis and Paul Huldschinsky; **costume supervisor**, Irene; **costumes**, Irene Sharaff; **makeup**, Jack Dawn; **sound**, Douglas Shearer; **camera**, George Folsey; **editor**, Albert Akst.

Judy Garland (**Esther Smith**); Margaret O'Brien (**Tootie Smith**); Mary Astor (**Mrs. Anne Smith**); Lucille Bremer (**Rose Smith**); June Lockhart (**Lucille Ballard**); Tom Drake (**John Truett**); Marjorie Main (**Katie, the Maid**); Harry Davenport (**Grandpa**); Leon Ames (**Mr. Alonzo Smith**); Henry Daniels, Jr. (**Lon Smith, Jr.**); Joan Carroll (**Agnes Smith**); Hugh Marlowe (**Colonel Darly**); Robert Sully (**Warren Sheffield**); Chill Wills (**Mr. Neely**); Donald Curtis (**Dr. Terry**); Mary Jo Ellis (**Ida Boothby**); Robert Emmet O'Connor (**Motorman**); Darryl Hickman (**Johnny Tevis**); Leonard Walker (**Conductor**); Victor Kilian (**Baggage Man**); John Phipps (**Mailman**); Mayo Newhall (**Mr. Braukoff**); Major Sam Harris (**Mr. March**); Sidney Barnes (**Hugo Borvis**); Myron Tobias (**George**); Kenneth Donner (**Clinton Badger**); Helen Gilbert (**Girl on Trolley**).

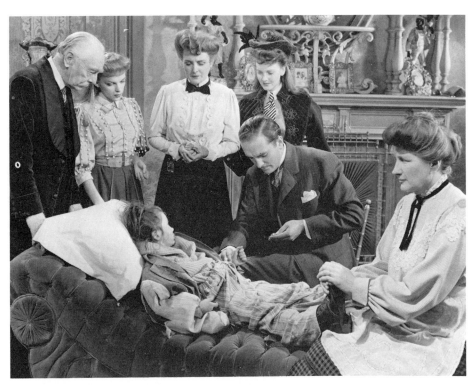

Harry Davenport, Judy Garland, Margaret O'Brien (on bed), Mary Astor, Donald Curtis, Lucille Bremer, and Marjorie Main in Meet me in St. Louis ('44).

SYNOPSIS

In turn-of-the-century St. Louis the Smith family of 5135 Kensington Avenue consists of Alonzo Smith, an attorney, his wife Anna, Grandpa, and the Smiths' five children: Alonzo ("Lon") Jr., Rose, Esther, Agnes, and little Tootie. Very much a part of the household is Katie the maid, who keeps everything and everyone pretty much in order.

Romance is the focal point of the older Smith children. Rose has a suitor away at school but still persistent in his courtship of her, and an older beau at home; Lon has a local belle at his beck and call; and Esther finds love in her new next-door neighbor, John Truett. As for Tootie, the youngest Smith offspring, she lives in a world of fantasy and fun, riding with Mr. Neely the iceman on his wagon, cavorting on Halloween when other youngsters laud her bravery, and even, on occasion, telling fibs that create misunderstandings among her elders.

When Mr. Smith announces he has a good business opportunity if he relocates himself and the family to New York City, the Smiths are downcast. Especially saddened is Tootie, who vents her frustrations and fear by smashing her beloved snowmen in the backyard. Finally, Mr. Smith realizes his family's contentment is more essential that a career promotion. He decides they will remain in St. Louis.

Happy again, the Smiths visit the World's Fair in a St. Louis suburb. All agree right then and there that it is the best city in America in which to live.

* * *

The romantic adventures of the Smith family of 5135 Kensington Avenue, from summer 1903 to spring 1904, are the charming basis of one of MGM's most memorable classics—**Meet Me in St. Louis.**

The nostalgic musical was based on Sally Benson's **The Kensington Stories.** Eight of the stories were published in the **New Yorker** magazine in 1941–42. Scripter Fred Finklehoffe had brought the beguiling if wispy tales to the attention of producer Arthur Freed, who in turn submitted the idea to Louis B. Mayer's story advisers, Lillie Messinger and Harriet Frank. And they in turn (observing, of course, the pecking order) presented the project in verbal form to Mayer. He was captivated by the there's-no-place-like-home aspect of the vehicle and outvoted those studio associates who thought the packaged concept lacked commercial viability.

As with most films, the genesis of **Meet Me in St. Louis** had many twists and turns. Freed assigned Finklehoffe to prepare a scenario in collaboration with Irving Brecher. (The two were then involved in **Anchors Aweigh**, 1945, and had to abandon that task.) Along the way several individuals contributed to the burgeoning scenario. When it was presented to Freed, his concept for the production changed. He now wanted to convey much of the plot line through song, dance, and music. When Freed reapproached Mayer, he outlined his expanding plan. The shrewd mogul approved the change of scheme, and the budget for the feature was increased drastically.

At the beginning the **Andy Hardy** Carvel Street set was to be the basis for **Meet Me in St. Louis**, but Mayer now agreed to a new slant. Freed was convinced that he required the talents of Lemuel Ayers, who had just designed the sets for the Broadway hit **Oklahoma!** Ayers joined the task force.

Judy Garland was the first choice of producer Arthur Freed and director George Cukor for the part of Esther Smith. But she was the lot's greatest star at the time and some forces at the studio feared it would be a career error to have her revert to being a teenage girl on screen. When Cukor had to leave the production to enter military service, replacement Vincente Minnelli continued the hearty fight to get Garland, and the opposition finally acquiesced. The rest of the cast was plucked principally from the expansive contract list: tot Margaret O'Brien as sister Tootie, Mary Astor as Mother,[1] Leon Ames as Father, Lucille Bremer (in her film debut) as sister Rose, Joan Carroll as sister Agnes, Henry Daniels, Jr. as Lon Jr., Harry Davenport as the grandfather, and Marjorie Main as the maid Katie. Initially cast as John Truett, the "Boy Next Door," was Van Johnson; he was later replaced by contract juvenile Tom Drake.

Meanwhile, the "St. Louis" street, marked by its American gothic homes with their gabled roofs, intricate bay windows, gingerbread decorations, and spreading lawns, was constructed. The major interior set, the Smith home, was constructed by Minnelli's wishes as a continuous set of rooms, rather than segmented in parts about the soundstage. The cost for the film's settings rose to over $208,000, an amount that staggered many MGM executives. (However, the St. Louis

[1]Astor had played Garland's mother in MGM's **Listen, Darling** (1938).

street set would prove a good investment, being utilized by Metro and other studios in the years to come.) Irene Sharaff then began coordinating her period costumes to blend with the (expensive) decor.

The score for **Meet Me in St. Louis** was entrusted to Hugh Martin and Ralph Blane, who had done Freed's **Best Foot Forward** (1943). For Garland they composed "The Boy Next Door," "Have Yourself a Merry Little Christmas," and "The Trolley Song." The first was a wistful love ballad, the second a poignant, bittersweet yuletide tune, made more memorable by its **mise-en-scène.** (The distraught six-year-old O'Brien realizes this is her last Christmas in St. Louis and nothing consoles her until her older sister, Garland, comes to comfort her with this near lullaby.) Ironically, Blane and Martin had not wanted to write a song about a trolley, but rather a song to be sung on such a vehicle. However, Freed pressured them to try and try and try again, until they came up with this rousing number, a tune which would become one of Garland's trademark songs. "Skip to My Lou" was (re)arranged by Martin and Blane and choreographed by Charles Walters for the Smiths' parlor party. This is followed by the cane-and-straw-hat strut by Garland and O'Brien to "Under the Bamboo Tree." From the Arthur Freed–Nacio Herb Brown repertoire, "You and I" was picked for Astor and Ames to "sing"; Freed dubbed the vocal for Ames and D. Markas for Astor. Obviously there was no question about using "Meet Me in St. Louis" (by Andrew B. Sterling and Kerry Mills), which was craftily woven into the proceedings with various members of the Smith household offering bits of the lyrics. One song that audiences did not see performed was "Boys and Girls Like You and Me" by Richard Rodgers and Oscar Hammerstein II. That selection had been originally written for the stage version of **Oklahoma!** but was deleted and later sold to Freed. It was shot at the World's Fair site with Garland being carried across a mud puddle by Drake. Later Freed decided it slowed down the mood of the picture too much, so it was discarded.

If minute attention was paid to each detail of the film, tremendous patience had to be exercised toward certain members of the cast. The players suffered from more than a normal rash of ailments. In the course of filming, Harry Davenport was bedded with a virus infection, Joan Carroll underwent an emergency appendectomy, Astor suffered from a bout of sinusitis, and Garland and O'Brien proved near impossible. Margaret's demanding mother would rush her actress daughter off the soundstage at the last moment—without warning—for a variety of (real) reasons: her child needed braces, her child was suffering from hay fever, her child needed a vacation (in the midst of the expensive shooting schedule), etc. As Mary Astor later recalled in her memoirs **A Life on Film** (1971), "Margaret O'Brien was at her most appealing (I might say 'appalling') age. . . . She was a quiet, almost too well behaved child, when her mother was on the set. When Mother was absent, it was another story and she was a pain in the neck."

Minnelli later recalled an incident involving the problematic O'Brien:

When Margaret O'Brien was very tiny and young her aunt and her mother used to prepare her for scenes. I never could find out what they said, but they would talk in her ear and whisper to her and she would listen with her eyes out on sticks and then she would go in and cry and get hysterical and do the scene. . . . One night when we were out on the back lot doing the scene in the backyard where she hysterically breaks up all the snowmen and cries and yells and screams and so forth, her mother came over to me and said, "Margaret and I have had a disagreement and she won't speak to me. And she wants **you** to prepare her." And I said, "My God, how do you do that?" She said, "Well, she has a little dog that she adores and you tell her that somebody is going to kidnap that dog and kill it." Well, I had to go over because she was waiting. It was very cold, and she was waiting with a blanket around her shoulders and I said, "Margaret, I hate to tell you this, but somebody is going to kidnap your little dog and shoot it, you know." And she said, "Will there be lots of blood?" And I went on and elaborated—and finally I said, "Turn 'em" and jerked the blanket off her and she went out there and did this hysterical scene all in one take. But I went home feeling like a dog. I never want to go through that again!

The crux of the shooting problems was Garland. She began the film with little enthusiasm for the low-keyed storyline or her central role. She took delight in mimicking the perfectionist director and in mocking her "sticky" dialogue. Her ailments—real and imaginary—played havoc with the schedule. She suffered from dental problems, from insomnia, and from bad management of her off-camera time. (Near the start of filming she was dating coplayer Drake. He recalled a few occasions when he escorted her home late at night. The next day Garland would either be tardy or not show at all for work.)

In **A Life on Film** Astor remembers losing her patience over Judy's emotional outbursts and her sudden decisions to seclude herself in her soundstage trailer:

I walked into her portable dressing room one tense morning, and she greeted me with her usual cheery, "Hi, Mom!" I sat down on the couch while she went on primping, and said, "Judy, what the hell's happened to you? You were a trouper—once." She stared at me. I went on, "You have kept the entire company out there waiting for two hours. Waiting for you to favor us with your presence. You know we're stuck—there's nothing we can do without you at the moment."

She giggled and said, "Yeah, that's what everybody's been telling me."

That bugged me and I said, "Well, then, either get the hell out on the set or **I'm** going home."

She grabbed me by the hand and her face crumpled up. "I don't **sleep,** Mom!"

And I said, "Well, go to bed earlier then—like we all have to do.

To Astor's credit, she would later admit she should have been more cognizant of the tremendous scope of Garland's problems and should have tried to refrain from her own outburst.

On the plus side, while the film musical was painfully taking shape, Garland was evolving a rapport with director Minnelli. Once she began to accept and understand his painstaking approach to filmmaking, they got along well during shooting; in fact, they began dating. Before the production was completed—and to the amazement of many, who thought the two personalities too contrasting and too conflicting—Judy and Minnelli were sharing living quarters.

Finally, on April 7, 1944, four months after filming began, **Meet Me In St. Louis** was completed. It was not released until December 31, 1944, after assorted front office debates as to whether the expensively mounted Halloween sequence should be cut from the picture. Fortunately the memorable segment, so central to the film's theme, remained intact. The critics were ecstatic about the color musical. Archer Winsten, **New York Post:** "At last MGM has gotten around to doing a musical memory book at once rich, tasteful, and a delight to experience. . . . The nicest part about it is that you feel the characters, not as quaint, costumed figures out of a past being commercialized for the easy laugh, but rather as people actually existing in those days." **Cue** magazine: "This brilliant Technicolored combination of **Life with Father** and **I Remember Mama** sparkles with tiny drama or chuckling comedy or screamingly funny farce." **Variety: "Meet Me in St. Louis** is the answer to any exhibitor's prayer. Perhaps accented in these days as ideal 'escapist' fare, it would be surefire in any period. It holds everything for the film fan."

Meet Me in St. Louis placed seventh on the National Board of Review's Ten Best Pictures list, won the "Outstanding Child Actress of 1944" Academy Award statuette for Margaret O'Brien, and grossed over $7.56 million in its initial release (on a cost of $1,707,561.14). The film has become one of the most beloved movies to emerge from Hollywood and has long been regarded as a special phenomenon to Judy Garland worshippers. Scenes from the film classic were featured in both **That's Entertainment!** (1974: "The Trolley Song") and **That's Entertainment: Part II** (1976: "Have Yourself a Merry Little Christmas"). As John T. McManus of **PM** prophetically wrote in his review of 1944, "If the archive keepers of film know their business, **Meet Me in St. Louis** should be in for a spell of immortality, too, as a technically excellent, warmly presented and charmingly produced item of musical Americana."

On April 26, 1959, CBS-TV offered a video version of **Meet Me in St. Louis,** using the musical score from the film. The cast included Jane Powell, Jeanne Crain, Tab Hunter, Walter Pidgeon, Myrna Loy, Patty Duke, and Ed Wynn. A stage adaptation of the motion picture, using additional songs composed by Hugh Martin and Ralph Blane, premiered at the St. Louis Municipal Opera on June 9, 1960.

THE MERRY WIDOW
1934—99 min. (TV title: THE LADY DANCES)

Producer, Irving Thalberg; **director,** Ernst Lubitsch; based on operetta **Die Lustique Witwe** by Franz Lehār, Victor Leon, and Leo Stein; **screenplay,** Samson Raphaelson and Ernst Vajda; **art directors,** Cedric Gibbons and Frederic Hope; **set decorator,** Edwin B. Willis; **gowns,** Adrian; **costumes,** Ali Hubert; **new lyrics,** Lorenz Hart and Gus Kahn; **music adapter,** Herbert Stothart; **choreography,** Albertina Rasch; **sound,** Douglas Shearer; **camera,** Oliver T. Marsh; **editor,** Frances March.

Maurice Chevalier (**Danilo**); Jeanette MacDonald (**Sonia**); Edward Everett Horton (**Ambassador Popoff**); Una Merkel (**Queen Dolores**); George Barbier (**King Achmed**); Minna Gombell (**Marcelle**); Ruth Channing (**Lulu**); Sterling Holloway (**Mischka**); Henry Armetta (**Turk**); Barbara Leonard (**Maid**); Donald Meek (**Valet**); Akim Tamiroff (**Maxim's Manager**); Herman Bing (**Zizipoff**); Lucien Prival (**Adamovitch**); Luana Walters, Sheila Mannors, Caryl Lincoln, Edna Waldron, and Lona Andre (**Sonia's Maids**); Patricia Farley, Shirley Chambers, Maria Troubetskoy, Eleanor Hunt, Jean Hart, Dorothy Wilson, Barbara Barondess, Dorothy Granger, Jill Dennett, Mary Jane Halsey, Peggy Watts, Dorothy Dehn, and Connie Lamont (**Maxim Girls**); Charles Requa, George Lewis, Tyler Brooke, John Merkyl, and Cosmo Kyrle Bellew (**Escorts**); Roger Gray, Christian Frank, Otto Fries, George Magrill, and John Roach (**Policemen**); Katherine Burke (**Prisoner**); Leonid Kinskey (**Shepherd**); George Baxter (**Ambassador**); Perry Ivins and Gino Corrado (**Waiters**); Paul Ellis (**Dancer**).

Jeanette MacDonald and Maurice Chevalier in The Merry Widow *('34).*

SYNOPSIS
When the attractive widow Sonia leaves the kingdom of Marshovia to reside in Paris, the king of the country is deeply disturbed. It seems she controls some fifty-two percent of Marshovia's wealth and the country's continued financial solvency depends largely on her spending her money there.

As punishment to playboy Prince Danilo (who was discovered in the queen's chambers), the king orders him to Paris. His mission is to woo Sonia and to see to it that she returns to Marshovia. If he fails, he will be court-martialed. In Paris Danilo finds Sonia at Maxim's, where the charming woman is masquerading as one of the bubbly cabaret girls. Although the two dance together and he falls prey to her beauty, neither is aware of the other's identity. Later they meet at an embassy ball in Marshovia. Sonia learns who Danilo is and what his mission in Paris is all about.

When she threatens to leave the country for-

ever, Danilo is court-martialed. She testifies at his trial, admitting that he did do everything in his power to woo her. However, he is convicted and put in jail. Later Sonia is persuaded to visit him in his cell and the king orders the guard not to allow her out until she agrees to wed him.

* * *

"That madman is making a filthy picture! All this business of a dirty old man kissing girls' feet and drooling over a closet of women's shoes! It's repulsive!" wailed star Mae Murray (of the beesting lips) to Irving Thalberg. The object of her scorn was filmmaker Erich von Stroheim, who was transforming the 1905 operetta **The Merry Widow** into a perverse study of the "decadence of Euro-

pean aristocracy"—and into one of the great classics of the MGM silent era.[1] The film (in which Clark Gable was an extra) was released in 1925 and proved a triumph for Murray, John Gilbert (overpoweringly dashing as Prince Danilo), and "the dirty Hun" (as Mae dubbed von Stroheim).[2] The title became a part of the Metro legend.

---

[1]There had been a 1912 two-reeler of **The Merry Widow** starring Alma Rubens and Wallace Reid.

[2]Von Stroheim soon left MGM. One day in Louis B. Mayer's office, arguing with the potentate about the sensuality of **The Merry Widow,** von Stroheim insisted, "All women are whores." When the Teutonic artist told

Nevertheless, Thalberg was never pleased with—in fact, he was somewhat offended by—the Freudian implications and fetishism of the opulent photoplay. He delighted in the prospect of creating a sound remake, exploiting the music and the charm of the beloved Lehar music.

Prime in Thalberg's mind for the part of Prince Danilo was Maurice Chevalier. The producer had admired the charming Frenchman ever since he and Norma Shearer had enjoyed him performing at the Casino de Paris during their European honeymoon. At that time (1927) Thalberg had screentested Chevalier, giving the footage to Chevalier after they failed to agree on contractual terms. Chevalier utilized the audition to win himself a contract at Paramount. After a string of romantic musicals (1929–34) for that company, Chevalier was contemplating a return to Paris. At this juncture Thalberg contacted him again, offering a plump financial pact. Chevalier accepted, and Ernst Lubitsch, who had directed several of the Frenchman's Paramount features, was signed to direct.

The search for a Sonia was more difficult. Joan Crawford pleaded with Louis B. Mayer for the part, but to no avail. Vivienne Segal and Lily Pons were considered, but Chevalier wanted Grace Moore, who had starred in MGM's **A Lady's Morals** and **New Moon,** both 1930 releases. The Metropolitan opera star had vacated MGM when her weight swelled over the 135-pound limit her contract stipulated; now Thalberg feared a repeat problem. Lubitsch finally vetoed her chances, finding her unsuitable. (She even offered to play the part for nothing, but to no avail. Meanwhile, she appeared in **One Night of Love,** 1934, at Columbia, and made a big splash with the public.)

Jeanette MacDonald, after a stay at Paramount, had just debuted at Metro in **The Cat and the Fiddle.** She was Lubitsch's choice for the aristocratic coquette. Thalberg approved, and she was appointed to the leading part. The decision was made over the objections of Chevalier, who had not hit it off well with Jeanette during their tandem Paramount films.

Literally dozens of melodies and several songs[3] crammed **The Merry Widow,** with arranger Herbert Stothart performing a leviathan task in welding all into a cohesive whole. Reviews varied. Thornton Delehanty **(New York Evening Post):** "The giddily romantic love story . . . has become, under Mr. Lubitsch's direction, a blithesome and cynical prank." Eileen Creehan **(New York Sun):** "Whatever it may have been in its heyday, **The Merry Widow** is now a frothy little farce, sumptuously costumed, elaborately set, and extremely uneven as entertainment. . . . It is as a comedy that Ernst Lubitsch has chosen to direct this celebrated old operetta." The British **Daily Film**

Mayer he would include his own mother in that generalization, Mayer, aghast, punched von Stroheim in the face and bodily tossed him out of the office. Von Stroheim later returned to the lot to join Greta Garbo in **As You Desire Me** (1932).

[3]The songs were: "Velia," "Maxim's," "Girls, Girls, Girls," and "The Merry Widow Waltz."

Fernando Lamas and Lana Turner in The Merry Widow *('52).*

Renter: "Albertina Rasch's ballet girls give the can-can, while the famous waltz is beautifully executed by a large crowd of dancers reflected in mammoth mirrors."

An expensive ($1,605,000) and perilously opulent production,[4] **The Merry Widow** did not prove a box-office success.[5] Business was particularly bad in the rural areas, where it was deemed too sophisticated and rich an offering. The film lost $113,000. **The Merry Widow** won only one Oscar: Best Interior Decoration, for Cedric Gibbons and Frederic Hope. Still, the film was worthwhile from Thalberg's point of view as an experiment in cinema elegance. John Baxter, in **Hollywood in the Thirties** (1968), examines the overall results:

Of all Lubitsch's operetta adaptations, **The Merry Widow** (1934) is the best. The film was made for Metro, but has all the Paramount polish, despite the problems Lubitsch had in getting Cedric Gibbons to fall in with his extravagant demands in the matter of sets. People

---

[4]Lubitsch made simultaneously a French-language version of **The Merry Widow,** with Chevalier and MacDonald in the lead roles.

[5]The film industry trade journal **Harrison's Reports** published, "When one remembers the fire and dash John Gilbert put into the part of the Prince, one's heart feels broken to see the 'butchering' that has been done by Mr. Chevalier. Aside from the fact that he has clowned the part, and that he lacks the dash and the gallantry that the Prince's part requires, he has a facial defect which, added to his poor enunciation, would prove sufficient to rob the picture of its dramatic intensity."

criticized Metro for allowing Lubitsch to change a frothy romance into a satire on the ludicrousness of sex, but the combination of disenchanted dialogue and the lush Lehar music (with lyrics by Rodgers, Hart and Kahn) gives this film a formal tension lacking in his earlier efforts. Chevalier plays the rake Danilo with style and charm, while MacDonald as the widow is at the height of her opulent pre-Raphaelite beauty. Her songs, especially "Velia," shot by the brilliant Oliver Marsh from a low angle, showing her spotted high on a balcony while in the foreground gypsy musicians play in half silhouette, are imaginatively directed, and her appearance in the film is, on balance, probably the peak of her career.

As for Chevalier, he soon departed MGM after this solo effort. Thalberg's desire to team him with Grace Moore in a film collapsed when Chevalier balked at Grace Moore receiving top billing (a demand issued by Columbia's Harry Cohn where Moore was under contract). Chevalier deserted Hollywood, not to return to MGM until **Gigi** (1958).

In 1952 MGM remade **The Merry Widow,** altering the storyline to fit the new leading players: Lana Turner (Crystal Radek); Fernando Lamas (Count Danilo); Una Merkel (this time playing Kitty Riley); Richard Haydn (Baron Popoff); and Thomas Gomez (King of Marshovia). It was produced by Joe Pasternak and directed by Curtis Bernhardt. The color production boasted Paul Francis Webster's new lyrics added to the Lehar music, and sets by Cedric Gibbons.

In **Lana Turner** (1976), Jeanine Basinger would write:

Turner and Lamas embody the ultimate in physical beauty à la Hollywood. She is stunning in Technicolor, and he, especially in tight pants, is the perfect Latin lover; not **too** oily and not **too** pretty, but handsome enough and smooth enough to fit the role of dream-prince. Although as a pair they lacked the humorous self-awareness of MacDonald and Chevalier, Turner and Lamas made the characters their own. By shifting the emphasis of the story, they created a sense of passion and frustrated love, which is what their version of the old property is all about. The casting of Lamas best illustrates this difference between the 1952 **Merry Widow** and the Lubitsch film; it is more Latin than French. It is therefore no less beautiful, but just a trifle less amusing, less sophisticated. To compensate, it has its own charms. . . .

Although some people feel Lana Turner's version of **The Merry Widow** is more fizzle than fizz, in terms of beauty of production, it is excellent. Visions of the dancers at Maxim's, gorgeous in scarlet and brilliant black . . . and the pink, white, and gold of the waltzers in a spectacular final number, linger in a viewer's memory.

The 1952 version, in which Trudy Erwin dubbed Lana Turner's singing, was only a modest hit. In the 1970s Ingmar Bergman announced that he was to direct a new version of **The Merry Widow** and that Barbra Streisand would star. The European-based project was abandoned later on.

Bobby); Vernon Downing **(Newspaper Man)**; Creighton Hale **(Husband)**; Tiny Kelly and Pat Flaherty **(Cops)**; Paul Bradley **(Defense Attorney)**; Gail Bonney **(Woman)**.

SYNOPSIS

In 1892 Australia, ten-year-old Annette Kellerman, the crippled daughter of music teacher Frederick Kellerman, regains the use of her legs by swimming. In the years that follow she becomes a champion swimmer and blossoms into a beautiful young woman.

Financial reverses compel Mr. Kellerman to accept a post at a London conservatory of music. Annette accompanies him, planning to study ballet dancing. Aboard ship they become acquainted with James Sullivan and Doc Cronnel, owners of a boxing kangaroo. Knowing of Annette's swimming prowess, Sullivan offers to manage her, but Mr. Kellerman frowns on professional swimming.

In London the Kellermans are disappointed when he learns there is no conservatory job for him and Annette is unable to obtain a dancing part. She then agrees to swim twenty-six miles down the Thames River as an exploitation stunt for Sullivan's kangaroo show. Her remarkable feat wins nationwide publicity and Sullivan persuades her to go to New York. He is confident he can book her into huge Hippodrome Theatre.

When Alfred Harper, the theatre's manager, is unable to use the act, Sullivan takes her to Boston for another marathon swim. There he engineers her arrest for appearing on the beach in a daring one-piece bathing suit. The judge acquits her of the charge of indecent exposure and the attendant publicity enables Sullivan to build her up as a sensational box-office attraction.

Meanwhile, Annette and Sullivan have fallen in love, but they part after a disagreement. He leaves to promote a flying daredevil while Annette soars to new heights as the star of a Hippodrome water ballet. In due time she accepts the marriage proposal of Alfred Harper but defers the wedding day until after she completes a Hollywood film. On the last day of shooting she is injured severely when the glass on the water tank bursts. Both Sullivan and Harper visit her at the hospital. When the latter realizes that she loves the promoter, he bows out of the situation gracefully.

* * *

When audiences cheered MGM's **That's Entertainment!** in 1974, few film clips won greater response than the magnificently gaudy, Busby Berkeley–directed water ballet of flames and hoops, torches and nymphets, and, of course, Esther Williams, from **Million Dollar Mermaid.** Of all of Esther's twenty-five Metro movies, this grand vehicle is perhaps the most fondly remembered and the most successful of all her cinema plunges.

Produced—lavishly—by producer Arthur Hornblow, Jr., **Million Dollar Mermaid** was directed by expert Mervyn LeRoy. In his memoirs **Take One** (1974), he recalls the front office thinking that led to this screen biography of Australian swim star Annette Kellerman:

There was a problem with what to do with a

MILLION DOLLAR MERMAID

1952 C—115 min. (British release title: THE ONE-PIECE BATHING SUIT)

Producer, Arthur Hornblow, Jr.; **director,** Mervyn LeRoy; **screenplay,** Everett Freeman; **music director,** Adolph Deutsch; **orchestrator,** Alexander Courage; **production numbers** staged by Busby Berkeley; **underwater choreography,** Audrene Brier; **art director,** Cedric Gibbons; **set decorators,** Edwin B. Willis and Richard Pefferle; **camera,** George J. Folsey; **editor,** John McSweeney, Jr.

Esther Williams **(Annette Kellerman)**; Victor Mature **(James Sullivan)**; Walter Pidgeon **(Frederick Kellerman)**; David Brian **(Alfred Harper)**; Donna Corcoran **(Annette at Age Ten)**; Jesse White **(Doc Cronnel)**; Maria Tallchief **(Pavlova)**; Howard Freeman **(Aldrich)**; Charles Watts **(Policeman)**; Wilton Graff **(Garvey)**; Frank Ferguson **(Prosecutor)**; James Bell **(Judge)**; James Flavin **(Conductor)**; Willis Bouchey **(Director)**; Adrienne D'Ambricourt **(Marie, the Housekeeper)**; Charles Heard **(Official)**; Clive Morgan **(Judge)**; Queenie Leonard **(Mrs. Graves)**; Stuart Torres **(Son)**; Leslie Denison **(Purser)**; Wilson Benge **(Caretaker)**; Elisabeth Slifer **(Soprano)**; Al Ferguson **(London

David Brian, Walter Pidgeon, and Esther Williams in Million Dollar Mermaid *('52).*

swimmer. The studio had tried several different approaches that had worked, in varying degrees. Mostly they were farfetched and the way they got Esther into the water (where she was unsurpassed) had all the subtlety of a kick in the head. It seemed to me that something more appropriate could be found for her.

Indeed, the life of Miss Kellerman,[1] splashed with Hollywood touches and color, was the perfect vehicle for Esther. The film treated her to two leading men (Victor Mature and David Brian), afforded her the honor of having studio veteran Walter Pidgeon play her father, and squeezed the shapely star into a parade of one-piece bathing suits. One of her most impressive outfits for the color film was a chain-mail bathing ensemble publicized as composed of some 50,000 gold flakes.

Two of the more outrageously spectacular numbers in this visually impressive feature are the fountain number and the smoke segment. In the fountain number Williams is in a tremendous water tank (allegedly on the stage of the New York Hippodrome Theatre) performing a specialty act. A canopy of four hundred streams of water shoot up thirty feet, creating a huge waterfall. Williams emerges from the center of the pool on top of a geyser and executes a lofty swan dive. The multihued lights playing on the water enhance the spectacle.

The smoke number would remain one of Berkeley's most outstanding cinema routines. As he described it:

I used one hundred boy and girl swimmers and for the background I had nothing but red and yellow smoke streams shooting up fifty feet. The effect was made by four hundred electrically controlled smoke pots. On each side of the pool, I had forty-foot-high ramps, from which the swimmers slid down at a terrific pace, standing up and carrying yellow lighted torches as they entered the water. I also had twelve long swings that swung down from high in the air through the smoke, and from which twelve girls and twelve boys simultaneously dived into the water. Esther was also the center of attention in this number. I dropped her from fifty feet into the mass of swimmers below, which exploded into a Ferris-wheel effect on the water. Then they all submerged, and gradually out of the water came Esther on a platform surrounded by beautiful girls. The closing effect was an array of five hundred lighted sparklers coming out of the water and forming a backdrop around the whole group.

Million Dollar Mermaid opened as the 1952 Christmas attraction at New York's Radio City Music Hall. While Bosley Crowther in the **New York Times** insisted that the film was "not the most brilliant romance or comedy that has been contrived for the girl," he did admit it was

"quite a splashy production that Metro has arranged to show off its elegant Miss Williams in a variety of one-piece bathing suits. From a comedy sequence describing a marathon swim in the Thames to a water ballet by Busby Berkeley, it does her proud in the aquatic scenes. Most resplendent of all the productions is that ultimate water ballet. . . . Blown up, as it is, to larger proportions on the Music Hall's Magnascope screen, the one number approaches Cinerama and far outclasses Billy Rose's Acquacade!"

Although **Million Dollar Mermaid** was a financial bonanza (it did a solid eight weeks of business at the Music Hall), it was the final peak of Esther Williams' screen career. None of her remaining Metro efforts—including **Dangerous When Wet** (1953), **Easy to Love** (1953; with water-ski and other aquatic numbers staged magnificently by Berkeley), and **Jupiter's Darling** (1955)—rekindled her dimming box-office appeal. In 1955 she departed the lot.

The swim star occupies a special niche in Metro's history, but she herself has been perennially disdainful of the studio, which spent a decade fashioning plush showpieces for her limited screen talents. In fact, she has never held her own abilities in very high repute: "I can't act, I can't sing, I can't dance. My pictures are put together out of scraps they find in the producer's wastebasket." When MGM invited their stellar alumni to the premiere of **That's Entertainment!** (1974), the lady who earned some $80 million for the corporation declined to attend.

MIN AND BILL
1930—66 min.

Director, George Hill; based on the novel **Dark Star** by Lorna Moon; **screenplay**, Frances Marion and Marion Jackson; **wardrobe**, Rene Hubert; **art director**, Cedric Gibbons; **sound**, Douglas Shearer; **camera**, Harold Wenstrom; **editor**, Basil Wrangell.

Marie Dressler **(Min)**; Wallace Beery **(Bill)**; Dorothy Jordan **(Nancy)**; Marjorie Rambeau **(Bella)**; Donald Dillaway **(Dick)**; DeWitt Jennings **(Groot)**; Russell Hopton **(Alec)**; Frank McGlynn **(Mr. Southard)**; Gretta Gould **(Mrs. Southard)**; Jack Pennick **(Merchant Seaman)**; Hank Bell **(Sailor)**; Henry Roquemore **(Bella's Stateroom Lover)**; Miss Vanessi **(Woman)**.

SYNOPSIS
Min is a hard-boiled proprietress of a sleazy California waterfront hotel. Her boyfriend is gruff but good-hearted fisherman Bill. She has brought up Nancy, a girl who was deserted by her mother many years prior. The local authorities attempt to persuade rough-and-ready Min that she is not a proper mother and that Nancy must be sent to school. Pressured by the truant officer and the prohibition officials (who have had her cafe under surveillance), Min dispatches Nancy to live with the school principal's family. Nancy insists she would rather remain with Min.

In the meantime, Bella, Nancy's real mother, a floozy, reappears. However, Min is soon able to convince Bella to return to San Francisco. Thereafter Min sacrifices to sponsor Nancy at a proper boarding school. There the girl falls in love with Dick, a wealthy youth who loves her in spite of her sketchy background. He plans to wed her.

Just then Bella, learning of her daughter's good luck, returns and tells Min she will reveal the girl's actual mother in the hopes of gaining some of Dick's money. In a struggle, Min's face is burned and she is forced to shoot Bella to stop her. Min is informed on by a jealous sailor. Later, as her daughter sails on her honeymoon, Min is led away to jail by the police.

* * *

Many glamorous teams caught audiences' fancies during the golden years at MGM: John Gilbert and Greta Garbo, Clark Gable and Joan Crawford, Gable and Jean Harlow, Gable and Lana Turner, William Powell and Myrna Loy, Jeanette MacDonald and Nelson Eddy, Spencer Tracy and Katharine Hepburn, among them. However, none inspired so supercharged an emotion in film attendees as did the tandem appearances of overweight, frumpy Marie Dressler and beer-bellied, gutsy Wallace Beery. Though actually teamed only twice (**Min and Bill** and **Tugboat Annie**, 1933), they worked a third and final time in the all-star **Dinner at Eight** (1933). In each entry the dynamic if unhandsome couple displayed their own brand of screen chemistry—rough, affectionate, and emotionally comic.

The first such pairing, **Min and Bill**, arrived at an opportune time for both stars. Dressler had managed a stunning comeback that climaxed with her performance earlier in the year in Garbo's **Anna Christie**. And Beery had just joined Metro following his acclaimed work in **The Big House**. The prison melodrama saved him from has-been status and impending financial disaster.

Based on Lorna Moon's novel **Dark Star, Min and Bill** rejoined Beery with director George Hill and Hill's scenarist wife, Frances Marion. Marion was a personal friend of Dressler's and had constantly reshaped scripts to help her regain professional prominence. The triumvirate of Beery, Hill, and Marion from **The Big House** joined with Dressler in offering an amazingly expansive bittersweet comedy. It allowed both stars to parade in tailor-made roles, Dressler as the battle-ax Min, the rough-and-rugged landlady of an unspeakable waterfront flytrap hotel, and Beery as a crude fishing-boat skipper.

Actually **Min and Bill** has a relatively tragic slant to its plot. However, audiences best remember the raucous comedy interludes. In one scene, Dressler and Dorothy Jordan (as her charge, Nancy) swoon in a runaway speedboat, which only scarcely avoids several catastrophes in Mack Sennett style. In another, the most crowd-pleasing

---

[1]Some of Annette Kellerman's films include: **A Daughter of the Gods** (1916), **The Honor System** (1917), **Queen of the Sea** (1918), and **The Art of Diving** (1920). When Australia's own "This Is Your Life" TV program paid tribute to Miss Kellerman in August 1975, both Esther Williams and Walter Pidgeon were on hand to represent Metro's picturization of her life.

Wallace Beery and Marie Dressler in Min and Bill *('30).*

of all, Dressler finds Beery flirting with Marjorie Rambeau[1] and attacks him with virtually everything within her grasp, including most of the furniture; she even heaves a pickax, which scarcely misses Beery's aghast face.

When **Min and Bill** debuted in November 1930 it did not please many critics with its plotline.[2] Mordaunt Hall **(New York Times)** labeled the film "unsavory" and judged, "It is regrettable that Miss Dressler and Mr. Beery should have been cast for the first time together in this far from pleasant film." Audiences, however, felt otherwise. **Min and Bill** became a great hit, thanks to the compelling, unglamorous star performances. At the fourth annual Academy Awards, the sixty-two-year-old Dressler found herself in competition with beauties Marlene Dietrich **(Morocco)**, Irene Dunne **(Cimarron)**, Ann Harding **(Holiday)**, and Norma Shearer **(A Free Soul)** for the Best Actress prize. Norma Shearer, winner the previous year for MGM's **The Divorcee**, presented the prize to "the grandest trouper of them all—the grand old firehorse of the screen"—Marie Dressler.

In the short time which followed, Marie Dressler became Mayer's favorite star at MGM. The mogul lavished her with royal treatment; in 1932 and 1933 she was the country's number-one box-office attraction.

As with many features of this period, **Min and Bill** was redone in foreign-language versions, none of which featured Dressler or Beery.

MRS. MINIVER
1942—134 min.

Producer, Sidney Franklin; **director,** William Wyler; based on the novel by Jan Struther; **screen-**

[1]The very talented Marjorie Rambeau had a strong career at MGM in the early 1930s, frequently cast as a floozy or gun moll (as in Beery's **The Secret Six**, 1931). Years later, in **Twenty Mule Team** (1940), there was an attempt to make Beery and her into a new Beery-Dressler team; instead, Marjorie Main, in a series of 1940s pictures, would become Beery's new partner. For Warner Bros. Rambeau would re-create one of Dressler's old roles, in **Tugboat Annie Sails Again** (1940).

[2]Shot on a thirty-eight-day production schedule at a cost of $327,000, **Min and Bill** earned a profit of $731,000.

play, Arthur Wimperis, George Froeschel, James Hilton, and Claudine West; **music,** Herbert Stothart; **song,** Gene Lockhart; St. Luke's Choristers—Ripley Dorr, director; **art directors,** Cedric Gibbons and Urie McCleary; **set decorator,** Edwin B. Willis; **gowns,** Kalloch; **men's wardrobe,** Gile Steele; **sound,** Douglas Shearer; **special effects,** Arnold Gillespie and Warren Newcombe; **camera,** Joseph Ruttenberg; **editor,** Harold F. Kress.

Greer Garson **(Mrs. Kay Miniver)**; Walter Pidgeon **(Clem Miniver)**; Teresa Wright **(Carol Beldon)**; Dame May Whitty **(Lady Beldon)**; Henry Travers **(Mr. Ballard)**; Reginald Owen **(Foley)**; Miles Mander **(German Agent's Voice)**; Henry Wilcoxon **(Vicar)**; Richard Ney **(Vincent Miniver)**; Clare Sandars **(Judy Miniver)**; Christopher Severn **(Toby Miniver)**; Brenda Forbes **(Gladys, the Housemaid)**; Rhys Williams **(Horace Perkins)**; Marie DeBecker **(Ada, the Cook)**; Helmut Dantine **(German Flyer)**; Mary Field **(Miss Spriggins)**; Tom Conway **(Man)**; St. Luke's Choristers **(Choral Voices)**; Paul Scardon **(Nobby)**; Ben Webster **(Ginger)**; Aubrey Mather **(George, the Innkeeper)**; Forrester Harvey **(Huggins)**; John Abbot **(Fred, the Porter)**; Connie Leon **(Simpson, the Maid)**; Billy Bevan **(Conductor)**; Oliver Smith **(Car Dealer)**; Charles Irwin **(Mac)**; Ian Wolfe **(Dentist)**; Thomas Louden **(Mr. Verger)**; Peter Lawford **(Pilot)**; Stanley Mann **(Workman)**; Billy Engle **(Townsman)**.

SYNOPSIS

In the summer of 1939 Kay Miniver purchases a costly hat at a London shop before making her way home to the countryside of Belham. When she arrives the train supervisor suggests using her name for a new species of rose which he has grown. She readily agrees and hurries home where she discovers that her architect husband Clem has just purchased a new automobile. They both laugh over their extravagances. Kay and Clem and their youngest children, Toby and Judy, welcome home older son Vin(cent) on his return from Oxford. Soon Vin encounters Carol Beldon, who has come to request that Kay ask Mr. Ballard to remove his "Miniver" rose from the flower show. Her reason is that her grandmother, Lady Beldon, has always won the competition and would be upset at losing. Vin and Carol are strongly attracted to each other and become engaged on the eve of his departure to serve in the recently declared war.

Both Kay and Clem do their share to aid in the war effort. While Clem and the other men of the village are away in their boats helping with the evacuation of Dunkirk, Kay experiences the war at home. A wounded German aviator is found in her yard and she later turns him over to the police.

Vin and Carol finally marry and return from their honeymoon to witness the flower competition, which Lady Beldon wins. However, she turns over her award to Mr. Ballard. The calm is interrupted by a German air raid, during which Carol is shot and killed by a low-flying plane. Belham is reduced to rubble, but the vicar speaks to his congregation in the semidestroyed church and spurs them to new faith in Great Britain's future.

"This is the people's war! It is our war! We are the fighters! Fight it then! Fight it with all that is in us! And may God defend the right!"

* * *

During World War II Hollywood, constrained to churn out timely propaganda, managed to produce a few war pictures that stand today as exemplary showpieces of the genre. Paramount's **Wake Island** (1942) realistically presented the grim life and unglamorous heroics of the American soldier. Totally different but far more powerful was Metro's classic **Mrs. Miniver**, a paean to England that somehow was translated into a piece of Americana. It was praised by **Time** magazine as "an almost impossible feat—a great war picture that photographs the inner meaning, instead of the outward realism of World War II."

Certainly nobody expected that **Mrs. Miniver** would score so potently. Based on Jan Struther's 1930s sketches for the **Times** (London), the property was scheduled originally as a vehicle for on-the-wane Norma Shearer. But the mature star's ego was in no condition to play the mother of a teenage boy. Ann Harding, also fortyish, was briefly considered before Louis B. Mayer beamingly presented the role to his "pet" Greer Garson (born 1908), the Irish redhead who already had a sizable following and two Oscar nominations.[1] Walter Pidgeon, who had performed well in tandem with Garson in **Blossoms in the Dust** (1941), was cast as Clem, Kay Miniver's stalwart architect husband. MGM borrowed Samuel Goldwyn's starlet Teresa Wright to play daughter-in-law Carol, and Richard Ney took the part of the Minivers' son Vin.

Even during production there were times when the studio feared the worst for its project. Director William Wyler, a notorious perfectionist, ruffled the egos of the stars. At the 1976 American Film Institute tribute to Wyler, Pidgeon related that he almost refused to make the film due to Wyler's reputation ("I shudder when I think of the fight I put up to get out of doing this picture!") and spent several days on the set just watching Wyler direct before he agreed to work with him. Cameraman Joseph Ruttenberg recently informed **Focus on Film,** "Wyler was . . . never, ever satisfied. . . . It was tough on the actors and Greer Garson got more and more angry until one Saturday morning she blew her stack, told Wyler what she thought of him, and walked off the set. It was quite a scene!" To add to the troubles, Garson began a romance with her movie "son," twenty-seven-year-old Richard Ney, that was closely monitored by the ever-vigilant Mayer. When an engagement resulted, Mayer called his favorite actress into his inner office and pleaded with her to delay the marriage until after **Mrs. Miniver** played its major engagements. Ever the "team player," Garson agreed, even in the face of the military draft that soon drew Ney into the navy.

All these problems were forgotten when **Mrs. Miniver** debuted at Radio City Music Hall on June

[1]Garson later related that Mayer acted out the entire part of **Mrs. Miniver** in his office to convince her to play it. She also claims she fainted after she left his chamber and realized what she had done.

Advertisement for Mrs. Miniver *('42).*

4, 1942. The ads blazed, "Two hours packed with a lifetime of soul-stirring drama." Response was phenomenal.[2] The picture enjoyed record-breaking business, eventually grossing some $5.5 million in distributors' domestic rentals. Howard Barnes **(New York Herald-Tribune)** endorsed, "There has been nothing to touch the understated eloquence of this magnificent and moving dramatization of the Battle of Britain. . . . A few works succeed in impinging on a time of crisis with stunning force and meaning. **Mrs. Miniver** is one of these." Even the world powers praised the picture. Hitler's

propaganda minister, Dr. Goebbels, cited the film as an "exemplary propaganda film for German industry to copy," and Winston Churchill ordered leaflets of the powerful closing speech (delivered in the film with terse power by Henry Wilcoxon) dropped over Allied and enemy lines.

As all expected, **Mrs. Miniver** was the big favorite at the fifteenth annual Oscar ceremonies held at the Hollywood Coconut Grove on March 4, 1943. The film won the Best Picture Oscar, defeating such competition as Warner Bros.' **Yankee Doodle Dandy** and Paramount's **Wake Island.** Garson won the Best Actress figurine (and gave the longest acceptance speech in Oscar's history); Teresa Wright earned the Best Supporting Actress Oscar (she was also competing with Garson that year for Best Actress for Goldwyn's **Pride of the Yankees);** Wyler triumphed as Best Director (he

was on a bombing raid over Germany the night of the ceremonies); Joseph Ruttenberg won for Best Black-and-White Cinematography; George Froeschel, James Hilton, Claudine West, and Arthur Wimperis won for Best Screenplay; and producer Sidney Franklin received the Irving G. Thalberg Memorial Award.[3]

The dynamic impact of **Mrs. Miniver** remained with the country throughout the war years. Garson and Pidgeon, who became the most celebrated romantic screen team of the 1940s, re-

[2]Endorsements came in from abroad. **The Scotsman** reported of **Mrs. Miniver,** "Of all the war films which have been seen in Edinburgh in 1940–41, this one gives the truest picture of life as people in London area knew it in 1940–41."

[3]Pidgeon was nominated for Best Actor but lost to James Cagney of **Yankee Doodle Dandy;** Henry Travers was nominated for Best Supporting Actor, but bowed to Van Heflin of MGM's **Johnny Eager;** Dame May Whitty was nominated for Best Supporting Actress, but lost to Miss Wright.

prised their Miniver characters on Cecil B. DeMille's "Lux Radio Theatre" on December 6, 1943, with Susan Peters and Ensign Henry Wilcoxon. A later return to the screen roles in Metro's **The Miniver Story** (1950), wherein Kay dies of cancer while Clem stands nobly by, was a disaster and a blow to the memories that many filmgoers held for the original.

Today **Mrs. Miniver** tends to draw sneers from the more cynical film historians, many of whom have no stomach for the war propaganda or the queenly histrionics of Garson. In a **Village Voice** piece of July 1975, critic Andrew Sarris labels the Minivers "a British version of the Hardy family." However, the powerful emotional expression cannot be attacked by even the most severe critic. The same Mr. Sarris acknowledges that "Wyler's directorial set piece in **Mrs. Miniver** is the bomb shelter scene in which meticulous composition and lighting (Garson shining gloriously in the foreground, Pidgeon dimly supportive in the background) illustrate the heroism and horror of a People's War."

It's sad but even the creative forces of **Mrs. Miniver** have taken potshots at their celebrated motion picture. Wyler returned from World War II, having seen the British people in action, to call his Oscar-winning work "synthetic." Greer Garson herself appeared at a screening in Annapolis, Maryland, in 1970 and apologized to the audience afterward, sheepishly smiling, "You have to understand, we really thought we were doing something important at the time." Such responses are unworthy of a film that Winston Churchill praised as being more powerful to the war effort than the combined work of six military divisions.

Clark Gable and Ava Gardner in Mogambo *('53).*

MOGAMBO
1953 C—116 min.

Producer, Sam Zimbalist; **director,** John Ford; based on the play by Wilson Collison; **screenplay,** John Lee Mahin; **art director,** Alfred Junge; **second-unit directors,** Richard Rosson, Yakima Canutt, and James C. Havens; **assistant directors,** Wingate Smith and Cecil Ford; **costumes,** Helen Rose; **sound,** Alexander Fisher; **camera,** Robert Surtees and Fredrick A. Young; **editor,** Frank Clarke.

Clark Gable **(Victor Marswell);** Ava Gardner **(Eloise Y. Kelly);** Grace Kelly **(Linda Nordley);** Donald Sinden **(Donald Nordley);** Philip Stainton **(John Brown Pryce);** Eric Pohlmann **(Leon Boltchak);** Laurence Naismith **(Skipper);** Dennis O'Dea **(Father Joseph);** Asa Etula **(Young Native Girl)** and: the Wagenia Tribe of Belgian Congo, the Samburu Tribe of Kenya Colony, the Bahaya Tribe of Tanganyika, and the M'Beti Tribe of French Equatorial Africa.

SYNOPSIS
While in Africa capturing wild animals for American zoos, white hunter Victor Marswell is visited in his jungle headquarters by brassy showgirl Eloise Y. Kelly, who has come to the area to be the guest of a wealthy maharaja. The globe-trotting playboy, however, has gone back to India, leaving Eloise at loose ends for a week until the steamer returns. She quickly succumbs to Marswell's virile charms and is glad when the arriving steamer breaks down.

Marswell allows Eloise to accompany him on a safari paid for by British archaeologist Donald Nordley and his wife Linda. Much to jealous Eloise's annoyance, Marswell and the aristocratic Linda become romantically inclined, although Nordley is unaware of the situation. In the course of the jungle trek the group confronts wild animals and belligerent natives. Nordley is particularly interested in capturing wild gorillas so that he can study their habits.

Marswell decides to tell Nordley of his growing love for Linda. Eloise tries to convince him that these feelings may just be an infatuation. Nevertheless, Victor proceeds to confess to the Britisher, stopping **only** when he realizes that the truth would hurt the husband too much.

Later Marswell saves Nordley from being mauled and perhaps killed by a rampaging gorilla. The hunter and Eloise then rendezvous and engage in drunken and romantic revelry. Linda happens upon the playful couple and in a jealous rage shoots Marswell, wounding him in the shoulder. Nordley comes rushing to Marswell's tent. To save the situation Eloise informs the archaeologist that Linda had shot Victor for being too ungentlemanly.

The Nordleys depart. Now alone with Eloise, Victor realizes her worth and asks her to remain with him.

* * *

Since its premiere in 1932, MGM's **Red Dust** had earned special notoriety in Hollywood sex annals because of its smoldering scenes with Gable, Jean Harlow, and Mary Astor. Certainly Gable had rarely enjoyed so impressive a part as the magnetic adventurer, and the star had reprised the role on the "Gulf Screen Guild" radio show (October 6, 1940) with Ann Sothern (in the Harlow part) and Jeffrey Lynn. But now the fifty-two-year-old actor's box-office power was sadly sagging, along with jowls, so Metro decided that a remake of **Red Dust** might prove an elixir to the aging star's appeal. Gable agreed to top billing in the film (as part of a packaged deal with **Never Let Me Go,** 1953) at just about the time Sylvia Ashley, his fourth wife, was receiving her provisional divorce from the King.

The new script (updated by **Red Dust**'s original writer, John Lee Mahin) was entitled **Mogambo** (a native expression meaning "to speak").

With surly triple-Oscar winner John Ford signed to direct,[1] Gable was placed back in his old part (more or less; he was no longer Dennis Carson, African plantation chief, but Victor Marswell, safari leader and hunter). Harlow had been dead for almost sixteen years; her part was transformed from a brazen whore named Vantine to a floundering showgirl by the name of Eloise Y. Kelly (a.k.a. "Honey Bear"), and Ava Gardner won the part. A very worn Mary Astor was in no condition to play again the bride whose passion overwhelms her, and Grace Kelly, the beautiful blonde who would become a MGM staple but spend most of her celebrated tenure in Hollywood on loanout, replaced Astor's "Babs." Kelly is cool, patrician Linda Nordley, whose spouse Donald (Donald Sinden, in the revised Gene Raymond role) appears far more interested in exploring the idiosyncrasies of gorillas than the assorted charms of his bride.

The cinema had matured in many ways since Harlow had asked that pet parrot in **Red Dust** if he had been eating cement. Producer Sam Zimbalist, encouraged by the success of **King Solomon's Mines** (1950), agreed to shooting in Technicolor on location and veteran Dark Continent guide Frank Allen led the MGM safari, which posted 175 white men and 350 natives at the filmmaking unit in Kenya with side trips to Tanganyika and Uganda.

Mogambo was also one of the very few Metro pictures devoid of a musical score (à la **Battleground**). Instead, director Ford ordered soundman Alexander ("Sash") Fisher to record the sounds of forty-three different animals and birds as well as thirty-five shouts, calls, and songs of natives, and these were blended into the soundtrack background.

However, because of all these modifications, the very element that had made **Red Dust** a classic was missing—the sexual tension. With screen censorship more restrictive in 1953 than it was in 1932, Mahin was forced to emasculate his original script. Thus audiences would never be certain of the sexual relationship between Gable and Kelly or between Gable and Gardner. In short, **Red Dust** was disemboweled.

No such censorship prevailed on the Kenya filming site. Frank Sinatra accompanied wife Ava, and the two fought and made up regularly. At one point Ava reportedly tossed away a mink coat Sinatra gave her as a peace offering. And Gable (who shot a crocodile and earned the nickname "Bwana" from the natives, who treasured the dead reptile's hide) became very close to Grace Kelly. The romance might have blossomed into a marriage, if Kelly had not felt the age difference between the two of them was too great.

Despite the toned-down sensuality of the remake, **Mogambo** performed extremely well when released in early fall 1953, following some soundstage work in England. Otis L. Guernsey, Jr. of the **New York Herald-Tribune** reported, "With Clark Gable, Ava Gardner, and Grace Kelly shedding purple light on Darkest Africa under John

Ford's rowdy direction, there is never a lazy moment in this Technicolor MGM safari . . . even the animals seem to have their tongues in their cheeks to match a script that is an adventurous joke all the way. . . . It is simply a jungle joyride, embellished with curves and spectacle." **Time** magazine offered, "Gable plays his he-man part with the bemused ease to be expected of a man who has done the same thing many times before; Grace Kelly's blonde beauty remains intact despite the remarkably silly lines she is made to say; and Ava romps delightfully with baby elephants and giraffes in the intervals between her pursuit of Gable." Gardner would win a Best Actress Oscar nomination, losing to Audrey Hepburn of Paramount's **Roman Holiday**; Grace Kelly's Best Supporting Actress bid was vanquished by Donna Reed of Columbia's **From Here to Eternity**.

Ironically, by the time **Mogambo** was released to good results (earning $4,688,000 in distributors' domestic rentals) and had proved a personal triumph for Gable, he had completed **Betrayed** (1954), his final film under his MGM contract.[2] He had already departed his longtime home base at Culver City, taking with him a studio pension worth $400,000. It was now too late to woo Gable back to the fold.

THE MORTAL STORM
1940—100 min.

Producers, Sidney Franklin and, **uncredited,** Victor Saville; **director,** Frank Borzage; based on the novel by Phyllis Bottome; **screenplay,** Claudine West, Anderson Ellis, and George Froeschel; **assistant director,** Lew Borzage; **art directors,** Cedric Gibbons and Wade Rubottom; **set decorator,** Edwin B. Willis; **gowns,** Adrian; **men's wardrobe,** Gile Steele; **makeup,** Jack Dawn; **music,** Edward Kane; **additional music,** Eugene Zador; **sound,** Douglas Shearer; **camera,** William Daniels; **editor,** Elmo Vernon.

Margaret Sullavan **(Freya Roth)**; James Stewart **(Martin Brietner)**; Robert Young **(Fritz Marlberg)**; Frank Morgan **(Professor Roth)**; Irene Rich **(Mrs. Roth)**; Maria Ouspenskaya **(Mrs. Brietner)**; William Orr **(Erich von Rohn)**; Robert Stack **(Otto von Rohn)**; Bonita Granville **(Elsa)**; Gene Reynolds **(Rudi)**; Russell Hicks **(Rector)**; William Edmunds **(Lehman)**; Thomas Ross **(Professor Werner)**; Ward Bond **(Franz)**; Esther Dale **(Marta)**; Fritz Leiber **(Oppenheim)**; Dan Dailey **(Holl)**; Robert O. Davis [Rudolph Anders] **(Hartman)**; Granville Bates **(Berg)**; Sue Moore **(Theresa)**; Harry Depp, Julius Tannen, and Gus Glassmire **(Colleagues)**; Dick Rich and Ted Oliver **(Guards)**; Dick Elliott **(Passport Official)**; Henry Victor and John Stark **(Gestapo Officials)**; Bert Roach **(Fat Man in Cafe)**.

SYNOPSIS
In 1933 Germany venerable Jewish Professor Roth celebrates his sixtieth birthday with his wife, two stepsons, Otto and Erich, and daughter Freya. Martin Brietner and Fritz Marlberg both love Freya. She chooses the latter, who, like her stepbrothers, is pro-Hitler.

At the birthday celebration the family hears that Hitler has become head of the militarized German state. This news splits the family politically and in time ends Freya's engagement to the radical Fritz. Freya discovers she really loves Martin, the farmer.

Professor Roth is later questioned by his students regarding Aryan supremacy and he dismisses the theory as irrational. The professor is fired from the university and sent to a concentration camp where he meets his death.

Mrs. Roth, Freya, and Rudi plan to join Martin in Austria. Their journey is interrupted by a Nazi inspection, during which one of the professor's manuscripts turns up in Freya's luggage. Fearing she might attempt to publish the work, the Nazis destroy the document and withhold Freya's passport. It makes her exit from the country impossible. Freya urges her mother and Rudi to continue without her.

Later Martin leaves Austria in hopes of sneaking Freya out of Germany. The lovers start a difficult journey across the snow-covered mountains to Austria and encounter a Nazi patrol led by Fritz. The soldiers open fire and kill Freya. She dies in Martin's arms as he carries her into the freedom of Austria.

* * *

In 1940 Adolf Hitler banned the showing of any MGM pictures in the Third Reich. The reason: **The Mortal Storm,** a stirring, bitter and dramatic attack on the "the mortal storm in which man finds himself today"—in short, Nazism.[1] Beginning with the evening in 1933 when Hitler took over the Hindenburg cabinet, **The Mortal Storm** proceeded to provide audiences with the most notable indictment of Nazi Germany since the release of 1939's **Confessions of a Nazi Spy** (Warner Bros.). The latter film had earned bomb threats for producer Jack L. Warner when premiered.

Based on the Phyllis Bottome novel of 1938, **The Mortal Storm** was directed by Frank Borzage, starred Margaret Sullavan in a prominent role—just as did 1938's **Three Comrades**, released by MGM. However, in that two-year span, the threat of Nazism had antagonized most Americans to the point that, with England already at war with the Axis powers, fear and hatred of the Third Reich had largely replaced controversy.

Producer Sidney Franklin assigned a powerful cast to the story. As Sullavan's lover, he cast her real-life friend James Stewart, who had been previously teamed with her in Universal's **Next Time We Love** (1936), MGM's **The Shopworn Angel**

---

[1]Ford would say, "I never saw the original picture. I liked the script and the story, I liked the setup and I'd never been to that part of Africa—so I just did it."

[2]Dore Schary's regime was continuing its economy wave by urging high-priced talent to depart the lot. Gable had demanded terms which for any future films for MGM would guarantee him a percentage of the profits plus salary.

[1]MGM was playing it careful by couching the film in the "safe" past of 1933 with Nazism more as a historical catalyst to the screen story than as a current threat. This was at a time before the U.S. was openly committed to World War II.

Irene Rich and Frank Morgan in The Mortal Storm *('40).*

MUTINY ON THE BOUNTY
1935—132 min.

Producer, Irving Thalberg; **associate producer**, Albert Lewin; **director**, Frank Lloyd; based on the novels **Mutiny on the Bounty** and **Men Against the Sea** by Charles Nordhoff and James Norman Hall; **screenplay**, Talbot Jennings, Jules Furthman, and Carey Wilson; **art directors**, Cedric Gibbons and Arnold Gillespie; **music**, Herbert Stothart; **song**, Gus Kahn, Bronislau Kaper, and Walter Jurmann; **marine director**, James Havens; **sound**, Douglas Shearer; **camera**, Arthur Edeson; **editor**, Margaret Booth.

Charles Laughton (**Captain William Bligh**); Clark Gable (**Fletcher Christian**); Franchot Tone (**Midshipman Roger Byam**); Dudley Digges (**Dr. Bachus**); Henry Stephenson (**Sir Joseph Banks**); Donald Crisp (**Burkitt**); Eddie Quillan (**Ellison**); Francis Lister (**Captain Nelson**); Spring Byington (**Mrs. Byam**); Maria Castaneda [Movita] (**Tehani**); Mamo Clark (**Maimiti**); Robert Livingston (**Young**); Douglas Walton (**Stewart**); Ian Wolfe (**Samuel**); DeWitt Jennings (**Fryer**); Ivan Simpson (**Morgan**); Vernon Downing (**Hayward**); Stanley Fields (**Muspratt**); Wallis Clark (**Morrison**); Dick Winslow (**Tinkler**); Byron Russell (**Quintal**); Percy Waram (**Coleman**); David Torrence (**Lord Hood**); John Harrington (**Mr. Purcell**); Marion Clayton (**Mary Ellison**); Hal LeSueur (**Millard**); Crauford Kent (**Lieutenant Edwards**); David Thursby (**McIntosh**); King Mojave (**Richard Skinner**); Doris Lloyd (**Cockney Moll**); Lionel Belmore (**Innkeeper**); Harry Cording (**Soldier**); Mary Gordon (**Peddler**); Herbert Mundin (**Smith**); Eric Wilton (**Captain of Board**); David Niven and James Cagney (**Extras**); Charles Mauu and Sam Wallace Driscoll (**Bits**).

SYNOPSIS
In 1787 HMS **Bounty** sets sail from England to transport breadfruit trees from the South Seas to the British West Indies as an inexpensive food for laborers. Commander of the ship is Captain William Bligh, a malevolent skipper whose watchword is, "They [the crew] respect one law—fear." Subsequently, the most minor infraction results in harsh penalty. Master mate Fletcher Christian tries to ease Bligh's inhuman behavior but is confronted by the captain's iron will. Relief to the relentless inhumanity briefly occurs when the **Bounty** arrives in Tahiti. While the crew completes its mission there, Christian falls in love with Maimiti, and Roger Byam is entranced with Tehani.

With their breadfruit trees secured, the crew sets sail again and Bligh's viciousness soon has the men disgruntled. When the sickly, alcoholic Dr. Bachus is ordered by Bligh to attend a flogging, he does so only to drop dead on deck. This causes Christian to lead the men in mutiny. They take over the **Bounty** and set Bligh and eighteen followers adrift in an open boat with limited supplies and a few nautical instruments.[1] A forty-

(1938), and MGM's **The Shop Around the Corner** (1940). Robert Young was surprisingly fine as the fanatical Hitler disciple who shoots Sullavan, his former love, in the name of duty.[2] Frank Morgan offered a pleasantly unmannered performance as the doomed professor who refused to support the theory of Aryan supremacy. The petite Maria Ouspenskaya sparkled as Mrs. Brietner, a woman who had endured other reigns of terrors. Then there was former silent-film star Irene Rich, now an MGM contractee, as the distraught mother attempting to remain calm and to lead her family to safety. Bonita Granville, who had scored so mightily in United Artists' **These Three** (1936) as the nasty gossip, had a very dramatic role here as the servant girl questioned by the unrelenting Nazi storm troopers. The terror she displayed as her inquisitors began to beat her, lent a harrowing note to the haunting proceedings.

When released in June 1940 **The Mortal Storm** did not indulge in a major anti-Nazi ad campaign. Instead, the promotional copy focused on the popular screen team of Sullavan and Stewart: "The most exciting picture. The love story of today. With the popular sweethearts of **The Shop Around the Corner.**" However, on June 12, 1940, at the time of the film's premiere, author Phyllis Bottome remarked, "The film will . . . live in my mind as the best possible medium for a message that the hour has made more pregnant now than ever. Without liberty there is no human life. With-

out the individual's complete acceptance of moral responsibility there is no such thing as human decency; there is only a shameful slavery enforced by inhuman cruelty." When the film opened in Stanton, Nebraska, the manager of the Rialto Theatre offered free admission to all fifth columnists who would make themselves known at the box office.

Critical reaction: Bosley Crowther (**New York Times**) wrote, "Strikes out powerfully with both fists at the unmitigated brutality of a system which could turn a small and gemutlich university community into a hotbed of hatred and mortal vengagle." Lee Mortimer (**New York Daily Mirror**): "Whatever the picture fails to return to MGM in profit will be more than made up in the form of personal satisfaction over a job well done." A few of the fourth estate mentioned that neither the cast nor the (MGM back lot) ambiance smacked very much of Germany, and that the scenario was overly sentimental and contrived.

Despite an expansive mounting and name players, **The Mortal Storm** was not a box-office winner. Apprehensive filmgoers were too busy coping with the actual headlines of Hitler's latest outrages. They were not willing to spend their leisure time or dollars beholding the bloodletting on screen. The sole honor afforded **The Mortal Storm** was that it placed tenth on **Film Daily**'s Ten Best Picture list.

In October 1940 MGM followed **The Mortal Storm** with another strongly anti-Nazi film, **Escape,** starring Norma Shearer, Robert Taylor, and Nazimova.

---

[2]At one point in the production MGM considered having the story end with Sullavan surviving.

---

[1]As he gets underway, Bligh snarls, "Casting me adrift 2500 from a port of call—you're sending me to my doom,

DeWitt Jennings, Dudley Digges, Charles Laughton, Herbert Mundin, Clark Gable, and Franchot Tone in Mutiny on the Bounty ('35).

nine-day open-boat voyage takes Bligh and his men to Timor in the Dutch East Indies while the mutineers return to idyllic Tahiti.

A year later Bligh takes command of the **Pandora** and seeks out the mutineers, some of whom retreated to uninhabited Pitcairn Island, between Chile and Australia. In 1790 they would burn and sink the **Bounty**, destroying their chance of leaving.

Meanwhile, Bligh arrests all the crewmen that he discovers on Tahiti, including Byam, who had remained loyal. Bligh attempts to catch the remaining mutineers and the **Bounty** but is thwarted when the **Pandora** wrecks on a reef.

A mutiny trial takes place in England. There Byam reveals Bligh's scores of injustices. Byam

suggests that captains could inspire loyalty "not by flogging their backs but by lifting their hearts." A result of the episode is the moderation of England's eighteenth-century maritime laws.

* * *

"One of the great adventures of all times lives again in a screen epic it took two years and two million dollars to make . . . a cast of thousands, including exotic native girls of Tahiti!" So read the promotional copy when MGM released **Mutiny on the Bounty** in November 1935. The studio had full right to boast. It had produced one of the most exciting and durable motion picture adventures of film history, and survived disaster, setback, and temperament to do so.

The film was based on the 1932 novel by Charles Nordhoff and James Hall, part of the sea trilogy that also comprised **Men Against the Sea** and **Pitcairn Island.** The actual **Bounty** mutiny of 1787 had long been a favorite of sea drama enthusiasts. Director Frank Lloyd, who had a special

love for the property, acquired the screen rights (with his agent Edward Small) for $12,500.[2]

When the production was first considered at Culver City, there was an immediate setback. Louis B. Mayer vetoed the project, reasoning there could be no appeal in a film in which the hero was a mutineer and in which there was no plot accommodation for the traditional romance. Irving Thalberg, however, was excited by the project, believing, "People are fascinated by cruelty, and that's why **Mutiny** will have appeal." With the production approval then forthcoming, Talbot Jennings, Jules Furthman, and Carey Wilson (among others) combined their talents to fashion the script.

---

eh? Well you're **wrong** Christian! . . . I'll live to see you—**all** of you—hanging from the highest yardarm in the British fleet!"

---

[2]There had been a 1933 cinema version of the saga, filmed in Australia with the title **In the Wake of the Bounty** and starring a then unknown named Errol Flynn as Fletcher Christian.

When Clark Gable, Oscar winner for Columbia's **It Happened One Night** (1934), was selected by Thalberg to portray Christian, the star was not thrilled. He told the executive:

Look, Irving. I'm a realistic kind of actor; I've never played in a costume picture in my life. Now you want me to wear a pigtail and velvet knee pants and shoes with silver buckles! The audience will laugh me off the screen. And I'll be damned if I'll shave off my moustache just because the British navy didn't allow them. This moustache has been damned lucky for me.

Reportedly, Gable changed his mind when studio executive producer Eddie Mannix pointed out that Christian was the only character in the epic who enjoyed a romance.

As for the monstrous Captain William Bligh, Metro first considered its Wallace Beery. But when he was judged "too American" the role went to Charles Laughton, Oscar winner for **The Private Life of Henry VIII** (1933) and portrayer of the incestuous Mr. Barrett in Thalberg's triumph, **The Barretts of Wimpole Street** (1934). Laughton was fascinated by the warped psyche of Bligh, but contracted with some trepidation for top billing over Gable. He felt the picture's real star was the ship. The third major lead, Midshipman Roger Byam, went to Franchot Tone when the initial choice, Robert Montgomery, refused to reschedule a long-planned vacation.

In early 1935 MGM began production. And there were problems. A special crew sailed the life-size re-creations of the **Bounty** and the **Pandora** on a 14,000-mile voyage to Tahiti and the South Sea Islands for location footage and the use of some 2,500 native extras. The fleet was handicapped by stubbornly inclement weather. Upon their return the filmmakers were shocked to discover that the entire footage was underexposed because the crew had failed to follow production manager Joe Cohn's orders to dehydrate the film in the tropical climate. The entire trip had to be repeated.

Early that summer the cast assembled off California's Catalina Island for principal shooting. Among the problems encountered was the sinking of a camera barge, drowning an assistant and destroying $50,000 worth of equipment. Then too the eighteen-foot midget reproduction of the **Bounty,** operated by two men in the hold (for a special sequence showing the ship floundering in a storm), was lost for several days when the storm became rougher than anticipated.

When nature was not being obstinate, humans were. Gable and Laughton did not work harmoniously. Thalberg had many disagreements with director Lloyd that necessitated the executive's leaving Culver City for the Catalina filming site. Charles Higham writes in his biography **Laughton** (1976):

Obsessed with details of the ship's rigging and sails, and concerned with sending his unfortunate cameraman, Arthur Edeson, to the tops of the masts to obtain effective shots, Lloyd left the actors virtually to their own devices. Both Charles and Gable complained by

telephone to Thalberg, who frequently came out to Catalina by seaplane, screaming at Lloyd that he was unsettling the stars. Lloyd screamed back, and the quarrels, conducted in front of cast and both film and ship's crew on deck at sea, surpassed those of Bligh and Fletcher Christian in the film.

During the first scene, in which Bligh read the Sunday prayer on the poop deck, the ship's company was fully assembled. . . . Bligh looked at the assembly and said, "Mr. Christian! You got this crew together, how would you describe them?" Christian replied, "In the main, sir, first-class seamen." Charles was under the impression he had played the scene correctly, but the moment it was over, Gable walked up to Lloyd and yelled very loudly, so that everyone could hear, "Laughton's treating me like an extra. He didn't even look at me when he addressed me! The audience won't see me in the sequence! Laughton hogged it!" Charles was furious, and Gable flatly refused to work any further that day. Lloyd canceled work and took Gable to his cabin. The cast could hear angry words through the bulkhead. Every now and again Gable was heard to say, "He's not playing to me, he's ignoring me!" In desperation, Lloyd called Thalberg, who flew over and held a midnight conference on board with Charles, Gable, and Lloyd, using Franchot Tone as an independent witness to give his own views. Thalberg forbade Gable to make any further objections, insisting that Lloyd's instructions must be carried out; but he also cautioned Charles to be sure to look Gable in the eye when he spoke to him, not glance sideways at the ocean.

There were many other problems, including Laughton's recurrent bouts with seasickness. Nevertheless, production continued and **Mutiny on the Bounty** was completed.

As the slouching, scowling, "seagoing disaster" Captain Bligh Laughton created one of the American screen's greatest villains.[3] His delivery of the line "Mr. Christian—come here!" is one of the most chilling mandates of the movies. Gable is his equal as the heroic Christian, powerful, commanding, and never more handsome. (As could be expected he played the hero in a very direct, masculine, nonfoppish manner.) His pose on the Tahitian beach is pure beefcake, and his famous love scene with native girl Maimiti on the sands, where superimposed waves crash and then fade back into their kiss, gave censors some cause to pause. Men and women in mid-1930s cinema were not permitted to be filmed in bed together, but Gable and Maimiti were awfully close together on the ground.

Critics were generally enthralled with the film. Perhaps Otis Ferguson **(New Republic)** summed it up best:

The putting together of static fragments into a live story is what is most wonderful about this picture anyway. Just as the most striking aspects of ships getting under way and standing in a line are sifted out and worked into a motion that is something more than the motion of vessels through water, so the details of various actions are made up into patterns and carried on from one to another. The action of the mutiny in particular has a brawling motion possible to no other art, with men pitched screaming out of the shrouds, blown down companionways, pinned to bulkheads, and just plain battered in a frenzy of released hatred. And the incidents leading up to the violent overthrow are made vivid in terms of the medium—the swish and pistol crack of the lash, the sweating, lean bodies, the terrible labor, and the ominous judgment from the quarterdeck. The ship and the ship's life open out here, but the film becomes grand by the virtue of something more than quarterdecks and hurlyburly. It is the reworking of a large tragedy—men not only against the sea but against their own forces, both universal and particular.

The **New York Daily Mirror** noted, "A man's picture, **Mutiny on the Bounty** also will entertain the women. . . . It has gentle, idyllic romance to balance its drama of brutality and greed. . . . For thrill, suspense, romance, beauty, horror and true drama, **Mutiny on the Bounty** tops all the recent film offerings."

Audiences agreed.[4] MGM reported a gross profit of $4,460,000 on the picture that cost $1,905,000. The Academy awarded Best Actor nominations to Gable, Laughton, and Tone; all three were defeated by Victor McLaglen (of **The Informer**). However, the film itself won the Best Picture Award, defeating such touted competition as Warner Bros.' **Captain Blood,** Paramount's **Lives of a Bengal Lancer,** RKO's **Top Hat,** United Artists' **Les Miserables,** and MGM's own **Broadway Melody of 1936, David Copperfield** and **Naughty Marietta.**

Mutiny on the Bounty would set the standard for future seafaring, swashbuckling screen efforts. But few could come close to matching the freewheeling, spirited genre classic.

---

[3]The real Captain William Bligh was not the excessively tyrannical monster of the film. Actually, Fletcher Christian had sailed with Bligh on two previous trips and they were on good terms right up to the time of the mutiny. Bligh was later made governor of New South Wales, where he became involved in another mutiny, but the hearing back in England found in his favor. He was elevated later to vice admiral and died in 1817 at the age of sixty-four. He is buried in the churchyard of Lambeth Palace.

[4]Amidst the expansive supporting cast are three performers of interest. Joan Crawford's brother, Hal Le-Sueur, was then under MGM contract (nepotism was not dead in Hollywood) and had the role of Millard. David Niven, having come to California in 1934, was seeking to make a foray into films. He was introduced to director Edmund Goulding, who in turn spoke to Irving Thalberg, who hired Niven to play an extra aboard the **Bounty.** Warner Bros. star James Cagney was sailing his yacht **Martha** near Catalina Island one day in 1935 and spotted the MGM troupe filming **Mutiny.** He signaled the ship, came aboard, and was rushed into a navy dress uniform. He thus became an extra for the crowd scene being shot that day. However, nobody to date has ever spotted the star in the release print of the picture.

EPILOGUE

For many years after **Mutiny**'s release, MGM planned to film sequels to the nautical adventure, but nothing materialized.[5] Then in the wake of a cycle of MGM remakes (**Ben-Hur** in 1959, **Cimarron** in 1960), it was decided to produce a color, widescreen version of the classic **Mutiny**. Producer Aaron Rosenberg hired scripter Eric Ambler to fashion a scenario for Marlon Brando as Fletcher Christian. The project was to commence filming on October 1, 1960, and to be budgeted at $6,000,000.

Before the venture was finally released in late 1962, the studio had invested some $18,500,000 in the would-be epic, and another approximately $10,000,000 in promotional and distribution fees. Scenarists, directors, and tempers had come and gone in the marathon efforts to ameliorate demanding Brando, to cope with the rainy season of Tahiti, and to fashion an ending for the 185-minute picture.

One of the greatest differences between the two versions was that Brando insisted Fletcher Christian should be presented as a foppish, aristocratic soul, whose battles with crude Captain Bligh (Trevor Howard) represent a class-difference struggle. In the 1962 rendition, Howard's Captain Bligh was only a distant relative of Charles Laughton's leering monster. The new Bligh was thoughtful, moody, unsophisticated, and believable, without being especially exciting. Other differences include:

1. The 1935 film dealt with two books of the trilogy; the 1962 version utilizes all three (including **Pitcairn Island**).
2. The 1962 version eliminates Midshipman Roger Byam (Franchot Tone), relating the mutiny through a flashback told by the **Bounty**'s gardener William Brown (Richard Haydn).
3. The new film ends with the death of Christian; an epilogue is used for TV airings, in which the gardener tells a sea captain that the crew was later exonerated.
4. In the 1962 version, Bligh does not confine Christian to the ship while at Tahiti; he orders him to make love to the chief's daughter to improve diplomatic relationships.
5. Christian's mutiny is more spontaneous in the 1962 edition; Bligh kicks a water ladle from the officer's hand as he is about to aid a sick man and this leads to the fracas.

Typical of the reviews for the 1962 **Mutiny** was that of the **New Yorker**: "[It] is a gaudy bauble of enormous size and negligible value, which only children will have the fortitude to sit through uncomplainingly." The 1962 **Mutiny** did receive seven Oscar nominations, but won no awards. The production grossed only $9,800,000 in U.S. and Canadian distributors' rentals and nearly caused the studio's financial downfall.

---

[5]In 1957 Twentieth Century–Fox released the low-budget **Women of Pitcairn Island**, starring Lynn Bari, Arleen Whelan, and James Craig. It detailed the account of widows and children of survivors of the **Bounty** combating lustful sailors and intruders.

As for the $750,000 motor-operated reproduction of the **Bounty**, which was constructed for the 1962 picture, today it is berthed at St. Petersburg, Florida. It is a permanent tourist attraction that fills most paying viewers with images of Gable and Laughton rather than their pedestrian replacements.

The **Bounty** saga has not ended. In the late 1970s, Dino De Laurentiis contracted with scenarist Robert Bolt to write a two-part version of what was described as "the best known yet least understood event in naval history." David Lean was announced to direct both **The Lawbreakers** and **The Long Arm,** based on the mutiny tale, with Phil Kellogg producing for Paramount release. So far this planned new version of the **Mutiny on the Bounty** account has not come to fruition.

NATIONAL VELVET
1944 C—125 min.

Producer, Pandro S. Berman; **director,** Clarence Brown; based on the novel by Enid Bagnold; **screenplay,** Theodore Reeves and Helen Deutsch; **music,** Herbert Stothart; **art directors,** Cedric Gibbons and Urie McCleary; **set decorators,** Edwin B. Willis and Mildred Griffiths; **assistant director,** Joe Boyle; **Technicolor consultant,** Natalie Kalmus; **sound,** Charles E. Wallace; **special effects,** Warren Newcombe; **camera,** Leonard Smith; **editor,** Robert J. Kern.

Mickey Rooney (**Mi Taylor**); Donald Crisp (**Mr. Brown**); Elizabeth Taylor (**Velvet Brown**); Anne Revere (**Mrs. Brown**); Angela Lansbury (**Edwina Brown**); Juanita Quigley (**Malvolia Brown**); Jackie "Butch" Jenkins (**Donald Brown**); Reginald Owen (**Farmer Ede**); Terry Kilburn (**Ted**); Alec Craig (**Tim**); Eugene Loring (**Mr. Taski**); Norma Varden (**Miss Sims**); Arthur Shields (**Mr. Hallam**); Dennis Hoey (**Mr. Grenford, the Farmer**); Aubrey Mather (**Entry Official**); Frederic Worlock (**Stewart**); Arthur Treacher (**Man with Umbrella**); Harry Allen (**Van Driver**); Stephen Bowson, Richard Haydel, and Murray Coombs (**Schoolboys**); Olaf Hytten (**Villager**); Leonard Carey (**Pressman**); Eric Wilton (**English Bookie**); Major Douglas Francis (**Track Official**); Donald Curtis (**American**).

SYNOPSIS

In Sussex, England, a butcher's daughter, Velvet Brown, encounters Mi Taylor, a wandering teenage jockey, in the village. She invites him to share dinner with her family. Velvet is fascinated with horses while her sister Edwina is boy crazy. The Browns take the jockey in and Mr. Brown gives him a job in the family shop.

Later Velvet enlists Mi's help in training "the Pi," a horse she has won in a raffle, to run in the Grand National. Mrs. Brown gives Velvet a hundred gold sovereigns she had won swimming the En-

Mickey Rooney and Elizabeth Taylor in National Velvet *('44).*

glish Channel years earlier. Now her daughter can pay the entrance fee for the race.

When the regular jockey cannot ride Pi, Velvet disguises herself as a boy and rides in the crucial race. Velvet is victorious but falls from the saddle as Pi crosses the finish line. The examining doctor discovers that Velvet is a girl, which disqualifies her.

No matter, since Velvet has realized her goal. The training session has renewed Mi's faith in himself and he plans to return to the road.

* * *

The beloved feature film that made a star Elizabeth Taylor had actually been in the planning stage almost a decade, though not at MGM. Enid Bagnold's 1935 novel originally was purchased by RKO's Pandro S. Berman as a vehicle for Katharine Hepburn. The production fell through there and **National Velvet** became a Paramount property, with talk of importing fourteen-year-old Britisher Nova Pilbeam to play the lead. Later, in 1937, it was sold to MGM amid rumors of Margaret Sullavan as Velvet and Spencer Tracy as her father. Still the property remained unrealized until its original champion, Pandro Berman, joined the Metro lot in 1940 and planned its actual making.

The pivotal role was of course that of Velvet Brown. There had been talk of giving Shirley Temple the role when she was at MGM in 1941, but negotiations fell through. More time passed. When Mrs. Sara Taylor learned of it, she brought daughter Elizabeth to see Berman. The girl was then the veteran of four films: **There's One Born Every Minute** (Universal, 1942), **Lassie Come Home** (MGM, 1943), **The White Cliffs of Dover** (MGM, 1944) and **Jane Eyre** (Twentieth Century–Fox, 1944). Her work in **Lassie Come Home** had won her a one-year Metro contract which was on its way to expiring.

Berman judged the going-on-twelve Elizabeth to be too thin and fragile for the demanding part. But three months later, after rigid training from her mother, Elizabeth was able to change Berman's mind and won the job. With top-billed Mickey Rooney as Mi, the homeless jockey who helps Velvet train her cherished horse, Donald Crisp and Anne Revere (borrowed from Fox) as Velvet's parents, and Metro newcomers Angela Lansbury (following her Cockney maid in **Gaslight**, 1944) and freckled Jackie ("Butch") Jenkins as her sister and brother, production began under Clarence Brown's direction on February 4, 1944.

Because of the climactic horse race and the dramatic effect it must have on the movie audience, Metro employed Australian jockey Snowy Baker to train Elizabeth to ride well; he also doubled for her in the dangerous steeplechase scenes.

When completed **National Velvet** convinced the front office that it was big box-office material, and the studio "prereleased" the film at Radio City Music Hall for the 1944–45 holiday audiences, though general release did not come until February 1945.[1] Wrote Howard Barnes (**New**

York Herald-Tribune), "**National Velvet** has heart and honesty. Eloquently performed and directed as a true motion picture, it is an entertainment which should have irresistible appeal for anyone who is not a horse hater." Bosley Crowther reported in his **New York Times** column, "This fresh and delightful Metro picture . . . tells by far the most touching story of youngsters and of animals since Lassie was coming home," and noted that "Mr. Brown has also drawn some excellent performances from his cast, especially from little Elizabeth Taylor, who plays the role of the horse-loving girl."

The film would win a Best Supporting Actress Oscar for Anne Revere.[2] Among those she defeated was her **Velvet** daughter Angela Lansbury, nominated for MGM's **The Picture of Dorian Gray.** However, it was the violet-eyed Miss Taylor who surmounted the charms of her horse and notorious scene-stealing costar Rooney (who entered military service after making this film) to become MGM's major adolescent star.

To win her role in **National Velvet,** Taylor was required to sign a long-term MGM pact. She would remain at the studio for seventeen years. For her thirteenth birthday the studio gifted her with the horse used in the film; thereafter, it was downhill for the fast-maturing Taylor during the remaining years of the dictatorial reign of Louis B. Mayer, whom she quickly grew to detest.

A great favorite with audiences,[3] **National Velvet** grossed $4,050,000 and has been frequently revived at children's matinees.[4] In 1946 there was a London stage version of the property

___

lage by the sea, its rolling hills and thatched cottages, and its plain, God-fearing family, **National Velvet** is the product of a bygone era in moviemaking. Following closely the structure of the popular Enid Bagnold novel, the movie is part horse story, part family portrait, scenes of training and riding are balanced by cozy family scenes, vignettes about young love and sermons from Mom on the virtues of courage and endurance."

[2]In **The Unkindest Cuts** (1972) Doug McClelland quotes Anne Revere on her Oscar win: " 'It came as a surprise, really. The odds were all against me. I was under contract to Fox, but the picture was MGM's, and MGM wasn't terribly interested in promoting an award for another studio's contract player. Nor was Fox anxious to push a picture made at Metro. Little Ann Blyth was the favorite for her performance in Warners' **Mildred Pierce.** My winning was such an upset, some of the papers the next day were still dazed and wrote things like, 'Anne Revere, who played the troublesome teenager in **Mildred Pierce,** won the Best Supporting Actress Academy Award last night.' I was very surprised.' "

[3]The British trade paper **Kine Weekly** reported of **National Velvet,** "The English atmosphere is more colourful than convincing—we have yet to see a girl wangle a mount—let alone be first past the post in the Grand National [the precedent was broken in 1977], but the delightful acting and the excellent horsemanship of Elizabeth, the soundness of the story's philosophy, and above all, the magnificently staged big race offset every extravagance and error in detail."

[4]In **It's Showtime** (United Artists, 1976), an animal-oriented version of **That's Entertainment,** clips are shown from Elizabeth Taylor's **National Velvet** and **Lassie Come Home.**

___

[1]In **Elizabeth Taylor** (1973) Foster Hirsch analyzes **National Velvet:** "With its picture-postcard English vil-

starring Tilsa Page as the intense young lady. Lori Martin would star as Velvet Brown in the 1960–62 NBC-TV series, with Arthur Space and Ann Doran as her parents, James McCallion as the handyman Mi, and a horse named King as Pi.

In 1977 Bryan Forbes announced that he would script and direct **International Velvet,** dealing with a grownup Velvet Brown who acquires custody of her fifteen-year-old orphaned niece. Tatum O'Neal was signed to play the American lass. Negotiations were undertaken to bring Elizabeth Taylor into the cast. She declined, as did Jean Simmons; afterward Forbes' actress wife Nanette Newman was assigned to the part. The $5,200,000 film emerged in mid-1978 as an undistinguished project. As the **Hollywood Reporter**'s Arthur Knight analyzed,

The original **Velvet,** of course, had just about everything—a heart-tugging story, gorgeously Technicolored scenery, horse-racing, and twelve-year old Elizabeth Taylor making her second [sic], and indelible, film appearance. It was the kind of lush, shrewdly calculated production that epitomized the heyday of MGM.

While one can only applaud the intentions behind this second coming, I can only say that I found it a gross miscalculation. After all, 1944 was a good many years ago, and I'm not at all sure that today's audiences are as familiar with the original as Forbes (and MGM) seems to assume. . . . Where **National Velvet** climaxed in a rousing horse race, Forbes has opted for the intricate, but essentially less dramatic maneuvers of dressage and show jumping, a sport that has yet to win a wide following in this country. As a result, his finale is more like watching a cricket match than a baseball game.

NAUGHTY MARIETTA
1935—106 min.

___

Producer, Hunt Stromberg; **director,** W. S. Van Dyke II; based on the operetta by Victor Herbert and Rida Johnson Young; **screenplay,** John Lee Mahin, Frances Goodrich, and Albert Hackett; **music adapter,** Herbert Stothart; **songs,** Herbert, Young, and Gus Kahn; **art director,** Cedric Gibbons; **assistant director,** Eddie Woehler; **costumes,** Adrian; **sound,** Douglas Shearer; **camera,** William Daniels; **editor,** Blanche Sewell.

Jeanette MacDonald (**Princess Marie de la Bonfain [Marietta]**); Nelson Eddy (**Captain Richard Warrington**); Frank Morgan (**Governor d'Annard**); Elsa Lanchester (**Madame d'Annard**); Douglass Dumbrille (**Prince de la Bonfain**); Joseph Cawthorn (**Herr Schuman**); Cecilia Parker (**Julie**); Walter Kingsford (**Don Carlos de Braganza**); Greta Meyer (**Fran Schuman**); Akim Tamiroff (**Rudolpho**); Harold Huber (**Abe**); Edward Brophy (**Zeke**); Jean Chatburn, Pat Farley, Jane Barnes, Kay English, Linda Parker, and Jane Mercer (**Casquette Girls**); Olive Carey (**Madame Renavant**); Dr. Edouard

Jeanette MacDonald, Nelson Eddy, and Frank Morgan in Naughty Marietta *('35).*

Lippe **(Bit)**; Walter Long **(Pirate Leader)**; Cora Sue Collins **(Felice)**; Guy Usher **(Ship's Captain)**; Harry Tenbrook **(Prospective Groom)**; Edward Keane **(Major Bonnell)**; Edward Norris and Ralph Brooks **(Suitors)**; Richard Powell **(Messenger)**; Wilfred Lucas **(Announcer)**; Arthur Belasco, Frank Hagney, Edmund Cobb, Edward Hearn, Tex Driscoll, Ed Brady, and Charles Dunbar **(Scouts)**.

SYNOPSIS

Princess Marie de la Bonfain, a red-haired beauty, is all aflutter to learn from her uncle, the Prince de la Bonfain, that she will become the victim of a diplomatic marriage, blessed by King Louis XV. Her bridegroom is to be the Spanish grandee Don Carlos de Braganza, a repulsive sort who inspires loathing in his fiancée's bosom.

Marie seeks an escape from this odious fate, and soon finds one. Her maid, Madame d'Annard, is about to leave for Louisiana as a "casquette girl" (a pretty lady selected by the king for export to the colonies to wed a settler, and provided by the crown with a dowry in a casquette—hence the name). The princess gives the maid the necessary money to wed her Marseilles sweetheart, then Marie embarks, in her place, on the voyage to the New World.

As the long trek nears its end, a band of lascivious pirates seize the ship, and the cutthroats take the girls ashore for their amusement. However, just before the pleasure begins, the sound of the singing Captain Richard Warrington and his Yankee Scouts is heard, and the women are rescued. Warrington is attracted by Marie's

beauty—"Nothing short of a wooden leg should have kept you from getting married," he informs her; but his dedication to soldiering soon separates them.

In New Orleans Marie and the other casquette girls are expected to choose husbands from the colonists, but the uncouth lot does nothing to stimulate Marie's desire. She falsely informs the governor that her virtue has been compromised. He blusteringly removes her from the group and casts her off to survive by her own means. Marie joins a marionette show, headed by the jolly Rudolpho, and there Warrington rediscovers her and realizes he loves her. Marie discovers she loves him. But before they can blissfully begin their romance, the governor's men arrest Marie. Her actual identity has been uncovered, and her uncle and Don Carlos have arrived to spirit her back to France. When Marie protests, her uncle promises that unless she weds Don Carlos, Warrington will be killed.

Surrendering to the awesome threats, Marie agrees to wed Don Carlos and attends a New Orleans ball with her uncle. Among the guests she discovers—Warrington! Marie communicates her love for him by singing the song she has written, "Ah, Sweet Mystery of Life," and he ecstatically joins her.

Learning of the danger Marie is suffering, Warrington persuades her to elope with him and escape into the wilderness, where the French villains can never discover them. Marie rapturously accepts, and with Warrington's trusted soldiers surrounding them, the couple depart the palace to begin life together.

* * *

Today, anything that has a suggestion of sentiment is quickly dismissed as corn. Frankly, what's wrong with it? Have we become so sufficient that we can live without sentiment? Sentiment, after all, is basic. Without it, there is no love, no life, no family."
Jeanette MacDonald, 1964

The oldest award in Hollywood's history is **not** the Academy Award, but the **Photoplay** magazine Gold Medal, described as the "only award in which the viewing public has the opportunity to speak its mind . . . a personal barometer to the true feelings of the American moviegoing public toward the movie product." Indeed, **Photoplay** almost always surpassed the Academy in pinpointing the public's favorite film and performers.

From 1934 to 1939, Metro-Goldwyn-Mayer proudly won **Photoplay's** accolade. In 1935, one of the cinema's greatest years, the champion was **Naughty Marietta.**[1] To some sophisticates, it was a curious choice. Though the operetta had been included among the dozen films nominated by the Academy for the Best Picture honor, it was never deemed major competition to such laureled works as RKO's **The Informer** (which won the New York Film Critics' Circle prize, as well as the National Board of Review's and the **New York Times'** top honor), and Metro's own **David Copperfield** (which topped the **Film Daily** Ten Best list) and **Mutiny on the Bounty** (which captured the Oscar). Nevertheless, no other film of that wondrously fruitful movie year so delightfully captivated the escapism-craving Great Depression public as this outdated, at times outrageous, operetta.

Today, the tandem operettas of Jeanette MacDonald and Nelson Eddy are regarded by some film followers as the acme of Hollywood "camp." In MGM's **That's Entertainment: Part II** the "tribute" to MacDonald and Eddy drew louder laughs than the offerings of comedy sector. Yet, there is in those films, for all the saccharine improbabilities, such enormous entertainment value and such irresistible artistry displayed by the two stars that only the most hapless cynic can remain totally derogatory. When **Naughty Marietta**, the first celluloid union of the team, was revived at New York City's Regency Theatre in late 1977, the **New Yorker** magazine reported, "It's an atrocity, of course, and one of the most spoofed of all the Jeanette MacDonald–Nelson Eddy operettas, and yet it has vitality and a mad sort of appeal. When the two profiles come together as they sing 'Ah, Sweet Mystery of Life,' it's beyond camp, it's in a realm of its own."

In 1935 the operetta vogue of movies was not new, but quite passé. In 1930 both Paramount and Warner Bros.–First National had cranked out a series of frothy songfests, soon kicked into oblivion by overabundance. Then Warner Bros.' **42nd**

[1]The **Photoplay** winners were: **The Barretts of Wimpole Street** (1934), **Naughty Marietta** (1935), **San Francisco** (1936), **Captains Courageous** (1937), the MacDonald-Eddy **Sweethearts** (1938), and **Gone With the Wind** (1939). MGM's streak ended in 1940 when the award was temporarily abandoned, through 1943.

Street (1933) started a new musical film vogue, but this time it focused on the garters and wisecracks of worldly chorus girls. It made the eyerolling of corseted sopranos in operettas appear hopelessly outdated.

But Louis B. Mayer felt differently. In 1933 he had contracted Jeanette MacDonald, a titian-haired, classically lovely, awesomely shrewd lady. She had risen from a Manhattan model of furs and lingerie to a Broadway player of major celebrity to a Paramount luminary, popular for her trilling in such operettas as 1930's **The Vagabond King** (opposite Dennis King) and her playing opposite Maurice Chevalier in **The Love Parade** (1930), **One Hour with You** (1932), and **Love Me Tonight** (1932). Mayer lavished professional attention on the soprano when she joined the Metro fold and offered her a choice of vehicles: Jerome Kern's **The Cat and the Fiddle** and Victor Herbert's and Rida Johnson Young's **Naughty Marietta**.[2] When Jeanette was not excited about either property, Mayer compensatorily ordered both films into production (and cast the star opposite Chevalier in 1934's **The Merry Widow,** as a replacement for Grace Moore).

Appointed producer of **Naughty Marietta** was Hunt Stromberg, who saw little promise in the melodrama. Mayer reminded him that the property was one of his favorites, and Stromberg went ahead. He was given a front office mandate to use Allan Jones in the male leading part. Jones, however, was in the midst of a Shubert Brothers' concert tour, and contractually unavailable, so Stromberg scouted for a new singer to fill the part. Hence, cast in the part of Captain Richard Warrington was blond Nelson Eddy, who had also joined the Metro roster in 1933. Eddy's enviable background in opera and concert tours could not compensate for his ill-at-ease look in front of the cameras in MGM's **Broadway to Hollywood** (1933), **Dancing Lady** (1933), and **Student Tour** (1934). In fact, despite much coaching in acting, the baritone had returned to the concert stage, expecting his MGM contract to lapse. But no sooner had he done so than he won the major screen assignment.

Producer Stromberg attempted to camouflage the dated facets of the story by mounting an opulent production. The various sets for the film covered thirty acres of the MGM back lot, and the cast members amounted to approximately one thousand—including such favorite character players as Frank Morgan, the bumbling, exasperated governor of Louisiana; Elsa Lanchester, the maid who merrily changes places with Jeanette; Douglas Dumbrille, the wicked uncle; Walter Kingsford as the doltish fiancé; and Akim Tamiroff as puppeteer Rudolpho.

Director W. S. Van Dyke II kept production swiftly moving; but he did allow William Daniels' camera to linger on the array of constructed set pieces and gathered props which gave the musical epic a lush historical flavor. For the departure number, sound apparatus was installed on the ship, with a chorus of 100 voices and a symphony orchestra between decks. Every aspect of the filming appeared immersed in elegance: Jeanette had an upholstered leaning board, decorated in pink satin and featuring her name, on which she leaned into relaxation at an oblique angle so as not to ruffle her array of Adrian costumes. Finally, the little dog in the picture called "Naughty Marietta" (who was just six weeks old) was provided a stand-in.

Of course, the aspect that made **Naughty Marietta** a box-office winner was the music. Jeanette's solos included "Chansonette" (with a chorus), "Prayer," "Italian Street Song," "Ship Ahoy" (in which she is joined for a bit by Tamiroff); Nelson launched into the famous "Tramp, Tramp, Tramp" with a male chorus, "The Owl and the Bob Cat," with the chorus, " 'Neath the Southern Moon," and "I'm Falling in Love with Someone." Together the costars duetted—unforgettably— "Ah, Sweet Mystery of Life."

MGM felt sure it had a bonanza when **Naughty Marietta** closed production. The film premiered in Washington, D.C., on March 8, 1935, before Supreme Court judges, thirty-five senators, and the Russian ambassador. On March 22, 1935, it opened at New York City's Capitol Theatre and enjoyed an enormous success.

Both stars reaped critical superlatives. The **Los Angeles Times** said that Jeanette "quite surpasses herself . . . invests her portrayal with charm and humanness" and the **New York Herald-Tribune** attested, "With all proper respect for Miss MacDonald, however, the triumph of the Van Dyke version is registered by Nelson Eddy. . . . Mr. Eddy has a brilliant baritone voice, he seems thoroughly masculine, he is engaging and good looking, and he gives the appearance of being unaffected. . . ." In addition to its **Photoplay** Gold Medal and the Academy Best Picture nomination, **Naughty Marietta** won an Oscar for Best Sound Recording (Douglas Shearer) and placed number four on the **Film Daily** Ten Best Pictures poll.

Thus began the glorious reign of Jeanette MacDonald and Nelson Eddy as the American cinema's greatest singing duo. The public demanded follow-ups, and MGM obliged with **Rose-Marie** (1936), **Maytime** (1937), **The Girl of the Golden West** (1938), **Sweethearts** (1938), **New Moon** (1940), **Bitter Sweet** (1940), and **I Married an Angel** (1942). On June 12, 1944, MacDonald and Eddy reprised their Princess Marie and Captain Warrington for Cecil B. DeMille's "Lux Radio Theatre."

A NIGHT AT THE OPERA
1935—92 min.

Producer, Irving Thalberg; **director,** Sam Wood; **story,** James Kevin McGuinness; **screenplay,** George S. Kaufman and Morrie Ryskind (uncredited additional material, Al Boasberg); **music,** Herbert Stothart; **songs,** Nacio Herb Brown and Arthur Freed; Bronislau Kaper, Walter Jurmann, and Ned Washington; **choreography,** Chester Hale; **art directors,** Cedric Gibbons and Ben Carre; **set decorator,** Edwin B. Willis; **wardrobe,** Dolly Tree; **sound,** Douglas Shearer, **camera,** Merritt B. Gerstad; **editor,** William Levanway.

Groucho Marx (**Otis B. Driftwood**); Chico Marx (**Fiorello**); Harpo Marx (**Tomasso**); Kitty Carlisle (**Rosa Castaldi**); Allan Jones (**Riccardo Baroni**); Walter Woolf King (**Rodolfo Lassparri**); Sig Rumann (**Herman Gottlieb**); Margaret Dumont (**Mrs. Claypool**); Edward Keane (**Captain**); Robert Emmet O'Connor (**Detective Henderson**); Billy Gilbert (**Peasant**); Frank Yaconelli (**Engineer**); Sam Marx (**Extra on Ship and at Dock**); Claude Peyton (**Police Captain**); Rodolfo Hoyos (**Count di Luna**); Olga Dane (**Azucena**); James Wolf (**Ferrando**); Ines Palange (**Maid**); Otto Fries (**Elevator Man**); William Gould (**Police Captain**); George Guhl (**Policeman**); Phillips Smalley and Selmer Jackson (**Committeemen**); Harry Allen (**Doorman**); Lorraine Bridges (**Louisa**); Alan Bridge (**Immigration Inspector**); Jack Lipson (**Bit**).

SYNOPSIS

"That's outrageous. If I were you, I wouldn't pay it," cracks Otis B. Driftwood to the wealthy Mrs. Claypool about an inflated dinner bill in a Milan restaurant. Flattered, if puzzled, by the advances of the eye-rolling, moustached Driftwood, she listens raptly to his concocted plan: invest her money in an opera company, supervised by Herman Gottlieb and headlined by sweet Rosa Castaldi and egomaniacal Rodolfo Lassparri. In exchange, Otis will introduce the dowager to New York society. She merrily agrees.

By the time the company boards the ocean liner for New York, others have joined them: Lassparri's dresser Tomasso; low-budget agent Fiorello, who has negotiated a contract with Driftwood to sign up Riccardo Baroni, the true love of Rosa (who is being pursued by the lascivious Lassparri); and the ingratiating Baroni himself.

Sheer insanity prevails thereafter. Aboard the luxury vessel, fifteen people crowd into Driftwood's tiny cabin, all tumbling out on top of Mrs. Claypool when she opens the door in anticipation of a rendezvous with Driftwood. Stowaways Fiorello and Tomasso elude capture in Manhattan by disguising themselves as bearded air heroes and they receive tributes at city hall. Their scheme goes awry when Tomasso spills water on his beard and it comes unhinged. Thereafter he is chased by Detective Henderson through assorted hotel rooms. Still later, Driftwood is fired by Mrs. Claypool, and Rosa is dismissed from the troupe when she resists Lassparri's lechery once too often.

Driftwood decides on a plot of vengeance. On the opening night of the opera, **Il Trovatore**, havoc erupts. Fiorello and Tomasso have made merry with the orchestra's sheet music and the overture becomes "Take Me Out to the Ball Game"; Driftwood runs up and down the aisles hawking peanuts in ballpark style; scenery flies asunder; Tomasso swings across the stage set à la Tarzan; Lassparri is kidnapped.

[2]**Naughty Marietta** was first performed on Broadway in 1910, with Emma Trentini and Orville Harrold starred for 136 performances.

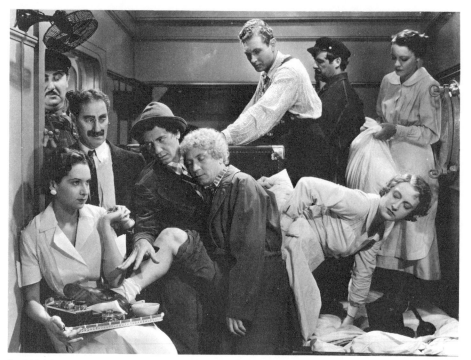

Jack Lipson, Groucho, Chico, and Harpo Marx, Allan Jones, and Frank Yaconelli in A Night at the Opera ('35).

formula, but when Thalberg offered them fifteen percent of the **gross** profits of the film, everything fell into proper place. James K. McGuinness outlined a story in which the irreverent Marxes would wreak havoc in the most dignified atmosphere of America's arts and sciences—the Metropolitan Opera House. The writers of **The Coconuts** and **Animal Crackers**, George S. Kaufman and Morrie Ryskind, were contracted by Thalberg and MGM to write the scenario.[1] Still, even after promising script drafts, the Marxes feared the project. They were sensitive over their Paramount firing. They now argued that **The Coconuts** and **Animal Crackers** had been their most successful shows because they had played them on the stage and had learned what was funny and which routines did not appeal to audiences. Thalberg found a solution—a six-week tour of Salt Lake City, Seattle, Portland, and Santa Barbara. During this stage trek all the material gathered for the project would be auditioned before live audiences, four times daily. In his autobiography, **Harpo Speaks** (1961), the author recalls:

So we hit the road with **A Night at the Opera.** Thalberg was so right. Some of the writers' favorite bits didn't get a snicker. They were cut. On the other hand, stuff that we ad-libbed on the stage, as in the stateroom scene, went into the shooting script. As written—a bunch of guys jamming into a stateroom for no very good reason—this bit failed to get a laugh on stage. The writers got very depressed over it and decided to cut it. We decided, however, to give it one more chance.

So this night we did it our way. Groucho, ordering a meal from a steward while being jostled into the corner of the jammed-up stateroom, said, "And a hard-boiled egg." I honked my horn. "Make it two hard-boiled eggs," said Groucho.

The audience broke up, and as simply as that, a dud became a classic. The stateroom scene is still the best remembered of any bit the Marx Brothers ever performed.

The stateroom scene, while the comic highlight of the film, was by no means the only classic

However, in the show-must-go-on tradition, Baroni and Rosa take over the leading parts. They prove to be the creative sensations of the bizarre evening.

* * *

In 1934 the professional situation looked dim for the Marx Brothers. They had enjoyed incredible success on Broadway in the 1920s in **The Coconuts** and **Animal Crackers.** Their foray into the movies was equally profitable. For Paramount's Long Island studio they made **The Coconuts** (1929), **Animal Crackers** (1930), **Monkey Business** (1931), **Horse Feathers** (1932), and **Duck Soup** (1933). But by the time of the last film comedy, their unique brand of insanity had apparently tired filmgoers. Their studio, boasting the acquisition of sensational Mae West, dropped the comedy team (which then also featured brother Zeppo). The brothers went their separate ways. Groucho was in Skowhegan, Maine, starring in a stock production of **Twentieth Century** when Chico phoned him. As Bob Thomas tells it in **Thalberg: Life and Legend** (1969):

Groucho received a telephone call from Hollywood. "What's new?" Chico asked cheerily.

Groucho, who had been spending his time in the Maine woods, was so struck by the absurdity of the inquiry that he replied, "———— you!" and hung up the phone.

The telephone rang again and it was Chico. "Now wait a minute—don't hang up" he said. "I want to tell you something. I've been playing bridge with Irving Thalberg, and he says he'd like to do some pictures with us. He

had to fight with Mayer, who thinks we're all washed up in pictures, but Irving is firm; he wants us to work with him."

"Okay, Chico," said Groucho. "I'll be back in a few weeks and we'll talk to him."

When Groucho returned to Hollywood, he discovered that meeting with the high-powered Thalberg was not as easy as he had anticipated. Groucho would later confide to Richard Anobile for **The Marx Bros. Scrapbook** (1973):

"He was a hard man to get to see. We would have an appointment to see him at 10 A.M. and 2 P.M. would roll around and he'd still be in conference or something. But we soon broke him of that! One time he was tied up past closing time and we were still waiting for him to see us. So, after his secretary left, we moved all of the filing cabinets and desks in front of his door so he couldn't get out. He was trapped in his office.

"The next time he still kept us waiting, so Harpo ran to the commissary and got some potatoes and we all went to his office, took off our clothes and began roasting the potatoes in the middle of his office.

"When Thalberg came, he found the three of us naked and sitting around a fire roasting potatoes in the middle of the room. He never kept us waiting again!"

Thalberg finally explained his theory to the Marxes, "I'd rather get half the laughs, and give the audience some story and romance to remember." The team at first was dubious of this movie

[1]To ensure the success of the scenario, Thalberg also hired 300-pound Al Boasberg, one of the top one-liner experts of the day. The inventive eccentric was frequently hired by comedian Jack Benny to bolster the comedian's weekly radio script, at a fee of $1,000 weekly. At one point in the refining of the Marx Brothers' script, Thalberg phoned Boasberg and begged to see the latest revisions. The latter said he was just leaving the studio office, but would leave the script there. Thalberg and the comedians rushed over to Boasberg's office, but could not find the script. Then Groucho noted something peculiar on the ceiling—it was the script, shredded into hundreds of one-inch strips and nailed individually to the ceiling. "It took us about five hours to piece it together," Groucho said. "But it was worth it, for it turned out to be the nucleus of one of the most famous scenes we've ever done—the stateroom scene."

sequence. There is the contractural war between Groucho and Chico:

GROUCHO: That's what they call a sanity clause.
CHICO: You can't fool me. There ain't no Sanity Claus.

There is the outrageous climax, with the Marxes kidnapping hambone star Walter Woolf King amidst flying scenery. Then there is the array of wild Marxian remarks dispensed by Groucho (to the stateroom steward, "Do you have any stewed prunes? Well, give 'em some hot coffee—that'll sober 'em up"). Interwoven into the zany fabric was the Thalberg-ordered romance between Allan Jones and Kitty Carlisle and their musical numbers. One bit that did **not** make it into the film was the proposed opening which had the three Marx Brothers bursting through the trademark MGM wreath and roaring in place of Leo the Lion. However, the studio hierarchy thought this gag might reflect badly on the company's prestige.

Despite all the prefilming preparations, **A Night at the Opera** took a long time in actual production. Director Sam Wood, never that certain about his ability to direct comedy, was insistent upon "perfection" in each scene. It resulted in some sequences being reshot twenty or thirty times. Contrary to the standard procedure of editing the film after production was completed, Wood felt that this type of picture required daily editing (and more retakes). This procedure endangered one of the comedians' best qualities—spontaneity. Realizing this problem, Wood urged his cast before each take, "Go in there and sell 'em a load of clams."

Ingenue Kitty Carlisle later commented on this picture:

Groucho would come up to me from time to time time to ask me, "Is this funny?" Then, totally deadpan, he'd try out a line. I'd say, "No, I don't think it is funny," and he'd go away absolutely crushed and try it out on everyone else in the cast. Chico was always playing cards in the back room and had to be called to the set. Harpo would work well until about eleven o'clock. Then he'd stretch out on the nearest piece of furniture and start calling at the top of his voice, "Lunchie! Lunchie!"

Although Carlisle termed the mood of the set "deadly earnest," Allan Jones had less pleasant memories of the filming. On the first day of filming Groucho welcomed Jones on the soundstage with "Hello, Sloucho." Jones asked what that meant. Groucho responded, "You're the fourth Marx Brother in this!" Things did not improve when the controversy arose over whether the dockside song "Alone" should remain in the picture. Jones went to Thalberg for arbitration. The producer decided to back Jones. "The Marx Brothers know comedy—you know music. I'll leave it in." Despite all the care lavished on it, **A Night at the Opera** almost flopped. Early previews received minimal laughs and a drastic several days were spent in the cutting room, tightening up the feature. However, when **A Night at the Opera** was finally released in December 1935, it was judged

to be, in the words of the **New York Daily Mirror**, "a riot of accidents. . . . There is so much joyous and inspired lunacy in **A Night at the Opera**, it shouldn't be missed." The **New York Evening Post** said, "None of their previous films is as consistently and exhaustingly funny, or as rich in comic invention and satire, as **A Night at the Opera**." The film broke admission records at New York's Capitol Theatre, and joined MGM's prestigious **Anna Karenina, Broadway Melody of 1936, The Great Ziegfeld, Rose-Marie, San Francisco,** and **A Tale of Two Cities** in the twenty-five top-grossing films of 1935–36. It earned $3 million profit.

MGM hastened to sign the three Marxes to studio contracts, and Thalberg put another comedy into production, **A Day at the Races** (1937). Thalberg died during production and supervision of the comedy was entrusted to director Sam Wood. The Marxes had tried out material for **At the Races** on the road and it proved a wise decision, as before.

With Thalberg no longer at the studio to intervene for the comedy team, the Marx Brothers thought of ending their Metro contract. However, they were persuaded to stay. Their remaining films[2]—**At the Circus** (1939), **Go West** (1940), and **The Big Store** (1941)—lacked the careful preparation and high-caliber mounting of their previous MGM efforts. When their MGM contracts expired, so had much of their cinema appeal.

A Night at the Opera has long been a cult favorite; the stateroom scene was included in Metro's **That's Entertainment: Part II** (1976). Many Marx Brothers buffs have watched the film dozens of times, including Mike Nichols. The latter met Groucho at a cinema colony party and the following conversation occurred:

NICHOLS: Groucho, I must tell you—I've seen **A Night at the Opera** seventeen times.
GROUCHO (very touched): Really?
NICHOLS: Yes, I just couldn't get over that love story between Allan Jones and Kitty Carlisle!

NIGHT MUST FALL
1937—117 min.

Producer, Hunt Stromberg; **director,** Richard Thorpe; based on the play by Emlyn Williams; **screenplay,** John Van Druten; **art director,** Cedric Gibbons; **music,** Edward Ward; **camera,** Ray June; **editor,** Robert J. Kern.
Robert Montgomery (**Danny**); Rosalind Russell (**Olivia**); Dame May Whitty (**Mrs. Bramson**); Alan Marshal (**Justin**); Merle Tottenham (**Dora**); Kathleen Harrison (**Mrs. Terence**); Matthew Boulton (**Belsize**); Eily Malyon (**Nurse**); E. E. Clive (**Guide**); Beryl Mercer (**Saleslady**); Winifred Harris (**Mrs. Laurie**).

---

[2]In 1938 they went over to RKO for **Room Service,** which was not a hit.

Robert Montgomery in Night Must Fall *('37).*

SYNOPSIS

In England charming Welsh page boy Danny has just murdered and decapitated a congenial, good-paying female guest at the hotel where he is employed. He buries the body in the nearby woods and retains the head in a hat box.

Danny moves on to the residence of wheelchair-bound Mrs. Bramson, who also takes a fancy to the handsome young man. Soon Danny becomes an adopted member of the household. On discovering the location of the family safe, he plots to kill the old woman.

Also residing with Mrs. Bramson is her niece Olivia, who later discovers Danny's homicidal background. Rather than report him to the police, Olivia protects him because she too has succumbed to his suave manner and good looks.

By chance Olivia leaves her aunt alone with Danny. She returns to discover Mrs. Bramson's corpse. She nearly realizes the same fate before her narrow escape and Danny's eventual apprehension by the authorities.

* * *

By 1937 Robert Montgomery had wearied of playing the ever-suave, often empty-headed vis-à-vis of Norma Shearer, Joan Crawford, and others at MGM. He began to campaign for more serious acting assignments. It must have been an embarrassment for the ambitious, intelligent star when the studio fanned his honest plea into a nationwide movie fan contest. "Do you want to see Robert Montgomery in serious dramatic roles, or in romantic comedy parts?" read the question. Cash prizes were promised to the authors of those letters best explaining their choice.

Even if movie enthusiasts had opted for Montgomery's turning to heavy dramatics, Metro had no real intentions of removing the actor from the profitable, debonair mold that had become his mainstay at the studio. However, the studio did not reckon with the determined star. In the autumn of 1936 Montgomery had seen the Broadway version of **Night Must Fall,** in which Emlyn Williams (who wrote the drama) and Dame May Whitty re-creacted their London stage parts. Montgomery was so impressed by the possibilities of the thriller as a vehicle for himself that he returned to California and nagged his employers to purchase the screen rights. Eventually they conceded, greatly hoping the venture would prove a disaster and teach the rebellious actor a much needed lesson.

In January 1937 filming began on the psychological drama. Seventy-two-year-old Dame May Whitty was signed to re-create her stage part of the hypochondriac who meets her death. (It was the beginning of a long MGM tenure for the distinguished British actress.) For the role of Olivia, Metro cast pert Rosalind Russell, who was eager to enlarge her repertoire of screen parts by undertaking an assignment of greater acting range than was her wont. The English street, cottage, and cricket-field settings were re-created on the studio back lot, inspired by photographs of the real items. In the stage versions of **Night Must Fall,** Williams utilized a Welsh accent; however, Montgomery, more at ease with another dialect, adopted an Irish lilt for his dialogue. Director Richard Thorpe also made an addition to the screen adaptation: a black cat which he felt would bring luck to the production.

When released in April 1937, **Night Must Fall** was regarded as a rare offering. Winston Burdett, **Brookly Daily Eagle** critic who was obviously conditioned to the gothic horrors of the Boris Karloff–Bela Lugosi nightmare tales from Universal, found the feature "a lethargic thriller which goes on for nearly two hours with barely any heightening of effect." But Bland Johaneson of the **New York Daily Mirror** begged to differ: "The most exhilarating shrouds of horror hang over **Night Must Fall.** It represents a provocative imagination, a skilled adapter, a sensitive director, a splendid acting job." Kate Cameron of the **New York Daily News** concurred, "The eerie atmosphere effects caught by the keen eye of the camera are of considerable help to heightening the suspense which Richard Thorpe's tight direction and brilliant editing of the picture produce on the screen as the story unravels."

When **Night Must Fall** opened at Grauman's Chinese Theatre in Hollywood on May 4, 1937 (a few days after the New York debut), Louis B. Mayer displayed his ire with Montgomery and his disgust with this sick film. He had handbills distributed to ticket purchasers disclaiming all responsibility for what the audience was about to see. This fact was reiterated in a special trailer, which preceded each showing of the film. However, when the positive reviews began appearing, Mayer did a fast turnabout. He stopped the leaflet-giving and the trailer showing.

Time magazine informed its readers, "Any picture in which Robert Montgomery, whose previous contribution to the screen has been a seven-year marathon of ingenuous charm, gives a first-rate performance in a different role, rates as at least a major surprise." This change-of-pace assignment won Montgomery an Oscar nomination, but he lost the Best Actor prize to Spencer Tracy (of MGM's **Captains Courageous**). The rumor yet persists that the Metro bosses, following the dictates of Mayer, ordered their workers not to vote for Montgomery. Dame May Witty was nominated for her impressive work, but she lost the Best Supporting Actress Award to Alice Brady of Twentieth Century–Fox's **In Old Chicago.** The National Board of Review, however, did select **Night Must Fall** as its number-one film of the year.[1]

Montgomery, who had played with Russell in **Forsaking All Others** (1934), and **Trouble for Two,** would hereafter appear with her in the comedy-cum-drama **Live, Love and Learn** (1937) and later in **Fast and Loose** (1939), a detective venture in the **Thin Man** vein. He would continue to wage a seesaw battle with the studio for more demanding acting assignments.

In 1964 MGM released its British-shot remake of **Night Must Fall,** starring Albert Finney, Susan Hampshire, and Mona Washbourne. Czech director Karel Reisz gave the proceedings a very sexual interpretation, but the film emerged awkward and weak.

NINOTCHKA
1939—110 min.

Producer-director, Ernst Lubitsch; based on the story by Melchior Lengyel; **screenplay,** Charles Brackett, Billy Wilder, and Walter Reisch; **art directors,** Cedric Gibbons and Randall Duell; **set decorator,** Edwin B. Willis; **gowns,** Adrian; **music,** Werner Heymann; **makeup,** Jack Dawn; **assistant director,** Horace Hough; **sound,** Douglas Shearer; **camera,** William Daniels; **editor,** Gene Ruggiero.

Greta Garbo (**Ninotchka [Lena Yakushova]**); Melvyn Douglas (**Count Leon Dolga**); Ina Claire (**Grand Duchess Swana**); Sig Rumann (**Michael Iranoff**); Felix Bressart (**Buljanoff**); Alexander Granach (**Kopalski**); Bela Lugosi (**Commissar Razinin**); Gregory Gaye (**Count Alexis Rakonin**); Richard Carle (**Vaston**); Edwin Maxwell (**Mercier**); Rolfe Sedan (**Hotel Manager**); George Tobias (**Russian Visa Official**); Dorothy Adams (**Jacqueline, Swana's Maid**); Charles Judels (**Pere Mathieu, the Cafe Owner**); Lawrence Grant (**General Savitsky**); Frank Reicher and Edwin Stanley (**Lawyers**); Peggy Moran (**French Maid**); Mary Forbes (**Lady Lavenham**); Armand Kaliz (**Louis, the Headwaiter**); Tamara Shayne (**Anna**); William Irving (**Bartender**); Bess Flowers (**Gossip**); Jody Gilbert (**Streetcar Conductress**); Kay Stewart and Jenifer Gray (**Cigarette Girls**).

---

[1] The British trade paper **Kine Weekly** judged, "Excellent serious entertainment, unique murder mystery skillfully adapted from the London stage success. Both pathological and psychological, the theme plays more on the senses than the emotions, yet, in spite of its subtle construction, continuous talk and great length, it holds with a relentless draw."

SYNOPSIS
In the 1930s the Soviet government sends Michael Iranoff, Buljanoff, and Kopalski to Paris to sell imperial jewels and use the funds to purchase needed farm equipment for the homeland.

The former owner of the jewels, Grand Duchess Swana, has her boyfriend, Count Leon Dolga, file a court suit to prevent the sale of her precious goods. When the Soviet government learns of the delay, it dispatches Lena Yakushova (Ninotchka) to Paris to untangle the problems.

She encounters the three comrades enjoying the high life of capitalistic Paris. Later Leon meets Ninotchka and, unaware of her identity or mission, falls in love with the stern foreigner. Later the duchess has her jewels stolen, but she agrees to relinquish her title to them if Ninotchka returns to Russia. Leon attempts to follow his newfound love to Moscow but cannot obtain the requisite passport.

The three comrades return to Russia and are promptly sent to Constantinople to sell furs. Ninotchka receives orders from Commissar Razinin to aid the trio. Upon arriving in Turkey Ninotchka learns that the three Russians plan to remain there permanently and open a restaurant. Leon is also there and wins Ninotchka as his wife.

* * *

When I first heard this joke I laughed myself sick! Here goes. A man comes into a restaurant. He sits down at the table and he says, "Waiter, bring me a cup of coffee without cream." Five minutes later the waiter comes back and says, "I'm sorry, sir, we have no cream. Can it be without milk?" . . . Oh, you have no sense of humor! None whatsoever. Not a grain of humor in you. There's not a laugh in you.

At which point dapper Melvyn Douglas topples over backward in his lunchroom chair—and Garbo laughs, and **laughs,** and LAUGHS in her most delightful screen performance as **Ninotchka.** The legendary satire on Communism was formulated into a Metro picture after a famous exchange between director Ernst Lubitsch[1] and the high-priced Swedish actress.

LUBITSCH: Greta, vy don't you tell those idiots in your studio to let us do a picture together? Gott, how I vould love to direct a picture vith you!
GARBO: You tell them, Ernst. I'm far too tired to talk to studio executives.

The film remains the finest vehicle of Garbo's celluloid mystique, a lasting tribute to her qualities as a screen enchantress. The picture is a fine sophisticated farce free of the heady mysticism of her **Mata Hari** (1932), **Anna Karenina** (1935), and other films, and a fine companion piece to the exquisite dramatics of her **Camille** (1936).

The pungent script, composed by Charles Brackett, Billy Wilder, and Walter Reisch (based

---

[1] At one point in pre-production when it seemed Ernst Lubitsch would not be available to direct **Ninotchka,** MGM began negotiations with William Wyler to direct the film.

Greta Garbo and Melvyn Douglas in Ninotchka *('39).*

number three in **Film Daily**'s poll of the best pictures, under United Artists' **Rebecca** and Twentieth Century–Fox's **The Grapes of Wrath**.

There would be one more Garbo picture, the poorly conceived **Two-Faced Woman** (1941), in which the star danced a rumba, swam, and glided on skis. **Time** magazine reported, "It is almost as shocking as seeing your mother drunk." Garbo thereafter went into temporary retirement, which became permanent. A legend had disappeared from MGM and the Hollywood scene.

Ninotchka's success would lead MGM to hatch **Comrade X** (1940), a copycat vehicle for Hedy Lamarr and Clark Gable. The **Ninotchka** story itself served as the source of Cole Porter's 1955 Broadway musical **Silk Stockings**, starring Hildegarde Neff and Don Ameche; Rouben Mamoulian directed the MGM musical version **Silk Stockings** (1957), with Fred Astaire and Cyd Charisse. A rather bizarre comedy offspring, **The Iron Petticoat** (MGM, 1956), featured Katharine Hepburn and Bob Hope. It was a disaster. Yet another variation of the **Ninotchka** story was Howard Hughes' **Jet Pilot**, starring John Wayne and Janet Leigh, which did not have its modest general release until 1958, several years after production had begun at the RKO facilities.

NORTH BY NORTHWEST
1959 C—136 min.

Producer, Alfred Hitchcock; **associate producer**, Herbert Coleman; **director**, Hitchcock; **screenplay**, Ernest Lehman; **production designer**, Robert Boyle; **art directors**, William A. Horning and Merrill Pye; **assistant director**, Robert Saunders; **music**, Bernard Herrmann; **makeup**, William Tuttle; **sound**, Franklin Milton; **special effects**, A. Arnold Gillespie and Lee LeBlanc; **camera**, Robert Burks; **editor**, George Tomasini.

Cary Grant (**Roger O. Thornhill**); Eva Marie Saint (**Eve Kendall**); James Mason (**Phillip Vandamm**); Jessie Royce Landis (**Clara Thornhill**); Leo G. Carroll (**The Professor**); Philip Ober (**Lester Townsend**); Josephine Hutchinson (**Handsome Woman**); Martin Landau (**Leonard**); Adam Williams (**Valerian**); Edward C. Platt (**Victor Larabee**); Robert Ellenstein (**Licht**); Les Tremayne (**Auctioneer**); Philip Coolidge (**Dr. Cross**); Patrick McVey and Ken Lynch (**Chicago Policemen**); Edward Binns (**Captain Junket**); Nora Marlowe (**Anna, the Housekeeper**); Alexander Lockwood (**Judge Anson B. Flynn**); Stanley Adams (**Lieutenant Harding**); Lawrence Dobkin (**Cartoonist**); Harvey Stephens (**Stockbroker**); Walter Coy (**Reporter**); Madge Kennedy (**Housewife**); Baynes Barron and Jimmy Cross (**Taxi Driver**); Tommy Farrell (**Elevator Starter**); Maudie Prickett (**Elise, the Maid**); Doris Singh (**Indian Girl**); Howard Negley (**Conductor**); Malcolm Atterbury (**Man on Road**); Helen Spring (**Woman at Auction**); Olan Soule (**Assistant Auctioneer**); Patricia Cutts (**Bit**); Dale Van Sickel (**Ranger**); Alfred Hitchcock (**Man Who Misses Bus**).

on the Melchior Lengyel story), began production at Culver City on May 19, 1939. It required fifty-eight days to shoot and combined elements that provided for faultless entertainment. Lubitsch later explained the Garbo approach to the classic picture: "During the first half of the story she is completely humorless. That is how we got our comedy, by showing humorous things happening to a humorless person. Then, after she meets Melvyn Douglas, she develops a sense of humor and becomes gay and frivolous."

The director exercised his acclaimed light touch against Cedric Gibbons sets, the latter ranging from the Eiffel Tower to sumptuous nightclubs to a drab Soviet apartment Ninotchka shares with her friend Anna (Tamara Shayne). The comedy boasted a superior cast: debonair Melvyn Douglas at his witty best; Sig Rumann, Felix Bressart, and Alexander Granach eccentrically amusing as Ninotchka's fun-seeking cohorts; and Bela Lugosi (fresh from a "comeback" as Ygor in Universal's **Son of Frankenstein**) in a brief appearance as the heroine's superior. Especially memorable was an aging, well-corseted Ina Claire as the exquisitely bitchy Grand Duchess Swana. It is her stinging repartee with Ninotchka that provides some of the film's best moments.

NINOTCHKA: You see, it would have been very embarrassing for people of my sort to wear low-cut gowns in the old Russia. The lashes of the Cossacks across our backs were not very becoming, and you know how vain women are.
SWANA: Yes, you're quite right about the Cossacks. We made a great mistake when we let

them use their whips. They had such reliable guns.

Ninotchka bowed at Radio City Music Hall in November 1939. The ad lines read "GARBO LAUGHS!" (recalling the ad campaign for her **Anna Christie**, 1930, when the studio announced, "GARBO TALKS!"). Other promotional tags stated, "What makes Garbo blush and laugh in **Ninotchka**? Don't pronounce it . . . see it!" The **New York Times'** Frank S. Nugent had to see the feature twice to decipher all the dialogue lost in the laughter of the packed house. He reported, "Garbo's **Ninotchka** is one of the sprightliest comedies of the year, a gay and impertinent and malicious show which never pulls the punch lines (no matter how far below the belt they may land) and finds the screen's austere first lady of drama playing in deadpan comedy with the assurance of a Buster Keaton." Howard Barnes (**New York Herald-Tribune**) revealed, "Now that she has done it, it seems incredible that Greta Garbo has never done comedy before **Ninotchka**. For in this gay burlesque of Bolsheviks abroad, the great actress reveals a command of comic inflection which fully matches the emotional depth or tragic power of her earlier triumphs. It is a joyous, subtly shaded, and utterly enchanting portrayal."

Ninotchka—a box-office revelation—was Oscar-nominated as Best Picture, and Garbo received her fourth and final nomination for Best Actress. MGM's **Gone With the Wind** and that epic's star, Vivien Leigh, however, were the victors. **Ninotchka** did place fourth in the National Board of Review's Ten Best Film list, and was

Cary Grant and Eva Marie Saint in North by Northwest *('59).*

known to Roger and enlists his help for a final showdown with the enemy. The denouement occurs in a scramble across the presidential facade of South Dakota's Mount Rushmore. The caper now closed, Roger and Eve continue their torrid romance.

* * *

Taking its title from **Hamlet** ("I am but mad north-northwest: when the wind is southerly I know a hawk from a handsaw"), this delicious spy thriller was a high point of 1950s cinema. Actually it was only the second choice of director Alfred Hitchcock, who had contracted with MGM to make **The Wreck of the Mary Deare** (1959). But after a month's work on that picture, he gave up attempting to produce a workable script and Michael Anderson replaced him on that project. According to Hitchcock, "Now it so happened that a New York journalist had given me an idea about an ordinary businessman being mistaken for a decoy spy. I took that and, with Ernie Lehman [the scripter with whom he had been collaborating on **Mary Deare**], worked up the whole thing. It took about a year to write."

Starring in the $4,000,000 production was Cary Grant, making his fourth Hitchcock feature. Eva Marie Saint, another in the succession of icy blonde actresses so favored by the director, was the "heroine," and James Mason was assigned to yet another villain's role. While shooting the color, VistaVision[1] (widescreen) picture in such location spots as Manhattan; Bakersfield, California; and Mount Rushmore, South Dakota.[2] Hitchcock pursued his objective of avoiding the mystery movie cliché.

The crop-dusting scene, staged out near Bakersfield here, was an example of avoiding the cliché. In ordinary circumstances, if they're going to put a man on the spot, they make him stand under a street lamp on a corner at night. The cobbles are washed by the recent rain. A black cat slithers along the wall. Somebody peers from behind a curtain. A black limousine goes by and—boom, boom, boom!—that's the cliché.

So I said, I won't do it that way. I'll make it in bright sunshine, without a tree or a house in sight. Thus the audiences are worked up much more: they know the man's put on the spot, but they're mystified as to where it's going to come from. I had him waiting and waiting. Then a car pulled up, a man got out, approached our hero, and said, "That's funny." "What is?" "There's a crop duster over there dusting a place where there are no crops." And with that he hops a bus and is off. Sure enough, the plane then dives on our hero and attacks him; no cliché.

SYNOPSIS

Because the Professor, a U.S. Central Intelligence operative, hopes to pressure an alien organization into action, he sets a fabricated "Mr. Caplan" on their trail. The espionage group's leader, Phillip Vandamm, mistakenly believes that Madison Avenue advertising executive Roger O. Thornhill is Caplan. He is kidnapped from the Hotel Plaza and taken to a Long Island mansion where he is forced to consume a bottle of bourbon. Then he is placed in a car with the expectation that he will drive himself to his death. He survives, to be arrested for drunken driving.

Later he traces the agents to the United Nations, where he is accused of murdering a man whom he has been questioning. Roger then escapes and begins the long trek (via the 20th Century Limited luxury train) across country, hoping to unravel the web of mystery. En route, he encounters Vandamm's mistress, icy cool Eve Kendall, whose assistance is not always dependable in Roger's attempts to remain alive. At one point, he is lured to a deserted midwestern prairie and attacked by a machine-gunning crop-dusting plane.

Thereafter, the Professor makes himself

---

[1]At one point the picture was to be a Paramount release, thus the MGM studio made use of its competitor's VistaVision process instead of employing its own CinemaScope lenses.

[2]Huge soundstage reproductions of the presidential faces were employed for much of the climactic chase.

Hitchcock has always insisted that **North by Northwest** was "one big joke," a point of view emphasized by the sophisticated tongue-in-cheek quality of the proceedings. One does not easily forget the amusement amidst tension in the elevator sequence in which Grant's on-screen mother, Jessie Royce Landis, turns to the two men her son says are would-be assassins, and asks benignly, "You gentlemen aren't **really** trying to kill my son, are you?" Or the double-edged repartee between the hero and heroine aboard the Chicago-bound train. Or the finale dissolve which sees the hero hanging precipitously over the side of Mount Rushmore's facade to rescue his lady fair, which scene then blends into one aboard the train where he is helping her to his upper berth from the one below.

One bit of comedy that appealed to the director was not incorporated into the action. "When Cary Grant was on Mount Rushmore," Hitchcock explained, "I would have liked to put him into Lincoln's nostril and let him have a sneezing fit."

Released in midsummer 1959, **North by Northwest** enjoyed unanimous critical applause. **Variety** called the film "the Alfred Hitchcock mixture as before—suspense, intrigue, comedy, humor. Seldom has the concoction been served up so delectably." **Saturday Review** praised the picture as "much the best Hitchcock that has come along in some years." British **Monthly Film Bulletin** lauded the "smooth defiance of logic, this wearing of implausibilities lightly, which gives the film its thoroughly entertaining unity, from Saul Bass's grille-like credits and the first brooding strains of Bernard Herrmann's score to the final shrug of defeat given by James Mason's polished, imperturbable mastermind." Enthusiastic reviews went to stars Cary Grant ("brings technique and charm to the central character"—**Variety**) and Eva Marie Saint ("emerges both the sweet heroine and a glamorous charmer"—**New York Times**) as well as to such spendid supporting performers as Mason, Landis, Carroll, and Martin Landau (the last especially effective in his sinister assignment). Hitchcock, of course, made his traditional cameo appearance, this time as a New York denizen who suffers the slamming of a bus door in his face.

North by Northwest grossed $6,362,000 and the studio was delighted with Hitchcock's success. However, the director shifted his operations to Universal City shortly after **North by Northwest**, where he directed **Psycho** (1960) and remained for a succession of other feature film productions.

NORTHWEST PASSAGE
1940 C—125 min.

Producer, Hunt Stromberg; **director,** King Vidor and **uncredited,** Jack Conway; based on the novel by Kenneth Roberts; **screenplay,** Laurence Stallings and Talbot Jennings; **assistant director,**

Robert Golden; **Technicolor consultants,** Natalie Kalmus and Henri Jaffa; **music,** Herbert Stothart; **art directors,** Cedric Gibbons and Malcolm Brown; **set decorator,** Edwin B. Willis; **makeup,** Jack Dawn; **sound,** Douglas Shearer; **camera,** Sidney Wagner and William V. Skall; **editor,** Conrad A. Nervig.

Spencer Tracy (**Major Robert Rogers**); Robert Young (**Langdon Towne**); Walter Brennan (**Hunk Marriner**); Ruth Hussey (**Elizabeth Browne**); Nat Pendleton (**Cap Huff**); Louis Hector (**Reverend Browne**); Robert Barrat (**Humphrey Towne**); Lumsden Hare (**Lord Amherst**); Donald MacBride (**Sergeant McNott**); Isabel Jewell (**Jennie Coit**); Douglas Walton (**Lieutenant Avery**); Addison Richards (**Lieutenant Crofton**); Hugh Sothern (**Jesse Beachacham**); Regis Toomey (**Webster**); Montagu Love (**Wiseman Clagett**); Lester Matthews (**Sam Livermore**); Truman Bradley (**Captain Ogden**); Andrew Pena (**Konkapot**).

SYNOPSIS

Langdon Towne, young artist, loves Elizabeth Browne and hopes to marry her. But the disapproval of her father, Reverend Mr. Browne, dashes his hopes and drives him to liquor. Unseemly conduct results in his leaving town, by request. He turns to pal Hunk Marriner for consolation. Both men meet Major Robert Rogers, head of the Rangers, which travel the 1759 frontier protecting the territories from ravaging Indians. Langdon and Hunk join the band, and set off for St. Francis to combat the vicious Indians.

The trip is a grueling ordeal. The Rangers scale mountains with heavy boats on their shoulders, cope with the insects and indelicacies of the swamps, and ford a river by forming a human chain. They finally reach their destination, where they engage in a bloody battle. They are victorious, burning the village and killing all the inhabitants.

The campaign, however, has seriously fatigued the hungry band, whose food supply and stamina have dwindled. The Rangers later trudge to Fort Wentworth, hoping to find aid from the British soldiers stationed there. But the fort is empty, and barren of food and supplies. Meanwhile, vengeful savages swell about the stockade, planning gruesome vengeance. Fortunately, the British arrive in time. The Indians are repulsed and the men return to Portsmouth as heroes.

Major Rogers announces a new expedition to the West, in search of the elusive Northwest Passage. However, Langdon, having proved his worth, remains in Portsmouth, to pursue his career as an artist and to marry Elizabeth.

* * *

The year 1939 was a big one for Westerns: Twentieth Century–Fox's **Jesse James,** United Artists' **Stagecoach,** Warner Bros.' **Dodge City** and **The Oklahoma Kid,** Paramount's **Union Pacific,** and Universal's **Destry Rides Again.** During the latter half of the year, MGM had a lavish outdoor tale in the works, though it was not released until 1940. The entry was **Northwest Passage,** from the bestselling novel of 1937 by Kenneth Roberts. It was one of the few films shot entirely in Technicolor during the 1930s and remains today a dramatic adventure saga. The project benefited greatly from top directors (King Vidor and uncre-

Walter Brennan, Spencer Tracy, and Robert Young in a publicity pose for Northwest Passage *('40).*

dited Jack Conway), a sterling cast (Spencer Tracy, Robert Young, Walter Brennan, et al.), and superb action sequences.

MGM purchased the screen rights to Roberts' oversized book in 1937. When shooting began in July 1939 in Idaho, producer Hunt Stromberg planned to film the picture in two separate parts. As King Vidor observed decades later:

Northwest Passage was a peculiar thing— it's a book in two parts. I made all the first part, which was the prologue; we were still supposed to do the second part of the book, and the producer, Hunt Stromberg, never could make up his mind about the second part. It would have been fun, because [in the first part] the man (Spencer Tracy) is built up to be a hero and the last part is his downfall. But they just couldn't see it. For a while they held the actors, I think for a couple of weeks, and said, "We'll have this fixed"—and I started shooting, believing they would send me the pages up there, and they never arrived. I went to New York for some reason and they had another director shoot the ending. So we came home. And then they released the prologue.

"Up there," in Oregon, the company for twelve weeks tolerated the elements and makeshift location headquarters to create the rousing yarn of eighteenth-century New England. The color photography of Sidney Wagner and William V. Skall was breathtaking, capturing the blues of the water and the greens of the forests with a vivid beauty.

Northwest Passage was released on February 23, 1940. It was a critical and commercial triumph. Philip T. Hartung of **Commonweal** reported, "Laurence Stallings and Talbot Jennings, in making a good screenplay from Kenneth Roberts' **Northwest Passage,** wisely limited themselves to the first part of the novel, the 1759 expedition of Rogers' Rangers to wipe out the Indians at St. Francis. Their script, Hunt Stromberg's production, King Vidor's dynamic direction, and the convincing acting of an almost all-male cast, led by Spencer Tracy, in another of those tremendously moving performances that win him Oscars, combine to make a patriotic, historic film of first caliber."

Northwest Passage placed eighth on the **Film Daily** Ten Best Picture poll of 1940. And it was, with **Another Thin Man, Babes in Arms, Gone with the Wind, Ninotchka,** and **The Women,** among the twenty-one top-grossing pictures of 1939–40.

In 1958–59 MGM-TV produced the video series "Northwest Passage." It starred Keith Larsen (Major Rogers), Buddy Ebsen (Sergeant Hunk Marriner), and Don Burnett (Ensign Langdon Towne). The half-hour show was telecast over NBC-TV.

ON THE TOWN
1949 C—98 min.

Producer, Arthur Freed; **associate producer,** Roger Edens; **directors,** Gene Kelly and Stanley Donen;

based on the play by Adolph Green, Betty Comden, and Leonard Bernstein, based on an idea by Jerome Robbins; **screenplay,** Comden and Green; **music,** Bernstein and Edens; **songs,** Bernstein, Comden, and Green; Edens, Comden, and Green; **music director,** Lennie Hayton; **orchestrator,** Conrad Salinger; **vocal arranger,** Saul Chaplin; **Technicolor consultants,** Henri Jaffa and James Gooch; **art directors,** Cedric Gibbons and Jack Martin Smith; **set decorators,** Edwin B. Willis and Jack D. Moore; **costumes,** Helen Rose; **makeup,** Jack Dawn; **sound,** Douglas Shearer; **camera,** Harold Rosson; **editor,** Ralph E. Winters.

Gene Kelly **(Gabey);** Frank Sinatra **(Chip);** Betty Garrett **(Brunhilde Esterhazy);** Ann Miller **(Claire Huddesen);** Jules Munshin **(Ozzie);** Vera-Ellen **(Ivy Smith);** Florence Bates **(Mme Dilyovska);** Alice Pearce **(Lucy Schmeeler);** George Meader **(Professor);** Bea Benaderet **(Brooklyn Girl);** Eugene Borden **(Waiter);** Hans Conried **(François);** Judy Holliday **(Voice of a Sailor's Date).**

SYNOPSIS
Sailors Gabey, Chip, and Ozzie are on a twenty-four hour leave in New York City. A poster for Miss Turnstiles, Ivy Smith, catches their eyes. Gabey determines to locate her during the brief furlough. En route, Chip encounters aggressive cabdriver Brunhilde Esterhazy and Ozzie discovers Claire Huddensen, a tap-dancing anthropologist researching her thesis "Modern Man, What Is It?" at the Museum of Natural History. They combine forces to search for Ivy, whom Gabey locates at a dance class in Carnegie Hall. They arrange an evening rendezvous, which Ivy breaks since she is committed to dancing with a hootch show at Coney Island. Serving as Gabey's substitute date is Hildy's bronchial roommate, Lucy Schmeeler.

All is resolved for the happy sextet when Gabey rediscovers Ivy at Coney Island.

* * *

On Thursday, December 29, 1949, Radio City Music Hall of New York City established a new record: a crowd estimated at 10,000, in a two-file line stretching seven blocks, queued up to purchase tickets for the Music Hall's holiday show. The attraction? MGM's **On the Town,** advertised as "Skirts, skyscrapers and scamperings are the theme as these three skittering scamps take highways and byways of the big city!" Innovative and lively, **On the Town** was one of the happiest hits of the Arthur Freed—MGM filming unit.

The property had long been an acquisition of MGM. The studio had purchased the screen rights to the musical for $250,000, in one of the first pre-Broadway production deals to be made. The show, with book and lyrics by Adolph Green and Betty Comden and music by Leonard Bernstein, had opened at the Adelphi Theatre on December 28, 1944, and it ran 463 performances. Viewing an early performance of the hit show was Louis B. Mayer. He left the theatre regretting having anything to do with the musical; it offered, he felt, no promise cinematically.[1] Freed felt differ-

ently, and after Comden and Green reported to Culver City to begin their contract in 1947, the producer assigned them to prepare the stage hit for a movie treatment.

Many problems faced the project. Immediately cast as the three gobs were Gene Kelly (who was to codirect and cochoreograph with Stanley Donen), Frank Sinatra, and Jules Munshin, the trio who had recently starred in Metro's **Take Me out to the Ball Game** (1949). Because of the men's varied personalities and talents, the original stage roles had to be restyled to accommodate the screen players. More delicate an impasse was Freed's dislike of most of Bernstein's stage music. Fortunately, Bernstein had little interest in the film project and Freed managed to return to him the rights to all his music from **On the Town,** while retaining four of the show tunes.[2] Comden and Green, at fees of $85,000 for book rewrites and $25,000 for new lyrics (as well as sixty percent of the $250,000 original purchase price), created a new score. The result: "On the Town" (featuring the six principals: Sinatra, Kelly, Munshin, Vera-Ellen, Betty Garrett, and Ann Miller), "Prehistoric Man" (Miller, Kelly, Munshin, Garrett, Sinatra), "You're Awful" (Garrett and Sinatra), "Main Street" (a Kelly–Vera-Ellen song and dance), "You Can Count on Me" (Miller, Garrett, **On the Town** stage veteran Alice Pearce, Kelly, Sinatra, and Munshin), "Pearl of the Persian Sea" (a cooch dance with Kelly, Sinatra, and Munshin posing as dancers), and the gag number "That's All There Is Folks."[3]

Perhaps the biggest hurdle which **On the Town** had to surmount was the creative forces' demand for location shooting in New York. When Manhattan's Regency Theatre held an MGM retrospective in the summer of 1977, Kelly reminisced about his favorite feature picture:

This film was a milestone—the first musical to be shot on location. We took the musical off the soundstage and showed that it could be realistic.

The idea of doing such a thing was anathema to the studio moguls. We shot a lot of it in New York and showed sailors getting off their ship in the Brooklyn Navy Yard and singing and dancing through the streets of New York. You can't imagine how crazy everybody thought this was at the time, but it changed the faces

---

[1] By the time **On the Town** went into actual production at MGM, Dore Schary had arrived on the lot as head of

production; he was antimusicals, feeling they were too luxurious for a studio's budget. However, he was advised to leave the Freed unit autonomous at this time; he complied.

[2] The Bernstein numbers remaining were: "I Feel Like I'm Not out of Bed Yet," "New York, New York," (Sinatra, Kelly, Munshin), "Miss Turnstiles Ballet" (Vera-Ellen), and "Come Up to My Place" (Garrett and Sinatra).

[3] One of the highlights of **On the Town** was the dream sequence. In 1979, Kelly would tell James Powers in an interview about that sensual segment that might have been censorship material. "There was nothing the censors could put their fingers on. The red color, the girl in black, and the sailor in white were very sensuous. The moves were sensuous. Yet I never laid a glove on her. There was nothing the censors could say. If they did, I could have said, 'What? Do you have a dirty mind?' But, yes, it was very sensual, and the colors did it.

Gene Kelly, Jules Munshin, Ann Miller, Frank Sinatra, and Betty Garrett in On the Town *('49).*

Zoo, Central Park, Carnegie Hall, the El subway, nightclubs, cabs, etc. As Stanley Donen recalls in Hugh Fordin's **The World of Entertainment** (1975):

> "In this film we tried a great many new things, aided as we were by the theme which was very cinematic. There was no stage, no theatre, simply the street. We never told ourselves, 'Now we're going to do something no one has ever done before.' We simply thought that this was the way one should deal with, one should conceive, a musical comedy. This is the way we felt—we didn't realize we were making any innovations."

On the Town was completed in a happy forty-seven days, on July 2, 1949, at a cost of $2,111,250. When released late in 1949, the movie enjoyed outstanding business and warm reviews. **Variety** rejoiced, "The pep, enthusiasm and apparent fun the makers of **On the Town** had in putting it together comes through to the audience and gives the picture its best asset. Picture is crammed with songs and dance numbers, the book is sufficient to carry it along, the Technicolor hues are top flight, and the cast hard working." **Time** magazine labeled **On the Town** "a film so exuberant that it threatens at moments to bounce right off the screen . . . leaves a happy impression that MGM has hit upon a bright new idiom for cinemusicals and a bright new directing team that knows how to use it."

On the Town won an Oscar for Roger Edens and Lennie Hayton for Best Scoring of a musical picture. The film grossed $4.4 million and has remained so popular on television and in retrospectives that there have been two off-Broadway stage revivals (both in 1959), a London revival in 1963, and a Broadway return in November 1971. "The picture has dated a bit," said Gene Kelly in 1977, "but it's the closest to my heart."

OUR VINES HAVE TENDER GRAPES
1945—105 min.

Producer, Robert Sisk; **director,** Roy Rowland; based on the book by George Victor Martin; **screenplay,** Dalton Trumbo; **music,** Bronislau Kaper; **art directors,** Cedric Gibbons and Edward Carfagno; **set decorators,** Edwin B. Willis and Hugh Hunt; **assistant director,** Horace Hough; **sound,** Douglas Shearer; **special effects,** A. Arnold Gillespie and Danny Hall; **camera,** Robert Surtees; **editor,** Ralph E. Winters.

Edward G. Robinson **(Martinius Jacobson);** Margaret O'Brien **(Selma Jacobson);** James Craig **(Nels Halverson);** Agnes Moorehead **(Ma Jacobson);** Jackie "Butch" Jenkins **(Arnold Hanson);** Morris Carnovsky **(Bjorn Bjornson);** Frances Gifford **(Viola Johnson);** Sara Haden **(Mrs. Bjornson);** Louis Jean Heydt **(Mr. Farrasen);** Francis Pierlot **(Minister);** Greta Granstedt **(Mrs. Farrasen);** Arthur Space **(Pete Hanson);** Elizabeth Russell **(Kola

of musicals and also influenced the New Wave in France.

When Mayer and Schary initially vetoed the idea of the location work, Freed persisted. Mayer finally agreed to allow the company five days in New York to shoot the bulk of the exterior sequences involving the principals. In the final run, the film managed to provide an exciting New York City travelogue of the Battery, Bronx, Brooklyn, the Statue of Liberty, Times Square, Fifth Avenue (on a double-decker bus), Radio City, the Bronx

Margaret O'Brien, Jackie ("Butch") Jenkins, James Craig, and Frances Gifford in Our Vines Have Tender Grapes *('45).*

Hanson); Dorothy Morris **(Ingborg Jensen);** Charles Middleton **(Kurt Jensen);** George Lloyd **(Farmer);** Arthur Hohl **(Ivar Svenson).**

SYNOPSIS

In southern Wisconsin's Norwegian farm community of Benson Junction, the Jacobson family—Martinius, Bruna, and little daughter Selma—live modestly but happily. Martinius is a strict father, but also compassionate—he comforts grief-stricken Selma after she accidentally kills a squirrel, and takes her to the train station in the middle of the night to see a circus elephant in transit.

Some excitement arrives with pretty Viola Johnson, the town's new schoolteacher. She finds romance with Nels Halverson, editor of the town newspaper. Though Viola loves Nels, she fears the thought of marriage, finding the simple life of the town dull. When Nels leaves for the service, Viola still has not come to terms with the placidity of her surroundings.

Nel's induction upsets Selma, but Martinius consoles her, assuring her that "peace on earth" is something one must fight for these days. Daughter Selma also needs dad's discipline when she fails to share her skates with cousin Arnold, his comfort after the death of retarded neighbor Ingborg Jensen, and his counsel after she and Arnold almost perish after rowing Martinius's metal bathtub into the spring freshet.

It is, however, Selma who teaches the town its most inspiring lesson. When Bjorn Bjornson's property is struck by lightning, bringing financial

ruin, Selma offers her prize Jersey calf. Martinius, overwhelmed by his daughter's generosity, scraps plans to build a new barn. He and all the neighbors sacrifice to help their unfortunate friend. Impressed by this town spirit, Viola decides she does belong in Benson Junction, and vows to become Nels' wife when he returns.

* * *

In **Our Vines Have Tender Grapes,** MGM reached four objectives: (1) supplying perennially snarling Edward G. Robinson[1] with a lovable, heartwarming role, (2) providing immensely popular Margaret O'Brien with another stellar assignment, (3) advancing the career and popularity of child star Jackie ("Butch") Jenkins of **The Human Comedy** (1943) and **National Velvet** (1944), and (4) producing a memorable piece of Americana.

The box-office hit, released shortly after V-J Day in September 1945, was based on episodes from George Victor Martin's book **Our Vines Have Tender Grapes.** The screenplay was by Dalton Trumbo, who scripted some of the war years' more

---

[1] In 1930 Edward G. Robinson had made **A Lady to Love** (1930) at MGM with Vilma Banky. Irving Thalberg was so impressed with the actor that he offered him a three-year contract for $1 million, but refused to concede that the performer could return to Broadway during this period. Robinson remained firm and negotiations were dropped. As he left the executive building, he realized what he had done, and he vomited. Thalberg gave the roles scheduled for Robinson to Wallace Beery. It was not until **The Last Gangster** (1937), by which time Thalberg was dead, that Robinson returned to the Metro lot.

inspirational films: Paramount's **The Remarkable Andrew** (1942), RKO's **Tender Comrade** (1943), and Metro's **A Guy Named Joe** (1943), and **Thirty Seconds over Tokyo** (1944). **Our Vines** would be Trumbo's last Hollywood film before being blacklisted in October 1947 as one of the "Hollywood Ten." In his 1974 posthumously published memoirs, **All My Yesterdays,** Robinson remembers how, fresh from bickering with vehement anti-Communists Joan Bennett and Raymond Massey at RKO while making Fritz Lang's **Woman in the Window,** he was much happier working on the Trumbo film:

> On my next picture I did not have to keep my mouth shut. It was written by Dalton Trumbo and was called **Our Vines Have Tender Grapes.** I'd known Trumbo for a long while; I knew he was hotheaded, wildly gifted, inordinately progressive, and, it seemed to me, intensely logical. My relationship with him professionally and socially became, not very many years later, a subject for official concern of the Congress.

Interestingly, **Our Vines** does contain elements which would later smack of Leftism to the House Committee on Un-American Activities. Ironically, they were the same concepts which at one time were held as purely American: the importance of concern for the good of all over individual concern; the nobility of self-sacrificing for the sake of the community; the divinity of sharing one's goods with his neighbor.

However, at the time most viewers deemed the film as wholesome entertainment, a vehicle enhanced by a superior group of actors, especially Robinson, O'Brien, and character actress Agnes Moorehead (who had excellent opportunities here to display a foreign accent and to be restrained and sympathetic).

When **Our Vines** visited the Radio City Music Hall, **PM** reported, "True to its entwining title, **Our Vines Have Tender Grapes** is a heartwarming and fulfilling story of life on a Wisconsin farm—done with deep sincerity, almost universally pleasing performances, and photography that loves the land and the people as it sees them." The **New York Times** praised Robinson as giving "one of the finest performances of his long and varied screen career" and the "remarkably natural" acting of Miss O'Brien and Master Jenkins.

Not to be overlooked in this 105-minute feature is Dorothy Morris, a consistently fine actress, here cast as the simpleminded neighbor Ingborg. MGM contractee Frances Gifford had been the "other woman" standing in the way of Esther Williams' romance with soldier Van Johnson in **Thrill of a Romance** (1945). In **Our Vines** she is the citified schoolmarm, displaying charming qualities that MGM never exploited fully. It was the first of her three assignments opposite James Craig. The two others were **She Went to the Races** (1945), in which Craig is a horse trainer and she a gal with a "scientific" system for beating the odds, and **Little Mr. Jim** (1946), wherein she is Butch Jenkins' mom whose death (midway through the film) so affects her GI husband, Craig, that he takes to alcohol and ignores their son.

PAT AND MIKE

1952—95 min.

Producer, Lawrence Weingarten; **director,** George Cukor; **story-screenplay,** Ruth Gordon and Garson Kanin; **art directors,** Cedric Gibbons and Urie McCleary; **set decorators,** Edwin B. Willis and Hugh Hunt; **assistant director,** Jack Greenwood; wardrobe for Miss Hepburn, Orry-Kelly; **music,** David Raksin; **makeup,** William Tuttle; **sound,** Douglas Shearer; **special effects,** Warren Newcombe; **montage,** Peter Ballbusch; **camera,** William Daniels; **editor,** George Boemler.

Spencer Tracy (**Mike Conovan**); Katharine Hepburn (**Pat Pemberton**); Aldo Ray (**Davie Hucko**); William Ching (**Collier Weld**); Sammy White (**Barney Grau**); George Mathews (**Spec Cauley**); Loring Smith (**Mr. Beminger**); Phyllis Povah (**Mrs. Beminger**); Charles Buchinsky [Bronson] (**Hank Tasling**); Frank Richards (**Sam Garsell**); Jim Backus (**Charles Barry**); Chuck Connors (**Police Captain**); Owen McGiveney (**Harry MacWade**); Lou Lubin (**Waiter**); Carl Switzer (**Bus Boy**); William Self (**Pat's Caddy**); Billy McLean, Frankie Darro, Paul Brinegar, and "Tiny" Jimmy Kelly (**Caddies**); Mae Clarke, Elizabeth Holmes, and Helen Eby-Rock (**Women Golfers**); Charlie Murray (**Line Judge**); Craufurd Kent (**Tennis Umpire**); King Mojave (**Linesman**); Don Budge, Helen Dettweiler, Betty Hicks, Beverly Hanson, Babe Didrikson Zaharias, Gussie Moran, Alice Marble, and Frank Parker (**Themselves**).

Spencer Tracy and Katharine Hepburn in Pat and Mike *('52).*

SYNOPSIS

Ebullient physical education instructor Pat Pemberton is employed at a modest California college and engaged to Collier Weld. The only hitch in their relationship is that Collier's presence at sports competitions unnerves Pat to the point where she performs poorly.

During a national golf tournament Pat encounters glib sports promoter Mike Conovan, who attempts to bribe Pat to lose. She refuses. Later she finds herself on a golf and tennis tour with Mike. She is playing her best in both sports until Collier joins up, which destroys her precision, and game. Collier walks in on what appears to be a compromising situation between Pat and Mike. He is so outraged that he abandons his athletic fiancée. Collier's absence convinces Pat that it is rough-and-tumble Mike whom she loves after all.

* * *

"Together again and it's no fib. Their funniest hit since **Adam's Rib!**" rhymed the advertisements for **Pat and Mike,** the seventh tandem vehicle of Spencer Tracy and Katharine Hepburn. Since that 1949 hit teaming, Tracy had enjoyed great popularity in **Father of the Bride** (1950) while Hepburn had experienced a Broadway and tour success in **As You Like It** and earned an Oscar nomination opposite Humphrey Bogart in **The African Queen** (1951).

Aided by the happy collaboration of **Adam's Rib** scenarists Garson Kanin and Ruth Gordon, and that picture's director, George Cukor, **Pat and Mike** was a leisurely, pleasant experience for the stars. It was shot almost entirely at the Riviera

Country Club in Pacific Palisades with costar Aldo Ray (on loan from Columbia) and a fleet of sports figures (Don Budge, Helen Dettweiler, Betty Hicks, Beverly Hanson, Babe Didrikson Zaharias, Gussie Moran, Alice Marble, and Frank Parker as themselves. (Chuck Connors, then a Los Angeles Angels' first baseman, appeared as a police captain.)

In Charles Higham's **Kate** (1975),[1] George Cukor recalls:

"The reason this comedy, and its predecessor **Adam's Rib,** worked was that none of us took ourself very seriously during the writing and preparation. We batted around ideas like tennis balls. We all **felt** the lines and situations, without any kind of ghastly solemnity. If we all laughed a line went in. I remember there was a scene in which Spencer massaged Kate's leg. No sex implied, but it was very sexy.

---

[1]Also in **Kate,** Aldo Ray shares this remembrance of the film:

"There was a scene in which I had to carry her [Hepburn] off a golf course, all the way into the clubhouse and up the stairs. I did it, the camera followed us in one take, and I deposited her on a couch as the scene ended. Then I whispered in her ear, 'I'm going to f—— you!' She said, shaking her head like a schoolmistress, 'You'll do no such thing! If you do, I'm going to call Spencer!' "

You sensed the empathy between these two. We had wonderful fun working out that scene."

There are many zesty moments in the breezy **Pat and Mike.** When someone asks Hepburn what her handicap is, her response is, "My fellow." Tracy's initial summation of Hepburn in this film is "An escaped fruit cake." In his book **Tracy and Hepburn** (1971), Garson Kanin relates the evolution of the motion picture's most famous vignette:

I had written a line for Mike to say when he first encounters and appraises Pat, an outstanding amateur golfer. With an eye toward turning her to pro and making her part of his stable, he hands her his card. She takes it and walks away. He speaks to his crony-assistant.

George [Cukor] shot it at a drinking fountain on the golf course. I drove out to watch because I particularly wanted to hear Spence say that line.

When the moment came, Kate walked away. Spencer got his cue and spoke. As he did so, he watched her leave (thus turning away from the camera), leaned over the drinking fountain, shot a stream of water into his mouth, and gave the operative word an extra twist of New Yorkese.

I was horrified. I felt that with all this the line would surely fail and that the moment would be wrecked. I mentioned it to George, who, in turn, spoke to Spencer. Take two. Exactly like the first, only more so. I left.

Months later, at the preview at the Capitol Theatre in New York I tensed as the moment approached. I need not have troubled. The line came.

"Not much meat on 'er," Spence (as Mike) commented. "But what there **is** is **cherce!**"

The theatre exploded.

This favorite dialogue bit was included in the Tracy-Hepburn tribute segment of **That's Entertainment: Part II** (1976).

Released in the summer of 1952, **Pat and Mike** did brisk box office as the stars received their usual critical plaudits. **Films in Review** reported, "This trifling moneymaker successfully provides the following opportunities: for Katharine Hepburn to display her golf prowess; for Spencer Tracy to prove that he can be illiterate and still have his heart of gold; for Ruth Gordon and Garson Kanin to write specious, amusing dialogue and to kid Miss Hepburn's spare physique; for director George Cukor to kid film gangsters, pugilists, and other stereotypes. It also provides an opportunity for almost anyone to have an entertaining hour and a half." The Kanins received an Oscar nomination for their script.

Pat and Mike was the final commitment on Hepburn's MGM contract. After this feature she left the lot, although she returned for **The Iron Petticoat** (1956) opposite Bob Hope, an effort she would certainly prefer to forget. Tracy remained at MGM for three more years, until his erratic, temperamental behavior on **Tribute to a Bad Man** (1956) got him fired by the Metro moguls. Tracy and Hepburn later acted together in Twentieth Century–Fox's **Desk Set** (1957) and in Columbia's **Guess Who's Coming to Dinner** (1967). The latter was Tracy's final film and Hepburn's second of three (to date) Oscar-winning performances.

THE PHILADELPHIA STORY

1940—112 min.

Producer, Joseph L. Mankiewicz; **director,** George Cukor; based on the play by Philip Barry; **screenplay,** Donald Ogden Stewart; **art directors,** Cedric Gibbons and Wade B. Rubottom; **set decorator,** Edwin B. Willis; **music,** Franz Waxman; **costumes,** Adrian; **assistant director,** Edward Woehler; **makeup,** Jack Dawn; **sound,** Douglas Shearer; **camera,** Joseph Ruttenberg; **editor,** Frank Sullivan.

Cary Grant (**C. K. Dexter Haven**); Katharine Hepburn (**Tracy Lord**); James Stewart (**Mike Connor**); Ruth Hussey (**Liz Imbrie**); John Howard (**George Kittredge**); Roland Young (**Uncle Willie**); John Halliday (**Seth Lord**); Virginia Weidler (**Dinah Lord**); Mary Nash (**Margaret Lord**); Henry Daniell (**Sidney Kidd**); Lionel Pape (**Edward**); Rex Evans (**Thomas**); Russ Clark (**John**); Hilda Plowright (**Librarian**); Lita Chevret (**Manicurist**); Lee Phelps

(**Bartender**); David Clyde (**Mac**); Claude King (**Willie's Butler**); Robert DeBruce (**Dr. Parsons**); Veda Buckland (**Elsie**); Dorothy Fay, Florine McKinney, Helen Whitney, and Hillary Brooke (**Main Liners**).

SYNOPSIS

Philadelphia society girl Tracy Lord is about to marry proper but stuffy George Kittredge. Ex-husband C. K. Dexter Haven arrives on the scene with reporter Macaulay ("Mike") Connor and photographer Liz Imbrie of **Spy Magazine** to cover the nuptials.

Tracy is displeased by the proposed press coverage but agrees when she learns that otherwise the magazine will print a titillating story about her father's dalliance with an actress.

Tracy becomes infatuated with Connor and the duo follow up a champagne drunk with a moonlight swim. It is hardly the behavior of a bride-to-be and Kittredge demands an explanation.

Now Tracy begins to see the situation realistically. She breaks her engagement to Kittredge, rejects Connor's hasty marriage proposal (knowing he belongs with Liz), and continues the wedding plans with her ex-husband now substituted as the new groom.

* * *

Good manners, sincerity, a touch of humanity—that would seem to be the diet—all else being equal—which determines a long life for a Hollywood star.

But, of course, every day there are people in perfect health who climb to the tops of high bridges, admire the view below—and jump off.

They seem to like it.

Perhaps Hepburn and the current corps of headstrong Terrible Turks rather fancy the diet too.

One thing is certain—they'll know for sure when they land.

The magazine was **Photoplay,** the date September 1935, and the article "Is Hepburn Killing Her Own Career?" Berating the RKO star's cavalier treatment of the press and her assorted bag of eccentricities, **Photoplay**'s forecast of a shattering "landing" appeared vindicated when in 1938 the infamous "Box Office Poison" list appeared. The blacklist included the names of Mae West, Marlene Dietrich, Kay Francis, Greta Garbo, Joan Crawford, Fred Astaire, and Hepburn. Her home lot believed the report. It offered Hepburn a B film, **Mother Carey's Chickens,** which forced her to sell her contract and take refuge at Columbia with director George Cukor, writer Donald Ogden Stewart, and star Cary Grant to do a remake of Philip Barry's **Holiday.** It flopped. In May 1938 Hepburn left Hollywood.

She would return in style.

On March 28, 1939, Katharine Hepburn became Broadway's greatest attraction of the season when she opened in Philip Barry's **The Philadelphia Story,** a project which the playwright tailor-made for the unique actress. Having paid twenty-five percent of the production cost, Hepburn took no salary. Instead, she accepted ten

Virginia Weidler and Katharine Hepburn in The Philadelphia Story *('40).*

percent of the gross; the play ran for 415 performances, with Joseph Cotten as her ex-spouse and Van Heflin as her reporter-suitor.

Hollywood executives were impressed by the audience appeal of **The Philadelphia Story** and when MGM made a bid for the movie rights, the studio had to deal with Hepburn herself. After touring in the comedy for 254 road performances (at twelve and a half percent of the gross), Hepburn accepted Louis B. Mayer's offer. She sold the studio screen rights for $250,000, with a guaranteed approval of director, costars, and script execution.

To nobody's surprise, Hepburn chose George Cukor to direct. Her friend Donald Ogden Stewart began work on the scenario. As neither Cotten nor Heflin was then known sufficiently to movie audiences, she picked Cary Grant (who demanded and got top billing, and donated all of his $137,500 salary to the British War relief) and "hot" MGM star James Stewart. The latter had been Oscar-nominated the previous year for his shining work in Columbia's **Mr. Smith Goes to Washington.**

The Philadelphia Story was lensed in eight weeks—five days under schedule—in the summer of 1940. Cukor later recalled in Charles Higham's **Kate** (1975):

"In the beginning, the producer, Joe Mankiewicz, had the entire play tape-recorded in New York, so that we would know the lines the audience laughed at. Well, it was rather pointless, really. You see, we had to make the laughs come from visual gags because so much of the wit of Barry was purely verbal, and too many complicated speeches would have slowed things up. Once or twice I clashed with Kate— she wanted to cry in the last scenes, because she had cried in the play . . . it had become a kind of stock in trade with her. I said, 'I don't think we'll cry this time round.' She was very unhappy, but she tried to do what I wanted, and then she said, 'All right, I won't cry.' The result was a much stronger scene. She was perfect as Tracy Lord—she was arrogant but sensitive, she was tough but vulnerable, she didn't care what people thought of her, they had to accept her on her own terms, or forget it. Of course, she was far more polished, more skillful than she had ever been before."

Though Metro trusted that **The Philadelphia Story** would be a hit, the extent of its smashing success was a major surprise. The picture broke all records of the Radio City Music Hall after its November 1940 premiere. It grossed $594,000 during its six-week engagement there. **Life** magazine judged, "In any screen year **The Philadelphia Story** would belong among the best funny pictures. Its people are recognizable humans. They drink, they make mistakes, they discuss their feelings, they even discuss such ideas as class differences and decide there aren't any. All this makes for adult entertainment." The **Philadelphia Record** concurred, **"The Philadelphia Story** is first and above all a Katharine Hepburn triumph. Not only does she know her character intimately, but she portrays her with humor, wis-

dom, and an emotional intensity that she hasn't displayed to screen audiences since **A Bill of Divorcement."** As the feature opened its initial play dates around the country, Hepburn returned to the touring company of the show, which closed in Philadelphia on February 15, 1941.

Placing third in the **Film Daily**'s Ten Best Pictures poll (under **Gone With the Wind** and Warner Bros.' **Sergeant York**), **The Philadelphia Story** won an Academy nomination for Best Picture. But United Artists' **Rebecca** won the prize. It was not one of MGM's better Oscar nights (February 27, 1941, at the Hollywood Biltmore Hotel); Stewart, apparently having haunted the voters' conscience after losing in 1939 for **Mr. Smith Goes to Washington,** represented **The Philadelphia Story**'s major win for his charming but hardly outstanding performance of Mike Connor. (Stewart was amazed and would claim he had voted for his friend, the favored Henry Fonda of Twentieth Century–Fox's **The Grapes of Wrath.**) Hepburn, however, the winner of the New York Film Critics Circle's Award for best actress for her Tracy Lord, was defeated by Ginger Rogers of RKO's **Kitty Foyle.** Ruth Hussey's Liz Imbrie was not expected to defeat Jane Darwell's Ma Joad of **The Grapes of Wrath** (and did not); Donald Ogden Stewart claimed an Oscar for Best Adaptation. George Cukor lost the Best Director prize to John Ford of **Grapes.**

The Philadelphia Story continued to be a media favorite. On July 20, 1942, in a special victory show for the government, "Lux Radio Theatre" presented the play with Hepburn, Grant, Hussey, Virginia Weidler (repeating her role as Hepburn's precocious younger sister), and Lieutenant James Stewart. On July 14, 1943, the "Lux Radio Theatre" offered Barry's work again, this time with Loretta Young, Robert Taylor, and Robert Young. Radio's "Theatre Guild of the Air" also presented an April 4, 1948, airing, with Stewart, John Conte, and Joan Tetzel. The picture's constant success in reissue later inspired the creation of **High Society** (1956), the Metro musical with Bing Crosby, Grace Kelly, and Frank Sinatra.

Finally, **The Philadelphia Story** became Hepburn's professional vindication. She not long after joined the MGM lot, began her celebrated screen work with Spencer Tracy, and remained a powerful box-office name. The 1940 film remains a special favorite with film disciples, mainly because of her near perfect performance. "When Katharine Hepburn sets out to play Katharine Hepburn," saluted **Life** magazine, "she is a sight to behold. Nobody is her equal."

THE PICTURE OF DORIAN GRAY
1945—107 min.[1]

---

[1]Technicolor sequence.

Producer, Pandro S. Berman; **director,** Albert Lewin; based on the novel by Oscar Wilde; **screen-**

play, Lewin; **art directors,** Cedric Gibbons and Hans Peters; **set decorators,** Edwin B. Willis and Hugh Hunt; **portrait,** Ivan Albright; **assistant director,** Earl McEvoy; **music,** Herbert Stothart; **sound,** William R. Edmondson; **camera,** Harry Stradling; **editor,** Ferris Webster.

George Sanders **(Lord Henry Wotton)**; Hurd Hatfield **(Dorian Gray)**; Donna Reed **(Gladys Hallward)**; Angela Lansbury **(Sybil Vane)**; Lowell Gilmore **(Basil Hallward)**; Peter Lawford **(David Stone)**; Richard Fraser **(James Vane)**; Reginald Owen **(Lord George Farmoor)**; Lydia Bilbrook **(Mrs. Vane)**; Morton Lowry **(Adrian Singleton)**; Douglas Walton **(Alan Campbell)**; Mary Forbes **(Lady Agatha)**; Robert Greig **(Sir Thomas)**; Lisa Carpenter **(Lady Henry Wotton)**; Moyna Macgill **(Duchess)**; Billy Bevan **(Chairman Malvolio Jones)**; Miles Mander **(Sir Robert Bentley)**, Devi Dga and Her Balinese Dancers **(Specialty Number)**; Sir Cedric Hardwicke **(Narrator)**; William Stack **(Mr. Erskine)**; Natalie Draper **(Mrs. Vandelear)**; Lillian Bond **(Kate)**; Alan Edmiston **(Cabby)**; Charles Coleman **(Butler)**; Carol Diane Keppler **(Gladys as a Child)**; Emily Massey **(Parker, the Nurse)**; Jimmy Conlin **(Piano Player)**; James Aubrey **(Cabby)**; Joe Yule **(Stage Manager)**; Rex Evans **(Lord Gerald Goodbody)**; Audrey Manners **(Lady Alice Goodbody)**; Renie Riano **(Lady Ruxton)**; Gibson Gowland **(Gibson, David's Driver)**; Toby Doolan and Major Sam Harris **(Club Members)**; Lee Powell and Will Patton **(Loaders)**; Frank O'Connor **(Butler)**; Mary Benoit and Elyse Brown **(Guests at Mayfair Tea).**

SYNOPSIS
In 1890 London, Malvolio Jones introduces hedonistic Dorian Gray to young, innocent East End music-hall performer Sybil Vane. Dorian and Sybil fall in love and he proposes marriage. Later he rejects her and she commits suicide. Pompous artist Basil Hallward is shocked by Dorian's heartless behavior. Through some mysterious means, the portrait of Dorian which Basil has painted grows old while the living subject remains apparently young.

Basil's niece, Gladys Hallward, a child when the portrait was painted, becomes engaged to the still youthful Dorian. The latter has been leading a secret life of debauchery and dissoluteness since having his mind corrupted by Lord Henry Wotton. Gladys is unaware that it is Dorian who has shot her uncle in a fit of rage or that he accidentally shot Sybil Vane's brother, who had traced his sister's debaucher to Gray's country residence.

Wholesome David Stone is in love with Gladys and is constantly protecting her. It is he who informs her of a discovery he has made in a locked room on the upper floor of Dorian's house. At the finale the dazzlingly youthful Dorian is seen stabbing his portrait before falling dead beside it. David and Gladys are now free to be united in marriage.

* * *

By the early 1940s the cinema genre of the fantastic had largely degenerated to the endless efforts of escapism-minded Universal Pictures,

Peter Lawford, Donna Reed, and Lowell Gilmore in The Picture of Dorian Gray *('45).*

where, in the words of director Mark Robson, "the prevailing idea of horror was a werewolf chasing a girl in a nightgown up a tree." Robson was then part of the Val Lewton production unit at RKO, which offered such entries as **The Cat People, The Leopard Man,** and **I Walked with a Zombie,** all well-regarded (then and now) mood pieces. The critical and popular reception of these films inspired other studios to put shockers into production. MGM, under the prompting of literary-minded Albert Lewin, chose Oscar Wilde's **The Picture of Dorian Gray,** the elegant morality tale written in 1891.[2]

With production supervised by Pandro S. Berman and a screenplay and direction by Lewin, **The Picture of Dorian Gray** was well filmed. George Sanders was obtained to play the pivotal part of Lord Henry Wotton, an epicurean whose libertine, satanic philosophies poison Mr. Gray's morality. Angela Lansbury, whose debut in **Gaslight** (1944) won her a Best Supporting Actress Oscar bid, was cast as the virginal Sybil Vane. Studio contractees Donna Reed and Peter Lawford joined the film as the young lovers (her role was not in Wilde's version). To portray the title role, Berman and Lewin selected Hurd Hatfield, a delicately featured, twenty-six-year-old actor who had appeared in **Dragon Seed** (1944). His rather expressionless face and flat voice somehow impressed the front office as ideal material for the enigmatic Dorian.

The result was superb. George Sanders, attractively goateed and garbed in the most splendid of London apparel, was an apt Lord Henry, delightfully delivering Wilde's epigrams: "To get back my youth, I'd do anything but take exercise, get up early, or act respectable"; "Isn't it monstrous the way people go about today saying things behind people's backs that are absolutely and entirely true." Lansbury proved to be a deeply moving and tragic Sybil, the pathetic figure who sings the haunting "Little Yellow Bird."[3] Hatfield was effective as the unemotional degenerate, a victim of greed for nature's riches.

Director Lewin created a series of notable vignettes: Sybil, sadly walking away from Dorian, a tear streaking her cheek after he has bid her to sleep with him, as he moodily plays the piano and lures the heartbroken girl back to him; Lord Henry casually congratulating Dorian on the news of Sybil's suicide and the notoriety her ruination will win for him. Most impressive is the first chilling glimpse of the "aged" portrait. As Gray reveals the picture to its creator, Basil Hallward, the camera lingers on the artist's fascinated reaction, fooling the audience into thinking the portrait will not be shown.[4] Then with a jolting crash of Herbert Stothart's music and a sudden splash of Technicolor photography, the vile, grotesque

portrait of the spiritually horrible Dorian suddenly fills the screen.

Permeating the entire production, narrated with élan by Sir Cedric Hardwicke, is the masterfully created aura of dreadful immortality. There are brief suggestions of the "dreadful place" in Whitechapel patronized by Gray and the disturbed look of the coachman when Gray directs him to head there. There are also the hints of the "boy in the guards who killed himself" reputedly after a scandalous affair with Dorian; David Stone's quietly spoken description of the portrait he has discovered in Dorian's secret room ("The eyes shine in an evil way that is indescribable!"); and the allusions to orgies and drug dens which manage to infest the feature with a tinge of depravity and moral decay.

Released in March 1945, **The Picture of Dorian Gray** received only the approval of the more broad-minded critics. Bosley Crowther **(New York Times)** was far from impressed: "Aside from the fact that Oscar Wilde would probably have split his portly sides laughing at the mawkish pomposity of the film . . . there is good and sufficient reason for a modern to do the same thing. As a matter of fact, one might venture to slip it a ribald razz." The **New Yorker** magazine found the film "a more or less dubious wedding of Oscar Wilde and MGM. There are the celebrated epigrams and the degenerating portraits, but there are also a couple of moderately intense love affairs which it is rather hard to believe the master had in mind."

Less stuffy critics found much to cheer in the offering. The **New York Herald-Tribune** wrote, "[it] has been brought to the screen with genuine distinction. . . . The picture is not always so delicate as the novel, but it recaptures most of the exoticism in a show which is well off the beaten road of Hollywood producing." The **New York Daily News** saluted MGM for taking "a bold step toward releasing the screen from the many taboos that have encompassed it." The film did solid box-office business and won Lansbury her second Best Supporting Actress nomination (she lost to Anne Revere who played her mother in MGM's **National Velvet**). An Oscar did go to cinematographer Harry Stradling, whose utilization of deep-focus and wide-angle lens seemed revolutionary at the time.

In 1970 Helmut Berger starred in a modern, specious Italian remake of the Wilde tale. A few years later there appeared the homosexual pornographic entry **The Portrait of Dorian Gray.** Neither effort affected the high standing of the 1945 classic.

---

[2]The studio had enjoyed success the previous year (1944) with its filming of Wilde's **The Canterville Ghost.**

[3]Lansbury's singing of this almost trademark song was reportedly dubbed.

[4]Ivan Albright painted the portrait.

THE PIRATE
1948—102 min.

Producer, Arthur Freed; **director,** Vincente Minnelli; based on the play by S. N. Behrman; **screenplay,** Albert Hackett, Frances Goodrich, and, **uncredited:** Joseph L. Mankiewicz, Joseph Than, Lillian Braun, Anita Loos, and Wilkie Mahoney; **songs,** Cole Porter; **music director,** Lennie Hayton; **instrumental arranger,** Conrad Salinger; **vocal arrangers,** Kay Thompson, Robert Tucker, and Roger Edens; **choreography,** Robert Alton and Gene Kelly; **Technicolor consultants,** Natalie Kalmus and Henri Jaffa; **art directors,** Cedric Gibbons and Jack Martin Smith; **set decorators,** Edwin B. Willis and Arthur Krams; **costume supervisor,** Irene; **costumes,** Tom Keogh and Mde Babara Karinska; **makeup,** Jack Dawn; **sound,** Douglas Shearer; **camera,** Harry Stradling; **editor,** Blanche Sewell.

Judy Garland (**Manuela**); Gene Kelly (**Serafin**); Walter Slezak (**Don Pedro Vargas**); Gladys Cooper (**Aunt Inez**); Reginald Owen (**The Advocate**); George Zucco (**The Viceroy**); Nicholas Brothers (**Specialty Dance**); Lester Allen (**Uncle Capucho**); Lola Deem (**Isabella**); Ellen Ross (**Mercedes**); Mary Jo Ellis (**Lizarda**); Jean Dean (**Casilda**); Marion Murray (**Eloise**); Ben Lessy (**Gumbo**); Jerry Bergen (**Bolo**); Val Setz (**Juggler**); Gaudsmith Brothers (**Themselves**); Cully Richards (**Trillo**).

SYNOPSIS

In the 1820s wide-eyed West Indian Manuela is enthralled by the romantic legends surrounding a pirate known as Black Macoco. She meets strolling player Serafin, who performs in the Town Square. He hypnotizes her and she performs a sultry song and dance. He is captivated by her beauty and pursues her but she rebuffs him.

It develops that Manuela is betrothed to the portly Don Pedro Vargas and will soon wed him. Serafin returns to the town disguised as Macoco and tells the townsfolk that his men have their village under siege. No harm will come to them, he insists, if they deliver the beautiful Manuela to him.

En route she discovers Serafin's ruse and a rough-and-tumble brawl erupts. Finally it is revealed that Don Pedro is the legendary Macoco, now retired. No matter, since by now Manuela has fallen in love with Serafin and runs off with him to join the troupe of players. They participate in the "Be a Clown" finale.

* * *

The Pirate is wildly, wonderfully eclectic. One gets the feeling that the director is trying to combine and set in motion everything that has ever delighted him in the visual arts. . . . It is a glorious and sophisticated entertainment, an immense, lavish production yet as enchantingly weightless as a daydream. The Garland and Kelly performances are extremely ambitious attempts at extending their usual ranges and are arguably the most satisfying of their respective careers. The screenplay is uncommonly witty in its satiric thrusts. . . . The huge, lovingly detailed production is, I'm certain, the closest Vincente Minnelli has ever come to realizing the abstract, deeply personal world of whirling forms and colors.

Joel Siegel, **Film Heritage,** Fall 1971

Judging by this relatively recent review, one would suspect that **The Pirate** was a resounding

Gene Kelly in The Pirate *('48).*

success when released in 1948. Not so. For once, the Arthur Freed—MGM unit went a bit too far in its marvelous artistry and created a movie which, cynical though it sounds, was almost too fine a motion picture for huge commercial appeal. With the cinema now a part of some college art courses, however, **The Pirate** has emerged from the studio vaults to become a special favorite of Metro musical lovers, with its superb Minnelli direction, star performances of Kelly and Garland, and music by Cole Porter.

During the 1942 Broadway season, Alfred Lunt and Lynn Fontanne had starred for 177 performances in S. N. Behrman's stylish comedy, **The Pirate.** MGM acquired the screen rights at that time for $225,026. Joseph Pasternak was assigned to produce the film as the straight comedy it was, with Henry Koster directing, and Joseph L. Mankiewicz providing the scenario. Then the property was shelved. It was briefly reactivated in 1944 when scenery and costume designer Lemuel Ayers suggested to Arthur Freed that **The Pirate** be filmed with a Cole Porter score. Finally, in 1945 Joseph Than and in 1946 Anita Loos, both under MGM contract, were brought into **The Pirate** project. At this point it was decided that Vincente Minnelli would direct, with Judy Garland starring. When it was discovered that the two writers had so revamped the stage play (itself based on the comedy **Der Seerauber** by German playwright Ludwig Fulda), a greatly upset Freed immediately put the husband-and-wife writing team of Frances Goodrich and Albert Hackett to work to resuscitate **The Pirate.**[1] Meanwhile, Cole Porter had submit-

ted several song numbers to Freed. At a $100,000 fee, it was felt that the composer could do better than he had, and Freed asked the famed songwriter to try again. By now, Gene Kelly, who had been released from World War II navy duty, was involved in the pending musical.

The Freed unit then went to work: choreographer Robert Alton, music conductor Lennie Hayton, orchestrator Conrad Salinger, vocal arranger Kay Thompson, and Freed's jack-of-all-trades associate, Roger Edens. In those plush moviemaking days, expense seemed to be no object. The wardrobe cost alone for the color feature was approximately $141,600.

The supporting cast included such MGM stock company regulars as Gladys Cooper (Garland's guardian-aunt) and Reginald Owen (the advocate). There were the additional talents of Walter Slezak as the corrupt local mayor, George Zucco as the viceroy, and the fantastic dancing Nicholas Brothers. Hope for success on the project was great, and this was further strengthened by the reunion of Garland and her **For Me and My Gal** (1942) costar, Kelly. The male lead was tailor-

---

[1]In 1979, Gene Kelly would relate the following about **The Pirate,** "What really hurt the picture was that Vincente Minnelli and I really outsmarted ourselves. **The Pirate** had been the only flop the Lunts had. We'd both seen it on Broadway, and we knew something had to be changed. S. N. Behrman's dialogue was brilliant, but we wanted to get in a lot of action and a lot of dash. So we said, 'Let's make it obvious that the pirate is being played like Douglas Fairbanks, Sr. and the actor is being played like John Barrymore. Not too obvious, just enough to let everybody in on it.' Gee, we were being so clever. Then all the reviews hit us, 'This cheap actor tries to imitate the great. . . .' and so forth. The reviews were all of that ilk. Minnelli and I had to skulk behind bushes."

made for Kelly as the ham actor, etched in the hero-lover vein of Douglas Fairbanks and John Barrymore.

But a pall soon hung over the production, from the time Garland began prerecording her numbers on December 27, 1946. In his memoirs, **I Remember It Well** (1975), director Minnelli recalls this difficult time when his marriage to Garland was not going well (despite the joy over the birth of their child Liza):

> She began to feel she wasn't functioning and turned again to the pills that had sustained her during past crises. I stood helplessly by, knowing she had started taking them again but unable to determine who was supplying them to her.
>
> I'd been very proud that Judy had been temperate in their use since our marriage. Yet, Judy's tolerance was lessened, and the periodic spells of illness began. There might have been a history of squabbles with the studio and fears by executives that she would be in no shape to perform, but her indomitable spirit always came through. It was as if she could sense the exact number of days the studio could shoot around her. She would report at the last possible moment, so that her pictures usually ended within both the allotted shooting schedule and the budget. Now, for the first time, she had failed her substitute fathers, the men at the studio. The shooting schedule had to be extended."

Minnelli's description of what happened during the filming and refilming of **The Pirate** is euphemistic at best. Garland's bouts of paranoia became so intense that at points in the filming she broke into fits and violently attacked her husband and costar Kelly, charging that their close working relationship was all at the expense of her star status. (Other witnesses to the filmmaking insisted that Minnelli, realizing his wife was incapable of giving her professional best, built up Kelly's role as a defense against allowing Garland to ruin the picture.) Hugh Fordin, in his book **The World of Entertainment** (1974), said that Garland was absent nearly a hundred out of 135 days of rehearsals, shootings, and layoff periods regarding **The Pirate.** Gossip columnist Hedda Hopper recalled that on one occasion she visited the set of **The Pirate** and found Garland in a state of hysteria in her trailer. Garland confided to the writer that she feared that everyone, including her mother, had turned against her. As Judy talked she became so emotionally overwrought that she had to be bodily lifted from the trailer and driven home from the studio, still wearing her costume and makeup.

In **Rainbow** (1975) Christopher Finch outlines some of the horrors the singing star experienced during the making of **The Pirate.** He relates how the studio and Louis B. Mayer urged her to resume consulting a psychiatrist. When Dr. Ernest Simmel, her regular psychiatrist, died, she tried another physician; the latter suggested she be placed in a private sanatorium. The choice was Compton, south of Los Angeles. Later Garland was admitted to the Riggs Foundation in Stockbridge,

Massachusetts, with the studio publicity department doing its best to camouflage the turbulent behavior of its beloved star.

While Garland was suffering horrendous emotional problems, Kelly was involved in creative tasks. It was he who urged Porter to write a clown number, which turned out to be "Be a Clown" (first performed in the film by Kelly and the Nicholas Brothers; later reprised by Garland and Kelly). To fulfill Kelly's desire to display part of his characterization through a ballet, Goodrich and Hackett revamped the script, and "The Pirate Ballet" came into being. Within the framework of this brilliant segment the storyline is resolved. Kelly is thought to be the pirate and is about to be executed. He begs to be given a last request— to give a public performance. His wild dance throws the crowd into a trance, leading the real Mack the Black to bound onto the stage. Slezak is captured and Kelly is freed.

There was much re-recording of Garland's numbers as her emotional condition seesawed. For the highlight of the film, "Be a Clown," on-the-set observers recall that for some bizarre reason Minnelli and Garland threw a fit of hysterical laughter, which the director was able to carry over into the mood of the filming. It was a great boon to the shooting, but it left soundstage participants feeling eerie. As for Porter, his relationship with Garland was strained. He was undergoing his own professional questioning, wondering whether **The Pirate** represented a decline. Judy had not liked "Be a Clown," which many had told Porter was the best thing he had ever written. When it came time to prerecord "You Can Do No Wrong," the situation between the two had deteriorated even further; she was no longer even civil to the acclaimed songwriter.

During the long shooting schedule of **The Pirate**—February to August 1947—Kelly completed **Living in a Big Way** (1947), a rather undistinguished Metro film he had begun for director Gregory LaCava before he went into the service. While the last retakes were being completed on **The Pirate,**[2] Garland had gone on to make **Easter Parade** (1948), which was to have reteamed her with Kelly (who broke an ankle and was replaced by Fred Astaire) and with director Minnelli (replaced, by orders of Mayer and Freed, with Charles Walters).

Only a most knowing soul would be able to spot any of the production problems in the release print of **The Pirate.** With its high spirits and marvelous use of color, the film abounds with rhythmic delights—Judy soloing "Love of My Life," "Mack

the Black,"[3] and "You Can Do No Wrong," and Kelly singing and dancing to "Nina" and "The Pirate Ballet." The aforementioned "Be a Clown" would suffer some paring when released in Southern cities. The segment of the song featuring the black specialty dancers, the Nicholas Brothers, was cut.[4]

When finally released, **The Pirate** won raves from the leading critics. The **New York World-Telegram:** "Eye-filling entertainment the stage can never match." **PM:** "Best big-time musical show presented on screen or on stage in years!" **Life** magazine: "If **The Emperor Waltz** [Paramount, 1948] is pure whipped cream, MGM's **The Pirate** is practically helium. . . . As directed by . . . Vincente Minnelli, a former scene designer, **The Pirate** makes probably the most striking use of Technicolor on record. But the movie's chief charm is its complete lightheartedness. Sets, songs, characters, and comedy are all devoted to pounding home a single message: it's silly to be serious." However, audiences of the day were not as appreciative of the "inside" humor and unique dazzle of the feature. **The Pirate,** which cost $3,768,496, earned only $2,956,000 in its initial release, representing a loss (after publicity and distribution charges) of some $2,290,000. Minnelli would state that the merchandising of the film had been all wrong, and Freed would say years later, "I think today **The Pirate** would be a hit. It was twenty years ahead of its time. . . . I think one of the reasons [it was a flop] was the public didn't want to see Judy as a sophisticate."

Among the current crop of enthusiastics for **The Pirate** is Jeanine Basinger. In **Gene Kelly** (1976) she decides that it is

> a winner on all counts, although no one thought so at the time. . . . Designed in seashell pinks, sea green, and a soft salmon color, **The Pirate** sets its tone at the very beginning, as romantic but childishly styled drawings by Doris Lee decorate a book the heroine . . . reads. . . . From the moment of his entrance atop a cargo box being swung off a ship, Kelly's colorful garb and even more colorful spiel mark him as that favorite among screen heroes—the beloved rogue. With dash and grace, and wearing curly hair and a moustache with a jaunty tilt at the tips, Kelly proves himself a deft comedian as well as a capable dancer. . . . As the girl who longs for a prince instead of a pumpkin [Slezak], Judy Garland is magnificent.

In the mid-1950s, when MGM was wetting its toes in the video medium, the studio produced the "The MGM Parade," a thirty-minute weekly ABC-TV show. As one of its offerings, it split **The Pirate** into three parts and presented it for home viewers. It was a novelty in the days before the major

[2]Among the many retakes ordered for **The Pirate** were some dictated by Louis B. Mayer. According to Hedda Hopper, it was Mayer's long-standing secretary Ida Koverman who alerted Mayer after a screening of some rushes that the picture contained some "hair-curling" scenes of a Kelly-Garland dance. Hopper would recall, "Gene and Judy had flung themselves too eagerly into the spirit of things. It looked like a torrid romance." Mayer is supposed to have shouted, "Burn the negative! If that exhibition got on any screen, we'd be raided by the police." The following day Kelly was dressed down by an angry Mayer for having nearly sabotaged the wholesome Garland-Kelly movie image.

[3]In the original play, the pirate's name was Estramundo. Porter requested the name be changed to Macoco because he had a friend by that name whose nickname was Mack the Black, and he had always wanted to compose a comic song about him.

[4]Also deleted were Garland's rendition of "Voodoo" and Porter's song "Manuela."

studios had sold their product catalog to the rival entertainment field.

THE POSTMAN ALWAYS RINGS TWICE
1946—113 min.

Producer, Carey Wilson; **director,** Tay Garnett; based on the novel by James M. Cain; **screenplay,** Harry Ruskin and Niven Busch; **art directors,** Cedric Gibbons and Randall Duell; **set decorator,** Edwin B. Willis; **music,** George Bassman; **orchestrator,** Ted Duncan; **assistant director,** Bill Lewis; **costume supervisor,** Irene; **sound,** Douglas Shearer; **camera,** Sidney Wagner; **editor,** George White.

Lana Turner (**Cora Smith**); John Garfield (**Frank Chambers**); Cecil Kellaway (**Nick Smith**); Hume Cronyn (**Arthur Keats**); Leon Ames (**District Attorney Kyle Sackett**); Audrey Totter (**Madge Gorland**); Alan Reed (**Ezra Liam Kennedy**); Jeff York (**Blair**); Charles Williams (**Doctor**); Cameron Grant (**Willie**); Wally Cassell (**Ben**); Morris Ankrum and William Halligan (**Judges**); Garry Owen (**Truck Driver**); Edgar Sherrod (**Man**); Edward Earle (**Doctor**); Byron Foulger (**Picnic Manager**); Sondra Morgan (**Matron**); Philip Ahlm, John Allan, Harold Miller, and Reginald Simpson (**Photographers**); Paula Ray (**Woman**); Tom Dillon (**Father McConnell**); James Farley (**Warden**); Joel Friedkin (**John X. McHugh**).

Hume Cronyn, Lana Turner, and John Garfield in The Postman Always Rings Twice *('46).*

SYNOPSIS
Young vagabond Frank Chambers drifts into the Twin Oaks, California, lunch stand and gas station owned by soft-touch Nick Smith. Once Frank glimpses Nick's young wife, Cora, he asks the very middle-aged man for a job which will keep him near the seemingly frustrated counterlady.

At first Cora treats Frank with contempt, but his physical presence gets the best of her. Soon they admit their mutual love and decide to run away together. But Cora does not want to give up the financial security provided by the diner. They plot to murder Nick. The first attempt fails, but the second succeeds. Nick is hit unconscious and pushed over a steep cliff in his automobile.

District attorney Kyle Sackett is suspicious of the accident and soon arrests the lovers. Thanks to devious courtroom tactics by Cora's attorney, Arthur Keats, the couple is released with a suspended sentence. However, the breakdown of trust and affection that occurred during the trial (when they were pitted against each other) continues. The two are still urged to wed by her lawyer, who insists it will look better to the authorities and to the public.

Later Cora discovers she is pregnant and makes an effort to develop a working marriage with Frank. But the couple is too engulfed in sus-

picion, fear, and emotional exhaustion. The situation is further complicated by Ezra Liam Kennedy, a blackmailing detective.

Frank and Cora return to the beach where they first yielded to their passion. Again they decide to dismiss the past and start fresh. However, just as they are nearing home, the car crashes and Cora dies. It is an accident, but Frank is convicted of Cora's death, allegedly motivated by Nick's insurance policy. One hope accompanies Frank to the gas chamber—that Cora, wherever she may be, will realize it was really an accident.

* * *

Lusciously framed in a doorway stands Lana Turner, clad in a white turban, halter, and shorts. She drops her lipstick and it rolls toward John Garfield. The camera follows back from the lipstick to her feet and pans up . . .

So begins one of the cinema's great unholy collaborations, and some of the screen's greatest sexual chemistry—the team of Turner and Garfield in MGM's **The Postman Always Rings Twice.**

The project had a long pre-production history. MGM acquired the screen rights to James M. Cain's smoldering novel of desire and greed not long after its publication in 1934. However, movie censorship prevented the filming of the tale as written, and several attempted adaptations were rejected. The property remained shelved for more than a decade. Meanwhile, the book was adapted to the stage by the author and presented on Broadway in 1936 with Richard Barthelmess, Mary Philips, and Joseph Greenwald. In 1939

there appeared **Le Dernier Tournant,** a French film version, with Fernand Gravet, Michel Simon, and Corinne Luchaire. Three years later Luchino Visconti made his Italian (new-wave) adaptation, **Ossessione,**[1] which featured Massimo Girotti, Clara Calamai, and Elio Marcuzzo.

Then in early 1945 producer-writer Carey Wilson evolved a scenario that would pass the censorship board, and the Hollywood production got under way. By this time Cain's works were proven box-office draws: Paramount's **Double Indemnity** (1944) and Warner Bros.' **Mildred Pierce** (1945).

For an actress whose career had soared mainly because of a well-filled sweater and swaying derriere in **They Won't Forget** (Warner Bros., 1937), many pulchritudinous roles at Metro, and scores of romantic adventures which titillated the gossips, Lana Turner provided a bravura performance as the white-clad Cora.[2] Her costarring with Garfield was inspired casting. Today Turner remembers the late Garfield as the best of her screen leading men. "He had terrific magnetism. The lines just bounced back and forth between us

---

[1]Because of copyright infringement suits, it was not until 1977 that the Italian feature had any American release.

[2]Lana is rarely out of white costume. There is the scene in which she affects a black robe as she fingers a knife while thinking of suicide; later she wears black again, this time to attend her mother's funeral.

in **The Postman Always Rings Twice**. It kept a gal on her toes." Besides the appropriately doltish performance of Cecil Kellaway, the supporting cast is filled with top character actors, including Leon Ames as the suspicious district attorney, Alan Reed as a blackmailer, and especially Hume Cronyn, who supplies some of the film's best moments in his battle of judicial wits and bluffing with the district attorney. It is Cronyn who is filled with such caustic quips as telling the lovers at their wedding, "I can only think of fifteen or twenty reasons why you shouldn't be happy."

The Postman Always Rings Twice won great critical endorsement after its May 1946 release. Bosley Crowther **(New York Times)** said, "Mr. Cain wrote—and Metro has pictured—a Greek tragedy in cheap modern dress, and Lana Turner and John Garfield have played it in an extraordinarily honest way. Sex and self-seeking are suggested quite plainly . . . but scriptwriters, director, and actors have not worked to sensationalize same." **Newsweek** magazine confided, "Within the limits of the movie medium, the film is as explicit as it can be in the relationship between the double-crossing lovers and their foolish victim." The **New York Daily News** revealed, "It isn't a pretty tale, but it has dramatic power, as directed by Tay Garnett and acted by the three principals and a good supporting cast." **Life** magazine picked **Postman** as the "Movie of the Week." The melodrama reaped $4,000,000 in distributors' domestic rentals.

Years later director Garnett reminisced about this highly regarded feature:

Yeah, I was rather pleased with it. . . . We almost didn't get Garfield. He went into the army, and we tested Cameron Mitchell. He did a great test, then Garfield was invalided out of the service—he had a bad ticker even then. It was a real chore to do **Postman** under the Breen Office, but I think I managed to get the sex across. I think I like doing it better that way. I'm not a voyeur, and I don't like all the body display that you get in pictures nowadays. I think that's just a crutch for untalented directors and writers.

Jeanine Basinger in **Lana Turner** (1976) appraised:

The Postman Always Rings Twice is loaded with hot, repressed sex. Everything that happens in the film depends on Turner and Garfield being able to generate that feeling. They can and do. When they play the jukebox and dance on a hot summer night, the Latin music in the shadowed room lit by a neon sign makes anything—including murder—seem not only possible but downright necessary.

The link between sex and violence which is now associated with Turner's private life makes **Postman** an even more disturbing film today. In a stunning scene in Garfield's room, she lures him to murder her husband with a closeup that is an image of Satan as a beautiful woman, electric with evil. Eyebrows arched with tension, mouth half-parted, voice whispering, Turner is overlaid with a silvery magnetism that shocks. Entirely gone now is that kittenish girl of her early career.

Regarding Lana's "historic," nearly all-white wardrobe, Garnett said:

The white clothing was something that Carey [Wilson] and I thought of. At that time there was a great problem of getting a story with that much sex past the censors. We figured that dressing Lana in white somehow made everything she did seem less sensuous. It was also attractive as hell. And it somehow took a little of the stigma off everything that she did. They didn't have "hot pants" then, but you couldn't tell it by looking at hers.

In 1972 MGM announced plans to remake **The Postman Always Rings Twice**. The update was to be called **Three-Cornered Circle** and star Jack Nicholson, with Hal Ashby directing. It was not until January 1980 that the project, reverting to the original title, got under way, as a Lorimar production, produced by Andrew Braunsberg, directed by Bob Rafelson, and starring Nicholson, Jessica Lange, and John Colicos.

PRIDE AND PREJUDICE
1940—117½ min.

Producer, Hunt Stromberg; **director,** Robert Z. Leonard; based on the novel by Jane Austen; **screenplay,** Aldous Huxley and Jane Murfin; **art directors,** Cedric Gibbons and Paul Groesse; **set decorator,** Edwin B. Willis; **gowns,** Adrian; **men's costumes,** Gile Steele; **makeup,** Jack Dawn; **choreography,** Ernst Matray; **technical adviser,** George Richelure; **camera,** Karl Freund; **editor,** Robert J. Kern.

Greer Garson **(Elizabeth Bennet)**; Laurence Olivier **(Mr. Darcy)**; Mary Boland **(Mrs. Bennet)**; Edna May Oliver **(Lady Catherine DeBurgh)**; Maureen O'Sullivan **(Jane Bennet)**; Ann Rutherford **(Lydia Bennet)**; Edmund Gwenn **(Mr. Bennet)**; Edward Ashley **(Wickham)**; Frieda Inescort **(Caroline Bingley)**; Heather Angel **(Kitty Bennet)**; Melville Cooper **(Mr. Collins)**; Karen Morley **(Charlotte Lucas)**; Marsha Hunt **(Mary Bennet)**; Bruce Lester **(Bingley)**; Marten Lamont **(Denny)**; E. E. Clive **(Sir William Lucas)**; May Beatty **(Mrs. Phillips)**; Marjorie Wood **(Lady Lucas)**; Gia Kent **(Miss DeBurgh)**; Gerald Oliver-Smith **(Fitz William)**; Vernon Downing **(Captain Carter)**; Buster Slaven **(Beck's Assistant)**; Wyndham Standing and Lowden Adams **(Committeemen)**; Clara Reid **(Maid in Parsonage)**.

SYNOPSIS

England circa 1810. Mrs. Bennet is constantly in a dither, attempting to wed her five, disparate daughters: Elizabeth, Jane, Lydia, Kitty, and Mary. Her vulgar methods of matchmaking are disliked by her husband, a true gentleman. Because they do not have a son, Mrs. Bennet also worries about their estate passing to a cold-hearted cousin, Mr. Collins, upon Mr. Bennet's death.

Excitement arrives in the forms of two rich and distinguished bachelors, Mr. Darcy and Mr. Bingley. Bingley is immediately attracted to Jane Bennet, but Mr. Darcy, a snob, looks down on everyone. Elizabeth Bennet, annoyed at Darcy's snobbishness, is determined to insult him. She antagonizes him by refusing to dance with him at a ball. This makes him take notice of her. Meanwhile, Jane and Bingley fall in love, but he is influenced adversely by his class-conscious sister, Caroline Bingley, and by Darcy. Thus Bingley decides to return to London, leaving Jane heartbroken.

While visiting a friend, Elizabeth again meets Darcy, who then acts kindly toward her. He asks her to marry him, stating that, as much as he dislikes her family, he cannot resist her charms. Elizabeth is infuriated and rejects his marriage bid. In the meantime, Mr. Collins, always trailing his meddlesome and demanding patroness, Lady Catherine DeBurgh (who is also Mr. Darcy's aunt), comes to visit the Bennets in order to see his future estate and to court Elizabeth. She rejects his pompous bid of marriage.

Then it is learned that Lydia has run off with the scoundrel soldier Wickham without first being married. Darcy finally comes to the aid of the Bennets. By bestowing an income on the scheming Wickham, he influences the cad to marry Lydia. Later Elizabeth agrees to wed Darcy. Mrs. Bennet is overjoyed for it now seems that all her daughters will soon be wed.

* * *

"This, by your leave, we proclaim the most deliciously pert comedy of old manners, the most crisp and crackling satire in costume that we . . . can remember ever having seen on the screen." The praise came from Bosley Crowther **(New York Times)** in response to the opening of **Pride and Prejudice** at Radio City Music Hall. Jane Austen's first novel, written between 1796 and 1797 and published in 1813, supplied the cinema with one of the first screen versions of a classic which did not alienate, bore, or sedatize audience. The reason: lavish production by Hunt Stromberg, marvelous star performances by Greer Garson and Laurence Olivier, and MGM opulence evident in every frame of celluloid.

Following a successful stage version of **Pride and Prejudice,** presented at Broadway's Music Box Theatre in 1935 (the treatment prepared by Helen Jerome), Irving Thalberg purchased the stage rights, although the novel was in the public domain. The sagacious producer felt the play's success could make for good publicity. Naturally, Thalberg pictured wife Norma Shearer in the part of Elizabeth Bennet. In 1938, even after Thalberg's death, MGM announced an upcoming production of **Pride and Prejudice** with Shearer in the lead role. At one brief point Clark Gable was considered for the role of Mr. Darcy, but he refused the possible assignment. For a brief period, Melvyn Douglas was considered for the role. Then in August 1939 Metro announced that Robert Donat would play the male lead and that George Cukor would direct. However, the British-based MGM star decided he would rather do a full season with the Old Vic and he rejected the screen offering.

As a substitute MGM turned to another Britisher, Laurence Olivier, who had acquitted himself so admirably in Samuel Goldwyn's **Wuthering Heights** (1939) and Alfred Hitchcock's **Rebecca** (1940). However, Olivier had his own ideas about his vis-à-vis. He suggested his longtime romance, actress Vivien Leigh. She was a logical choice, since she had appeared in MGM's **A Yank at Oxford** (1938; filmed in England), **Gone With the Wind** (1939; for which she won a Best Actress Oscar), and **Waterloo Bridge** (1940). But Louis B. Mayer was set on Garson to play Elizabeth Bennet, and so she did—admirably.[1]

The Aldous Huxley–Jane Murfin script used dialogue taken directly from Austen, an authoress "as brittle as Huxley, Noel Coward, and a whole package of saltiness." The art and research department reproduced Longbourn, the Bennet home, using architecture and furnishings of the Queen Anne period. However, the costuming department, realizing that fashions were far more attractive three or four decades beyond Austen's early nineteenth-century setting, created the apparel to suit the later time and to impress filmgoers. There was, in fact, during production a hesitancy by the studio to emphasize the period aspect of the feature. This fact was reflected by the rather bizarre ad copy which promoted the feature upon release: "Five charming sisters (age 16 to 24) . . . on the gayest, merriest manhunt that ever snared a bewildered bachelor. . . . Girls . . . take a lesson from these husband hunters!"

However, on its merits, **Pride and Prejudice** proved an enormous hit. Howard Barnes **(New York Herald-Tribune)** reported, "In handsomely mounted and leisurely sequences it does a first-rate job of re-creating the manners and conventions as well as the outer show of the period. . . . Here is a tasteful and faithful screen version of a definitely dated literary work." Archer Winsten **(New York Post)** labeled the entry "one of the most delightfully contemporary pictures imaginable." And the **Times'** Crowther noted, "It isn't often that a cast of such uniform perfection is assembled. Greer Garson is Elizabeth—'dear, beautiful Lizzie'—stepped right out of the book, or rather out of one's fondest imagination: poised, graceful, self-contained, witty, spasmodically stubborn, and as lovely as a woman can be. Laurence Olivier is Darcy, that's all there is to it—the arrogant, sardonic Darcy whose pride went before a most felicitous fall. Mary Boland is a completely overpowering Mrs. Bennet." The siblings—Maureen O'Sullivan, Ann Rutherford, Heather Angel, and Marsha Hunt—were all lauded, as were such players as Edna May Oliver (as Lady Catherine), Edmund Gwenn (as Mr. Bennet), and Melville Cooper (as Mr. Collins). There were some critical quarters, however, who insisted that Cooper and Hunt (she as the bespectacled Mary) allowed their roles to flow into caricature. But this was perhaps the fault more of the script and direction than of the players themselves. (To give an idea of the attitude here, it should be noted that at one point Phil Silvers was tested for the part of Mr. Collins!)

Commercially, **Pride and Prejudice** per-

Melville Cooper and Greer Garson in Pride and Prejudice *('40).*

formed far better than Metro had dared hope.[2] It became one of the very few films to play more than three weeks at Radio City Music Hall (**Snow White**, **Rebecca**, and **All This, and Heaven Too** had also garnered this honor; **Pride** was held for four weeks). Yet for all its critical and public acclaim, **Pride and Prejudice** was not nominated in any major category for an Oscar. It did win a prize for Best Black and White Interior Decoration (Cedric Gibbons and Paul Groesse).

Pride and Prejudice played an important factor in the mounting popularity of Greer Garson, who rapidly filled the gap of the declining Greta Garbo and Shearer as Metro's class actress attraction. Incidentally, billed twelfth in the credits was Karen Morley (as Charlotte Lucas). She had been one of MGM's most serviceable leading ladies in the early thirties, playing everything from the bitch who destroys Wallace Beery in **Flesh** (1932) to the screaming blonde ingenue of **The Mask of Fu Manchu** (1932).

As for the disgruntled Vivien Leigh, she and beau Laurence Olivier wed before they starred in United Artists' **That Hamilton Woman** (1941). Then the couple returned to England for the duration of the World War II years.

In 1947 MGM producer Arthur Freed planned a musical version of **Pride and Prejudice**.[3] First

Sally Benson, then Sidney Sheldon, scripted scenarios. However, the screen project was later abandoned.

PRIVATE LIVES
1931—92½ min.

Director, Sidney Franklin; based on the play by Noel Coward; **screenplay,** Hans Kraly and Richard Schayer; **continuity,** Claudine West; **camera,** Ray Binger; **editor,** Conrad A. Nervig.

Norma Shearer **(Amanda Chase Paynne);** Robert Montgomery **(Elyot Chase);** Reginald Denny **(Victor Paynne);** Una Merkel **(Sibyl Chase);** Jean Hersholt **(Oscar);** George Davis **(Bellboy).**

SYNOPSIS
Elyot Chase and Amanda have been divorced for two years and now have each remarried. Both have selected practical spouses: he has wed Sibyl and Amanda is now Mrs. Victor Paynne.

---

[1] Garson had been hired by Olivier to appear in the play **Golden Arrow,** which played London's West End in 1935; she appeared on British TV in the late thirties as Juliet to Olivier's Romeo.

[2] The British trade newspaper, **Kine Weekly,** assessed of **Pride and Prejudice,** "Period comedy of manners preserving gracefully and faithfully the gentle yet defiant spirit of Jane Austen's immortal novel of English country life in the early part of the 19th century."

[3] On March 19, 1959, **First Impressions** debuted at the Alvin Theatre. This Broadway musical version of **Pride and Prejudice** was based on the Austen novel and the Helen Jerome play, with music and lyrics by Robert Goldman, Glenn Paxton, and George Weiss. As directed by Abe Burrows (who provided the book), it starred Polly Bergen (Elizabeth Bennet), Farley Granger (Mr. Darcy), Hermione Gingold (Mrs. Bennet), and Christopher Hewett (Mr. Collins). Despite its many charming qualities, the show did not have a long run.

Robert Montgomery and Norma Shearer in Private Lives *('31).*

It happens that each couple honeymoons in a French hotel, the same one where Elyot and Amanda spent their honeymoon years before. No sooner do Elyot and Amanda see each other there than they realize they are still very much in love with each other. They run away to a Swiss chalet, leaving a note informing their spouses of their drastic step.

Elyot and Amanda are happy for a time but they begin to quarrel again. The abandoned wife and husband, who have followed them, come upon the couple amidst a bitter fight.

The next morning the two couples make up and decide to forgive each other. But at the breakfast table the practical husband and the practical wife quarrel. This amazes both Elyot and Amanda for they thought they were the only ones who quarreled. And so they run off again, promising never to part.

* * *

In his unrelenting effort to showcase the talents of his patrician wife Norma Shearer and to boost the still infant sound cinema to a higher level of literacy, Irving Thalberg found an admirable vehicle in **Private Lives**. The sophisticated farce by Noel Coward opened on Broadway[1] on

January 27, 1931, at the Times Square Theatre with the following cast:

Elyot Chase . . . . Noel Coward
Amanda Chase Paynne . . . . Gertrude Lawrence
Victor Paynne . . . . Laurence Olivier
Sibyl Chase . . . . Jill Esmond

The froth ran in New York for 248 performances. Thalberg, who purchased the screen rights, found the stage rendition impeccable and had a film made of a performance to guide the work of the MGM artists who were set for the project: director Sidney Franklin; stars Norma Shearer and Robert Montgomery, as the slightly mad couple who divorce and remarry; and Reginald Denny and Una Merkel as the dullard mates whom the split couple have teamed up with for the present.

The screenplay by Hans Kraly and Richard Schayer retained most of the plot structure and wit of the Coward original, although the film's ending was relocated from Paris to a snug Alpine chalet. **Private Lives** enjoyed a smooth production, save for one incident. In the famous fight

scene between Amanda and Elyot, a comic highlight of the play and the movie in which the couple brawl about a room and sprawl over a sofa, Shearer "lost control." She landed so deft a punch on Montgomery's face that he plummeted backward and fell through a screen. Though the actress was greatly upset by her display of strength, Franklin was so amused by the sight that he retained the scene in the completed picture.

Private Lives was released at Christmas time 1931. It won the gratitude of the critics when it discovered that the film had not sacrificed any of Coward's brisk adult dialogue in deference to the lowbrow masses.[2] **Motion Picture** magazine, swiping at Norma's heavy melodramatics of **The Divorcee** (1930) and **A Free Soul** (1931), noted, "Norma Shearer matches Robert Montgomery's well-known flair for light comedy and, after the posey dramatics of late, reveals herself as a charming comedienne." **Photoplay** magazine: "Well, they've kept them all in—those swell lines of the Noel Coward play. And they're both there—those two, grand, impossible delightful characters. . . . Norma Shearer and Robert Montgomery are excellent. . . . A wild farce idea made snappy by a sparkling and at times questionable dialogue." **Time** magazine: "In this production directed by Sidney Franklin, Norma Shearer and Robert Montgomery play through the almost actor-proof situations of the comedy with savoir faire which equals if it does not excel that of their predecessors—author Noel Coward and Gertrude Lawrence." (Several reviewers noted that Shearer frequently imitated Lawrence's mannerisms from the play with almost too much fidelity, leaving little room for her own personality to emerge on screen.)

After **Private Lives** had opened in England, the **Times** (London) reported, "Mr. Robert Montgomery seems rather taken aback to discover that his lines, usually so amiable, have, in this instance, taken on a catty and quite ungentlemanly venom."

This was the fourth of five screen teamings of Shearer and Montgomery. Previously they had joined forces in **Their Own Desire** (1929), **The Divorcee** (1930), and **Strangers May Kiss** (1931). They would appear together once more on the MGM soundstages, in the Irving Thalberg–produced **Riptide** (1934), a rather soggy finale for one of the screen's most sophisticated acting pairs.

QUEEN CHRISTINA
1933—100 min.

Producer, Walter Wanger; **director**, Rouben Mamoulian; **story**, Salka Viertel and Margaret P. Levine; **screenplay**, Viertel and H. M. Harwood; **dialogue**, S. N. Behrman; **art directors**, Alexander Toluboff and Edwin B. Willis; **music**, Herbert Stothart; **costumes**, Adrian; **sound**, Douglas Shearer; **camera**, William Daniels; **editor**, Blanche Sewell.

---

[1]Coward and Lawrence had played the roles in London in September 1930 for a brief engagement. Over the

years the play has been revived frequently on Broadway and on tour. In the film **Star!** (1968) Julie Andrews as Gertrude Lawrence and Daniel Massey as Noel Coward re-created the balcony scene from the play.

[2]Filmed on a forty-day schedule, **Private Lives** cost $500,000 and earned a $256,000 profit.

Greta Garbo **(Christina)**; John Gilbert **(Don Antonio)**; Ian Keith **(Magnus)**; Lewis Stone **(Oxenstierna)**; Elizabeth Young **(Ebba)**; C. Aubrey Smith **(Aage)**; Reginald Owen **(Prince Charles)**; Georges Renavent **(French Ambassador)**; Gustav von Seyffertitz **(General)**; David Torrence **(Archbishop)**; Ferdinand Munier **(Innkeeper)**; Akim Tamiroff **(Pedro)**; Cora Sue Collins **(Christina as a Child)**; Edward Norris **(Count Jacob)**; Lawrence Grant and Barbara Barondess **(Bits)**; Paul Hurst **(Swedish Soldier)**; Ed Gargan **(Fellow Drinker)**; Major Sam Harris **(Nobleman)**.

Greta Garbo and John Gilbert in Queen Christina *('33).*

SYNOPSIS

In the seventeenth century Queen Christina of Sweden rejects marriage to Prince Charles, despite the fact that he is a hero to the people. Her former lover, the crafty Magnus, favors the marriage and is disappointed at her politically unsound decision.

One day while riding in the snow she meets Don Antonio, the newly arrived ambassador from Spain. Later she encounters him again at an inn. He does not realize that beneath her boy's clothing she is a woman. Because the tavern is overcrowded, they are forced to share a room that night. He soon discovers his companion is female, but is unaware of her identity.

In the ensuing days they fall in love and Christina wants to marry him and resettle in Spain. Once Antonio discovers she is the queen, he explains that he had been dispatched to arrange a marriage between her and the Spanish king.

Magnus learns of the growing relationship between Antonio and Christina and causes the Swedes to turn against the Spanish ambassador. Christina sends Antonio away, abdicates her title, and plans to keep a rendezvous with her foreign lover. Arriving at the designated spot, she discovers Antonio slain by Magnus in a duel.

A sorrowful Christina departs for Spain with her lover's body, never to return to her beloved homeland.

* * *

The silent cinema had no other love team more glorious than that of Greta Garbo and John Gilbert. Their torrid romances of **Flesh and the Devil** (1927), **Love** (1927), and **A Woman of Affairs** (1929) were filled with some of the motion picture's greatest and most passionate love scenes, reputedly kindled by Gilbert's actual infatuation with Garbo. (He is said to have proposed to the Swede, who in a moment of romantic candor laughed and replied, "But, Johnny, you're such a **boy.**")

Then came the talkies. No other star ever suffered the humiliation that befell Gilbert as the primitive sound recording techniques abused his dialogue in **His Glorious Night** (1929), **Way for a Sailor** (1930), and other films. Audiences who only months before swooned and applauded his powerful, restrained, dashing performances, now squealed in derision. This painful turnabout delighted Louis B. Mayer, who despised the free-living, free-thinking Gilbert and took pains to accent the star's downfall so as to embarrass the

actor into breaking his million-dollar Metro contract. Gilbert was removed from **Grand Hotel** (1932), in which he was to reunite with Garbo, and replaced by John Barrymore. Gilbert's announced role in **Red Dust** (1932) was suddenly given to Clark Gable. The lot tried assorted psychological ploys[1] which, while driving Gilbert from a heavy drinker to an alcoholic, could not prevent him from cashing his hefty weekly paycheck.

Two MGM powers remained faithful to the fallen Gilbert. One was producer Paul Bern, who chose Gilbert to be his best man at his July 3, 1932, wedding to Jean Harlow. Bern promised his friend he would find something to launch Gilbert back into prominence despite Mayer's vindictiveness. However, after Bern's suicide of Labor Day 1932, Gilbert's only friend in power was Greta Garbo. Still, their personal relationship was not without complications. While Gilbert's career had fractured, Garbo's had soared after **Anna Christie** (1930) and she continued to reveal to her worshippers new alluring facets through her divine melancholia in **Grand Hotel** and her luscious sensuality in **Mata Hari** (1932). In addition, Gilbert had suffered a painful divorce from stage and screen star Ina Claire, whose theatre-trained tones tortured him. In August 1932 he had wed Metro starlet Virginia Bruce, all of which es-

tranged his personal contact with his Swedish costar.

Nevertheless, Garbo, shocked by the cruelty which marked Gilbert's downfall, decided to do something to aid his professional plight. The answer—the part of Don Antonio in **Queen Christina,** her latest MGM vehicle. Leslie Howard was the lot's, and Garbo's, initial choice. He refused. Franchot Tone, Nils Asther, and Bruce Cabot were then considered before Laurence Olivier was contracted. However, after arriving back in Hollywood, Olivier was vetoed by Garbo and he returned to Broadway and a production of **The Green Bay Tree.** At this point Garbo directed the studio to call Gilbert down from the Beverly Hills Tower Road mansion he shared with Virginia Bruce and he began his fifth film with Garbo.[2]

Historical accuracy was glaringly absent in Metro's screen biography of Queen Christina (1626–89). She was actually a squat, unattractive woman who savored foul stories and slept with her lady-in-waiting. Too, Garbo rather disagreeably dominated the entire production, from approving a director (Rouben Mamoulian) to deciding against ardent embraces in the film, since her leading man was again married.

Publicity abounded concerning Garbo's on-camera masquerade as a boy, Lewis Stone's seventh and final appearance opposite Garbo, and such dialogue as:

CHANCELLOR: You cannot die an old maid.
CHRISTINA: I have no intention to. I shall die a bachelor.

All of which served as buildup to **Queen**

---

[1]Over the years, Hollywood observers have insisted that MGM once called for Gilbert to appear in full evening dress late one night on the back lot, where he was thrown into a swimming pool throughout the evening. The humiliation went on until dawn as the director insisted with each take that it had to be done yet again. Gilbert, determined to draw every penny of his contracted salary, gulped liquor between takes and charmingly suffered the harassment.

---

[2]Garbo and Gilbert had made cameo appearances in **A Man's Man** (1929).

Christina's preview in mid-December 1933. Garbo attended. She sneaked into the theatre early, alone, and left the same way.

Reviews of the costume drama were mixed. **Modern Screen:** "One of the great pictures of the past few years, this historical epic makes a sustained drive for artistry . . . an unending series of exceptional scenes, packed with fine characterizations and good direction. A triumph for Garbo, a comeback for Gilbert . . . you cannot afford to miss it." **Variety:** "Chief fault with **Queen Christina** is its lethargy. It is slow and ofttimes stilled. This is perhaps good cinematic motivation, according to Mamoulian's standards, in order to establish the characteristic contrasts between the queen."

Gilbert, looking weary in heavy makeup and his wig, was dominated by Garbo, whose name highlighted the marquees and the reviews. His MGM contract expired with **Queen Christina**. He made only one more feature film, Columbia's **The Captain Hates the Sea** (1934). Following a divorce that year from Virginia Bruce, Gilbert embraced alcohol with a passion, which led to a fatal heart attack on January 9, 1936. Mayer could scarcely contain a smile at the funeral, and Garbo left the theatrics to Marlene Dietrich, who had had a recent romance with the actor. The German actress nearly collapsed in the church aisle.

Since each new Garbo picture was deemed a prestigious event, the studio did its best to promote her offerings to the public. Despite the mixed feelings of the critics, the public endorsed this historical romantic yarn, turning **Queen Christina** into one of the studio's profitable ventures of the 1933–34 period, along with **The Barretts of Wimpole Street, Chained, Riptide,** and **Sons of the Desert.**[3]

Word of mouth did a great deal to enhance the marketability of **Queen Christina**. Filmgoers were equally enchanted with the emotional import of such scenes as Garbo touching and examining each item of the inn bedroom that she has shared with Gilbert. And few could forget the finale in which an enigmatic-faced Garbo stands at the bow of the ship that carries her and the body of her lover to Spain.[4]

The life of Queen Christina would continue to fascinate filmmakers years after the Garbo feature was released. In 1974 Warner Bros. distributed **The Abdication,** starring Liv Ullmann as the trouble-prone monarch. The narrative focused on her stay in Rome and her sudden passion for Cardinal Azzolino (Peter Finch). The picture was a commercial and artistic disaster, dimming not one whit the celluloid memory of Garbo as the magnetizing queen of Sweden.

---

[3]Filmed on a sixty-eight-day schedule, **Queen Christina** cost $1,144,000 and earned a profit of $632,000.

[4]For this well-remembered scene, director Mamoulain advised Garbo, "I want your face to be a blank sheet of paper. I want the writing to be done by every member of the audience. I'd like it if you could avoid blinking your eyes, so that you're nothing but a beautiful mask."

QUO VADIS
1951 C—171 min.

Producer, Sam Zimbalist; **director,** Mervyn LeRoy; based on the novel by Henryk Sienkiewicz; **screenplay,** John Lee Mahin, S. N. Behrman, and Sonya Levien; **art directors,** William A. Horning, Cedric Gibbons, and Edward Carfagno; **set decorator,** Hugh Hunt; **costumes,** Herschel McCoy; **music,** Miklos Rozsa; **historical adviser/English hymn lyrics,** Hugh Gray; **choreography,** Marta Obolensky and Auriel Millos; **camera,** Robert Surtees and William V. Skall; **editor,** Ralph E. Winters.

Robert Taylor **(Marcus Vinicius);** Deborah Kerr **(Lygia);** Leo Genn **(Petronius);** Peter Ustinov **(Nero);** Patricia Laffan **(Poppaea);** Finlay Currie **(Peter);** Abraham Sofaer **(Paul);** Marina Berti **(Eunice);** Buddy Baer **(Ursus);** Felix Aylmer **(Plautius);** Nora Swinburne **(Pomponia);** Ralph Truman **(Tigellinus);** Norman Wooland **(Nerva);** Peter Miles **(Nazarius);** Geoffrey Dunn **(Terpnos);** Nicholas Hannen **(Seneca);** D. A. Clarke-Smith **(Phaon);** Rosalie Crutchley **(Acte);** John Ruddock **(Chilo);** Arthur Walge **(Croton);** Elspeth March **(Miriam);** Strelsa Brown **(Rufia);** Alfredo Varelli **(Lucan);** Roberto Ottaviano **(Flavius);** William Tubbs **(Anaxander);** Pietro Tordi **(Galba);** Lia DeLeo **(Pedicurist);** Sophia Loren **(Extra);** Elizabeth Taylor **(Guest);** Walter Pidgeon **(Narrator).**

SYNOPSIS

In the first century A.D. Marcus Vinicius, commander of the victorious Roman legions, returns to Rome after his conquests in Britain. He is honored by the Empress Poppaea. Soon he meets and falls in love with Lygia, a Christian hostage and the daughter of a defeated king. She spurns him because of his pagan ways.

He then contrives to have Lygia given to him as a slave. But she still refuses to yield to him and he frees her from her guard through the assistance of servant Ursus. Later Marcus follows Lygia to a meeting of the Christians where a sermon by the apostle Peter gives him a better understanding of her religious beliefs. She eventually falls in love with Marcus and consents to become his wife. However, he leaves her in anger when she refuses to abandon her Christian faith.

Yet when the mad Emperor Nero sets fire to Rome, Marcus rushes to Lygia's rescue. The two are seized with other Christians when Nero places the blame of the fire on the adherents of Christ. Marcus and Lygia are married by Peter in a dungeon while they await their slaughter in the arena. Empress Poppaea, maddened by her unrequited love for Marcus, decides to torture him by making him watch Lygia threatened with death by an infuriated bull. Nero has promised the crowd that if Lygia's friend Ursus can kill the rampaging animal, he will free Lygia. Marcus breaks out of his bonds, leaps into the arena, and rouses the crowd against Nero when he fails to free Lygia. It sets off the revolt that culminates in the death of Nero and Poppaea.

* * *

Robert Taylor with director Mervyn LeRoy on the set of Quo Vadis *('51).*

For nearly a decade after its production, the Metro extravaganza **Quo Vadis** occupied a special niche in the corporation's rich history: it ranked only behind **Gone With the Wind** (1939) as the studio's greatest box-office attraction. Even today, after the release of such champion grossers as **Doctor Zhivago** (1965), **Ben-Hur** (1959), and **2001: A Space Odyssey** (1968), **Quo Vadis** rests high among MGM's all-time hits.[1] It is a fact often forgotten by many Metro-philes, who dwell on the halcyon Garbo-Harlow-Gable days and the plush period of the Arthur Freed musicals.

There had been several silent film versions of the Henryk Sienkiewicz novel: a twelve-minute 1902 French edition; a nine-reel Italian epic in 1912, which was imported to the United States as a prestigious road-shown film in 1913, and another Italian entry in 1924, which would enjoy American distribution in a silent (1925) and a sound-effects (1929) version. In the late 1930s, MGM planned its own version, with preparation being made to send a company to Italy under the aegis of associate producer-director Robert Z. Leonard. However, the World War II situation prevailed and the Hunt Stromberg project was abandoned for the duration. Then, in the late forties,[2] Metro reactivated its plans for **Quo Vadis,** setting up another of the increasingly bitter battle royals between Louis B. Mayer and Dore Schary. The latter insisted on a cerebral production, intending to draw parallels between the Roman emperor Nero and modern dictators. On the other hand, the more simplistic-minded Mayer wanted a traditional production (much in the vein that Frank Ross was planning elsewhere for **The Robe**). It

---

[1]The MGM top ten: **Gone With the Wind** (1939), **Doctor Zhivago** (1965), **Ben-Hur** (1959), **2001: A Space Odyssey** (1968), **The Dirty Dozen** (1967), **Ryan's Daughter** (1970), **Quo Vadis** (1951), **How the West Was Won** (1962), **Mutiny on the Bounty** (1962), and **Cat on a Hot Tin Roof** (1958).

[2]An apocryphal story has it that Hollywood would certainly have turned out a version of **Quo Vadis** much sooner, had it not been for a producer's jittery query, "But who would we get to play Quo?"

was Mayer's notion to emphasize the glamour and the splendor of ancient, decadent Rome.

For a time it appeared that Schary had won again. A company headed by producer Arthur Hornblow, director John Huston, and stars Gregory Peck and Elizabeth Taylor went to Rome in 1949 to begin shooting. However, many MGM traditionalists feared Rome, where the 1920s' **Ben-Hur** had caused such terrible and costly production nightmares. It appeared their superstitions were vindicated when **Quo Vadis** shut down production and the company returned to Hollywood. The approximate cost for the debacle was $2 million.

Mayer cherished the opportunity to prove he could succeed where Schary had failed. By early 1950 a newly conceived production was being planned. Mayer's trusted director Mervyn LeRoy was offered the job; he agreed if producer Sam Zimbalist was assigned to the mammoth project. To top the cast, Mayer favorites Robert Taylor (as the Roman legionnaire Marcus Vinicius) and Deborah Kerr[3] (as Lygia the Christian hostage-slave) were signed. Peter Ustinov continued on in his previously announced role of the mad Nero (played in the 1924 Italian version by Emil Jannings).[4]

Again the Metro troupe was dispatched to Rome, setting up headquarters in the Cinecitta Studios where production costs were relatively low and extras could be hired very cheaply.[5] Tony Thomas in **Ustinov in Focus** (1971) writes:

The logistics involved in producing a film of this magnitude were staggering. There were over two hundred speaking parts, many hundreds of workmen, and tens of thousands of extras. The company was managed along military lines, with group captains assigned certain numbers of extras, for whom they were responsible from beginning to end, everything from makeup to wages. **Quo Vadis** was the first color film made at the Cinecitta Studio in Rome, and Mervyn LeRoy winces at the memory: "They knew nothing about color, not even the fact that they had to use two and three times the intensity of lighting. When the cameras turned over for the first time, they went backward. They had put the switches in wrong. I never forgot that."

As for packaging this epic, LeRoy would say

that the toughest problem on **Quo Vadis** was the use of lions for the arena:

I had rounded up every lion in Europe, from circuses and zoos, about one hundred and twenty of them. I also got all the lion tamers I could find and dressed them as Christians—I was afraid the lions would actually eat people. On the day of shooting the arena sequence I had six thousand extras in the stands. I explained to the cast and crew that I would fire four pistol shots. The first to be ready, the second to start turning the cameras, the third for confirmation that the cameras were turning, and the fourth for the crowds to start roaring. I had eight cameras. I told the trainers in the arena they would have to fend for themselves. I fired the shots and the gates opened—all the lions charged into the arena, they looked up at the sun and went back in. I didn't know what to do. I got all the trainers together and asked for their advice. They said to starve the lions for two weeks. I didn't like the sound of that but I agreed. So for two weeks we worked on other scenes as these lions growled in the background. I thought, "My God, they'll eat everybody." Anyway, after two weeks we restaged the scene. I fired my shots, the gates opened, and out poured these roaring, starving lions. And they did exactly the same thing—looked up at the sun and went back in. I never did get the shots I wanted. I had to double-expose some of the shots of people running and lions coming out, and the only way I could get shots of the lions attacking people was to take some of the Christians' costumes and stuff them with raw meat. I then reversed the shots of the lions backing away. I never did get it the way I wanted.

Amidst the chaos and frustrations of creating this historical mélange, LeRoy maintained a jocular relationship with actor Ustinov. Says LeRoy:

I used to kid Peter. He was always clowning on the set and sometimes he would get a little hammy on camera. But he's easy to pull down, all you do is to tell him he's overdoing it. Once, I yelled to my assistant, "Bill, get the shredded-wheat set." Peter looked up, "What do you mean 'shredded-wheat set'?" I said, "Well, if you're going to eat the scenery, we might as well make it edible."

In his **Ustinov in Focus**, author Thomas writes:

Ustinov has one particularly effective scene in **Quo Vadis**. Always petulant and always imaging himself to be an artist—a singer, composer, poet—Nero retreats for a while, then calls his cabinet and his confidants together to unveil a large model of a new city, Neropolis: "Attend me, attend me all. My lack of consideration for you during the past few days in keeping you from my presence forces me to impress upon you, once again, the tribulations of the true artist. When I play and sing, I have

visions of things I never dreamed existed. The world is mine, and mine to end. . . . This is a day for sincerity, let me open my soul to you. Do you think I do not know there are people in Rome who call me a matricide, a wife killer, call me a monster, tyrant; but there is something they do not realize—a man's acts may be cruel while he himself is not cruel. And there are moments, my dear Petronius, when music caresses my soul. I feel as gentle as a child in a cradle. Yet, there are those who say I am mad. I'm only seeking. The flatness and misery of common life depresses me. I seek because I must be greater than man, because only then will I be the supreme artist. You know why I condemned both my wife and my mother to death? I did it in order to lay at the gates of an unknown world the greatest sacrifice a man can put. Now, I thought, doors will open beyond which I will catch a glimpse of the unknown. Let it be wonderful or let it be awful. So long as it is uncommon." Thus Nero rationalizes his ambitions for changing the face of the earth.

After six months of filming in Rome at a cost of nearly $7 million, the Technicolor **Quo Vadis** completed its main shooting. Postproduction work was accomplished at Metro's British and Culver City studios. Walter Pidgeon was assigned to deliver the voice-over narration and Miklos Rozsa's complex music score was added to the film.

Miklos Rozsa, whose first film scores for MGM included **Adam's Rib** (1949), **Madame Bovary** (1949), and **The Asphalt Jungle** (1950), has written extensively about his preparations for this gigantic film. In James L. Limbacher's **Film Music: From Violins to Video** (1974), he relates the assistance provided by George Schneider, the librarian at MGM who unearthed every possible reference to the period that could be located. "We reconstructed these [antique instruments] from Roman statues (in the Vatican and Naples museums), antique vases and bas-relief on columns and tombstones, giving exact measurements for all details."

Rozsa then noted:

To select music for a historical picture of the Middle Ages, for instance, would have been an easy task, as there is a wealth of material available. But this is not the case with Roman music from the year A.D. 64. . . . There is absolutely no actual record of any music of the classic times of Roman history. . . . In **Quo Vadis** there were three distinguishable styles in which music had to be created. Firstly, the music of the Romans, such as the songs of Nero and the slave girl Eunice, sacrificial hymns of the Vestal, marches and fanfares. Secondly, the hymns of the Christians; and thirdly, the music performed by the slaves, which I call the Roman Empire music. As nothing remains of Roman music, this had to be recreated by deduction. . . . The orchestration of the music performed on scene was another problem. None of the old instruments were available and, therefore, the archaic sound had to be created with our modern instruments. I

---

[3]Actor Alec Guinness, who had been originally introduced to fledgling actress Audrey Hepburn by actor-coach Felix Aylmer with whom Hepburn was studying, suggested to Mervyn LeRoy that Hepburn be considered for the role of Lygia in **Quo Vadis**. However, LeRoy insisted he required a name actress for the leading part.

[4]Peter Ustinov had been contacted and tested in 1949 to play the role of Nero in **Quo Vadis**. When a year after his satisfactory audition for the film had passed, he happened to hear that Metro was still considering him for the showy role, but was concerned that he might be too young for the assignment. He telegraphed the studio, "If you wait much longer I shall be too old. Nero died at 31." MGM responded, "Historical research has proved you correct. The part is yours."

[5]One of the extras is a prestardom Sophia Loren; a reminder of the original production is the presence of Elizabeth Taylor in a crowd bit.

Buddy Baer and Deborah Kerr in Quo Vadis

ing lifestyles of the pious followers of Christ and the pagan disciples of the mad Nero. According to MGM promotional material, the burning of Rome was a major achievement of colossal proportion:

For three months a crew of twenty men labored continuously to mix thousands of gallons of inflammable liquid and then lay two miles of pipe to conduct it. Ten huge tanks . . . were built. Into them were poured 4,000 gallons of fuel oil, 2,000 gallons of gasoline, 3,000 gallons of a special alcohol mixture, and more than a ton of napthalene. In addition, fifty 20-gallon tanks of butane gas were connected to the set.

Next it was necessary to lay two miles of small iron pipe to carry these inflammables to 127 doors and windows in the four-block area. Each pipe passed through an elaborate control board which held a system of 275 valves, every one numbered corresponding to a door or a window.

Nero burned Rome in six days but it took MGM 24 nights to complete the job. During these nights of filming the special effects unit of 94 men on the assignment stood behind the cameras . . . As flames would be called for to pour from Window Number Two or Door Number Ten, the proper valve was pressed to start the flow of inflammable liquid from the storage tanks.

A company from the Rome Fire Department stood by throughout filming of the dangerous scenes. They were there just in case. Fortunately, however, their services were not needed, the 2,000 actors involved moving in and out of the flaming buildings without mishap—something they certainly were not able to do in Nero's day.

In its day **Quo Vadis** was considered such a bold example of lush movie-making that few filmgoers minded the cardboard appearances of the characters, the pretentiousness of the dialogue, the contrasting acting styles of the Hollywood, British, and Italian performers, and the occasionally unconvincing special effects. For all its grandeur MGM had never been in the vanguard of visual special effects, especially those dealing with rear projection, glass shots, etc. There is an especially bad example of transposed action near the finale of **Quo Vadis** involving Finlay Currie's Apostle Peter and his religious experience of a vision of Christ, which leads him to inquire, "Quo vadis, Domine?" ("Wither goest Thou, Lord?")

Bosley Crowther in the **New York Times** outlined the mixed feelings of the highbrow for this mammoth production. He said the feature was

. . . a perfection of spectacle and of hippodrome display with a luxuriance of made-to-order romance in a measure not previously seen. . . . We have a suspicion that this picture was not made for the overly sensitive or discriminate. It was made, we suspect, for those who like grandeur and noise—and no punctuation. It will probably be a vast success.

He was correct. Audiences responded to the spectacle en masse, particularly fascinated with

used a small Scottish harp, the clarsach, and this delicate instrument gave a remarkably true likeness to the sound of the lyre and antique harp. For military music, cornets, mixed with trumpets and trombones, gave the roughness of the early brass instruments. Bass flute and English horn replaced the sound of the aulos. Our modern percussion instruments come close to the antique ones and therefore it was safe to use tambourines, jingles, drums of different shapes and sizes, and cymbals. Bowed stringed instruments, however, could not be used. . . . [as] they would have been completely anachronistic. For music that was supposed to be performed by a large group of players I took the liberty of using the string group of the orches-

tra playing pizzicato to reinforce the main body of the orchestra.

Hugh Gray, who was the historical adviser on the project, provided the English words to the unharmonized hymns of the Christians.

When released in November 1951, **Quo Vadis** was distributed as a road-show attraction. Placards in front of the first-run theatres showing the "colossal" color feature informed potential patrons of every excitement that awaited them, detailing each spectacle within the course of the 171-minute feature. The highlights of the picture, of course, were the legionnaires' return to the Italian capitol, the burning of Rome, the killing of the Christians in the arena, and the contrast-the evil Poppaea (Patricia Laffan) leaving the bound Kerr to the mercy of the mad bull and forcing Taylor to watch, followed by the contest between the enraged animal and the oversized Christian slave Ursus (Buddy Baer).

Quo Vadis placed eighth in the **Film Daily** Ten Best Picture Poll for the year, and ninth in the National Board of Review's list. The Academy nominated it for Best Picture, but the epic lost to MGM's **An American in Paris,** which, along with Paramount's **A Place in the Sun,** was that year's big Oscar winner. Ustinov lost a Best Supporting Actor bid to Karl Malden of **A Streetcar Named Desire** (Warner Bros.). But, with general audiences, **Quo Vadis** was a top favorite. It grossed $12.5 million in distributors' domestic rentals and $25 million in worldwide rentals.

Quo Vadis was credited with making Hollywood spectacular-conscious. MGM put **Ivanhoe** (1952) into production, with Robert Taylor and Elizabeth Taylor starred, and the next year offered Robert Taylor in **Knights of the Round Table** (the studio's first CinemaScope film). Columbia produced **Salome** (1953) with Rita Hayworth. Twentieth Century–Fox released **David and Bathsheba** (1951), with Gregory Peck and Susan Hayward, and Frank Ross' long-cherished project **The Robe** (1953) and its 1954 sequel, **Demetrius and the Gladiators.** It also inspired producer Zimbalist to plan production of **Ben-Hur,** which would finally enter active production in Rome in 1958 and usurp **Quo Vadis's** number-two slot on the MGM profits list.

It is poetically proper that the star of this MGM milestone[6] was Robert Taylor, who became one of the great champions of Mayer and Metro throughout his career. Said Taylor:

> Some writers have implied that Mayer was tyrannical and abusive, and a male prima donna who outacted his actors. As I knew him, he was kind, fatherly, understanding, and protective. He gave me picture assignments up to the level that my abilities could sustain at the time, and was always there when I had problems. I just wish today's young actor had a studio and boss like I had. [The studio] groomed us carefully, kept us busy in picture after picture, thus giving us exposure, and made us stars. My memories of L.B. will always be pleasant, and my days at MGM are my happiest period professionally.

As such, **Quo Vadis** must have had special significance for Taylor; by the time it was released, Louis B. Mayer had been ousted from his post of authority. This spectacular film was one of the final testimonials to his talents. (It was

---

[6]It is interesting to compare the 1932 Paramount film **The Sign of the Cross,** a Cecil B. DeMille spectacular, with **Quo Vadis.** In the earlier film, Roman soldier Fredric March spurns "the wickedest woman in the world," Poppaea (played by Claudette Colbert), while Nero (played in effeminate fashion by Charles Laughton) capers about. The plot similarity is keen. There is even an episode in which a nude Christian girl is tied to a pillar, left to the paws of a savage gorilla—a vignette quite similar to the famous bull sequence of **Quo Vadis.**

Robert Taylor, Deborah Kerr, Buddy Baer, and Peter Miles in Quo Vadis

also during Taylor's Rome sojourn that rumors reached his wife, Barbara Stanwyck, that her spouse was playing the romantic field; they would lead to their divorce.)

Astute filmgoers have noted that four sequences from **Quo Vadis,** along with footage from Lana Turner's **The Prodigal** (1955), were woven into the proceedings of Metro's **Atlantis, the Lost Continent** (1961).

RANDOM HARVEST
1942—124 min.

Producer, Sidney Franklin; **director,** Mervyn LeRoy; based on the novel by James Hilton; **screenplay,** Claudine West, George Froeschel, and Arthur Wimperis; **music,** Herbert Stothart; **art director,** Cedric Gibbons; **camera,** Joseph Ruttenberg; **editor,** Harold F. Kress.

Ronald Colman **(Charles Ranier);** Greer Garson **(Paula);** Philip Dorn **(Dr. Jonathan Benet);** Susan Peters **(Kitty);** Reginald Owen **(Biffer);** Edmund Gwenn **(Prime Minister);** Henry Travers **(Dr. Sims);** Margaret Wycherly **(Mrs. Deventer);** Bramwell Fletcher **(Harrison);** Arthur Margetson **(Chetwynd);** Jill Esmond **(Lydis, Chet's Wife);** Marta Linden **(Jill, Kitty's Mother);** Pax Walker **(Sheila);** Clement May **(Beddoes);** Arthur Shields **(Chemist);**

David Cavendish **(Henry Chilcotte);** Norma Varden **(Julia);** Ann Richards **(Bridget);** Elisabeth Risdon **(Mrs. Lloyd);** Ivan Simpson **(The Vicar);** Charles Waldron **(Mr. Lloyd);** John Burton **(Pearson);** Rhys Williams **(Sam);** Alec Craig **(Comedian);** Henry Daniell **(Heavy Man);** Marie DeBecker **(Vicar's Wife);** Mrs. Gardner Crane **(Mrs. Sims);** Aubrey Mather **(Sheldon);** Montague Shaw **(Julia's Husband);** Lumsden Hare **(Sir John);** Frederic Worlock **(Paula's Lawyer);** Wallis Clark **(Jones);** Harry Shannon **(Badgeley);** Arthur Space **(Trempitt);** Una O'Connor **(Tobacconist);** Ian Wolfe **(Registrar);** Olive Blakeney **(Woman);** Peter Lawford **(Soldier).**

SYNOPSIS
In the excitement caused by the armistice of World War I, Charles Ranier, a shell-shocked amnesia victim, wanders out of a British asylum and makes his way to Medbury. Because of his odd manner and dress, he is recognized as a patient by music-hall dancer Paula. Sympathetic, she befriends the man and takes him to a country village where she restores his faith in himself.

He develops his talent as a writer and he and Paula soon wed. A child is born to them. One day Charles goes to Liverpool to inquire about a position. He is struck down by a vehicle while crossing the street. The accident and the ensuing shock restore his memory but his two years with Paula vanish.

Ronald Colman and Greer Garson in
Random Harvest *('42).*

He returns to his wealthy family and within a few years has become a leading industrialist. Meanwhile, Paula, after years of suffering and the loss of her child, locates Charles through the assistance of Dr. Jonathan Benet, a kindly psychiatrist. She manages to become Charles' secretary, but he does not show any signs of recognition. Dr. Benet advises Paula not to reveal herself.

She is thus forced to stand by while Kitty, Charles' youthful niece, becomes involved romantically with him. Kitty and Charles become engaged; but later Kitty calls off the marriage when her womanly instinct warns her that somewhere in Charles' past, there was another woman. More lonely than ever, Charles comes to depend on Paula. He offers her marriage in name only and she accepts. Under her guidance he becomes a political leader, but her efforts to recapture their past fails. She decides to take a long trip, but before sailing, she visits the cottage where she and Charles had been happy. Meanwhile, Charles has gone to Medbury to settle a labor strike and there piece by piece his past comes back to him. He retraces his steps to the cottage, where he and Paula joyfully reunite.

* * *

Could eloquent Greer Garson match the enormous success of **Mrs. Miniver** (1942)? Could dashing Ronald Colman, sans a major box-office hit since Paramount's **The Light That Failed** (1939), recapture major stardom? Metro's **Random Harvest** supplied an affirmative to both of these questions. The story of the loves of an amnesiac was based on James Hilton's exceedingly popular 1940 novel and it became one of the most successful and memorable features of the World War II years.[1]

Random Harvest was produced by Sidney Franklin, who would win the Irving Thalberg Award that year for **Mrs. Miniver**; Mervyn LeRoy directed. In her biography of her father, **Ronald Colman: A Very Private Person** (1975), Juliet Benita Colman quotes LeRoy:

"When **Random Harvest** came along, Ronnie and Greer were the first choice for the roles; it could have been written for them. (The film still holds the record for the longest run at the Radio City Music Hall in New York.)

"There was nothing of the ham in him. He'd always make a lot of suggestions about script and dialogue, always good ideas. He'd never be definite about it though; he didn't want to hurt you, and you didn't want to hurt him, so we would walk around the set and talk things over. . . .

". . . **Random Harvest**, which was all shot at MGM, cost around two million. (Today it would cost over five.) Sidney Franklin (the producer) and I worked so well together, and we all got on so well, it was a wonderful picture to make. When we did the last scene at the cottage gate, which was also the last scene we filmed, Ronnie said to me, 'This is one picture I hate to finish!' "[2]

For Greer Garson, **Random Harvest** was a special boon. It allowed the beautiful redheaded star to emote in another powerful role, demonstrating again that the mantle of special studio stardom had passed from Greta Garbo to Garson. (At this juncture Joan Crawford was still hanging on at the lot.) Morever, this film included a musical interlude—"The Imitation of Harry Lauder"—in which Garson charmingly sang and danced in a skimpy kilt, revealing a very shapely pair of legs. This episode won the elaborate feature its major publicity, despite the predominating love story. Yet as Garson recently remarked of the high-stepping episode, "They usually cut it out on television so they can sell more dog food and deodorant—very depressing."

Also seen to fine advantage in the picture is Susan Peters, cast as Kitty, Colman's love who breaks their engagement when she suspects a potentially damaging threat to their romance in his past. LeRoy cast the young actress after seeing her Warner Bros. test (where she had been under contract) for **Kings' Row**. Her success in the part led to an MGM buildup before a gun accident crippled her and her career.

Random Harvest opened at Christmas time 1942 and collected mainly rave reviews.[3] **Time** magazine: "**Random Harvest** is a first-rate film made from James Hilton's second-rate novel of the same name. It is distinguished by (1) a moving love story, (2) the unveiling of Miss Garson's interesting legs." The **New York Herald-Tribune**, although finding that "the subject matter and treatment are definitely unworthy of the acting," praised the stars: "Colman has never been more

stoically appealing . . . Miss Garson is radiantly persuasive as the girl from the music hall who marries him twice." The **New York Times** likewise labeled **Random Harvest** "a strangely empty film" but heralded the leads: "Miss Garson and Mr. Colman are charming; they act perfectly." The recurrent themes of the cherry blossoms, the music "O, Perfect Love," and the powerful performances of the stars made **Random Harvest**, despite its length and ponderousness, a great financial success. It grossed $4.5 million in distributors' domestic rentals.

Falling short of the **Mrs. Miniver** grosses by $1 million, **Random Harvest** was defeated by **Mrs. Miniver** at the Academy Awards. Just as the earlier-made film won the Best Picture prize, so Garson's Oscar nomination that year came for **Miniver** (and she won). Colman was nominated for Best Actor, but lost to James Cagney of **Yankee Doodle Dandy** (Warner Bros.), and Susan Peters lost the Best Supporting Actress Oscar to Teresa Wright (**Mrs. Miniver**). **Random Harvest** did place first on **Film Daily**'s 1943 Ten Best Picture Poll (in 1943 rather than 1942 because of its late calendar release), and Garson, at the glorious peak of her screen popularity, won England's **Picturegoer** magazine Gold Medal for her Paula.

In **The Great Romantic Films** (1974), Lawrence J. Quirk says of this well-mounted feature:

True, in some aspects the picture defies the rules of logic. The coincidences and happenstances are worked up too patly, the psychology is shaky, and the MGM music department poured on the molten melodic fudge so determinedly that at times the dialogue was drowned out—a frequent drawback in MGM dramas of the period. But with suave, sensitive Ronald Colman and tender, womanly Greer Garson up front, and a story that purged the emotions while vitiating abstract analysis, who was there to quibble? Few did.

RASPUTIN AND THE EMPRESS

1932—133 min. (British release title: RASPUTIN—THE MAD MONK

Producer, Bernard Hyman; **directors**, Richard Boleslawski and, uncredited, Charles Brabin; **story-screenplay**, Charles MacArthur; **music**, Herbert Stothart; **art directors**, Cedric Gibbons and Alexander Toluboff; **costumes**, Adrian; **assistant director**, Cullen Tate; **sound**, Douglas Shearer; **camera**, William Daniels; **editor**, Tom Held.

John Barrymore (**Prince Paul Chegodieff**); Ethel Barrymore (**Empress Alexandra**); Lionel Barrymore (**Rasputin**); Ralph Morgan (**Emperor Nikolai**); Diana Wynyard (**Natasha**); Tad Alexander (**Alexis**); C. Henry Gordon (**Grand Duke Igor**); Edward Arnold (**Doctor**); Gustav von Seyffertitz (**Dr. Wolfe**); Anne Shirley (**Anastasia**); Jean Parker (**Maria**); Sarah Padden (**Landlady**); Henry Kolker (**Chief of Secret Police**); Frank Shannon (**Profes-**

---

[2]LeRoy also said, of both Colman and Garson, "Between the two of them, the English language was never spoken more beautifully on film."

[3]William Whitebait in **New Statesman** presented a British evaluation. "**Random Harvest** is a very long, emotional, earnest, well-acted Hollywood-English drama. . . . In fact, I rather enjoyed this film, though it reeks of the studio, and every landscape looks as though one could put one's foot through it. Devonshire, especially, is precarious."

---

[1]Colman had previously appeared in the screen version of James Hilton's **Lost Horizon** (Columbia, 1937) and Garson had been in Hilton's **Goodbye, Mr. Chips** (1939).

Ethel Barrymore and Ralph Morgan (center) in Rasputin and the Empress *('32).*

sor Propotkin); Frank Reicher (German-Language Teacher); Hooper Atchley (Policeman); Leo White and Lucien Littlefield (Revelers); Mischa Auer (Butler); Dave O'Brien and Maurice Black (Soldiers); Charlotte Henry (Princess).

SYNOPSIS

Peasants are filling the streets of imperial Russia violently protesting the royal rule of Czar Nicholas and his empress, Czarina Alexandria. Prince Paul Chegodieff struts into the court to warn the rulers that certain reforms must be decreed if a bloody revolution is to be avoided.

As the ineffectual czar plans his new policies, his son, Crown Prince Alexis, a hemophiliac, suffers a fall and appears doomed to die. However, the lovely Natasha, lady-in-waiting to the czarina and the romance of Chegodieff, sends for Rasputin. The latter is a wide-eyed "holy man" of peasant stock who promises to stop the boy's bleeding. He does so by hypnotic powers. Overwhelmed by his miraculous talents, the czarina insists that Rasputin remain at court. The "mad monk" is only too happy to oblige.

Rasputin immediately plots his rise to the top power position in Russia. Meanwhile, he seduces the ladies of the court, enjoys wild parties, insults royalty, and belches at imperial affairs. Chegodieff, determined to eradicate his power, plots assassination attempts. He finally employs the court doctor to inject enough poison "to kill five men" into cakes to be served at one of Rasputin's orgies. The monk devours the pastry, but then recognizes Chegodieff's butler. He seeks out the hiding prince and takes him to the cellar to

shoot him. However, at the fatal moment, the poison takes some effect and Chegodieff attacks Rasputin. The two wage a lengthy physical brawl that ceases when the prince drags his adversary out into the winter night and drowns him in the icy river.

The czar publicly rebukes Chegodieff, but privately expresses his deep-felt gratitude, sending the assassin into safe exile. Natasha accompanies the prince and they face a promising future together. However, the royal family, convinced that their people will never harm them, remain in Russia. There the 1917 Revolution succeeds and the Bolsheviks condemn them to their doom.

* * *

"You need not worry about Mrs. Colt. Our sister will be standing right before the camera—in front of us," quipped John Barrymore (1882–1942) as his celebrated sister Ethel (1879–1959) arrived in the West to join him and brother Lionel (1878–1954) for MGM's Rasputin and the Empress. For the first time officially[1] in their theatrical and cinema careers, all three Barrymores were to join thespianic forces. It resulted in one of the greatest all-out battles of scene-stealing, mugging, posturing, and scenery-chomping yet recorded on Hollywood celluloid.

Brothers Lionel and John, each on MGM contract, had appeared together on stage in Peter Ibbetson (1917) and The Jest (1919), and had played together with splendid results in MGM's 1932 releases, Arsene Lupin and Grand Hotel.

---

[1]Actually the Barrymore trio had acted together in an impromptu benefit in Baltimore circa 1916 for a family impoverished by a fire.

Ethel had never trod the boards with her brothers and, with an attitude toward the cinema that at best was cavalier, had not made a motion picture since The Divorcee (1919). When Metro envisioned its project dealing with the intrigues of the Russian court of 1917, the image of Lionel as the evil Rasputin, John as the dashing assassin Prince Paul, and Ethel as the doomed czarina, it seemed inspired casting. Ethel agreed to join her brothers—she was chronically short of ready funds—and did so only with the demand that she work no longer than eight weeks.[2] (It was midsummer and she wished to return to New York's theatrical environs by fall.) Lionel, fearing the potential fireworks of such a union, set the tone of the filming when he queried publicly, "What poor, unsuspecting maniac of a director is going to take on this job?"

With Charles Brabin, a personal friend of Ethel's, supplying the initial answer to Lionel's question, Rasputin did not have a tranquil start. The script was rejected by the Barrymores, leading to Charles MacArthur thereafter beginning scenario rewrites on a daily basis. Sometimes he supplied the pages the morning they were to be shot, so as to honor Ethel's ironclad eight-week agreement.

Ethel, who played the mature czarina with an abundance of imperious eye-rolling and hand-wringing, sniped at the script and vetoed all directorial suggestions with a sniffed, "I knew her majesty personally." More dramatically, Lionel and John declared histrionic war. As Rasputin, Lionel delighted in his seduction of the court maidens, hypnotism of the hemophiliac Crown Prince Alexis, and assorted peasant gaucheries that upset the royal court. John, stuck with a typically dashing heroic part, envied his brother's flavorful character assignment. "The Great Profile" had always been happiest in screen roles like Dr. Jekyll and Mr. Hyde (1920—regarded as the greatest cinema version yet recorded), Svengali (1931), and The Mad Genius (1931).

John retaliated for his hero's pose by employing every scene-diverting trick in his extensive repertoire. When Lionel's character belches after a serving of borscht, John pops his magnificent eyes in comic astonishment. While Lionel's Rasputin orates passionately, "In less than a year, I will be Russia!" John's Prince Paul struts about parrying with a sword. The situation got so bad that Lionel skulked off the set, went to a studio pay phone, called the director, and told him to warn John about his larceny "lest at the close of this scene I be tempted to lay one on him!" Their acting match reached a climax in the assassination scene, in which, as Lionel slowly (oh, so slowly) dies of John's poison cakes, John cackles and shrieks. The two then battle for an interminable time. When the scene in which John finally drowns Lionel was lensed, set designer Cedric

---

[2]Of the three Barrymores, John was the best paid on the picture. He received $150,000. Lionel continued to draw his weekly MGM check of $1,500, and Ethel received $57,500, spending all of it and more on a lavish Beverly Hills abode and on her family, who accompanied her on the "vacation."

Gibbons created a masterful outdoor scene through which a river actually ran. John became so moved as he screamingly dragged his brother to his watery ruin that he himself fell backward into the river. Lionel remained on the fabricated terra firma while the crew dived in to save the floundering star.

The script problems and fraternal high jinks caused production to sag on the prestigious **Rasputin**. Ethel, blaming the problems on the slow-working Brabin, and intent that she not remain in Hollywood any longer than absolutely necessary, finally marched to a set telephone one day. She called the front office and declaimed in stentorian tones, "See here, Mayer, let's get rid of this Brabin or Braybin or what's-his-name." Her former friend walked off the set and the picture.

Another friendly acquaintance of Ethel's, Richard Boleslawski, took over, But even his friendship with Ethel could not convince her to remain and complete the unfinished production when her eight weeks were over. She vacated her leased mansion, and returned East. In a parting shot she insulted her own performance ("I look like Tallulah's [Bankhead] burlesque of me"), her brothers ("Nothing more than overpublicized and overpaid factory hands"), and Hollywood in general ("The whole place is a set, a glaring, gaudy, nightmarish set, built up in the desert"). Ethel would return to Hollywood in the forties and win a Best Supporting Actress Oscar for RKO's **None but the Lonely Heart** (1944).

Using newsreel footage and inventing some new scenes, Boleslawski required two months after Ethel's departure to tie up the loose ends of **Rasputin**. When production finally ceased after 104 days of work, the film had cost over $1,000,000.[3]

"Never has the talking screen offered so mysteriously fascinating a story as that of Rasputin, uncrowned ruler of a dynasty; worshipped as a saint by empress and emperor, feared by men, superhuman in his hypnotic power over women." Such read MGM's advertising copy for the period drama when it was released in late 1932. To the amazement of all, critical reaction was generally snide. The **New York Herald-Tribune** summed up, "It achieves one feat which is not inconsiderable. It manages to libel even the despised Rasputin." Rasputin's actual assassin, Prince Felix Youssoupoff, and his wife, Princess Irina, felt even more strongly than the critics and sued the studio (largely because of the inference that Rasputin had sexually ravaged Irina).[3] The film was subsequently withdrawn and the princess received an estimated $750,000 in "damages," while Ethel crowed in Manhattan that she had warned MGM, as soon as she read the script, that this would happen.

Before its withdrawal, **Rasputin** enjoyed sufficient box-office returns that MGM suffered only a slight loss ($185,000) on its return. Largely overlooked in the Barrymore fireworks were fine

performances by charming Diana Wynyard (who would work with John Barrymore in **Reunion in Vienna,** Ralph Morgan (as the czar), Tad Alexander (as the ill young prince), and Jean Parker (as Duchess Maria). The cinema would treat the subject of Rasputin many times, notably in 1965's **Rasputin, The Mad Monk** (with Christopher Lee in the title role) and 1971's **Nicholas and Alexandra** (with Tom Baker as Rasputin).

In February 1976 the Friends of the Museum of the City of New York held an invitational screening of **Rasputin and the Empress.** Ethel Barrymore's daughter Ethel Colt (since deceased) was hospitalized and could not attend, but asked Helen Hayes to deny completely the rumors that there was temperament on the set. "Mother and Uncle Lionel and John were far too professional for that sort of nonsense. When you are acting with peers, as they were well aware of, you give the best that is in you, and that's what they did." It was a testimony that must have been difficult for the invited audience to accept as **Rasputin** exposed three majestically talented actors childishly competing with one another in the spirit of a Thanksgiving Day football game.

RED DUST
1932—83 min.

Supervisor, Hunt Stromberg; **director,** Victor Fleming; based on the play by Wilson Collison; **screenplay,** John Lee Mahin and, **uncredited,** Howard Hawks; **art director,** Cedric Gibbons; **gowns,** Adrian; **sound,** Douglas Shearer; **camera,** Harold G. Rosson; **editor,** Blanche Sewell.

Clark Gable **(Dennis Carson);** Jean Harlow **(Vantine);** Gene Raymond **(Gary Willis);** Mary Astor **(Barbara Willis);** Donald Crisp **(Guidon);** Tully Marshall **(McQuarg);** Forrester Harvey **(Limey);** Willie Fung **(Hoy).**

SYNOPSIS
Dennis Carson and assistants Guidon and McQuarg operate a rubber plantation in Indochina. Escaping prostitute Vantine arrives by boat from Saigon and Carson permits her to remain until she can plot her exit from the country. In the ensuing days they have a brief affair which concludes at week's end when the next boat arrives. Aboard are Gary and Barbara Willis. Carson has hired Gary as the plantation's new engineer.

Vantine's hopes to leave on the vessel are shattered when the craft proves inoperable. She returns to the plantation, becoming distressed that Carson and Barbara are now romantically involved. Carson respects Gary and decides to terminate his relationship with Barbara, by reinitiating his affair with Vantine. In a moment of hysteria Barbara shoots Carson. Vantine saves the situation by explaining that Carson had made lewd advances to the engineer's resisting wife.

The Willises depart and Vantine nurses Carson back to health.

* * *

Despite the frequent double standards that pervaded Hollywood in general and MGM in particular in the early thirties (and thereafter), the studio maintained that a leading lady must convey the image of class, no matter what type of role she might perform on screen. Greta Garbo, Norma Shearer, and Joan Crawford conformed to this standard. But when garishly lacquered and brazenly unbridled Jean Harlow was signed by Metro in early 1932, word quickly spread that she would never last there. MGM had no place for "tramps."

When Howard Hughes' Caddo Company had sold Jean's contract to MGM for $60,000, the latter's top executives felt she was just a piece of transient baggage who might bring some added revenue to the studio and who would then disappear from sight. Irving Thalberg thought her cheap and Louis B. Mayer referred to her as "a freak whore." But within six months of receiving the first of her $1,250 per week Metro paychecks, Harlow had scored in **The Beast of the City** (1932) as gangster moll Daisy and then proved her cinematic worth again in **Red-Headed Woman** (1932). Through such achievements—as well as having just wed Paul Bern (Thalberg's top assistant)—Jean was cast as the tawdry jungle doxy in **Red Dust.**

The property, based on an unsuccessful 1928 Broadway venture, had been kicking around MGM for about a year. It was originally scheduled to be a John Gilbert vehicle, in hopes of reviving his sagging movie career. Frenchman Jacques Feyder was to direct. Just as filming was to start, picture supervisor Hunt Stromberg was alerted by scripter John Lee Mahin that he had just seen contractee Clark Gable in a new MGM picture and he would be far better than Gilbert in the role. Stromberg soon agreed. Gilbert was replaced as was director Feyder (by Victor Fleming). Harlow and Gable had worked together the previous year in the well-regarded gangster yarn **The Secret Six,** but had generated little rapport on or off the set. This time around Gable was far more thoughtful of the twenty-one-year-old bride.

Red Dust was shot largely on Metro's back lot tropic set under the tough direction of Fleming. The director was a perfectionist in the love scenes, exhaustively devising angles and actions that would overpower the audience, and at the same time not offend the Hays office. He succeeded admirably.

In the midst of production (which had been delayed while scripter Mahin revamped the scenario to appease Gable, who thought the story too crude), tragedy and unexpected publicity converged on **Red Dust.** On Labor Day 1932 Jean Harlow, MGM, and the country were shocked by what has become one of the great Hollywood death stories: Paul Bern's suicide. His naked body, drenched in Jean's perfume, was discovered with a .38 bullet in the brain. The inferences, repercussions, and innuendos could have filled books. The emotional condition of the grieving widow threatened

---

[3]MGM had changed John Barrymore's character's name from Youssoupoff to Chegodieff to avoid just such a suit.

Jean Harlow, Clark Gable, and Donald Crisp in Red Dust *('32).*

completion of the film.[1] As Fleming remarked when Harlow stoically returned to work, "How are we going to get a sexy performance with **that** look in her eyes?"

However, production resumed. Harlow, aided by the kindness of her coworkers—including cinematographer Hal Rosson, whom she would wed the following year—completed her role. In November 1932 **Red Dust** was released and became a sensation because of its tawdry sex scenes and the chemistry of the three major attractions.[2] **Time** magazine reported, "Given **Red Dust**'s brazen moral values, Gable and Harlow have full play for their curiously similar sort of good-natured toughness. The best lines go to Harlow. . . . Her effortless vulgarity, humor, and slovenliness make a noteworthy characterization as good in the genre as the late Jeanne Eagels' Sadie Thompson." The **New York Herald-Tribune** wrote, "The flagrantly blonde Miss Harlow, who hitherto has attracted but intermittent enthusiasm from this department, immediately becomes one of its favorites

by her performance in **Red Dust.**" Indeed, Harlow was well-nigh irresistible as Vantine. Her bathing in a rain barrel (to Astor as Gable stands by, "Oh, good morning! You're just in time to see the trained seal. Hey, Denny, scrub my back!"), reading Gable a children's bedtime story ("A chipmunk and a rabbit—hey, I wonder how **this** comes out!"), and cleaning the parrot's cage ("What've you been eating—cement?") were gems of bawdy humor.

Red Dust would lead to four more Gable-Harlow outings. The jungle plot line would be revamped by Metro for **Congo Maisie** (1940), with Ann Sothern in the Harlow role pared down to the Maisie series character, John Carroll in the Gable part, and Shepperd Strudwick and Rita Johnson as the married couple. An official remake appeared titled **Mogambo** (1953), produced for MGM by Sam Zimbalist and directed by John Ford. The new version was shot in Africa, with Gable recreating the lead (now as a white hunter) and playing opposite Ava Gardner (in the Harlow role) and Grace Kelly (in Astor's assignment).

---

[1]At one point after Bern's death, Louis B. Mayer invited Tallulah Bankhead to his Culver City offices. She had just completed her "six rancid pictures" at Paramount and Mayer was considering replacing Harlow with Tallulah if the inquest proved the platinum blonde was destroyed as a bankable movie star. To win Tallulah's sympathy, Mayer acted out "his discovery" of Bern's body for Bankhead. The latter merely walked out of the mogul's office.

[2]Shot on a forty-four-day schedule, **Red Dust** cost $408,000 and earned a profit of $399,000.

ROMEO AND JULIET
1936—127 min.

Producer, Irving Thalberg; **director,** George Cukor; based on the play by William Shakespeare; **adapter,** Talbot Jennings; **music,** Herbert Stothart; **art directors,** Cedric Gibbons, Oliver Mes-

sel, and Frederic Hope; **set decorator,** Edwin B. Willis; **choreography,** Agnes DeMille; **artistic consultant,** Messel; **literary consultants,** Professor William Strunk, Jr. and James Tucker Murray; **costumes,** Messel and Adrian; **camera,** William Daniels; **editor,** Margaret Booth.

Norma Shearer **(Juliet);** Leslie Howard **(Romeo);** Edna May Oliver **(Nurse);** John Barrymore **(Mercutio);** C. Aubrey Smith **(Lord Capulet);** Basil Rathbone **(Tybalt);** Andy Devine **(Peter);** Henry Kolker **(Friar Laurence);** Violet Kemble-Cooper **(Lady Capulet);** Ralph Forbes **(Paris);** Reginald Denny **(Benvolio);** Maurice Murphy **(Balthasar);** Conway Tearle **(Prince of Verona);** Virginia Hammond **(Lady Montague);** Robert Warwick **(Lord Montague);** Vernon Downing **(Samson Capulet);** Ian Wolfe **(Apothecary);** Carlyle Blackwell, Jr. **(Tybalt's Page);** Anthony March **(Mercutio's Page);** Anthony Kemble-Cooper **(Gregory Capulet);** John Bryan **(Friar John);** Katherine DeMille **(Rosalind);** Wallis Clark **(Town Watch);** Charles Bancroft and José Rubio **(Noblemen);** Dorothy Granger and Lita Chevret **(Bits).**

SYNOPSIS
In the splendor of fifteenth-century Verona, Italy, the families of Montague and Capulet continue the feud that has made bitter enemies of their families. En route to the cathedral, the factions mock one another until swords clash. The prince of Verona terminates the disturbance. He threatens banishment or death to those guilty of perpetuating the violent feud.

Meanwhile, the young heir of the Montagues, Romeo, attends uninvited a ball hosted by Lord Capulet. There he dances with the Capulets' lovely Juliet, becoming so obviously infatuated with her that he incurs the wrath of Juliet's cousin, the hot-blooded Tybalt. Violence is avoided, but Romeo enters the Capulet garden later that evening. He overhears Juliet soliloquizing of her infatuation for Romeo; the young couple fall joyously in love, and are soon married by Friar Laurence.

However, the shadow of the feud precludes their happiness. The strutting Tybalt later that day provokes a fight with Romeo, who in turn greets his arrogance with a mild salutation. This ires Romeo's bawdy friend Mercutio, who fatally loses a sword fight with Tybalt. Romeo takes up Mercutio's sword, pursues Tybalt, slays him, and is later banished to Mantua by the prince of Verona. However, before he leaves, Friar Laurence and Juliet's nurse arrange for the newlyweds to spend the night together.

The following day, after Romeo flees, Lord Capulet announces that Juliet is to wed Count Paris. Juliet rushes to Friar Laurence for advice. He supplies her with a potion that will cause her to display all the symptoms of death for forty hours. As her family lays her to rest in the family crypt, Friar Laurence sends word of the scheme to Romeo. However, the young husband learns of the death before he receives the friar's message. He rushes back to the tomb and swallows a vial of poison. When Juliet awakens, she finds the corpse of her bridegroom. With a dagger, she joins him in death. Friar Laurence informs the

Norma Shearer in Romeo and Juliet *('36).*

families of the woeful tragedy. The Montagues and Capulets mourn together the untimely end of their children as the prince of Verona intones.

> For never was a story of more woe,
> Than this of Juliet and her Romeo.

* * *

"Thalberg was a sweet guy—but he could piss ice water," stated Eddie Mannix, veteran MGM troubleshooter and producer. It was an apt description, especially in regard to the brilliant Thalberg's invincible convictions about a cinema property's artistic and commercial appeal and his unabating adoration of the talents of his wife, Norma Shearer. When the two beliefs merged, no obstacle—be it a crude Louis B. Mayer, a roaringly drunk John Barrymore, or an aghast studio finance department—could stand in his way. This was lavishly illustrated by the 1936 production of the exquisite **Romeo and Juliet.**

Although Shakespeare had been a favorite of international filmmakers since 1899, when a film record of Sir Herbert Beerbohm Tree's **King John** at London's Her Majesty's Theatre was produced, the Bard had become a controversial commodity among 1930s film producers.[1] In 1935 Warner Bros. had lavishly produced **A Midsummer Night's**

---

[1] The U.S. screen had not ignored Shakespeare. In 1916 Metro had released a version of **Romeo and Juliet** with Francis X. Bushman and Beverly Bayne, while Fox released one simultaneously, with Theda Bara and Harry Hilliard. In 1929 United Artists released **The Taming of the Shrew,** a talkie with Douglas Fairbanks and Mary Pickford. MGM's **Hollywood Revue of 1929** contained the **Romeo and Juliet** balcony scene, played by John Gilbert and Norma Shearer. John Barrymore had brilliantly raved as Richard III, giving the soliloquy from **Henry VI,** part 3, in Warner Bros.' **Show of Shows** (1929).

Dream on the Burbank lot, starring James Cagney, Olivia de Havilland, and Mickey Rooney, along with a diverse sampling from the studio contract list. The costly production, later critiqued as "more Barnum and Bailey than Shakespeare," barely recouped its cost. It convinced Louis B. Mayer that Shakespeare was persona non grata at Culver City.

Thalberg violently disagreed. Stimulated by the challenge to produce Shakespeare's classic with taste and fidelity, he high-pressured the picture into production, vowing to Mayer that he would complete the project for $900,000. Demanding that Thalberg keep to this financial limit, Mayer approved the project.

There was never any question in Thalberg's concept as to who must portray Juliet. "I believe Norma can play anything and do it better than anyone else. . . . Juliet and Marie Antoinette will mark the end of Norma Shearer's acting career. Too many stars stay on camera too long. I want her to bow out at her highest point." Miss Shearer began working daily with Shakespearean actress-coach Constance Collier to meet the challenge of a thirty-one-year-old actress playing a fourteen-year-old girl. Mrs. Frances Robinson-Duff, New York's most famous drama coach, actor Rollo Peters, and choreographer Agnes DeMille also lent their advice to Norma.

Romeo was less easy to cast.[2] Thalberg's first choice was Fredric March, who immediately refused the offer. Clark Gable was also considered, and soon replied, "I don't look Shakespeare, I don't talk Shakespeare, I don't like Shakespeare, and I won't do Shakespeare." At this point Thalberg, after briefly considering Britisher Robert Donat, approached Leslie Howard, then under Warner Bros. contract. The forty-six-year-old Englishman also refused, at first. "A woman, to be interesting," said Howard, "does not have to be anything but in love. . . . But a man who does nothing but love! If he is as young as Romeo is reputed to be, we do not take him seriously. And if he is as old as the average actor has to be to have the necessary experience for this role, he is a bore." The rather difficult Howard soon changed his mind when he learned that Jack Warner would not lend him to Metro anyway. Howard then mischievously decided he wanted the assignment.[3]

Thalberg handpicked the supporting cast. John Barrymore, off screen for nearly two years dallying with alcohol, dissipation, and a Hunter College girl named Elaine Barrie, was signed to play Mercutio. So desperate was Barrymore for finances that he accepted the studio's offer of $20,000, only three years after he was making $150,000 per film on his Metro contract. Basil Rathbone[4] was cast to portray the villainous Tybalt, and such "name" character players as C. Aubrey Smith, Edna May Oliver, Reginald Denny, Ralph Forbes, and even roly-poly Andy Devine (as the servant Peter) joined the company.

Thalberg strove for perfection in every department. George Cukor was set to direct. Talbot Jennings (**Mutiny on the Bounty**) fashioned a screenplay that was supposed to contain not a single line not written by Shakespeare himself. Shakespearean scholars William Strunk, Jr. of Cornell and James Tucker Murray of Harvard were imported to Hollywood for constant technical advice ("Your job is to protect Shakespeare from us," Thalberg told them). An entire technical crew flew to Verona to photograph the fifteenth-century relics, reproduced on MGM's lot.[5] Agnes DeMille cho-

reographed the dances for the Capulet Masque. As **Time** magazine noted approvingly, "Producer Irving Thalberg did everything except recall Shakespeare from the grave."

It soon became obvious that **Romeo and Juliet** could not be completed for $900,000. And because of the high jinks of Barrymore, it seemed the picture might not be finished at all. The aging actor was brilliant as Mercutio. But all too often he arrived on the set drunk, sprinkling Shakespeare's lines with obscenities and unable to follow instructions from dueling master Fred Cavens. At one point a frustrated Thalberg asked William Powell to replace the actor, but Powell had a high regard for the star and refused the offer. So Barrymore remained and was spasmodically marvelous. He delivered the famous "Queen Mab" speech in one glorious take.

Finally, at a cost of $2,066,000 **Romeo and Juliet** closed production. Released in August 1936, the film won bravos from the major reviewers. Wrote Frank S. Nugent (**New York Times,**) "Metro the Magnificent has loosed its technical magic upon Will Shakespeare and has fashioned for his **Romeo and Juliet** a jeweled setting in which the deep beauty of his romance glows and sparkles and gleams with breathless radiance."

Time magazine observed: "[It] proved that the cinema has at last grown up. To intelligent cinema addicts, it will be no great shock to learn that the best actors currently functioning in the U.S. act the play as well as it can be acted; that the most expensive sets ever used for **Romeo and Juliet** are by far the most realistic and hence the most satisfactory; and that the camera—which can see Juliet as Romeo saw her and vice versa—greatly facilitates the story. As for the play itself, which is by far the best part of the production, it remains what it has always been, the best version ever written of Hollywood's favorite theme, Boy Meets Girl."

And **Newsweek** magazine added, "A large gold watch should also be tossed to Irving Thalberg (Miss Shearer's husband) for his part in reversing the movies reputation for emasculating the classics."

Of the stars, Norma Shearer won splendid reviews. "With a sense that this memory will endure the longer, do we recall Miss Shearer's tender and womanly perverse Juliet" (**New York Times**). "Shearer's Juliet can rub elbows with any modern interpretation of the damsel, from [Jane] Cowl to [Katharine] Cornell. . . . No one of the current crop of cinema satellites could have touched her performance with an eleven-foot pole . . . she presents a gentle, unsophisticated Juliet that should last in the popular imagination long after the celluloid has cracked and shriveled" (**Newsweek**).

Howard's performance was less approved, his notices varying. The **New York Times** found him a "pliant and graceful Romeo," but **Newsweek** lamented, "The only weak spot in the ensemble, Howard enunciates beautifully and tiptoes about in the best of taste, but with all the

passionate fervor of a potato." **Newsweek** went on to cheer the supporting players, "Edna May Oliver barks and squeals in her finest hoity-toity way through the part of the nurse. . . . It seems incredible that Barrymore's bawdy raillery will actually go uncensored. Basil Rathbone looks down Tybalt's patrician nose in the approved fashion."

The British trade publication **Kine Weekly** praised, "The film is unquestionably a masterpiece, a worthy monument to the genius of Shakespeare, a graceful tribute to the vision of Irving Thalberg, its sponsor, an unforgettable emotional experience, and to be more mundane, a graceful compliment to each and every box office."

Audiences were less agog. **Romeo and Juliet** lost $922,000, the only serious deficit for a Thalberg film. Still, the production won MGM all the prestige Thalberg had sought and did garner Academy nominations in the areas of Best Picture (Metro's **The Great Ziegfeld** won), Best Actress (Luise Rainer of **Ziegfeld** won), and Best Supporting Actor, for Rathbone (Walter Brennan for United Artists' **Come and Get It** won).

Years later George Cukor reflected on his direction of **Romeo and Juliet**. He sighed, "It was unfamiliar territory for me, I suppose. It's one picture that if I had to do over again, I'd know how. I'd get the garlic and the Mediterranean into it."

ROSE-MARIE

1936—113 min. (TV title: INDIAN LOVE CALL)

Producer, Hunt Stromberg; **director,** W. S. Van Dyke II; based on the musical play by Otto Harbach and Oscar Hammerstein II; **screenplay,** Frances Goodrich, Albert Hackett, and Alice Duer Miller; **music director,** Herbert Stothart; **songs,** Harbach, Hammerstein, and Rudolf Friml; Gus Kahn, Stothart, and Friml; Kahn and Stothart; Sam Lewis, Joe Young, and Harry Akst; Shelton Brooks; totem-pole dance staged by Chester Hale; operatic sequences staged by William von Wymetal; **art directors,** Cedric Gibbons and Joseph Wright; **set decorator,** Edwin B. Willis; **sound,** Douglas Shearer; **camera,** William Daniels; **editor,** Blanche Sewell.

Jeanette MacDonald (**Marie DeFlor**); Nelson Eddy (**Sergeant Bruce**); James Stewart (**John Flower**); Reginald Owen (**Meyerson**); Allan Jones (**Romeo**); Gilda Gray (**Bella**); George Regas (**Boniface**); Robert Greig (**Cafe Manager**); Una O'Connor (**Anna**); Lucien Littlefield (**Storekeeper**); Alan Mowbray (**Premier**); David Niven (**Teddy**); Herman Bing (**Mr. Daniels**); Aileen Carlyle (**Susan**); Mary Anita Loos (**Corn Queen**); Dorothy Gray (**Edith**); James Conlin (**Joe**); Edgar Dearing (**Mounted Police**); Halliwell Hobbes (**Mr. Gordon**); Russell Hicks (**Commandant**); Rolfe Sedan and Jack Pennick (**Men**); Leonard Carey (**Louis**); Pat West (**Traveling Salesman**); Milton Owen (**Stage Manager**); Bert Lindley (**Trapper**).

---

[2]In his memoirs, **My Wicked Wicked Ways** (1959), Errol Flynn says he tested for the part as Romeo.

[3]To obtain Howard, MGM had to arrange a deal in which Howard and Paul Muni were promised a picture apiece at Culver City, and Metro loaned Warner Bros. the services of Clark Gable and Robert Montgomery.

[4]Rathbone was an expert on the play, having performed the part of Paris in England, and acted Romeo both at Stratford-on-Avon and opposite Katharine Cornell on Broadway and on tour.

[5]The Verona Square set also appeared in **The Firefly** (1937) as Spain, **A Lady without Passport** (1950) as

Havana, and **Diane** (1956) as sixteenth-century France, and others.

Nelson Eddy and Jeanette MacDonald in Rose-Marie *('36).*

SYNOPSIS

Marie DeFlor, celebrated opera soprano, is enjoying a hugely successful concert tour of Canada. However, a personal problem makes her even more temperamental than usual: her brother John has been imprisoned for participation in a holdup. Marie hopes to request the premier of Canada, who has become an ardent admirer of her talents, to issue an appeal for her brother. But before she can do so, a grimy Indian guide, Boniface, calls at her elegant suite and informs her that John has escaped from prison, is wounded, needs help—and has killed a mountie. With all her savings, Marie abandons her tour and sets out for the Canadian wilderness, with Boniface as a guide, to aid her imperiled brother.

Not much time elapses before the shifty Boniface steals Marie's purse and leaves her stranded. To survive, she finds employment in a bawdy dance hall, where her refined soprano draws disrespectful responses from the uncouth patrons. However, under the tutelage of Bella, a honky-tonk entertainer, Marie vulgarizes her act sufficiently to maintain her job. Marie is performing there when Sergeant Bruce enters and recognizes the star. Sergeant Bruce's mission at this time is to find and capture John Flower.

When Marie leaves the saloon, Bruce follows and offers to assist her in recovering her lost purse. Together they go to the land where the Indians stage their dances, and there they find Boniface, who coweringly returns the purse and

agrees to resume his job as her guide. By this time Bruce has deducted that Marie must be the sister of his prey. When she departs with Boniface, he trails them.

Once again Boniface, fearful of the pursuing mountie, abandons Marie, and Bruce assumes responsibility for her. They are soon in love. But when Marie unwittingly leads Bruce to John, duty demands that Bruce arrest the criminal and return him to justice. Marie, deeply distraught, resumes her tour.

The emotional anguish soon overcomes the singer. While singing **Tosca** she collapses, suffers a complete breakdown, and appears to lose all desire to recover. However, her understanding manager, Meyerson, sends for Sergeant Bruce. The mountie returns to her side, and Marie recaptures her will to live—and love. She and the mountie face a new future together.

* * *

On November 18, 1959, the operetta spoof **Little Mary Sunshine** opened with little publicity, and less money in the box office. The book, music, and lyrics for this off-Broadway show were by Rick Besoyan, and the principal characters were Little Mary (Eileen Brennan), a posturing, eyelid-flapping, lethally flamboyant soprano, and Captain ("Big Jim") Warington (William Graham), a stiff, stolid baritone usually at the mercy of his upstaging costar. To the amazement of all, **Little Mary Sunshine** became the talk of the town and a hit which ran for three and a half years.

The reason for its popularity was obvious. The little spoof was not so much a show as a mock tribute to Jeanette MacDonald and Nelson Eddy's glorious screen teamings—especially **Rose-Marie.** For the more mature theatregoers, MacDonald and Eddy personified Hollywood's golden age, especially its unabashed schmaltz; for the new generation freshly exposed to the MGM film library, which had been sold to television (**Rose-Marie** had received its New York City TV premiere on September 19, 1958), they were the corniest artists of the outmoded movies. Whatever reverence or irreverence would attend **Rose-Marie** (or **Indian Love Call,** as it is entitled in telecasts), this operetta was doubtless the supreme teaming of the "Iron Butterfly" and the "Singing Capon"— the most luminous cinema beacons of the depression era.

Otto Harbach's and Oscar Hammerstein II's **Rose-Marie** was anything but fresh in 1935. The original stage production had opened at New York's Imperial Theatre on September 2, 1924, starring Dennis King, Mary Ellis, and Arthur Deacon, and it ran 557 performances.[1] MGM, having filmed the operetta **The Merry Widow** as a silent photoplay, followed suit, with a silent **Rose-Marie,** starring Joan Crawford as Marie, James Murray as the outlaw trapper, and House Peters as the mountie. When MGM announced plans to refilm **Rose-Marie,** it was scheduled as a vehicle for Grace Moore.[2] When she was unavailable, Louis B. Mayer happily replaced her. The substitute was Jeanette MacDonald. It provided his cherished leading lady with a new major assignment.

The talent force of **Rose-Marie** was a reprise of the very successful **Naughty Marietta.** In addition to the same stars, there were the identical producer (Hunt Stromberg), director (W. S. Van Dyke II), and music director (Herbert Stothart), as well as another screenplay constructed by Frances Goodrich and Albert Hackett. With "One-Take" Van Dyke in command, the company embarked on a location trip to Lake Tahoe in California's High Sierras, where seventeen boxcars transported the Hollywood equipment, chuck wagons served the meals, and over seven hundred Indians filled the extra ranks.

There are several reasons why **Rose-Marie** has evolved into the definitive MacDonald-Eddy feature. The musical selections are outstanding, and both stars' voices are extravagantly treated. Miss MacDonald sings selections from the operas **Roméo et Juliette** and **Tosca,** shares "Pardon Me, Madame" with a chorus and nine soloists, charmingly performs "Three Blind Mice" with her echo, and, totally delightful in a honky-tonk sequence with famed "Shimmy" wiggler Gilda Gray, romps

---

[1]In the original stage production, the hero was **not** the mountie but the outlaw, a plot line which remained in the 1928 MGM silent-film version.

[2]It took some time before Miss MacDonald replaced Grace Moore as the most highly touted of Hollywood's operatic singers. At the funeral of Irving Thalberg in September 1936, it was Miss Moore who was asked to sing the Psalm of David at the Synagogue B'nai B'rith. Miss MacDonald was among the mourners.

through popular renditions of "Dinah" and "Some of These Days." Eddy renders "The Mounties," a virile chant reminiscent of **Naughty Marietta**'s "Tramp, Tramp, Tramp" song, bolstered by the booming voices of his male chorus. He sings "Just for You" and, of course, the title number. Then there is the celebrated duet "Indian Love Call," which, released as a single record with **Naughty Marietta**'s "Ah, Sweet Mystery of Life" on the second side, sold over a million copies. The supporting cast is excellent, featuring Allan Jones (in his second feature film), James Stewart as the outlaw brother of Jeanette and Eddy's prey, and David Niven in a brief spot as a rejected suitor of MacDonald. For comedy relief there are Una O'Connor as Anna and accented Herman Bing as Mr. Daniels.

The crowning touch, however, to **Rose-Marie** is the fact that both stars appear to be luxuriating in their now clichéd professional shortcomings: Miss MacDonald was never more posingly coquettish, Eddy never more stolidly wooden. As opera star Marie DeFlor, regal songbird not above bitching, she appeared at times to be spoofing her status as MGM's pampered prima donna. By now approaching her mid-thirties, deftly concealing a hint of corpulence with corsets and astute tailoring, wearing cotton-candy-colored wigs under her favored feathered bonnets, the star strutted about the lot with the patrician hauteur of a peacock, sometimes whisking into Mayer's office unannounced, prattling to her enraptured employer for hours, while artists with appointments angrily sighed at their watches. Though hardly the little ingenue anymore, she still primped and preened (engagingly) before the camera, acting with the bravura coyness of a novice juvenile at a sold-out Saturday matinee, shrewdly instructing the cameraman to favor her left profile and the lighting man to eradicate the touches of a double chin. While the amazing and talented lady possessed the saving grace of a splendid sense of humor which tinged her affectedness with a patina of fun, the MGM lot largely regarded her as very much the Iron Butterfly—a reputation which almost cost her Clark Gable as leading man in **San Francisco**, released later in 1936.

"I've handled Indians, African natives, South Sea Islanders, rhinos, pygmies, and Eskimos and made them act—but not Nelson Eddy," complained director Van Dyke on one occasion. Indeed, if Miss MacDonald sought a naive, easy-to-dominate vis-à-vis, Eddy fit the bill perfectly. It has been reported that, on the set of **Maytime** (1937), John Barrymore once ended Miss MacDonald's scene-stealing with a snarled, "If you wave that loathsome chiffon rag you call a kerchief once more while I'm speaking, I shall ram it down your gurgling throat!" Eddy was not as astute, and his titian-haired screen mate cornered the majority of the flattering camera angles, at times even managing to position Eddy so that the back of his head was toward the camera. The simple fact was that the baritone was extremely self-conscious while acting before the cameras. His being accident-prone did not help matters. In **Naughty Marietta**, while gazing with rapture at Miss MacDonald on one take, he walked into a prop tree; attempting to mount a horse with

heroic élan on location for **Rose-Marie**, he leaped right over the steed and landed in a bush.

Eddy's mannequinlike Sergeant Bruce, encircled by Miss MacDonald's parading Marie DeFlor, reminds one of the later MGM team of Greer Garson and Walter Pidgeon, where that lady enjoyed the heavy dramatics and an attentive cinematographer while the male provided flattering deference. In that instance, however, the very unpretentious, very professional Pidgeon knew exactly what he was doing. Eddy rarely realized how much scene larceny his top-billed costar practiced until he viewed the daily rushes.[3]

If these touches tarnish **Rose-Marie** today, the cynics were few indeed when the motion picture premiered at New York City's Capitol Theatre (where **Naughty Marietta** had played) on January 31, 1936. The ad line read, "A pampered pet of the opera meets a rugged Canadian mountie." The **New York Times** reported, "As blithely melodious and rich in scenic beauty as any picture that has come from Hollywood. . . . let Jeanette MacDonald and Nelson Eddy sing an operetta's love songs and we care not who may write its book. In splendid voice, whether singing solo or in duet, they prove to be fully as delightful a combination here as they were in the film of Victor Herbert's **Naughty Marietta**, which was so welcome a contribution to last year's film calendar." The singing of the stars, the lovely location shots of the High Sierras, the marvelous "Totem Tom Tom" dance (staged by Chester Hale), all provided the type of rich escapism which captivated Depression-fatigued moviegoers. **Rose-Marie** appeared on the top twenty-five moneymakers list of 1935–36, sharing the honor with **Anna Karenina, Broadway Melody of 1936, The Great Ziegfeld, A Night at the Opera, San Francisco, A Tale of Two Cities,** and others.

In 1954 MGM released a CinemaScope color remake of **Rose-Marie.** Ann Blyth was no substitute for Miss MacDonald, and Howard Keel felt his part of the mountie was that of "a blithering idiot." The comedy relief of Marjorie Main and Bert Lahr could not disguise the ineptitudes of the latest version of the now very dated operetta.

A half a dozen MacDonald-Eddy outings still remained for their fans: **Maytime** (1937), **The Girl of the Golden West** (1938), **Sweethearts** (1938) **New Moon** (1940), **Bitter Sweet** (1940), and **I Married an Angel** (1942). However, it was **Rose-Marie** which provided Miss MacDonald with the opportunity to perform cinema opera, which boosted Eddy's fan mail to 6,000 letters per week, and which gave cinemagoers the cherished image of MacDonald in slacks, flannel shirt, and incongruous high heels, and Eddy in impeccable mountie attire canoeing together in the splendor of the great outdoors to the strains of "Indian Love Call."

When Jeanette MacDonald died in 1965, her

---

[3]Eddy did recognize major competition on this production in the presence of Allan Jones. After viewing Jones' superb work opposite MacDonald in the **Roméo et Juliette** and **Tosca** operas-within-the-film sequences, Eddy provided Stromberg with an ultimatum: cut down Jones' on-camera part, or face "difficulties" with Eddy in the future. Jones' role was ensuingly abbreviated.

will left one possession to Nelson Eddy—a print of **Rose-Marie.**

SAN FRANCISCO
1936—115 min.

Producers, John Emerson and Bernard H. Hyman; **director,** W. S. Van Dyke II; **story,** Robert Hopkins; **screenplay,** Anita Loos; **assistant director,** Joseph Newman; **music director,** Herbert Stothart; **music,** Edward Ward; **songs,** Gus Kahn, Bronislau Kaper, and Walter Jurmann; Arthur Freed and Nacio Herb Brown; **art directors,** Cedric Gibbons, Arnold Gillespie, and Harry McAfee; **set decorator,** Edwin B. Willis; **choreography,** Val Raset; operatic sequences staged by William von Wymetal; **gowns,** Adrian; **sound,** Douglas Shearer; **montages,** John Hoffman; **camera,** Oliver T. Marsh; **editor,** Tom Held.

Clark Gable **(Blackie Norton)**; Jeanette MacDonald **(Mary Blake)**; Spencer Tracy **(Father Mullin)**; Jack Holt **(Jack Burley)**; Jessie Ralph **(Mrs. Burley)**; Ted Healy **(Mat)**; Shirley Ross **(Trixie)**; Margaret Irving **(Della Bailey)**; Harold Huber **(Babe)**; Al Shean **(Professor)**; William Ricciardi **(Signor Baldini)**; Kenneth Harlan **(Chick)**; Roger Imhof **(Alaska)**; Charles Judels **(Tony)**; Russell Simpson **(Red Kelly)**; Bert Roach **(Freddie Duane)**; Warren Hymer **(Hazeltine)**; Edgar Kennedy **(Sheriff)**; Adrienne d'Ambricourt **(Madame Albani)**; Nigel DeBrulier **(Old Man)**; Mae Digges and Nyas Berry **(Dancers)**; Tudor Williams and Tandy MacKenzie **(Singers)**; Tom Mahoney **(Captain of Police)**; Gertrude Astor **(Drunk's Girl)**; Jason Robards, Sr. **(Father)**; Vernon Dent **(Fat Man)**; Anthony Jowitt **(Society Man)**; Carl Stockdale **(Salvation Army Man)**; Richard Carle, Oscar Apfel, Frank Sheridan, and Ralph Lewis **(Members of Founders' Club)**; Don Rowan **(Coast Type)**; Jack Kennedy **(Old Irishman)**; Chester Gan **(Jowl Lee)**; Flora Finch, Rhea Mitchell, King Baggott, Jean Acker, and Naomi Childers **(Bits)**.

SYNOPSIS
San Francisco, New Year's Eve 1905. A fire blazes in a Barbary Coast hotel, leaving Mary Blake, a penniless singer, wandering the raucous streets. In her hapless travels she meets Blackie Norton, roguish owner of the Paradise Cafe. Learning that she is a singer, he asks to see her legs. "A little thin for down here," he judges, but is impressed by her "pretty fair set of pipes." He hires her to sing in his establishment.

Blackie is interested in politics and is running for city supervisor on a platform promising to destroy the Barbary Coast's firetrap buildings. This incurs the displeasure of Coast magnate Jack Burley, who further antagonizes Blackie by becoming infatuated with Mary and enticing her to sign with his new Tivoli Opera House. Mary, enamored of Blackie, refuses. However, after a chat with Trixie, one of Blackie's old flames, naive Mary fears Blackie will soon discard her. She informs Father Tim Mullin, Blackie's old boyhood

Clark Gable, Jeanette MacDonald, and Spencer Tracy in San Francisco *('36).*

pal and perennial boxing foe, that she is leaving to sign with Burley.

Enraged, Blackie orders the sheriff to arrive at the Opera House the night of Mary's debut to present an injunction and close down the performance. However, when Blackie hears how beautifully Mary sings the part of Marguerite in **Faust,** he knocks out the sheriff to prevent the injunction from being delivered. He then asks Mary to marry him, and demands she return to the Paradise. Mary is soon back at Blackie's establishment and about to make her entrance in black tights and scandalous costume when Father Tim enters. He is shocked by Mary's daring apparel and informs Blackie, "You can't marry a woman and sell her immortal soul"—and for his words of advice he is punched in the nose by Blackie. Shocked, Mary walks out, as does Father Tim. Meanwhile, the out-of-patience customers begin destroying the furnishings.

Mary returns to Burley and stars in **La Traviata.** However, she learns of Burley's scheme to destroy Blackie completely. She tries to warn Norton but he rebuffs her. Even after she wins his club a prize at the annual Chicken's Ball (singing a fiery rendition of "San Francisco"), Blackie throws the trophy cup to the floor and humiliates her.

Then comes the earthquake of 1906. In the horrors Burley is killed, and Blackie fears that Mary may be among the thousands of corpses. Wandering through the ruins, he hears her singing "Nearer My God to Thee" to a mother and her dead child. He asks Father Tim how to pray—for he has found religion along with his real love. The three personalities united, they march off, the survivors behind them, to build a new—and decent—San Francisco.

* * *

San Francisco, guardian of the Golden Gate, stands today as a queen among seaports . . . industrious, mature, respectable . . . but perhaps she dreams of the queen and city she was . . . splendid and sensuous, vulgar and magnificent . . . that perished suddenly with a cry still heard in the hearts of those who knew her at exactly 5:13 A.M., April 18, 1906. . . .
Foreword, **San Francisco**

After the premiere of **The Great Ziegfeld** (1936), audiences and studio officials alike believed that Metro-Goldwyn-Mayer had unleashed its box-office sensation of the year with the $3 million production of the life and times of Florenz Ziegfeld and his Glorified American Girls. Hence, it was something of a surprise to the entertainment world when, only two and a half months after **The Great Ziegfeld**'s release, Metro premiered a film that actually outdistanced **Ziegfeld** in popularity, critical appeal, and profits. **San Francisco** was a rowdy welding of a plot crammed with sin, corruption, sex, and religion. It boasted a cast of Clark Gable, Jeanette MacDonald, and Spencer Tracy, and a sensational climax featuring as terrifying a screen finale as has ever appeared in motion pictures.

The idea for the film, which became MGM's greatest moneymaker in its twelve-year history, was nurtured by writer Robert Hopkins. He was shrewd enough to enlist the aid of MGM star Jeanette MacDonald. She was riding the crest of renewed movie popularity gendered by her vastly popular **Naughty Marietta** (1935) and **Rose-Marie** (1936)—each costarring Nelson Eddy. Hopkins dispatched Jeanette to Louis B. Mayer's tabernacle where the outgoing star backed up her request for the production with the notion that Clark Gable should be her leading man. Gable, having just been Oscar-nominated for his work in **Mutiny on the Bounty** (1935), was adamant about **not** doing the film. He regarded the soprano star as a prima donna (having heard "tales" from his pal Nelson Eddy); besides, he disliked the part. Gable lamented that the scenario called upon him merely to stand about while Jeanette, as Mary Blake, sang in his direction. Anita Loos relaxed Gable's apprehensions by investing her screenplay with much more business for Gable's Blackie Norton and the star finally acquiesced. Spencer Tracy completed the star triangle as Father Tim Mullin.[1] Vigorous Jack Holt was assigned the role of unscrupulous Jack Burley, and the resourceful, scene-stealing Jessie Ralph was cast as his all too understanding mother. With many-silent screen names on relief in this Depression era, Metro launched a highly publicized campaign to cast many of these unfortunates in small parts in **San**

Francisco. Among them: King Baggott and Rhea Mitchell, who had been directed by W. S. Van Dyke II in **The Hawk's Lair** (1918); Flora Finch, who worked often with comedian John Bunny; Naomi Childers, a former Vitagraph star; and Jean Acker, the first wife of Rudolph Valentino. Also, D. W. Griffith, an old friend and former boss of Van Dyke, was briefly employed by the lot to direct a symphony scene.

Van Dyke took on the directing post and the mammoth feature got under way. The scenario provided ample showcasing of MacDonald's musical talents as she sang "Il Était un Roi de Thule" and "The Jewel Song" from **Faust,**[2] "The Battle Hymn of the Republic," "The Holy City," "Near My God to Thee," "Would You" (the Arthur Freed–Nacio Herb Brown song which was later included in 1952's **Singin' in the Rain),** "San Francisco," and others. The film abounds in salty vignettes, such as the boisterous goings-on in the Paradise gambling hall operated by the ruthless Gable. There is the heroine being romanced by both Gable and Holt, besides many touching scenes—for example, Jessie Ralph explaining to MacDonald just how she feels about San Francisco, her son, and her own past.

And, of course, there is the famed climax, a telescoped re-creation of the nightmarish San Francisco earthquake. In **50 Classic Motion Pictures** (1970), David Zinman tells of the filming of this classic sequence:

Van Dyke shot most of the twenty-minute scene inside the studio. He used outdoor shots only as background for montages. One of the most startling views shows the sidewalk splitting. This was done by building an elevated stage with two platforms. As cables pulled the platforms apart, hoses pumped water into the opening space. On the screen, it looked as if the earth had suddenly opened.

Most of the special effects work was supervised by the uncredited James Basevi, who the following year helped to create the sensational sequences of MGM's **The Good Earth** and United Artists' **The Hurricane.** Ironically, with all the seemingly inevitable doom of the climax, the only dangerous accident of **San Francisco** occurred in a Paradise Cafe scene, in which Gable was dancing with Margaret Irving and Jack Holt was time-stepping with MacDonald. A wall collapsed; Gable pushed Irving out of the way and the prop wall fell on top of him. Gable was not injured, but since the visuals made him look like a supergod to have survived, the laugh-provoking sequence was later snipped from the film.

When premiered on June 25, 1936, **San Francisco** appeared destined for box-office glory, and indeed it was. It surpassed **Ben-Hur** (1925) as the studio's greatest moneymaker, topped **The Great**

---

[1]Anita Loos reminisced to **Film Fan Monthly** in 1967: "Sometimes you had to be clever to get your point over [with the Production Code office]. . . . I know in one case it vastly improved a picture. It was **San Francisco,** and there was a scene where Clark Gable hauled off and socked a priest, played by Spencer Tracy. The Johnson Office said you cannot have Clark Gable sock a priest, it's unthinkable. So I went away and got to pondering about how I could fix the scene. So I figured out that the priest could floor Gable any time he wanted to. He was a much cleverer boxer than Gable. That proved that when Clark hit him he could have killed Clark, but didn't do it, which made his character stronger as a priest, and it was accepted by the censor. In order to prove this situation I opened the picture with a scene of two men boxing and you saw Spencer Tracy sock Gable and knock him out. And then when they got dressed you saw that one of them was a priest. That scene wouldn't have been in if I hadn't had to outsmart the censor.

[2]During a rehearsal of one of the operatic numbers for **La Traviata,** MacDonald took a curtain call within the scene and the curtain, supposedly pulled back for her exit, got caught in her skirts, yanking them back and up into the air. She had to call for help. She said to the laughing extras, "Maybe they can use this situation for the next Marx Bros. picture."

Clark Gable in San Francisco.

Ziegfeld in grosses (over $4,000,000), and, until **Gone With the Wind** (1939), occupied the number-one spot in MGM's moneymakers list. The **New York Sun** noted, "With those earthquake scenes, with Miss MacDonald's golden voice and beauty, with the dimpled Mr. Gable in a he-man role, and with Mr. Tracy quietly humorous, quietly powerful as the understanding priest, **San Francisco** does not have to worry." The **New York Times** wrote in awe of the climactic episode, "The earthquake is a shattering spectacle, one of the truly great cinematic illusions; a monstrous, hideous, thrilling debacle with great fissures opening in the earth, buildings crumbling, men and women apparently being buried beneath showers of stone and plaster, gargoyles lurching from rooftops, water mains bursting, live wires flaring, flame, panic, terror . . ."

In a 1977 **Films in Review** article, Paul Caster overcomes moviegoers' traditional awe of **San Francisco** and mentions two particularly "amusing" examples of unintentionally funny (or so they seem today) sections of the classic film:

When Gable, overjoyed at MacDonald's survival, asks Tracy, "Tim, I want to pray. How do I pray?" Spencer simply tells him to say, "Thanks." Whereupon poor Clark falls to his knees, clasps his hands, looks skyward and says, "Thanks, God. [And then in a close-up] I **really** mean it!"

This latter affirmation was enough to make an audience squirm. Certainly it sounds more like Louis B. Mayer than Anita Loos and possibly it was. . . .

Gable is determined to stop MacDonald from singing in Jack Holt's opera house, and has obtained an injunction, to be served by Edgar Kennedy. Holt asks if there is any possibility of diverting Kennedy from his objective, but Gable responds with a negative shake of his head. To impress Holt with Kennedy's lack of warmth and understanding, he offers this marvelous character portrait:

"Why, he's so mean he'd shut off the air in a baby's incubator, just to watch the little sucker squirm!"

How that line got by Louis B. Mayer, who could be horrified by a scene in which Andy Hardy failed to express enthusiasm for the dinner his mother had served him, must remain one of the mysteries of Hollywood.

San Francisco placed fourth in the **Film Daily** Ten Best Picture Poll and won the **Photoplay** Gold Medal of 1936. It was Oscar-nominated as Best Picture of the Year, losing to Metro's **The Great Ziegfeld**. Tracy, who had also garnered fine reviews for **Fury** (1936)—made at MGM after **San Francisco** but released before it—was nominated for Best Actor, but lost to Paul Muni of **The Story of Louis Pasteur** (Warner Bros.). Douglas Shearer did accept an Oscar for **San Francisco** for Best Sound Recording.

In addition to its glories, **San Francisco** provided MGM and audiences with a perfect male team in Gable and Tracy. The two stars worked together with fine virile chemistry, perhaps in part because Gable envied Tracy's versatility while Tracy resented Gable's sex appeal. MGM would

pair the men again in **Test Pilot** (1938) and **Boom Town** (1940).

The studio owed a vote of thanks to MacDonald, who implored so long to get the film made and who waited on the sidelines until Gable was free to participate in it. She also suffered the ignominy of being ignored by Gable whenever the **San Francisco** cameras were not filming (as would Greer Garson of **Adventure,** 1945); he had no patience for high-toned ladies.

Not to be outdistanced by rajah Louis B. Mayer, Darryl F. Zanuck, the next few years, would deal with celluloid holocausts in **In Old Chicago** (1938), **Suez** (1938), and **The Rains Came** (1939), all three films starring Tyrone Power. Neither these nor the aforementioned Samuel Goldwyn production, **The Hurricane,** could match MGM's mixture of gloss, slick splendor, and staged excitement.

THE SEARCH
1948—105 min.

Producer, Lazar Wechsler; **director,** Fred Zinnemann; **screenplay,** Richard Schweizer in collaboration with David Wechsler; **additional dialogue,** Paul Jarrico; **music,** Robert Blum; **technical adviser–military liaison,** Therese Bonney; **camera,** Emil Berna; **editor,** Hermann Haller.

Montgomery Clift **(Ralph Stevenson);** Aline MacMahon **(Mrs. Murray);** Jarmila Novotna **(Mrs. Malik);** Wendell Corey **(Jerry Fisher);** Ivan Jandl **(Karel Malik);** Mary Patton **(Mrs. Fisher);** Ewart G. Morrison **(Mr. Crookes);** William Rogers **(Tom Fisher);** Leopold Borkowski **(Joel Makowsky);** Claude Gambier **(Raoul Dubois).**

SYNOPSIS
The narrative opens with youngsters, typical of thousands of homeless waifs who have been wandering lost among the ruins of World War II–torn Europe, being brought to an UNRRA camp in Germany for displaced children. Nine-year-old-Karel Malik—a Czechoslovakian youth separated from his mother since the age of five when they were sent to a concentration camp—is like the other kids at the reception center. He distrusts everyone, even those now trying to help him. But, unlike the others, the harrowing experiences have left him an amnesia victim, unable to remember his name or to speak anything except "I don't know" in German.

While being sent to another camp, he and several other children break out of a Red Cross ambulance because they fear they are being taken to a gas chamber. Karel hides among the ruins of the city and is presumed to have drowned when his hat is retrieved from the river. Days later he is found famished by Ralph Stevenson, an American soldier, who takes him to his place where he gains the youth's confidence. Ralph learns to love the child and teaches him to speak English. When his efforts to identify the boy prove fruitless, he decides to take him back to the U.S.

Ivan Jandl and Leopold Borkowski in The Search *('48).*

Meanwhile, Mrs. Malik has been carrying on a long search for her son, trekking from one European relief center to another in a futile search to identify him. She finally reaches the center from which he escaped and learns that he is presumed drowned. She refuses to abandon her quest. Months later Ralph, preparing to return home, brings Karel to the UNRRA center to remain until he can send for him. Mrs. Murray, an alert official there, recognizes him as the youth in question. Through her efforts, Mrs. Malik and Karel are reunited.

* * *

"A major revelation in our times" was how Bosley Crowther of the **New York Times** described **The Search**, Loew's most internationally successful film of 1948, and certainly its most powerful. Like other movie studios in the post–World War II years, MGM was then beginning to explore European locales for authentic scenic backdrops. This globe-trotting served two purposes: it provided the new crop of realism-seeking filmgoers with realistic settings rather than costly Hollywood fabrications; and it allowed the studios to tap distribution funds which had remained frozen in various Continental countries since the war years.

The Search gave moviegoers their first perusal of the talented Montgomery Clift. As Ralph Stevenson, he is the sensitive GI who befriends little Karel Malik (Ivan Jandl) after the boy's nightmarish existence. Others in the cast were Metropolitan Opera soprano Jarmila Novotna as the tireless mother of the lost boy, Wendell Corey as Clift's pal, and Aline MacMahon (in very solid support) as the sympathetic UNRRA supervisor.

In his March 24, 1948, **Times** review, Crowther continued:

. . . a picture which may prudently be said to be as fine, as moving, and as challenging as any the contemporary screen provides. . . . Our earnest wish is that it might be seen by every adult in the United States. . . . Unquestionably, the remarkable performance of a little Czech lad named Ivan Jandl as the principal figure in the drama is vital to the spirit of the whole. For this youngster, who was found by Mr. Zinnemann in a school group in Prague, has such tragic expression in his slight frame, such poetry in his eyes and face, and such melting appeal in his thin voice that he is the ultimate embodiment of the sorrow-inflicted child. . . . As the American officer who "adopts" him, the young American actor, Montgomery Clift, gets precisely the right combination of intensity and casualness into the role, and Aline MacMahon is crisply professional yet compassionate as an UNRRA worker.

The Search earned Academy Awards for Richard Schweizer and David Wechsler in the area of Best Motion Picture Story; Ivan Jandl won a miniature Oscar as the outstanding juvenile performer of 1948. Clift was nominated for Best Actor but lost to Laurence Olivier of **Hamlet** (a J. Arthur Rank release). The National Board of Review placed **The Search** third in its Ten Best list of 1948.

For Clift, **The Search** was the public debut of a very promising film career that remained largely unfulfilled during his tragic life. Actually, he had made Howard Hawkes' Western **Red River** before **The Search**, but that United Artists' picture was released after the MGM entry. As a result of his two 1948 screen performances, Clift was featured in a **Life** magazine cover story for its De-

cember 6, 1948 issue; **Look** magazine bestowed on him its Achievement Award and stated that he was "the most promising star on the Hollywood horizon"; and **Motion Picture Herald** listed the actor as a "star of tomorrow." However, it would not be MGM who placed the budding star under contract, but Paramount. His only other MGM film would be the trouble-plagued historical epic **Raintree County** (1957).

The year 1948 would also see the very talented Fred Zinnemann leave the lot. His other feature that year was the taut low-budget thriller **Act of Violence,** with Van Heflin, Robert Ryan, Janet Leigh, and Mary Astor. Artistically he had developed tremendously since directing short subjects at the studio and then debuting as a feature film director with Van Heflin's **Kid Glove Killer** and Edward Arnold's **Eyes in the Night,** both 1942. In 1953 he and Clift would be professionally reunited for **From Here to Eternity** (Columbia).

SEE HERE, PRIVATE HARGROVE
1944—101 min.

Producer, George Haight; **directors,** Wesley Ruggles and, **uncredited,** Tay Garnett; based on the book by Marion Hargrove; **screenplay,** Harry Kurnitz; **music,** David Snell; **song,** Frank Loesser and Ted Grouya; **art directors,** Cedric Gibbons and Stephen Goosson; **set decorators,** Edwin B. Willis and Ralph Hurst; **assistant director,** Barney Glazer; **sound,** John F. Dullam; **camera,** Charles Lawton; **editor,** Frank E. Hull.

Robert Walker (**Marion Hargrove**); Donna Reed (**Carol Halliday**); Robert Benchley (**Mr. Halliday**); Keenan Wynn (**Private Mulvehill**); Bob Crosby (**Bob**); Ray Collins (**Brody S. Griffith**); Chill Wills (**Sergeant Cramp**); Marta Linden (**Mrs. Halliday**); Grant Mitchell (**Uncle George**); George Offerman, Jr. (**Private Orrin Esty**); Edward Fielding (**General Dillon**); Donald Curtis (**Sergeant Heldon**); William "Bill" Phillips (**Private Bill Burk**); Douglas Fowley (**Captain Manville**); Morris Ankrum (**Colonel Forbes**); Mickey Rentschler (**Sergeant**); Frank Faylen (**MP**); Jack Luden (**Doctor**); Maurice Murphy (**Lieutenant**); Dennis Moore (**Executive Officer**); Rod Bacon (**Field Operator**); Connie Gilchrist and Louis Mason (**Farming Couple**); Harry Strang (**Captain**); Mantan Moreland (**Porter**); Mary McLeod (**Girl Clerk**); Blake Edwards (**Another Field Operator**); James Warren (**Executive Officer**); Eddie Acuff (**Captain Hammond**).

SYNOPSIS

Marion Hargrove is a cub reporter on the **Charlotte News.** Like many other young Americans during World War II, he is drafted into the army. In the service he makes friends with three other privates: Mulvehill, who has a knack of turning everything he does to his advantage; Bill Burk, a diamond-in-the-rough from New Jersey; and Orrin Esty, a serious baby-face young man.

Blundering Hargrove daily finds himself on KP duty at Fort Bragg, North Carolina, but Sergeant Cramp vows he will make a soldier of him—no matter what! Later Hargrove spots Carol Halliday, a beautiful New York girl, at the camp canteen. It is love at first sight. Mulvehill pretends he has a dating bureau and sells Hargrove a date with Carol for $5.00. When she learns of the ruse she is at first angry, and then amused by it all. Soon she is enamored of ingenuous Marion. They plan to meet the next week, but Marion's actions earn him KP duty. Next they agree to rendezvous in New York.

Further into the training regimen he becomes an acting corporal, but during a practice warfare maneuver, he unwittingly delivers his howitzer to the "enemy" and loses his rank. Hargrove believes he has also lost his leave privilege, so he spends all his money on his pals. Then he gets the leave permit and has to borrow from Mulvehill, to whom he signs over his future paychecks and any revenue from the unsold book he has been writing at camp.

In New York he dates Carol and tries to sell his book. Back at camp he and Mulvehill, through the latter's instigation, get "soft" jobs in the public relations department. As a result the two men are labeled yellow by their buddies. News came that Marion's book has been sold for publication and he receives a $300.00 advance, but he is still depressed by the low esteem in which his fellows hold him and Mulvehill. The two arrange to transfer back to their old battalion and are part of a group being sent to the war zone.

* * *

"The first great rookie comedy of the war. . . . It's a dream of a picture! The book had America in stitches! You'll come apart at the seams."

Since Hollywood's service films were very rarely a laughing matter, at least intentionally, there was considerable interest when MGM filmed Marion Hargrove's humorous book. **See Here, Private Hargrove** detailed his adventures as an army inductee at Fort Bragg, North Carolina.

The comedy starred "new face" Robert Walker as the title character and he gave a charmingly hilarious performance. The black-and-white film spotlighted the woes that plagued the lives of drafted young men during the war: KP duty, practice warfare maneuvers, and the unavoidable characters who inhabit every army base—the bellicose sergeant (here played at top volume by Chill Wills), the conniver (craftily interpreted by Keenan Wynn). Also on hand was the lovely Donna Reed, then a flourishing ingenue at Metro. She was the camp canteen girl who inspired Walker's bumbling infatuation.

After **See Here** was well into production, the front office became leery of presenting a too jocular view of military life. The studio felt the picture should also contain scenes of "significance, importance, and relevance." The last third of the film was then reoriented. But at the initial previews, the heterogeneous picture displeased audiences with its downbeat ending. The hierarchy reconsidered its original concepts and decided that a comedy approach throughout was the proper key to success. However, by now director Wesley Ruggles was in England for the J. Arthur

Robert Walker and Donna Reed in See Here, Private Hargrove *('44).*

Rank organization. He requested Tay Garnett to direct the retakes. There was much grumbling on the set when Garnett took over control, but eventually the situation smoothed out. As Garnett later recalled, "I realized that the air had cleared for **Hargrove** when I began to hear stagehands referring to it as 'my picture.' "

The last-minute switches in tempo proved effective with the public and the critics. "With Robert Walker playing Hargrove like a veteran trouper," wrote Howard Barnes in his **New York Herald-Tribune** review after the film's March 1944 premiere, "and such excellent supporting performers as Robert Benchley, Keenan Wynn, Ray Collins, and Chill Wills adding a wide range of clowning embellishments to the proceedings, it is a singularly satisfying show. . . . Harry Kurnitz has composed a fresh and funny continuity from the Marion Hargrove book and Wesley Ruggles has directed it as though he were actually reporting on a period of small adventures of basic training."

So successful was **See Here, Private Hargrove** (it was one of the top twenty-five money-makers of the 1943–44 season) that MGM released in 1945 **What Next, Corporal Hargrove?** The follow-up was supervised by Richard Thorpe and starred Walker, Wynn, and Wills in their original parts. An unofficial remake of the 1944 film appeared with Warner Bros.' **The Girl He Left Behind** (1956), starring Tab Hunter and Natalie Wood.

As for the real-life Marion Hargrove, he later became a Hollywood scriptwriter.

SEQUOIA

1934—75 min.[1] (Reissue title: MALIBU)

Producer, John W. Considine, Jr.; **director,** Chester M. Franklin; based on the novel **Malibu** by Vance Joseph Hoyt; **adapters,** Ann Cunningham, Sam Armstrong, and Carey Wilson; **dialogue,** Wilson; **music,** Herbert Stothart; **camera,** Chester Lyons; **editor,** Charles Cochberg.

---

[1]Filmed in Sepia.

Jean Parker **(Toni Martin)**; Russell Hardie **(Bob Alden)**; Samuel S. Hinds **(Matthew Martin)**; Paul Hurst **(Bergman)**; Ben Hall **(Joe)**; Willie Fung **(Sang Soo)**; Harry Lowe, Jr. **(Feng Soo)**.

SYNOPSIS

The narrative deals with Malibu, a deer, and Gato, a puma, who are reared together by Toni Martin. She wants to prove that under the proper surroundings these two animals can be taught to be friends instead of natural enemies. Toni had found Gato when he was a cub, his mother having been caught in a trap and died. Throughout the chronicle is the haunting question whether the two animals will revert to natural type, despite their special upbringing. While domiciled at the Martin household the growing Gato does steal out at night to prey on neighboring animals. However, the puma's response to Malibu and to his human friends is always warm and affectionate.

When Gato and Malibu are grown, Toni sets them free, hoping the two animals will not forget each other. Her theory proves true. On one occasion the cruel guide-trapper Bergman sets out to kill foraging Malibu. Gato, lurking nearby, realizes the danger. At the crucial moment, he springs on Bergman and holds him while Malibu escapes. Gato then follows Malibu and they both drink from a stream. Malibu occasionally licks Gato to show his feelings. At another time Toni is out swimming, accompanied by Feng Soo, son of the cook Sang Soo. Toni leaves the boy on shore tied to Malibu's baby son. The boy runs away, dragging the young deer with him and sometimes visa versa. Suddenly a rattler appears and Feng Soo throws a stick at it. Malibu arrives to trample the rattler to death. On yet another occasion Malibu spots Bergman rounding up deer to be used for a hunt. Malibu leaps into the enclosure and shows the animals how to jump the stiles. Perhaps the best illustration of the human quality of the animals occurs when Malibu's mate is killed by Bergman's trap. Both Malibu and her baby deer stand by the trap until Malibu thinks it is time to leave. Then he pushes the young one away from the dead animal and the two reluctantly depart.

Although there is some romantic interaction between Toni Martin and Bob Alden, the highlight of the film is the death of the crafty Bergman, for which Malibu and Gato are responsible.

* * *

The lion's share of credit for developing live-action animal pictures into a cinematic art belongs to Walt Disney, but Metro's **Sequoia** was itself a splendid entry. The Sepia-lensed feature was a mature if emotional study which presented animals not as savage predators, but as intelligent, gentle creatures. Though given the studio go-ahead because of the great success of **Trader Horn** (1931), this film in no way resembled its violent predecessor. Steamy Africa was replaced by the cool and quiet High Sierras, and the snarling, screeching monsters of the jungle were supplanted by a deer named Malibu and a puma called Gato. Together they formed one of the classic animal sagas of the screen.

Sequoia was nurtured to completion by Ches-

Jean Parker and puma in Sequoia *('34).*

ter Franklin, the director, who spent a year in the Sierras with cameraman Chester Lyons preparing the offbeat story. Not to be overlooked was the adept human acting of Jean Parker as the beautiful naturalist who sought to prove that the deer and the puma can live together peaceably. Then there was Paul Hurst (five years later shot in the face by Vivien Leigh as he stalked her in the decaying Tara of **Gone With the Wind**) as a brutal trapper. It is his demise at the paws of Malibu and Gato which elicits cheers from audiences.

The human performers aside, the film principally centers on the marvelous adventures of the two contrasting animals. The scenes of their loyalty and love for one another—the deer licking the puma, the puma pouncing on the evil Hurst to allow the deer to escape his snare—as well as some thrilling sequences (Malibu saving a baby from a rattlesnake), and a heartbreaking one (Malibu and her young finding Malibu's mate dead in a trap), were novelties to audiences. It was regarded as a fascinating new direction for the Hollywood cinema.

MGM was somewhat baffled as how best to promote **Sequoia,** which was scheduled for release in late 1934. The studio finally decided to advertise the film in the tradition of **Trader Horn,** with some absurdly misleading copy: "A girl goddess of nature leads the animals against man. . . . The theme was so daring, so exciting, that nothing since **Trader Horn** could equal its brilliant novelty." Nevertheless, when **Sequoia** opened at New York's Capitol Theatre, it found a large audience and critical acclaim. Andre Sennwald wrote in the **New York Times:**

If **Sequoia** were only the technical triumph of making the biblical lion and lamb lie down

together, Mr. Franklin could be applauded for his success in arranging a unique practical joke. But the film possesses genuine artistic distinction and it encompasses an emotional cycle that is more profoundly touching than most human make-believe . . . a remarkable picture . . . when the Academy of Motion Picture Arts and Sciences comes to judge the best performances of the year it can hardly afford to neglect Malibu and Gato.

So well does **Sequoia** survive that under the new title of **Malibu** it is frequently revived for Saturday matinee series.

Franklin, the older brother of MGM producer-director Sidney Franklin, would helm one more picture in his long career: Metro's **Tough Guy** (1936), with Jackie Cooper and Rin Tin Tin, Jr. But, MGM never made proper use of contractee Jean Parker. She had shown great promise as the little Duchess Maria in **Rasputin and the Empress** (1932), and on loan to RKO shone as the angelic Beth who dies in **Little Women** (1933). She would leave the studio in 1935; her best film thereafter was **The Ghost Goes West** (1936) opposite Robert Donat.

SEVEN BRIDES FOR SEVEN BROTHERS
1954 C—102 min.

Producer, Jack Cummings; **director,** Stanley Donen; based on the story "The Sobbin' Women" by Stephen Vincent Benét; **screenplay,** Albert Hack-

ett, Francis Goodrich, and Dorothy Kingsley; **art directors,** Cedric Gibbons and Urie McCleary; **set decorators,** Edwin B. Willis and Hugh Hunt; **choreography,** Michael Kidd; **songs,** Johnny Mercer and Gene dePaul; **music directors,** Adolph Deutsch and Saul Chaplin; **costumes,** Walter Plunkett; **assistant director,** Ridgeway Callow; **sound,** Douglas Shearer; **camera,** George Folsey; **editor,** Ralph E. Winters.

Jane Powell (**Milly**); Howard Keel (**Adam Pontabee**); Jeff Richards (**Benjamin Pontabee**); Russ Tamblyn (**Gideon Pontabee**); Tommy Rall (**Frank Pontabee**); Howard Petrie (**Pete Perkins**); Virginia Gibson (**Liza**); Ian Wolfe (**Reverend Elcott**); Marc Platt (**Daniel Pontabee**); Matt Mattox (**Caleb Pontabee**); Jacques d'Amboise (**Ephraim Pontabee**); Julie Newmeyer [Newmar] (**Dorcas**); Nancy Kilgas (**Alice**); Betty Carr (**Sarah**); Ruta Kilmonis [Lee] (**Ruth**); Norma Doggett (**Martha**); Earl Barton (**Harry**); Dante DiPaolo (**Matt**); Kelly Brown (**Carl**); Matt Moore (**Ruth's Uncle**); Russell Simpson (**Mr. Bixby**); Marjorie Wood (**Mrs. Bixby**); Dick Rich (**Dorcas' Father**); Anna Q. Nilsson (**Mrs. Elcott**); Larry Blake (**Drunk**); Lois Hall (**Girl**); Jarma Lewis (**Lem's Girlfriend**); Walter Beaver (**Lem**); Sheila James (**Dorcas' Sister**).

SYNOPSIS

In the Oregon territory of the 1850s, frontier farmer Adam Pontabee rides into the distant town for a very good reason; he wants a wife. He sets his amorous sights on Milly, a waitress in the town's cafe, and he clumsily proposes to her. Attracted to the handsome farmer, she accepts, unaware that Adam shares their future love nest with six brothers.

Arriving at the farm Milly learns the truth as Adam's bewhiskered siblings introduce themselves to her. She puts aside her initial anger and vows to teach the brothers cleanliness and manners. But it is an uphill fight. At a barn-raising, where the bachelor brothers become wide-eyed when they see a bevy of single girls, the boys show off by engaging in a fracas with the pack of town boys who tried to humiliate them.

Returning home, the brothers cannot forget the girls. When they confide their woes to Adam, he tells them about the "sobbin' women"—that is, the Sabine women of Rome—about whom he has just read in one of Milly's books. He proposes that the boys, following the example of their Roman predecessors, sneak into town and kidnap the girls they want. Their abduction scheme is a total success, aided by a chance avalanche which blocks off the pursuing townspeople.

Upon their return, the boys rush to tell Milly the news. She is angered when she learns what has happened. Adam, hurt by her remarks, departs for his hunting cabin, unaware that Milly is pregnant. He remains away for the winter, during which the captive girls look longingly at the boys and the boys peek amorously at the girls.

Finally come the spring thaws. The brothers begin courting the girls seriously, and Adam returns contritely to Milly and his newborn baby. But the thawing also melts the snow and the townsfolk rush to the Pontabee farm to retrieve the girls. Upon their arrival, the vigilantes hear the crying of Milly's baby. Reverend Elcott asks the kidnapped girls whose "wee babe" he hears. All six girls reply "Mine!" With shotguns at their backs, the six Pontabee brothers join Adam as happily married men.

* * *

The early 1950s found MGM justifying large outlays for screen rights to stage hits or musical classics such as **Annie Get Your Gun** (1950), **Showboat** (1951), and **Kiss Me Kate** (1953) with elaborate screen mountings. However, there emerged from the Metro portals in 1954[1] a zesty musical that was original in origin, inexpensively produced on the back lot, and would become a box-office champion.

Stanley Donen, who in tandem with Gene Kelly or on his own had produced several inspired MGM musical packages already, rose to the occasion with this celluloid package. With songs by Johnny Mercer and Gene DePaul[2] and choreography by Michael Kidd, the picture boasted only two star names—Jane Powell, who had been graduated from the juvenile chores she began at the studio in **Holiday in Mexico** (1946), and Howard Keel, stalwart baritone workhorse whom producer Jack Cummings had especially requested for the pivotal part of frontiersman Adam. Playing the six brothers were carefully chosen, proven dancers. There were Jacques d'Amboise of the New York City Ballet, Marc Platt of the Radio City Music Hall Ballet Corps, Tommy Rall (who had been a featured dancer in Metro's **Kiss Me Kate** and who later scored on Broadway in **Milk and Honey),** and film dancer and actor Matt Mattox (his singing voice was dubbed by Bill Lee). In addition, there were studio contractees Russ Tamblyn, whose dancing was on a professional par with his cohorts, and Jeff Richards, beefcake juvenile who spent most of the dancing numbers watching and encouraging his on-screen siblings. All the men were dyed redheads for the picture. MGM picked relative unknowns to play the "brides," including blonde newcomer Ruta Kilmonis, who later changed her surname to Lee, and a twenty-three-year-old brunette Amazon beauty named Julie Newmeyer, who later became a Broadway sensation as Julie Newmar of **The Marriage-Go-Round** (1958).

Although they might have seemed an unlikely combination, tall Keel and petite Powell proved amazingly adept together, he with his masculine verve and rich singing, she being pretty and spunky, and with a clearly pitched high tone that reverberated well on the soundstages. The highlight of the film was the barnraising sequence, a lengthy dance scene divided into two sections:

Norma Doggett, Ruta Lee, Virginia Gibson, Betty Carr, Tommy Rall, Matt Mattox (in air), Jacques d'Amboise (rear), Nancy Kilgas, Russ Tamblyn, Jeff Richards, and Kelly Brown (extreme right) in Seven Brides for Seven Brothers ('54).

the acrobatics and then the choreographed fight. As Douglas McVay describes in **The Musical Film** (1967), "Here, everything—music, terpsichore, the incredibly agile and energetic male and female corps, George Folsey's CinemaScope, Ralph Winters' editing and Donen's **mise-en-scène**—united to produce the best square dance ever."

One major complaint against the film was the use of murky AnscoColor, which tended to negate the intended expansiveness of the widescreen process. Then too it was obviously filmed on the back lot and soundstages, diluting the intended effect of the robust outdoors. (Metro had pulled the same stunt with the far more expensively scaled **Brigadoon,** 1954, directed by Vincente Minnelli on a very artificial plane on soundstage sets.)

However, the public responded favorably to **Seven Brides** and the summer 1954 release grossed $6,298,000. Keel, who had earned only about $10,000 for his work on the picture, was rewarded by MGM with a new $3,000 per week contract. Adolph Deutsch and Saul Chaplin received an Oscar for Best Scoring of a Musical Picture. Stanley Donen would direct two more musicals for the studio: **Deep in My Heart** (1954), which he cochoreographed, and **It's Always Fair Weather** (1955), codirected with Gene Kelly.

Seven Brides served to stem temporarily the decline of the studio's musical cycle. It is well remembered even today for its gusto. The film was also an uncredited inspiration behind the 1968–70 ABC-TV series "Here Come the Brides," with Robert Brown and Joan Blondell. In 1978 Jane

Powell and Howard Keel began an extensive tour in a musical stage version of **Seven Brides,** which was adapted from the screen by Al Kasha and David Landay, with additional songs by Kasha and Joel Hirschhorn. The road engagements began in mid-1978 to less than enthusiastic endorsements and closed in Miami Beach in February 1979, proving once again that show business magic cannot be tampered with or recreated.

THE SHOP AROUND THE CORNER
1940—97 min.

Producer-director, Ernst Lubitsch; based on the play **Parfumerie** by Nikolaus Laszlo; **screenplay,** Samson Raphaelson; **music,** Werner Heymann; **art directors,** Cedric Gibbons and Wade Rubottom; **set decorator,** Edwin B. Willis; **sound,** Douglas Shearer; **camera,** William Daniels; **editor,** Gene Ruggiero.

James Stewart **(Alfred Kralik);** Margaret Sullavan **(Klara Novak);** Frank Morgan **(Matuschek);** Joseph Schildkraut **(Ferencz Vadas);** Sara Haden **(Flora);** Felix Bressart **(Perovitch);** William Tracy **(Pepi Katena);** Inez Courtney **(Ilona);** Charles Halton **(Detective);** Charles Smith **(Rudy);** Sarah Edwards and Gertrude Simpson **(Woman Customers);** Grace Hayle **(Plump Woman);** Charles Arnt **(Po-**

---
[1]MGM would have produced the film five years earlier, but producer Joshua Logan held an option on Benét's story, which he planned to convert into a Broadway musical.

[2]The songs: "Wonderful, Wonderful Day" (sung by Powell), "Bless Your Beautiful Hide" (Keel), "When You're in Love" (Keel and Powell), "Goin' Courtin' " (Powell and the boys), "Lonesome Polecat" (the boys), "Sobbin' Women" (Keel and the boys), "June Bride" (Marc Platt and the girls), "It's Spring, Spring, Spring" (the boys and the girls), and "Barn-raising Ballet" (the boys and the girls).

Margaret Sullavan and James Stewart in a pose for The Shop Around the Corner *('40).*

liceman); William Edmunds (**Waiter**); Mary Carr (**Grandmother**); Mabel Colcord (**Aunt Anna**); Renie Riano, Claire DuBrey, Ruth Warren, Mira McKinney, and Joan Blair (**Customers**); Edwin Maxwell (**Bit**).

SYNOPSIS

Alfred Kralik is the head clerk at Matuschek's speciality shop in tranquil, pre–World War II Budapest. He escapes the humble nature of his job by becoming the pen pal of a young lady who has advertised in the newspaper for a correspondent sharing an interest in "developing mentally." During the Christmas rush Matuschek finds his employees (including suave natty dresser Ferencz Vadas, browbeaten Perovitch, and cheery Ilona) overworked, so he hires Klara Novak to assist them.

Alfred and Klara immediately ire each other, and argue incessantly throughout the day over anything and everything. Alfred's exasperation is eased when he finally sets up a time and place to meet his pen pal. He arrives and discovers the girl to be—Klara. Alfred decides not to betray his identity but to pretend he has run into Klara there by sheer coincidence. She is bored by his small talk and asks him to leave, for she is expecting a friend—who does not arrive.

Meanwhile, Matuschek discovers that his wife is enjoying an affair with one of his employ-

ees. As Alfred is the only worker who has ever been invited to the house, Matuschek accuses him of adultery and fires him from his post. Crushed, Alfred leaves the store. Matuschek, however, soon learns that his spouse has been dallying not with Alfred, but with Vadas. Ashamed, Matuschek attempts to shoot himself. Saved by the messenger boy, he instead enters a hospital for a rest and contritely rehires Alfred, this time assigning him to be general manager.

Klara has meanwhile become attracted to Alfred, and he has fallen in love with her. Finally, he reveals himself as the man who filled her postal box 237 with so many wonderful letters, and they joyfully begin a promising romance.

* * *

Masterfully stylistic director Ernst Lubitsch once reflected on the three best (in his own opinion) feature films of his career. For "pure style," he chose Paramount's **Trouble in Paradise** (1932), which starred Kay Francis, Herbert Marshall, and Miriam Hopkins. For satire, Lubitsch believed he was never "sharper" than in Metro's Greta Garbo vehicle **Ninotchka** (1939). And as for "human comedy," he selected MGM's **The Shop Around the Corner**. "Never did I make a picture in which the atmosphere and the characters were truer than in this picture."

There was indeed much to admire in this ninety-seven minute confection, based on Nikolaus Laszlo's play **Parfumerie**. The motion picture

featured the third teaming of James Stewart and Margaret Sullavan; the stars had been yoked in Universal's **Next Time We Love** (1936) and in MGM's **The Shopworn Angel** (1938). (They would be teamed one final time, in MGM's **The Mortal Storm**, also released in 1940.) In their first two films together, Miss Sullavan had been top-billed over her lanky costar, but now Stewart was the top attraction. His triumph in Columbia's **Mr. Smith Goes to Washington** boosted his cinema stock tremendously. (It would rise even higher when he won an Oscar for his performance in MGM's **The Philadelphia Story,** 1940.)

There was in support of the two stars a gallery of splendid character players, all at their best: Frank Morgan, free of familiar blustery mannerisms and deftly amusing as cuckolded Budapest store owner Matuschek; Joseph Schildkraut, dapper and wolfish as the impeccably attired adulterer Ferencz Vadas; mousey Felix Bressart (who had earlier played one of the wide-eyed Russian trio in Lubitsch's **Ninotchka**) as put-upon clerk Perovitch; and perky Inez Courtney as the cheerful Ilona.

Then, too, the film benefited from the incisive Lubitsch charm. As critic Andrew Sarris noted in his book **Interviews with Film Directors** (1967), "In a Lubitsch film, the play is not the thing—it is but a device wherewith he can reveal people to us—their petty bickerings, their foibles and weaknesses, vanities, desires, dreams, disillusionments, in the 'human-all-too-human' comedy of life." It is just this device which exposes the various aspects of Stewart's Alfred Kralik and Sullavan's Klara Novak, who transcend their job routines, self-images, and prejudices, to discover their love for each other.

Opening at New York's Radio City Music Hall on January 25, 1940, **The Shop Around the Corner** drew praise for the aforementioned Lubitsch quality. The **New York Herald-Tribune**'s Howard Barnes assessed, "The plot of the new Music Hall offering does not make much of a claim on one's photoplay memories, but the characters and the incidents have been so brilliantly treated that the film becomes disarming and beguiling comedy." Barnes also saluted Stewart for "his great gift for shy understatement" and Miss Sullavan, who "once more . . . . shows that she has few colleagues who can match her for crowding a line or scene with emotional intensity, even when it is a minor situation." **Variety** summarized, "It's smart and clever, but still packaged with easily understandable situations and problems of middle-class folk."

Stewart's last MGM film before enlisting in the U.S. Air Force would be **Ziegfeld Girl** (1941). After his World War II military duty he chose not to return to Metro as a contract star, but to freelance in the "new" Hollywood. Sullavan completed her six-film pact with MGM with **Cry Havoc** (1943); thereafter she devoted her attentions primarily to the stage. Her last movie was Columbia's **No Sad Songs for Me** (1950).

MGM revamped **The Shop Around the Corner** into the 1949 color musical **In the Good Old Summertime**, starring Judy Garland and Van Johnson. In 1963 there appeared a Broadway musical, **She**

Loves Me, based on the 1940 film, with songs by Jerry Bock and Sheldon Harnick. Daniel Massey, Barbara Cook, Jack Cassidy, and Barbara Baxley filled the Stewart, Sullavan, Schildkraut, and Courtney roles for 301 performances. The story appeared ready for another screen adaptation when in 1970 plans were announced to film **She Loves Me** as a vehicle for Julie Andrews, to be directed by Blake Edwards. However, the production was later abandoned by a foundering MGM.

SHOW BOAT
1951 C—108 min.

Producer, Arthur Freed; **associate producers,** Ben Feiner, Jr. and, **uncredited,** Roger Edens; **director,** George Sidney; based on the musical play by Jerome Kern and Oscar Hammerstein II and the novel by Edna Ferber; **screenplay,** John Lee Mahin and, **uncredited,** George Wells and Jack McGowan; **music director,** Adolph Deutsch; music numbers staged and directed by Robert Alton; **orchestrator,** Conrad Salinger; **vocal arranger,** Robert Tucker; **songs,** Hammerstein and Kern; **art directors,** Cedric Gibbons and Jack Martin Smith; **set decorators,** Edwin B. Willis and Alfred Spencer; **makeup,** William Tuttle; **costumes,** Walter Plunkett; **special montage director,** Peter Ballbusch; **special effects,** Warren Newcombe; **camera,** Charles Rosher; **editor,** Albert Akst.

Kathryn Grayson (**Magnolia Hawks**); Ava Gardner (**Julie Laverne**); Howard Keel (**Gaylord Ravenal**); Joe E. Brown (**Captain Andy Hawks**); Marge Champion (**Ellie May Shipley**); Gower Champion (**Frank Schultz**); Robert Sterling (**Stephen Baker**); Agnes Moorehead (**Parthy Hawks**); Adele Jergens (**Cameo McQueen**); William Warfield (**Joe**); Leif Erickson (**Pete**); Owen McGiveney (**Windy McClain**); Frances Williams (**Queenie**); Regis Toomey (**Sheriff Ike Vallon**); Frank Wilcox (**Mark Hallson**); Ian MacDonald (**Drunk Sport**); Fuzzy Knight (**Troc Piano Player**); Emory Parnell (**Jake Green**); Chick Chandler (**Herman**); Joyce Jameson and Lyn Wilde (**Chorus Girls**); Annette Warren (**Singing Voice of Julie**); Edward Keane (**Hotel Manager**); Tom Irish (**Bellboy**); Jim Pierce (**Doorman**); William Tannen (**Man with Julie**); Anna Q. Nilsson (**Seamstress**); Bert Roach (**Drunk**); Earle Hodgins (**Bartender**); Ida Moore (**Old Lady**); Alphonse Martell (**Headwaiter**).

SYNOPSIS
The **Cotton Blossom,** an elegant riverboat, travels up and down the Mississippi River, helmed by Captain Andy Hawks and his shrewish wife Parthy, and featuring a top entertainer in the curvaceous form of Julie Laverne. When Julie rebuffs the sexual advances of Pete, a laborer on the boat, he informs the sheriff that she is a mulatto and wed to a white husband, hence guilty of the crime of miscegenation. Julie escapes the sheriff and thereby loses her employment with Captain Andy's paddle wheeler.

Meanwhile, Captain Andy's daughter, Magnolia, becomes infatuated with Gaylord Ravenal, a devil-may-care gambler dandy. Gaylord himself falls in love with Magnolia and the two are wed, Gaylord sacrificing his gambling and taking a job as an actor on the **Cotton Blossom.** However, his old instinct quickly surfaces, and the marriage soon flounders as Gaylord again indulges his gambling passions.

However, by the story's end, Gaylord and Magnolia, through the efforts of the tragic Julie, reconcile and leave on the **Cotton Blossom** to begin their love life anew.

* * *

A long and celebrated heritage followed Edna Ferber's novel **Show Boat** after its publication in 1926. On December 27, 1927, the Jerome Kern–Oscar Hammerstein II musical version opened on Broadway, and in 1929 there followed Universal's half-talking version, which utilized a mostly new score. In 1936 Universal released the classic version directed by James Whale, which used the full score (although the number "Why Do I Love You?" ended up on the cutting-room floor). The expansive screen musical starred Irene Dunne and Allan Jones, and employed stage version members Charles Winninger (as Captain Andy) and Helen Morgan (as Julie). The Universal film was one of the last productions of Carl Laemmle, Jr. When "Junior" and his father, "Uncle Carl" Laemmle, lost control of the studio to new management at the time of the film's release, the new brass, seeking quick ways to win dividends, sold the movie rights to **Show Boat** to MGM as part of a 1938 three-picture pact.

Metro had planned to use **Show Boat** as a vehicle for the screen team of Jeanette MacDonald and Nelson Eddy, but that did not come to pass. In the mid-1940s Arthur Freed became enamored of the **Show Boat** property as a project for his studio unit. To test the feasibility of remaking **Show Boat,** Freed suggested that MGM back a Broadway revival (January 5, 1946) of the venerable musical, and he also—quite logically—included selections from **Show Boat** in the fabricated Jerome Kern screen biography **Till the Clouds Roll By** (1946).

Freed and his associate Roger Edens were not satisfied with the plot maneuverings of Hammerstein's "book" for the stage play. They did not want Magnolia and Gaylord to be separated for two decades and finish the story as an elderly couple. Moreover, the film producers thought Julie should have a more central part in the narrative and not disappear from the story so abruptly. Scripter John Lee Mahin, noted for handling such Clark Gable vehicles as **Red Dust** (1932), **Test Pilot** (1938), and **Boom Town** (1940), was the principal scenarist in charge of executing Freed's dictates. Meanwhile, the studio had to cope with the Breen Office, which reminded the filmmakers that under the existing production code, no film story was to deal with miscegenation. However, the 1936 film version had set a precedent and the Breen Office had to bow to it.

There was little question about using Howard Keel (who had scored so mightily in Freed's **Annie Get Your Gun,** (1950) as Gaylord, or about casting resident vocalist Kathryn Grayson as Magnolia.[1] But there was great debate as to who would play the expanded role of Julie. Freed initially wanted Judy Garland for the job, but after replacing her in **Annie Get Your Gun** and **Royal Wedding** (1951), the studio saw no other alternative but to fire her from the lot. Meanwhile, new studio head Dore Schary thought Dinah Shore would be admirable in the part and verbally promised it to her. Freed talked the songstress out of the idea and pushed for his own choice, Ava Gardner. The beauteous actress was screen-tested, lip-synching to a Lena Horne recording from the score. She was as unenthusiastic about the assignment as was the studio.

Energetic, imaginative Edens located young black baritone William Warfield from reviews of a powerful Town Hall recital debut he made, and advised Freed to cast him as Joe, the deckhand. Joe E. Brown, the inspiration for Edna Ferber when she initially wrote **Show Boat,** was hired as Captain Andy. Contract players Agnes Moorehead (as Parthy) and Marge and Gower Champion (new to the stock company) were assigned to the film, and Robert Sterling, Adele Jergens, and Leif Erickson rounded out the major roles.

At first it was hoped to photograph **Show Boat,** under George Sidney's direction, on location on the Mississippi River. But this expensive concept was discarded and it was decided to use the **Tarzan** jungle lake on the back lot. Since it would be near impossible to find a floating showboat usable for the principal filming, Jack Martin Smith convinced Cedric Gibbons and the others to construct one. It was perhaps the most expensive single prop ever built: 171 feet in length, 34 feet in the beam, 57 feet to the top of its stacks, and with a 19½-foot paddle wheel. The lake was drained, and the three-deck vessel was built on steel pontoons, at a cost of $126,468.[2] In the interim Walter Plunkett completed the period costumes for the color musical, at a cost of $98,725.

As with the **Show Boat** sequences in **Till the Clouds Roll By,** Robert Alton was choreographer, Conrad Salinger was the orchestrator, Adolph Deutsch the music director, and Roger Edens the overall supervisor. This time Bobby Tucker handled the vocal arrangement (a task which had been overseen by Kay Thompson on the Kern screen biography). One of the major prerecording problems was whether or not to allow Gardner to sing her own vocals. The studio insisted she should not. Said a bitter Ava years later in an interview with Rex Reed:

I really tried in **Show Boat** but that was MGM crap. Typical of what they did to me there. I wanted to sing those songs—hell, I've still got a Southern accent—and I really thought Julie should sound a little like a Negro since she's supposed to have Negro blood. Christ,

[1] Grayson had played Magnolia in the **Show Boat** sequences of **Till the Clouds Roll By** (1946).

[2] The **Cotton Blossom** long bobbed in "the lake" on MGM's back lot (3). Though very expensive to construct, it was hardly ever employed again; it was used as background for **Desperate Search** (1952).

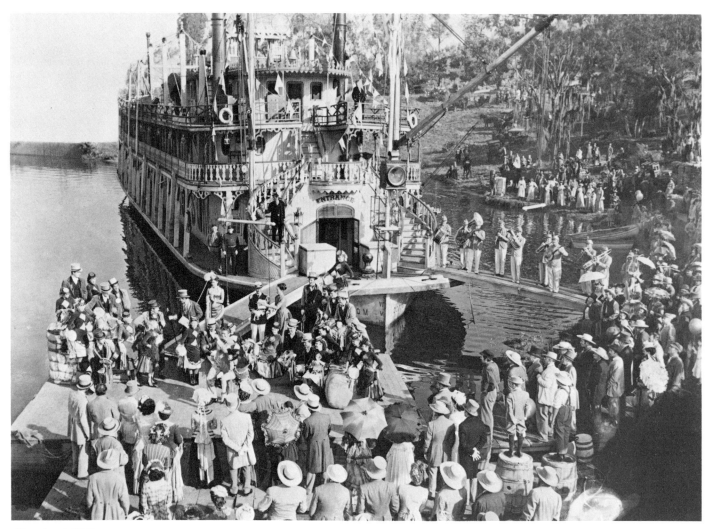

Showboat *('51).*

those songs like "Bill" shouldn't sound like an opera. So, what did they say? "Ava, baby, you can't sing, you'll hit the wrong keys, you're up against real pros in this film, so don't make a fool of yourself." **Pros!**

Gardner remained adamant, but as a precaution the filmmakers tested voice dubbers and settled on Annette Warren, who made recordings of each of Ava's numbers.

On the other hand, there was absolutely no problem with Warfield or his big number "Ol' Man River." His first take was also the final one; it was that good and moving. (When Louis B. Mayer heard the playback he reputedly broke into tears.) The filming (November 17, 1950, to January 9, 1951, with retakes in early February and March 1951) was not without problems: the fog (both natural and artificial) had to be maintained at a consistency for daily shooting; the **Cotton Blossom** caught fire and had to be repainted and re-

furbished, at a cost of $67,000; and director Sidney became indisposed and Edens had temporarily to replace him.

Right up to the time of the first preview—in Pacific Palisades on March 22, 1951—it was undecided whether to leave in Gardner's singing of "Can't Help Lovin' That Man" and "Bill" (by Kern, Guy Bolton, and P. G. Wodehouse). After the audience reaction to the showing, Gardner's singing voice track was removed, and Warren's inserted. (However, in the "soundtrack" album, Gardner's voice is used, and as she says, "I still get royalties on the goddamn records I did.") Before the film bowed, Freed, Edens, and Sidney did some drastic cutting to tighten up the storyline so that the separation and reunion of Magnolia and Gaylor would not last so long on camera. While the major numbers remained intact in the film— "Make Believe," "You Are Love," "Why Do I Love You," "Life Upon the Wicked Stage," "Ol' Man River," "I Might Fall Back on You," and Julie's

numbers—deleted were "Nobody Else but Me,"[3] "I Have the Room Above," and "Ah Still Suits Me."

Show Boat was released in midsummer 1951. It was fast evident that the story had not at all lost its audience appeal. Bosley Crowther of the **New York Times** wrote that, while the picture was familiar already to a generation of moviegoers, never had the story enjoyed "anything like the visual splendor and richness of musical score as are tastefully brought together in the re-creation of the show. As a matter of fact, it is doubtful if even its first performance on the stage surpassed, except in novelty and freshness, this faithful translation that Metro has done." Made at a cost of $2,295,429, the musical would gross more than $8,650,000.

Though far more successful financially, **Show Boat** was upstaged by the premiere of MGM's **An**

---

[3]Written for the 1946 Broadway revival.

American in Paris four months later. The latter film won the Academy Award for Best Picture and assorted other plaudits, including the Irving G. Thalberg Award for producer Freed.

SINGIN' IN THE RAIN
1952 C—103 min.

Producer, Arthur Freed; **associate producer,** Roger Edens; **directors,** Gene Kelly and Stanley Donen; **story-screenplay,** Adolph Green and Betty Comden; suggested by the song "Singin' in the Rain" by Freed and Nacio Herb Brown; **music director,** Lennie Hayton; music numbers staged and directed by Kelly and Donen; **orchestrators,** Conrad Salinger, Wally Heglin, and Skip Martin; **vocal arrangers,** Jeff Alexander and Edens; **songs,** Freed and Brown; Comden, Green, and Edens; **Technicolor consultants,** Henri Jaffa and James Gooch; **art directors,** Cedric Gibbons and Randall Duell; **set decorators,** Edwin B. Willis and Jacques Mapes; **costumes,** Walter Plunkett; **makeup,** William Tuttle; **sound,** Douglas Shearer; **special effects,** Warren Newcombe and Irving Ries; **camera,** Harold Rosson and John Alton; **editor,** Adrienne Fazan.

Gene Kelly (**Don Lockwood**); Donald O'Connor (**Cosmo Brown**); Debbie Reynolds (**Kathy Selden**); Jean Hagen (**Lina Lamont**); Millard Mitchell (**R. F. Simpson**); Rita Moreno (**Zelda Zanders**); Douglas V. Fowley (**Roscoe Dexter**); Cyd Charisse (**Dancer**); Madge Blake (**Dora Bailey**); King Donovan (**Rod**); Kathleen Freeman (**Phoebe Dinsmore**); Bobby Watson (**Diction Coach**); Dan Foster (**Assistant Director**); Tommy Farrell (**Sid Phillips, the Assistant Director**); Margaret Bert (**Wardrobe Woman**); Mae Clarke (**Hairdresser**); Judy Landon (**Olga Mara**); John Dodsworth (**Baron de la May de la Toulon**); Bill Lewin (**Bert, Villain in Western**); Dennis Ross (**Don as a Boy**); Richard Emory (**Phil, the Cowboy Hero**); Julius Tannen (**Man on Screen**); Dawn Addams and Elaine Stewart (**Ladies in Waiting**); Wilson Wood (**Vallee Impersonator**); Dave Sharpe and Russ Saunders (**Fencers**); Joi Lansing, Charles Evans, William Lester, and Dorothy Patrick (**Audience**); Jac George (**Orchestra Leader**).

SYNOPSIS
Don Lockwood, vaudevillian-turned-movie-stunt-man-turned-star, and Lina Lamont, blonde, egomaniacal, and idiotic, are the greatest stars of the Hollywood silent cinema. Though Don can scarcely abide the narcissistic, screechy-voiced Lina, he plays her wooer to the press to solidify their screen image.

Enjoying his stellar status with old vaudeville partner Cosmo Brown, a studio musician, Don becomes very attracted to Kathy Selden. She feels that movies are a bastard art and refuses to be impressed by the screen celebrity. Don is ensuingly delighted when his "legitimate" friend, as a hired performer, jumps out of a cake to Charleston in skimpy attire at a party. She further charms

Gene Kelly in Singin' in the Rain *('52).*

him when, throwing a cake at Don who has irritated her, she misses him and scores a bull's-eye on Lina's lacquered face.

At the party R. F. Simpson, chief of Monumental Pictures where Don and Lina are under contract, shows a talking picture. With sound revolutionizing Hollywood, Simpson decided the latest Lockwood-Lamont vehicle, **The Dueling Cavalier,** must have sound. Thus director Roscoe Dexter tries to outfit the company with sound but problems abound. Lina takes a most unfeminine pratfall when her microphone wires tangle and she trips. Later, the worst disaster of all occurs. At the preview the audience howls at the poor sound synchronization and at Lina's horrid speaking voice.

It appears that the screen love team is doomed. But Cosmo comes up with a novel idea—why not transform **The Dueling Cavalier** into a musical and have Kathy, now Don's girlfriend, dub Lina's voice? The result is terrific; so great, in fact, that Lina bullies Simpson into restricting Kathy's screen career to being Lina's movie voice.

It appears the bitchy Lina will triumph. However, at the premiere, an enormous success, the audience gives the stars a tremendous ovation and shouts for Lina to sing! Kathy is rushed behind the curtain to perform "Singin' in the Rain" as Lina pantomimes in front of the curtain. Meanwhile, Don, Cosmo, and Simpson, all having the same vengeful thought, yank up the curtain. The audience shrieks with laughter at Lina's vocal secret. Lina makes a hasty exit and Don informs the audience that it was Kathy whose voice they applauded that night.

Consequently, Don Lockwood and Kathy Sel-

den are the new stellar love team of Monumental Pictures.

* * *

"I've made a lot of films that were bigger hits and made a lot more money, but now they look dated. But this one, out of all my pictures, has a chance to last." So spoke Gene Kelly in 1977. "The picture was made with love. We weren't putting down Hollywood. And everything in it is true," added the dancing-singing star. "It all really happened when movies went into sound."

The genesis of **Singin' in the Rain** was a strange one. Betty Comden and Adolph Green won the assignment of writing a musical script that would employ Arthur Freed and Nacio Herb Brown tunes. Most of the songs available had been written during Hollywood's transition from silents to sound, so the scenarists decided to create a movie-based satire set in that era.

The scripters toyed with the idea of musicalizing an old Metro classic—**Bombshell** (1933) received special consideration. And with resident baritone Howard Keel then very popular, the team also thought of writing a saga of a Western star who becomes a singing cowboy with the advent of talkies.[1] But the disastrous effects of sound on the silent-film industry kept coming into discussion. The writers would say later: "We remembered particularly the downfall of John Gilbert, the reigning king of the silent screen in 1928, whose career was finished off by one single talking picture, in which, with his director's encour-

---

[1]Keel would make a comedy about a cowboy star who enjoys a comeback when his old films are shown on TV. It was entitled **Callaway Went Thataway** (1951).

agement, he improvised his own love scene, insisting on the phrase 'I love you,' repeated many times with growing intensity, exactly as he had done it the year before in front of the silent camera."

As the property evolved, the Gilbert role underwent a sex change; he became Lina Lamont, the silver screen bitch whose monstrosity of a voice is dubbed over by sweet-toned ingenue Kathy Selden. The satiric, light tone of the film appeared to require a song-and-dance performer, not Howard Keel. Comden and Green timidly sent the script to Gene Kelly, who was just completing **An American in Paris.** They expected a certain no from the exhausted artist.

Instead, Kelly appeared enthralled by the story and the role of Don Lockwood. He gave his full-hearted support. Donald O'Connor was added as Cosmo,[2] Debbie Reynolds as Kathy, Jean Hagen as Lina.[3] The songs included "Would You?" "Singin' in the Rain," "All I Do Is Dream of You," "I've Got a Feeling You're Fooling," "Wedding of the Painted Doll," "Should I?" "Make 'em Laugh," "You Were Meant for Me," "You Are My Lucky Star," "Fit as a Fiddle and Ready for Love," "Good Morning," "Moses," and "Beautiful Girl."[4]

Preparations for this spoof of the old Hollywood were extensive. As reported in Hugh Fordin's **The World of Entertainment** (1975):

Turning the clock back on Hollywood was not as simple as it might look to the casual observer. Randall Duell and set decorator Jacques Mapes spent months unearthing designs for the actual cubicle to house the cameras. Those early microphones had to be recreated from originals long since relegated to museums. Old Cooper-Hewitt stage lights were built to specifications and early recording and dubbing equipment was reproduced. Twenty-

[2]Oscar Levant was the original choice. However, the writers, Kelly, and director Stanley Donen begged for Donald O'Connor, as they wanted a dancer.

[3]Nina Foch, fresh from her Milo Roberts' role in **An American in Paris,** was tested without any positive results. Among the others wanting the Lina Lamont role was MGM contractee Jane Greer.

[4]The tunes were all "veterans" of MGM pictures. "Would You?" had been in **San Francisco**; "Singin' in the Rain" in **Hollywood Revue of 1929** and **Little Nellie Kelly** (as well as Universal's **Hi, Beautiful**); "All I Do Is Dream of You" in **Sadie McKee, Broadway Melody of 1936** (in French, and deleted), and **Andy Hardy Meets Debutante**; "I've Got a Feeling You're Fooling" in **Broadway Melody of 1936**; "Wedding of the Painted Doll" in **The Broadway Melody**; "Should I?" in **Lord Byron of Broadway**; "You Were Meant for Me" in **The Broadway Melody, Hollywood Revue of 1929,** as well as Warner Bros' **Show of Shows** and Twentieth Century–Fox's **You Were Meant for Me**; "You Are My Lucky Star" in **Broadway Melody of 1936, Babes in Arms,** and **Born to Sing**; "Good Morning" in **Babes in Arms**; "Beautiful Girl" in **Stage Mother** and **Going Hollywood.**

"Fit as a Fiddle" had appeared in Warner Bros' **College Coach**; "Make 'em Laugh" (the last song written by the team of Freed and Brown, was an unabashed copy of Cole Porter's "Be a Clown") was especially created for O'Connor for this picture; "Moses" was written by Comden, Green, and Roger Edens.

five-year-old still photos of the MGM studio played an important role in duplicating the studio of Monumental Pictures. Even an old glass soundstage, last remaining relic of the early days, was pressed into service. The stage, for many years used as a building for the construction of equipment, was emptied, and once again, those glass walls heard the grinding of an old silent camera and the inevitable 'Hearts and Flowers,' played as mood music by musicians on the set. For the mansion occupied by Kelly, as an early-day movie star, Duell-Mapes used the same tables, chairs, rugs, and chandeliers that graced the rooms in which Gilbert and Garbo romanced in **Flesh and the Devil.** Debbie Reynolds even used Andy Hardy's old jalopy.

While there were prevailing high spirits on the set, there were also problems, most of them supplied by Debbie Reynolds.[5] The nineteen-year-old former Miss Burbank of 1948 was cast in this expensive musical, after appearing in MGM's **Three Little Words** (1950) and **Mr. Imperium** (1951). It was a gamble by Kelly and Donen, and her early lack of professionalism proved a trial. Kelly said recently, "There were times when Debbie Reynolds was more interested in playing the French horn somewhere in the San Fernando Valley or going to a Girl Scout meeting. She didn't realize she was a movie star all of a sudden." Miss Reynolds herself admitted:

I was so confused. It seemed dumb to me that people were killing themselves—reporting to the studio at 6 A.M. six days a week and shooting until midnight. I didn't know anything about show business. I learned a lot from Gene. He is a perfectionist and a disciplinarian—the most exacting director I've ever worked for. And he has a good temper. Every so often he would yell at me and make me cry. But it took a lot of patience for him to work with someone who had never danced before. It's amazing that I could keep up with him and Donald O'Connor. This little girl from Burbank sure had a lot of spirit.

It took more than Debbie's **joie de vivre** to keep her momentum. Ironically, while Debbie was playing a girl who dubs for a star, she herself was dubbed in the singing by Betty Royce. The irony was compounded by the fact that Jean Hagen was an exceptionally talented actress with great vocal skill, whereas Debbie was handicapped by what director Donen called "that terrible Western noise"; hence, Jean dubbed Debbie dubbing Jean.

A special highlight of **Singin' in the Rain** was the "Broadway Rhythm" ballet, featuring a vampy Cyd Charisse as the guest artist. Gene Kelly would

[5]In 1974 at a New York City benefit for the Collective for Living Cinema, Debbie Reynolds would say about **Singin' in the Rain,** "The kiss at the end of that picture was my first French kiss. I didn't know what it was, but now I've learned to like them. Oh, could I tell you some stories about Gene Kelly!" On a more serious note, the actress mentioned that her vocals were dubbed without her knowledge; MGM did it while Debbie was on a personal appearance tour of Loew's theatres.

comment in 1979 at an American Film Institute symposium re the "Broadway Rhythm" ballet:

Donald O'Connor and I needed a third duet together, and the studio wanted it. But we found out that Donald had another contract; he was to get on "The Colgate Comedy Hour" on a certain date. We had already shot a scene where Donald and I tell the producer, modeled after Arthur Freed, how great the dance scene is going to be, and then the camera moves toward a blank screen. We had that, but no Donald O'Connor—and Debbie Reynolds wasn't a strong enough dancer to carry a pure dance scene alone. So we got Cyd Charisse and just wrote a whole new ballet and stuck it in. That's how it came about. We had to have a number there. We never meant it to be that long, but since we were introducing a new character into the show, we had to keep adding to it and adding to it. It went on for hours, it seems.

The ballet took a month to rehearse and two weeks to shoot, at a cost of $600,000. Jeanine Basinger in **Gene Kelly** (1976) reflects:

"Broadway Rhythm" provides Kelly with a chance to metamorphose from a comically exaggerated hick dancer into a sleekly tuxedoed success. Thus, the two halves of his persona are both given a chance, and the development of one out of the other is cleverly presented in a short space of choreographic time. Kelly dances in several styles again, although the emphasis is more on tap than on ballet, the opposite of the emphasis in **An American in Paris.** The ballet also pairs Kelly for the first time with Cyd Charisse, who functions equally well as a lowdown funky gold-digger and as Kelly's romantic vision of her as a loving feminine presence.

Singin' in the Rain opened in April 1952. It was one of the last Metro features to have the stamp of approval of Louis B. Mayer. The longtime mogul was officially replaced by Dore Schary on June 22, 1951, three days after **Singin' in the Rain** began shooting.

Bosley Crowther **(New York Times)** wrote of the film, "This song-and-dance contrivance is an impudent, offhand comedy about the outlandish making of movies back in the sheik-and-flapper days when they were bridging the perilous chasm from silent to talking films. . . . At times it reaches the level of first-class satiric burlesque."

The color feature abounds in sparkling moments: Kelly's classic rain dance ("The real work for this one was done by the technicians who had to pipe two city blocks on the back lot with overhead sprays, and the poor cameraman who had to shoot through all that water. All I had to do was dance"); O'Connor's "Make 'em Laugh" song-aerobatic dance routine (one of the top crowd pleasers of **That's Entertainment!** (1974); the gaiety of Debbie Reynolds; and the magnificent hammy performance of Jean Hagen. Her Lina Lamont of Lilyan Tashman fashion and Minnie Mouse voice won her a Best Supporting Actress

Oscar nomination and nearly stole the entire picture. **Singin' in the Rain** would gross $7,655,000 in distributors' domestic rentals.

At the American Film Institute forum, Gene Kelly would reminisce about **Singin' in the Rain:**

Donald O'Connor was always making us laugh, and so I said, "Let's do a number called 'Make 'Em Laugh.' " It was all improvisation. The difficulty of doing choreography for it was that Donald was a spontaneous artist and comedian, and he never could do anything the same twice. And so to put it on the same beat, my assistants, Carol Haney and Jeannie Coyne, and I would sit there with a note pad, and he would just do tricks, and we'd put them on one beat. We'd say, "Do it again" or "No, you did that on the first beat," and so he would adjust for the first beat.

He was so funny that we couldn't contain ourselves. There was no way a director or choreographer could say, "Do it this way and it will be funnier." There's no way you can write that stuff. The dummy he uses in the dance, for example, was lying on a rehearsal stage next door to us. We walked in there one day, and Donald started to fool around with it. For half an hour we just roared with laughter. Finally we said, "Well, let's put that in the number." To get the beats where he'd slap his head on the musical counts was most difficult.

All of that number came right out of Donald. None of it was imposed on him, except for the finish. I wanted him to do the trick that he had done as a little boy in vaudeville. So we got his brother over to rehearse him with a rope to get his confidence back and then to break through the wall at the end. The rest was all his, and it was unbelievable. We had to throw out twenty minutes of it.

The musical continues to win disciples. In 1971 the **New Yorker** magazine reported. "This exuberant and malicious satire of Hollywood in the late twenties is perhaps the most enjoyable of all movie musicals. Gene Kelly, Donald O'Connor, and Debbie Reynolds are the stars, assisted by Jean Hagen as an imbecile movie queen, Millard Mitchell as a producer, Cyd Charisse as a dancer, and Rita Moreno as a flapper-actress."

Kelly today says of the feature, "Fifty years from now, it may seem dated or silly. Who knows? But I still like it myself. It still makes me laugh.

SOME CAME RUNNING
1958 C—134 min.

Producer, Sol C. Siegel; **director,** Vincente Minnelli; based on the novel by James Jones; **screenplay,** John Patrick and Arthur Sheekman; **music,** Elmer Bernstein; **song,** Sammy Cahn and James Van Heusen; **art directors,** William A. Horning and Urie McCleary; **set decorators,** Henry Grace and Robert Priestley; **color consultant,** Charles K. Hagedon; **makeup,** William Tuttle; **costumes,** Walter Plunkett; **assistant director,** William

McGarry; **sound,** Franklin Milton; **camera,** William H. Daniels; **editor,** Adrienne Fazan.

Frank Sinatra **(Dave Hirsh);** Dean Martin **(Bama Dillert);** Shirley MacLaine **(Ginny Moorhead);** Martha Hyer **(Gwen French);** Arthur Kennedy **(Frank Hirsh);** Nancy Gates **(Edith Barclay);** Leora Dana **(Agnes Hirsh);** Betty Lou Keim **(Dawn Hirsh);** Larry Gates **(Professor Robert Haven French);** Steven Peck **(Raymond Lanchak);** Carmen Phillips **(Rosalie);** Connie Gilchrist **(Jane Barclay);** Ned Wever **(Smitty);** John Brennan **(Wally Dennis).**

SYNOPSIS

Following a wanderlust career as a writer and a stint in the U.S. Army, Dave Hirsh returns to his hometown of Parkman, Illinois, accompanied by an unpublished manuscript and a mirthful whore named Ginny Moorhead, who loves him. Dave inspires various reactions upon his arrival: resentment from stuffy, successful businessman brother Frank, who is carrying on an affair with his jewelry shop assistant Edith Barclay; snobbish indifference from his sister-in-law Agnes; sexual attraction from college instructor Gwen French, who also finds appeal in Dave's writing; and friendship from carefree gambler Bama Dillert, who adopts Dave as a carousing crony in the world of cards, whiskey, and women. Bama, incidentally, is dying of diabetes and, being superstitious, never removes his hat for fear of bad luck.

Dave and Gwen soon form a romance, as she

Frank Sinatra and Connie Gilchrist in Some Came Running *('58).*

succeeds in selling his writing to the **Atlantic Monthly.** However, Gwen suffers from frigidity, and when Dave fails to thaw her reserve by proposing marriage, the writer embarks on a binge with Bama and the ever-patient Ginny.

In Terra Haute, Dave discovers his niece Dawn, who ran away from home when she learned of her father's affair with his secretary. Dave returns the runaway to her home, lambastes her parents for their hypocrisy, and marries the earthy Ginny—a union of which even Bama disapproves.

At a carnival, a former flame of Ginny's arrives and jealously aims his gun at Dave; Ginny fatally blocks the shot. At the funeral Bama, in an ultimate tribute, removes his hat.

* * *

Since his Oscar-winning role in **From Here to Eternity** (1953), Frank Sinatra had progressively become a bigger and bigger cinema star. Since his amazingly deft dramatic performance in **The Young Lions** (1958), Dean Martin was becoming more respected as a major talent and less remembered as Jerry Lewis's stooge. And since **Around the World in 80 Days** (1956), Shirley MacLaine was maturing into one of the screen's most charming females. Hence, it was a profitable venture for MGM to team the three stars in **Some Came Running,** based on the bestselling novel by James Jones, author of **From Here to Eternity.** As directed by Vincente Minnelli, the project offered the three personalities tailor-made assignments: Sinatra as a disillusioned, aimless writer,[1] Martin as a carousing gambler, and MacLaine as a hell-raising, heart-of-gold tramp, not above self-sacrifice of any degree.

In **I Remember It Well** (1974) Minnelli recalls the novel that inspired the film:

The James Jones novel was long and rambling, heavily populated, but I felt the main characters were interesting and well thought out. I never met Jones, nor was he otherwise involved in the production, so our adaptation would be purely our own.

Jones, however, had described the theme of the book as being about "the separation between human beings—the fact that no two people ever totally get together; that everyone wants to be loved **more** than they want to love." Why he should take seven years and 1,266 pages in which to state that premise was a subject of some controversy when the book was published the previous January.

John Patrick and Arthur Sheekman trimmed the novel into a relatively compact screenplay. With superb performers Arthur Kennedy and Martha Hyer added to the scenario, the company or **Some Came Running** traveled to Madison, Indiana, where Minnelli reveled in locating garish, honky-tonk-type backgrounds for his story of "cheap low lives not without charm." If the denizens of Madison did not resent the implication that their town was a hotbed of similar breeds, they soon resented Sinatra and his inimitable

style of antagonizing the public. In his book **Sinatra** (1976), columnist Earl Wilson lists assorted episodes which later earned Sinatra a shellacking not only from the Hoosiers of Indiana, but also from **Time** magazine:

Girls were brought in to entertain the stars. Strolling the streets with a drink in his hand, Frank commented picturesquely about the native girls, saying he preferred the importees. Declining to visit the local country club, he crossed the river into Kentucky with Dean Martin to hunt a floating crap game.

In the morning "his eyes would look like two urine spots in the snow," a studio publicist said, "and when I saw his hangover look I would keep walking."

Frank was said to have referred to local women as "broads, finks and old hags!"

. . . Because he was Sinatra, Frank was accused of ripping phones off walls, pushing people, and other misbehavior that was never proved.

After three madly publicized weeks in Madison, the company moved back to Culver City where, at Sinatra's command, shooting ran daily from 12 to 8 rather than 9 to 5 ("Performers work better in the afternoon and the girls looked better," reasoned Sinatra). The picture proceeded to a smooth completion and, upon its release in late 1958 (producer Sol Siegel was confident that the film had Oscar possibilities, so he managed a few qualifying 1958 bookings before general distribution in 1959), critical reaction was almost ridiculously diversified. **Time,** curiously ired by Sinatra's Madison peccadilloes, attested that only the season's **The Vikings** and **A Farewell to Arms,** released shortly before **Some Came Running,** "were even more absurdly awful" than Metro's release. **Time** attacked the film's assumptions that "small towns are places in which respected people lead secret lives of shocking depravity, rich men are usually stuffed shirts, a man who cannot hold his liquor is less than a man, the boss usually sleeps with his secretary, teachers are frigid, prostitutes have hearts of gold, bars are interesting places, there is honor among thieves, culture is for the birds, Hemingway and Faulkner are the greatest writers who ever lived." But even **Time** in its diatribe had to admit there were "occasional flickers of brilliant overacting by Shirley MacLaine."

On the other hand, **Variety** said the lengthy film was "certainly one of the most exciting pictures of the season" and praised the "sardonic and compassionate acting" of Sinatra, the "grace and humor" of Martin, the "shattering performance" of MacLaine, the "playing of a high order," of Hyer, the "fine character study" of Kennedy, and nearly every facet of the "brilliantly directed" film.

Oscar nominations did ensue for MacLaine (for whom the picture was a special triumph even though she lost to Susan Hayward of **I Want to Live!**), Arthur Kennedy (his fifth Academy Award nomination; he lost to Burl Ives of **The Big Country**), and Martha Hyer, who gave the film's finest performance (she lost to Wendy Hiller of **Separate**

Tables); her seduction by Sinatra gave the picture its most subtle, memorable vignette. Some wags felt Miss Hyer deserved a special award for her tasteful, above-and-beyond-the-call-of-duty defenses of Sinatra during the various atrocities in Madison. Not to be overlooked was Elmer Bernstein's pulsating score, which underlined the contrasting dramatic moments within the film.

The public sided with the critics who had cheered **Some Came Running.** The picture joined **North by Northwest** as MGM's top earners of the 1958–59 season, the Minnelli film grossing $4,392,000.

STATE OF THE UNION
1948—124 min. (British release title: THE WORLD AND HIS WIFE)

Producer, Frank Capra; **associate producer,** Anthony Veiller; **director,** Capra; based on the play by Howard Lindsay and Russel Crouse; **screenplay,** Veiller and Myles Connolly; **art directors,** Cedric Gibbons and Urie McCleary; **set decorator,** Emile Kuri; **music,** Victor Young; **assistant director,** Arthur S. Black, Jr.; **costumes,** Irene; **sound,** Douglas Shearer; **special effects,** A. Arnold Gillespie; **camera,** George J. Folsey; **editor,** William Hornbeck.

Spencer Tracy **(Grant Matthews);** Katharine Hepburn **(Mary Matthews);** Van Johnson **(Spike McManus);** Angela Lansbury **(Kay Thorndyke);** Adolphe Menjou **(Jim Conover);** Lewis Stone **(Sam Thorndyke);** Howard Smith **(Sam Parrish);** Maidel Turner **(Lulubelle Alexander);** Raymond Walburn **(Judge Alexander);** Charles Dingle **(Bill Hardy);** Florence Auer **(Grace Orval Draper);** Pierre Watkin **(Senator Lauterback);** Margaret Hamilton **(Norah);** Irving Bacon **(Buck);** Patti Brady **(Joyce);** George Nokes **(Grant, Jr.);** Carl Switzer **(Bellboy);** Tom Pedi **(Barber);** Tom Fadden **(Waiter);** Charles Lane **(Blink Moran);** Art Baker **(Leith);** Rhea Mitchell **(Jenny);** Arthur O'Connell **(Reporter);** Marion Martin **(Blonde Girl);** Stanley Andrews **(Senator);** Dave Willock **(Pilot);** Dell Henderson **(Broder);** Francis Pierlot **(Josephs);** Roger Moore, Gene Coogan, Wilson Wood, Harry Anderson, Charles Coleman, Stanley Price, and Jack Boyle **(Photographers);** Bert Moorhouse and Thornton Edwards **(Men).**

SYNOPSIS

When Grant Matthews makes a bid for the Republican presidential nomination, his estranged wife, Mary, returns to him and they play the charade of being a very happily wed couple.

It is, however, a sad ordeal for Mary. She sees her husband fall in love with ambitious newspaper publisher Kay Thorndike. Moreover, on the advice of crafty campaign manager Jim Conover, Grant steadily discards his idealism to snare the nomination.

Mary's emotions climax at a dinner party. Fearing she has lost Grant to Kay's clutches and thus having nothing to lose, she makes an impassioned speech, lambasting the pomposity and

---

[1]At one juncture in early 1957 Marlon Brando was being touted for the lead role in **Some Came Running.**

hypocrisy of the politicians present. Grant, lamenting what has happened to his life and his ideals, leaves Kay. He returns to Mary, calling himself "unworthy." Thereafter he confesses his indiscretions to the public and retires from the presidential contest.

* * *

In October 1947 the historic Hollywood anti-Communist hunt was launched. Political dramas, never the most profitable of screen efforts, suddenly appeared a taboo subject. Thus, only by courage, class, and an inordinate amount of bureaucratic maneuvering did **State of the Union** reach the screen. It was an amazing feat to occur in what was perhaps Hollywood's most reactionary era.

The Howard Lindsay–Russel Crouse play had opened on Broadway at the Hudson Theatre on November 14, 1945, starring Ralph Bellamy and Ruth Hussey (an ex-MGM contractee). It played 765 performances and was a sellout on tour. The screen rights were acquired by Liberty Pictures, a corporation established by directors Frank Capra, William Wyler, George Stevens, and producer Samuel Briskin. The independent outfit originally planned to release nine features through RKO, the first being **It's a Wonderful Life** (1946). However, when Capra presented RKO with a $2.8 million budget for **State of the Union,** the studio balked and the proposed film appeared doomed.

Enter MGM. Spencer Tracy had long wanted to play the Bellamy role of Grant Matthews. In the tradition of **Gone With the Wind,** Metro offered their star and financing in exchange for Liberty's distribution rights. Capra agreed and was delighted with the leading stars provided by the studio: Tracy and Claudette Colbert, the latter having won an Oscar for Capra's **It Happened One Night** (1934).

But Claudette never played a scene in the picture. In his autobiography, **The Name Above the Title** (1971), Capra recalls why:

And here she comes into my office looking as cute and bright and stand-offish as she did fourteen years ago in **It Happened One Night.** She had matured into a real top star now; her price, two hundred thousand dollars per picture!

"Frank," she opened up businesslike, "I just read my contract. You left out that I was not to work one minute after five o'clock on any day."

"What? You never mentioned five o'clock"

"I must have. My agent puts it into all my contracts now. My doctor says I get too tired." Her agent was her brother, and her doctor was her husband.

"Claudette, this is a big, expensive picture. I **can't** tie my hands to a seven-hour shooting day—"

"Frank, those are **your** problems. I have to quit work at five. And if it isn't in my contract I won't sign it."

She did not sign it. With shooting to commence the following Monday, Claudette walked out of the office after being ordered by Capra to return her $15,000 wardrobe. When Capra phoned

Adolphe Menjou, Katharine Hepburn, and Spencer Tracy in State of the Union *('48).*

Tracy with the bad news, the star suggested Katharine Hepburn.[1] "The bag of bones has been helping me rehearse. Kinda stops you, Frank, the way she reads the woman's part. She's a real theatre nut, you know. She might do it for the hell of it." By Monday morning, Hepburn was contracted and shooting had begun.

Capra continues "In **State of the Union** my hardest directing job was trying to keep four other great pros—Adolphe Menjou, Van Johnson, Angela Lansbury, and Lewis Stone—from stealing too many scenes from the two champs." However, there was another rather touchy problem. While Hepburn had spoken out against the "smear campaign" of HUAC chairman J. Parnell Thomas, Menjou had happily cooperated with the committee. He voiced the view that if Communism came to America, he would move to Texas, because "Texans would shoot them on sight." With reporters anxious to stir up friction on the set, Capra ordered the soundstage closed as Hepburn and Menjou performed their tandem scenes with stony silence. It was a sad contrast to their pleasant working rapport years before in RKO's **Morning Glory** (1933) and **Stage Door** (1937).

State of the Union premiered in May 1948 at the Capitol Theatre in Washington, D.C. President Harry S. Truman and daughter Margaret were in the audience. Reviews were mixed. **Time** magazine: "To sustain the illusion of interest, wonder-worker Capra relies on a blaze of star power. . . . But Tracy, as in all his recent pictures, lacks fire; Hepburn's affectation of talking like a woman simultaneously to steady a loose dental brace sharply limits her range of expression; Johnson, playing a Drew Pearsonish columnist, is no more effective than Pearson would be playing Johnson; Menjou (in a double-breasted vest) is rather more Menjou than politician. Only Lansbury, whom Metro has long dieted on lean parts, does any real acting. As the adderish lady publisher, she sinks a fine fang." On the other hand, Howard Barnes of the **New York Herald-**

[1]Hepburn had been among the stars—Helen Hayes and Margaret Sullavan were the others—who had rejected the Pulitzer Prize–winning play when it was originally being cast for the stage.

Tribune, praised the work as "a triumphant film, marked all over by Frank Capra's artistry." And the **New York Times'** Bosley Crowther added, "Mr. Tracy is glib and delightful as the gentleman who would rather be right than be the Republican candidate for president and Miss Hepburn is charming as his wife."

Today, **State of the Union** maintains less of its political wallop and serves more as another example of the Tracy-Hepburn talents. As Capra wrote, when they "played a scene, cameras, lights, microphones, and written scripts ceased to exist. And the director did just what the crews and other actors did—sat, watched, and marveled."

THE STRATTON STORY
1949—106 min.

Producer, Jack Cummings; **director,** Sam Wood; **story,** Douglas Morrow; **screenplay,** Morrow and Guy Trosper; **music director,** Adolph Deutsch; **art directors,** Cedric Gibbons and Paul Groesse; **set decorators,** Edwin B. Willis and Ralph S. Hurst; **assistant director,** Sid Sidman; **makeup,** Jack Dawn; **technical adviser,** Monty Stratton; **costumes,** Helen Rose; **sound,** Douglas Shearer and Charles E. Wallace; **montage,** Peter Ballbusch; **special effects,** A. Arnold Gillespie and Warren Newcombe; **camera,** Harold Rosson; **editor,** Ben Lewis.

James Stewart (**Monty Stratton**); June Allyson (**Ethel**); Frank Morgan (**Barney Wile**); Agnes Moorehead (**Ma Stratton**); Bill Williams (**Gene Watson**); Bruce Cowling (**Ted Lyons**); Eugene Bearden (**Western All-Stars Pitcher**); Bill Dickey and Jimmy Dykes (**Themselves**); Rogert Gist (**Larnie**); Mervyn Shea (**White Sox Catcher**); Pat Flaherty (**Western All-Stars Manager**); Captain F. G. Somers (**Giants Manager**); Mitchell Lewis (**Conductor**); Michael Ross (**Pitcher**); Florence Lake (**Mrs. Appling**); Anne Nagel (**Mrs. Piet**); Barbara Wooddell (**Mrs. Shea**); Alphonse Martel (**Headwaiter**); Holmes Herbert (**Doctor**); Lee Tung Foo (**Waiter**); Kenneth Tobey (**Detroit Pitcher**); Charles B. Smith (**Theatre Usher**).

SYNOPSIS
Barney Wile, a former big leaguer and now a hobo, sees Monty Stratton win a sandlot game in Greenville, Texas, and tells him he should try out with a major league team. Stratton invites Wile to spend the winter as a helping hand on the family farm and during the next few months—between farm chores—Barney coaches Monty on the fine points of pitching.

With the coming of spring Monty, over the objections of his practical-minded mother, hitchhikes to California with Wile. There, Jimmy Dykes, the White Sox manager and an old acquaintance of Wile's, gives Stratton a tryout. The newcomer is signed to a contract. During training Monty meets and falls in love with Ethel. Professionally

James Stewart and June Allyson in The Stratton Story *('49).*

he does not fare so well. He is knocked out of the box by the New York Yankees on his first professional appearance and is sent to a farm team for seasoning. Recalled, after he makes an impression in the minor leagues, Monty marries Ethel and returns to Chicago. There he becomes the freshman sensation of the league and by the next season wins great fame. He also becomes the father of a son. A brilliant future awaits.

But tragedy strikes. Monty, while hunting on the farm, accidentally shoots himself in the leg. The limb has to be amputated to save his life. Stratton loses all interest in living until he sees his young toddler trying to take his first steps. He resolves to learn to walk, and soon masters the use of an artificial leg.

Through Ethel's prodding he regains his pitching form, and now refuses to concede that he cannot make a successful comeback. He arranges to play in an all-star game and pitches well, helping his team win. The acclaim of the crowd renews his courage to carry on in the old style.

* * *

MGM had suffered a jarring shock after World War II when James Stewart, who had risen through the studio grooming process to become one of the lot's great stars, refused to re-sign with the company. Stewart was seeking contracts elsewhere which would eventually allow him percentage-of-the-profits deals. Louis B. Mayer was aghast at such a demand—surely such a move would eventually destroy the industry! Nevertheless, under such terms Stewart returned to MGM to replace Van Johnson in one of Hollywood's

greatest hits of the late forties. It was the screen biography of Monty Stratton, whose baseball career was stymied—temporarily in 1938—by the loss of a leg in a hunting accident.

Produced by Jack Cummings, **The Stratton Story** was directed by Sam Wood, who had so poignantly controlled Samuel Goldwyn's **The Pride of the Yankees**, the 1942 film about Lou Gehrig. **The Stratton Story** benefited from a number of excellent points: June Allyson in perhaps her best homey performance as Stratton's patient wife; Frank Morgan as Barney Wile, the big leaguer-turned-hobo who discovers Stratton's talents on a Greenville, Texas, sandlot; the presence of Agnes Moorehead as the ballplayer's devoted mother; and, especially, the restrained, powerful performance of Stewart himself. The actor's constant control of the part, which might easily have toppled into bathos (especially in the sequence where Stratton is inspired to try again by the sight of his little son taking his first steps), was superb. It ranks as one of the star's finest hours, certainly making all the hours of baseball practice worthwhile for Stewart.

There was a Radio City Music Hall premiere for **The Stratton Story** when it was released in May 1949. Bosley Crowther recorded for the **New York Times**:

Call it luck or what you will, but the circumstances which took Van Johnson off the mound and brought James Stewart in as the star of **The Stratton Story** was the best thing that has yet happened to Mr. Stewart in his postwar film career. For in the new picture

. . . [he] gives such a winning performance that it is almost impossible to imagine anyone else playing the role of the Chicago White Sox pitcher. . . . it would be gross injustice to slight the affecting contribution of June Allyson as Mrs. Stratton, or the good taste evidenced by the authors and the fine direction provided by Sam Wood . . . Monty Stratton is one of the few living persons to have his life dramatized by Hollywood. Moreover, he is that even rarer individual who may view with pride the manner in which his story has been set before the world to bring comfort and courage to the afflicted and to remind the rest of us just how well off we are.

The Stratton Story would gross $4 million in distributors' domestic rentals. It would place fifth in the **Film Daily** Ten Best Picture Poll, and win the **Photoplay** Gold Medal of 1949 for actor Stewart, and for best picture. Douglas Morrow won an Oscar for the Best Motion Picture Story.

The year 1949 was important to Stewart not only for the career-propelling **The Stratton Story**, but also because the longtime bachelor first married—Gloria Hatrich McLean, a nonprofessional, who had two small sons by her previous marriage. Stewart and Allyson would be reunited twice: Universal's **The Glenn Miller Story** (1954) and Paramount's **Strategic Air Command** (1955), both directed by Anthony Mann. In the latter Stewart plays a ball player again, this time one called back into active military service.

Sam Wood, the director of **The Stratton Story**, would make one more film, MGM's **Ambush** (1950), starring Robert Taylor. The picture maker, who had helmed such Metro features as Joan Crawford's **Paid** (1930), the Marx Brothers' **A Night at the Opera** (1935) and **A Day at the Races** (1937), and Clark Gable's **Command Decision** (1948), died on September 22, 1949, at the age of sixty-five.

SUMMER HOLIDAY
1948 C—92 min.

Producer, Arthur Freed; **director**, Rouben Mamoulian; based on the play **Ah, Wilderness!** by Eugene O'Neill; **screenplay**, Frances Goodrich and Albert Hackett; **adapters**, Irving Brecher and Jean Holloway; **songs**, Harry Warren and Ralph Blane; **music director**, Lennie Hayton; **orchestrator**, Conrad Salinger; **choreography**, Charles Walters; **vocal arrangers**, Robert Tucker and Blane; **Technicolor consultants**, Natalie Kalmus and Henri Jaffa; **art directors**, Cedric Gibbons and Jack Martin Smith; **set decorators**, Edwin B. Willis and Richard Pefferle; **costumes**, Irene and Walter Plunkett; **makeup**, Jack Dawn; **sound**, Douglas Shearer; **camera**, Charles Schoenbaum; **editor**, Albert Akst.

Mickey Rooney (**Richard Miller**); Gloria De-Haven (**Muriel**); Walter Huston (**Nat Miller**); Frank Morgan (**Uncle Sid**); Jackie "Butch" Jenkins (**Tommy Miller**); Marilyn Maxwell (**Belle**); Agnes Moorehead (**Cousin Lillie**); Selena Royle (**Mrs. Miller**); Michael

Kirby (**Arthur Miller**); Shirley Johns (**Mildred Miller**); Hal Hackett (**Wint**); Anne Francis (**Elsie Rand**); John Alexander (**Mr. Macomber**); Virginia Brissac (**Miss Hawley**); Howard Freeman (**Mr. Peabody**); Alice MacKenzie (**Mrs. Macomber**); Don Garner (**Gilbert Ralston**); Ruth Brady (**Crystal**); Emory Parnell (**Bartender**); Wally Cassell (**Salesman**); Terry Moore (**Hatcheck Girl**); Francis Stevens and Budd Fine (**Farmers**); Louise Colombet, Blanche Rose, Margaret Fealey, and Nell Spaugh (**Old Painting Characters**); Oliver Blake (**Scorekeeper**); Margaret Bert (**Mrs. Nichols**).

SYNOPSIS

In 1906, in a small Connecticut town, the Millers are a typical American family: Nat Miller is the newspaper editor, Mrs. Miller is a busy but well-satisfied wife and mother, seventeen-year-old Richard is the high school valedictorian with revolutionary ideas about how to make a better world, Tommy is the precocious younger brother, Cousin Lillie is the spinster aunt, and Uncle Sid is a bachelor cousin whose weakness for drink once caused Lillie to break their engagement.

Richard is disillusioned when ordered to stay away from schoolmate Muriel. It seems her puritanical father caught Richard kissing her. The matter is made all the worse when Muriel sends Richard a note denouncing him. As a result he joins an older boy on a date with two burlesque queens. Richard's companion is Belle, who gets him drunk and, after making him spend all his money, has him thrown out of the saloon.

The Millers are shocked when Richard staggers home drunk. As a disciplinary measure he is confined to his room. Later, in a talk with his father, Richard assures Mr. Miller that he has done nothing to be ashamed of and promises not to associate with such women again.

Soon Richard is reconciled with Muriel. Meanwhile, Uncle Sid, having sworn off drinking, is accepted by Cousin Lillie.

* * *

When **Take Me Along,** the Broadway musical version of Eugene O'Neill's **Ah, Wilderness!** opened October 22, 1959, at New York's Shubert Theatre for the first of 448 performances,[1] it was largely forgotten that the opus was **not** the initial musicalization of O'Neill's superb account of Americana. MGM had performed the task with charm and color with **Summer Holiday,** a motion picture which boasted a pleasant Harry Warren–Ralph Blane score, lush direction by Rouben Mamoulian, and a competent cast including Mickey Rooney, Walter Huston, Frank Morgan, Marilyn Maxwell, and Gloria DeHaven. Nevertheless, this unique, quaint screen musical was a financial disaster when originally released—it lost well over $1 million—and it has been largely forgotten over the years because of such profitable studio releases as **Ziegfeld Follies, The Harvey Girls,** and **On the**

Agnes Moorehead, Mickey Rooney, Walter Huston, Jackie ("Butch") Jenkins (rear), Gloria DeHaven, and Selena Royle in Summer Holiday *('48).*

Town. However, the feature has recently become, in this age of revivals, a favorite—like its partner-in-losses, **Yolanda and the Thief,** the musical which was also too different for its time.

When Rouben Mamoulian first told Eugene O'Neill of Metro's plans to musicalize his Theatre Guild masterpiece of 1933, the playwright responded, "How can you?"[2] Mamoulian himself had been wary of the idea when producer Arthur Freed suggested the idea across the commissary table in December 1945. The director of such screen classics as **Hallelujah!, Applause,** 1931's **Dr. Jekyll and Mr. Hyde,** and 1940's **The Mark of Zorro** acquiesced. He felt the humanity of the Danville, Connecticut, family of 1906 could be colored, not dimmed, by a musical treatment. Mamoulian, who at one time had been banned by Louis B. Mayer from the Metro lot because of his reputation for being a fiercely independent director, exhaustively enlisted the special aids of all departments at MGM. Interviewed by Charles Higham and Joel Greenberg for **The Celluloid Muse** (1969), Mamoulian recalled:

> "I had a conference ahead of shooting with every department and I wanted to capture the quality of Americana. With the yellows and light greens of Grant Wood and Curry, and similar painters, I didn't want any contrasting colors at all, just tints within a very narrow chromatic range. Cedric Gibbons, the art di-

rector, told me he liked the idea, but that Louis B. Mayer preferred bright colors; insisted on them, in fact. I told him not to worry.

> "We had Charles Schoenbaum as cameraman. We had shot half of the picture, and we hit a scene in a bar in which Mickey Rooney as the young boy in the story sees a floozy get bigger and bigger and redder and redder; he's drunk, and she's overpowering to him, she's his first woman. We had to change gelatins, and I said to Schoenbaum, 'I don't like that red shadow on the wall.' And he said, 'I can't see a red shadow at all. It's green.' It turned out this top color cameraman was color-blind! And the sound man at the studio, Douglas Shearer, brother of Norma, was deaf!"

A superior cast was assembled: Walter Huston as Nat Miller, Mickey Rooney as Richard (he had appeared in MGM's 1935 **Ah, Wildnerness!** as Tommy, a role played here by freckled Jackie "Butch" Jenkins, studio veteran Frank Morgan as heavy-drinking Uncle Sid, Agnes Moorehead as spinster Lillie, Sid's long-suffering romance; Marilyn Maxwell as saloon tart Belle;[3] ingenue Gloria DeHaven as Rooney's love Muriel; and contract character actress Selena Royle as Rooney's and Jenkins' mother.

Mamoulian learned a surprising thing about the different approaches of the pros and the newcomers, as related in Hugh Fordin's **The World of Entertainment** (1975):

[1]The music was by Bob Merrill, and the cast included Jackie Gleason as Sid, Walter Pidgeon as Nat, Robert Morse as Richard, Una Merkel as Elsie, Eileen Herlie as Lillie, and Arlene Golanka as Belle.

[2]**Ah, Wilderness!** opened October 2, 1933, at the Guild Theatre in New York, playing 285 performances. Original cast members included George M. Cohan as Nat, Gene Lockhart as Sid, and Elisha Cook, Jr. as Richard.

[3]Years later Marilyn Maxwell recalled working with star Rooney, "I expected to get lost in the shuffle, but he gave me everything."

"I was rehearsing Huston, Moorehead, Morgan, Royle, all the great acting troupers for hours, and finally I said, 'That's enough.'

"'Please let's try it again,' said Huston.

"'No, that's enough, Walter, now take it easy, sit down. I'm doing to rehearse the love scene with Mickey and Gloria.'

"So they all sat down, the heavy artillery, and on came the two kids who knew from nothing, really.

"'Let's go through the scene.'

"Suddenly it occurred to me, Oh, my God, what a long way I have to go with Gloria DeHaven. I have to feed it to her by the teaspoonful.

"'Now try it again and do it with one thing in mind.'

"'Well, you know, Mr. Mamoulian, you shouldn't rehearse me too much, because, you know, if you rehearse me too much I get stale.'

"'Well, I'll try not to get you stale.'"

Perfectionist Huston was much amused; thereafter he greeted DeHaven by asking, "Gloria, are you stale?"

With the score[4] by Warren and Blane featuring the songs "Our Home Town," "Afraid to Fall in Love," "Dan-Dan-Danville High," "The Stanley Steamer," "Independence Day," "While the Men Are All Drinking," "You're Next," "Weary Blues," and "The Sweetest Kid I Ever Met," **Summer Holiday** suffered through a none too smooth production. In the summer of 1946 a nasty strike involving the Teamster's Union and the IATSE (the stagehands' union) erupted, and Huston and Royle refused to cross picket lines unless the conflict was settled. Production finally closed on October 15, 1946, after 113 days of production and a cost of $2,258,235 ($404,708 over budget).

Release of the unpromising film was delayed until spring 1948. The colorful splash of Americana received lukewarm critical reviews and found few enthusiasts. After years of topping the popularity polls, the no longer adolescent Rooney (he was then 26) was beginning to slip in box-office popularity, especially after his years away from filmmaking while in the military service. The cumulative effect of his too familiar screen image was evident in Bosley Crowther's **New York Times**' review, which complained that the musical feature "has been stripped down to a vehicle for Mickey Rooney's use—all of which sounds, for Mr. O'Neill's drama, like a fate somewhat worse than death . . . where the youngster in the play was a human, he is simply Mr. Rooney in this film." While Crowther admired the "humor and sensual quality" of Maxwell's episode, and found Huston "magnificently sapient and adroit," Morgan "leisurely and funny," Royle "nice," Butch Jenkins "spry," Moorehead "prissy," and DeHaven "crisply

prim and pretty," his potshots at Rooney dominated the reviews. Other critics, oblivious to Mamoulian's more subtle touches (especially the astute use of Technicolor), were generally underwhelmed, and **Summer Holiday** lost $1.46 million in its original release.

The perennial popularity of O'Neill's story of the Miller family has inspired revivals of **Summer Holiday.** Now the film, many decades after its first distribution, is applauded for the innovativeness apparent in its quality production and the overall attractiveness of its cast. As Fordin summarizes the film in **The World of Entertainment,** "Artistically it must be considered a milestone in the history of screen fare. It presented a departure from conventional patterns, and the formula soon became an accepted language in the entertainment world, on the screen as well as on the stage. On Freed's credit sheet it was a failure, but a failure of quality."

SUMMER STOCK

1950 C—109 min. (British release title: IF YOU FEEL LIKE SINGING)

Producer, Joe Pasternak; **director,** Charles Walters; **story,** Sy Gomberg; **screenplay,** George Wells and Gomberg; **music directors,** Johnny Green and Saul Chaplin; **choreography,** Nick Castle, Gene Kelly, and Walters; **orchestrators,** Conrad Salinger and Skip Martin; **stager of "Happy Harvest,"** Roger Edens; **songs,** Mack Gordon and Harry Warren; Gordon, Warren, Jack Brooks, and Chaplin; Harold Arlen and Ted Koehler; **costumes,** Walter Plunkett; **Gloria DeHaven's costumes,** Helen Rose; **art directors,** Cedric Gibbons and Jack Martin Smith; **camera,** Robert Planck; **editor,** Albert Akst.

Judy Garland **(Jane Falbury);** Gene Kelly **(Joe D. Ross);** Eddie Bracken **(Orville Wingait);** Gloria DeHaven **(Abigail Falbury);** Marjorie Main **(Esme);** Phil Silvers **(Herb Blake);** Ray Collins **(Jasper G. Wingait);** Carleton Carpenter **(Artie);** Nita Bieber **(Sarah Higgins);** Hans Conried **(Harrison I. Keath);** Paul E. Burns **(Frank);** Carol Haney, Arthur Loew, Jr., and Jimmy Thompson **(Members of Stock Company);** Bette Arlen and Bunny Waters **(Show Girls);** Erville Alderson **(Zeb);** Almira Sessions **(Constance Fliggerton);** Kathryn Sheldon **(Amy Fliggerton);** Michael Chapin and Teddy Infuhr **(Boys);** Cameron Grant, Jack Daley, and Reginald Simpson **(Producers);** Eddie Dunn **(Sheriff).**

SYNOPSIS

Jane Falbury is an impoverished farm owner in Connecticut. She awaits the arrival of her younger sister Abigail, to help gather the crops. Jane is furious when Abigail, an aspiring actress, arrives with a summer-stock company headed by Joe D. Ross. The latter is Abigail's boyfriend and he and the troupe hope to put on a new musical show in the farm barn.

Learning that Joe and his group have in-

vested all their money to stage the show, Jane agrees to let them remain on the farm provided they help housekeeper Esme with the chores. The presence of actors at Jane's farm perturbs Orville Wingait, her boyfriend, as well as Jasper G. Wingait, his father and owner of the local general store. Soon Jane and Joe are attracted to each other, but in consideration of Abigail, Jane remains aloof.

Complications arise when, several days before the opening of the show, Abigail and Joe argue. She returns to New York. Joe is desperate for a replacement leading lady and calls on Jane to assume the demanding part. She agrees, despite the objections of Orville, who hurries to Manhattan to bring Abigail back to Connecticut.

During the next few days of intense rehearsing Jane and Joe realize they love each other. Abigail and Orville return on opening night, but Abigail refuses to interfere when she observes that Jane and Joe are truly in love. The show is a hit and all are happy. Even Abigail and Orville have found romance with each other.

* * *

Waterloo at MGM was inevitable for Judy Garland. Her growing emotional problems and bouts of ill health had combined to make her an increasingly hazardous risk to any film production. Shooting **The Pirate** (1948) had been a near overwhelming trial for the Arthur Freed–MGM unit, and **Easter Parade** (1948) was not much better; but at least the latter project was a financial and artistic success. Because Garland had enjoyed a harmonious working relationship with Fred Astaire in **Easter Parade,** it was decided to reteam them in **The Barkleys of Broadway** (1949), but eventually it was necessary to replace her (with Ginger Rogers) while Judy sought to recuperate. Then came her fiasco with **Annie Get Your Gun** (1950). After she was removed from the musical and replaced by Paramount's Betty Hutton, Garland was shipped to Peter Bent Brigham Hospital in Boston to undergo amphetamine and barbiturate withdrawal. It was an extremely painful experience for the frightened actress. When her health had improved sufficiently she was allowed visits from her director-husband Vincente Minnelli and from their little daughter Liza. Another visitor was Arthur Freed. He informed Judy that MGM wanted her back and that a script was awaiting her return.

The vehicle was **Summer Stock,** to be produced by Joe Pasternak. At one point, it had been hoped to reunite Mickey Rooney with Garland in the venture, but he had left the lot by the time the musical could get into production. Then Pasternak turned to Gene Kelly, a Garland favorite, who had been with her in **For Me and My Gal** (1942), **The Pirate,** and initially **Easter Parade** (before he broke his ankle and was replaced by Astaire). Everything was done to provide Garland with a sense of security. Charles Walters, who had directed her in **Easter Parade** and **The Barkleys of Broadway** (before she left the cast), was assigned to the project, as was old friend Phil Silvers, and such Garland (working) pals as Johnny Green and Saul Chaplin, both involved with the film's music. Also in the cast was Marjorie

---

[4]Deleted from release prints were the songs "Omar and the Princess" (a song and ballet sequence with Rooney and DeHaven, inspired by Richard Miller's love of **Rubiyat**), "Wish I Had a Braver Heart" (a DeHaven solo), Huston's first rendition of "Spring Isn't Everything" and "Never Again" (a duet with Moorehead and Morgan; the latter was petrified of singing and was very bad at it).

Main, the rambunctious on-screen (but very understanding off-screen) soul who had supported Judy in **Meet Me in St. Louis** (1944) and **The Harvey Girls** (1946).

What promised to be a relaxed situation soon deteriorated into chaos. For starters, MGM insisted that a psychiatrist (one who had dealt with Garland in Boston) be on the set at all times to oversee the star's mental condition. The situation embarrassed Judy, who begged to be left alone and not to be publically humiliated. Adding to her problems was her weight. She was in obvious need of dieting and when she did so, it led to an increase in the use and dependence on drugs, all of which made her emotionally unstable again. Soon the unreliable Garland of old was in the fore. She would report to the studio late, some days not showing up at all. She required the consultation of Minnelli at any given moment. When she could bring herself to concentrate on the script and filming, she became depressed. She had decided that the project was a waste of her talents; that it was merely a continuation of the **Babes on Broadway** (1941) type of movie.

Director Walters later recalled:

God, she was a problem on that picture—her nerves were shot, there was the weight thing, everything. We never knew what time she'd come in—or whether she was prepared for anything when she did. She'd come storming in and say, "Looky, buddy. If you expect any acting out of me today, forget it!" And I had to sort of josh her out of it, had to pretend that I didn't care if she worked or not. "Let's just have a cup of coffee and talk a bit," I'd say. There's a number in that picture, "Friendly Star," which I think is one of the best things she ever did. . . . We were moving in for a giant close-up, Judy looked up with those great liquid eyes of hers and it was the most fantastic shot in the world. "Cut," I yelled. "Will someone please hand me a towel. I've just come!" Now that might be thought indelicate, but Judy loved that kind of foolishness. . . . You always had to keep her spirits high. Once you had her in the mood for work, you had to keep her there. Not that it was always easy. What was the number on the tractor? Oh, "Howdy, Neighbor!" The days we spent on that. I can see her sitting on that damn thing mumbling, "What am I doing here? Please send for Vincente to take me home."

At one juncture, when Garland's absences and inability to work plagued production too greatly, Pasternak went to Louis B. Mayer hoping to unburden himself of the set's problems. Pasternak wanted to scrap the project, but Mayer refused. "Judy Garland," he said, "has made this studio a fortune in the good old days and the least we can do is to give her one more chance. If you stop production now, it will finish her." (Ironically, Mayer himself was well on the way to being finished at the studio.)

The film limped to completion. The rough cut of **Summer Stock** failed to impress. Pasternak would remark:

Marjorie Main and Judy Garland in Summer Stock *('50).*

When the picture was over, we discovered we needed another number. She had lost about fifteen or twenty pounds between the two months before we had finished cutting the picture and the time she did the last number—"Get Happy"—and looked so beautiful that everybody thought it was a stock shot. When we previewed the picture with an audience, they didn't care what she looked like. They loved her. I don't think any actress was as loved by the American public as Judy.

Summer Stock appeared in the late summer of 1950. **Time** magazine observed:

Summer Stock, no great shakes as a cinemusical, serves nonetheless as a welcome reminder of Judy Garland's unerring way with a song. Ill, and in and out of trouble with her studio, actress Garland has been off the screen since last year's **In the Good Old Summertime.** A rest cure left her chubbily overweight for her first return performance. But none of it seems to have affected her ability as one of Hollywood's few triple-threat girls. Thanks to actress Garland's singing, dancing, and acting (and some imaginative dancing by Gene Kelly) the picture seems considerably better than it is.

There is much to recommend within **Summer Stock.** Silvers joins with Kelly in the jocular "Dig, Dig, Dig for Your Dinner" and "Heavenly Music." In the latter the duo are garbed as broken-toothed hillbillies, sporting fake feet that are many times the normal size. Kelly performs the production number "All for You," does a solo dance, "You Wonderful You," on an empty stage (a favorite gimmick of his), and leads Garland about the dance floor in the "Portland Fancy" routine. One of the artistic highlights of the film is Kelly's (self-choreographed) dance using a squeaky floorboard and a dropped newspaper as his only props. If Garland's tractor number ("Howdy, Neighbor") is bucolic, her "If You Feel Like Singing, Sing" folksy, and her "Friendly Star" poignant, then the "Get Happy" segment is exuberant. Dressed in leotards, a man's tuxedo jacket, and a black fedora pushed down over one eye, she commands everyone's presence with her singing and dancing. The scene would be a highlight of the feature. In **That's Entertainment!** (1974) cohostess Liza Minnelli stated on camera that this song-and-dance segment was one of Judy's all-time favorite movie routines.

By the time it was decided to add "Get Happy" to the filming schedule, choreographer Nick Castle had left the production; director Walters choreographed the segment. Meanwhile, Garland had gone to Santa Barbara with a hypnotist to help her lose weight, and she returned home some fifteen pounds slimmer. According to cocomposer Saul Chaplin, she prerecorded the song in three takes. In **Rainbow** (1975) Christopher Finch says:

When she came on the set for the shooting of "Get Happy" she was in a somewhat manic state. . . . The dancers had good reason to notice this since Judy was in a mood to convey to them certain notions she felt could only be spoken in a whisper. She pointed to a member of the crew—a small, inoffensive man who had been at the studio for years—and began to recite accusations against him under her breath. "He's been after my body since I was thirteen years old" was the general drift of her monologue. Eventually, she called the man over and, as soon as he was within range, high-kicked him in the teeth. Then she went about her business, more brilliant than ever, committing the difficult routine to film in a couple of takes.

Summer Stock became a money earner.[1] Garland departed for a rest in Carmel, California (as a substitute against returning to Boston for further psychiatric treatment). Despite the studio's promise to allow her sufficient vacation, she was at her retreat for less than three weeks, when she was paged by Metro. June Allyson had become pregnant and could not perform in the musical **Royal Wedding** (1951) with Fred Astaire. Garland reluctantly reported for rehearsals on May 23, 1950. Within a few weeks—by June 17, 1950—her behavior, illness, and tardiness had led the studio to remove her from the company payroll. It was the end of her nearly fifteen-year tenure at MGM.

SUSAN AND GOD
1940—117 min. (British release title: THE GAY MRS. TREXEL)

Producer, Hunt Stromberg; **director,** George Cukor; based on the play by Rachel Crothers; **screenplay,** Anita Loos; **art director,** Cedric Gibbons; **costumes,** Adrian; **music,** Herbert Stothart; **sound,** Douglas Shearer; **camera,** Robert Planck; **editor,** William H. Terhune.

Joan Crawford (**Susan Trexel**); Fredric March (**Barry Trexel**); Ruth Hussey (**Charlotte**); John Carroll (**Clyde Rochester**); Rita Hayworth (**Leonora Stubbs**); Nigel Bruce (**Hutchins Stubbs**); Bruce Cabot (**Michael O'Hara**); Rose Hobart (**Irene Burrows**); Rita Quigley (**Blossom Trexel**); Norma Mitchell (**Paige**); Romaine Callender (**Oliver Leeds**); Marjorie Main (**Mary**); Aldrich Bowker (**Patrick**); Constance Collier (**Lady Wiggam**); Herbert Evans (**Bronson**); Cece Broadhurst (**Cowboy Joe**); Richard O. Crane (**Bob**); Don Castle (**Attendant**); Dan Dailey, Jr. (**Homer**); Louis Payne (**Dave**); Gloria DeHaven (**Enid**); Joan Leslie, Susan Peters, David Tillotson, and William Lechner (**Guests**).

SYNOPSIS
Society matron Susan Trexel embraces a new religious movement while touring Europe. Upon returning to her aristocratic Long Island home, she attempts to convert her luxury-loving pals to the new fad. However, they remain unenthusiastic.

Her interference results in rifts between friend "Hutchie" Stubbs and his much younger, actress wife, Leonora. Within short order, the proselytizing, domineering Susan has disjointed

[1]In November 1978, Edward A. Montanus, president of MGM-TV, announced that the studio was planning a TV series based on **Summer Stock.** It never came to be.

Joan Crawford and John Carroll in Susan and God *('40).*

Leonora's potential affair with ex-stage partner Clyde Rochester. Moreover, interfering Susan has almost convinced an unwilling Hutchie to leave his overamorous new spouse.

This newfound ardor of Susan's—the latest in a series of causes for her—further estranges her husband (who becomes attracted to Charlotte) and makes her remiss in her maternal interest in daughter Blossom. Barry implores Susan to resume their life together for Blossom's sake.

In time, Susan rises above her spiritual distraction and realizes her husband and daughter's urgent need for her.

* * *

One of the lively gossip items of Culver City in 1939 had been the bitchy battles of Norma Shearer and Joan Crawford as they played their few tandem scenes in **The Women.** Crawford, long bitter over the queenly treatment afforded Shearer during Irving Thalberg's tenure,[1] was in the forefront of the MGM habitués who harbored a hatchet for Norma's Sidney Guilaroff–treated scalp. To Crawford's delight, her own career was experiencing a vitalizing metamorphosis after her triumph in **The Women** and the reteaming with Clark Gable in **Strange Cargo** (1940). On the other hand, Shearer was drifting into what promised to be an early screen retirement.

Hence, it was especially pleasing to Joan

[1]Shearer had snared **A Free Soul** (1931), for example, a scenario tailor-made for Crawford.

Crawford when, in early 1940, Norma Shearer vetoed the cinema version of Rachel Crothers' hit play. Shearer reasoned it would seem unglamorous for her to play the mother of a teenager. When Crawford was approached to accept the job, she replied in what has become a classic Hollywood remark, "I'd play Wallace Beery's grandmother if it was a good part." Thus she eagerly took on the role of the vain, religiously fanatic Susan Trexel.

A dream part for a picaresque actress, Susan had been interpreted on Broadway by no less than Gertrude Lawrence. The New York opening took place on October 7, 1937, and the drama ran 288 performances. To create the screen version, the same team that made **The Women** was reunited: producer Hunt Stromberg, director George Cukor, scenarist Anita Loos, and star Crawford. To adapt the property "properly" for the screen, Loos made several adjustments in the original. More comic scenes were added, and salty characters were made a more definite part of the proceedings, including Marjorie Main's gardener's wife, Constance Collier's Lady Wiggam, and Nigel Bruce's bumbling Hutchie Stubbs. Also, the parts of the husband and daughter (played on Broadway by Paul McGrath and Nancy Kelly) were enlarged for Fredric March (who indubitably demanded such a revision) and Rita Quigley.

For the smallish but flashy part of Leonora Stubbs, director Cukor had his own choice. He remembered testing a pert actress at Columbia

Pictures when he was casting for the younger sister of Katharine Hepburn in **Holiday** (1938). "She was too young for that part, but I thought her attractive and gifted," Cukor recalled. He now had the opportunity to use her on camera, and so Rita Hayworth was borrowed from Columbia. Hayworth and the seasoned Crawford would have a good scene together in which the latter unctuously offers a greeting to her guest, the new bride: "Why, you're too, too lovely, my dear. And Hutchie was such a bachelor, too. But I can quite see how you did it. Hutchie, she's marvelous!" Later Rita radiates her own intensity when she begins (but unfortunately is interrupted) an undulating rumba.

In analyzing this film with the wisdom of his perspective, Stephen Harvey in **Joan Crawford** (1974) observes:

> Crawford had never encountered anything like Susan before. Usually Crawford was surrounded by a handful of fascinated men. Here Fredric March is the bone of contention, and Crawford risks losing him to the attractive and more youthful Ruth Hussey. Crawford heroines generally are obsessed with their labyrinthine private lives to the utter exclusion of the outside world. Susan is so absorbed in vague causes and other people's affairs that she completely neglects her duties to her insecure daughter and bibulous husband....
>
> The script itself is glib and breezy, quite resembling **The Philadelphia Story** [directed by Cukor] in tone. Also, the relationships explored are rather more illicit than the movies usually permitted in 1940. Ruth Hussey's other woman is really the nicest person in the movie, and she is complemented by an assortment of lushes, gigolos, and adulteresses.

Unfortunately, despite its many positive facets, **Susan and God** emerged on the screen as an uneasy blend of satire and emotional drama. The transitions were difficult for both players and viewers. When the high-toned feature opened in June 1940, Bosley Crowther (**New York Times**) advised his readers:

> If ever a woman needed a beating—but good—that woman is the Susan Trexel of Joan Crawford in **Susan and God**. In the early part of the picture there are bright and promising glimmers when it looks as though it might all build up to a funny satire on the high-class evangelism and on the foibles of the so-called upper class, in a manner reminiscent of **The Women**. . . [but] the whole picture drifts away in a cloud of sentiment and melancholy.

Despite Fredric March's bombastic speech here and there, some effective (if all too typical) fumbling by Nigel Bruce, and the radiant presence of prestardom Rita Hayworth, **Susan and God** remains primarily a Joan Crawford vehicle. And it is one in which she is not totally effective. Her performance is very much and very obviously a copy of Gertrude Lawrence's New York stage work, and would have fared better with more of Crawford's own individual aggressiveness and spark.

As Stephen Harvey summed up in his study of the actress, "She does everything possible to hide her basic down-to-earth quality, but the effort shows—despite her wide-eyed, breathless delivery Crawford simply isn't the sort of ethereal creature called for." Actually the part required Claudette Colbert, who for her home lot, Paramount, would translate another Gertrude Lawrence stage success to the screen, in **Skylark**, 1941.

In a year (1940) when the screen had an abundance of riches, **Susan and God** would be only a lukewarm success financially. However, it did provide Crawford fans with another glimpse of their star in an important transitional stage. Far more popular would be Crawford's follow-up, the splendid melodrama **A Woman's Face** (1941), also directed by George Cukor.

A TALE OF TWO CITIES
1935—121 min.

Producer, David O. Selznick; **director,** Jack Conway; based on the novel by Charles Dickens; **screenplay,** W. P. Lipscomb and S. N. Behrman; **music,** Herbert Stothart; **art directors,** Cedric Gibbons and Fredric Hope; **set decorator,** Edwin B. Willis; revolutionary sequences staged by Val Lewton and Jacques Tourneur; **camera,** Oliver T. Marsh; **editor,** Conrad A. Nervig.

Ronald Colman (**Sydney Carton**); Elizabeth Allan (**Lucie Manette**); Edna May Oliver (**Miss Pross**); Blanche Yurka (**Madame DeFarge**); Reginald Owen (**Stryver**); Basil Rathbone (**Marquis St. Evremonde**); Donald Woods (**Charles Darnay**); Henry B. Walthall (**Dr. Manette**); Walter Catlett (**Barsad**); Fritz Leiber, Sr. (**Gaspard**); H. B. Warner (**Gabelle**); Mitchell Lewis (**Ernest DeFarge**); Claude Gillingwater (**Jarvis Lorry**); Billy Bevan (**Jerry Cruncher**); Isabel Jewell (**Seamstress**); Lucille LaVerne (**La Vengeance**); Tully Marshall (**Woodcutter**); Fay Chaldecott (**Lucie, the Daughter**); Eily Malyon (**Mrs. Cruncher**); E. E. Clive (**Judge in Old Bailey**); Lawrence Grant (**Prosecuting Attorney in Old Bailey**); Donald Haines (**Jerry Cruncher, Jr.**); Ralf Harolde (**Prosecutor**); Edward Hearn (**Leader**); Ed Peil, Sr. (**Cartwright**); Richard Alexander (**Executioner**); Cyril McLaglen (**Headsman**); Nigel DeBrulier (**Aristocrat**); Walter Kingsford (**Victor, the Jailer**); Rolfe Sedan (**Dandy Who Is Condemned**); Tempe Pigott and Dale Fuller (**Old Hags**); Montague Shaw (**Chief Registrar**); Billy House (**Border Guard**); Jimmy Aubrey (**Innkeeper**).

SYNOPSIS

In late eighteenth-century France, cynical, unhappy Sydney Carton falls in love with the lovely Lucie Manette. Her emotions for Sydney, however, are mostly platonic, for she has fallen in love with Charles Darnay. The latter, who looks a good deal like Carton, is the nephew of the Marquis St. Evremonde, a sneering French aristocrat. His cruel treatment of the French peasants has awak-

Donald Woods and Ronald Colman in A Tale of Two Cities ('35).

ened talk of revolution among the masses. Shortly after Darnay moves to England, sickened by his uncle's wickedness, St. Evremonde's coach runs over a little boy—Evremonde's sole concern is for his prize horses.

The peasants are inflamed. The dastardly deed becomes their rallying point. The father of the dead boy crashes into Evremonde's mansion and murders the aristocrat in his bed. The blood-lust quickens, and soon aristocrats are brought by tumbrel to the guillotine where the peasants cheer each decapitation with devilish glee. Especially conspicuous, in the front row of the executions, is Madame DeFarge, who revels in the macabre and vindictive "entertainment." With Evremonde the most hated name in France, she plots and succeeds in luring Darnay back to France where he is condemned to death by the tribunal.

Throughout these world-shaking events, Carton has maintained his love for Lucie. His devotion to her and her little girl moves him to exchange places with lookalike Darnay. A seamstress recognizes him in the dungeon. But she helps him keep his secret as he shares his feelings with her throughout the long night before their execution.

The next morning Carton goes to the guillotine. His final words are, "It is a far, far better thing that I do than I have ever done; it is a far far better rest that I go to than I have ever known."

* * *

During the banner cinema year of 1935, three of Metro's top producers worked to the hilt to outdo one another with a blockbuster motion picture which would end the year on a pinnacle. Irving Thalberg busied himself with **Mutiny on the Bounty**, Hunt Stromberg cinematized Eugene O'Neill's **Ah, Wilderness!**, and the indefatigable David O. Selznick followed his laurel-laden **David Copperfield** (1935) with another Charles Dickens' title, **A Tale of Two Cities**. Only months before, Warner Bros. had been eager for its star Leslie Howard to perform the dual-role lead of the classic adventure story. When he refused, the studio sold its preparatory package to the eager Mr. Selznick.

Although lensed previously by several silent-film companies, this was to be the debut of the sound version of the beloved property. Dickens' narrative of the heartache and viciousness in France of the 1790s fascinated Selznick tremendously. Simultaneously the concept disturbed him. He had discovered in his laborious efforts to bring **David Copperfield** to the screen that Dickens was not an author who transferred to the cinema readily. In Rudy Behlmer's **Memo from David O. Selznick** (1972), a letter to MGM assistant story editor Kate Corbaley summed up the filmmaker's growing apprehensions:

"It is amazing that Dickens had so many brilliant characters in **David Copperfield** and so few in **A Tale of Two Cities**. . . . The book is sheer melodrama and when the scenes are put on the screen, minus Dickens' brilliant narrative passages, the mechanics of melodramatic construction are inclined to be more than apparent, and in fact, to creak. . . .

". . . Since the picture is melodrama, it must have pace and it must pack a wallop."

To ensure this, Selznick carefully selected the talents for the film: director Jack Conway, who had impressed Selznick with his work on the producer's **Viva Villa!** (1934), scripters W. P. Lipscomb and S. N. Behrman (the latter a great favorite of Selznick's because of his ability to write flowing dialogue); and a superb cast. Happily contracted to play Sydney Carton was Ronald Colman, then under contract to Darryl F. Zanuck's Twentieth Century Productions. Ever the perfectionist, Selznick even had his qualms about the debonair, swashbuckling star. ("Bear in mind that we have Colman playing the role and that there is the difficulty of getting him as anything but a rather gay, casual Colman—as he has always been.")

In **Ronald Colman: A Very Private Person** (1975), his daughter Juliet Benita Colman relates:

Ronnie knew Dickens' novel virtually by heart and had longed to play the role of Carton for many years. Seven years before he was finally cast for the film, in an interview with a magazine writer, he said: "In Sydney Carton, he [Dickens] conceived a character that only a genius would know; a whimsical, sardonic, bitterly disillusioned fellow who successfully—or almost so—masks his emotions beneath an unmoved exterior. Dickens wrote of this man with a glorious power. He has lived for me since the first instant I discovered him in the pages of the novel. . . . It has a charm that is greater than magnificence, the charm of intimacy in the midst of spectacle."

Care went into the selection of the other key talents: British import Elizabeth Allan in her finest screen moments as Lucie Manette; Basil Rathbone in the brief but memorable assignment as the wicked Marquis St. Evremonde; Isabel Jewell,[1] superb in atypical casting as the timid seamstress who precedes Colman to the guillotine; and, most memorable of all, Blanche Yurka as the infamous Madame DeFarge. In 1969 the actress told Mel Schuster for **Film Fan Monthly**:

"It was Nazimova who was responsible for my getting the part of Madame DeFarge in **A Tale of Two Cities**. We had never met, but when the part was offered to her, she felt it was not right for her and told them the only person she knew who could properly play the part was Blanche Yurka. I was the sixty-seventh and last actress to test for the part and, as Aline MacMahon put it, I had the plum role of the season."

Selznick invested a painstaking and expensive five months on the production. Though he actually resigned from MGM on June 27, 1935, he agreed to work for a flat fee at Culver City to

finalize work on **Anna Karenina** and **A Tale of Two Cities**. **A Tale** abounds with memorable sequences: Rathbone agitatingly inquiring as to the health of his horses after they had trampled a peasant boy to death; the brawl between Yurka's DeFarge and Edna May Oliver's Miss Pross; Colman's tenderness in the climax to Jewell's fearful seamstress.

A Tale of Two Cities was released very late in 1935, the last of the trio of epics that year from Metro. Critical appeal was bountiful.[2] Andre Sennwald (**New York Times**) reported, "For more than two hours, it crowds the screen with beauty and excitement. . . . The drama achieves a crisis of extraordinary effectiveness at the guillotine, leaving the audience quivering under its emotional sledge-hammer blows. . . . Ronald Colman gives his ablest performance in years as Sydney Carton and a score of excellent players are at their best in it." The powerful playing, alternating with magnetizing scenes of spectacle (including a thrilling battle of the Bastille), made the feature a potent box-office attraction.

Released too late to qualify for 1935 Academy Award honors, **A Tale of Two Cities** was among the entries nominated for Oscar's Best Picture of 1936; it lost to MGM's **The Great Ziegfeld**. It did place sixth on the Film Daily 1936 Ten Best Picture Poll, and was among the twenty-five top-grossing films of the 1935–36 season.

A Tale of Two Cities was Selznick's final production at MGM (although his **Gone With the Wind** would be released by the studio). As he departed the lot to form his own Selznick International Pictures, Louis B. Mayer bade his son-in-law goodbye by stomping and screaming, "You'll fail! You'll fail!" Selznick's calmly replied, "I'm thirty-two. I can afford to fail."

TARZAN THE APE MAN
1932—99 min.

Director, W. S. Van Dyke II; based on the character created by Edgar Rice Burroughs; **screenplay,** Cyril Hume; **dialogue,** Ivor Novello; **camera,** Harold Rosson and Clyde DeVinna; **editors,** Ben Lewis and Tom Held.

Johnny Weissmuller **(Tarzan)**; Neil Hamilton **(Harry Holt)**; Maureen O'Sullivan **(Jane Parker)**; C. Aubrey Smith **(James Parker)**; Doris Lloyd **(Mrs. Cutten)**; Forrester Harvey **(Beamish)**; Ivory Williams **(Riano)**.

SYNOPSIS

In quest of the sacred elephant burial ground and its treasure of ivory tusks are famed safari leader

---

[1]Jewell's desire to win the role had irked director Conway. He was familiar with the blonde actress' wisecracking screen image and refused to test her. She so persisted that Selznick himself ordered her to be auditioned; he gave her the part. She would reteam with Colman in Columbia's **Lost Horizon** (1937).

[2]The British trade paper **Film Weekly** judged, "The Dickens story retold with great restraint and dominated by Ronald Colman's fine portrait of Sydney Carton. The other players are well chosen, the settings and the Revolutionary scenes are vastly imposing, but the plot is somewhat out of balance."

James Parker, his young associate Harry Holt, and Parker's daughter Jane. She is fascinated by the prospects of the adventure and has begged to go on the dangerous trek. In the ensuing days of travels to the unexplored Mutia Escarpment, the horrors of the jungle reveal themselves: they include ravenous crocodiles, belligerent hippopotamuses, and baying animals creeping only feet away from the nightly campfire. However, most startling of all to the band is a strange cry, which the natives guess to be a hyena; Parker insists it is a human yell.

The mystery is solved shortly thereafter. Some mischievous hippos pursue the hunters' path. The cry is sounded again and an athletic white man appears, garbed only in a loincloth. Strangely, the hippos obey his command and leave the hunters alone. However, the stranger appears fascinated with the lovely Jane. Later, while Parker and Holt are distracted, he swoops down and carries her off by means of vines. They try to communicate—the stranger calls himself Tarzan, and soon is reveling in introductions: "Jane—Tarzan. Jane—Tarzan. Jane—Tarzan . . ." After spending the night in Tarzan's treehouse, Jane further acquaints herself with Tarzan and his pet chimpanzee Cheetah. Days later, when she rejoins her father and the smitten Holt, she appears to be a changed young woman. She is no longer fearful of the jungle wilds, but respectful.

Tarzan now leads the expedition, and reveals himself to be a superb athlete in the water, on the vines, and in contest with the animals. The party is later captured by savage pygmies, who jubilantly begin lowering the prisoners into a pit holding a giant gorilla. Tarzan, who remained at liberty, attacks with stampeding elephants and stabs the gorilla to death. Saved from a grisly fate, the hunters now follow a wounded elephant—through a waterfall—to the long-sought elephants' graveyard.

Upon reaching the rich remains of the animals, Parker, exhausted by the expedition and his injuries, dies. The party buries him there and Jane intones, "He found what he was looking for. . . . I know that somewhere—wherever great hunters go—he's happy."

As they head back to civilization, Jane realizes that Holt can offer her only riches of a material kind. In contrast, Tarzan can provide her with the beauties of an unmolested nature. Holt leaves with the promise from Jane that she and Tarzan will lead his next safari. Tarzan and Jane embark together on a new and wondrous existence.

* * *

My lines read like a backward two-year-old talking to his nurse. Once I was following my elephant by vine when he stopped. I ran into his ass and broke my nose.
Johnny Weissmuller

I was never more consistently sick and miserable in all my life. . . . I was never without an ache or a pain. I was never completely or comfortably warm. And I was never without a bite from one of those monkeys. I always had

Advertisement for Tarzan the Ape Man ('32).

the same average—one fresh bite, one about half-healed, and one scar.
Maureen O'Sullivan

Such are the none too romantic reminiscences of the stars of what is arguably the greatest escapism ever offered by the motion pictures—the **Tarzan** series—here, the applauded adventures of MGM's Johnny Weissmuller and Maureen O'Sullivan. Though there have been approximately fifty screen versions (and burlesques) of the exploits of Edgar Rice Burrough's ape man, the MGM Weissmuller-O'Sullivan series, complete with Cheetah, the toothless crocodiles, the chanting natives (courtesy of black actors residing in Los Angeles), and the Culver City back lot Africa, still comes immediately to mind when the legendary literary–motion picture–radio–television–cartoon character is discussed.

By 1932 the character Tarzan, which had been conceived in a 1912 magazine story sold for $700 by author Edgar Rice burroughs, had pounded his Caucasian chest through twenty-six books and eight motion pictures. That year **Tarzan** came to radio with a series of 364 prerecorded fifteen-minute episodes starring Joan Burroughs Pierce (Burroughs' daughter) and husband, former **Tarzan** actor Jim Pierce. Also in 1932 United Features Syndicate began its "Tarzan" comic strip, originally drawn by Hal Foster.

It was at this time that MGM, having enjoyed huge grosses with **Trader Horn** (1931), recognized in **Tarzan** a perfect excuse to cash in on the public

interest in Africa adventure. There was also the ulterior motive of wanting to utilize leftover footage from **Trader Horn.** W. S. Van Dyke II, who had guided the earlier MGM jungle epic to completion, was set to direct the new adventure. He was promised that there would be no painful location junket to the wild interiors of Africa, as with **Trader Horn.**

For the lead actor Van Dyke wanted "a man who is young, strong, well built, reasonably attractive but not necessarily handsome, and a competent actor." The nominees: Charles Bickford, John Mack Brown, Clark Gable, Joel McCrea, Tom Tyler, and Bruce Bennett (then known as Herman Brix—he almost won the assignment). However, while Cyril Hume was working on the scenario, he noticed Johnny Weissmuller swimming in a Hollywood hotel pool. The twenty-seven-year-old had represented the U.S. in the 1924 and the 1928 Olympics, winning a total of five gold medals. Weissmuller, who had appeared briefly in **Glorifying the American Girl** (Paramount, 1929), passed his MGM screen test. But he was then under contract with the BVD company to publicize its underwear and swimwear. BVD agreed to allow Metro to contract Weissmuller. However, MGM had to promise the corporation a pick of its female roster to fill BVD swimsuits for advertisements. (Jean Harlow, Joan Crawford, and Marie Dressler were among the studio contractees who later donned the BVD togs.)

Contracted to play Jane was Maureen O'Sullivan, the twenty-one-year-old Irish actress who had played in such Fox films as **Just Imagine**

(1930) and **A Connecticut Yankee** (1931). She joined MGM thereafter and would have nine releases in 1932, including three for Universal, one for RKO, and one for low-budget Patrician-Films. Her Metro assignments that year included **Payment Deferred,** starring Charles Laughton, and the role of Madeline, the fiancée of Norma Shearer's illegitimate son, in **Strange Interlude.** It would be the **Tarzan** project that gave her the needed career boost.

With such solid supporting players as Neil Hamilton, C. Aubrey Smith, and Forrester Harvey filling out the cast, **Tarzan the Ape Man** began production. Much of the three months of production took place at Toluca Lake in North Hollywood. The filmmakers employed a liberal amount of **Trader Horn** footage for atmosphere shots. The company dispatched a bus to recruit unemployed local blacks who were willing to screech and scream as natives for $12 a day (double pay if they had to work near animals). A fleet of animal trainers was hired to supervise the numerous monkeys, chimpanzees, crocodiles, hippopotamuses, rhinoceroses, etc., required for the film. Created for this 1932 feature was the unique apeman cry. Its origin is described by David Zinman in **Saturday Afternoon at the Bijou** (1973):

> To produce it, technicians ingeniously blended a whole series of unconnected sounds. They reportedly mixed a camel's bleat, a hyena's yowl played backward, the pluck of a violin string, a soprano's high C and Weissmuller's bellowing at the top of his lungs. Then, they played them at a fraction of a second after one another, thus creating a weird jungle call that become Weissmuller's trademark. Amazingly, Weissmuller learned to imitate it.

During the production of **Tarzan the Ape Man,** Metro had to deal with a legal crisis. Independent producer Sol Lesser had acquired the rights to make a **Tarzan** feature, which rights Burroughs had optioned to another independent filmmaker back in 1928. Because Burroughs had never voided the agreement, Lesser had legal precedent to enforce it. He brought the $10,000 option money to an astonished Burroughs and the latter was required to accept it. Lesser then had a court decide if his option was truly legitimate; it declared that it was legal. Terrified by the possible competition to its expensively mounted feature, MGM's attorneys contacted Lesser, who for a fee agreed to postpone his project.

When released in March 1932, **Tarzan the Ape Man** proved to be a sensation. Most of the critics and the general public did not mind that MGM's Tarzan bore little resemblance to Burroughs' original character (who was actually a cultivated, articulate English lord).[1] Thornton Delehanty **(New York Evening Post)** was enthusiastic:

> However credible or interesting Tarzan may be on the printed page, I doubt very much if he

[1]Many years later Johnny Weissmuller was asked to analyze the secret of his **Tarzan** success. "My grunt," he confided.

Johnny Weissmuller in Tarzan the Ape Man.

emerges in such splendor as he does in the person of Johnny Weissmuller, who makes his bow to the moviegoing public. And as Tarzan he will probably remain bowing through a whole series of these pictures, even though the public may clamor to see him in Clark Gable roles. There is no doubt that he possesses all the attributes, both physical and mental, for the complete realization of this son-of-the-jungle role. With his flowing hair, his magnificently proportioned body, his catlike walk, and his virtuosity in the water, you could hardly ask anything more in the way of perfection. . . .

Single-handed he attacks lions and tigers; he leaps off a tree onto the back of a waterbuck and throws it with one twist of the neck; he makes a herd of elephants as subservient as a troupe of trained fleas.

When released in England, the lofty **New Statesman**'s critic Francis Birrell admitted, "**Tarzan** has a hundred percent entertainment value, and gains enormously over such pictures as **Trader Horn** by never pretending to provide accurate information. It is just a terrific piece of gusto in the romantic manner."

The film soon joined **Emma, Grand Hotel, Hell Divers,** and **Mata Hari** in the category of MGM's top grossers of the season.[2] The National Board of Review chose it as one of the Ten Best pictures of the year. The studio ensured (in the precode days) that the film had its provocative side to lure patrons. Both O'Sullivan and Weissmuller were scantily clad, and it did not take an adult to realize that their relationship was not sanctioned by the clergy. As one of the ad lines for the film read, "Girls—would you live like Eve if you found the right Adam?" It all helped to boost revenue for the $1 million production.

As a result of **Tarzan the Ape Man,** MGM picked up Weissmuller's option. (**Photoplay** magazine had definitively stated that he was "the topnotch heart-flutterer of the year.") As part of the contractual agreement, which paid him an eventual $2,000-plus weekly, Weissmuller was persuaded to divorce singer-dancer Bobbe Arnst, whom he had wed in 1930. (The studio later approved his romantic liaison with tempestuous Lupe Velez because she was at one time in the early thirties being groomed for studio stardom. The couple married in 1933, and divorced in 1938 amidst stormy scenes and courtroom arguments.) Metro was soon promoting Weissmuller as "the only man in Hollywood who's natural in the flesh and can act without clothes."

While MGM was preparing the next Tarzan film, Lesser completed his own project, starring Buster Crabbe.[3] **Tarzan the Fearless** was released in 1933 by Principal Pictures as both a feature and a twelve-chapter serial. Because of Burroughs' contractual-copyright freedom, there would be other non-MGM **Tarzan** films in the thirties: Principal's **Tarzan and the Green Goddess** (1938) with Herman Brix and Twentieth Century–Fox's **Tarzan's Revenge** (1938) with Glenn Morris.

However, MGM's series remained far and away the most popular, with five more features following: **Tarzan and His Mate** (1934), **Tarzan Escapes** (1936; remembered for the sequence in which the natives bind prisoners to crossed trees, then rip them in two as the trees are released);[4] **Tarzan Finds a Son!** (1939, which introduced Johnny Sheffield as Boy); **Tarzan's Secret Treasure** (1941), and **Tarzan's New York Adventure** (1942). In the course of these follow-ups, several noticeable changes in the entries were evident: the film industry's Production Code office insisted that the lead players not be so scantily dressed and that a high decorum regarding their joint life be employed (thus, for example, when they have a son, it is the orphaned offspring of two Britishers); less and less care was taken with production values, and more and more stock footage from

past films was used; and Weissmuller continued to grow heftier, Sheffield older, and O'Sullivan more bored. In a 1975 interview with Kingsley Canham for **Focus on Films** magazine, O'Sullivan said:

"To turn briefly to a subject with which I am very bored by today: Cedric Gibbons started **Tarzan and His Mate,** but he was just not a director, so Jack Conway stepped in and finished it, although they both got the credit—probably something to do with Gibbons' contract. It was very hard to tell how long the **Tarzan** films were in the making. The first was made in three months and then, when it was a hit, the second took a year and then they were always making them. They turned them out perpetually, one after another; it was just an endless stream. I was more fortunate—or perhaps Johnny Weissmuller did not care; no, I don't think Johnny cared . . . he was identified as Tarzan and that was that—but I could do and did do other things. Often I would be making three different films in one day. Perhaps I would shoot some scenes in the morning, then go on to **The Barretts of Wimpole Street** in the afternoon, and then some small film like **The Bishop Misbehaves** in the evening. But always they were shooting those **Tarzan** films, so I would have no idea how long each one took."

In 1943 Sol Lesser–RKO acquired the **Tarzan** series, as well as the screen services of Weissmuller and Sheffield, and the entries continued. Weissmuller finally abandoned the part after **Tarzan and the Mermaids** (1948). He went on to a **Jungle Jim** low-budget series at Columbia, and Sheffield starred in **Bomba the Jungle Boy** programmers at Allied Artists.

Tarzan returned to MGM in 1957 in the form of Gordon Scott, who starred in **Tarzan and the Lost Safari** and 1958's **Tarzan's Fight for Life.** In 1959 MGM released a "remake" of **Tarzan the Ape Man,** an inept retelling starring Denny Miller as Tarzan and Joanna Barnes as Jane. Later MGM excursions into the **Tarzan** legend included **Tarzan Goes to India** (1962) and **Tarzan's Three Challenges** (1963), with Jock Mahoney. Although numerous film–TV–cartoon Tarzans have come and gone—Lex Barker, Mike Henry, Ron Ely, et al.—none has matched the flamboyant savagery of Weissmuller's performance in the gaudy, irresistibly entertaining **Tarzan** epics.

Incidentally, as in the tradition of "Let me take you to the Casbah" and "Play it again, Sam," "Me, Tarzan—you, Jane" was never actually spoken on screen. The real words were simply "Tarzan—Jane." Maureen O'Sullivan explains:

I was deathly afraid of height. And one day, Johnny Weissmuller and I had to cower in the high branches of a tree for one of our scenes. Johnny was a practical joker. He knew I was afraid of height. So he began to shake our branch and I screamed.

Recognizing her wail as a variation on his famous cry, Weissmuller intoned, "**Me,** Tarzan—**you,**

Jane." Van Dyke liked it and the line was retained—without the pronouns.

TEA AND SYMPATHY
1956 C—122 min.

Producer, Pandro S. Berman; **director,** Vincente Minnelli; based on the play by Robert Anderson; **screenplay,** Anderson; **art directors,** William A. Horning and Edward Carfagno; **music,** Adolph Deutsch; **costumes,** Helen Rose; **assistant director,** Joel Friedman; **camera,** John Alton; **editor,** Ferris Webster.

Deborah Kerr (**Laura Reynolds**); John Kerr (**Tom Robinson Lee**); Leif Erickson (**Bill Reynolds**); Edward Andrews (**Herb Lee**); Darryl Hickman (**Al**); Norma Crane (**Ellie Martin**); Dean Jones (**Ollie**); Jacqueline DeWit (**Lilly Sears**); Tom Laughlin (**Ralph**); Ralph Votrian (**Steve**); Steven Terrell (**Phil**); Kip King (**Ted**); Jimmy Hayes (**Henry**); Richard Tyler (**Roger**); Don Burnett (**Vic**); Mary Alan Hokanson (**Mary Williams**); Don Kennedy (**Dick**); Peter Miller (**Pete**); Bob Alexander (**Pat**); Michael Monroe (**Earl**); Byron Kane (**Umpire**); Harry Harvey, Jr. and Bobby Ellis (**Boys**); Saul Gorss and Dale Van Sickel (**Men**); Del Erickson (**Ferdie**).

SYNOPSIS

Tom Robinson Lee, now a successful writer, returns to his prep school alma mater for a reunion and reminisces. He recalls his troubled stay at the New England establishment. There was Laura Reynolds, wife of an instructor-housemaster.

Laura is touched and somewhat amused by the puppylike devotion shown to her by young Tom, who lives in her dormitory. She is shocked when fellow students began to deride Tom unmercifully, nicknaming him "sister boy" because he would rather listen to classical music than play ball or swim. Only his roommate Al defends him. Laura is horrified when Tom's father, Herb Lee, upbraids the boy for not acting more manly, and when her husband, Bill, declines to help the student. The hopeless bewilderment that grows in the boy alarms Laura.

John Kerr and Deborah Kerr in Tea and Sympathy *('56).*

---

[2]Filmed on a sixty-day schedule at a cost of $660,000, **Tarzan the Ape Man** earned a profit of $919,000.

[3]Crabbe had been tested in 1931 for the MGM **Tarzan** film, but was never seriously considered for the role. In 1933 he appeared as the star of Paramount's Tarzanesque feature, **King of the Jungle.**

[4]Much of **Tarzan Escapes** was reshot when Metro feared it was too gruesome for the family trade; director Richard Thorpe added much new footage to the picture.

Meanwhile, she too is lonely because Bill Reynolds, despite his outward show of masculinity, is a failure as a husband. Unsubtle Bill warns Laura not to get involved in Tom's plight, and reminds her that she is supposed to give the students only "tea and sympathy." Nevertheless, when she learns that Tom has been goaded into dating the disreputable Ellie Martin—a rendezvous that would cause him to risk expulsion but cause the others to see him as a "man"—Laura uses every pretext to keep him from meeting the girl. However, Tom keeps the date, but runs away from Ellie in revulsion.

This leads him to believe that he is really a "sister boy," and in despair he unsuccessfully attempts suicide. Laura, feeling deeply Tom's siege of misery and humiliation, offers herself to him to prove his manliness. Because of this incident she separates from her husband.

Now, in the present, Tom, who has married and has children of his own, can appreciate fully the sacrifice Laura made to save him.

* * *

Robert Anderson's play **Tea and Sympathy** is a sad and stinging study of a young man taunted in a private school by his peers. While they equate his sensitivity with homosexuality, it is the housemaster's wife who shows him compassion. When the drama bowed on Broadway on September 30, 1953, at the Ethel Barrymore Theatre, it was deemed adult stage fare and ran for 712 performances. Its success made the property movie material, but the controversial theme was highly unorthodox for mid-1950s' cinema.

Producer Pandro S. Berman acquired the screen rights for an MGM production and vowed, despite the censorship problems that the subject matter would entail, to supply the film rendition with an excellent—and true—adaptation. Berman contracted the original stage stars: Deborah Kerr as lonely Laura Reynolds, Leif Erickson as her bullying and inadequate spouse Bill, and John Kerr as the tortured boy. Robert Anderson was signed to write the scenario. The director was Vincente Minnelli, who in his memoirs **I Remember It Well** (1974) quotes a letter of Anderson's, explaining the underlying concept of the drama:

"Of course the meanings of the play are various . . . the chief one being that we must understand and respect the differences in people. . . . Along with this is the whole concept of what manliness is. I attack the often movie-fostered notion that a man is only a man if he can carry Vivien Leigh up a winding staircase. I stump for essential manliness which is something internal, and consists of gentleness, consideration, and other qualities of that sort, and not just of brute strength. Another point, of course, is the tendency for any mass of individuals to gang up on anyone who differs from it . . . if there is nothing to persecute in the individual, they will invent something. That is the only way they can show their strength and solidarity. . . . Also a major point is that when a person is in terrible trouble, we have to give him more than tea and sympathy, we have to give them part of ourselves, no matter what the cost."

In preparing the campus setting for **Tea and Sympathy,** art director Edward Carfagno turned to standing sets on the Metro back lot. The schoolhouse which had been built for Eddie Cantor's **Forty Little Mothers** (1940), had later been revamped for **Good News** (1947), and then for **The Cobweb** (1955) was transformed to represent a sanatorium. For **Tea and Sympathy** Carfagno added a domed cupola and a clock tower to the structure.

The screen adaptation forced Anderson to soften the play's original epithet-filled dialogue.[1] "Sister-boy" is the worst of the names hurled at the focal character in the film. Anderson compensated for these losses by adding to most effective cinematic sequences: one detailing a bonfire pajama raid in which the schoolboys sadistically humiliate Tom; the other focuses on Tom's visit to the town whore (Norma Crane), an experience which so horrifies him that he attempts suicide. Still, the censors did score a victory by insisting that following the famous love-making between Laura and Tom, there be read a letter of apology from the "fallen" Laura for her extramarital sexual act. This postscript badly dampens the effectiveness of the film, which did a masterly job of retaining the power focus of the play original.

"The drama is here in all its aspects," wrote Bosley Crowther of the **New York Times** in his September 28, 1956, review. "Throughout, Mr. Kerr's performance of the lad is incredibly sure, as sensitive as a fine mechanism and yet reflective of the callowness of youth. And Miss Kerr, who is no relative, reveals as the housemaster's wife one of the most genuine and tender female characters we have seen on the screen in a long, long time. . . . Because the letter at the end, which brings the story into a ten-years-later reminiscent frame, is so prudish and unnecessary, we strongly suggest that you leave after Miss Kerr has reached her hand gently toward the boy and spoken the unforgettably poignant line, 'Years from now, when you talk about this—and you will—be kind.'"

Though a solid box-office success, **Tea and Sympathy** was regarded by many as rather daring cinema material, even for 1956. As such this adventure in controversial filmmaking received no major critical honors, save for placing ninth on **Film Daily**'s Ten Best Pictures list.

When Deborah Kerr returned to MGM to make **Tea and Sympathy,** she was no longer under contract to the studio, but a freelancing performer. When she left the home lot after **Julius Caesar** (1953) she stated, "I suffered from too much respect for the boss. I took for granted that the heads of studios, with all their experience, knew

---

[1]Author Robert Anderson would later admit about **Tea and Sympathy:** "The picture didn't come off as well as we had hoped . . . we had to make too many changes for censorship. We kept fooling ourselves that we were preserving the integrity of the theme, but we lost some of it. I feel that the stage production was indeed beautiful, and brought out the harshness and whatever bite the play possessed, while the film bordered on the pretty. But it serves its purpose in preserving the performances of Deborah and Jack Kerr and Leif Erickson."

instinctively what was best for me. It took me six years to learn that perhaps they didn't." She would later play in the following MGM releases: **The Journey** (1959), with Yul Brynner; **Count Your Blessings** (1959), with Rossano Brazzi and Maurice Chevalier; **The Night of the Iguana** (1964), with Richard Burton and Ava Gardner; **Eye of the Devil** (1967), with David Niven; and **The Gypsy Moths** (1969), with Burt Lancaster.

TEST PILOT
1938—118 min.

Producer, Louis D. Lighton; **director,** Victor Fleming; **story,** Frank Wead and, **uncredited,** Howard Hawks; **screenplay,** Vincent Lawrence and Waldemar Young; **music,** Franz Waxman; **art directors,** Cedric Gibbons and John Detlie; **set decorator,** Edwin B. Willis; **wardrobe,** Dolly Tree; **montage,** Slavko Vorkapich; **camera,** Ray June; **editor,** Tom Held.

Clark Gable (**Jim Lane**); Myrna Loy (**Ann Barton**); Spencer Tracy (**Gunner Sloane**); Lionel Barrymore (**Howard B. Drake**); Samuel S. Hinds (**General Ross**); Arthur Aylesworth (**Frank Barton**); Claudia Coleman (**Mrs. Barton**); Gloria Holden (**Mrs. Benson**); Louis Jean Heydt (**Benson**); Ted Pearson (**Joe**); Marjorie Main (**Landlady**); Gregory Gaye (**Grant**); Virginia Grey (**Sarah**); Priscilla Lawson (**Mabel**); Dudley Clements (**Mr. Brown**); Henry Roquemore (**Fat Man**); Byron Foulger (**Designer**); Frank Jaquet (**Motor Expert**); Roger Converse (**Advertising Man**); Billy Engle (**Little Man**); Brent Sargent (**Movie Leading Man**); Mary Howard (**Movie Leading Woman**); Douglas McPhail (**Singing Pilot in Cafe**); Forbes Murray, James Flavin, Hooper Atchley, Dick Winslow, Ray Walker, Richard Tucker, Don Douglas, and Frank Sully (**Pilots in Cafe**); Fay Holden (**Saleslady**); Tom O'Grady (**Bartender**); Syd Saylor (**Boss Loader**).

SYNOPSIS

One of the greatest assets of the airplane company owned and operated by Howard B. Drake is daredevil test pilot Jim Lane. With his mechanic and close pal Gunner Sloane, Jim sets out to test the new Drake "Bullet" on a coast-to-coast flight.

Engine trouble forces Jim to land in Kansas, on the Barton farm. He is immediately attracted to Ann Barton, a pert beauty who returns his infatuation. When his plane is repaired, he takes Ann to Pittsburgh, marries her, and then asks Drake for a week off for his honeymoon. Concerned about his plane, Drake bellows a refusal and fires his ace pilot. The latter, in turn, embarks on a five-day drinking spree. A shocked Ann is about to leave her new husband. However, Gunner finds Jim, sobers him up, and brings him back to his wife. They reconcile. Drake also seeks an end to the quarrel and soon Jim is a very happy, employed newlywed.

Meanwhile, General Ross, who once booted Lane from the army because of his wild night life, wants Jim to test the new B-17 bomber. With sandbags loaded to equal the weight of guns, bombs, and crew, Jim, with Gunner in tow, tries to boost the plane to 30,000 feet. He almost succeeds but the plane suddenly collapses into a terrifying nosedive. The sandbags explode from the rear compartment, pinning Gunner beneath them. As the plane speeds to earth, Jim tries to free his friend. However, Gunner, determined that Jim not lose his life also, kicks Jim from the plane. As Jim parachutes to safety, the B-17 perishes in a spectacular crash. Jim rushes to cradle the corpse of his sacrificial pal.

Jim is so saddened by the death of Gunner that he no longer can serve as a test pilot. However, Drake and Ross determine to rehabilitate the crushed man as a flight instructor. Jim begins a new career, finding happiness in the love of Ann—and in the birth of his baby boy.

* * *

Early one morning in January 1938 Spencer Tracy steered his convertible off Washington Boulevard and into the gateway of MGM. To his surprise, he could not even get near the portals. A mob of Clark Gable fans had earlier congregated there to wait for their idol's car. As it approached they surrounded it and begged for autographs, causing a star-studded traffic jam. The worshippers so completely ignored Tracy that the sensitive actor stood up in his car, threw a mock bow in Gable's direction, and catcalled, "Long live the king! And now, for Christ's sake, let's get inside and go to work!"

When the MGM crew heard of the incident, a prop department fashioned a cardboard crown lined with rabbit's fur and Gable was mockingly crowned in the studio commissary. Columnist Ed Sullivan saw headlines in the incident, and with complete sobriety, asked his readers to vote for the king and the queen of Hollywood. The winners—MGM's Clark Gable and Myrna Loy. During all this, Gable, Loy, and the belligerent Tracy were working together in what became one of MGM's most profitable, popular escapisms of the 1930s— **Test Pilot.**[1]

Test Pilot, a paean to aviation and to the chemistry of its stars, was mostly shot at March Field in the desert near Riverside, California. The company was headed by Gable's favorite man's picture director, Victor Fleming. With the cooperation of the army—a benefit not enjoyed by **Hell's Angels** (1930) and **Dawn Patrol** (1930)—it was a grand production, sometimes with eighteen cameras and 100 planes in the air. Special emphasis was placed on the new bomber craft, the Boeing B-17 "Flying Fortress," which was to

Advertisement for Test Pilot *('38).*

become the most famous bomber plane of World War II.

Tracy had accepted his part in **Test Pilot** with trepidation. His friend, critic J. P. McEvoy, later described the character of Gunner Sloane (as well as Tracy's part in 1940's **Boom Toom**) as "the good-natured goof who loses the girl to Gable." As had happened when they toiled together in **San Francisco** (1936), the two stars worked amicably, but were wary of each other. Gable was envious of Tracy's scene-stealing prowess and likely Oscar (an honor he at the time was only weeks away from acquiring for **Captains Courageous)** and Tracy was resentful of Gable's immense popularity. As Warren G. Harris wrote in **Gable and Lombard** (1974):

Gable was much better liked around the set than Tracy, who tended to lose his violent Irish temper at the least provocation. One morning Tracy turned up nursing a bad hangover, his face looking very tired, his hair a mess. The makeup man tried to fix him up before he went in front of the camera, but Tracy told him to go away. Later, after Tracy had seen the rushes, he berated the makeup man, "Why the hell can't you make me look as good as Gable?"

Despite all the high jinks and bouts of depression, the problems of the company were never glimpsed in **Test Pilot** as the two actors worked perfectly on screen with Loy and with each other.

In **Long Live the King** (1975), author Lynn Tornabene quotes Myrna Loy concerning an ad-

venture of Gable, director Fleming, engineer Al Menasco, and flier Paul Mantz (unit director of the film's flight sequences):

"Vic and Clark and Al were going to Catalina one afternoon; Paul was going to fly them over in a B-17, maybe let Clark take the controls for a while. They asked Spence to go, but he wouldn't and they figured he was afraid. Spence was so angry with them I asked him why he didn't go. At first he just said he didn't want to. Later he told me he wouldn't go because he was on the wagon. He said, 'I couldn't go with those bastards; they're going to get drunk.'

After dinner they all came back very full of themselves. Spence walked right past them without talking, and the next morning, didn't show up for work. I told Clark what had happened and he was terribly chagrined. He wouldn't have gone, ever, if he had known why Spence wouldn't go. After that, we tried to track down Spence, but he got away. He went on a twenty-four-hour drinking spree."

Released in April 1938, **Test Pilot,** with the "King" and "Queen" of Hollywood, as well as one of the cinema's most accoladed actors, was solidly profitable. As **Boxoffice** magazine reported, "This one looks as if it's heading for 'wow' grosses. In star value it has Clark Gable, Myrna Loy, and Spencer Tracy and their performances rank well with anything they have so far done. In the case of Gable and Loy, probably their best here." **Time** magazine offered, "Credit for blending this grounded mental conflict with the melo-

[1]Gable saw to it that young Virginia Grey, a longtime close pal of the star, had a part in this film, as she did in Gable's **Idiot's Delight** (1939).

During the making of **Test Pilot,** Gable was friendly with Paul Mantz, unit director of the flight scenes; Ray Moore, Gable's flying stunt stand-in; and engineer Al Menasco. Their adventures sorely tried Spencer Tracy, who was "trying" to reform his usual wild behavior. However, after one Gable spree, Tracy became so annoyed (or jealous) of the trio that the next day he went out on a twenty-four-hour drinking caper of his own.

drama of wings in the air, screaming struts, and whining motors goes to director Victor Fleming. Not the least of his accomplishments was to exact performances that verge on reality from pert, actressy Myrna Loy and loud, slam-bang Clark Gable. From amenable, sandy Spencer Tracy, currently cinema's No. 1 actor's actor, director Fleming got what he wanted without coaxing." **Test Pilot** was Oscar-nominated as Best Picture but lost to Columbia's **You Can't Take It with You.** There followed a number of highly promoted aviation films, such as Warner Bros.' 1938 remake of **The Dawn Patrol** and its 1939 **Wings of the Navy.**

On May 25, 1942, "Lux Radio Theatre" offered a version of **Test Pilot** with Robert Taylor, Rita Hayworth, and Robert Preston starred.

THAT'S ENTERTAINMENT!
MGM–United Artists, 1974 C—132 min.

Executive producer, Daniel Melnick; **producer-director-script,** Jack Haley, Jr.; **additional music adapter,** Henry Mancini; **music supervisor,** Jesse Kaye; **assistant directors,** Richard Bremerkamp, David Silver, and Claude Binyon, Jr.; **film librarian,** Mort Feinstein; **sound re-recording,** Hal Watkins, Aaron Rochin, Lyle Burbridge, Harry W. Tetrick, and William L. McCaughey; **camera,** Gene Polito, Ernest Laszlo, Russell Metty, Ennio Guarnieri, and Allan Green; **opticals,** Robert Hoag and Jim Liles; **editors,** Bud Friedgen and David E. Blewitt.

Fred Astaire, Bing Crosby, Gene Kelly, Peter Lawford, Liza Minnelli, Donald O'Connor, Debbie Reynolds, Mickey Rooney, Frank Sinatra, James Stewart, and Elizabeth Taylor **(Narrators-Hosts).**

Extracts from: **The Hollywood Revue of 1929** ("Singin' in the Rain"—Cliff Edwards); **Speak Easily** ("Singin' in the Rain"—Jimmy Durante); **Little Nellie Kelly** ("Singin' in the Rain"—Judy Garland); **Singin' in the Rain** ("Singin' in the Rain"—Gene Kelly, Donald O'Connor, and Debbie Reynolds); **Broadway Melody** ("Broadway Melody"—Charles King); **Rosalie** ("Rosalie"—Eleanor Powell); **Rose-Marie** ("Indian Love Call"—Jeanette MacDonald and Nelson Eddy); **The Great Ziegfeld** ("A Pretty Girl Is Like a Melody"—Dennis Morgan [dubbed by Allan Jones] and Virginia Bruce); **Broadway Melody of 1940** ("Begin the Beguine"—Fred Astaire and Eleanor Powell); **It Happened in Brooklyn** ("The Song's Gotta Come from the Heart"—Frank Sinatra and Jimmy Durante); **Cynthia** ("Melody of Spring"—Elizabeth Taylor); **Thousands Cheer** ("Honeysuckle Rose"—Lena Horne); **Take Me Out to the Ball Game** ("Take Me Out to the Ball Game"—Frank Sinatra and Gene Kelly); **Words and Music** ("Thou Swell"—June Allyson); **Good News** ("Varsity Drag" and "French Lesson"—June Allyson and Peter Lawford); **Two Weeks with Love** ("Aba Daba Honeymoon"—Debbie Reynolds and Carleton Carpenter); **A Date with Judy** ("It's a Most Unusual Day"—Elizabeth Taylor, Jane Powell, Wallace Beery, Selena Royle, Robert Stack, George Cleve-

land, Scotty Beckett, Jerry Hunter, and Leon Ames); **The Harvey Girls** ("On the Atcheson, Topeka and Santa Fe"—Judy Garland and Ray Bolger); **Free and Easy** ("It Must Be You"—Robert Montgomery and Lottice Howell); **The Hollywood Revue** ("I've Got a Feelin' for You"—Joan Crawford); **Reckless** ("Reckless"—Jean Harlow [dubbed by Virginia Verrell]); **Suzy** ("Did I Remember?"—Jean Harlow and Cary Grant); **Born to Dance** ("Easy to Love"—James Stewart and Eleanor Powell); **Idiot's Delight** ("Puttin' on the Ritz"—Clark Gable); **Broadway to Hollywood** (montage dance number—Mickey Rooney); **Broadway Melody of 1938** ("You Made Me Love You"—Judy Garland); **Babes in Arms** ("Babes in Arms"—Douglas McPhail and chorus); **Babes on Broadway** ("Hoedown"—Judy Garland and Mickey Rooney); **Strike Up the Band** ("Do the La Conga"—Judy Garland and Mickey Rooney); **Babes on Broadway** ("Waitin' for the Robert E. Lee" and "Babes on Broadway"—Judy Garland and Mickey Rooney); **Strike Up the Band** ("Strike Up the Band"—Judy Garland and Mickey Rooney); **Ziegfeld Follies** ("The Babbitt and the Bromide"—Gene Kelly and Fred Astaire); **The Barkleys of Broadway** ("They Can't Take That Away from Me"—Fred Astaire and Ginger Rogers); **Dancing Lady** ("Rhythm of the Day"—Fred Astaire and Joan Crawford); **The Band Wagon** ("I Guess I'll Have to Change My Plans"—Fred Astaire and Jack Buchanan); **Royal Wedding** ("Sunday Jumps"—Fred Astaire); **The Barkleys of Broadway** ("Shoes with Wings On"—Fred Astaire); **Royal Wedding** ("You're All the World to Me"—Fred Astaire); **The Band Wagon** ("Dancing in the Dark"—Fred Astaire and Cyd Charisse); **Pagan Love Song** ("Pagan Love Song"—Esther Williams); **Bathing Beauty** (production number—Esther Wil-

liams); **Million Dollar Mermaid** (production number—Esther Williams); **Three Little Words** ("I Wanna Be Loved by You"—Debbie Reynolds [dubbed by Helen Kane] and Carleton Carpenter); **Small Town Girl** ("I Gotta Hear That Beat"—Ann Miller; **The Toast of New Orleans** ("Be My Love"—Mario Lanza and Kathryn Grayson); **Singin' in the Rain** ("Make 'em Laugh"—Donald O'Connor); **Show Boat** ("Cotton Blossom"—cast; "Make Believe"—Kathryn Grayson and Howard Keel; "Ol' Man River"—William Warfield); **The Band Wagon** ("By Myself"—Fred Astaire); **The Pirate** ("Be a Clown"—Gene Kelly and the Nicholas Brothers); **Living in a Big Way** (dance number—Gene Kelly); **The Pirate** ("Mack the Black"—Gene Kelly); **On the Town** ("New York, New York"—Frank Sinatra, Gene Kelly, and Jules Munshin); **Anchors Aweigh** ("The Worry Song"—Gene Kelly and Jerry the Mouse); **Singin' in the Rain** ("Singin' in the Rain" and "Broadway Melody"—Gene Kelly); **In the Good Old Summertime** ("In the Good Old Summertime"—Judy Garland, Van Johnson, and Liza Minnelli); **La Fiesta Santa Barbara** ("La Cucaracha"—The Gumm Sisters with Judy Garland); **Every Sunday** ("Opera Versus Jazz"—Judy Garland and Deanna Durbin); **Broadway Melody of 1938** (dance—Judy Garland and Buddy Ebsen); **The Wizard of Oz** ("We're Off to See the Wizard"—Judy Garland; "If I Only Had a Brain"—Judy Garland, Ray Bolger, Jack Haley, and Bert Lahr; "Over the Rainbow"—Judy Garland); **Meet Me in St. Louis** ("The Trolley Song"—Judy Garland; "Under the Bamboo Tree"—Judy Garland and Margaret O'Brien; "The Boy Next Door"—Judy Garland) **Summer Stock** ("Get Happy"—Judy Garland); **Going Hollywood** ("Going Hollywood"—Bing Crosby); **High Society** ("Well, Did You Evah!"—Bing Crosby and Frank Sinatra;

Host Bing Crosby in That's Entertainment! *('74).*

"True Love"—Bing Crosby and Grace Kelly); **Hit the Deck** ("Halleluja"—Kay Armen, Debbie Reynolds, Jane Powell, Ann Miller, Tony Martin, Russ Tamblyn, and Vic Damone); **Seven Brides for Seven Brothers** ("Barnraising Ballet"—cast); **Gigi** ("Gigi"—Louis Jourdan; "Thank Heaven for Little Girls"—Maurice Chevalier); and **An American in Paris** ("An American in Paris"—Gene Kelly and Leslie Caron).

By 1974, 10202 West Washington Boulevard in Culver City had become one of the film industry's most chilling mausoleums. Though the Metro-Goldwyn-Mayer Studios had produced some major box-office films throughout the sixties and early seventies, the majority of them—**Dr. Zhivago** (1965), **The Dirty Dozen** (1967), **2001: A Space Odyssey** (1968), **Ryan's Daughter** (1970)—were filmed abroad. In later years the studio's product was not even released by MGM, but by United Artists. There were well-publicized funereal touches, such as the lamentable MGM "Auction" where such pieces of memorabilia as Judy Garland's **Wizard of Oz** slippers were sold to affluent buffs, and the destruction of back lot landmarks, such as the **Hardy** family home and **Tarzan's** jungle. The British branch of MGM closed, amalgamating with EMI in 1970; the lot announced the curtailment of feature production and appeared to place its major interest in the Las Vegas Grand Hotel, which opened at Christmas 1973. On the fiftieth anniversary of the studio's opening, new president Frank E. Rosenfelt (an attorney) sought to quiet some of the tongue-clucking concerning the fate of "Hollywood's most prodigal studio." He announced, "One of our principal objectives will be to provide a climate at MGM which will attract creative filmmakers. . . . Contrary to recent public speculation, the roar of Leo the Lion will not be reduced to a weak meow."

Far more effective, however, in winning the sadly humbled studio some painfully needed respect was the release in May 1974 of **That's Entertainment!** It was the Jack Haley, Jr.—weaved anthology of the 1928–58 musical highlights of Metro's history. The film became a show business phenomenon. **Variety** would rejoice, "While many ponder the future of Metro-Goldwyn-Mayer, nobody can deny that it has one hell of a past."

In widescreen 70-mm and remixed stereophonic sound, the "sensational" retrospective" boasted clips from over a hundred movies and was tied together by eleven star narrators in specially filmed introductions. They themselves provided an endearing glance into the heritage of Metro by their attitudes, comments, and vanities. A still slim but aged Fred Astaire introduced clips of friend Gene Kelly, with Kelly returning the favor for Astaire; Liza Minnelli solemnly introduced a segment dedicated to her mother (with some especially fascinating clips of Judy with Deanna Durbin in their premiere short, **Every Sunday**); Peter Lawford gave the lead-in to the college-type youth musicals, in which he so self-consciously played in **Good News** (like Astaire in his segment, which showed the deteriorated train station set from **The Band Wagon** both then and now, so Lawford wan-

Hostess Debbie Reynolds in That's Entertainment!

dered amidst the remnants of the Tate College locale); Debbie Reynolds spoke of the studio's penchant for casting unknowns in major roles (as she was in **Singin' in the Rain**); James Stewart employed his usual self-parody in introducing musical efforts of nonmusical performers (including his attempted serenade to Eleanor Powell, "So Easy to Love," from **Born to Dance**); a poignantly aged Donald O'Connor strolled by the decaying standing pool set formerly graced by Esther Williams in a segment dedicated to that aquatic wonder; Bing Crosby introduced his "Well, Did You Evah!" from **High Society**; Frank Sinatra opened and closed the film; and a stunningly photographed Elizabeth Taylor, who generally speaks of her eighteen MGM years with scarcely disguised sarcasm, betrayed her attitude here and there between the lines, her violet eyes glinting now and then as she delivered her antiseptic piece.

That's Entertainment! contained segments which caused audiences alternately to cheer (O'Connor's "Make 'em Laugh" from **Singin' in the Rain,** the "Pretty Girl" extravaganza from **The Great Ziegfeld**, Eleanor Powell's tapping on that oversized, awe-inspiring set of **Rosalie**, Astaire's off-the-wall and ceiling hoofing from **Royal Wedding**), to smirk (Harlow painfully lip-synching to Virginia Verrill's dubbing in **Reckless**, Gable performing his 'Puttin' on the Ritz" in straw hat and cane with chorus girls as Norma Shearer rolls her eyes in **Idiot's Delight**), and to marvel (especially at the Busby Berkeley fire-and-water ballet starring Esther Williams from **Million Dollar Mermaid** (the film's top crowd-pleaser, which would have been a far better climax for the film than the cut ballet from **An American in Paris** which closed the film rather anticlimactically.

Most of the surviving MGM alumni were delighted with the attention promised them with the

spring 1974 release of **That's Entertainment!** The majority turned out for the gala premiere celebration: over fifty survivors were on hand. Those who preferred to stay at home included Greta Garbo (of course). Greer Garson and Walter Pidgeon (perhaps miffed that **musicals** were the meat of the film), and, strangely enough, the film's most revived star, Esther Williams (for reasons made more clear with the release of **That's Entertainment: Part II**).

Critical reaction was one of pure ecstasy to the methodical presentation, which offered audiences the finest quality of prints available from the selected pictures. Not only were newly minted prints utilized, but the sound department did everything it could to reproduce the fidelity of the original soundtracks, enhanced for today's sophisticated audio equipment. One of the catchy gimmicks utilized throughout the film was the switching from black-and-white films to color product, from the regular screen to widescreen, and from (enhanced) mono to stereo sound. It did a good deal to keep audience interest from lagging.

Variety exhausted the adjectives: "Outstanding, stunning, sentimental, exciting, colorful, enjoyable, spirit-lifting, tuneful, youthful, invigorating, zesty, respectful, heartwarming, awesome, cheerful, dazzling, and richly satisfying." The **Hollywood Reporter** noted, "Those lavish musical films are genuine American folk art, masterfully made and performed, and uncluttered by neurotic agony. Their purpose was to create pleasure, a form of entertainment the movies have, hopefully, only temporarily set aside."

The 132-minute anthology was a revelation[1]

---

[1]Metro, like the other studios, had frequently issued short subjects to the theatres detailing segments of its product history, as well as such fuller-length entries as

for young film fans who have had little exposure to the grand old days, and a nostalgia orgy for the older patrons, many of whom had not ventured into a movie theatre in years.[2] The full-length film became the ninth greatest grosser in MGM's history—$10,800,000.

Finally, it should be noted that the name of Louis B. Mayer is singled out in an opening credit card. Though maligned by many, and hardly the sort of man who demonstrated the cardinal virtues (as revealed in numerous entries in this book), Mayer indeed deserved the tribute paid him by this film, which owed so much to his courage and foresight.

Astaire and Cyd Charisse); **Seven Brides for Seven Brothers** ("Lonesome Polecat"—Howard Keel); **Lovely to Look At** ("Smoke Gets in Your Eyes"—Kathryn Grayson, Marge Champion, and Gower Champion); **Easter Parade** ("Easter Parade"—Fred Astaire and Judy Garland; "Steppin' Out with My Baby"—Fred Astaire; "A Couple of Swells"—Fred Astaire and Judy Garland); **Going Hollywood** ("Temptation"—Bing Crosby and Fifi D'Orsay); **Listen, Darling** ("Zing Went the Strings of My Heart"—Judy Garland); **Cabin in the Sky** ("Taking a Chance on Love"—Ethel Waters and Eddie "Rochester" Anderson); **Born to Dance** ("Swingin' the Jinx Away"—Eleanor Powell); **New**

Moon ("Stouthearted Men"—Nelson Eddy; "Lover Come Back to Me"—Nelson Eddy and Jeanette MacDonald); **Hollywood Party** ("Inka Dinka Doo"—Jimmy Durante); **Girl Crazy** ("I Got Rhythm"—Judy Garland and Mickey Rooney); **Songwriters Revue** ("Songwriters Revue of 1929"—Jack Benny); **The Broadway Melody** ("Wedding of the Painted Doll"—original troupe); **Lady Be Good** ("Lady Be Good"—Ann Sothern and Robert Young); **Broadway Serenade** ("Broadway Serenade"—Lew Ayres and Al Shean; "For Every Lonely Heart"—Jeanette MacDonald); **Words and Music** ("The Lady Is a Tramp"—Lena Horne; "Manhattan"—Mickey Rooney, Tom Drake, and Marshall Thompson); **Three**

THAT'S ENTERTAINMENT: PART II

(MGM–United Artists, 1976) C—133 min.

Producers, Saul Chaplin and Daniel Melnick; **new sequences director**, Gene Kelly; **commentary**, Leonard Gershe; **production designer**, John De-Cuir; **music director–music arranger**, Nelson Riddle; **music supervisor**, Harry V. Lojewski; **special lyrics**, Howard Dietz and Saul Chaplin; **assistant director**, William R. Poole; **animators**, Hanna-Barbera Productions; **sound**, Bill Edmondson; **sound-recording**, Hal Watkins and Aaron Rochin; **camera**, George Folsey; **editors**, Bud Friedgen and David Blewitt; **contributing editors**, David Bretherton and Peter C. Johnson.

Fred Astaire and Gene Kelly (Hosts).

Extracts from: **The Band Wagon** ("That's Entertainment"—Fred Astaire, Nanette Fabray, Oscar Levant, Jack Buchanan, Cyd Charisse; "Triplets"—Astaire, Fabray, Buchanan); **For Me and My Gal** ("For Me and My Gal"—Judy Garland and Gene Kelly); **Lady Be Good** ("Fascinatin' Rhythm"—Eleanor Powell); **Broadway Melody of 1936** ("I've Got a Feeling You're Fooling"—Robert Taylor); **Two-Faced Woman** ("La Chica Chaca"—Greta Garbo); **The Belle of New York** ("I Wanna Be a Dancin' Man"—Fred Astaire); **Lili** ("Hi-Lili, Hi-Lo"—Leslie Caron); **The Pirate** ("Be a Clown"—Judy Garland and Gene Kelly); **Kiss Me Kate** ("From This Moment On"—Ann Miller, Tommy Fall, Carol Haney, Bobby Van, Bob Fosse, and Jeanne Coyne); **Silk Stockings** ("All of You"—Fred

Co-hosts Fred Astaire and Gene Kelly in That's Entertainment: Part II *('76).*

The MGM Story (1951) and **MGM's Big Parade of Comedy** (1964). For many years, Loew's theatres around the country had recurring operetta series, featuring many of the Jeanette MacDonald–Nelson Eddy musicals, and there is still a MGM matinee series encompassing such children's features as **National Velvet**, **Sequoia**, the **Lassie** films, etc.

[2] There were some miffed filmgoers who resented the unfair showcasing of Joan Crawford in an awkward dance sequence (from **Hollywood Revue of 1929**); the snippet of Jeanette MacDonald-Nelson Eddy from **Rose-Marie**, which displayed them to disadvantage; and the strange exclusion of Ann Sothern, who was one of MGM's brightest and most accomplished singing performers for a decade.

Little Words ("Three Little Words"—Fred Astaire and Red Skelton); **The Great Waltz** ("Tales from the Vienna Woods"—Fernand Gravet and Miliza Korjus); **Singin' in the Rain** ("Good Morning"—Gene Kelly, Debbie Reynolds, and Donald O'Connor; "Broadway Rhythm"—Gene Kelly and Cyd Charisse); **An American in Paris** ("Concerto in I"—Oscar Levant; "I Got Rhythm"—Gene Kelly; "Our Love Is Here to Stay"—Gene Kelly and Leslie Caron; "I'll Build a Stairway to Paradise"—Georges Guetary); **Meet Me in St. Louis** ("Have Yourself a Merry Little Christmas—Judy Garland and Mar-

garet O'Brien); **Love Me or Leave Me** ("Ten Cents a Dance"—Doris Day and James Cagney); **The Tender Trap** ("The Tender Trap"—Frank Sinatra); **Till the Clouds Roll By** ("Ol' Man River"—Frank Sinatra; "The Last Time I Saw Paris"—Dinah Shore); **Anchors Aweigh** ("I Fall in Love Too Easily"—Frank Sinatra; "I Begged Her"—Frank Sinatra and Gene Kelly); **It Happened in Brooklyn** ("I Believe"—Frank Sinatra, Jimmy Durante, and Billy Roy); **High Society** ("You're Sensational"—Frank Sinatra and Grace Kelly; "Now You Has Jazz"—Bing Crosby and Louis Armstrong); **The**

Merry Widow (1934) ("Maxim's" and "Girls, Girls, Girls"—Maurice Chevalier; "The Merry Widow Waltz"); **The Merry Widow** (1952) ("Can-Can"—Gwen Verdon and dancers); **Invitation to the Dance** ("Sinbad"—Gene Kelly); **Small Town Girl** ("Take Me to Broadway"—Bobby Van); **Annie Get Your Gun** ("There's No Business Like Show Business"—Betty Hutton, Howard Keel, Keenan Wynn, and Louis Calhern); **It's Always Fair Weather** ("I Like Myself"—Gene Kelly); **Gigi** ("I Remember It Well"—Maurice Chevalier and Hermione Gingold); **The Barkleys of Broadway** ("Bouncin' the Blues"—Fred Astaire and Ginger Rogers); **Easy to Love** ("Water Ski Ballet"—Esther Williams); **Bud Abbott and Lou Costello in Hollywood** (Bit); **Adam's Rib** (Spencer Tracy and Katharine Hepburn); **A Day at the Races** (The Three Marx Brothers); **A Night at the Opera** (The Three Marx Brothers); **A Tale of Two Cities** (Bit); **Bombshell** (Jean Harlow); **Boom Town** (Spencer Tracy and Clark Gable); **Boys Town** (Spencer Tracy and Mickey Rooney); **China Seas** (Robert Benchley); **Dancing Lady** (Bit); **David Copperfield** (W. C. Fields); **Dinner at Eight** (Jean Harlow); **Gone with the Wind** (Vivien Leigh and Clark Gable); **Goodbye, Mr. Chips** (Bit); **Grand Hotel** (Greta Garbo and John Barrymore); **Billy Rose's Jumbo** (Jimmy Durante); **Lassie Come Home** (Roddy McDowall); **Laurel and Hardy's Laughing Twenties** (Bits); **Ninotchka** (Greta Garbo); **Pat and Mike** (Spencer Tracy and Katharine Hepburn); **The Philadelphia Story** (Katharine Hepburn and Cary Grant); **Private Lives** (Bit); **Saratoga** (Jean Harlow and Clark Gable); **Strange Cargo** (Bit); **Tarzan the Ape Man** (Johnny Weissmuller); **The Thin Man** (William Powell); **Two Girls and a Sailor** (Bit); **White Cargo** (Bit); **Without Love** (Bit); **Ziegfeld Girl** (Bit); and scenes from the travelogues: **Hong Kong, Hub of the Orient; Stockholm, Pride of Sweden; Beautiful Banff and Lake Louise; Land of the Taj Mahal, Colorful Guatemala; Japan, in Cherry Blossom Time; Ireland, the Emerald Isle; Switzerland, the Beautiful; Picturesque Udaipur; Old New Orleans; A Day on Treasure Island; Madeira, Island of Romance; Copenhagen, City of Towers.**

Television ad for That's Entertainment: Part II.

With the high-grossing success of **That's Entertainment!** (1974), a sequel appeared inevitable. After all, much rich cinematic material still remained untapped. Thus when Culver City issued a publicity release that another all-star anthology of great Metro moments was being assembled, few were taken aback. Especially enticing to film enthusiasts was the news that the new documentary would embrace not only musicals, but also great scenes of the big stars in their finest movies. The report inspired wild conjecture about which vignettes would be included: Clark Gable confronting Charles Laughton in **Mutiny on the Bounty**? A suspenseful Greer Garson and Walter Pidgeon in the bombing-raid shelter from **Mrs. Miniver**? The three Barrymores displaying flamboyant dash in **Rasputin and the Empress**? Jean Harlow and Wallace Beery swapping venomous insults in **Dinner at Eight**?

Suffice it to say that none of these classic

moments appeared. Indeed, **That's Entertainment: Part II** proved a huge disappointment to most viewers. While containing brief—very brief—glimpses of such Metro legends as Tarzan, Nick and Nora Charles, Greta Garbo, Laurel and Hardy, the 1976 release functioned principally as a vehicle for two of the lot's aging and most active veterans, Fred Astaire and Gene Kelly. Although the film—**not** packaged by Jack Haley, Jr.—exposed a prodigious amount of talent, and managed again to overwhelm less-erudite film lovers, **That's Entertainment: Part II** emerged more as a testimony to Kelly's and Astaire's charisma (and egos) than as a sweeping survey of MGM's fifty glorious years.

"Even if it's a dud, it's a compendium of history," said Kelly, who "directed" the bridge sequences featuring himself and Astaire. (One of the few joys in the film was the opening credits, which falsely promised that the presentation would have some originality of concept; the title cards were executed in a variety of genre styles, which have become delightful clichés over the decades). The 133 minutes[1] contained a salute to Spencer Tracy and Katharine Hepburn, and to Jeanette MacDonald and Nelson Eddy, and several studio travelogues (amusing more for the requisite "Now we bid a fond farewell" closing than for their contents), but gave brutally short shrift to other classic moments and vintage stars. Greer Garson was glimpsed long enough to say "Goodbye, Mr. Chips"; Walter Pidgeon was seen for a second or two from one of his **Nick Carter** programmers; the unforgettable Greta Garbo–John Barrymore love scene from **Grand Hotel** was unmercifully scanned for a few brief lines; Laurel and Hardy (whose appearance brought sighs of joy from many audiences) were shown driving a car—then disappearing permanently; and so forth.

A bit more time was devoted to **Gone With the Wind,** and there were sections focusing on Frank Sinatra's Metro stay (although nothing was included from his MGM finale-fiasco, **Dirty Dingus McGee,** 1970), the stateroom scene from the Marx Brothers' **A Night at the Opera,** and Eleanor Powell at her most glorious in "Swingin' the Jinx Away" from **Born to Dance.** However, with exasperating steadiness, the film kept returning to the talents of Astaire and Kelly, awesome indeed, but tiresome when overexposed to the detriment of the other talents involved. The film reverted so often to the two hosts' sequences that Kelly, obviously unable to think of a new line to introduce Fred's next vignette, simply said, "Here you are again, Fred!"

Once again, MGM went to great pains to promote the new anthology. The studio arranged for several of Mike Douglas' TV talk shows to concentrate on the film, with many guest appearances by studio veterans.[2] The world premiere was held

on Astaire's birthday, May 10, 1976 (he turned 77), at New York's Ziegfeld Theatre, for the benefit of the Film Society of Lincoln Center.

Some critics were "overwhelmed" by the package. Rex Reed: "A glittering extravaganza of music and excitement. Will dazzle, amuse, and make the heart beat faster!" Charles Champlin, **Los Angeles Times:** "A half century of MGM genius. A super rich dessert." Kevin Saunders, WABC-TV: "Hollywood as it was in extravagant abundance and splendor. It's all there!" However, Geoff Brown of the discriminating British **Monthly Film Bulletin** noted that "quality never keeps up with quantity. . . . The random arrangement of the clips only emphasizes the lack of thought behind the project." As for the ever-present hosts, the **New York Times'** Vincent Canby wrote, "They are still vital talents, but they should sue the makeup men who have attempted to erase the years of their careers under layers of paint and borrowed hair."

Several veteran Metro stars went on a cross-country promotional tour and then flew to Europe to do the same (following the publicity pattern of **That's Entertainment!**), but one ex-MGM star[3] took a different tack. In September 1976, in Los Angeles Superior Court, Esther Williams sued MGM for $1 million for breach of contract and invasion of privacy. Terming the two pictures "unwarranted exploitations," she charged that the film studio had no legal right to utilize sequences in a new film without consulting her about it or offering to share profits from the reissue, or both. She cited her 1951 and 1955 pacts with MGM covering the films: **Million Dollar Mermaid, Dangerous When Wet, Pagan Love Song,** etc. Trying to fathom her action, some insisted that the ex-MGM star never forgave the company for letting her leave the fold in 1955 (following **Jupiter's Darling**) with hardly a goodbye or a thank-you. The matter was settled privately.

Lucrative, but not nearly as popular as the 1974 film, **That's Entertainment: Part II** appears to be the studio's last attempt to anthologize its history, at least for some time to come.

the 'A' company." Ann Miller, complete with her trademark boa and lavish hair arrangement, was at odds with Janis Paige over the merits of the old MGM contract system; Ann was a staunch supporter, while Janis lamented the lack of "freedom." Debbie Reynolds finally intervened as a tactful peacemaker. Sammy Cahn (his sequence cut in the film) appeared to sing a tribute with Paul Anka to the tune of "My Way" to Astaire and Kelly (who were Mike's cohosts), both of whom grinned stoically through the dismal lyrics.

Only joyously frank Pidgeon directly remarked the specious quality of the tribute. After Douglas' none too successful interviews with Walter, Garson (twirling a rose), Kelly, Astaire, and Mervyn LeRoy (apparently intimidated by Walter's cracks), Pidgeon lamented, "Why don't we end this and have a drink?"

[3]Another annoyed star was Elizabeth Taylor. She felt it unethical of MGM to promote her as a part of the **That's Entertainment: Part II** proceedings, and then barely show her in the footage used.

---

[1]Among the sequences cut from **That's Entertainment: Part II** were Sammy Cahn as a cohost and segments from **Seven Brides for Seven Brothers.**

[2]Many rare moments occurred on the "Mike Douglas Show." The host, on one occasion, asked Gene Kelly if he had ever worked with Greer Garson and Walter Pidgeon; Kelly replied somewhat snidely, "Oh, no, they were

THE THIN MAN
1934—91 min.

Producer, Hunt Stromberg; **director,** W. S. Van Dyke II; based on the novel by Dashiell Hammett; **screenplay,** Albert Hackett and Frances Goodrich; **assistant director,** Les Selander; **art directors,** Cedric Gibbons and David Townsend; **set decorator,** Edwin B. Willis; **costumes,** Dolly Tree; **music director,** Dr. William Axt; **sound,** Douglas Shearer; **camera,** James Wong Howe; **editor,** Robert J. Kern.

William Powell **(Nick Charles);** Myrna Loy **(Nora Charles);** Maureen O'Sullivan **(Dorothy Wynant);** Nat Pendleton **(Lieutenant John Guild);** Minna Gombell **(Mimi Wynant);** Porter Hall **(McCauley);** Henry Wadsworth **(Tommy);** William Henry **(Gilbert Wynant);** Harold Huber **(Nunheim);** Cesar Romero **(Chris Jorgenson);** Natalie Moorhead **(Julia Wolf);** Edward Brophy **(Joe Morelli);** Thomas Jackson, Creighton Hale, Phil Tead, Nick Copeland, and Dink Templeton **(Reporters);** Ruth Channing **(Mrs. Jorgenson);** Edward Ellis **(Clyde Wynant);** Gertrude Short **(Marion);** Clay Clement **(Quinn);** Cyril Thornton **(Tanner);** Robert E. Homans **(Bill, the Detective);** Raymond Brown **(Dr. Walton);** Douglas Fowley and Sherry Hall **(Taxi Drivers);** Polly Bailey and Dixie Laughton **(Janitresses);** Arthur Belasco, Ed Hearn, and Garry Owen **(Detectives);** Fred Malatesta **(Headwaiter);** Rolfe Sedan and Leo White **(Waiters);** Ben Taggart **(Police Captain);** Pat Flaherty **(Cop–Fighter).**

SYNOPSIS

Inventor Clyde Wynant disappears and his distraught daughter Dorothy implores Nick Charles to help her locate her father.

At first Nick, a retired sleuth on holiday, is reluctant but finds his interest kindled by the discovery of the body of Clyde's secretary, Julia Wolf. Along with his chic wife, Nora, Nick undertakes the case and soon discovers a corpse at the inventor's shop. The victim is Clyde.

Later Nick and Nora congregate all the suspects at a dinner party. There he reveals that the inventor's lawyer, McCauley, is the murderer. The attorney, aided by Julia, had been robbing the inventor. The latter, in turn, discovered their plot and was killed for his knowledge. The lawyer later murdered Julia because she knew too much about the caper.

Her father's name cleared, Dorothy is content and plans to wed Tommy.

* * *

It is amazing even today to contemplate that **The Thin Man,** one of most popular film series to flow from MGM in the thirties and forties, was almost aborted at conception by Louis B. Mayer.[1]

---

[1]Decades later the husband-and-wife screenwriting team of Albert Hackett and Frances Goodrich would relate about scripting **The Thin Man.** "We were hesitant about tackling a detective story—but the director, Mr. Van Dyke, said, 'I don't care anything about the mystery stuff, just give me fine scenes between Nick and Nora.'"

In planning the Dashiell Hammett novel for the screen, director W. S. Van Dyke II pictured two stars as the gilt-edged, mutually insulting, marvelously chemical Nick and Nora Charles: William Powell and Myrna Loy.[2] Mayer was apprehensive. To prove his point, Van Dyke reminded his boss that he had just directed Powell and Loy in **Manhattan Melodrama** (1934) and that they had worked very well together. More important, he referred to Powell's past interpretations of sleuth Philo Vance (at Paramount and Warner Bros.) as substantiation that he could well handle the new detective image. Finally, after agreeing to film the picture on a particularly rigid production schedule (of sixteen days), the director received reluctant studio approval.

In this initial **The Thin Man**—the title refers to tall, gangly Edward Ellis, not to Powell's character—the two leads, as Van Dyke anticipated, proved delightful foils for each other: both urbane, both slightly patrician, both blessed with divinely barbed tongues. Their exchanges alone were worth the price of admission, even without the bonus of the who-dun-it aspects.

NORA: What are you going to give me for Christmas? I hope I don't like it.
NICK: Well, you'll have to keep them anyway. There's a man at the aquarium who said he wouldn't take them back.

NORA: I think it's a dirty trick to bring me all the way to New York just to make a widow out of me.
NICK: You wouldn't be a widow long.
NORA: You bet I wouldn't.
NICK: Not with all your money.

NICK: I'm a hero. I was shot twice in the **Tribune.**
NORA: I read you were shot five times in the tabloids.
NICK: It's not true. He didn't come anywhere near my tabloids.

Powell and Loy would occupy a unique niche in MGM screen couples. They did not overemphasize sex appeal, as did Clark Gable and Jean Harlow; they were not noble and grand, like Greer Garson and Walter Pidgeon; and they did not bounce with youthful energy, like Mickey Rooney and Judy Garland. But they were fun—sophisticated, dry, and unobtrusively sensual. Although they would perpetuate their popularity together in other MGM films—**The Great Ziegfeld** (1936), **Libeled Lady** (1936), **Love Crazy** (1941), and more—the characters of Nick and Nora Charles always accommodated their tandem performing best. Another special novelty of these characterizations was that both individuals were equal. Nora never allowed herself to be subservient to Nick, unless she chose to be—quite something in the days

Myrna Loy, William Powell, Porter Hall, and Minna Gombell in The Thin Man *('34).*

before woman's liberation was commonly accepted.

MGM released the picture with the following promotional copy: "It's a pleasure to tell you! Filming an important novel like The Thin Man is a privilege and honor! M-G-M did it with gay excitement, mixing each hair-raising thrill with fun and frolic. A prediction. We think you'll describe it as the best movie of the season!"[3]

"I shot it in sixteen days [actually eighteen], retakes and all. And that sweet smell of success was in every frame," said Van Dyke of his "modest" effort, which was released in June 1934. Richard Watts, Jr. **(New York Herald-Tribune)** was enthusiastic: "Vigorous, resourceful, and nervously moving, it combines brashness with excitement and emerges as a triumph of cinema mystery narration."

Aiding the audience appeal of the movie was the Charles' pet dog, Asta. As Loy remembered later, "He was a wirehair terrier and they were not popular at all at the time. His name was really Skippy and he was highly trained to do all of his tricks for a little squeaky mouse and a biscuit. He'd do anything for that reward. But the minute his scenes were over, it was definitely verboten to hug him or have any further contact with him off the set."

Both the film and Powell won Academy Award nominations. The Best Picture that year was **It Happened One Night** (Columbia) and the Best Ac-

tor Oscar went to that comedy's Clark Gable. **The Thin Man,** which would gross over $1 million, placed sixth on the **Film Daily** Ten Best Picture Poll and ninth on the National Board of Review's top ten selections.

William K. Everson, in his tome **The Detective in Film** (1972), wrote of Powell's Nick and Loy's Nora: "Their devotion to each other was obvious, and they had **fun.** They also satisfied a kind of wish fulfillment from audiences in those rather grim days in that they solved the Depression by completely ignoring it rather than by offering patronizing platitudes or artificial solutions."

In 1936 Powell and Loy reprised their **Thin Man** roles on "Lux Radio Theatre" (June 18) and also that year were reunited with writer Dashiell Hammett, director W. S. Van Dyke II, and producer Hunt Stromberg for **After the Thin Man.** When the followup picture opened on Christmas Day at New York City's Capitol Theatre, Howard Barnes **(New York Herald-Tribune)** wrote, "If After the Thin Man tends to confirm the theory that sequels never measure up to their originals, it is still an absorbing and glibly amusing photoplay . . . a brisk-paced and intriguing mixture of violence and brash fooling. It is not as engaging as **The Thin Man,** but it recaptures a great deal of its notable prototype's bright, insouciant quality."

While other studios, and even MGM were turning out screwball detective films in rank imitation of **The Thin Man,** Metro continued carefully with its lucrative series. At one point in 1938 it

---

In three weeks they turned out the script, including five fine interchanges between the two lead characters.

[2]At one point in pre-production the studio considered casting Edward Ellis, who was later assigned to the title role of Clyde Wynant, to portray Nick Charles.

---

[3]Filmed at a cost of $231,000, **The Thin Man** earned a profit of $729,000.

considered having Melvyn Douglas (or Reginald Gardiner) and Virginia Bruce take over the Nick and Nora Charles screen roles, because of Powell's recurring physical ailments. However, Powell and Loy returned on-camera in **Another Thin Man** (1939), **Shadow of the Thin Man** (1941), **The Thin Man Goes Home** (1944), and **Song of the Thin Man** (1947).

Although Peter Lawford and Phyllis Kirk would attract a huge following when they became the television Nick and Nora Charles (1957–59), Powell and Loy remain the definitive sleuths of Dashiell Hammett's novel.[4]

THIRTY SECONDS OVER TOKYO
1944—138 min.

Producer, Sam Zimbalist; **director,** Mervyn LeRoy; based on the book by Ted W. Lawson and Robert Considine; **screenplay,** Dalton Trumbo; **music,** Herbert Stothart; **art directors,** Cedric Gibbons and Paul Groesse; **set decorators,** Edwin B. Willis and Ralph S. Hurst; **assistant director,** Wally Worsley; **sound,** Douglas Shearer and John F. Dullam; **special effects,** A. Arnold Gillespie, Warren Newcombe, and Donald Jahraus; **camera,** Harold Rosson and Robert Surtees; **editor,** Frank Sullivan.

Van Johnson (**Captain Ted W. Lawson**); Spencer Tracy (**Lieutenant Colonel James H. Doolittle**); Robert Walker (**David Thatcher**); Phyllis Thaxter (**Ellen Lawson**); Tim Murdock (**Dean Davenport**); Scott McKay (**Davey Jones**); Gordon McDonald (**Bob Clever**); Don DeFore (**Charles McClure**); Robert Mitchum (**Bob Gray**); John R. Reilly (**Shorty Manch**); Horace [Stephen] McNally (**Doc White**); Donald Curtis (**Lieutenant Randall**); Louis Jean Heydt (**Lieutenant Miller**); William "Bill" Phillips (**Don Smith**); Douglas Cowan (**Brick Holstrom**); Paul Langton (**Captain "Ski" York**); Leon Ames (**Lieutenant Jurika**); Moroni Olsen (**General**); Benson Fong (**Young Chung**); Dr. Hein Kung Chuan Chi (**Old Chung**); Kay Williams, Peggy Maley, Hazel Brooks, Myrna Dell, and Elaine Shepard (**Girls in Officers' Club**); Dorothy Ruth Morris (**Jane**); Ann Shoemaker (**Mrs. Parker**); Ching Wah Lee (**Guerrilla Charlie**); Morris Ankrum (**Captain Halsey**); Steve Brodie (**MP**); Harry Hayden (**Judge**); Blake Edwards (**Officer**); Robert Bice (**Jig White**); Bill Williams (**Bud Felton**); Alan Napier, Selena Royle, and Jacqueline White (**Bits**).

SYNOPSIS
Captain Ted W. Lawson, a World War II army pilot, learns he is to be part of a surprise attack on

---

[4]Craig Stevens and Jo Ann Pflug would appear as the detective couple in an ill-fated 1975 entry on "ABC Wide World of Mystery." In the Neil Simon screen spoof, **Murder by Death** (1976), David Niven and Maggie Smith did a send-up of the Charleses as Dick and Dora Charleston.

Robert Walker, Van Johnson, and Spencer Tracy in Thirty Seconds over Tokyo *('44).*

Japan in revenge for the Japanese raid on Pearl Harbor. Lieutenant Colonel James H. Doolittle visits the prospective flyers and explains the dangerous mission. He then asks any man who feels he does not want to risk his life in so perilous a mission to drop out without fear of ridicule. None does.

In April 1942 the B-25 twin-engine Mitchell bombers take off from the U.S. aircraft carrier **Hornet.** The surprise attack is a success but a costly one. Some of the planes return to the ship, but many are destroyed or lost at sea. Lawson's plane, the **Ruptured Duck,** crashes off the coast of China. Ted makes his way inland but his injuries result in the amputation of the lower part of one of his legs.

Nevertheless, with the help of his friend David Thatcher, fellow crewmen, and the gallant Chinese people themselves, Lawson manages to make his way back to Allied lines.

He is reunited with Doolittle, who commends him for his bravery, and with his wife, Ellen.

* * *

Considerable resentment built up against Hollywood during the World War II years for its overglamorized heroics in war films. So much bad feeling developed that the studios became somewhat shy of depicting actual battles on the screen. At MGM, there were only a few exceptions to this rule: **Bataan** (1943) was one and, far more successful, **Thirty Seconds over Tokyo** was another. The depiction of the April 1942 raid of B-25 Mitchell bombers over Tokyo was produced by Sam Zimbalist and directed by Mervyn LeRoy with

relative realism and much accuracy. The only jibe tossed by critics was that it required 138 minutes to tell the story of the half-minute title.

Based on the popular book written by pilot Ted W. Lawson (with journalist Bob Considine), **Thirty Seconds over Tokyo** almost did not have Spencer Tracy headlining the cast. Having made **A Guy Named Joe** (1943) and **The Seventh Cross** (1944; as an escapee from a German concentration camp), he felt he should not follow with another war film. Moreover, Tracy was reticent about impersonating the famous Lieutenant Colonel James H. Doolittle. It took a good deal of convincing by director LeRoy to get Tracy to agree to this "cameo" job. He accepted the task partly because he knew his presence would give box-office strength to the project, and he wanted his pal Van Johnson to succeed in his first starring role in a major drama.

Tracy performed his chore with dignity and was actually on camera for only a minimal amount of time.[1] The major acting chores fell to Johnson and Robert Walker, both involved in the preparations for the raid.

Thirty Seconds over Tokyo was released in November 1944, some two and a half years after the actual raid. It was approved of by the critics, many of whom had become hostile toward Hollywood's prior efforts to pictorialize the Allied

---

[1]The **New York Herald-Tribune** endorsed, "Spencer Tracy plays Doolittle as only he could do it, bringing a cynical but deep emotional power to a part which might have eluded most Hollywood actors."

cause. Bosley Crowther (**New York Times**) reported, "Told with magnificent integrity and dramatic eloquence. . . . As the re-created picture of one of our boldest blows in this war and as a drama of personal heroism, it is nigh the best yet made in Hollywood . . . a most stimulating and emotionally satisfying film." **Newsweek** magazine: "One of Hollywood's finest war films to date. . . . Director Mervyn LeRoy achieves sustained drama . . . as Lawson, Van Johnson comes through with the most effective performance of his career." Though Dalton Trumbo sentimentalized the story (in approved MGM fashion) in occasional episodes, most critics endorsed his handicraft, if for no other reason than that it introduced in the part of Lawson's wife Phyllis Thaxter. Her appealing work gained her an MGM contract. (She again would be with Johnson—but not as his wife—in **Weekend at the Waldorf**, 1945 and with Tracy in **The Sea of Grass** 1947, as his teary-eyed daughter.)

Thirty Seconds over Tokyo placed eighth in the National Board of Review's Ten Best picture list. It won an Oscar for Best Special Effects (A. Arnold Gillespie, Donald Jahraus, Warren Newcombe, and Douglas Shearer). Of all the mid-1940's war films with the accent on combat, **Thirty Seconds over Tokyo** was the top financial draw. It grossed $4,500,000 in distributors' domestic rentals.

In assessing this genre of picture, Norman Kagan in **The War Film** (1974) lauds **Thirty Seconds** as a "brilliantly filmed sequence of a low-level attack on Tokyo, starting with a carrier take-off in the middle of a storm to a plunge at zero altitude over ocean and enemy to a crash landing on the China coast. After seeing the pilot's [Johnson] warm, personal life and boundless energy, the amputation of his leg under primitive conditions is all the more tragic and humiliating."

Spotted in the cast of **Thirty Seconds over Tokyo** are Robert Mitchum (Bob Gray), Stephen McNally (Doc White), Bill Williams (Bud Felton), and Blake Edwards (Officer), who later became a director-producer. Kay Williams, one of the girls in the officers club, is the MGM contractee who would wed Clark Gable.

TOPPER
1937—98 min.

Producer, Hal Roach; **associate producer,** Milton H. Bren; **director,** Norman Z. McLeod; based on the story "The Jovial Ghosts" by Thorne Smith; **screenplay,** Jack Jevne, Eric Hatch, and Eddie Moran; **music,** Edward Powell and Hugo Friedhofer; **music supervisor,** Marvin Hatley; **music arranger,** Arthur Morton; **song,** Hoagy Carmichael;

art director, Arthur Rouce; **set decorator,** W. L. Stevens; **wardrobe supervisor,** Ernest Schraps; gowns for Miss Bennett, Irene; gowns for Miss Burke, Howard Schraps; **sound,** Elmer Roguse; **camera effects,** Roy Seawright; **camera,** Norbert Brodine; **editor,** William Terhune.

Constance Bennett (**Marion Kerby**); Cary Grant (**George Kerby**); Roland Young (**Cosmo Topper**); Billie Burke (**Henrietta Topper**); Alan Mowbray (**Wilkins**); Eugene Pallette (**Casey**); Arthur Lake (**Elevator Boy**); Hedda Hopper (**Mrs. Stuyvesant**); Virginia Sale (**Miss Johnson**); Theodore von Eltz (**Hotel Manager**); J. Farrell MacDonald (**Policeman**); Elaine Shepard (**Secretary**); Doodles Weaver and Si Jenks (**Rustics**); Three Hits and a Miss (**Themselves**); Donna Dax (**Hatcheck Girl at Rainbow Nightclub**); Hoagy Carmichael (**Bill, the Piano Player**); Claire Windsor and Betty Blythe (**Ladies**).

SYNOPSIS

Rich, young, carefree Marion and George Kerby lead a pleasant but idle life, managing to enjoy their frivolous existences to the fullest. While driving at a reckless speed they crash into a tree and are killed. Their spirits rise from their bodies and they conclude that before they can enter heaven, they have to do at least one good deed.

They pick banker Cosmo Topper, henpecked by his demanding wife Henrietta, and hope to teach him how to live and enjoy himself. They drive him almost frantic by putting him into em-

barrassing positions, but he soon enjoys the madcap way of life very much. Henrietta, though, strongly disapproves of his bizarre actions and causes him to leave home.

While driving with the ghostly Kerbys he meets with an auto accident and is taken to his home. Henrietta nurses him and admits she is glad to have him back. She confesses she will now live any sort of life he wants. The ghosts, satisfied with their work, depart the earth.

* * *

For a decade Hal Roach had operated his subsidiary Metro unit, characterized by the economical and beloved comedy shenanigans headlined by Laurel and Hardy. It was not until 1937 that Roach finally ventured into sophisticated, top-budget comedy. The film was **Topper,** assisted by the talents of director Norman Z. McLeod and top farceurs Constance Bennett (too long engulfed in playing sin-drenched movie heroines), Cary Grant, Roland Young, and Billie Burke. The result was one of the biggest comedy hits of the thirties.

Actually, when producer Roach first approached Grant to play in the screwball comedy, he hoped to have Jean Harlow and W. C. Fields as the debonair Britisher's costars. Grant reluctantly agreed to the package, at a salary of $50,000, fearful that the public would not react favorably to a tale of zany ghosts. Then Harlow died and negotiations with Fields and his agent proved fruitless. At this point Constance Bennett (top-billed) and Roland Young entered the picture.

Topper proved to be a very spirited exercise.

Advertisement for Topper *('37).*

As the madcap Kerbys who must accomplish one good deed before they can enter heaven, Grant and Bennett were in top form. They were a near perfect team, and exuded a style similar to that of William Powell and Myrna Loy sans insults. What made the film so joyous and kept the audience interest so high was the engaging contrast between the carefree, fun-loving Kerbys and the staid establishment-prone Toppers. The transformation of banker Cosmo Topper from a henpecked routine-minded crank into a yeasty soul takes up most of the film's action.

Throughout the picture director McLeod relied a good deal on special-effects wizard Roy Seawright. The latter accomplished the task of fading the ghostly leads in and out, thereby upsetting conventions and giving Topper a new lease on life. There is the scene where the invisible Kerbys assist the soused Topper from the hotel lobby; on another occasion the couple rearrange Topper's disheveled appearance in a courtroom; and again, the time when irreverent Marion unleashes chaos in a bank and later in a boutique. Still further into the proceedings, George battles portly house detective Eugene Pallette, and later on George pushes Topper's chair about a room gendering at once consternation and hilarity. At the finale, Grant and Bennett, astride Topper's rooftop, bid him goodbye and drift from sight.

When **Topper** opened at New York's Capitol Theatre, it proved to be a most appealing attraction. The feature helped to demonstrate Grant's capacity for farce and gave Bennett a new lease on cinema popularity. Added to the flattering reviews she won for her ethereal Marion Kerby was some racy publicity: as a promotional gimmick Constance had autographed a pair of her silk panties. The item had been displayed in the Capitol Theatre's lobby to entice the audiences. Shoftly after the film's premiere in August 1937, the panties were stolen and the management replaced them with an unautographed pair. A few days later, a package containing the missing inscribed undergarment arrived at the Capitol. Included within were a dollar bill and the signature, "An ashamed father."

In the Oscar sweepstakes, **Topper**'s Roland Young was nominated for Best Supporting Actor, but he lost to Joseph Schildkraut of **The Life of Emile Zola** (Warner Bros.)

The next year Roach produced—for MGM release—**Merrily We Live** (1938) starring Constance Bennett. She was joined in the proceedings by such **Topper** alumni as director Norman Z. McLeod, scripters Eddie Moran and Jack Jevne, special-effects creator Roy Seawright, and cast members Billie Burke and Alan Mowbray. It did not match its predecessor in quality or box-office returns. By the time that Roach had produced **Topper Takes a Trip** (1939), he had shifted his distribution contract from MGM to United Artists. Young, Burke, and Mowbray joined Bennett in recreating their original assignments, but Grant, having moved into the top echelon of stardom, was too busy to accept Roach's offer for the follow-up film. For the 1941 **Topper Returns** (United Artists), Burke and Young were back again, but now Marion Kerby was played by Joan Blondell.

The 1953 video series would star Robert Sterling and Anne Jeffreys as the ghostly Kerbys, with Leo G. Carroll and Lee Patrick as the Toppers. In 1979 Kate Jackson and Andrew Stevens starred as that couple in a TV movie version.

TORTILLA FLAT
1942—105 min.

Producer, Sam Zimbalist; **director,** Victor Fleming; based on the novel by John Steinbeck; **screenplay,** John Lee Mahin and Benjamin Glazer; **music,** Franz Waxman; **songs,** Waxman and Frank Loesser; **art directors,** Cedric Gibbons and Paul Groesse; **set decorator,** Edwin B. Willis; **makeup,** Jack Dawn; **sound,** Douglas Shearer; **special camera effects,** Warren Newcombe; **camera,** Karl Freund; **editor,** James E. Newcom.

Spencer Tracy **(Pilon)**; Hedy Lamarr **(Dolores "Sweets" Ramirez)**; John Garfield **(Danny)**; Frank Morgan **(The Pirate)**; Akim Tamiroff **(Pablo)**; Connie Gilchrist **(Mrs. Torelli)**; Henry O'Neill **(Father Ramon)**; Allen Jenkins **(Portagee Joe)**; John Qualen **(Jesus Maria)**; Sheldon Leonard **(Tito Ralph)**; Donald Meek **(Mr. Cummings)**; Harry Burns **(Torelli)**; Mercedes Ruffino **(Mrs. Morales)**; Roque Ybarra **(Alfredo)**; Nina Campana **(Señora Teresina Cortez)**; Arthur Space **(Mr. Jones)**; Tim Ryan **(Rupert Hogan)**; Charles Judels **(Joe Machado)**; Betty Welles **(Cosca)**; Yvette Duguay **(Little Girl)**; Harry Strang **(Fireman)**; Walter Sande **(Foreman)**; Louis Jean Heydt **(Young Doctor)**; Emmett Vogan **(Doctor)**.

SYNOPSIS

Tortilla Flat is a tiny West Coast fishing village, populated by wanderers and rustics. Among them is Danny, a young man who suddenly becomes wealthy when he inherits two houses. With the newly won affluence comes boldness; he romances the village beauty, Dolores. Generous Danny allows his scoundrel friend Pilon and his gang of ne'er-do-wells—Pablo, Portagee Joe, and Jesus Maria—to move into one of the new homes.

Pilon is soon up to no good. He plans to rob a nearby eccentric known as "the Pirate," rumored to have a bundle of money. However, in executing the robbery, Pilon learns from the selfless old man that the money is being saved to buy a candlestick for St. Francis. Pilon abandons his thievery. However, he does become romantically attracted to Dolores. Soon a tension builds between him and Danny as both pursue the redheaded beauty.

Tragedy strikes the village when a fire destroys one of Danny's homes. Danny himself is later hurt in a fight. When Pilon realizes how valuable his friendship with Danny is, he does something for Danny he has never done for anyone else in his whole life—he gets a job. Using the money to help buy Danny a boat, Pilon steps away from the love triangle. Danny and Dolores plan to wed.

* * *

The works of John Steinbeck had made for some cinema bonanzas: United Artists' **Of Mice and Men** (1939) and Twentieth Century–Fox's **The Grapes of Wrath** (1940) had garnered laurels and profits. MGM took notice. The studio decided to cast its lot with the Pulitzer Prize–winning author.[1] The result was the moving and sincere **Tortilla Flat,** based on the author's 1935 novel.

It was a very conscientious production. Victor Fleming's direction caught the flavor of the poverty-stricken California village.[2] John Garfield, on loanout from Warner Bros., was an admirable choice for the good-hearted Danny. Herein Tracy, now the prime actor on the lot (since most of the able-bodied younger performers had joined the military service), attacked his first accent-oriented role since his Academy Award-winning Manuel of **Captains Courageous** (1937). Tracy was rematched with Hedy Lamarr, his costar of the trouble-plagued **I Take This Woman** (1940). In **Tortilla Flat** she gave a most polished performance; it is hard to believe that she is the same actress who later in the year wiggled and writhed so pathetically as the infamous Tondelayo of **White Cargo** (1942).

Studio stock player Frank Morgan did something he had not done since **Port of Seven Seas** (1938): he dropped most of his trademark mannerisms, including the sputtering and awesomely timed takes. Freed from these tricks, he offered a quite moving performance as the Pirate, the dog-loving lounger who hoards his savings only to spend them on a candlestick for his beloved St. Francis. Character names Akim Tamiroff (on loan from Paramount), Allen Jenkins, and John Qualen (memorable as Muley in **The Grapes of Wrath**) provided zesty flavoring to the film, as did MGM's own Connie Gilchrist. This time she appeared as the Mexican Mrs. Torelli, the one who performs a dance with Tracy within the film.

There was only one problem with this production. The film was just what Steinbeck had written—a simple story of mundane people living leisurely in a drab setting. Could such material be of sufficient interest to a public which had just marched off to war? To ensure appeal, MGM cheated a bit with the advertisements and made the film sound like a cinema fiesta worthy of the Brazilian Bombshell, Carmen Miranda:

> This way to **Tortilla Flat!** Follow this sign and you'll come to the place where life is happy, and wine, women, and song make a fiesta of every day! It's the gay paradise on the Pacific. . . . It's warming as the California sun . . . heady as spring wine . . . romantic as the tinkle of a guitar in the moonlight.

MGM received a welcome assist from the critics after the film opened in May 1942. **Newsweek** magazine reported:

---

[1]In September 1937 Paramount planned to produce a musical screen version of **Tortilla Flats**, with a Mexican background and George Raft in the lead.

[2]Victor Fleming had previously directed Tracy in **Captains Courageous** (1937), **Test Pilot** (1938), and the 1941 abandoned sequences for **The Yearling**. He would later direct Tracy in **A Guy Named Joe** (1943).

Allen Jenkins, Connie Gilchrist, Akim Tamiroff (rear), Spencer Tracy, Hedy Lamarr, and John Garfield in Tortilla Flat *('42).*

Probably nothing short of a documentary film, people with anonymous paisanos, and photographed on the grassy hills overlooking Monterey, could hope to catch all the earthy, amoral spirit of John Steinbeck's **Tortilla Flat.** . . . Victor Fleming, the director, makes the most of its atmosphere and ingratiating attitudes, and an exceptionally strong cast. . . . The result is an unusual film that creates a reasonable fascimile of the Steinbeck flavor.

However, box-office earnings were **not** in keeping with the earlier Steinbeck film adaptations. There were no Oakie camps as in **The Grapes of Wrath,** no hulking, pathetic moron as in **Of Mice and Men** with sensationalistic overtones to pull in audiences; just sincerity and restrained, good acting. It was not enough. **Tortilla Flat,** while not a financial failure, was a sharp disappointment. John Steinbeck's works would not be filmed again at Culver City.

It should be noted **Tortilla Flat** did rate a Best Supporting Actor nomination for Frank Morgan[3] (he lost to Van Heflin of MGM's **Johnny Eager**). Also, for one of the rare times in her screen career, Hedy Lamarr, in what she herself deems her best performance, rated flattering reviews. One wonders, even today, what professional fate would have awaited Lamarr had **Tortilla Flat** been a popular success and the studio had thereafter searched for more quality roles for her.

---

[3]Morgan had previously been nominated in the Best Actor category for United Artists' **Affairs of Cellini** (1934), losing to Clark Gable of **It Happened One Night** (Columbia).

TRADER HORN
1931—123 min.

Director, W. S. Van Dyke II; based on the novel by Alfred Aloysius Horn and Ethelreda Lewis; **adapters,** Dale Van Every and John Thomas Neville; **screenplay,** Richard Schayer; **dialogue,** Cyril Hume; **sound,** Andrew Anderson; **camera,** Clyde DeVinna; **editor,** Ben Lewis.

Harry Carey **(Trader Horn);** Edwina Booth **(Nina Trend);** Duncan Renaldo **(Peru);** Mutia Omoolu **(Rencharo);** Olive Fuller Golden [Olive Carey] **(Edith Trend);** C. Aubrey Smith **(Trader).**

SYNOPSIS
Deepest, darkest Africa. Heading down a jungle river are Trader Horn, veteran hunter, and Peru, the tenderfoot son of his old partner. Arriving in a native village to accomplish some trading, young Peru learns of the predilictions of the natives when he sees a spread-eagle corpse dangling from a post. The trading ceases when the bellicose Masai tribe arrives, forcing the two white men to make a hasty retreat to their boat.

In their travels, Horn and Peru meet missionary Edith Trend, she being in search of the daughter she lost in Africa some twenty years before. She believes she will find her at the Falls where her husband was killed by the natives. Undaunted by the white men's warnings, she sets out for her dangerous destination. When Horn and Peru themselves reach the Falls a few days later, they find Edith Trend's ravaged body. Now Horn decides to find the daughter himself.

However, both men are captured. After a bloodthirsty celebration marked by natives performing wild dances, the White Goddess appears. She orders the hordes to tie the white men to crosses, turn them upside down, and burn them. But an old civilized feeling reawakens inside her and, instead, she orders the men freed—and escapes with them.

In addition to the pursuing natives, the fleeing Caucasians face a python, leopards, lions, crocodiles, near starvation, and fierce pygmies. However, with the help of the loyal native Rencharo, who loses his life in order that his master may go free, all return to safety.

There is one more problem. Both Horn and Peru have fallen in love with the White Goddess (Nina Trend). However, moved by his magnanimous philosophy, "I'll still be beholdin' the wonders of the jungle that'll never grow old before your eyes, the way a woman does," Horn gives up the girl to Peru, and the young lovers board a boat for civilization.

* * *

For decades, Metro-Goldwyn-Mayer has been chastised by various film historians who have spun stories of the unspeakable fate suffered by actress Edwina Booth, the curvaceous starlet with the copious golden tresses. While slaving in the steaming African wilds for **Trader Horn,** some insist she became infected by some foul native poison and went insane. Others claim the starlet was long in a state of near death. Another faction has written that Edwina Booth died after enduring the horrors of the Congo, but that her demise was well camouflaged by the Metro publicists. The truth is, Edwina Booth was alive as of 1980 and living in West Hollywood. She was still refusing all interviews seeking the true story of the production of **Trader Horn.**

Fascinated by the bestselling book **Trader Horn,** Irving Thalberg had won Louis B. Mayer's reluctant approval to dispatch a company to Africa to shoot the tale of real-life adventurer Alfred Aloysius Horn. The original choice for the role was Wallace Beery. However, the gruff star refused the prospect of traipsing about the African veldt. Thalberg then contracted Harry Carey, veteran movie lead. The actor was having professional and financial problems, his ranch having been destroyed by the St. Francis Dam break. Thalberg offered him $600 weekly, aware the former Western star had been earning $2,500 weekly at one peak time. Duncan Renaldo was picked to play Peru and twenty-year-old Edwina Booth[1] won MGM's highly publicized search for a starlet to be the White Goddess who dazzlingly appears in the savage African environs. To direct, Thalberg appointed W. S. Van Dyke because of his reputation for fast shooting.

On May 1, 1929, the company (including Carey's actress wife and children) arrived in East Africa and headed for the jungle interior. Thus began seven months of wild adventures; savage animals, hostile natives, tropical diseases all

---

[1]She had previously appeared in Paramount's **Manhattan Cocktail** (1928) and MGM's **Our Modern Maidens** (1929).

Mutia Omoolu, Duncan Renaldo, Edwina Booth, and Harry Carey in Trader Horn *('31).*

1930–31, but lost the Oscar to RKO's **Cimarron**.

So fascinated was the U.S. public by the wilds of Africa that in 1932 Metro began the adventures of **Tarzan the Ape Man**. However, Johnny Weissmuller, Maureen O'Sullivan, and the rest of the cast never placed a bare foot in Africa in the entire series. Metro had learned not to risk the wrath of the Congo. Years later, with excellent guides, modern medical supplies, and transportable luxuries, Metro **would** return to Africa for **King Solomon's Mines** (1950) and **Mogambo** (1953).

As for Edwina Booth, she did indeed return alive from Africa—and sued MGM successfully when the after effects of a tropical disease failed to disappear. With Harry Carey she appeared in the Mascot serials **The Vanishing Legion** (1931) and **The Last of the Mohicans** (1932), and was in the Monogram low-budget picture **Midnight Patrol** (1932). Shortly thereafter she retired from filmmaking. Few today would recognize the very mature woman working at the Mormon temple in West Hollywood as the once glorious White Goddess of the screen.

In 1973 MGM released a new **Trader Horn**, starring Rod Taylor, Anne Heywood, and Jean Sorel. As directed by Reza S. Badiyi in color, and using footage from **Mogambo** and **King Solomon's Mines**, the remake bore faint resemblance to the plot line or impact of the Metro original. Also surfacing in the 1970s was **Trader Horny**, a pornographic entry.

combined to make life a nightmare for the troupe. The additional horror of the sound truck toppling into the waters at Mombasa compounded the miseries. Van Dyke, fortified with cases of gin, refused to be intimidated by it all and continued seeking beautiful locations and placing his actors in melodramatic episodes. Finally the company turned homeward; the completed reels were sent ahead. Mayer was aghast at the mess of footage which flickered on the screen before him. When the cast arrived in New York late in 1929, they were informed on the dock that **Trader Horn** had terminated production. The film was to be scrapped and they all were fired.

Meanwhile, Metro producers Bernard Hyman and Paul Bern were still captivated by the offbeat project. They saved the reels from destruction and convinced Thalberg to resume production. The cast was summoned, and for nearly a year the company worked in secret.[2] The knowledge, Thalberg feared, that some of the footage was newly shot around Culver City and in Mexico would detract from the box-office appeal.

Filmed on a 115-day shooting schedule at a cost of $1,322,000, **Trader Horn** earned a profit of $937,000. Some of the promotional copy for

the film included: "The MGM Miracle Picture. . . . After two years while an impatient world waited, the motion picture industry has come through with its most amazing achievement. . . . The world's newspapers have recorded the perils of the Metro-Goldwyn-Mayer Company on its 14,000-mile journey into darkest Africa to bring you the supreme romance, the stirring adventures, the savage thrills of Trader Horn's true story!"

When released in February 1931, **Trader Horn** was a sensation. The **New York Times** reported, "For this sort of excitement there has been nothing like it seen on the screen and in picturing the incidents this film has the latitude offered it by fiction, or borrowed truths." The **Times'** Mordaunt Hall added, "This shrewdly fashioned jungle melodrama proved to be thoroughly exciting to the spectators . . . and it seemed as though many of them were a bit nearer than they ever wanted to be to a big-game hunt. For not only were the wild beasts perceived in their full fierceness, but their cries and growls and roars were heard from the screen as they never have been before." Only the more astute observers were aware of the difference between the authentic-shot footage and that restaged in North America. **Trader Horn** became one of the greatest MGM successes of the season.[3] It was nominated as the Best Picture of

TUGBOAT ANNIE
1933—88 min.

Associate producer, Harry Rapf; **director,** Mervyn LeRoy; based on the stories by Norman Reilly Raine; **adapters,** Zelda Sears and Eve Green; **additional dialogue,** Raine; **art director,** Merrill Pye; **set decorator,** Edwin B. Willis; **camera,** Gregg Toland; **editor,** Blanche Sewell.

Marie Dressler (**Annie Brennan**); Wallace Beery (**Terry Brennan**); Robert Young (**Alec Brennan**); Maureen O'Sullivan (**Pat Severn**); Willard Robertson (**Red Severn**); Tammany Young (**Shif'less**); Frankie Darro (**Alec as a Boy**); Jack Pennick (**Pete**); Paul Hurst (**Sam**); Oscar Apfel (**Reynolds**); Robert McWade (**Mayor of Secoma**); Robert Barrat (**First Mate**); Vince Barnett (**Cabby**); Robert E. Homans (**Old Salt**); Guy Usher (**Auctioneer**); Willie Fung (**Chow, the Cook**); Hal Price (**Mate**); Christian Rub (**Sailor**); Major Sam Harris (**Onlooker**).

[2] Harry Carey honorably agreed to continue work for his usual fee of $600 a week; but his wife Olive, who appeared as the missionary mother of Edwina Booth, demanded the fee of $1,000 a week—the fee Thalberg had planned to pay Marjorie Rambeau. Mrs. Carey received the amount when it was found that Rambeau could not match the long shots of Olive from the African location trek.

[3] As a "follow-up" to **Trader Horn**, MGM in 1933 released **Eskimo**, directed by W. S. Van Dyke, with Hunt Stromberg as associate producer. It was based on Peter Freuchen's books on the Eskimos and filmed in northern Alaska with a cast composed largely of Eskimos, as well as the native actor Mala. The studio promoted the fea-

ture as "successor to **Trader Horn's** Thrills" and proclaimed its "Stampede of thousands of caribou! . . . Hand-to-hand fight with savage wolf! . . . Actual blood-curdling sounds of breaking of the ice flows! . . . The fearless hunter leaps on the back of the whale! . . . His savage strength was stronger than the white man's chains!"

SYNOPSIS

Hard-working Annie Brennan runs a tugboat and is known all along the waterfront as a tough but good-hearted woman. She receives little help from her blowhard husband Terry, who is good-natured but given to drink and laziness. It is Annie who ensures that their son Alec completes school; she is especially proud when he is made captain of a ship.

Alec is in love with Pat Severn, the daughter of shipowner Red Severn; Pat in turn loves Alec. Alec has hopes of doing things for his mother, such as making a comfortable apartment for her, but she loves the **Narcissus** and her rugged way of life too much. Alec is disgusted by his father's continued drunkenness and insists that Annie leave him. When she refuses, he says he will not see her again.

Meanwhile, Terry rams the family tugboat in a chase for a case of liquor and the boat is later sold at auction. It is to be used as a garbage hauler. Annie is made the captain, and since she needs the job badly, she swallows her pride and accepts the assignment.

One stormy night while at sea dumping garbage, she notes distress signals from her son's ship. By working furiously and endangering their lives—Terry even going into the boiler to fix a leak—Annie and Terry reach Alec's vessel in time. Terry is decorated for his action, the tugboat is repaired and given back to Annie, and there is a family reunion.

* * *

In 1933 MGM placed two movies in the eleven top-grossing films of the year. One was **Rasputin and the Empress,** the glorious spectacle of the three Barrymores trying to out-scene-steal one another with manic glee; the other was **Tugboat Annie.** The latter was the second Marie Dressler–Wallace Beery teaming, a delight instituted by 1930's immensely popular **Min and Bill.** Based on a series of magazine stories by Norman Reilly Raine, the film offered both stars tailor-made characterizations: Marie as irrepressible Annie Brennan, Pacific Coast drudge, and Wally as her crude husband Terry, who never struck his mate " 'cept in self-defense."

Directed by Mervyn LeRoy, the film was a mixture of husband-wife slapstick, with especially memorable lethal glances from Marie toward the sottish Wally. It is the interaction of the two leads which elevates the story well above its pulp-fiction origin. Balancing the continuing battle between the rambunctious couple is the mother-son relationship. Robert Young plays, with winning innocuousness, her offspring, ambitious to become a merchant marine officer but not above listening to his mother's counsel. Rounding out the subplot is Maureen O'Sullivan, as the girl Young adores. In true **Romeo and Juliet** tradition, she is the daughter of his parents' rival.

When **Tugboat Annie** premiered in August 1933, it captivated the critics and public alike.[1]

Wallace Beery in Tugboat Annie *('33).*

"Miss Dressler is admirable, giving a genuinely human touch to her role. As for Mr. Beery's performance, he is very amusing when showing Terry's penchant for strong drink, particularly in the scene where his brain becomes so muddled that the task of dressing is almost impossible." The studio promoted the feature with the ad line, "America's sweethearts—together again. . . . The 'greatest lovers' of **Min and Bill** reunited—and laugh-time is here again."

When the sentimental comedy of a warhorse and a slob opened in London, the **Times** reported, "Both Miss Dressler and Mr. Beery have that exceptional power of making a comic point with complete certainty, of isolating it, and the next moment of making with the same certainty an effect that wins a sympathetic response deeper

than laughter. Always—and it is their supreme merit—they have abounding life."

Dressler and Beery later appeared in the all-star **Dinner at Eight** (1933) but were not on camera as a team. Any plans to reunite the unique acting pair were cut short by Dressler's death of cancer on July 28, 1934. At which time **Photoplay** magazine editorialized:

It is the greatest of all tributes to Marie Dressler to say that her appeal was universal. . . . I do not care what your status in life may be, of one thing I am certain: if you ever saw Marie

---

[1]Tugboat Annie was shot on a forty-three-day shooting schedule at a cost of $613,000 and earned a profit of $1,212,000.

[2]As a result of Beery's boisterous appearance in **Tugboat Annie,** MGM rewrote his contract, giving the actor even more favorable terms.

Dressler on the screen she went straight to your heart. That was because the shining qualities that made her so beloved by everyone that knew her personally were revealed—every word, gesture, and facial expression—in her film interpretations.

As for the **Narcissus,** the tugboat of the tale, it was later skippered by Beery in MGM's **Barnacle Bill** (1941), in which Marjorie Main (touted as Marie Dressler's successor) was his costar. For many years thereafter the vessel floated in "the lake" (MGM's largest body of back lot water), sadly listing to port.

The character of Tugboat Annie was later reprised for Warner Bros.' **Tugboat Annie Sails Again** (1940), with Marjorie Rambeau in the title role and Alan Hale as her mate. For Republic's **Captain Tugboat Annie** (1945), Jane Darwell and Edgar Kennedy were the leads. The 1957 syndicated TV series starred Minerva Ureca.

THE UNHOLY THREE

1930—75 min.

Director, Jack Conway; based on the story and the novel by Tod [Clarence Aaron] Robbins; **continuity-dialogue,** J. C. Nugent and Elliott Nugent; **art director,** Cedric Gibbons; **wardrobe,** David Cox, **sound,** Anstruther MacDonald and Douglas Shearer; **camera,** Percy Hilburn; **editor,** Frank Sullivan.

Lon Chaney (**Echo**); Lila Lee (**Rosie**); Elliott Nugent (**Hector**); Harry Earles (**Midget**); John Miljan (**Prosecuting Attorney**); Ivan Linow (**Hercules**); Clarence Burton (**Regan**); Craufurd Kent (**Defense Attorney**).

Lon Chaney, Ivan Linow, and Harry Earles in The Unholy Three ('30).

SYNOPSIS

In a sleazy carnival, Echo, aided by the monstrous strongman Hercules, and the sneering Midget, performs as a ventriloquist while his cohorts fleece the audience. When his partners start a fight with a patron, the police close the carnival, and Echo seeks a new outlet for his wickedness.

The new front is a petshop. There Echo disguises himself as an old lady, Hercules poses as his son-in-law, Midget pretends to be a baby, and Rosie, who has prospered as a pickpocket for Echo's gang, enacts his daughter. In the bizarre shop—the menagerie boasts a huge and thoroughly unpleasant gorilla—Echo discovers a new way to con the public. By throwing his voice for assorted parrots, he establishes a reputation as selling the city's most exciting collection of talking birds. The store attracts a wealthy clientele and the gang robs the customers when they make deliveries.

The perfect arrangement crumbles when Rosie falls in love with Hector, a timid clerk who works in the shop unaware of its perverse nature. When Hercules and Midget later commit a murder, the police trace the crime to the petshop. There-

after the desperate rogues hide the stolen goods in Hector's room. The clerk is soon arrested and appears doomed to die in the electric chair. However, Echo—disguised as the old lady—takes the witness stand in defense of Hector. But at the end of the testimony, he slips—and speaks in his own voice. His disguise is unveiled on the stand.

That the unsavory Midget and Hercules have met their demises—Midget killed by Hercules and Hercules by the rampaging gorilla—moves the court to show clemency to Echo. He is sentenced to only five years in prison. Hector and Rosie bid him farewell at the train station.

* * *

I, Lon Chaney, being first duly sworn, depose and say: In the photoplay entitled **The Unholy Three,** produced by Metro-Goldwyn-Mayer Corporation, all voice reproductions which purport to be reproductions of my voice, to wit, the ventriloquist's, the old woman's, the dummy's, the parrot's, and the girl's, are actual reproductions of my own voice, and in no place in said photoplay was a "double" or substitute used for my voice.

Save for Charles Chaplin, the last great star of the silents to venture into the ominous talking era was Lon Chaney. Though Chaney's most famous successes—**The Hunchback of Notre Dame** (1923) and **The Phantom of the Opera** (1925)— were produced by Universal, Chaney later became an MGM contract star. Culver City was the situs of such classic films as his **London After Midnight** (1925) and **Mr. Wu** (1927). One of Chaney's greatest movie triumphs was **The Unholy Three** (1925), in which the "Man of a Thousand Faces"

reveled as a carnival shyster who spends most of the footage disguised as a meek old lady. In preparing for his sound debut, Chaney selected this feature, hoping a repeat of his role as Echo would establish him as the talkie screen's "Man of a Thousand Voices."

It was during a fishing jaunt to his cabin in the High Sierras that Chaney practiced the various vocal characterizations—human, animal, and dummy—which he employed in the remake. Jack Conway replaced the original director, Tod Browning, and directed with pace and humor. Ivan Linow took on the Hercules part, played in the original by Victor McLaglen. Harry Earles, who two years later would be lusting after Olga Baclanova in Browning's **Freaks,** repeated his role of the sadistic Midget who masquerades with a minimum of infant charm as a baby. Lila Lee could not measure up to the vampy Rosie O'Grady of Mae Busch of the 1925 version, though Elliott Nugent (who also worked on the dialogue) was appropriately bewildered and innocuous as the none too observant Hector.

Chaney strove long and tirelessly on the production; he was rightfully proud of his efforts. He requested the studio attorney to prepare an affidavit which vowed to audinece that all five voices used in the picture were the star's. When released early in July 1930, **The Unholy Three** was a triumph. The **New York Times** printed:

Mr. Chaney has made a further contribution to the modern motion picture—although it may be a bit indelicate to mention it here. Like the two dozen students who swam the Hellespont and so ruined the beautiful legend forever, he has destroyed the effect of the phrase, "See your favorite actor; he speaks." For while others were proudly proclaiming the finding of a forgotten note, he quietly went fishing and came back with five. The industry will never be the same again.

The future of Chaney as a major star of the talkie medium seemed secure. Universal began negotiations to borrow him for the star role of its forthcoming **Dracula.** But, ironic tragedy struck. Chaney's career was cut short by throat cancer. As audiences marveled at his performance in the sinister **The Unholy Three,** Chaney was spending his last days at his beloved hideaway cabin. Suffering from pneumonia and anemia, he was rushed back to St. Vincent's Hospital in Los Angeles. There, shortly after midnight, on August 26, 1930, he died. Irving Thalberg would comment, "He was great, not only because of his God-given talent, but because he used that talent to illuminate certain dark corners of the human spirit." Added Tod Browning, "He was the hardest-working person in the studio." Several of the roles planned for Chaney were later readapte for MGM's new contract star, Wallace Beery.

VALLEY OF DECISION
1945—111 min.

Producer, Edwin H. Knopf; **director,** Tay Garnett; based on the novel by Marcia Davenport; screenplay, John Meehan and Sonya Levien; **music,** Herbert Stothart; **art directors,** Cedric Gibbons and Paul Groesse; **set decorators,** Edwin B. Willis and Mildred Griffiths; **assistant director,** Marvin Stuart; **special effects,** A. Arnold Gilllespie and Warren Newcombe; **camera,** Joseph Ruttenberg; **editor,** Blanche Sewell.

Greer Garson **(Mary Rafferty);** Gregory Peck **(Paul Scott);** Donald Crisp **(William Scott);** Lionel Barrymore **(Pat Rafferty);** Preston Foster **(Jim Brennan);** Gladys Cooper **(Clarissa Scott);** Marsha Hunt **(Constance Scott);** Jessica Tandy **(Louise Kane);** Dan Duryea **(William Scott, Jr.);** Reginald Owen **(McCready);** Marshall Thompson **(Ted Scott);** Barbara Everest **(Delia);** John Warburton **(Giles, Earl of Moulton);** Mary Currier **(Mrs. Gaylord);** Arthur Shields **(Callahan);** Russell Hicks **(Mr. Gaylord);** Geraldine Wall **(Kate Shannon);** Norman Ollestead **(Callahan's Son);** Evelyn Dockson **(Mrs. Callahan);** Connie Gilchrist **(Cook);** Willa Pearl Curtis **(Maid);** Richard Abbott **(Minister);** Dean Stockwell **(Paulie);** Joy Harrington **(Stella);** Anna Q. Nilsson **(Nurse);** Mike Ryan **(Timmie at Age Seven);** Sherlee Collier **(Clarrie).**

SYNOPSIS
In 1880 Pittsburgh, Mary Rafferty becomes a servant in the home of William Scott, despite the opposition of her father, Pat Rafferty, who had been crippled in an accident in Scott's steel mill. Mary endears herself to Clarissa, William Scott's

Greer Garson and Gregory Peck in Valley of Decision ('45).

wife, and to the four children: Paul, Constance, William Jr., and Ted.

Eventually love comes to Mary and Paul, but she decides not to wed him because of her lowly position. But when Mr. Scott learns of this, he brings the two together. Mary's joy, however, turns to sadness because of a mill strike. The rebellion has been encouraged by her dad. When Mr. Scott sends for the strike leaders, Mary, fearing bloodshed, arranges a peace meeting between the owner and the strikers. Because of a misunderstanding, the strikebreakers arrive in the midst of the meeting. Pat Rafferty, enraged, incites the strikers, and in the ensuing battle both he and Mr. Scott are killed. Grief-stricken, Mary withdraws from Paul's life.

Ten years later Paul, wed to childhood sweetheart Louise Kane, is leading an unhappy life because of Louise's constant nagging. When Clarissa Scott is stricken with a heart attack, she calls for Mary, much to the annoyance of Louise, who fears that Paul's love for Mary might flame anew. After the death of Mrs. Scott, William, Constance, and Ted vote to sell the steel mill, despite Paul's plea that it remain in the family. Mary, to whom Mrs. Scott has left her share of the mill, sides with Paul and saves the mill by inducing Constance to change her vote. Incensed by Mary's action, Louise insults her. Paul, angered, breaks with his wife and, indicating a divorce, reunites with Mary.

* * *

By 1945 Greer Garson had enjoyed a stellar reign at MGM, one which few actresses have experienced in Hollywood. Not only did the redheaded celebrity own the title Queen of the Culver City lot, but she had also scored a record four consecutive Oscar nominations for Best Actress: **Blossoms in the Dust** (1941), **Mrs. Miniver** (1942—she won), **Madame Curie** (1943), and **Mrs. Parkington** (1944). The Irish-born beauty had also

won England's **Picturegoer** magazine Gold Medal for three consecutive years: **Blossoms in the Dust, Mrs. Miniver,** and **Random Harvest.** She was the proverbial darling of reviews. As critic James Agate wrote in 1943, "I am inclined to think the time has come to recognize Greer Garson as the next best film actress to Bette Davis."

Garson's fifth consecutive Academy Award nomination was for her portrayal of Mary Rafferty in MGM's **Valley of Decision.** It was a sprawling, clichéd yarn (she is a servant who falls in love with her employer's handsome son) embellished by the panting close-ups and classy histrionics of its leading lady.

In his autobiography, **Light Your Torches and Pull Up Your Tights** (1973), director Tay Garnett (who had monitored Garson's performance in **Mrs. Parkington**) described the expensive production and the picture's working atmosphere:

We had a formidable cast for **Valley.** Opposite Greer was the brilliant newcomer from Broadway, Gregory Peck; other superlative talents were Lionel Barrymore, Jessica Tandy, Gladys Cooper, Donald Crisp, and Marshall Thompson[1] (his first picture, which gave no clue to his eventual association with a cross-eyed lion named Clarence).

We worked on a happy set. By that time Greer and I had become firm friends. Lionel Barrymore and I always hit it off beautifully— he got a kick out of knowing that his younger brother John, Gene Fowler, and I occasionally [had] applied a bright coat of paint to the local scene. Donald Crisp and I had been friends since the old Writer's Club days, and Gladys Cooper had always enjoyed Instant Popularity.

Placed in Pittsburgh, the adaptation of the Marcia Davenport novel of love, sacrifice, and uplifting emotions also afforded excellent opportunities for Dan Duryea to smirk as the no-good son, and for cinematographer Joseph Ruttenberg to approximate the grimy mill atmosphere of Pittsburgh.

Of all the Garson box-office blockbusters, **Valley of Decision** was the most successful, outgrossing even **Mrs. Miniver.** It reaped $5,560,000 in its initial spring 1945 release. Garson won the aforementioned Oscar bid, but the winner that year was the star of Warner Bros.' **Mildred Pierce.** Ironically it was triumphant Joan Crawford whom Garson had a few years before replaced as the top distaff star on the Metro lot. **Valley of Decision** won the **Photoplay** Gold Medal of 1945. It also placed fourth on the **Film Daily** Ten Best Picture Poll of the season, and was Metro's highest-grossing feature of the year.

With this winner Garson reached her apex as a major screen attraction. The overtouted **Adven-**

---

[1]Actually Metro contractee Hume Cronyn had been withdrawn from the studio's **The Clock** (1945) to play Peck's brother in **Valley.** However, only when he appeared on the soundstage did the obvious become clear—he was far shorter than Peck; so Marshall Thompson was assigned to play the brother. Meanwhile, Keenan Wynn had been cast in Judy Garland's **The Clock,** and Cronyn had to wait for reassingment.

ture (1945), with Clark Gable, splattered her appealing dignity by inferring that on screen she could be a sailor's pickup. Only **Julia Misbehaves** (1948), with Walter Pidgeon, really clicked thereafter. Her costar, Gregory Peck, prospered, however. He had enough talent and drive to reject Louis B. Mayer's offer of a lucrative contract—and thereby to inspire a legend. Reputedly a teary-eyed Mayer had fallen to his knees to beg Peck to accept the pact. Asked in 1976 by interviewer Roy Pickard if the incident were fact, the star replied, "Yes, he did. It's true, but I think he used to do it every day. Sometimes for two performances. . . . He did actually cry when I said no, but he enjoyed crying, I think, and had a thoroughly good time."

VIVA VILLA!
1934—115 min.

Producer, David O. Selznick; **directors,** Jack Conway and Howard Hawks; suggested by the book by Edgcumb Pinchon and O. B. Stade; **screenplay,** Ben Hecht; **assistant directors,** Art Rosson and John Waters; **music consultant,** Juan Aguilar; **music,** Herbert Stothart; **art director,** Harry Oliver; **set decorator,** Edwin B. Willis; **costumes,** Dolly Tree; **technical advisers,** Carlos Novarro and Matias Santoyo; **sound,** Douglas Shearer; **camera,** James Wong Howe and Charles G. Clarke; **editor,** Robert J. Kern.

Wallace Beery (**Pancho Villa**); Fay Wray (**Teresa**); Leo Carrillo (**Diego**); Donald Cook (**Don Felipe de Castillo**); Stuart Erwin (**Johnny Sykes**); George E. Stone (**Chavito**); Joseph Schildkraut (**General Pascal**); Henry B. Walthall (**Francisco Madero**); Katherine DeMille (**Rosita**); David Durand (**Bugle Boy**); Phillip Cooper (**Villa as a Boy**); Frank Puglia (**Pancho's Father**); Charles Stevens, Steve Clemento, Pedro Regas, and John Merkel (**Pascal's Aides**); Harry Cording (**Majordomo**); Francis McDonald (**Villa's Man**); Clarence Hummel Wilson (**Jail Official**); Nigel DeBrulier (**Political Judge**); Sam Godfrey (**Prosecuting Attorney**); Julian Rivero (**Telegraph Operator**); Mischa Auer (**Military Attaché**); Francis X. Bushman, Jr. (**Calloway**); André Cheron (**French Reporter**); William von Brincken (**German Reporter**); Chris-Pin Martin and Nick DeRuiz (**Peons**); Arthur Treacher (**British Reformer**); H. B. Warner (**Bit**).

SYNOPSIS
Young Pancho Villa witnesses his father being whipped to death by a soldier because he protested the seizure of the peons' land by tyrannical Porfirio Díaz. The boy avenges his father's death by stabbing the soldier and then flees to the hills.

Villa grows into a Robin Hood-like character who attacks the wealthy and aids the poor. During a raid Villa encounters American Johnny Sykes, and they develop a long friendship.

Wealthy Don Felipe de Castillo and his sister Teresa are sympathetic to the revolutionary's cause and invite Villa to meet Francisco Madero, intellectual leader of the peons. Madero succeeds in enlisting Villa's aid in overthrowing Díaz.

Villa teams with General Pascal to overrun the Díaz forces. The tyrant later abdicates and Villa names Madero president. Madero then suggests that Villa and his men disband since Pascal will now fill the role of military adviser.

When Villa blackjacks a bank teller, Pascal arranges to have his rival executed. Madero intercedes, granting Pancho a pardon if he will leave Mexico. With Villa gone, Pascal assassinates Madero and assumes power. Villa returns for a second revolution, which proves to be a bloody ordeal. Don Felipe and Teresa refuse to join the vengeful Villa. Later Teresa is killed by a stray shot from one of Villa's men.

Eventually Villa captures Pascal and orders his men to pour honey over the general so that the ants can eat him alive. Villa becomes president for only a short while. He is shot by Don Felipe, the latter avenging his sister's murder.

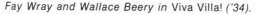

* * *

MGM prided itself that its "epics" were produced with speed, smoothness, and élan. Such was not the case with **Viva Villa!**

Suggested by the book by Edgcumb Pinchon and O. B. Stade concerning the escapades of Mexico's prodigal hero Pancho Villa (1877–1923), the film boasted a screenplay by Ben Hecht. The largely fictional project starred Wallace Beery as the legendary Pancho and Lee Tracy as Johnny Sykes, the latter Villa's American newspaperman ally and mouthpiece. Under Howard Hawks' direction, the company in November 1933 traveled to Mexico where 10,000 miles of countryside would be covered for location filming.

Problems began immediately. Between 500 and 6,000 extras were employed daily and were paid only fifty cents a day; the minimum fee should have been $1.00. Prominent Mexicans resented that Beery—largely regarded as a comic actor—should be assigned the role of the heroic Villa. (Beery had his own problems: his wife Rita was quite ill and he kept his private plane in constant readiness in case he had to return home quickly.)

The coup de grace occurred on Sunday morning, November 19, 1933. Lee Tracy, one of Hollywood's Olympian drinkers, was in his hotel suite, recovering from a night of carousing in the bordertown clubs. He awoke to the sounds of a Mexican parade in the street below. What actually happened has inspired many versions. Hollywood legend insists that Tracy, with only a blanket covering his naked body, wandered out onto his hotel balcony, lost his blanket, and urinated on a band of soldiers marching below. Shocked Mexican officials had Tracy arrested. The actor's behavior became the biggest news in Mexico—and at MGM. Disgusted by the publicized episode and fearful of the rumored boycott of all Metro pictures by south-of-the-border audiences, Louis B. Mayer ordered Tracy back to MGM. On November 23, 1933, he fired him. Tracy's comment, "Tell Hollywood to go to hell! I'm going back to the stage!" Stuart Erwin was rushed into the Sykes' part, which was revamped so as not to tax the comedian's limited histrionic acumen.

If all these high jinks were not enough, the

Fay Wray and Wallace Beery in Viva Villa! *('34).*

plane carrying the location footage back to Culver City crashed en route. Every frame of film was destroyed.

Undaunted, MGM decided to put the pieces back together. Jack Conway replaced the frazzled Hawks as director. (Hawks had refused to testify in Culver City against Lee Tracy, which angered Mayer.) Fay Wray was signed for the vacated role of Teresa. Conway completed the shooting in Hollywood on January 12, 1934.

The results proved worthy of all the effort.[1] The film is exciting and colorful, and Beery's portrayal of Pancho is expert. The actor provides an effective mixture of sheepish child and sadistic tyrant. In the latter capacity he is the one who orders the execution of his peacock rival, General Pascal (played to odious perfection by Joseph Schildkraut). Villa orders Pascal staked to an ant hill and smeared with honey to provide a feast for the insects! "Put it on his ears, his eyes, his nose, his mouth—put it every place on him—**every** place!" commands Pancho. Conway brings this chilling sequence to a comic finale when, after some grisly shots of vultures coming to roost as the general screams his last, Pancho's chief lieutenant (Leo Carrillo) visits Pancho and smiles, "I got his boots!"

To cap his performance, Beery performed a touching death scene. He lies mortally wounded on a butchershop floor and asks Johnny Sykes to create for him his dying words:

SYKES: Pancho Villa spoke for the last time. He said . . . he said . . .

PANCHO: Hurry Johnny, Johnny—what were my last words?

SYKES: "Goodbye, my Mexico," said Pancho Villa. "Forgive me for my crimes. Remember, if I sinned against you, it was because I loved you too much."

PANCHO: Forgive me? Johnny . . . what I done wrong?

When **Viva Villa!** premiered in the spring of 1934, MGM had the 1,225-square-foot billboard over the Criterion Theatre on Broadway painted with the likeness of Beery's face. Both public and critics cheered the film. The **New York World-Telegram** reported, "Ben Hecht has spun a savagely realistic, stirring, and dramatic picture of Pancho Villa's life . . . with Wallace Beery giving a magnificent performance in the role of Mexican hero bandit." Many were surprised that Beery was not nominated for an Academy Award; he did win the best actor prize of the 1934 Venice Film Festival. The picture itself was Oscar-nominated, but lost to Columbia's **It Happened One Night.**

Beery later reprised his Pancho characterization on "Lux Radio Theatre" on October 10, 1938, with costars Noah Beery and Ellen Drew.

In 1962, Robert Preston starred in the pre-Broadway production of **We Take the Town,** a musical version of the Pancho Villa story. It never reached New York City.

---

[1]Filmed on a sixty-five day schedule, **Viva Villa!** cost $1,022,000 and earned a profit of $87,000.

WATERLOO BRIDGE
1940—103 min.

Producer, Sidney Franklin; **director,** Mervyn LeRoy; based on the play by Robert E. Sherwood; **screenplay,** S. N. Behrman, Hans Rameau, and George Froeschel; **art directors,** Cedric Gibbons and Urie McCleary; **set decorator,** Edwin B. Willis; **gowns,** Adrian; **men's costumes,** Gile Steele; **music,** Herbert Stothart; ballet staged by Ernst Matray; **sound,** Douglas Shearer; **camera,** Joseph Ruttenberg; **editor,** George Boemler.

Vivien Leigh (**Myra Lester**); Robert Taylor (**Captain Roy Cronin**); Lucile Watson (**Lady Margaret Cronin**); C. Aubrey Smith (**Duke**); Maria Ouspenskaya (**Mme Olga**); Virginia Field (**Kitty**); Leo G. Carroll (**Policeman**); Clara Reid (**Mrs. Bassett**); Steffi Duna (**Lydia**); Leonard Mudie (**Parker**); Herbert Evans (**Commissionaire**); Halliwell Hobbes (**Vicar**); Ethel Griffies (**Mrs. Clark**); Gilbert Emery (**Colonel**); David Clyde (**Barnes, the Butler**); Janet Shaw (**Maureen**); Virginia Carroll (**Sylvia**); Florence Baker (**Beatrice**); Elsie Prescott (**Cockney Woman**); Bob Winkler (**Boy**); Norma Varden (**Hostess**); Fred Sassoni (**Newsboy**); Kathryn Collier (**Barmaid**); Dennis d'Auburn (**Generous Man**); Wilfred Lucas (**Elderly Huntsman**).

SYNOPSIS

In September 1939, forty-eight-year-old Colonel Roy Cronin of the British army finds himself in a London blackout as he drives through to Waterloo Station on his way to France. He has never married. He gets out of the vehicle and walks on the new Waterloo Bridge, which has replaced the old structure damaged in World War I. He twists a tiny ivory figure charm in his fingers; it is a key to the past.

By flashback the story shifts to 1917. Captain Cronin, the scion of an old Scottish family, is on Waterloo Bridge as the air-raid warning sounds. He is passed by a group of chattering young women. One of the girls drops her purse. He helps her retrieve the spilled contents and then guides her to the safety of a bomb shelter. She is Myra Lester, a twenty-three-year-old dancer from Birmingham in Madame Olga's international ballet company. That night he sees her perform **Swan Lake** and later invites her to supper at the Candlelight Club. Both agree it is love at first sight. He then obtains the permission of his uncle the duke, commanding officer of his regiment, to marry Myra. But before the wedding can take place, his regiment is ordered to the French front.

The very afternoon she is meeting Roy's mother for tea she reads in the newspapers that he has fallen in action. Disillusioned and unable to find employment, she follows the lead of her roommate Kitty and becomes a street prostitute to make a living.

Months later she is at Waterloo Station to pick up a soldier. There Roy Cronin (who had been a prisoner of war during this time) spots her. His joy is great for he believes she has been waiting

Robert Taylor and Vivien Leigh in Waterloo Bridge *('40).*

for him. He escorts her to his family's estate in Scotland. Their engagement is announced. However, Myra realizes she could never be comfortable as the wife of her social better, especially with her lurid past. She confesses her sins to Lady Margaret and then hastily returns to London. Roy follows in pursuit and learns the truth from Kitty. They search in vain for Myra. Meanwhile, amidst the pell-mell of a foggy night on Waterloo Bridge, she deliberately steps in front of a Red Cross van and is killed.

Roy is left with his memories.

* * *

While the role of Scarlett O'Hara bequeathed to Vivien Leigh instant worldwide celebrity and an Academy Award, it also presented a serious professional problem—how could she possibly follow it on screen with an assignment of equal merit. Having contracted with **Gone With the Wind** producer David O. Selznick, Miss Leigh initially examined the script for his forthcoming adaptation of **Rebecca** (1940). Not only was she enticed by the dramatic title role, but she was also excited by the possibility of playing opposite her husband-to-be, Laurence Olivier. Though Selznick went to considerable trouble to convince himself to cast his new star in that choice part, he finally surrendered to his perfectionism. He informed the British actress that she was not right for the film; Joan Fontaine was given the screen opportunity instead.

Both Selznick and Leigh, however, agreed that the role of Myra Lester, dancer-turned-prostitute-turned-suicide, of **Waterloo Bridge** would be "right" for the star. In fact, the Robert Sherwood play, previously filmed at Universal in 1931 with Mae Clarke and Douglass Montgomery,[1] was being designed by MGM scenarists S. N. Behrman, Hans Rameau, and George Roeschel as a tandem vehicle for Leigh and Olivier. (Since 1939's **Wuthering Heights,** Olivier had been an acclaimed Hollywood box-office figure.) This turn of events soothed the actress's sensitivities, and she looked forward to commencing work on the melodrama.

The bubble was soon pricked. Greer Garson, a Louis B. Mayer favorite and a new Metro star because of **Goodbye, Mr. Chips,** requested that Olivier be her leading man in **Pride and Prejudice,** (1940). Mayer coddlingly agreed, and cast his favored Robert Taylor as Roy Cronin.[2] The delighted,

---

[1]In the late 1930s, David O. Selznick had acquired the screen rights to **Waterloo Bridge** from Universal and he, in turn, sold the film property to MGM at the same time he concluded an agreement with Metro that Vivien Leigh should portray the female lead.

As was studio custom then, MGM acquired all of Universal's extant prints of the 1931 **Waterloo Bridge** and the motion picture was long thought lost until the Musuem of Modern Art in New York City managed to acquire a print from the Metro vaults for a Universal retrospective late in 1977.

[2]In the British-filmed MGM release, **A Yank at Oxford,** starring Robert Taylor and Maureen O'Sullivan, Vivien Leigh had endured a supporting role, since at that time the Metro hierarchy felt she was an unproven commodity at the U.S. box office.

ultrahandsome Mr. Taylor said, "When I was just about convinced I had been forgotten, MGM handed me the script of **Waterloo Bridge.** It was an actor's dream and the role fitted me better than a pair of custom-made shoes!" Miss Leigh was not of the same opinion; in Anne Edwards' **Vivien Leigh: A Biography** (1977), the author quotes a letter of the actress in which she writes, "Robert Taylor is the man in the picture and as it was written for Larry, it's a typical piece of miscasting." Virginia Field, a standout as Kitty in a superb supporting cast (Lucile Watson, C. Aubrey Smith, Maria Ouspenskaya, Leo G. Carroll), recalled a few years ago, "Miss Leigh was completely upset from start to finish of the picture. She was furious at having her Laurence Olivier pulled from the cast. . . . [She] pouted and knitted unforgivingly to the end of shooting."

Apparently Olivier was less supportive of his mate than she was of him. In an interview with Scott Eyman of **Focus on Film** (1976), the film's cinematographer, Joseph Ruttenberg, disdainfully remembered Olivier's visits to the set. "Vivien Leigh was charming, charming, but that husband [sic] of hers, Olivier, was awful—always criticizing her acting, her technique. He tore her down."

Metro's **Waterloo Bridge** was an expensive, expansive production, produced by Sidney Franklin and directed by Mervyn LeRoy (who later teamed for **Mrs. Miniver,** 1942). In a 1977 **Films in Review** article William K. Everson, characterized the 1940 version:

Comparison with the 1940 version is the most direct way to stress the simplicity and honesty of the original. The first remake, a big, glossy, MGM spectacular, designed as a showcase follow-up for Vivien Leigh after **Gone With the Wind,** was undeniably entertaining, well crafted, and richly romantic, beautifully mounted and photographed; it contained some memorable sequences, and Mervyn LeRoy directed it with style and taste. But first and foremost, it was a deluxe MGM production, clearly dominated by Louis B. Mayer's own production code—as well as the official one—and by the desire to present their new star with a flattering role. Initially, it was all updated by giving it a World War II framework. The basic story was still relegated to World War I, but within a flashback device which somehow had the effect of softening tragedy into nostalgia. Secondly, the characters were ugraded into MGM aristocracy. The soldier, as played (and quite well) by Robert Taylor, was no longer a mere enlisted man but an officer, and his parents were promoted to the nobility (C. Aubrey Smith was a duke!), living in quarters as far removed from reality as those of Mr. and Mrs. Miniver, MGM's conception of Britain's **middle** class. The not particularly talented chorus girl of the original was now presented with a **Red Shoes**-like problem—she is a brilliant young ballet dancer who is told she can only succeed if she sticks to her art and shuts out love. Morally, she is as pure as all MGM heroines of the period, taking to prostitution (and then in a brief and subtly suggestive scene) only when

she believes her officer to be dead, and life no longer has any meaning for her.

Whatever the MGM transformation, the result was a well-played, powerfully assembled film, almost too skillfully concocted to be described as a tearjerker, which is its logical classification. In his **New York Times** review, Bosley Crowther wrote, "Let there be no doubt about it, Vivien Leigh is as fine an actress as we have on the screen today. Maybe even the finest, and that's a lot to say. . . . Miss Leigh shapes the role of the girl with such superb comprehension, progresses from the innocent fragile dancer to an empty, bedizened streetwalker with such surety of characterization and creates a person of such appealing naturalness that the picture gains considerable substance as a result." Taylor also drew praise for his "surprisingly flexible and mature performance," and his career enjoyed a revitalization because of the film's popularity. (It did far more for him than the lushly mounted outdoor epic **Billy the Kid,** 1941, which was geared to enhance his masculine image, and to erase, it was hoped, some of the pretty-boy stigma that had hounded him in the thirties.)

Sherwood's play experienced yet another cinema rendering, also courtesy of Metro—1956's **Gaby.** Leslie Caron, John Kerr, Cedric Hardwicke, and Taina Elg played the leads, and Curtis Bernhardt directed the CinemaScope color production. But the storyline had little impact on mid-1950s audiences, and **Gaby** proved to be, unlike its cinematic predecessors, a box-office mediocrity.

WEEKEND AT THE WALDORF
1945—130 min.

Producer, Arthur Hornblow, Jr.; **director,** Robert Z. Leonard; suggested by the play **Grand Hotel** by Vickie Baum; **adapter,** Guy Bolton; **screenplay,** Sam and Bella Spewack; **art directors,** Cedric Gibbons and Daniel B. Cathcart; **set decorators,** Edwin B. Willis and Jack Bonar; **choreography,** Charles Walters; **music–music director,** Johnny Green; **orchestrator,** Ted Duncan; **vocal arranger,** Kay Thompson; **songs,** Sammy Fain, Ted Koehler, and Pepe Guizar; **assistant director,** William Lewis; **costume supervisor,** Irene; **sound,** Douglas Shearer; **special effects,** Warren Newcombe; **camera,** Robert Planck; **editor,** Robert J. Kern.

Ginger Rogers **(Irene Malvern)**; Walter Pidgeon **(Chip Collyer)**; Van Johnson **(Captain James Hollis)**; Lana Turner **(Bunny Smith)**; Robert Benchley **(Randy Norton)**; Edward Arnold **(Martin K. Edley)**; Leon Ames **(Henry Burton)**; Warner Anderson **(Dr. Campbell)**; Phyllis Thaxter **(Cynthia Drew)**; Keenan Wynn **(Oliver Webson)**; Porter Hall **(Stevens)**; Samuel S. Hinds **(Mr. Jessup)**; George Zucco **(Bey of Aribajan)**; Xavier Cugat and His Orchestra **(Themselves)**; Lina Romay **(Juanita)**; Bob Graham **(Singer)**; Michael Kirby **(Lieutenant John Rand)**;

Cora Sue Collins (**Jane Rand**); Rosemary DeCamp (**Anna**); Jacqueline DeWit (**Kate Douglas**); Frank Puglia (**Emile**); Charles Wilson (**Hi Johns**); Irving Bacon (**Sam Skelly**); Miles Mander (**British Secretary**); Nana Bryant (**Mrs. H. Davenport Drew**); Russell Hicks (**McPherson**); Naomi Childers (**Night Maid**); Ruth Lee (**The Woman**); Byron Foulger (**Barber**); Franklyn Farnum, Bess Flowers, and Ella Ethridge (**Guests**).

SYNOPSIS

At the posh New York hotel assorted lives become intertwined during the course of a weekend. Screen star Irene Malvern learns from her maid Anna that the latter is mixed up with a would-be crook; Irene agrees to speak to the young man in hope of changing his ways. Through a chain of circumstantial evidence she confuses war correspondent Chip Collyer with the jewel thief and he does not dissuade her of the mixup; he pretends to be a crook named Duke. Later his true identity is learned and both Irene and Chip admit they are in love.

Meanwhile, Cynthia Drew is about to call off her wedding, believing her fiancé Dr. Campbell is in love with Irene. The movie star convinces the girl of her error by telling her that she is actually wed—secretly—to Chip. The information, told in confidence, is soon spread throughout the hotel.

As for hotel stenographer Bunny Smith, her ambitions are to live on Park Avenue. But she meets air force captain James Hollis, who is not expected to survive a serious operation. Later Bunny receives an offer of a lavish living style if she will become the mistress of Martin K. Edley, a crafty con artist, However, while talking with Captain Hollis at the Starlight Roof, she realizes that she loves him and that he is the man for her.

As the weekend draws to a close, Chip releases Irene from his "claim" on her, but she in turn agrees to meet him in London where she plans to marry him. Captain Hollis learns that with good luck he may survive the operation. If he does, he and Bunny plan to wed. Cynthia and Dr. Campbell depart on their honeymoon. Cub reporter Oliver Webson, with the aid of Chip, manages to foil Edley's plot to fleece the Bey of Aribajan by means of a fake oil stock promotion. As for gossip columnist and bon vivant Randy Norton, his scottie dog has triplets.

* * *

There's Ginger Rogers, a movie star in town for the premiere of her latest picture. She's so worn out, she cries over nothing. She's never married or had a divorce. She has no children, not even a dog. All she's ever done is work.

There's Walter Pidgeon, a tall, exhausted foreign correspondent. He's been around the world watching men die in large numbers. On Monday, after the weekend, he'll start flying around the world again. What a debilitating life!

There's Van Johnson, a combat pilot on his way to Walter Reed Hospital, where he has a 50–50 chance of surviving an operation to remove a chunk of shrapnel near his heart. He

Walter Pidgeon, Ginger Rogers, Lana Turner, and Van Johnson in a promotional shot for Weekend at the Waldorf ('45).

has no family at all. Nobody gives a darn whether he lives or dies, and that's bad because the doctor has said that he has to want to live.

That leads us to tasty Lana Turner, the public stenog who wants more than anything to move from 10th Avenue to Park. And if the oil tycoon Edward Arnold, who has missed jail by narrow margins in the past, can pull off his deal with a goat-toting Prince of Araby, she may get that swanky address.

If the **New York Post**'s rundown of **Weekend at the Waldorf** (". . . exactly what it takes to make a tired, gloomy person happy," wrote reviewer Archer Winsten) sounds curiously familiar, it is supposed to—sort of. The 130-minute soap opera of stars and tinsel was a 191-page Sam and Bella Spewack rewrite of Vicki Baum's **Grand Hotel**, so definitively filmed by the studio thirteen years before. True, there was nobody declaiming "I want to be alone," no gloomy scar-faced doctor cynically sneering "Nothing ever happens," and certainly no acting worth remembering or reviving.[1] Still, in its day it was "a smart, up-to-the-

minute and thoroughly entertaining story" (**New York Daily News**) which substituted Xavier Cugat for moody art and Robert Z. Leonard's dazzle for Edmund Goulding's character study. It enjoyed a nine-week showcase run at Radio City Music Hall, and went on to become the sixth largest grossing film of 1945 (earning $4,370,000 in distributors' domestic rentals).

Updated to 1945, as the war was nearing a satisfactory end for the Allies, **Weekend** performed a facelift on the original Baum characters that made them almost unrecognizable. To present the new set of people the story time frame was expanded from the thirty-six hours of the original to a three-day weekend period. Rather than a suicidal Grusinskaya, the beautifully miserable form of Garbo, we meet Irene Malvern, a fatigued, weepy, wisecracking actress played by top-billed, aloof Ginger Rogers. In the course of

---

Hotel. Smart-mouthed Irene Malvern (Rogers) retorts, "Why . . . that's right out of **Grand Hotel.**" "Yes," responds Pidgeon dryly, "and we're off to see the Wizard." Still later in the film, some fun is made with the name of Pidgeon's character, allowing for references to another MGM past hit. Movie star Miss Malvern says on two occasions to the war correspondent, "Goodbye, Mr. Chip . . . Collyer."

---

[1] At one point in the picture, Pidgeon's character begins to quote one of John Barrymore's speeches from **Grand**

the proceedings she models a bevy of costumes (by Irene) which easily outdistance her frigid acting. As one reviewer of the day recorded, her ensembles included "a cocktail outfit with the new dolman sleeves and harem-style pantalettes under a trailing wraparound skirt; and a nightgown with no visible connective tissue over an expanse of possibly six inches of marvelous midriff." The only facet of Rogers' appearance to garner criticism was her occasionally unflattering hairstyle. As Jeanine Basinger would recall in **Lana Turner** (1976), "In one scene, she wears a hairdo like an Italian sausage with a gold hoop hanging out of it."

A very flirtatious Walter Pidgeon, whose charming insouciance here gave a far more accurate picture of the real-life Hollywood party-favorite Pidgeon than his rather stodgy stooges of the Greer Garson epics, was less lucky with his wardrobe. As a war correspondent, his prime props were a standard-issue trenchcoat and a wry smile. His character had none of the underworld rogue qualities of the John Barrymore counterpart. Lana Turner, whose stenographer Bunny Smith made material success seem like a far more agreeable problem than did Joan Crawford's languid-eyed Flaemmchen, had her opportunity to sparkle in a costume that would make any ten working girls envious.[2] During the Starlight Roof club sequence she models a white-sequined strapless gown, radiating youthful stardom and a beauty that qualify her for MGM status rather than casting credibility.

"This is the kind of production in which Van Johnson's name is fourth on the list of credits," noted the impressed **New York Sun**. He was about as far removed from Lionel Barrymore's dying middle-age clerk as could be conceived. He was light years younger, far more handsome, and instead of the brooding, teach-me-how-to-be-happy pose of Barrymore, Johnson was permitted to display his famous freckle-face smile at almost every possible opportunity. Though Wallace Beery's bombastic Preysing was not to be found, Edward Arnold provided an effectively lewd heavy, subtly propositioning the almost susceptible stenographer. Replacing the cynical Lewis Stone figure was acid-tongue gossip columnist Randy Norton (Robert Benchley), a man with a penchant for too much drink and for caring for his pregnant scottie dog.

With the confection further sugarcoated by Xavier Cugat's bongo band and vocalist Lina Romay, and songs ("And There You Are" and "Guadalajara") by Sammy Fain, Ted Koehler, and Pepe Guizar, film fans with good memories had to remind themselves that **Grand Hotel** was not only the inspiration but the model for this ultra-sleek escapism.

---

[2] Ever since the casting of this film was first announced, there have been those who insisted that Ginger Rogers—who won an Academy Award as secretary **Kitty Foyle** (1940)—should have played Bunny Smith and that Lana Turner would have been more suitable as the glamorous movie star. However, since the Irene Malvern assignment called for the actress to be world-weary, it was too soon in Turner's life and career for her to appropriate that pose successfully.

"Most interesting aspect of the picture, and almost as entertaining as the stories, is the astonishing realism of the Waldorf sets, as recreated by MGM's set designer Cedric Gibbons and staff" (**Cue** magazine). Just as the original **Grand Hotel** register of characters had been homogenized to suit the Hollywood wholesome casting choices of MGM, 1940s-style, so the story's hotel locale was Americanized to play upon the filmgoer's dream of gracious living—that is, to mingle with the beautiful and elite people at the luxurious Waldorf-Astoria Hotel in New York City. Unlike Paramount for **The Stork Club** (1945) or Twentieth Century–Fox for **Billy Rose's Diamond Horseshoe** (1945), MGM was **not** forced to pay its movie setting original any premium for the privilege of exploiting its glamorous fame. According to a **Newsweek** magazine piece at the time, Waldorf spokesman Lucius Boomer was so gratified by the studio's treatment of his hotel that he charged Metro no fee. "In this case," reported the magazine, "the publicity is more than worth its weight in royalties." Such was the case when the plushest of Hollywood film factories set out to showcase the Tiffany of American hotels.

WHISTLING IN THE DARK
1941—77 min.

Producer, George Haight; **director,** S. Sylvan Simon; based on the play by Lawrence Gross and Edward Carpenter; **screenplay,** Robert MacGunigle, Harry Clork, and Albert Mannheimer; **art director,** Cedric Gibbons; **camera,** Sidney Wagner; **editor,** Frank E. Hull.

Red Skelton (**Wally Benton**); Ann Rutherford (**Carol Lambert**); Virginia Grey (**Fran Post**); Conrad Veidt (**Joseph Jones**); Rags Ragland (**Sylvester**); Eve Arden (**Buzz Baker**); Don Douglas (**Gordon Thomas**); Paul Stanton (**Jennings**); Don Costello (**Noose Green**); William Tannen (**Robert Graves**); Reed Hadley (**Beau Smith**); Lloyd Corrigan (**Harvey Upshaw**); Henry O'Neill (**Phillip Post**); George Carleton (**Deputy Commissioner O'Neill**); Inez Cooper (**Stewardess**); Emmett Vogan (**Producer**); Leon Tyler (**Gerry**); Dorothy Adams (**Mrs. Farrell**); Brick Sullivan, Al Hill, and Robert Homans (**Policemen**).

SYNOPSIS

Joseph Jones, head of a gang conducting a fake cult by means of which they lure wealthy women to their premises, is enraged when he learns that a certain man stands in his way of inheriting $1,000,000, a sum left by one of his deceased followers. Since he does not wish to commit open murder and knows of no way to get rid of the intended victim, Jones decides to follow the advice of his men—to kidnap Wally Benton. The latter conducts a radio program on crime stories which he concocts himself.

Jones' scheme is to force Wally to think up a plot by means of which they can kill the bene-

ficiary and not leave any telltale clues. At first Wally refuses, but when Jones has his henchmen kidnap Benton's sweetheart, Carol Lambert, and his sponsor's daughter, Fran Post, Wally accedes to his captors' wishes. The plan he works out is for one of Jones' men to follow the intended victim on a plane and to put poison in the mouthwash he uses.

Left in the hideout with just one of the henchmen, Wally, Carol, and Fran hit upon an idea to wrap up the caper. Since Jones has torn out the phone box, they connect the telephone wires to a radio and in that way are able to contact the phone operator. By leading the gangland stooge to believe they are pretending to give a broadcast, they get their message across to the authorities and the intended victim is saved. Soon the police arrive and rescue them.

* * *

For all the stellar attributes of MGM in 1940, there was one rather conspicuous void in its lineup—contractees devoted to the art of the slapstick and physical-humor feature films. With the Marx Brothers soon to depart the lot, studio executives were anxious to remedy the situation.[1]

It was director Frank Borzage who told Louis B. Mayer of a redheaded young clown who was already a veteran of radio, Warner Bros. two-reel Vitaphone shorts, vaudeville, and a single feature picture, RKO's **Having Wonderful Time** (1938). After viewing Red Skelton's screen test, Mayer offered Skelton a studio contract.

As expected, the newcomer to the lot began his stay at Culver City with a disciplined buildup. He was the clown of Walter Pidgeon's naval air squadron in **Flight Command** (1940) and created the part of gangly orderly Vernon Briggs in **The People vs. Dr. Kildare** (1941). Then came a B film which proved to be a box-office sleeper and established Skelton as Metro's answer to Mr. Bob Hope. **Whistling in the Dark** was a mixture of thrills and chuckles much in the style of the Paramount-Hope outings. The property had previously been filmed by MGM as a 1933 release, with Ernest Truex as a pint-size mystery expert, Una Merkel as his girl, and Edward Arnold as the head of a band of crooks.

Metro's update starred Skelton as a radio sleuth, Ann Rutherford (Polly Benedict of the **Andy Hardy** series), and Teutonic Conrad Veidt. Director S. Sylvan Simon provided an admirable mixture of all the touches which were so acceptable to audiences of the day: screaming attractive girls (including Virginia Grey and Eve Arden in the concoction), smooth and sinister villainy deliciously served by the masterly Veidt, and Skelton abounding in wild farce, comic sprawls, and terrified yells. All this in a plot involving a series of sliding walls and eerie cellars in the spooky hideout of the bad guys. Abetting the future star prankster was Metro contractee Rags Ragland, the burlesque veteran who would bolster so many studio

---

[1] Robert Benchley, who had been making an engaging series of shorts at MGM, departed the studio in 1941 for Paramount. Throughout the thirties and well into the fifties, Pete Smith's production unit at Metro made a series of educational-experimental-comedy shorts, most of the later ones featuring Dave O'Brien.

Virginia Grey and Red Skelton in Whistling in the Dark *('41).*

offerings before his untimely death in 1946 of uremic poisoning.

"To the cheerfully swelling list of bright new film comedians you may add the rosy name of one Richard (Red) Skelton," wrote Bosley Crowther of the **New York Times.** "For Metro has really turned up an impressive young Bob Hopeful in the person of this jaunty chap with wavy blond hair and wild expressions. . . . The screen needs smooth comics like this one. Where there is Hope, there is Skelton, too."

Whistling in the Dark proved far more successful than MGM dared to hope. After Skelton played orderly Briggs for one more time in **Dr. Kildare's Wedding Day** (1941), the comedian enjoyed a stellar Metro campaign. He was spotlighted in such musicals as **Lady Be Good** (1941) and **Panama Hattie** (1942), both with Ann Sothern, **Ship Ahoy** (1942) and **I Dood It** (1942), both with Eleanor Powell, and, as an official star clincher, the Technicolor **Du Barry Was a Lady** (1943) with Lucille Ball. There were also two more reprisals of his sleuth Wally Benton: **Whistling in Dixie** (1942) and **Whistling in Brooklyn** (1943), both directed by S. Sylvan Simon and each featuring Ann Rutherford and Rags Ragland.

Skelton served thirteen years at Metro, and remains one of the noteworthy examples of that studio's style of developing screen talent. In 1977, during a week-long stint as cohost of "The Mike Douglas Show," Skelton revealed elaborate plans to create a school to develop future "clowns" (as Skelton always refers to himself), training them very much after the pattern used by the late, lamented MGM.

THE WHITE CLIFFS OF DOVER
1944—126 min.

Producer, Sidney Franklin; **director,** Clarence Brown; based on the poem "The White Cliffs of Dover" by Alice Duer Miller; **screenplay,** Claudine West, Jan Lustig, and George Froeschel; **music,** Herbert Stothart; **art directors,** Cedric Gibbons and Randall Duell; **set decorators,** Edwin B. Willis and Jacques Mesereau; **costumes,** Irene; **makeup,** Jack Dawn; **technical adviser,** Major Cyril Seys Ramsey-Hill; **sound,** Charles E. Wallace; **special effects,** Arnold Gillespie and Warren Newcombe; **camera,** George Folsey; **editors,** Robert J. Kern and Al Jennings.

Irene Dunne (**Susan Dunn Ashwood**); Alan Marshal (**Sir John Ashwood**); Frank Morgan (**Hiram Porter Dunn**); Roddy McDowall (**John Ashwood II as a Boy**); Dame May Whitty (**Nanny**); C. Aubrey Smith (**Colonel**); Gladys Cooper (**Lady Jean Ashwood**); Peter Lawford (**John Ashwood II at Age Twenty-four**); Van Johnson (**Sam Bennett**); John Warburton (**Reggie**); Jill Esmond (**Rosamund**); Brenda Forbes (**Gwennie**); Norma Varden (**Mrs. Bland**); Elizabeth Taylor (**Betsy at Age Ten**); June Lockhart (**Betsy at Age Eighteen**); Charles Irwin (**Farmer Kenney**); Jean Prescott (**Mrs. Kenney**); Tom Drake (**American Soldier**); Isobel Elsom (**Mrs. Bancroft**); Edmond Breon (**Major Bancroft**); Miles Mander (**Major Loring**); Ann Curzon (**Miss Lambert**); Steven Muller (**Gerhard**); Norbert Muller (**Dietrich**); Molly Lamont (**Helen**); Lumsden Hare

(**The Vicar**); Arthur Shields (**Benson**); Emily Fitzroy (**Spinster in Boardinghouse**); Guy D'Ennery (**Curate in Boardinghouse**); Ethel Griffies (**Woman on Train**); Elton and Eldon Burkett (**Twins in Boardinghouse**); Alec Craig (**Billings**); Ian Wolfe (**Skipper**); Bunny Gordon (**John at Six Months**); Gavin Muir (**Captain Griffiths**); Charles Coleman (**Captain Davis**).

SYNOPSIS
In pre–World War I times, American Susan Dunn visits England with her small-town newspaper publisher father, Hiram Porter Dunn. There she falls in love with a young nobleman, Sir John Ashwood. After a whirlwind courtship they are married. Their honeymoon is interrupted when war is declared and he leaves for France. Both manage to see each other at Dieppe during one of John's furloughs. On Armistice Day Susan learns of his death in action. She decides to remain in England to rear her son, John, whom the deceased officer never saw.

Years later, Mr. Dunn, fearing a new war, urges Susan to return to America with her boy. When Lady Jean Ashwood, her mother-in-law, dies and Susan finds herself and young John alone on the estate, she decides to accept her father's advice. But John II reminds her that his dad would have liked her to carry on the family tradition. Thus she decides to remain in England, although she fears her son may someday meet her husband's fate.

The year 1942 finds Susan a Red Cross commandant in a London hospital. Among the wounded servicemen brought in from a raid on Dieppe is her son. He is mortally wounded. Informed that he has only some four hours to live, she comforts him in his last moments. He dies as she stands before an open window, describing to him a parade of American soldiers. They are the first contingent to land in England, having come, like the generation before them, to fight for "a peace that will stick."

* * *

The Allied cause of America and England during the harrowing days of World War II inspired Hollywood not only to develop propaganda pieces for U.S. morale, but also to produce portraits— or idealized portraits—of the British, our noble compatriots in the united cause. MGM'S **Mrs. Miniver** (1942) had performed this task magnificently, with Oscar-winning élan, the compliments of President Roosevelt and Prime Minister Churchill, and a box-office gross of $5.5 million. In search of a property to duplicate **Miniver**'s awesome success, that film's producer, Sidney Franklin, found material in Alice Duer Miller's poem, "The White Cliffs of Dover." It was the account of a woman who sacrifices both her husband and her son to the war cause. The picture was a major step in further solidifying U.S.–British goodwill, at least in most quarters on the American side of the Atlantic.

Since **Mrs. Miniver** had benefited by the star performance of Greer Garson, producer Franklin sought another top Hollywood name to portray Susan Ashwood. The choice was Irene Dunne, then at work in MGM's **A Guy Named Joe** (1943). (Be-

Irene Dunne and C. Aubrey Smith in The White Cliffs of Dover *('44).*

England, but no one can deny that the studio hasn't tried hard and often. Take **Goodbye, Mr. Chips, Mrs. Miniver, Random Harvest,** and now **The White Cliffs of Dover**. . . . Anglophile though the first three pictures were, the new one is more so with knobs on." The **New York Times**: "Such a tribute to English gentility as only an American studio would dare to make. . . . For such folks as like to think of England and America as being symbolically bound by such ties, say, as Lady Astor's, **The White Cliffs of Dover** should be a comforting film." When the tear-drenched romantic drama debuted in bomb-torned England, the British **Spectator** editorialized, "Such films like **The White Cliffs of Dover** (it is an outstanding example of a common type) are not malicious in intention but represent rather a friendly gesture gone badly wrong. Surely it should be possible for one of our British representatives to encourage the makers of such films to take a look at England for themselves before they go into production."

Despite its shortcomings, **The White Cliffs** is an admirable example of the slick machinery of MGM filmmaking expertly at work. Dunne provides her usual sterling performance, interpreting the self-sacrificing wife-mother with a depth of characterization not found in the screenplay. And where else but at MGM (who else could afford such a roster of players) could one find such authentic British types as Dame May Whitty, C. Aubrey Smith, Gladys Cooper, Isobel Elsom, Ethel Griffies, Brenda Forbes, et al., to give the picture the desired (albeit fictional) English flavor. As such, the picture did appeal to the American ideal of its English cohorts and the public's approval was reflected at the box office with a domestic gross of $4,050,000.

THE WIZARD OF OZ
1939 C—101 min.[1]

Producer, Mervyn LeRoy; **directors,** Victor Fleming and **uncredited:** Richard Thorpe, George Cukor, and King Vidor; based on the book by L. Frank Baum; **screenplay,** Noel Langley, Florence Ryerson, Edgar Allan Woolf, and **uncredited:** Herman Mankiewicz, Ogden Nash, Herbert Fields, Samuel Hoffenstein, Jack Mintz, Sid Silvers, and John Lee Mahin; **art directors,** Cedric Gibbons and William A. Horning; **set decorator,** Edwin B. Willis; **music,** Herbert Stothart; **songs,** E. Y. Harburg and Harold Arlen; **music numbers** staged by Bobby Connolly; **associate conductor,** George Stoll; **orchestral-vocal arrangers,** George Bass, Murray Cutter, Paul Marquardt, and Ken Darby; **character makeup,** Jack Dawn; **sound,** Douglas Shearer; **special effects,** Arnold Gillespie; **camera,** Harold Rosson; **editor,** Blanche Sewell.

Judy Garland **(Dorothy Gale);** Frank Morgan **(Professor Marvel [The Wizard]);** Ray Bolger **(Hunk [The Scarecrow]);** Bert Lahr **(Zeke [Cowardly**

cause of Van Johnson's automobile accident, **Joe** was delayed in production and Dunne found herself simultaneously working on two major features. She called the situation "unbearable" but worthwhile.)

Said the ever ladylike Dunne of **The White Cliffs,** "I don't think it smacks of propaganda, but if it does, then I'm glad. I feel everything possible should be done to cement friendship between the two nations that are most alike and speak the same language." Supporting the actress in her showcase performance were Alan Marshal as her spouse, Roddy McDowall and Peter Lawford as the son (as a boy and at age twenty-four), **Miniver** alumnus Dame May Whitty, **A Guy**

Named Joe veteran Van Johnson, and Elizabeth Taylor[1] (whose footage as a coquettish country girl is trimmed from prints shown on television currently). Clarence Brown directed the 126-minute inspirational saga.

Released in May 1944, **The White Cliffs of Dover** did not fare as well critically as MGM hoped, despite the lavish budget and care expended on the project. **Newsweek** magazine, "Whether Metro-Goldwyn-Mayer has always done right by England is a matter of opinion, even in

[1]Taylor and Dunne would be reunited on screen in Warner Bros.' **Life with Father** (1947).

[1]Opening and closing scenes in Sepia.

Lion]); Jack Haley (**Hickory [Tin Woodman]**); Billie Burke (**Glinda**); Margaret Hamilton (**Miss Gulch [The Witch]**); Pat Walshe (**Nikko**); Charley Grapewin (**Uncle Henry**); Clara Blandick (**Auntie Em**); Toto (**The Dog**); The Singer Midgets (**The Munchkins**); Jerry Maren (**A Munchkin**).

SYNOPSIS

Dorothy Gale, pert Kansas farm girl, is upset because the wealthy local shrew, Miss Gulch, has threatened to take away her mischievous little dog, Toto. Back at the farm, owned by her Auntie Em and Uncle Henry, the three farmhands offer Dorothy advice. Hunk suggests she use her brains and avoid Miss Gulch's house; Zeke tells her not to be afraid; and Hickory offers his help—after all, "One day, they're going to build a statue of me in this town." Nevertheless, when Miss Gulch arrives with a sheriff's order to take the dog, all of Dorothy's friends are powerless. Toto, however, escapes from the basket on the back of Miss Gulch's bicycle and returns to Dorothy. She, in turn, decides to take her beloved little dog and run away from home.

Soon Dorothy encounters Professor Marvel, a gypsy charlatan who, by means of his crafty chicanery, convinces Dorothy that her Auntie Em is ill and needs her. The girl races home, but not before a tornado forces the family to take shelter underground. Dorothy, looking for them, races into the house, and the winds knock out a window which hits her on the head.

Suddenly, Dorothy discovers herself high in the clouds as the tornado twists the house into the air. Dorothy and Toto observe a witch race by on her broomstick outside the window. Suddenly the house plops down in a colorful new land where the beautiful witch Glinda appears. Glinda informs Dorothy that her house has fatally fallen upon the wicked Witch of the East, and all of Munchkinland, where Dorothy has landed, comes out of hiding to offer gratitude and to rejoice. In the midst of the jubilation of the tiny Munchkins, there is a ghastly puff of smoke. The horrid Wicked Witch of the West appears, terrifying the Munchkins and intent on retrieving her dead sister's magical ruby slippers.

Glinda, however, transfers the shoes to Dorothy's feet. The Wicked Witch vanishes in a rage, not before vowing doom for the frightened girl and her barking dog. Glinda assures Dorothy safety, and she and the Munchkins direct Dorothy to follow the Yellow Brick Road to locate the one power who can grant her wish to return home—the Wizard of Oz.

Dorothy soon finds friends. In a cornfield, a Scarecrow, somehow reminiscent of Hunk, speaks to Dorothy of his great wish for a brain. Farther on, in the forest a Tin Woodman, resembling Hickory, is saved from rusting by Dorothy and the Scarecrow, and he sings of his craving for a heart. And in a fearsome wooded area populated by lions and tigers and bears, a Zeke-like Cowardly Lion weeps over his lack of bravery. All three join forces to seek Oz's aid. Although the Wicked Witch plagues their long journey—she tosses a fireball

at the Scarecrow and plunges Dorothy and the Lion into a deep sleep in a field of poppies— Glinda watches over them and eventually they arrive in the wonderful Emerald City of Oz.

After beholding the city's wonders, Dorothy and her refreshed friends are finally granted an audience with the wondrous Oz. "The Great Oz has every intention of granting your requests," he assures them, as soon as they perform one small

task—bringing Oz the broomstick of the Wicked Witch of the West (who has been cackling in the skies above Oz, writing "Surrender Dorothy" in broomstick vapor). The nervous band begins its fearsome trek. Soon, flying monkeys, slaves of the Witch, swoop down to carry Dorothy and Toto off to the castle, pummeling the three friends into helplessness.

The Witch is unable to remove Dorothy's ruby

The Wizard of Oz *on television.*

slippers—Glinda's power prevents it—and the gorgon turns over a huge hourglass, informing Dorothy that, when the sand runs out, the girl will die. Meanwhile, Toto escapes, finds the trio, and leads them to the Witch's castle. There, disguised as the evil one's soldier goblins, they enter the fortress. They rescue Dorothy, but the Witch traps them all on a parapet where she sets the Scarecrow afire. Dorothy tosses a bucket of water on her straw friend, and splashes the Witch. The latter shrieks in horror and begins to melt! "My beautiful wickedness!" she wails as she is reduced to a puddle. To Dorothy's surprise, the Witch's soldiers thank her for disposing of the loathsome hag, and happily give the group the broomstick to take back to the Wizard.

Back at Oz the travelers are crushed when the Wizard procrastinates in supplying the favors he has promised. As he rages at their impatience, Toto trots over to a curtain and pulls it back. The disclosure reveals that the "great and powerful" Oz is merely a blustery old man, very like Professor Marvel. "Pay no attention to that man behind the curtain!" roars the Wizard before admitting he is simply a "humbug." Still, he does not fail the faithful. The Scarecrow receives his brain in the form of a diploma ("Doctor of Thinkology"); the Tin Man gets his heart, a large heart-shaped testimonial watch; and the Lion is supplied bravery symbolized by a medal. As for Dorothy, he promises to escort her, by balloon, back to Kansas.

All of Oz turns out to see the Wizard leave the Emerald City, entrusting the Metropolis to the care of the wise Scarecrow, the compassionate Tin Man, and the courageous Lion. However, when Toto jumps from the balloon basket to chase a cat, Dorothy follows to retrieve her frisky companion and the balloon takes off without her. "Stay with us, then, Dorothy," pleads the Lion. "We all love ya. . . . We don't want ya to go." However, just then Glinda appears and informs Dorothy she could have returned to Kansas at any time by means of her magic slippers, but she had to learn for herself that "there's no place like home." Dorothy bids goodbye to the Tin Man ("Now I know I've got a heart," he says, " 'cause it's breaking"), the Lion, and the Scarecrow. She clicks her slippers together and repeats the words, "There's no place like home . . . There's no place like home."

Suddenly Dorothy is back in Kansas. She is in her bed with Auntie Em and Uncle Henry at her bedside. Professor Marvel appears to ask about her recovery from the accident, and Hunk, Zeke, and Hickory all approach the bed. She tells them of the wonderful, terrible place she visited, where they all were, a place they gently dismiss as a dream. Assuming that her injury will persuade her aunt and uncle not to let Toto be taken away again, Dorothy rejoices, "I love you all, and—oh, Auntie Em—there's no place like home!"

* * *

Already in advanced production as we go to press, it is acclaimed by those who have been privileged to see it thus far as comparable to the showmanship surprise of **Snow White and the Seven Dwarfs. The Wizard of Oz,** however, is performed by flesh and blood characters.

Jack Haley, Judy Garland, and Ray Bolger in The Wizard of Oz.

A brilliant array of screen stars has been gathered by Producer Mervyn LeRoy. Glittering pageantry, lilting musical numbers, spectacular settings and gorgeous costumes, beautiful girls, and elaborate dancing specialties are combined in a glorified extravangaza. Far greater than any stage presentation could ever be is **The Wizard of Oz,** all-color picturization of L. Frank Baum's beloved book, read by millions the world over. The galaxy of talent and its elaborate features make it unquestionably the greatest musical spectacle the industry has ever seen.

From the four-page promotional spread for MGM's **The Wizard of Oz,** in **Film Daily Yearbook,** 1939

Most of the cinema magic which won legendary acclaim and receipts for Metro's Leo the Lion now haunts east-of-midnight TV movie shows. For rather modest rentals to local stations, the ghosts of Clark Gable challenging Charles Laughton, William Powell quipping with Myrna Loy, John Barrymore wooing Greta Garbo, and Jean Harlow bobbing in a rain barrel appear on video screens.

Among the feature films long relegated to the insomniac hours are six of MGM's seven top-grossing pictures of 1939: **Goodbye, Mr. Chips; Another Thin Man; Babes in Arms; Ninotchka; Northwest Passage;** and **The Women. Gone with the Wind,** of course, made television history when it finally aired as a bicentennial event of 1976. Yet the recent accolade offered this box-office champion almost pales before the love feast which annually greets the showing of 1939's **The Wizard of Oz.**[2] In twenty years of theatrical engagements it earned only $4 million in domestic rentals. Now in its third decade as a once-a-year television event, **Oz** presently reaps $800,000 per network TV showing.

"Oh, what delight awaits us all!" cried the posters for **The Wizard of Oz** when it premiered in August 1939. Indeed, the marvelous fantasy charm of **The Wizard of Oz** has touched the lives of countless viewers over the past forty-plus years until it has become not so much a film as a phenomenon, a miniculture which has spawned toys, cartoons, an all-black Broadway version **(The Wiz),** which has become one of the most successful stage shows in history (and was itself turned into a 1978 feature film). Nobody was much surprised when, at the pathos-filled MGM auction of 1970, the most exciting moments surrounded the bidding on the ruby slippers of Judy Garland's Dorothy.[3]

Just before Lyman Frank Baum died in Hollywood on May 6, 1919, he sighed, "Now we can

---

[2]**Gone With the Wind** was recently acquired by CBS-TV network for a $35 million fee, which allows it to make showings of the epic an annual event, like **The Wizard of Oz.**

[3]At the MGM auction, Judy's ruby slippers were sold for $15,000; the purchaser remained anonymous, his bidding done by lawyer Richard Wonder. The Cowardly Lion suit brought $2,400 from Dr. Julius Marini, West Covina, California, doctor. Ray Bolger had kept his Scarecrow costume since production closed and was still able to wear it as late as 1970. The Tin Man costume was never found. Jack Haley was not interested anyway. "Where would I put it? Down in the basement? 'Hey, come on down, see my Tin Man suit!' "

cross the Shifting Sands." It was an area very well known to the millions of children and adults who had loved the Oz stories he had been writing since 1900 when **The Wonderful Wizard of Oz** experienced its first printing (with thirteen other **Oz** books following). Baum's creation gendered a 1903 Broadway stage production, as well as two silent-screen versions: one in 1910 from Polyscope Productions, and a 1925 Larry Semon Company effort which featured Oliver Hardy as corpulent Tin Woodman. (Baum, quite a showman, had created the Oz Film Manufacturing Company in 1914, but his productions were ensnared in distribution problems and the company soon collapsed, its facilities sold to Universal Pictures.) In 1934 Samuel Goldwyn purchased the screen rights to the **Oz** stories for $40,000, and planned to transform it into an Eddie Cantor vehicle. Goldwyn still owned the unrealized property when in 1937 Walt Disney amazed the industry and much of the world via the incredible success of **Snow White and the Seven Dwarfs.** That animated, color feature went on to tally a domestic gross of $16 million and caused other studios to plan fantasy films to delight—lucratively—the moviegoing public.

The **Oz** stories struck MGM as a capital idea. The pivotal character was the Kansas girl Dorothy, and on contract was a very promising little singer named Judy Garland, especially attractive to the front office at a time when the nation's top boxoffice star was Twentieth Century–Fox's Shirley Temple, and Universal's salvation from bankruptcy was young soprano Deanna Durbin. MGM defeated other film company bidders for Goldwyn's rights to the **Oz** property with the top offer of $75,000.

Who persuaded Louis B. Mayer to buy the screen rights? That has long been a very bitter question: producer Mervyn LeRoy has insisted it was his idea, while his associate producer, Arthur Freed, attested that his insights spurred Mayer to make the deal. At any rate, at the start of 1938 MGM began preparations for the filming. As the screenplay formulated under the care of Noel Langley, Florence Ryerson, and Edgar Allan Woolf (Herman Mankiewicz and others had drafted various screen treatments), and E. Y. Harburg and Harold Arlen created the songs, the adventures of filming began—with some twists and turns worthy of Baum's bizarre imagination. Various imbroglios touched virtually every major talent involved on the elaborate production.

The Director. Originally set to direct **Oz** was Norman Taurog, noted for his ability to coax mature performances out of often-immature actors. Nevertheless, when shooting began on October 12, 1938, Richard Thorpe, who had just directed Robert Montgomery's startling performance in **Night Must Fall** (1937), was handling the important film. However, twelve days later, he was fired, and in typical MGM style was whisked away to Palm Springs by studio public relations director Howard Strickling to avoid embarrassing questions from the press while George Cukor took over.[4] Cukor, whose approach to the film project

The Witch (Margaret Hamilton) singes the Scarecrow (Ray Bolger) with a ball of fire in The Wizard of Oz.

was cavalier at best ("I was brought up on grander things. I was brought up on Tennyson"), stayed for three days. Finally, LeRoy managed to drag Victor Fleming, "the man's man" director of such vintage Metro pieces as **Red Dust** (1932), **Captains Courageous** (1937), and **Test Pilot** (1938), to Mayer's Santa Monica beach mansion. There the studio executives persuaded the director to take over the picture. Fleming reluctantly agreed, according to friends, to please his little daughter.

The Wizard. One of MGM's top favorites had his heart set on playing the Wizard—Wallace Beery. He craved the part to impress his little adopted daughter, Carol Ann. However, Beery had reached the point in his career at Metro where his crass behavior and rudeness ("Get Beery in and get him out!" became Mayer's dictum) had mired him in B vehicles. Ed Wynn was offered the part as first choice. He turned it down as being too small a role for a star of his magnitude. So did W. C. Fields. Fields wanted $100,000 for the role; Metro offered him $75,000. Besides, he was too busy preparing the script for his upcoming Universal vehicle with Edgar Bergen and Charlie McCarthy, **You Can't Cheat an Honest Man** (1939). Finally, Frank Morgan, a Metro contractee since 1933, was assigned the colorful role after he allegedly begged for a screen test. Morgan, who

would report each day for work with a miniature bar, also would play in the movie the Doorman of Emerald City, the Carriage Driver, and the Guard of Oz's palace.

Dorothy. While MGM from the beginning saw **Oz** as a starmaking vehicle for Judy Garland, some powers on the lot felt the offbeat story required a major box-office name. Mayer approached Darryl F. Zanuck of Twentieth Century–Fox to determine if a loanout of Shirley Temple was conceivable. It was not. Universal refused to consider a temporary loss of Deanna Durbin. Hence, Judy Garland began her work as Dorothy Gale, but under a fancy blonde wig and heavy cherubic makeup. It was Cukor, during his brief stint on the picture, who scrapped the fairytale appearance, told Judy to stop acting in a "fancy-schmancy way," and arranged the basic Kansas farm girl appearance and character. (The simplicity was aided by the MGM costuming department, which harnessed the sixteen-year-old's rapidly developing figure in special halters. Ironically, poster art for the film would later feature curvaceous, ruby-lipped Dorothy, provocatively skipping in a skirt cut above her knees!)

In 1938 Judy was still away from the period in her life when she would become the pill-racked neurotic who sputtered across concert stages. She was very much then a young professional. As Jack Haley informed **TV Guide** in 1970, "What I remember most is how she used to love to laugh. She was full of laughter. And pep. She didn't need pills. . . . The pills started when she turned out

---

[4]LeRoy told Aljean Harmetz, in her book **The Making of the Wizard of Oz** (1977), that Thorpe was removed from the film because "to make a fairy story, you have to think like a kid," Nevertheless, there were no complaints with the way Thorpe directed Mickey Rooney's **The Adventures of Huckleberry Finn** at MGM in 1939.

pictures faster than Metro could make money on them."

The Scarecrow. The role of the worthless crow-scarer who dreams of a brain was deeply desired by lanky Ray Bolger, the vaudeville-Broadway eccentric dancer whose Metro contract had placed him in such films as **The Great Ziegfeld** (1936), **Rosalie** (1937), and **Sweethearts** (1938). Hence, he was crushed when the part went to Buddy Ebsen, who was also on the studio payroll and had scored mightily in **Broadway Melody of 1938.** Bolger was cast as the Tin Woodman. Even as Ebsen reported for costume fittings, Bolger pleaded with LeRoy for a switch in roles, and finally succeeded. The actor was delighted with the part but, like his costars, exhausted by the requirements. "We'd get up at 5 A.M. to be at makeup by 7. . . . We were so grotesque Metro wouldn't let us eat in the commissary." Nor could he even go to the bathroom with a clear conscience. "They sewed straw into my sleeves and my boots, and then they stuffed straw in the belly and the legs and the shoulders. If I opened up my costume, all the straw fell out, and then they had to put it back so it matched the way it had looked in the last shot. I didn't even take my costume off for lunch most of the time, because it was such a mess to put on again."

The Tin Woodman. Buddy Ebsen good-naturedly accepted the switch in casting—he had no preference—but he soon had reason to regret the decision. "I was a guinea pig," he recalled of the makeup efforts, which, because of the aluminum dust, coated his lungs and nearly killed him. After work on the day of October 22, 1938, ten days after production began, Ebsen returned home. "After dinner I took a breath and nothing happened." He spent two weeks in Los Angeles' Good Samaritan Hospital where, despite the demands of an irate studio behind schedule on a major picture, doctors carefully tended his alarming condition. Finally, MGM forgot about Ebsen (his contract option was later dropped and he fell into a career decline which lasted until Walt Disney's "Daniel Boone" TV series of 1956) and borrowed Jack Haley from Twentieth Century–Fox to portray the milquetoast Tin Man who yearns for a heart. Haley deemed the engagement "the most horrendous job in the world," and his memories of his most notable performance are anything but affectionate:

My costume was agony. I couldn't bend in that Tin Man thing. When I wasn't working, I was on a reclining board. . . . The only chance I had all day to get out of that costume was when Judy had to go to school. When her teacher came on the set and said "Judy—school," that was the highlight of our day. We'd all be yelling, "Where's my dresser? Where's my dresser?"

The Cowardly Lion. " 'Put up your dukes! Put up your paws!' Can you imagine Bert doing that?" mused E. Y. Harburg as the **Oz** libretto developed. Indeed, Lahr, a Broadway favorite (he had worked with Bolger in the 1934 revue **Life Begins at 8:40,** a Harburg-Arlen credit) who had never really clicked in films, was the first and only choice for

The Witch (Margaret Hamilton) materializes in The Wizard of Oz.

the part of the king of beasts unblessed by bravery. In **Notes on a Cowardly Lion** (1970) by Lahr's son, John, Harburg relates the special reasons Lahr won the part:

"When the Cowardly Lion admits that he lacks courage, everybody's heart is out to him. He must be somebody who embodies all this pathos, sweetness, and yet puts on this comic bravura. Bert had that quality to such a wonderful degree. It was in his face; it was in his talk; it was in himself."

The neurotic Lahr reveled in his role of the blustery Lion, adding bits of business and lines from his Broadway performances (for instance, his line "Put 'em up! Put 'em uuup!" was lifted from his role as Gink Shiner of **Hold Everything,** 1928). None of the rigors of the filmmaking seemed to perturb Lahr, who had to wear one hundred pounds of costume (his tail was operated by a crew member in the catwalks with a fishing rod). Nor was Lahr hampered by Frank Morgan's warning, "Bert, you're going to be a great hit in this picture. But it's not going to do you a damn bit of good—you're playing an **animal.**"

The Wicked Witch of the West. Edna May Oliver was the original front-office choice for the nasty witch, but she was unavailable (busy in John Ford's **Drums Along the Mohawk** at Twentieth Century–Fox). Another contender was Gale Sondergaard, the first female winner of the Best Supporting Actress Oscar for Warner Bros.' **Anthony Adverse** (1936). The striking Miss Sondergaard,

then on contract to Metro, was tapped to provide a novel interpretation of the horrible witch. As she later told **Film Fan Monthly:**

"Mervyn LeRoy had a sudden thought . . .to make a glamorous witch instead of an ugly witch. We actually did the costumes—a high, pointed hat, but of sequins, a very glamorous sequined gown. She was to be the most glamorous, but wicked sort of witch. And we got into testing for it, and it was absolutely gorgeous. And then, I suppose Mervyn got to remembering that this was a classic by now, and the children who read it, and grownups too, were going to say, 'That isn't the way it was written!' And everybody agreed you could not do that to **The Wizard of Oz.**"

Hence, hatch-faced Margaret Hamilton won the part; the makeup department provided her with the wart-pocked nose and pointy chin of the cackling gorgon. Miss Hamilton holds great affection for the film and her role (having reprised it in several stage productions over the decades), though no other **Oz** veteran has the valid reasons she has to detest the adventure: the fiery special effect when she disappeared from Munchkinland burned the skin off her right hand, singed her right eyebrow and eyelashes, and scalded her chin, nose, and forehead. Not long afterward, Miss Hamilton understandably refused to mount a "flying broomstick," which she was assured was safe; the ensuing explosion sent her stand-in, Betty Danko, to the hospital for eleven days (the

Frank Morgan, Judy Garland, Charley Grapewin, Ray Bolger, Jack Haley, Bert Lahr, and Clara Blandick in the finale to The Wizard of Oz.

Witch's hat and wig were found days later in the soundstage rafters).

Glinda, the Good Witch. Originally Metro contractee Helen Gilbert was to play the benign spirit, but she was AWOL from the lot on a romantic mission. Billie Burke, another studio player, was then cast in the job. The ex–Mrs. Ziegfeld was quite fragile by this time, both physically and temperamentally, and her brief solo to the Munchkins ("Come out, come out, wherever you are . . .") was dubbed by Lorraine Bridges.

The Munchkins. "This unholy assemblage of pimps, hookers and gamblers infested the Metro lot and all of the community," wrote Hugh Fordin in **The World of Entertainment** (1975) of the 124 midgets assembled by Leo Singer of "Singer's Midgets" fame. On the set they played with knives, propositioned the stars, and chased the

lot's showgirls, and provided the cast with outrageous anecdotes that became legendary. Lahr had a special favorite story about the midgets, when they were appearing as the Witch's monkeys:

I remember one day when we were supposed to shoot a scene with the Witch's monkeys. The head of the group was a little man who called himself "the Count." He was never sober. When the call came, everybody was looking for the Count. We could not start without him. And then, a little ways off the stage, we heard what sounded like a whine coming from the men's room. Somebody investigated. They found the Count. He got plastered during lunch, and fell in the latrine and couldn't get himself out.

The cast was less amused when the midgets,

fearful they would not receive the overtime due them for retakes in the scenes in which they flew on wires to capture Dorothy's group, went on strike to ensure payment. The Screen Actors Guild had to settle the fracas.

With Charley Grapewin and Clara Blandick (a substitute for May Robson and Janet Beecher) added as Uncle Henry and Auntie Em, and a female cairn terrier named Terry playing Toto (under the training of Carl Spitz), **The Wizard of Oz** required 136 days of shooting.[5] Arnold Gillespie's

[5]According to Doug McClelland's **Down the Yellow Brick Road** (1976), "Early drafts of the **Wizard** script had funny girl-lady Fanny Brice, singer Betty Jaynes, and Kenny Baker penciled in as a witch, a princess, and a prince, respectively, characters written out of the final screenplay."

special-effects staff was, of course, constantly busy, creating such celluloid magic as the tornado-tossed farmhouse (a three-foot tall model, dropped on a sky-colored floor, with the film then run backward), the tornado's center (a muslin-covered drum thirty-five feet in diameter), and a melting witch (created via dry ice and an elevator). Production was nearly completed when Victor Fleming was removed from the picture to take up the challenge of **Gone With the Wind,** and King Vidor, uncredited, completed the project, including the Sepia-filmed Kansas scenes at the beginning and the end. As Vidor would recall for the Public Broadcasting System TV series, "The Men Who Made the Movies":

> Victor Fleming was a good friend, and he took me around to all the sets that had been built and went through the thing. He left that night, and I took over—it was, as I remember, about two and a half weeks, three weeks possibly. Which included the "Somewhere Over the Rainbow." It's run all the time, and whenever I hear it, I get a tremendous kick out of knowing I directed that scene. . . . I did some of the cyclone scenes, and "We're Off to See the Wizard." . . . But I did not want any credit, and as long as Victor was alive, I kept quiet about it.

On July 18, 1939, **The Wizard of Oz** previewed at the Westwood Village Theatre. It was decided to cut "The Jitterbug," a major production number dominated by Lahr's Lion and publicized in the **Film Daily** ad as "a colorful dancing number amid the strange 'Jitter Trees' " (it had taken five weeks to produce). The studio seers also determined to eliminate Garland singing "Over the Rainbow." Freed argued vehemently that the latter number should remain, but was vetoed by producers Sam Katz ("This score is above the heads of children"), Jack Robbins ("Who'll buy the sheet music?"), and Mayer himself ("It's too sad"). Fortunately, "Over the Rainbow" remained, and it was a very special part of **The Wizard of Oz** when it premiered at Grauman's Chinese Theatre on August 17, 1939. The same day it opened at Loew's Capitol Theatre in New York City, and Frank S. Nugent reported in his **New York Times'** review, "Not since Disney's **Snow White** has anything quite so fantastic succeeded half so well. . . . It is all so well intentioned, so genial, and so gay that any reviewer who would look down his nose at the fun-making should be spanked and sent off, supperless, to bed."

Oz placed seventh on **Film Daily**'s Ten Best list of 1939. It was Academy Award-nominated for Best Picture (winner being **Gone With the Wind**) and won two Oscars: Best Original Score (Herbert Stothart) and Best Song (Arlen and Harburg's "Over the Rainbow").[6] The film proved very popular with audiences—sixty policemen were called on duty at New York's Capitol Theatre as over 37,000 people jammed the first day's seven shows—and

its initial release grossed $3,017,000 (at a production cost of $3.7,000[7]) Re-releases in 1948, 1949, and 1954–55 proved lucrative, and **Variety** now lists **Oz** on the all-time box-office list, with a gross of $4 million in U.S. and Canadian distributor rentals.

Interestingly, **The Wizard of Oz** would evolve as a part of American folklore, not in theatres, but on television. It first aired on CBS-TV on November 3, 1956, at a lease price of $225,000. Thereafter, showings of the feature became an annual event. In 1967 NBC attained the video rights when CBS-TV dropped its option, and in 1976 CBS-TV regained the rights, currently paying $800,000 per year to televise the film five times between 1976 and 1980. **The Wizard of Oz** now occupies eleventh place in the list of top-rated theatrical movies aired on network television.

Over the years the MGM movie has spawned other film adaptations: the animated **Journey Back to Oz** (1962), which featured the voices of Liza Minnelli (Dorothy), Mickey Rooney (the Scarecrow), Milton Berle (the Cowardly Lion), Margaret Hamilton (Aunt Em), Ethel Merman (Mombi, the Bad Witch), Danny Thomas (the Tinman), and Rise Stevens (Glinda, the Good Fairy); **Wizard of Oz** (1976), a pornographic film by Bill Osco and starring Kristine DeBell; and, of course, **The Wiz** (1978), featuring Diana Ross as Dorothy and Lena Horne as the Good Witch.

In an age of rampant cynicism, especially among children, it is amazing that **The Wizard of Oz** retains so loving an audience and has not toppled into the realm of camp. Apparently, MGM produced a nearly foolproof piece of escapism for many generations to enjoy; and one hopes that they will fully appreciate its theme, as expressed by Scarecrow Ray Bolger, "There's no place like home. . . . Everybody has a heart. Everybody has a brain. Everybody has a soul."

WOMAN OF THE YEAR
1942—112 min.

Producer, Joseph L. Mankiewicz; **director,** George Stevens; **screenplay,** Ring Lardner, Jr., and Michael Kanin; **art directors,** Cedric Gibbons and Randall Duell; **set decorator,** Edwin B. Willis; **music,** Franz Waxman; **costumes,** Adrian; **assistant director,** Robert Golden; **makeup,** Jack Dawn; **sound,** Douglas Shearer; **camera,** Joseph Ruttenberg; **editor,** Frank Sullivan.

Spencer Tracy **(Sam Craig)**; Katharine Hepburn **(Tess Harding)**; Fay Bainter **(Ellen Whitcomb)**; Reginald Owen **(Clayton)**; Minor Watson **(William Harding)**; William Bendix **(Pinkie Peters)**; Gladys Blake **(Flo Peters)**; Dan Tobin **(Gerald)**; Roscoe Karns **(Phil Whittaker)**; William Tannen **(Ellis)**; Ludwig Stossel **(Dr. Martin Lubbeck)**; Sara

Haden **(Matron at Refugee Home)**; Edith Evanson **(Alma)**; George Kezas **(Chris)**; Henry Roquemore **(Justice of the Peace)**; Cyril Ring **(Harding's Chauffeur)**; Ben Lessy **(Punchy)**; Johnny Berkes **(Pal)**; Duke York **(Football Player)**; Winifred Harris **(Chairlady)**; Joe Yule **(Building Superintendent)**; Edward McWade **(Adolph)**; Michael Visaroff **(Guest)**; Jimmy Conlin and Ray Teal **(Reporters)**; William Holmes **(Man at Banquet)**.

SYNOPSIS
Dynamic Tess Harding, daughter of diplomat William Harding and herself the international affairs columnist for a major New York City newspaper, calls for the abolition of the game of baseball for the duration of World War II. Sportswriter Sam Craig, of the same journal, takes great offense at her stance. A feud breaks out between the two in their respective columns, a battle which eventually leads to their meeting in the office of newspaper editor Clayton. Sam enters as Tess, sitting on Clayton's desk, is tending to a stocking; an immediate attraction sparks between the two journalists.

Tess survives her first baseball game through Sam's tutelage, and he manages to sneak out of one of her oppressively sophisticated parties. However, their love grows and, to the amazement of their common acquaintances, the two are soon married.

The union, though, early shows signs of crumbling. Tess has no flair for domesticity and her career ambitions irk Sam, who yearns for Tess at least to make an attempt at being a good wife. The very day that Tess realizes her woeful inadequacies as a spouse she is selected Woman of the Year.

William Harding, meanwhile, reweds, and Tess attends the ceremony. The words of the wedding vows impress her anew, and she returns to her husband, determined to live up to her concept of the domesticated wife. It is not as easy as she believes. She manages to make a shambles of a breakfast—a toaster launches bread into the air, a mixer molests the eggs, and a coffeepot erupts. Sam, however, reassures her that he never expected her to throw away her entire career, only to provide him with the love and care he wants from a wife. The two begin again their stimulating union.

* * *

In 1938 Walt Disney released a clever cartoon, **Mother Goose Goes Hollywood,** delightfully lampooning popular film stars in the guise of nursery rhyme favorites. One sequence presented "Rub-a-Dub-Dub" with the three men in the tub being Charles Laughton in his Captain Bligh togs from **Mutiny on the Bounty,** and Freddie Bartholomew and Spencer Tracy in character as Harvey and Manuel from Metro's **Captains Courageous.** However, sharing the tub with these three gentlemen was Katharine Hepburn, jaw jutting, teeth bared, pantaloons exposed. Undoubtedly, few members of the 1938 filmgoing audience contemplated that Hepburn, then under the eclipse of the box-office poison list, and Tracy, triumphant through his Oscar-winning portrayals in **Captains**

---

[6]None of the principals received Oscar nominations, although Judy Garland received a special miniature statuette from the Motion Picture Academy of Arts and Sciences as the year's outstanding juvenile.

[7]In December 1939 the London Board of Censors banned showings of **The Wizard of Oz** for children, reasoning that the witches in the film would frighten the youngsters.

Spencer Tracy and George Kezas in Woman of the Year *('42).*

Courageous and **Boys Town,** would proceed to become perhaps the greatest man-woman acting team in the history of the American cinema. In fact, at the time that **Mother Goose Goes Hollywood** was playing in movie houses, Tracy was approaching the distinction of becoming the Academy's only Best Actor winner in two consecutive years, while Hepburn was being offered the lead in **Mother Carey's Chickens** by home lot RKO.

However, in the 1938–41 period Hepburn's professional status underwent many changes, notably, the mammoth success of Broadway's **The Philadelphia Story,** and the star's duplication of its success in MGM's 1940 screen adaptation costarring Cary Grant and James Stewart. After this magnificent screen comeback, Hepburn departed on a stage tour of **The Philadelphia Story,** keeping watch for a promising screenplay as a proper follow-up to her 1940 film.

It was friend Garson Kanin (who later damaged his long-standing friendship with the actress by the publication of his self-serving memoirs, **Tracy and Hepburn,** 1971) who presented to Hepburn a script entitled **The Thing About Women.** The scenario was written by Ring Lardner, Jr., and was based on the life of his sportswriter father and his relationship with Dorothy Parker. Kanin entered upon military service at this time, but his brother Michael joined the project. Through numerous conferences, in which Lardner, Kanin, and Hepburn pooled ideas, there evolved the script of **Woman of the Year.** Lanky Hepburn then put on her four-inch high heels, met with diminutive mogul Louis B. Mayer, and won through intimidation a deluxe contract (as she had with **The Philadelphia Story**), receiving a check for

$211,000 ($100,000 for herself, $50,000 for each writer, and $11,000 for her commission and agent fees) and director-costar approval. Part of the deal provided that Hepburn would become part of the Metro star family of performers. Her choice for director was George Stevens (who had guided her in 1935's **Alice Adams** and 1937's **Quality Street**); her choice for costar was Spencer Tracy.

Both luminaries admired each other enormously. Hepburn cherished Tracy's Manuel of **Captains Courageous** ("I never can face the end without weeping so!") and his **Dr. Jekyll and Mr. Hyde;** and Tracy had in fact wanted Hepburn to play **both** the Lana Turner and Ingrid Bergman parts in **Jekyll** (an idea deemed ridiculous by Mayer and director Victor Fleming). The fact that Tracy was in Florida on location for **The Yearling** temporarily stymied Hepburn's request, but when that production collapsed under a series of problems (not the least of which was Tracy's disagreeable temperament),[1] he returned to Culver City and prepared to star in the new feature.

The meeting of Tracy and Hepburn as they prepared to begin **Woman of the Year** has become one of Hollywood's most oft-quoted stories. As Herman Mankiewicz tells it:

I was walking into the commissary one day when Kate and Spencer met for the first time in the corridor. Kate said, "I'm afraid I'm a little tall for you, Mr. Tracy." I turned to her and said, "Don't worry, Kate, he'll soon cut you down to size."

---

[1]Gregory Peck inherited Tracy's part in **The Yearling** when production resumed four years later.

The supporting cast for **Woman of the Year** boasted such pros as Fay Bainter, Minor Watson, Reginald Owen, Roscoe Kahns, and William Bendix. But their scene-stealing abilities bowed here to the histrionics of this singular acting duo. In Charles Higham's **Kate** (1975) the author records Hepburn's reminiscences of the first scene she played with Tracy:

"I accidentally knocked over a glass. Spencer handed me a handkerchief, and I took his handkerchief and I thought, 'Oh, you old so-and-so, you're going to make me mop it up right in the middle of a scene.' So I started to mop it, and the water started to go down through the table. I decided to throw him by going down under the table, and he just stood there watching me. I mopped and mopped, and George Stevens kept the camera running. Spencer just smiled. He wasn't thrown at all."

In the same book George Stevens recalls the experience:

"From the beginning of the picture, and their relationship, Spencer's reaction to her was a total, pleasant, but glacial putdown of her extreme effusiveness. He just didn't get disturbed about doing things immediately; she wanted to do a hundred and one things at once; he was never in a hurry. She loved to rehearse, to do everything except hang the arc lights; he loved to do nothing except 'be' the part, if possible on the first take. She 'worried the bone'; he just took it and padded off with it. Slowly."

Released in January 1942, **Woman of the Year** proved one of the top Metro grossers of the 1941–42 season (along with **Honky Tonk, Mrs. Miniver,** and **Somewhere I'll Find You**) and collected a bevy of laudatory reviews. **Time** magazine: "Actors Hepburn and Tracy have a fine old time in **Woman of the Year.** They take turns playing straight for each other, act one superbly directed love scene, succeed in turning several batches of cinematic corn into passable moonshine. As a lady columnist, she is just right; as a working reporter, he is practically perfect." **New York World-Telegram**: "The title part is played by Miss Hepburn, who has never looked more beautiful. It is played with such humor, resourcefulness and contagious spirit that I think it is even better than her performance in **The Philadelphia Story,** and that was just as fine as anything could be. No less satisfactory is Mr. Tracy. There isn't a false note in his characterization of the sportswriter. And the things he can do with a gesture, with a smile, are nobody's business. . . . What an actor!" **Baltimore Sun**: "[Hepburn's] performance is a constant pleasure to watch. Mr. Tracy is an excellent foil for her in this particular instance. His quiet masculine stubbornness and prosaic outlook on life is in striking contrast with her sparkle and brilliance. They make a fine team, and each complements the other."

Woman of the Year placed ninth on the **Film Daily** Ten Best Pictures list, won Hepburn her fourth Oscar nomination (she lost to Greer Garson's Kay Miniver), and won an Oscar for Ring

Lardner, Jr., and Michael Kanin for Best Original Screenplay.

In the spring of 1943, Tracy and Hepburn reprised **Woman of the Year** in a half-hour "Screen Guild Theatre" broadcast. (Aside from a 1946 movie short for the American Cancer Society, it was their only joint acting work outside the medium of feature films.) In 1951 Bette Davis and George Brent would star in a radio series based on **Woman of the Year**. In 1981 Lauren Bacall starred in a Broadway musical adaptation of the 1942 feature.

There are many delightful episodes within **Woman of the Year**; Hepburn's first baseball game ("If the batter were smart he'd stoop down and fool the pitcher"); Tracy's discomfort at Hepburn's elegant soirée; the misadventure over the "adopted" Greek boy refugee; Hepburn's marvelously slapdash venture into connubial bliss and her battle with the kitchen appliances, her arch enemy; etc. All this found a ready reception with audiences, whose demand occasioned the production of the eight Tracy-Hepburn films which followed.

Hepburn herself explained the team's appeal:

"We balanced each other's natures. We were perfect representations of the American male and female. The woman is always pretty sharp, and she's needling the man, sort of slightly like a mosquito. The man is always slowly coming along, and she needles, and then he slowly puts out his big paw and slaps the lady down, and that's attractive to the American public. He's the ultimate boss of the situation, and he's very challenged by her. It isn't an easy kingdom for him to maintain. That—in simple terms—is what we did."

notorious repute. As the judges, the defense attorney, and the public prosecutor call the witnesses to the stand, the following tale unfolds.

When Anna was five, the right side of her face was badly burned when her brilliant but drunken father inadvertently set fire to their house. The jeers her scars invited over the years caused the woman to develop a bitter hatred of the world. Using a restaurant as a front, she and a batch of rogues (including Bernard and Christina Dalvik and Herman) operate a lucrative blackmailing operation. When the dapper Torsten Barring steals love letters from the promiscuous Vera Segert, he enlists Anna to handle the blackmailing, and then, unrepelled and perhaps even attracted by her scarred profile, engages her in her first love affair.

When Anna visits Vera, the cuckolded Dr. Segert arrives home unexpectedly. Anna turns her ankle in her rush to escape. Observing her facial affliction, Dr. Segert, a noted plastic surgeon, challenges Anna to undergo a drastic operation. She accepts and Segert's skill triumphs.

Ecstatic, Anna returns to her lover, who has a new mission for her: journey to Europe to become the governess to little Lars Erik, who blocks Torsten's inheritance of the massive wealth of Consul Barring—and kill the boy. Anna arrives but is unable to fulfill the task because of the kindness of the consul and the love of young Lars. Soon both Torsten and Dr. Segert (recently divorced) arrive on the scene and Anna still refuses to kill the boy.

At the Barring mansion Torsten reveals himself as a madman, with dreams of world power. That night Torsten absconds with Lars. Anna and Segert pursue him and then she shoots him.

Back in court, Anna's guiltlessness surfaces when the consul's jealous maid, Emma, reveals a note she stole from the pocket chess set Anna gave the consul as a birthday gift. The note tells of Anna's plan to kill herself so as to avoid her gruesome task.

Her innocence now demonstrated, Anna is free to embark on a new life with Segert.

* * *

During 1941 a few MGM screen goddesses were experiencing declining careers, Norma Shearer and Greta Garbo being two cases in point. Their professional fade-out seemed the more certain with the ascent of such new studio and public favorites as Lana Turner, Greer Garson, and (given a fresh lease of screen life) Katharine Hepburn.

Not all the Metro distaff veterans, however, were ailing. Joan Crawford was enjoying a new cycle of popularity. She had been delightful as the devouring bitch of **The Women** (1939), the religious fanatic of **Susan and God** (1940), and as Gable's enticer of **Strange Cargo** (1940). Astute Crawford then set her mascara eyes on a property that had been a play in France, **Il Etait une Fois**, and a film in Sweden, **En Kvinnas Ansikte** (1938), with Ingrid Bergman. Crawford persuaded director George Cukor to join her campaign to film the story of a scarred villainness who is saved from disfigurement and immorality by a suave plastic surgeon. Louis B. Mayer was perplexed by the no-

Conrad Veidt, Joan Crawford, Donald Meek, and Connie Gilchrist in A Woman's Face *('41).*

A WOMAN'S FACE
1941—105 min.

Producer, Victor Saville; **director,** George Cukor; based on the play **Il Etait une Fois** by Francis DeCroisset; **screenplay,** Donald Ogden Stewart; **art director,** Cedric Gibbons; **music,** Bronislau Kaper; **costumes,** Adrian; **sound,** Douglas Shearer; **camera,** Robert Planck; **editor,** Frank Sullivan.

Joan Crawford (**Anna Holm**); Melvyn Douglas (**Dr. Segert**); Conrad Veidt (**Torsten Barring**); Reginald Owen (**Bernard Dalvik**); Albert Bassermann (**Consul Barring**); Marjorie Main (**Emma**); Donald Meek (**Herman**); Connie Gilchrist (**Christina Dalvik**); Richard Nichols (**Lars Erik**); Osa Massen (**Vera Segert**); Charles Quigley (**Eric**); Henry Kolker (**Judge**); George Zucco (**Defense Attorney**); Henry Daniell (**Public Prosecutor**); Robert Warwick and Gilbert Emery (**Associate Judges**); Sarah Padden (**Police Matron**); Rex Evans (**Notary**); Doris Day and Mary Ellen Popel (**Girls at Party**); Lionel Pape (**Einer**); Gwille Andre (**Gusta**); Cecil Stewart (**Pianist**); Veda Buckland (**Nurse**).

SYNOPSIS
On trial in Stockholm for the murder of Torsten Barring is Anna Holm, a former blackmailer of

tion, but Crawford and Cukor triumphed. **A Woman's Face** entered production.

A super "woman's picture," a superb melodrama, **A Woman's Face** costarred Melvyn Douglas as the deft surgeon and Conrad Veidt (in his second Hollywood picture after his American debut in Metro's **Escape**, 1940) as the suavely evil madman. Years later Crawford fondly remembered the production:

> What worried George Cukor was my emotionalism. He anticipated that wearing a scar could affect me as wearing a cape has been known to affect some actors. To offset the possibility, he rehearsed the very life out of me. Hours of drilling, with cameras and lights lined up for the opening sequence in the courtroom, then Mr. Cukor had me recite the multiplication tables by twos until all emotion was drained and I was totally exhausted, my voice dwindled to a tired monotone. "Now," Mr. Cukor said, "Now, Anna . . . tell us the story of your life."

Cukor recalled:

> Conrad Veidt, who played the villain Torsten Barring, was absolutely charming to work with, not at all like the parts he usually assumed. He always looked like the wickedest man in the world, yet he was really very gay and funny. I'd be awful with him and say, "No, no, let's not have any of that UFA acting." Everybody liked him very much. He would do everything with great gusto. . . .
>
> . . . Albert Bassermann, the venerable German actor who played Torsten Barring's uncle, did not speak one word of English. He learned his entire part phonetically. He knew, really, what it was all about, but I would have to explain things to him in my wretched German. He would read it aloud first in English, and if his inflection was sometimes wrong I'd correct him; and his ear was so impeccable that he would get the correct inflection immediately. . . .
>
> . . . In the first half of the picture, when Joan Crawford played a facially scarred criminal, I thought she displayed great gifts. It wasn't difficult to extract that standard of performance out of her. She's a very accomplished actress and she realized that the part was "twisted." Right before every scene, in fact, she'd try to "twist" herself mentally.

The set was a congenial one. When Crawford was happy, relaxed, and unintimidated (which she was **not** in such films as **Grand Hotel**, 1932, and **The Women**, 1939), she could be charming company. Connie Gilchrist remembered the coffee and cakes served by the "wonderful" star during the picture's filming. Awed by superstar Crawford, Gilchrist (a contract featured player) was not able to accept the lady's mandate to call her "Joan" until, after being called "Miss Crawford" once again by Gilchrist, Crawford intoned, "My name is Joan! If you don't call me Joan, I'm going to call you 'Miss Kill-Christ!'" Said Gilchrist, "After that, it was strictly a first-name basis."

Released in May 1941—publicized as "a psychological study of a woman's soul—**A Woman's Face** did not draw big box-office crowds until De-troit exhibitors began advertising the film as the story of "a scarred she-devil," "a soulless woman," and "a female monster." Profits skyrocketed and MGM followed suit in its ads. The result was a triumph for Crawford.

Variety stated, "Miss Crawford has a strongly dramatic and sympathetic role . . . which she handles in top-notch fashion"; **Photoplay** magazine judged, "Outstanding. . . . You'll find yourself completely held by the gripping intensity of this. Joan Crawford is magnificent." The splendid support offered by Douglas, one of the few actors ever to mix debonair polish with strong acting skills; Veidt, impeccably evil; and Bassermann, Main, Meek, and, especially, Osa Massen (as the slinky adultress) provided the narrative with sincerity and dynamics.

Despite this success, Joan Crawford would star in only three more features for MGM before vacating the contract rolls in 1943: **When Ladies Meet** (1941), with colead Robert Taylor and major competitor Greer Garson; **Reunion in France** (1942), in which she skirted Nazis with John Wayne; and **Above Suspicion** (1943), with romance by Fred MacMurray and menace by Basil Rathbone and Conrad Veidt (the latter's last film; he was shortly after stricken by a fatal heart attack).

Never docile, Crawford took suspensions to avoid assignments she scorned (such as **Cry Havoc**, 1943). She concluded before leaving, "The consensus of opinion among the top brass was that I was washed up again." Contracted at Warner Bros. at one-third of her MGM salary, she was rumored to be finished as a top-echelon star. Then the seemingly indestructible actress turned the Bette Davis hand-me-down **Mildred Pierce** (1945) into an Oscar-winning comeback.

On November 2, 1942, "Lux Radio Theatre" presented **A Woman's Face**, with Ida Lupino as Anna, Brian Aherne as Dr. Segert, and Conrad Veidt repeating his interpretation of the sinister Torsten Barring.

THE WOMEN
1939—132 min.[1]

Producer, Hunt Stromberg; **director,** George Cukor; based on the play by Clare Boothe; **screenplay,** Anita Loos, Jane Murfin, and, **uncredited:** F. Scott Fitzgerald, Sidney Franklin, and Donald Ogden Stewart; **art directors,** Cedric Gibbons and Wade B. Rubottom; **set decorator,** Edwin B. Willis; **music,** Edward Ward and David Snell; **costumes,** Adrian; **sound,** Douglas Shearer; **camera,** Oliver T. Marsh and Joseph Ruttenberg; **editor,** Robert J. Kern.

Norma Shearer **(Mary Haines)**; Joan Crawford **(Crystal Allen)**; Rosalind Russell **(Sylvia Fowler)**; Mary Boland **(Countess DeLage)**; Paulette Goddard **(Miriam Aarons)**; Joan Fontaine **(Peggy Day)**; Lucile Watson **(Mrs. Morehead)**; Phyllis Povah

---

[1]Technicolor sequences.

(Edith Potter); Florence Nash **(Nancy Blake)**; Virginia Weidler **(Little Mary)**; Ruth Hussey **(Miss Watts)**; Muriel Hutchison **(Jane)**; Margaret Dumont **(Mrs. Wagstaff)**; Dennie Moore **(Olga)**; Mary Cecil **(Maggie)**; Marjorie Main **(Lucy)**; Esther Dale **(Ingrid)**; Hedda Hopper **(Dolly Dupuyster)**; Mildred Shay **(Helene, the French Maid)**; Priscilla Lawson and Estelle Etterre **(Hairdressers)**; Ann Morriss **(Exercise Instructress)**; Mary Beth Hughes **(Miss Trimmerback)**; Marjorie Wood **(Saide)**; Virginia Grey **(Pat)**; Cora Witherspoon **(Mrs. Van Adams)**; Veda Buckland **(Woman)**; Charlotte Treadway **(Her Companion)**; Theresa Harris **(Olive)**; Vera Vague **(Receptionist)**; May Beatty **(Fat Woman)**; Hilda Plowright **(Miss Fordyer)**; Judith Allen **(Miss Archer, the Model)**; Dorothy Sebastian and Renie Riano **(Saleswomen)**; Josephine Whittell **(Mrs. Spencer)**; Lillian Bond **(Mrs. Erskine)**; Carole Lee Kirby **(Theatrical Child)**; Natalie Moorhead **(Woman in Modiste Salon)**; Marie Blake **(Stockroom Girl)**; Dorothy Adams **(Miss Atkinson)**; Carol Hughes **(Salesgirl at Modiste Salon)**; Peggy Shannon **(Mrs. Jones)**.

SYNOPSIS

Mary Haines is a happy, contented lady, secure in the love of her wealthy husband, Stephen, and her young daughter, Little Mary. Though she is unaware that her husband is in the midst of a passionate affair with a redheaded perfume salesgirl named Crystal Allen, her catty girlfriends learn the news from beauty parlor manicurist Olga. Scarcely able to contain their delight over the affair, Sylvia Fowler and Edith Potter shrewdly make an appointment for Mary to visit Olga. As they hoped, Olga tells her customer the latest gossip.

Heartbroken, Mary soon ignores the advice of her mother, Mrs. Morehead, to say nothing to Stephen. Mary also confronts Crystal in the latter's dressing room at a swank dress salon. The result is a divorce, as Mary departs for Reno. En route she meets Countess DeLage, an oft-married aging playgirl, and Miriam Aarons, a Vanities showgirl who just happens to have her claws in Sylvia's husband.

Staying in Reno at the ranch of garrulous Lucy, Mary is amused by the arrival of Sylvia and the ensuing catfight between Miriam and Sylvia when the latter realizes it is Miriam who stole her husband. But Mary is crushed to learn that Stephen has married Crystal.

Upon her return, however, Mary learns from her daughter that Stephen is miserable being wed to Crystal. The latter madly spends money and is soon dallying with Buck, a singing cowboy who met the countess in Reno, wed her, and became a radio star.

Ecstatic that Stephen's new union is failing, Mary dresses in her finest and rushes to a party where drunken Buck blurts out his affair with Crystal in front of most of the gathering—including Stephen. Crystal announces plans to wed Buck, bragging that he is worth more than Stephen Haines will ever possess. The countess then wails that it is she who is sponsoring Buck's radio show, as nobody else would give the untalented man a job. Crystal, crestfallen, admits defeat and

Virginia Weidler and Joan Crawford in The Women *('39).*

plans to return to the perfume counter. As she bids farewell to her girlfriends, she spits out, "There's a word for you ladies, but it's seldom used in high society—outside of a kennel."

Mary exultantly rushes to a repentant Stephen.[2]

* * *

On December 26, 1936, **The Women,** Clare Boothe's all-female play of love and bitchery (mostly bitchery), opened at Broadway's Ethel Barrymore Theatre with the following leading players:

Mary	Margalo Gillmore
Crystal	Betty Lawford
Sylvia	Ilka Chase
Miriam	Audrey Christie
Edith	Phyllis Povah

[2]Several variations of the finale were filmed. One that was discarded showed Stephen's shadow against the wall, as Mary rushes to him.

Countess DeLage	Margaret Douglass
Lucy	Marjorie Main
Mrs. Morehead	Jessie Busley

The unique comedy ran for 657 performances and was named best play of the season by the Burns-Mantle staff. In September 1937 it was announced that producers Max Gordon and Harry Goetz intended that Gregory LaCava direct the screen version of **The Women** and that Claudette Colbert star in it. However, when control of the project came into MGM's domain, the situation changed. Direction was entrusted to George Cukor. Anita Loos and Jane Murfin provided the final screenplay,[3] and Cukor stocked the cast with

[3]As with many Hollywood pictures, the screen credits for scenarists do not reveal all the talent involved. In 1938 F. Scott Fitzgerald had worked alone on the adaptation of **The Women,** then with Sidney Franklin, later with Donald Ogden Stewart. Jane Murfin took over the writing chores, and she was later replaced by Anita Loos. It is

some of Hollywood's most adored: Norma Shearer as Mary,[4] stoical lady who is victimized by her philandering spouse and her harpy girlfriends; Joan Crawford, replete with a dyed-red coiffure, as the predatory Crystal who destroys Mary's home and almost her husband; Mary Boland as the oft-wed Countess DeLage, ever cooing "Toujour l'amour!"; Paulette Goddard, on loan from David O. Selznick, as Miriam, Broadway chorus girl who snares the husband of superfeline Sylvia, Mary's chief tormentor. For this last part, Cukor had difficulty reaching a casting decision. Rosalind Russell, who had spent several years at MGM playing snooty patricians, begged for the role. Reluctant Cukor tested her five times; when Rosalind bur-

said that some of Fitzgerald's dialogue remains in the release print.

[4]When Hollywood first talked of casting **The Women,** Paramount's Claudette Colbert was the initial choice to play Mary Haines.

lesqued Sylvia in the last audition, Cukor gave her the part already "promised" to Ilka Chase (from the stage version). Both Phyllis Povah and Marjorie Main were signed to re-create their stage characterizations.

In a delightful touch, the opening credits of **The Women** represent each leading character as an animal before dissolving into a close-up of the star. The result, in order of billing: Shearer, a fawn; Crawford, a leopard; Russell, a panther; Boland, a chimp; Goddard, a fox; Joan Fontaine (as Mary's loyal friend Peggy), a lamb; Lucile Watson (as Mary's wise mother), an owl; Phyllis Povah (as Mary's many-daughtered chum), a cow; Virginia Weidler (as Mary's precocious daughter), a doe; and Main, a donkey.

The very amusing 132 minutes of film boasts a wicked brawl between Goddard and Russell in which the latter fights dirty by yanking at Paulette's tresses, pulling down her shorts, and biting her on the leg ("I gotta be careful of hydrophobia!" wails Paulette); a Technicolor Fashion Show sequence featuring opulent Adrian creations; and a barrage of playwright Boothe's acid lines—"Come on, Countess, chin up! Both of them"; "He says, 'I gotta go home tomorrow, Baby!' And I says, 'Why?' And he says, 'My family always expects me home on Easter.' So I says, 'What do they expect you to do? Lay an egg?'"

The Women was highlighted by the confrontations of Shearer and Crawford,[5] in which the unabashed Crystal, using Mary's husband's charge accounts to purchase for herself a new, stunning wardrobe, trades snipes with her adversary:

MARY: I'm glad you understand the streak of sentiment, Miss Allen—because its beauty is something you'll never know.

CRYSTAL (showing her the door): This happens to be **my** room, Mrs. Haines.

MARY: It's yours, yes, for the time being, like everything else you've got. May I suggest if you're dressing to please Stephen, not that one. He doesn't like such **obvious** effects.

CRYSTAL: Thanks for the tip. But when anything I wear doesn't please Stephen—I take it off!

The scenes between Shearer and Crawford carried a special punch, for the two stars were waging an ugly feud during production. Long resentful of the special treatment her competitor had enjoyed during her years as Mrs. Thalberg, pugnacious Crawford battled Shearer from the start of filming. Nothing was sacred. Shearer kept

---

[5]In a tribute to the late Joan Crawford, George Cukor stated in the **New York Times** in May 1977:

"In the role of bitchy, opportunist shop girl in **The Women,** she knew perfectly well that she would be surrounded by formidable competition from the rest of the all-female cast, many of whom were playing funnier—and certainly more sympathetic—parts. Yet she made no appeals for audience sympathy; she was not one of those actresses who have to keep popping out from behind their characters signaling, 'Look, it's sweet, lovable me, just pretending to be a tramp.'"

Cukor does not repeat the well-known tale of how hard Crawford had to fight to convince the disinclined Metro hierarchy to give her the important assignment.

Crawford waiting in Sidney Guilaroff's hairdressing parlor, arriving four hours late, during which time Guilaroff was unable to attend to the second-billed stars. There were squabbles between the two ladies regarding clothes, camera angles, and dialogue. At the finale of shooting, Norma treated the company to a celebration party; Joan and chum Goddard refused to attend.

Released early in the fall of 1939, **The Women** took a place as one of the year's happiest hits. All the leading ladies won critical ovations, with Russell scoring a special triumph as archbitch Sylvia ("It was **The Women** that gave my career its greatest impetus. As a dramatic actress I had at last been given the opportunity to show that I could play comedy also"). However, **The Women** was also the last real success savored by Norma Shearer. While Crawford would go on to make several important ventures at the studio in the early forties, Shearer would star in only three more vehicles for the home lot: **Escape** (1940), **We Were Dancing** (1942), and **Her Cardboard Lover** (1942). The last two ventures were disappointments on every level. Thereafter she entered upon a lavish retirement as the wife of skiing instructor Martin Arrouge.

The reviews were generally enthusiastic. **Variety:** "Miss Shearer delivers a sparkling performance . . . Miss Crawford, is ruthless and tough-shelled . . . Rosalind Russell contributes a highlight characterization. . . ." **New Republic:** "It is a holiday from Hays [censorship office] all right; there is more wicked wit than Hollywood has been allowed since **The Front Page.**" **Film Daily:** "Smart brilliant play becomes sure-fire screen fare finely produced and acted." **New York Times:** "The tonic effect of Metro-Goldwyn-Mayer's film of Clare Boothe's **The Women** is so marvelous we believe every studio in Hollywood should make at least one thoroughly nasty picture a year."

In 1956 MGM followed the lead of other studios that were remaking their old properties. It transformed its elite **The Women** into a mediocre musical entitled **The Opposite Sex.** Adding insult to injury, the studio diluted playwright Boothe's intent by grafting several male roles to the proceedings. The new version featured June Allyson (as the heroine), Joan Collins (Crystal), Dolores Gray (Sylvia), Ann Sheridan (Amanda—a variation of Peggy), Ann Miller (Gloria—a version of Miriam), Joan Blondell (Edith), Charlotte Greenwood (Lucy), Agnes Moorehead (the Countess), and such male players as Leslie Nielsen, Jeff Richards, Sam Levene, and Jim Backus. The widescreen color feature, produced by Joe Pasternak and directed by David Miller, was not a box-office bonanza.

A major revival of **The Women** opened on Broadway at the 46th Street Theatre on April 25, 1973, with an impressive cast:

Mary	Kim Hunter
Crystal	Marie Wallace
Sylvia	Alexis Smith
Miriam	Rhonda Fleming
Edith	Dorothy Loudon
Countess	Jan Miner
Lucy	Polly Rowles
Mrs. Morehead	Myrna Loy

Whatever the reasons—perhaps catty women losing their appeal as women's liberation became less novel, or maybe the oft-revived 1939 film being too vivid in the public's mind—this edition of **The Women** closed after only sixty-three performances.

In the spring of 1978 producer Jon Peters announced he and MGM would produce a contemporary version of **The Women** which would be re-scripted by Polly Platt. The project has yet to become a reality.

THE YEARLING
1946 C—134 min.

Producer, Sidney Franklin; **director,** Clarence Brown; based on the novel by Marjorie Kinnan Rawlings; **screenplay,** Paul Osborn; **art directors,** Cedric Gibbons and Paul Groesse; **set decorator,** Edwin B. Willis; **music,** Herbert Stothart; **Technicolor consultants,** Natalie Kalmus and Henri Jaffa; **assistant director,** Joe Boyle; **sound,** Douglas Shearer; **special effects,** Warren Newcombe; **camera,** Charles Rosher, Leonard Smith, and Arthur Arling; **editor,** Harold F. Kress.

Gregory Peck (**Pa Baxter**); Jane Wyman (**Ma Baxter**); Claude Jarman, Jr. (**Jody Baxter**); Chill Wills (**Buck Forrester**); Clem Bevans (**Pa Forrester**); Margaret Wycherly (**Ma Forrester**); Henry Travers (**Mr. Boyles**); Forrest Tucker (**Lem Forrester**); Donn Gift (**Fodderwing**); Daniel White (**Millwheel**); Matt Willis (**Gabby**); George Mann (**Pack**); Arthur Hohl (**Arch**); June Lockhart (**Twink Weatherby**); Joan Wells (**Eulalie**); Jeff York (**Oliver**); B. M. Chick York (**Doc Wilson**); Houseley Stevenson (**Mr. Ranger**); Jane Green (**Mrs. Saunders**); Victor Kilian (**Captain**); Robert Porterfield (**Mate**); Frank Eldredge (**Deckhand**).

SYNOPSIS

In Florida, shortly after the Civil War, the Baxter family are having a struggle to survive on their meager earnings from the soil. Pa Baxter hopes to raise a money crop that will enable him to build a well outside his door, thus easing his wife's burden. However, it does not seem likely that this will come true. Their son, Jody, the only one of four children to have survived the rigors of pioneer life, begs for a pet to relieve the loneliness of his solitary boyhood. However, Ma denies the request, explaining that the pet would put a further drain on the family's limited resources.

When Pa, bitten by a rattlesnake, hurriedly kills a doe and uses its heart and liver to draw out the poison, Jody is permitted to adopt the doe's orphaned fawn. It makes life more pleasant for Jody, who spends his days caring for the crop. As the fawn grows into a yearling, the animal becomes a great liability because of the damage it does to crops. The yearling's destructiveness eventually threatens the family's very existence. Pa is compelled to order Jody to shoot the animal.

Unable to kill his pet, Jody turns the yearling loose in the scrub, but the animal soon returns

Claude Jarman, Jr., Gregory Peck, and Jane Wyman in a publicity pose for The Yearling *('46).*

write the scenario. It was not until 1941 that director Victor Fleming took a company of Spencer Tracy, Anne Revere, and Gene Eckman (a child actor picked after numerous tests for the part of Jody) to Florida for location shooting. Problems abounded: insects, ravenous pigs, Fleming's bouts with both Tracy and producer Franklin, and the fawn growing too fast. Even the corn caused problems, having to look a certain way for particular scenes and hence having to be grown indoors, then stored, until required. The bellicose Fleming finally left the project, and King Vidor was asked to take over. When he realized that he had too little time to acquaint himself with the script, he too abandoned the film. A saddened Franklin shelved the project at a loss of over $500,000.

In 1942 Franklin sought to resume production with Roddy McDowall (of Twentieth Century–Fox's **How Green Was My Valley,** 1941) as Jody. But it was a false restart. There were further abortive plans in 1944. Finally, in 1946, with Clarence Brown directing, **The Yearling** resumed production. This time it starred Gregory Peck[1] (who had just given an Oscar-nominated performance in Twentieth Century–Fox's **The Keys of the Kingdom**), Jane Wyman (who had recently scored as Ray Milland's love interest in Paramount's **The Lost Weekend**), and Claude Jarman, Jr., as Jody, chosen after a well-publicized perusal of 19,000 youths. The Tennessee lad had never before acted. To avoid the fate which befell the last fawn, Brown picked sixteen different fawns to represent the story's little "Flag."

Years later, Anne Revere recalled for Doug McClelland's **The Unkindest Cuts** (1972):

> "We were in Florida for about ten days. I don't know that we shot any real scenes. We did a lot of testing. Spence was to play Penny Baxter, who was called that because he was small. Remember, these were poor people to whom a little spilled milk was a tragedy. I recall they put Spence on a huge horse that looked like it could win the Preakness, hoping the animal's size would make Spence seem smaller. They got me up in lifts and big bosoms. Oh, it was all terrible! I'm glad the filming didn't go on. I wasn't ready to play Ma Baxter then. After I did **Velvet** under his direction in '45, Clarence Brown tested me for the **Yearling** he was preparing then. I was ready then. But they wanted someone sexy to appear opposite the rising young actor Gregory Peck, who already had risen over six feet in height—so they got Jane Wyman and took all the sexiness out of her! I didn't especially like the movie. It was too pretty."

There were numerous emotional and exciting episodes in **The Yearling:** the hunting of a savage bear named "Slewfoot" with a vicious fight be-

to the farm. Then Ma, of necessity, shoots and wounds the pet. Jody is forced to put the yearling out of its misery. Embittered, he runs away from home but returns after three days of starvation and hardship.

He is now more mature and fully aware that practicality, not viciousness, motivated his parents in demanding that he dispose of the yearling.

* * *

"It isn't often that there is realized upon the screen the innocence and trust and enchantment that are in the nature of a child and the yearning love and anxiety that a father feels for his boy. . . .

But we've got to hand it to Metro and to everyone who helped to visualize **The Yearling**. . . . They have caught the rare sentiments and beauties in this picture." Bosley Crowther's words of praise in the **New York Times** are exemplary of the acclaim won by **The Yearling,** one of Metro's top moneymakers of the company's history, and a dream of producer Sidney Franklin which took five often-disastrous years to bring to a superb completion.

Marjorie Kinnan Rawlings' Pulitzer Prize–winning novel of 1938 began its cinematization that year when MGM assigned John Lee Mahin to

---

[1]Peck had starred the previous year in MGM's **Valley of Decision** opposite Greer Garson. Metro studio head Louis B. Mayer said of Peck, that he had made stars of "Judy and Mickey and Gable and Garbo" and that he could transform Peck into "the greatest of them all." After **The Yearling,** Peck would return to MGM for the lugubrious **The Great Sinner** (1949).

tween Pa and Jody's dog, and that beast;[2] the chilling snakebite scene in which Peck kills Flag's mother to use her heart and liver as an antidote to the poison; and the heartbreaking climax in which Wyman, to protect the family's crop, shoots the yearling. Then Jarman's Jody is forced to kill the poor animal to end its suffering. This arousing scene is one of the most tear-inducing vignettes of the cinema. (When Wyman took her daughter Maureen to see the completed film, the girl could not forgive her mother after the picture was over. Said Wyman, "My child wouldn't speak to me for two weeks because I shot the deer.")

When released late in 1946, **The Yearling** was of enormous critical and audience appeal.[3] Crowther of the **Times** paid tribute to director Brown ("has revealed both his heart and his intelligence in keeping the whole thing restrained"), Peck's "simple dignity and strength," Wyman's "credulity and sympathy," and, especially, Master Jarman, who "achieved a child characterization as haunting and appealing as any we've ever seen."

The Yearling was Oscar-nominated for Best Picture, but was outdistanced by Samuel Goldwyn's **The Best Years of Our Lives.** Gregory Peck lost the Best Actor Oscar to Fredric March of **The Best Years of Our Lives,** and Olivia de Havilland of Paramount's **The Heiress** was victorious over Wyman and others in the Best Actress category. **The Yearling** Oscars did go to Charles Rosher, Leonard Smith, and Technicolor specialist Arthur Arling (Best Color Cinematography); to Cedric Gibbons, Paul Groesse, and Edwin B. Willis (Best Color Interior Decorations); and to Claude Jarman, Jr., who won a miniature statuette as the outstanding child star of the year. The film placed fourth in **Film Daily**'s Ten Best picture poll and won such tributes as the **Redbook** Motion Picture Award. **The Yearling** grossed $5.2 million in distributors' domestic rentals.

YOUNG DR. KILDARE
1938—81 min.

Director, Harold S. Bucquet; based on characters created by Max Brand; **screenplay,** Willis Goldbeck and Harry Ruskin; **art directors,** Cedric Gibbons and Malcolm Brown; **set decorator,** Edwin B. Willis; **music,** David Snell; **camera,** John Seitz; **editor,** Elmo Vernon.

---

[2]A scene in which the brutal Slewfoot mauls a pig was judged to be so disturbing by Gus Eyssell, managing director of Radio City Music Hall where the film debuted, that he demanded the scene be deleted. MGM finally agreed and ordered the segment excised from the two hundred Technicolor prints about to be processed; ninety prints had already been made containing the controversial mauling.

[3]Costar Gregory Peck would many years later admit, "I would have liked **The Yearling** better had its Walt Disney aspects been pushed into the background. It was much too lushly done." More recently Peck commented about the film, "The boy cried too much."

Lew Ayres (**Dr. James Kildare**); Lionel Barrymore (**Dr. Leonard Gillespie**); Lynne Carver (**Alice Raymond**); Nat Pendleton (**Joe Wayman**); Jo Ann Sayers (**Barbara Chanler**); Samuel S. Hinds (**Dr. Stephen Kildare**); Emma Dunn (**Mrs. Martha Kildare**); Walter Kingsford (**Dr. Walter Carew**); Nella Walker (**Mrs. Chanler**); Pierre Watkin (**Mr. Chanler**); Truman Bradley (**John Hamilton**); Monty Woolley (**Dr. Lane Portous**); Don Castle (**Bates**); Donald Barry (**Collins**); Marie Blake (**Sally, the Switchboard Operator**); Leonard Penn (**Stuart Walden**); Virginia Brissac (**Landlady**); Clinton Rosemond (**Conover**); Nell Craig and Barbara Bedford (**Nurses**); Grace Hayle (**Stout Lady**); Emmett Vogan (**Detective Heerman**); Murray Alper (**Waiter**); Jack Murphy and Cyril Ring (**Interns**); Howard Hickman (**Dr. Harris**).

SYNOPSIS

When Dr. James Kildare returns to his small hometown as a full-fledged doctor, his parents are happy for they feel he will now work with his country-doctor father in a joint practice. But Jim Kildare has other ideas. Although he does not want to offend his parents, he knows that he must find out where he belongs in the scheme of life.

As such he joins a large New York City hospital as an intern for $20 per month. This action makes his sweetheart, Alice Raymond, unhappy, but she does not stop him. At Blair General Hospital Dr. Kildare is noticed by Dr. Leonard Gillespie, a brilliant diagnostician. But because of the continual caustic remarks Dr. Gillespie makes, Dr. Kildare believes that he dislikes him.

Later Dr. Kildare gets into trouble because of his stand in a case involving Barbara Chanler, the young daughter of wealthy parents. The hospital authorities, guided by the eminent authority on mental cases, Dr. Lane Portous thought the girl was unbalanced, but Dr. Kildare, having talked to her, knows there is a legitimate basis for her mental problems. He investigates and finds out the circumstances surrounding her past. He is then able to talk to her and make the young woman realize she has imagined many things. In that way he brings her back to a normal emotional state.

But Dr. Kildare, despite his good deed, is dismissed from the hospital staff on the grounds of insubordination. He prepares to return home, but Dr. Gillespie, who appreciates Dr. Kildare's talents, chooses him as his new assistant.

* * *

There might not have been many interns who were as noble as Dr. James Kildare of New York's Blair General Hospital, but then there were few families as wholesome as the Hardys and few dogs as brilliant as Lassie. The MGM **Dr. Kildare–Dr. Gillespie** series proved to be one of the lot's most popular continuing entries, displaying the idealized conception of American life as dictated by Louis B. Mayer. The emotional, melodramatic, sentimental ingredients of the **Kildare** films won a following which allowed the series to survive a major Hollywood–World War II controversy and which permitted the company to utilize the films—

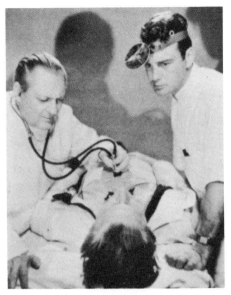

Lionel Barrymore and Lew Ayres in Young Dr. Kildare *('38).*

as with the **Hardy** series—as a training ground for newly contracted players.

It was not at MGM but at Paramount where the screen legend of Dr. James Kildare began. The film was the 1937 feature **Internes Can't Make Money,** the director Alfred Santell, the stars Joel McCrea and Barbara Stanwyck, and the plot revolving about the dedication and stoicism of the young members of the medical profession. Receipts were quite good. MGM, in search of a new series (the **Hardys** had just begun), recognized a number of appealing aspects in the **Kildare** adventures: (1) a glamorization of the young doctors of America, (2) a subject matter which could lead in all sorts of directions, and (3) the possibility of casting Mayer's favorite actor, Lionel Barrymore, in a recurring part. In fact, the role could be designed to allow him to perform in the wheelchair, which had become a physical necessity. With Lionel ensconced in the part of the senior doctor, the crusty Gillespie, Harold S. Bucquet (of the **Crime Does Not Pay** short subjects) directing, and the production accent on economy,[1] Metro signed Lew Ayres to star as Dr. James Kildare. The sensitive-featured actor, who had shown such promise as Greta Garbo's lover of MGM's **The Kiss** (1929) and the star of Universal's **All Quiet on the Western Front** (1930), had suffered a severe career slide in ensuing cinema efforts. He had even tried directing (Republic's **Hearts in Bondage** in 1936) without notable success. However, an acclaimed performance in Columbia's **Holiday** (1938; as Katharine Hepburn's bored, ever-so-rich brother) led Metro to sign him and to slate the handsome performer for B unit leads. (He began his contract with 1938's **Rich Man,**

---

[1]It was not until 1934 that MGM began to make B pictures. But at the high-class studio, even a programmer had to display a slick quality. Said Mayer, "If it's an MGM film, it has to look like an MGM film."

Poor Girl.) Twenty-nine-year-old Ayres took on the title role of **Young Dr. Kildare** with minimal enthusiasm. He remembered later, "When I saw the preview, it made me pretty miserable. Frankly, I thought it was terrible."

MGM promoted the film with: "While sirens scream . . . and adventure lies dead ahead . . . ride with the ambulance interns of a great hospital! Learn the secrets of Men in White and the Women they love . . . in the split-second drama of **Young Dr. Kildare** . . . and the mystery of the girl in sables!"

In the October 28, 1938, **New York Times'** review of Frank S. Nugent, **Young Dr. Kildare** won a sincere endorsement: "With the film of A. J. Cronin's **The Citadel** just around the corner, Metro stole some of its own thunder yesterday by presenting **Young Doctor Kildare** at the Music Hall. [It was a sign of industry faith in the programmer to have it bow at such a prestigious showcase theatre.] It is a rather fine picture in most respects, quiet in tone and performance, happily free from the clichés of most men-in-white dramas. Credit it, too, with cementing the comeback of Lew Ayres, happily cured of a rash of brashness, and with proof of Lionel Barrymore's ability to run away with a picture even when he is chained to a wheelchair." MGM, pleased with the crucial response and the lucrative public endorsement, proceeded with the **Kildare** series, which was to earn the studio huge profits.

Young Dr. Kildare introduced several characters who became regulars in the follow-ups: Nat Pendleton (as ambulance driver Joe Wayman), Samuel S. Hinds (as Jim's dad, small-town Dr. Stephen Kildare), Emma Dunn (as Mrs. Martha Kildare, Jim's mother), and Walter Kingsford (as Blair General Hospital's Dr. Walter Carew). The next entry, **Calling Dr. Kildare** (1939), which became a popular American expression of the era, featured rapidly advancing MGM ingenue Lana Turner as a gangster's moll, and added more characters to the series: Alma Kruger (as nurse Molly Byrd), and most notably, Laraine Day (as Nurse Molly Lamont, who becomes Kildare's sweetheart).

The subsequent installments flowed profitably: **The Secret of Dr. Kildare** (1939), in which Gillespie learns he has cancer—the film added Frank Orth and George Reed as interns Mike and Conover; 1949's **Dr. Kildare's Strangest Case, Dr. Kildare Goes Home,** and **Dr. Kildare's Crisis;** 1941's **The People vs. Dr. Kildare** (which introduced Red Skelton as clumsy orderly Vernon Briggs) and **Dr. Kildare's Wedding Day** (in which Laraine Day, about to become Mrs. James Kildare, is instead hit by a truck and dies after telling her bereaved fiancé, "This is going to be much easier for me than it is for you. Poor sweet Jimmy"); and 1942's **Dr. Kildare's Victory.**

At this point a crisis confronted the **Kildare** series: Ayres, who had been seen in other MGM products—**Ice Follies of 1939** with Joan Crawford, **Broadway Serenade** (1939) with Jeanette MacDonald, **Remember?** (1939) with Greer Garson, and **Maisie Was a Lady** (1941) with Ann Sothern—announced that he was a conscientious objector. He stated that he would not fight in World War II and that he was willing to "praise the Lord, but **not** pass the ammunition." The general public—remember this was when patriotism was still de rigueur— was aghast. **Variety** labeled the actor "a disgrace to the industry." MGM president Nicholas Schenck huffed, "As far as I'm concerned, I am no party of interest one way or the other. Lew Ayres is washed up with us since he's washed himself up with the public." After a B potboiler, **Fingers at the Window,** already in production when the "news" broke, Ayres left MGM in considerable disgrace. He later served twenty-two months of exemplary, courageous duty with the Army Medical Corps at the Pacific beachhead invasions of Hollandia, Leyte, and Luzon. After the war he returned to picture making, but never again to gain the popularity he once had.

Meanwhile, MGM's Blair General Hospital functioned without Dr. James Kildare; 1942's **Calling Dr. Gillespie** focused on Barrymore's growling and an appealing new contractee named Donna Reed. And 1943's **Dr. Gillespie's New Assistant** introduced Van Johnson as Dr. Randall ("Red") Adams, as well as Keye Luke as Dr. Lee Wong Howe, the latter a regular in all subsequent entries. Johnson and Barrymore starred in 1943's **Dr. Gillespie's Criminal Case** (which featured Margaret O'Brien), 1944's **Three Men in White** (containing a young Ava Gardner), and 1944's **Between Two Women** (with Gloria DeHaven). The series ended with 1947's **Dark Delusion,** without Johnson (James Craig was the new young doctor) but with Barrymore, who when asked how long he wanted to go on playing Dr. Gillespie, replied "I hope until hell freezes over."

However, **Dark Delusion** ended the film series. But a whole new lease on popularity began for Dr. James Kildare in the September 27, 1961, premiere of NBC-TV's "Dr. Kildare" series, starring Richard Chamberlain in the title role and Raymond Massey as Dr. Gillespie. The show ran for five seasons. A 1972 syndicated teleseries, "Young Dr. Kildare," featured Mark Jenkins in the title role and Gary Merrill as his mentor, Dr. Leonard Gillespie.

ZIEGFELD FOLLIES
1946 C—110 min.

Producer, Arthur Freed; **directors,** Vincente Minnelli and, **uncredited:** George Sidney, Norman Taurog, Robert Lewis, Lemuel Ayers, and Roy Del Ruth; **sketches,** Pete Barry, Harry Tugend, George White, and David Freedman; **choreography,** Robert Alton, Eugene Loring, and Charles Walters; **vocal arranger,** Kay Thompson; **orchestrators,** Conrad Salinger and Wally Heglin; **music director,** Lennie Hayton; **music adapter,** Roger Edens; **songs;** Freed and Harry Warren; Freed and Earl Brent; Ralph Blane and Hugh Martin; Philip Braham and Douglas Furber; Brent and Edens; Ralph Freed and Edens; Ira and George Gershwin; **Technicolor consultants,** Natalie Kalmus and Henri Jaffa; **art directors,** Cedric Gibbons, Jack Martin Smith, Merrill Pye, and Lemuel Ayers; **set decorators,** Edwin B. Willis and MacAlper; **costume supervisor,** Irene; **puppet costumes,** Florence Bunin; **costumes,** Irene Sharaff and Helen Rose; **makeup,** Jack Dawn; **sound,** Douglas Shearer; **camera,** George Folsey, Charles Rosher, and Ray June; **editor,** Albert Akst.

William Powell **(Florenz Ziegfeld);** Bunin Puppets **(Themselves);** "Here's to the Ladies": Fred Astaire, Lucille Ball, Cyd Charisse; "A Water Ballet": Esther Williams; "Number, Please": Keenan Wynn **(Phone Caller);** La Traviata: James Melton and Marion Bell; "Pay the Two Dollars": Victor Moore and Edward Arnold **(Themselves);** Ray Teal **(Special Officer);** Joseph Crehan **(Judge);** William B. Davidson **(Presiding Judge);** Harry Hayden **(Warden);** Eddie Dunn and Garry Owen **(Officers);** "This Heart of Mine": Astaire **(The Imposter);** Lucille Bremer **(The Princess);** Count Stefenelli **(The Duke);** Naomi Childers **(The Duchess);** Helen Boice **(The Countess);** Robert Wayne **(Retired Dyspeptic);** Charles Coleman **(The Major);** Feodor Chaliapin **(The Lieutenant);** Sam Flint **(The Flunky);** Shirlee Howard, Natalie Draper, Katherine Booth, Lucille Casey, Eve Whitney, Elaine Shepard, Frances Donelan, Aileen Haley, Aina Constant, and Helen O'Hara **(Girls);** "A Sweepstakes Ticket": Fanny Brice **(Norma);** Hume Cronyn **(Monty);** William Frawley **(Martin);** Arthur Walsh **(Telegraph Boy);** "Love": Lena Horne; "When Television Comes": Red Skelton; "Limehouse Blues": Astaire **(Tai Long);** Bremer **(Moy Ling);** Robert Lewis **(Chinese Gentleman);** Dante Dipaolo, Robert Chetwood, Jack Purcell, Herb Luri, Walter Stane, Edward Brown, Milton Chisholm, Jack Regas, Bert May, Richard D'Archy, Alex Romero, Don Hulbert, Ricky Ricardi, Robert Trout, Bill Hawley, Rita Dunn, Charlotte Hunter, Patricia Lynn, Ruth Merman, Melba Snowden, Patricia Jackson, Marilyn Christine, Wanda Stevenson, Judi Blacque, Virginia Hunter, Sean Francis, Dorothy Gilmore, and Doreen Hayward **(Ensemble);** Eugene Loring **(Costermonger);** Harriet Lee **(Singer in Dive);** Cyd Charisse **(Chicken);** "A Great Lady Has an Interview": Judy Garland **(The Star);** Rex Evans **(The Butler);** "The Babbitt and, the Bromide": Astaire and Gene Kelly; "There's Beauty Everywhere": Kathryn Grayson and the Ziegfeld Girls.

SYNOPSIS
The musical revue opens with Florenz Ziegfeld, the late Broadway producer, in his palatial apartment in heaven. He dreams of once more creating a Ziegfeld Follies, this time using the talent and resources available today. His dream begins with: "Here's to the Ladies," a lavish production number featuring Fred Astaire, Lucille Ball, and a host of shapely chorus girls. Esther Williams follows with "A Water Ballet," in which she gives a graceful exhibition of her swimming talents. Keenan Wynn is next in "Number, Please," an amusing skit about his difficulties with a telephone operator. Then come James Melton and Marion Bell in an opulent opera number in which they sing "Brindisi" from **La Traviata.** They are followed by "Pay the Two Dollars," a venerable stage skit in which Victor Moore finds himself in all sorts of trouble with the law because his lawyer, Edward

Arnold, insists that he appeal a $2.00 fine for a subway violation. Next is a dance poem, "This Heart of Mine," set in a ballroom where Princess Lucille Bremer becomes enchanted with jewel thief Fred Astaire. Thereafter there is "A Sweepstakes Ticket," in which a married couple (Fanny Brice and Hume Cronyn) have a mixup over the ownership of a winning sweepstakes ticket with their landlord, William Frawley. Lena Horne then sings "Love," followed by the comedy skit, "When Television Comes," which finds Red Skelton as an inebriated TV announcer. Fred Astaire and Lucille Bremer dance to "Limehouse Blues," a dramatic Oriental-toned pantomime, which contrasts to Judy Garland performing "A Great Lady Has an Interview," a song-and-dance satire on a very affected actress. Fred Astaire and Gene Kelly unite for a lively song-and-dance number, "The Babbitt and the Bromide." In the finale, Kathryn Grayson and the Ziegfeld Girls sing "There's Beauty Everywhere."

* * *

When Florenz Ziegfeld died, crushed by debt, in 1932, his dying words reportedly were (in delirium), "Curtain! Fast music! Lights! Ready for the last finale! Great! The show looks good! The show looks good!" In those dying breaths, the great showman certainly never imagined that his last mandate would be predominately fulfilled not by the stage, but by the theatre's brutal competitor, the movies—MGM to be precise.[1]

The name Ziegfeld had proven a bonanza for Metro, through its Oscar-winning **The Great Ziegfeld** (1936) with William Powell's urbane portrayal of the title role, Luise Rainer's Academy-honored playing of Anna Helm, and a series of exquisitely opulent production numbers; and **Ziegfeld Girl** (1941), starring the gorgeous trio of Hedy Lamarr, Judy Garland, and Lana Turner. The third, last, and highest-grossing film pairing of MGM and Ziegfeld was **Ziegfeld Follies**. Although it proved another enormous success for the studio, it might have consoled the departed Flo as being one of the cinema's most troublesome and costly celluloid excursions.

Ziegfeld Follies was conceived as a special confection to celebrate MGM's 1944 twentieth anniversary. Louis B. Mayer allowed producer Arthur Freed a $3 million budget, with the film to contain no plot, but rather be a series of musical and comedy skits, à la Metro's **Hollywood Revue of 1929**. Production began in January 1944; on November 1, 1944, the Technicolor, 273-minute result (which had shed director George Sidney en route to completion, at Sidney's request; Vincente Minnelli was the replacement) previewed at the Westwood Village Theatre with the following lineup of screen attractions:

1. "Ziegfeld Days"—an introduction performed by the Bunin Puppets.
2. "Meet the Ladies"—a luscious extravaganza featuring Fred Astaire, Cyd Charisse, and

Judy Garland in "A Great Lady Has an Interview" number from Ziegfeld Follies *('46).*

most attractively, a plumed, pink-gowned Lucille Ball flailing a whip at black-clad, fishnet-stockinged, pantherlike chorines, all against the background of a swirling merry-go-round.
3. "Honolulu"—a water ballet featuring James Melton singing and Esther Williams' swimming (mostly underwater).
4. "If Swing Goes, I Go Too"—a Fred Astaire number.
5. "The Pied Piper"—a comedy skit featuring Jimmy Durante.
6. "If Television Comes"—Red Skelton as a dyspeptic TV announcer, performing his popular "Guzzler's Gin" routine he had originally used in his MGM screen test.
7. "A Cowboy's Life"—a western number sung by operatic tenor James Melton.
8. "Liza"—Avon Long singing to Lena Horne and ten dancers.
9. "Baby Snooks"—Fanny Brice performing her old standby specialty characterization.
10. "This Heart of Mine"—the Harry Warren-Arthur Freed tune, a magnificent pavilion set, a **Raffles** theme, and the combined talents of Astaire and Freed's new favorite, Lucille Bremer.
11. "Death and Taxes"—a comedy skit played by Durante, Edward Arnold, and Stephen McNally.
12. "Pay the Two Dollars"—another comedy skit, this one performed by Victor Moore and Edward Arnold, ironically borrowed from **George White's Scandals of 1931**.
13. "Love"—a sultry number sung by Lena Horne.

14. **La Traviata**—Melton and soprano Marion Bell singing "Brindisi" from the opera.
15. "The Sweepstake Ticket"—comedy skit featuring Brice, Hume Cronyn, and William Frawley. (It was the only number in the film actually to derive from a **Ziegfeld Follies**.)
16. "Limehouse Blues"—a stunning production segment, filmed on the overhauled **The Picture of Dorian Gray** London street set, with Bremer as an Oriental harlot, Astaire as her victim, in a thirteen-minute number which required eighteen days of rehearsal, two days of recording, ten days of shooting, and $228,225.66 of financing.
17. "A Great Lady Has an Interview"—Judy Garland as the gloriously affected Madame Crematon talking to the press between poses, in a marvelous takeoff on MGM's then reigning queen, Greer Garson. (The number was created especially for La Garson herself, who visited Freed's house with her mother and spouse Richard Ney to listen to the piece. Mother said, "Well, I don't think so." Ney said, "No, it's not for you dear." And Garson went home.)
18. "The Babbitt and the Bromide"—The only tandem screen dancing of Astaire and Gene Kelly to that date, originally written by the Gershwins for Fred and sister Adele for the 1927 Broadway show **Funny Face**. The lamentable, simpleminded number (which cost $78,725.70 to shoot, with six days of rehearsal, one day of prerecording, and four days of filming) saw the pair singing to each other in the number as young men, mature men, and bearded angels. Kelly has said of the ludicrous

[1]It was reported that MGM acquired the film, radio, and television rights to the title **Ziegfeld Follies** from Billie Burke Ziegfeld and Lee Shubert at a $100,000 price. The sellers retained the stage rights.

Fred Astaire and Gene Kelly in "The Babbitt and the Bromide" number from Ziegfeld Follies.

From December to February 1945 added scenes and retakes were shot (some by Norman Taurog). The inserted material included: Keenan Wynn's comedy skit **Number, Please** (which had been done originally by Fred Allen in the 1930 Broadway revue **Three's a Crowd**); Virginia O'Brien's comic vocal turn, "Bring on Those Wonderful Men!"—added to the opening sequence of Ball and her panther women; and Kathryn Grayson's finale vocal selection "There's Beauty Everywhere" (substituted for the Melton, Astaire, Bremer, et al. hodgepodge). To frame the array of skits, footage was shot of William Powell as a celestial Ziegfeld, dreaming of producing yet one more show.[3] At last, on April 8, 1946, after over two years of effort and $3,240,816.86 of cost, **Ziegfeld Follies** was ready for national release.

Reviews of the feature film varied. The **New York Daily News**' Kate Cameron praised the mélange as "a great big beautiful hunk of entertainment . . . . as elaborate and stunning a revue as the master himself ever devised." The **New York Journal-American**'s Rose Pelswick labeled the opus "one of those super-dazzling spectacles that MGM does so well." **PM** dismissed the film as "nothing more or less than a parade of celebrity short subjects," while Alton Cook (**New York World-Telegram**) regretted that the **Follies** contained "all those stars and not one really star act."

The top crowd-pleasers of the show were Esther Williams' ballet, Skelton's drunk routine, Garland's send-up of the big star, and the unique "Limehouse Blues" number. Actually, it was Astaire—in his first Technicolor feature—who proved the pivotal force of the potpourri, being in four numbers.

In its initial release **Ziegfeld Follies** grossed over $5,340,000. It was the last time the studio would exhume the great Ziegfeld's name and reputation; postwar tastes, postwar economy, and postwar Hollywood made such extravaganzas less a potential reality and more a happy memory.[4]

last sequence, "I thought I looked like a klotz!"

19. "There's Beauty Everywhere"—Astaire, Bremer, Charisse, Melton, and the chorus in a grand finale enhanced by a lavish spray of bubbles which emitted so noxious a gas that the studio fire brigade was called to stage 27. (Because the bubbles proved so troublesome, the intended Astaire-Bremer dance finale to the vocal accompaniment of Melton's singing was ruined and had to be mostly deleted.)

The preview reaction was a highly uneven one. The excessive length of the picture caused even the most susceptible audiences to fidget and squirm, and back at Culver City, cuts were ordered. Since most of the comedy material had proven very flat, the Durante sketches and Brice's

Baby Snooks routine were snipped. Astaire, displeased with the result of "If Swing Goes . . . ," volunteered that it be cut. Lena Horne–Avon Long's "Liza" was trimmed from the print, as was Melton's cowboy song and his section of the Esther Williams' water ballet. (The deletions represented over $300,000 of filmed footage.)[2]

---

[2]"Will You Love Me in Technicolor as You Do in Black and White?" was prerecorded by Judy Garland and Mickey Rooney but not used in the film; other numbers planned for the **Follies** but **not** used were: "Fireside Chat," with Garland, Ann Southern, and Lucille Ball; "Pass That Peace Pipe," with June Allyson, Gene Kelly, Nancy Walker, and chorus; "Reading of the Play," with Garland and Frank Morgan; "As Long As I Have My Art,"

with Garland and Rooney; "Glorifying the American Girl," with Ball, Marilyn Maxwell, Lucille Bremer, Lena Horne, and Elaine Shephard; "A Trip to Hollywood," with Jimmy Durante, Ball, and Maxwell; "Fairy Tale Ballet," with Katharine Hepburn, Margaret O'Brien, and Jackie ("Butch") Jenkins; and "You're Dream-Like," based on the Howard Dietz and Arthur Schwartz song.

[3]**Ziegfeld Follies** had a special premiere in Boston on August 20, 1945. As a result of the mixed audience reaction, it was decided to hold back release while additional cuts, switching of scenes, and new sequences were considered. After seven months of pandemonium, the film—as seen in Boston—was released.

[4]On May 21, 1978 NBC-TV presented a three-hour television movie entitled **Ziegfeld: The Man and His Women**, starring Paul Shenar as The Great Showman who supervised twenty-one Broadway shows between 1907–31. The TV-movie created such **Follies** musical numbers as "A Pretty Girl Is Like a Melody," "Nobody," "By the Light of the Silvery Moon," "Poor Butterfly," and "If You Knew Susie." Kay Gardella (**New York Daily News**) judged it to be ". . . a big, colorful, old-fashioned musical with all the assets and liabilities of that endangered species of entertainment."

ABOUT THE STAFF

JAMES ROBERT PARISH, Los Angeles-based writer, was born in Cambridge, Massachusetts. He attended the University of Pennsylvania and graduated as a Phi Beta Kappa with an honors degree in English. He is a graduate of Pennsylvania Law School and a member of the New York Bar. As president of Entertainment Copyright Research Co., Inc., he headed a major research facility for the media industries. Later he was a film interviewer for show business trade papers. He is the author of many books, including *The Fox Girls*, *The RKO Gals*, *Actors TV Credits*, *The Tough Guys*, *The Jeanette MacDonald Story*, *The Elvis Presley Scrapbook*, and *The Hollywood Beauties*. Among those he has co-written are *The MGM Stock Company*, *The Debonairs*, *Liza!*, *The Leading Ladies*, *Hollywood Character Actors*, *The Funsters*, *The Great Spy Pictures*, *The Forties Gals*, and *The Hollywood Reliables*.

GREGORY W. MANK is a graduate of Mount St. Mary's College, with a B.A. in English. He is the author of *It's Alive! The Classic Cinema Saga of Frankenstein* and has written several articles for *Films in Review*, *Cinefantastique*, and *Film Fan Monthly*, and has been associated with Mr. Parish on *Hollywood Players: The Forties*, *Hollywood Players: The Thirties*, *The Tough Guys*, *Great Child Stars*, *The Hollywood Beauties*, *The Funsters*, *The Hollywood Reliables*, and many others. He has been a contributing author to the anthologies *The Real Stars* and *Masterpieces of Cinema*, and is presently at work on two new books: *Classics of Terror* and *The Hollywood Hissables*. Mr. Mank is active in the theatre as both an actor and instructor. He is a college teacher and lives in Pennsylvania with his wife Barbara and family.

RICHARD G. PICCHIARINI is a freelance theatre and film researcher living on New York's Upper West Side. He has contributed frequently to *Playbill* magazine. He has acted off-Broadway as well as in regional theatre. Among other works, he has contributed to such books as *The Great Western Pictures* and *The Hollywood Beauties*.

JOHN ROBERT COCCHI was born in Brooklyn where he currently resides. He is one of America's most respected film researchers. He has been the New York editor of *Boxoffice* magazine and is now a free lance consultant on media research. He was research associate on *The American Movies Reference Book* (and Supplement), *The Fox Girls*, *Good Dames*, *The Tough Guys*, *The Hollywood Reliables*, and many others. He has written cinema history articles for *Film Fan Monthly*, *Screen Facts*, and *Films in Review*. He is the author of *The Western Picture Quiz Book* and is co-founder of one of New York City's leading film societies.

The late FLORENCE SOLOMON was born in New York, attended Hunter College, and then joined Ligon Johnson's copyright research office. Later she was director for research at Entertainment Copyright Research Co., Inc., and then became a reference supervisor at ASCAP's Index Division. Ms. Solomon collaborated on such works as *The American Movies Reference Book*, *TV Movies*, *Film Actors Guide: Western Europe*, *Hollywood Character Actors*, *The Hollywood Reliables*, and many others. She was the niece of the noted sculptor, Sir Jacob Epstein.

DeWITT BODEEN was born in Fresno, California. After graduation from UCLA he was an actor and playwright at the Pasadena Playhouse. In 1941 he was placed under contract at RKO as a screenwriter. His first project, *Cat People*, was a hit. Two other films that he wrote for producer Val Lewton—*Curse of the Cat People* and *Seventh Victim*—are highly regarded today as cult films. Among his other screenwriting credits are *The Yellow Canary*, *The Enchanted Cottage*, *Night Song*, and *I Remember Mama*, the last three for producer Harriet Parsons. He has collaborated on the scenarios for *Mrs. Mike* and *Billy Budd* and has written more than fifty teleplays. He is the author of *From Hollywood*, *More From Hollywood*, and the novel *13 Castle Walk*; co-author of *The Films of Cecil B. DeMille* and *The Films of Maurice Chevalier*; and associate editor for the reference volume *Who Wrote the Movie (and What Else Did He Write)?*

INDEX

A

Abel, Walter, 68
Adoree, Renee, xx-xxi
Albert, Eddie, 104
Albertson, Frank, 68, 101
Alexander, Kathryn, 22
Allan, Elizabeth, 42, 52, 203
Allyson, June, 15, 60, 73, 74, 84, 85, 122, 197, 198
Alton, John, 3
Alton, Robert, 9, 20, 24, 95
Ames, Leon, 5, 26, 114, 122, 135, 167, 226
Ames, Preston, 18
Anderson, Eddie ("Rochester"), 41-42
Anderson, Judith, 45-46
Anderson, Maxwell, 26
Anderson, Warner, 30, 51
Andrews, Robert D., 23
Antik, Alan, 3
Arden, Eve, 228
Arlen, Harold, 12, 41, 200, 230
Armen, Kay, 211
Armetta, Henry, 5
Armstrong, Louis, 41, 97-98
Arnaud, Leo, 12, 14, 35, 39, 56, 65, 133
Arnaz, Dezi, 23-24
Arness, James, 26
Arnheim, Gus, 12
Arnold, Edward, 9-10, 50, 101, 103, 104, 108, 109, 176, 226, 240
Asher, Irving, 31
Astaire, Fred, 18-21, 39-40, 56-57, 210, 212, 244, 246
Astor, Mary, 122, 135, 136, 178
Atwill, Lionel, 33-34
Aumont, Jean-Pierre, 121
Austin, Renee, 14
Axt, William, 2
Ayers, Lemuel, 244
Ayres, Lew, 243-44
Aylmer, Felix, 58

B

Backus, Jim, 161
Baclanova, Olga, 65-66
Bainter, Fay, 14, 109, 236
Ball, Lucille, 244
Bamattre, Martha, 3
Bankhead, Talullah, 7, 76, 77
Baron, Dick, 14
Barrymore, Diana, 16
Barrymore, Ethel, 176-78
Barrymore, John, 53-54, 86, 87, 131, 133, 176-78, 179, 181
Barrymore, Lionel, 2, 39, 41-42, 44-45, 47, 49, 52, 54, 66-68, 86, 87, 93, 99, 100, 176-78, 208, 223, 243
Bartholomew, Freddie, 7, 8, 36, 44-45, 52-53
Bassman, George, 14, 64
Beaumont, Harry, 36
Beaumont, Lucy, 66
Beavers, Louise, 32, 65
Beckett, Scotty, 210
Bedford, Barbara, 14, 73

Beery, Wallace, 29-30, 46-49, 53-55, 86, 87, 140-41, 220, 221, 224, 225, 233
Behrman, S.N., 7
Benchley, Robert, 48, 186, 226
Bendix, William, 236
Bennett, Compton, 112
Bennett, Constance, 217
Bennett, Joan, 61
Benny, Jack, 38, 61, 99
Beresford, Evelyn, 9
Bergerac, Jacques, 71, 72, 118
Bergman, Ingrid, 70, 71
Berkeley, Busby, 10, 12-15, 41, 64, 73, 74, 139-40
Berlin, Irving, 9, 10, 56-57, 89, 94, 125
Berman, Pandro S., 30, 61, 100, 106, 107, 148, 163, 207, 208
Bernard, Joe, 1
Bernstein, Elmer, 195
Bickford, Charles, 6-7, 50-51
Bing, Herman, 89, 91, 133, 137, 181
Blackmer, Sidney, 97
Blake, Madge, 1, 3
Blandick, Clara, 231
Blondell, Joan, 37
Blue, Ben, 64
Blyth, Ann, 87, 88
Blythe, Betty, 7, 100
Boemler, George, 1, 11
Boardman, Nan, 3
Boland, Mary, 168, 239
Boleslawski, Richard, 176, 178
Bolger, Ray, 89, 95-97, 230
Bond, Ward, 74, 93, 144
Booth, Edwina, 219, 220
Borden, Eugene, 3
Borgnine, Ernest, 12, 17-18
Borzage, Frank, 144
Boswell, Hugh, 22
Bowman, Lee, 23
Boyd, Stephen, 26
Boyer, Charles, 70, 71
Boyle, Charles, 5
Brabin, Charles, 176
Bracken, Eddie, 200
Bracy, Sidney, 7
Brando, Marlon, 110, 111
Brazzi, Rossano, 122
Brecher, Irving, 12, 64, 134
Bremer, Lucille, 135, 244
Bren, Milton H., 217
Brennan, Walter, 17-18, 68, 157
Brent, Earl, 5
Breon, Edmund, 70, 81
Bressart, Felix, 31, 154, 189
Brewster, Carol, 20
Brian, David, 105, 106
Briggs, Donald, 44
Briggs, Harlan, 133
Brocco, Peter, 88
Brodie, Steve, 5, 216
Brooks, Rand, 12
Brooks, Richard, 30, 45-46
Brophy, Edward, 46, 48, 65, 67
Brown, Charles, 12
Brown, Clarence L., 6, 7, 8, 57-58, 66-68, 103, 104, 105, 106, 148, 229, 241

H

I

N

O

T

U

V